Lecture Notes in Computer Science 4478

Commenced Publication in 1973
Founding and Former Series Editors:
Gerhard Goos, Juris Hartmanis, and Jan van Leeuwen

Joan Martí   José Miguel Benedí
Ana Maria Mendonça   Joan Serrat (Eds.)

Pattern Recognition and Image Analysis

Third Iberian Conference, IbPRIA 2007
Girona, Spain, June 6-8, 2007
Proceedings, Part II

Springer

Volume Editors

Joan Martí
University of Girona
Campus Montilivi, s/n., 17071 Girona, Spain
E-mail: joanm@eia.udg.es

José Miguel Benedí
Polytechnical University of Valencia
Camino de Vera, s/n., 46022 Valencia, Spain
E-mail: jbenedi@dsic.upv.es

Ana Maria Mendonça
University of Porto
Rua Dr. Roberto Frias, s/n, 4200-465 Porto, Portugal
E-mail: amendon@fe.up.pt

Joan Serrat
Centre de Visió per Computador-UAB
Campus UAB, 08193 Belaterra, (Cerdanyola), Barcelona, Spain
E-mail: joan.serrat@cvc.uab.es

Library of Congress Control Number: 2007927717

CR Subject Classification (1998): I.4, I.5, I.7, I.2.7, I.2.10

LNCS Sublibrary: SL 6 – Image Processing, Computer Vision, Pattern Recognition, and Graphics

ISSN   0302-9743
ISBN-10   3-540-72848-1 Springer Berlin Heidelberg New York
ISBN-13   978-3-540-72848-1 Springer Berlin Heidelberg New York

Springer is a part of Springer Science+Business Media

springer.com

© Springer-Verlag Berlin Heidelberg 2007
Printed in Germany

Typesetting: Camera-ready by author, data conversion by Scientific Publishing Services, Chennai, India
Printed on acid-free paper   SPIN: 12070374   06/3180   5 4 3 2 1 0

Preface

We welcome you to the 3rd Iberian Conference on Pattern Recognition and Image Analysis (IbPRIA 2007), jointly promoted by AERFAI (Asociación Española de Reconocimiento de Formas y Análisis de Imágenes) and APRP (Associção Portuguesa de Reconhecimento de Padrões). This year, IbPRIA was held in Girona, Spain, June 6–8, 2007, and was hosted by the Institute of Informatics and Applications of the University of Girona. It followed the two successful previous editions hosted by the Universitat de les Illes Balears (2003) and the Institute for Systems and Robotics and the Geo-systems Center of the Instituto Superior Técnico (2005).

A record number of 328 full paper submissions from 27 countries were received. Each of these submissions was reviewed in a blind process by two reviewers. The review assignments were determined by the four General Chairs, and the final decisions were made after the Chairs meeting in Girona, giving an overall acceptance rate of 47.5%. Because of the limited size of the conference, we regret that some worthy papers were probably rejected.

In keeping with the IbPRIA tradition of having a single track of oral presentations, the number of oral papers remained in line with the previous IbPRIA editions, with a total of 48 papers. The number of poster papers was settled to 108.

We were also very honored to have as invited speakers such internationally recognized researchers as Chris Williams from the University of Edinburgh, UK, Michal Irani from The Weizmann Institute of Science, Israel and Andrew Davison from Imperial College London, UK.

For the first time, some relevant related events were scheduled in parallel to the IbPRIA main conference according to the Call for Tutorials and Workshops: Antonio Torralba from MIT, USA and Aleix Martínez from Ohio State University, USA taught relevant tutorials about object recognition and Statistical Pattern Recognition, respectively, while the "Supervised and Unsupervised Ensemble Methods and Their Applications" workshop and the first edition of the "Spanish Workshop on Biometrics" were successfully developed.

We would like to thank all the authors for submitting their papers and thus making these proceedings possible. We address special thanks to the members of the Program Committee and the additional reviewers for their great work which contributed to the high quality of these proceedings.

We are also grateful to the Local Organizing Committee for their substantial contribution of time and effort.

Finally, our thanks go to IAPR for support in sponsoring the Best Paper Prize at IbPRIA 2007.

The next edition of IbPRIA will be held in Portugal in 2009.

June 2007   Joan Martí
                                                                    Ana Maria Mendonça
                                                                    José Miguel Benedí
                                                                    Joan Serrat

Organization

IbPRIA 2007 was organized by AERFAI (Asociación Española de Reconocimiento de Formas y Análisis de Imágenes) and APRP (Associação Portuguesa de Reconhecimento de Padrões), and as the local organizer of this edition, the Computer Vision and Robotics Group, Institute of Informatics and Applications, University of Girona (UdG).

General Conference Co-chairs

Joan Martí	University of Girona, Spain
José Miguel Benedí	Polytechnical University of Valencia, Spain
Ana Maria Mendonça	University of Porto, Portugal
Joan Serrat	Universitat Autònoma de Barcelona, Spain

Invited Speakers

Chris Williams	University of Edinburgh, UK
Michal Irani	The Weizmann Institute of Science, Israel
Andrew Davison	Imperial College London, UK

National Organizing Committee

Marc Carreras
Xavier Cufí
Jordi Freixenet
Rafael García
Xavier Lladó
Robert Martí
Marta Peracaula
Pere Ridao
Joaquim Salvi
Marcel Alofra
Elisabet Batlle
Anna Bosch
François Chung
Andrés El-Fakdi
Jordi Ferrer
Emili Hernández
Maryna Kudzinava
Arnau Oliver
Jordi Palau
Ricard Prados

Narcís Palomeras
David Raba
David Ribas
Miquel Villanueva

Program Committee

Lourdes Agapito	Queen Mary University of London, UK
Helder Araújo	University of Coimbra, Portugal
Hervé Bourlard	EPFL, Switzerland
Patrick Bouthemy	IRISA, France
Joachim Buhmann	ETH Zurich, Switzerland
Horst Bunke	University of Bern, Switzerland
Hans Burkhard	University of Freiburg, Germany
Francisco Casacuberta	Polytechnical University of Valencia, Spain
Vicent Caselles	Universitat Pompeu Fabra, Spain
Aurélio Campilho	University of Porto, Portugal
Luís Corte-Real	University of Porto, Portugal
Hervé Delinguette	INRIA, France
Pierre Dupont	Université catholique de Louvain, Belgium
Marcello Federico	ITC-irst Trento, Italy
Marco Ferreti	University of Pavia, Italy
Ana Fred	Technical University of Lisbon, Portugal
Andrew Gee	University of Cambridge, UK
Vito di Gesú	University of Palermo, Italy
Edwin R. Hancock	University of York, UK
Francisco Mario Hernández Tejera	Universidad de Las Palmas, Spain
Laurent Heutte	Université de Rouen, France
José Manuel Iñesta Quereda	Universidad de Alicante, Spain
Jorge Marques	Technical University of Lisbon, Portugal
Hermann Ney	University of Aachen, Germany
Wiro Niessen	University of Utrecht, The Netherlands
Francisco José Perales	Universitat de les Illes Balears, Spain
Nicolás Pérez de la Blanca	University of Granada, Spain
Fernando Pérez Cruz	Universidad Carlos III, Spain
Maria Petrou	Imperial College, UK
Pedro Pina	Technical University of Lisbon, Portugal
Armando Pinho	University of Aveiro, Portugal
Ioannis Pitas	University of Thessaloniki, Greece
Filiberto Pla	University Jaume I, Spain
Alberto Sanfeliu	Polytechnical University of Catalonia, Spain
Gabriella Sanniti di Baja	Istituto di Cibernetica CNR, Italy

Pierre Soille   Joint Research Centre, Italy
Karl Tombre   LORIA, France
M. Inés Torres   University of the Basque Country, Spain
Jordi Vitrià   Universitat Autònoma de Barcelona, Spain
Joachim Weickert   Saarland University, Germany
Reyer Zwiggelaar   University of Wales, Aberystwyth, UK

Reviewers

Maria José Abasolo   University of the Balearic Islands, Spain
Antonio Adán   Universidad de Castilla La Mancha, Spain
Francisco Jávier López Aligué University of Extremadura, Spain
René Alquézar   UPC, Spain
Joachim Buhmann   ETH Zurich, Switzerland
Juan Carlos Amengual   UJI-LPI, Spain
Hans Burkhard   University of Freiburg, Germany
Ramon Baldrich   Computer Vision Center, Spain
Jorge Pereira Batista   ISR Coimbra, Portugal
Luis Baumela   UPM, Spain
Alexandre Bernardino   Instituto Superior Técnico, Portugal
Lilian Blot   University of East Anglia, UK
Imma Boada   University of Girona, Spain
Marcello Federico   ITC-irst Trento, Italy
Michael Breuss   Saarland University, Germany
Jaime Santos Cardoso   INESC Porto, Portugal
Modesto Castrillón   Universidad de Las Palmas de Gran Canaria,
                              Spain
Miguel Velhote Correia   Instituto de Engenharia Biomédica, Portugal
Xevi Cufí   University of Girona, Spain
Jorge Alves da Silva   FEUB-INEB, Portugal
Hans du Buf   University of Algarve, Portugal
Óscar Deniz   Universidad de Las Palmas de Gran Canaria,
                              Spain
Daniel Hernández-Sosa   Universidad de Las Palmas de Gran Canaria,
                              Spain
Olga Duran   Imperial College, UK
Claudio Eccher   ITC-irst Trento, Italy
Arturo De la Escalera   Universidad Carlos III de Madrid, Spain
Miquel Feixas   Universitat de Girona, Spain
Francesc J. Ferri   Universitat de València, Spain
David Fofi   Le2i UMR CNRS 5158, France
Jordi Freixenet   University of Girona, Spain
Maria Frucci   Institute of Cybernetics "E. Caianiello", Italy
Cesare Furlanello   ITC-irst Trento, Italy
Miguel Ángel García   Universidad Autónoma de Madrid, Spain
Rafael García   University of Girona, Spain

Joao Silva Sequeira	Instituto Superior Técnico, Portugal
Margarida Silveira	Instituto Superior Técnico, Portugal
Joao Manuel R.S. Tavares	Universidade do Porto, Portugal
Antonio Teixeira	Universidade de Aveiro, Portugal
Javier Traver	Universitat Jaume I, Spain
Maria Vanrell	Computer Vision Center, Spain
Javier Varona	Universitat de les Illes Balears, Spain
Martin Welk	Saarland University, Germany
Laurent Wendling	LORIA, France
Michele Zanin	ITC-irst Trento, Italy

Sponsoring Institutions

MEC (Ministerio de Educación y Ciencia, Spanish Government)
AGAUR (Agència de Gestió d'Ajuts Universitaris i de Recerca, Catalan Government)
IAPR (International Association for Pattern Recognition)
Vicerectorat de Recerca en Ciència i Tecnologia, Universitat de Girona

Table of Contents – Part II

Table of Contents – Part I

Robust Automatic Speech Recognition Using PD-MEEMLIN

Igmar Hernández[1], Paola García[1], Juan Nolazco[1], Luis Buera[2],
and Eduardo Lleida[2]

[1] Computer Science Department, Tecnolgico de Monterrey,
Campus Monterrey, México
[2] Communications Technology Group (GTC), I3A, University of Zaragoza, Spain
{A00778595,paola.garcia,jnolazco,}@itesm.mx, {lbuera,lleida}@unizar.es

Abstract. This work presents a robust normalization technique by cascading a speech enhancement method followed by a feature vector normalization algorithm. To provide speech enhancement the Spectral Subtraction (SS) algorithm is used; this method reduces the effect of additive noise by performing a subtraction of the noise spectrum estimate over the complete speech spectrum. On the other hand, an empirical feature vector normalization technique known as PD-MEMLIN (Phoneme-Dependent Multi-Enviroment Models based LInear Normalization) has also shown to be effective. PD-MEMLIN models clean and noisy spaces employing Gaussian Mixture Models (GMMs), and estimates a set of linear compensation transformations to be used to clean the signal. The proper integration of both approaches is studied and the final design, PD-MEEMLIN (Phoneme-Dependent Multi-Enviroment Enhanced Models based LInear Normalization), confirms and improves the effectiveness of both approaches. The results obtained show that in very high degraded speech PD-MEEMLIN outperforms the SS by a range between 11.4% and 34.5%, and for PD-MEMLIN by a range between 11.7% and 24.84%. Furthemore, in moderate SNR, i.e. 15 or 20 dB, PD-MEEMLIN is as good as PD-MEMLIN and SS techniques.

1 Introduction

The robust speech recognition field plays a key rule in real environment applications. Noise can degrade speech signals causing nocive effects in Automatic Speech Recognition (ASR) tasks. Even though there have been great advances in the area, robustness still remains an issue. Noticing this problem, several techniques have been developed over the years, for instance the Spectral Subtraction algorithm (SS) [1]; and in the last decade, SPLICE (State Based Piecewise Linear Compensation for Enviroments) [2], PMC (Parallel Model Combination) [3], RATZ (multivariate Gaussian based cepstral normalization) [4] and RASTA (the RelAtive SpecTrAl Technique) [5]. The research that followed this evolution was to make a proper combination of algorithms in order to reduce the noise effects. For example, a good example is described in [6], where the core scheme is composed of a Continuous SS (CSS) and PMC.

J. Martí et al. (Eds.): IbPRIA 2007, Part II, LNCS 4478, pp. 1–8, 2007.

Persuing the same idea, a combination of the speech enhanced signal (represented by the SS method) and a feature vector normalization technique (PD-MEMLIN [7]) are presented in this work to improve the recognition accuracy of the speech recognition system in highly degraded environments [8,9]. The first technique was selected because of its implementation simplicity and good performance. The second one is an empirical vector normalization technique that has been compared against some other algorithms [8] and has obtained important improvements.

The organization of the paper is as follows. In Section 2, a brief overview of the SS and PD-MEMLIN. Section 3 details the new method PD-MEEMLIN. In Section 4, the experimental results are presented. Finally, the conclusions are shown in Section 5.

2   Spectral Subtraction and PD-MEMLIN

In order to evaluate the proposed integration, an ASR system is employed. In general, a pre-processing stage of the speech waveform is always desirable. The speech signal is divided into overlaped short windows, from which a set of coefficients, usually Mel Frequency Cepstral Coefficients (MFCCs)[10], are computed. The MFCCs are feeded to the training algorithm that calculates the acoustic models. The acoustic models used in this research are the Hidden Markov Models (HMMs), which are widely used to model statistically the behaviour of the phonetic events in speech [10]. The HMMs employ a sequence of hidden states which characterises how a random process (speech in this case) evolves in time. Although the states are not observable, a sequence of realizations from these states can always be obtained. Associated to each state there is a probability density function, normally a mixture of Gaussians. The criteria used to train the HMMs is the Maximum Likelihood, thus, the training process becomes an optimization problem that can be solved iteratively with the Baum and Welch algorithm.

2.1   Spectral Subtraction

The Spectral Subtraction (SS) algorithm is a simple and known speech enhancement technique. This research is based on the SS algorithm expressed in [9]. It has the property that it does not requiere the use of an explicit voice activity detector, as general SS algorithms does. The algorithm is based on the existance of peaks and valleys in a short noisy speech time subband power estimate [9]. The peaks correspond to the speech activity and the valleys are used to obtain an estimate of the subband noise power. So, a reliable noise estimation is obtained using a large enough window that can pemit the detection of any peak of speech activity.

As shown in Figure 1, this algorithm performs a modification of the short time spectral magnitude of the noisy speech signal during the process of enhancement. Hence, the output signal can be considered close to the speech clean signal when

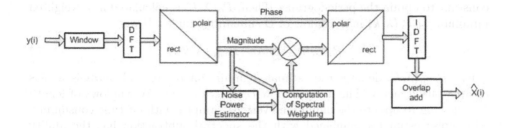

Fig. 1. Diagram of the Basic SS Method Used

synthesized. The appropriate computation of the spectral magnitude is obtained with the noise power estimate and the SS algorithm. Let, $y(i) = x(i) + n(i)$, where $y(i)$ is the noisy speech signal, $x(i)$ is the clean speech signal, $n(i)$ is the noise signal and i denotes the time index, $x(i)$ and $n(i)$ are statistically independent.

Figure 1 depicts the spectral analysis in which the frames in the time domain data are windowed and converted to frequency domain using the Discrete Fourier Transform (DFT) filter bank with W_{DFT} subbands and with a decimation/interpolation ratio named R [9]. After the computation of the noise power estimation and the spectral weightening, the enhanced signal can be transformed back to the time domain using the Inverse Discrete Fourier Transform (IDFT).

For the subtraction algorithm it is necessary to estimate the subband noise power $P_n(\lambda, k)$ and the short time signal power $\overline{|Y(\lambda, k)|^2}$, where λ is the decimated time index and k are the frequency bins of the DFT. A first order recursive network is used to obtain a short time signal power as shown in Equation 1.

$$\overline{|Y(\lambda, k)|^2} = \gamma * \overline{|Y(\lambda - 1, k)|^2} + (1 - \gamma) * |Y(\lambda, k)|^2. \tag{1}$$

Afterwards, the subtraction algorithm is accomplished using an oversubtraction factor $osub(\lambda, k)$ and a spectral flooring constant $(subf)$ [12]. The $osub(\lambda, k)$ factor is needed to eliminate the musical noise, and it is calculated as a function of the subband Signal to Noise Ratio $SNR_y(\lambda, k)$, λ and k (for a high SNR and high frequencies less $osub$ factor is required, for low SNR and low frequencies the $osub$ is less). The $subf$ constant helps the resultant spectral components from going below a minimum level. It is expressed as a fraction of the original noise power spectrum. The final relation of the spectral subtraction between $subf$ and $osub$ is defined by Equation 2.

$$|\hat{X}(\lambda, k)| = \begin{cases} \sqrt{subf * P_n(\lambda, k)} & \text{if } |Y(\lambda, k)| * Q(\lambda, k) \leq \sqrt{subf * P_n(\lambda, k)} \\ |Y(\lambda, k)| * Q(\lambda, k) & otherwise \end{cases} \tag{2}$$

where $Q(\lambda, k) = (1 - \sqrt{osub(\lambda, k) \frac{P_n(\lambda, k)}{|Y(\lambda, k)|^2}})$.

The missing element, $P_n(\lambda, k)$, is computed using the short subband signal power $P_y(\lambda, k)$ in a representation based on smoothed periodograms, as denoted by $P_y(\lambda, k) = \xi * P_y(\lambda - 1, k) + (1 - \xi) * |Y(\lambda, k)|^2$ where ξ represents the smoothing constant to obtain the periodograms. Then, $P_n(\lambda, k)$ is calculated as a weighted minimum of $P_x(\lambda, k)$ in a window of D subband samples. Hence,

$$P_n(\lambda, k) = omin \cdot P_{min}(\lambda, k), \tag{3}$$

where $P_{min}(\lambda, k)$ denotes the estimated minimum power and $omin$ is a bias compensation factor. The data window D is divided into W windows of length M, allowing to update the minimum every M samples without time consuming. This noise estimator combined with the spectral subtraction has the ability to preserve weak speech sounds. If a short time subband power is observed, the valleys correspond to the noisy speech signal and are used to estimate the subband noise power.

The last element to be calculated is the $SNR_y(\lambda, k)$ in Equation 4 that controls the oversubtraction factor $osub(\lambda, k)$.

$$SNR_y(\lambda, k) = 10 log \left(\frac{P_y(\lambda, k) - min(P_n(\lambda, k), P_y(\lambda, k))}{P_n(\lambda, k)} \right) \tag{4}$$

Up to this stage $osub(\lambda, k)$ and $subf$ can be selected and the spectral substraction algorithm can be computed.

2.2 PD-MEMLIN

PD-MEMLIN is an empirical feature vector normalization technique which uses stereo data in order to estimate the different compensation linear transformations in a previous training process. The clean feature space is modelled as a mixture of Gaussians for each phoneme. The noisy space is split in several basic acoustic environments and each environment is modelled as a mixture of Gaussians for each phoneme. The transformations are estimated for all basic environments between a clean phoneme Gaussian and a noisy Gaussian of the same phoneme.

PD-MEMLIN approximations. Clean feature vectors, x, are modelled using a GMM for each phoneme, ph

$$p_{ph}(x) = \sum_{s_x^{ph}} p(x|s_x^{ph})p(s_x^{ph}), \tag{5}$$

$$p(x|s_x^{ph}) = N(x; \mu_{s_x^{ph}}, \Sigma_{s_x^{ph}}), \tag{6}$$

where $\mu_{s_x^{ph}}$, $\Sigma_{s_x^{ph}}$, and $p(s_x^{ph})$ are the mean vector, the diagonal covariance matrix, and the a priori probability associated with the clean model Gaussian s_x^{ph} of the ph phoneme.

Noisy space is split into several basic environments, e, and the noisy feature vectors, y, are modeled as a GMM for each basic environment and phoneme

$$p_{e,ph}(y) = \sum_{s_y^{e,ph}} p(y|s_y^{e,ph})p(s_y^{e,ph}), \tag{7}$$

$$p(y|s_y^{e,ph}) = N(y; \mu_{s_y^{e,ph}}, \Sigma_{s_y^{e,ph}}), \tag{8}$$

where $s_y^{e,ph}$ denotes the corresponding Gaussian of the noisy model for the e basic environment and the ph phoneme; $\mu_{s_y^{e,ph}}$, $\Sigma_{s_y^{e,ph}}$, and $p(s_y^{e,ph})$ are the mean vector, the diagonal covariance matrix, and the a priori probability associated with $s_y^{e,ph}$.

Finally, clean feature vectors can be approximated as a linear function, f, of the noisy feature vector for each time frame t which depends on the basic environments, the phonemes and the clean and noisy model Gaussians: $x \approx f(y_t, s_x^{ph}, s_y^{e,ph}) = y_t - r_{s_x^{ph}, s_y^{e,ph}}$, where $r_{s_x^{ph}, s_y^{e,ph}}$ is the bias vector transformation between noisy and clean feature vectors for each pair of Gaussians, s_x^{ph} and $s_y^{e,ph}$.

PD-MEMLIN enhancement. With those approximations, PD-MEMLIN transforms the Minimum Mean Square Error (MMSE) estimation expression, $\hat{x}_t = E[x|y_t]$, into

$$\hat{x}_t = y_t - \sum_e \sum_{ph} \sum_{s_y^{e,ph}} \sum_{s_x^{ph}} r_{s_x^{ph}, s_y^{e,ph}} p(e|y_t) p(ph|y_t, e) p(s_y^e|y_t, e, ph) p(s_x^{ph}|y_t, e, ph, s_y^e), \tag{9}$$

where $p(e|y_t)$ is the a posteriori probability of the basic environment; $p(ph|y_t, e)$ is the a posteriori probability of the phoneme, given the noisy feature vector and the environment; $p(s_y^{e,ph}|y_t, e, ph)$ is the a posteriori probability of the noisy model Gaussian, $s_y^{e,ph}$, given the feature vector, y_t, the basic environment, e, and the phoneme, ph. To estimate those terms: $p(e|y_t)$, $p(ph|y_t, e)$ and $p(s_y^{e,ph}|y_t, e, ph)$, (7) and (8) are applied as described in [8]. Finally, the cross-probability model, $p(s_x^{ph}|y_t, e, ph, s_y^{e,ph})$, which is the probability of the clean model Gaussian, s_x^{ph}, given the feature vector, y_t, the basic environment, e, the phoneme, ph, and the noisy model Gaussian, $s_y^{e,ph}$, and the bias vector transformation, $r_{s_x^{ph}, s_y^{e,ph}}$, are estimated in a training phase using stereo data for each basic environment and phoneme [8].

3 PD-MEEMLIN

By combinig both techniques, PD-MEEMLIN arises as an empirical feature vector normalization which estimates different linear transformations as PD-MEMLIN, with the special property that a new enhanced space is obtained by applying SS to the noisy speech signal. Furthermore, this first-stage enhancement produces that the noisy space gets closer to the clean one, making the gap smaller among them. Figure 2 shows PD-MEEMLIN architecture.

Next, the architecture modules are explained:

- The SS-enhancement of the noisy speech signal is performed, $|\hat{X}(\lambda, k)|$, $P_n(\lambda, k)$ and $SNR_y(\lambda, k)$ are calculated.
- Given the clean speech signal and the enhanced noisy speech signal, the clean and noisy-enhanced GMMs are obtained.

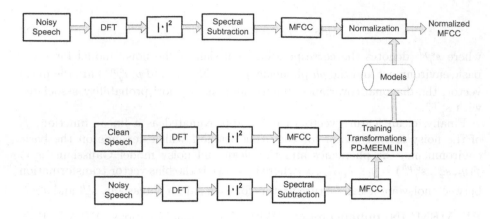

Fig. 2. PD-MEEMLIN Architecture

- In the testing stage, the noisy speech signal is also SS-enhanced and then normalized using PD-MEEMLIN.
- These normalized coefficients are forwarded to the decoder.

4   Experimental Results

All the experiments were performed employing the AURORA2 database [13], clean and noisy data based on TIDigits. Three types of noises were selected: Subway, Babble and Car from AURORA2, that go from -5dB to 20dB SNR. For every SNR the SS parameters $osub$ and $subf$ needs to be configured. The parameter $osub$ takes values from 0.4 to 4.6 (0.4 for 20dB, 0.7 for 15dB, 1.3 for 10dB, 2.21 for 5dB, 4.6 for 0dB and 4.6 for -5dB) and $subf$ values 0.03 or 0.04 (all SNR levels except 5dB optimised for 0.04). The phonetic acoustic models employed by PD-MEEMLIN are obtained from 22 phonemes and 1 silence. The models set is represented by a mixture of 32 Gaussians each. Besides, two new sets of each noise were used, PD-MEEMLIN needs one to estimate the enhanced-noisy model, and onother to obtain the normalized coefficients. The feature vectors for the recognition process are built by 12 normalized MFCCs followed by the energy coefficient, its time-derative Δ and the time-acceleration $\Delta\Delta$. For the training stage of the ASR system, the acoustic models of 22 phonemes and the silence consist on a three-state HMMs with a mixture of 8 Gaussians per state. The combined techniques show that for low noise conditions i.e. $SNR=10$, 15 or 20 dB, the difference between the original noisy space and the one approximated to the clean is similar. However, when the SNR is lower (-5dB or 0dB) the SS improves the performance of PD-MEMLIN. Comparing the combination of SS with PD-MEMLIN against the case where no techniques are applied, a significant improvement is shown. The results described before are presented in Tables 1, 2 and 3. The Tables show "Sent" that means complete utterances

Table 1. Comparative Table for the ASR working with Subway Noise

Subway SNR	ASR Sent %	ASR Word %	ASR+SS Sent %	ASR+SS Word %	ASR+PD-MEMLIN Sent %	ASR+PD-MEMLIN Word %	ASR+PD-MEEMLIN Sent %	ASR+PD-MEEMLIN Word %
-5dB	3.40	21.57	10.09	34.22	11.29	37.09	13.29	47.95
0dB	9.09	29.05	20.18	53.71	27.07	61.88	30.87	69.71
5dB	17.58	40.45	32.17	70.00	48.15	80.38	51.65	83.40
10dB	33.07	65.47	50.95	83.23	65.83	90.58	70.13	91.86
15dB	54.45	84.60	64.84	90.02	78.92	94.98	78.22	94.40
20dB	72.83	93.40	76.52	94.56	85.91	97.14	86.71	97.30

Table 2. Comparative Table for the ASR working with Babble Noise

Babble SNR	ASR Sent %	ASR Word %	ASR+SS Sent %	ASR+SS Word %	ASR+PD-MEMLIN Sent %	ASR+PD-MEMLIN Word %	ASR+PD-MEEMLIN Sent %	ASR+PD-MEEMLIN Word %
-5dB	4.60	23.08	7.59	29.78	8.49	29.54	6.69	37.79
0dB	11.29	30.41	15.98	44.49	23.48	55.72	20.08	59.50
5dB	20.58	44.23	30.37	65.11	48.75	80.55	49.25	83.70
10dB	40.86	72.85	50.25	80.93	74.93	94.20	69.33	91.48
15dB	69.03	90.54	69.93	90.56	84.12	96.86	81.32	95.54
20dB	82.42	96.17	83.52	95.84	88.91	98.09	88.01	97.98

Table 3. Comparative Table for the ASR working with Car Noise

Car SNR	ASR Sent %	ASR Word %	ASR+SS Sent %	ASR+SS Word %	ASR+PD-MEMLIN Sent %	ASR+PD-MEMLIN Word %	ASR+PD-MEEMLIN Sent %	ASR+PD-MEEMLIN Word %
-5dB	3.10	20.18	10.49	28.87	6.79	25.90	13.89	44.31
0dB	8.09	26.18	18.58	46.70	23.58	52.67	35.16	70.47
5dB	14.99	35.34	31.47	66.50	51.95	82.34	58.64	86.30
10dB	28.77	58.13	54.25	82.72	70.83	92.15	70.93	91.90
15dB	57.84	84.04	68.03	90.51	82.02	96.16	81.42	95.86
20dB	78.32	94.61	81.42	95.30	87.01	97.44	87.81	97.77

percentage correctly recognised, and "Word" indicates the words percentage correctly recognised. The gap between the clean and the noisy model, for the very high degraded speech, had been shortened due to the advantages of both techniques. When PD-MEEMLIN is employed the performance is between 11.7% and 24.84% better than PD-MEMLIN, and between 11.4% and 34.5% better than SS.

5   Conclusions

In this work a robust normalization technique, PD-MEEMLIN, has been presented by cascading a speech enhancement method (SS) followed by a feature vector normalization algorithm (PD-MEMLIN). The results of PD-MEEMLIN show a better performance than SS and PD-MEMLIN for a very high degraded speech. This improvement is made by the enhancement of the noisy models employed by PD-MEMLIN, which are close to the original clean model.

References

1. Boll, S.: Suppression of Acoustic Noise in Speech Using Spectral Subtraction. IEEE Trans ASSP 27, 113–120 (1979)
2. Droppo, J., Deng, L., Acero, A.: Evaluation of the Splice Algorithm on the Aurora2 Database. In: Proc. Eurospeech, vol. 1 (2001)
3. Gales, M.J.F., Young, S.: Cepstral Parameter Compensation for HMM Recognition in Noise. Speech Communication 12(3), 231–239 (1993)
4. Moreno, P.J., Raj, B., Gouvea, E., Stern, R.M.: Multivariate-Gaussian-Based Cepstral Normalization for Robust Speech Recognition. Department of Electrical and Computer Engineering & School of Computer Science. Carnegie Mellon University
5. Hermansky, H., Morgan, N.: RASTA Processing of Speech. IEEE Transactions on Speech and Audio Processing 2(4), 578–589 (1994)
6. Nolazco-Flores, J., Young, S.: Continuous Speech Recognition in Noise Using Spectral Subtraction and HMM adaptation. In: ICASSP, pp. I.409–I.412 (1994)
7. Buera, L., Lleida, E., Miguel, A., Ortega, A.: Multienvironment Models Based LInear Normalization for Speech Recognition in Car Conditions. In: Proc. ICASSP (2004)
8. Buera, L., Lleida, E., Miguel, A., Ortega, A.: Robust Speech Recognition in Cars Using Phoneme Dependent Multienvironment LInear Normalization. In: Proceedings of Interspeech. Lisboa, Portugal, pp. 381–384 (2005)
9. Martin, R.: Spectral Subtraction Based on Minimum Statistics. In: Proc. Eur. Signal Processing Conf. pp. 1182–1185 (1994)
10. Huang, X., Acero, A., Hon, H.-W.: Spoken Language Processing, pp. 504–512. Prentice Hall PTR, United States (2001)
11. Martin, R.: Noise Power Spectral Density Estimation Based on Optimal Smoothing and Minimum Statistics. IEEE Transactions on Speech and Audio Processing, vol. 9(5) (2000)
12. Berouti, M., Schwartz, R., Makhoul, J.: Enhancement of Speech Corrupted by Acoustic Noise. In: Proc. IEEE Conf. ASSP, pp. 208–211 (1979)
13. Hirsch, H.G., Pearce, D.: The AURORA Experimental Framework for the Performance Evaluations of Speech Recognition Systems Under Noisy Condidions. In: ISCA ITRW ASR2000, Automatic Speech Recognition: Challenges for the Next Millennium, Paris, France (2000)

Shadow Resistant Road Segmentation from a Mobile Monocular System

José Manuel Álvarez, Antonio M. López, and Ramon Baldrich

Computer Vision Center and Computer Science Dpt.,
Universitat Autònoma de Barcelona
Edifici O, 08193 Bellaterra, Barcelona, Spain
{jalvarez,antonio,ramon}@cvc.uab.es
http://www.cvc.uab.es/adas

Abstract. An essential functionality for advanced driver assistance systems (ADAS) is road segmentation, which directly supports ADAS applications like road departure warning and is an invaluable background segmentation stage for other functionalities as vehicle detection. Unfortunately, road segmentation is far from being trivial since the road is in an outdoor scenario imaged from a mobile platform. For instance, shadows are a relevant problem for segmentation. The usual approaches are ad hoc mechanisms, applied after an initial segmentation step, that try to recover road patches not included as segmented road for being in shadow. In this paper we argue that by using a different feature space to perform the segmentation we can minimize the problem of shadows from the very beginning. Rather than the usual segmentation in a color space we propose segmentation in a shadowless image which is computable in real–time using a color camera. The paper presents comparative results for both asphalted and non–asphalted roads, showing the benefits of the proposal in presence of shadows and vehicles.

1 Introduction

Advanced driver assistance systems (ADAS) arise as a contribution to traffic safety, a major social issue in modern countries. The functionalities required to build such systems can be addressed by computer vision techniques, which have many advantages over using active sensors (e.g. radar, lidar). Some of them are: higher resolution, richness of features (color, texture), low cost, easy aesthetic integration, non–intrusive nature, low power consumption, and besides, some functionalities can only be addressed by interpreting visual information. A relevant functionality is road segmentation which supports ADAS applications like road departure warning. Moreover, it is an invaluable background segmentation stage for other functionalities as vehicle and pedestrian detection, since knowing the road surface considerably reduces the image region to search for such objects, thus, allowing real–time and reducing false detections.

Our interest is real–time segmentation of road surfaces, both non–asphalted and asphalted, using a single forward facing color camera placed at the windshield of a vehicle. However, road segmentation is far from being trivial since the

J. Martí et al. (Eds.): IbPRIA 2007, Part II, LNCS 4478, pp. 9–16, 2007.

Fig. 1. Roads with shadows

road is in an outdoor scenario imaged from a mobile platform. Hence, we deal with a continuously changing background, the presence of different vehicles of unknown movement, different road shapes with worn–out asphalt (or not asphalted at all), and different illumination conditions. For instance, a particularly relevant problem is the presence of shadows (Fig. 1). The usual approaches found in the literature are ad hoc mechanisms applied after an initial segmentation step (e.g. [1,2,3]). These mechanisms try to recover road patches not included as segmented road for being in shadow. In this paper we argue that by using a different feature space to perform the segmentation we can minimize the problem of shadows from the very beginning. Rather than the usual segmentation in a color space, we propose segmentation in a shadowless image, which is computable in real–time using a color camera. In particular, we use the grey–scale illuminant invariant image introduced in [4], $\mathcal{I}$ from now on.

In Sect. 2 we summarize the formulation of $\mathcal{I}$. Moreover, we also show that automatic shutter, needed outdoors to avoid global over/under–exposure, fits well in such formulation. In order to illustrate the usefulness of $\mathcal{I}$, in Sect. 3 we propose a segmentation algorithm based on standard region growing applied to $\mathcal{I}$. We remark that we do not recover a shadow–free color image from the original, which would result in too large processing time for the road segmentation problem. Section 4 presents comparative road segmentation results in presence of shadows and vehicles, both in asphalted and non–asphalted roads, confirming the validity of our hypothesis. Finally, conclusions are drawn in Sect. 5.

2   Illuminant Invariant Image

Image formation models are defined in terms of the interaction between the spectral power distribution of illumination, surface reflectance and spectral sensitivity of the imaging sensors. *Finlayson et al.* [4] show that under the assumptions of *Planckian illumination*, *Lambertian surfaces* and having three different *narrow band sensors*, it is possible to obtain a shadow–free color image. We are not interested in such image since it requires very large processing time to be recovered. We focus on an illuminant invariant image ($\mathcal{I}$) that is obtained at the first stage of the shadow–free color image recovering process. We briefly expose here the idea behind $\mathcal{I}$ and refer to [4] for details.

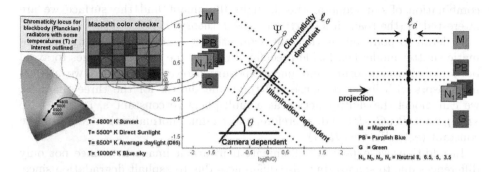

Fig. 2. Ideal log–log chromaticity plot. A Lambertian surface patch of a given chromaticity under a Planckian illumination is represented by a point. By changing the color temperature of the Planckian illuminator we obtain a straight line associated to the patch. Lambertian surface patches of different chromaticity have different associated lines. All these lines form a family of parallel lines, namely Ψ_θ. Let ℓ_θ be a line perpendicular to Ψ_θ and θ the angle between ℓ_θ and the horizontal axis. Then, by projection, we have a one–to–one correspondence between points in ℓ_θ and straight lines of Ψ_θ, so that ℓ_θ preserves the differences regarding chromaticity but removes differences due to illumination changes assuming Planckian radiators.

Let us denote by R, G, B the usual color channels and assume a normalizing channel (or combination of channels), e.g. without losing generality let us choose G as such normalizing channel. Then, under the assumptions regarding the sensors, the surfaces and the illuminators, if we perform a plot of $r = \log(R/G)$ vs. $b = \log(B/G)$ for a set of surfaces of different chromaticity under different illuminants, we would obtain a result similar to the one in Fig. 2. This means that we obtain an axis, ℓ_θ, where a surface under different illuminations is represented by the same point, while moving along ℓ_θ implies to change the surface chromaticity. In other words, ℓ_θ can be seen as a grey–level axis where each grey level corresponds to a surface chromaticity, independently of the surface illumination. Therefore, we obtain an illuminant invariant image, $\mathcal{I}(\mathbf{p})$, by taking each pixel $\mathbf{p} = (x, y)$ of the original color image, $I_{RGB}(\mathbf{p}) = (R(\mathbf{p}), G(\mathbf{p}), B(\mathbf{p}))$, computing $\mathbf{p}' = (r(\mathbf{p}), b(\mathbf{p}))$ and projecting $\mathbf{p}'$ onto ℓ_θ according to θ (a camera dependent constant angle). The reason for $\mathcal{I}$ being shadow–free is, roughly, that non–shadow surface areas are illuminated by both direct sunlight and skylight (a sort of scattered ambient light), while areas in the umbra are only illuminated by skylight. Since both, skylight alone and with sunlight addition, can be considered Planckian illuminations [5], areas of the same chromaticity ideally project onto the same point in ℓ_θ, no matter if the areas are in shadow or not.

Given this result, the first question is whether the working assumptions are realistic or not. In fact, *Finlayson et al.* [4] show examples where, despite the departures from the assumptions that are found in practice, the obtained results are quite good. We will see in Sect. 4 that this holds in our case, i.e., the combination of our camera, the daylight illuminant and the surface we are interested in (the road) fits pretty well the $\mathcal{I}$ theory.

A detail to point out is that our acquisition system was operating in automatic shutter mode: i.e., inside predefined ranges, the shutter changes to avoid both global overexposure and underexposure. However, provided we are using sensors with linear response and the same shutter for the three channels, we can model the shutter action as a multiplicative constant s, i.e., we have $sI_{RGB} = (sR, sG, sB)$ and, therefore, the channel normalization removes the constant (e.g. $sR/sG = R/G$).

In addition, we expect the illumination invariant image to reduce not only differences due to shadow but also differences due to asphalt degradation since, at the resolution we work, they are pretty analogous to just intensity changes. Note that the whole intensity axis is equivalent to a single chromaticity, i.e., all the patches of the last row of the Macbeth color checker in Fig. 2 (N_i) project to the same point of ℓ_θ.

3   Road Segmentation

With the aim of evaluating the suitability of the illuminant invariant image we have devised a relatively simple segmentation method based on region growing [6], sketched in Fig. 3. This is, we do not claim that the proposed segmentation is the best, but one of the most simplest that can be expected to work in our problem. We emphasize that our aim is to show the suitability of $\mathcal{I}$ for road segmentation and we think that providing good results can be a proof of it, even using such simple segmentation approach.

The region growing uses a very simple *aggregation criterium*: if $\mathbf{p} = (x, y)$ is a pixel already classified as of the road, any other pixel $\mathbf{p}_n = (x_n, y_n)$ of its 8–connected neighborhood is classified as road one if

$$diss(\mathbf{p}, \mathbf{p}_n) < t_{agg} \ , \tag{1}$$

where $diss(\mathbf{p}, \mathbf{p}_n)$ is the dissimilarity metric for the aggregation and t_{agg} a threshold that fixes the maximum dissimilarity to consider two connected pixels as of the same region. To prove the usefulness of $\mathcal{I}$ we use the simplest dissimilarity based on grey levels, i.e.,

$$diss_\mathcal{I}(\mathbf{p}, \mathbf{p}_n) = |\mathcal{I}(\mathbf{p}) - \mathcal{I}(\mathbf{p}_n)| \ . \tag{2}$$

Of course, region growing needs initialization, i.e., the so–called *seeds*. Currently, such seeds are taken from fixed positions at the bottom region of the image (Fig. 3), i.e., we assume that such region is part of the road. In fact, the lowest row of the image corresponds to a distance of about 4 meters away from the vehicle, thus, it is a reasonable assumption most of the time (other proposals require to see the full road free at the start up of the system, e.g. [1]).

In order to compute the angle θ corresponding to our camera, we have followed two approaches. One is the proposal in [7], based on acquiring images of

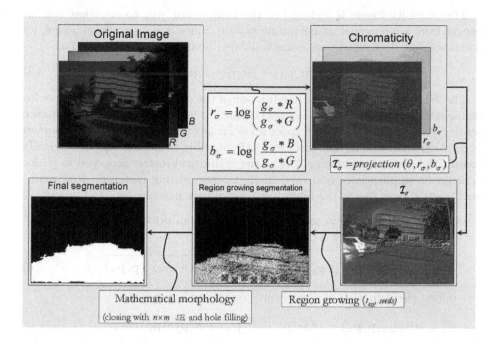

Fig. 3. Proposed algorithm. In all our experiments we have fixed values for the algorithm parameters: $\sigma = 0.5$ for Gaussian smoothing (Gaussian kernel, g_σ, discretized in a 3×3 window for convolution '$*$'); $\theta = 38°$; $t_{agg} = 0,007$ and seven *seeds* placed at the squares pointed out in the region growing result; structuring element (SE) of $n \times m = 5 \times 3$. Notice that we apply some mathematical morphology just to fill in some small gaps and thin grooves.

the Macbeth color checker under different day time illuminations and using the (r,b)–plot to obtain θ. The other approach consists in taking a few road images with shadows and use them as positive examples to find θ providing the best shadow–free images for all the examples. The values of θ obtained from the two calibration methods basically give rise to the same segmentation results. We have taken θ from the example–based calibration because it provides slightly better segmentations. Besides, although not proposed in the original formulation of $\mathcal{I}$, before computing it we regularize the input image I_{RGB} by a small amount of Gaussian smoothing (the same for each color channel).

4   Results

In this section we present comparative results based on the region growing algorithm introduced in Sect. 3 for three different feature spaces: intensity image (I; also called luminance or brightness); hue–saturation–intensity (HSI) color space; and the illuminant invariant image ($\mathcal{I}$).

The intensity image is included in the comparison just to see what can we expect from a monocular monochrome system. Since it is a grey level image, its corresponding dissimilarity measure is defined analogously to Eq. (2), i.e.:

$$diss_I(\mathbf{p}, \mathbf{p}_n) = |I(\mathbf{p}) - I(\mathbf{p}_n)| \ . \tag{3}$$

The HSI space is chosen because it is one of the most accepted color spaces for segmentation purposes [8]. The reason is that by having separated chrominance (H & S) and intensity (I) such space allows reasoning in a closer way to human perception than others. For instance, it is possible to define a psychologically meaningful distance between colors as the cylindrical metric proposed in [8] for multimedia applications, and used in [1] for segmenting non–asphalted roads. Such metric gives rise to the following dissimilarity measure for HSI space:

- Case *achromatic pixels*: use only the definition of $diss_I$ given in Eq. (3).
- Case *chromatic pixels*:

$$diss_{HSI}(\mathbf{p}, \mathbf{p}_n) = \sqrt{diss_{HS}^2(\mathbf{p}, \mathbf{p}_n) + diss_I^2(\mathbf{p}, \mathbf{p}_n)} \ , \tag{4}$$

taking the definition of $diss_I$ from Eq. (3), and given

$$diss_{HS}(\mathbf{p}, \mathbf{p}_n) = \sqrt{S^2(\mathbf{p}) + S^2(\mathbf{p}_n) + S(\mathbf{p})S(\mathbf{p}_n)\cos\varphi} \ ,$$

being $\qquad \varphi = \begin{cases} diss_H(\mathbf{p}, \mathbf{p}_n) & \text{if } diss_H(\mathbf{p}, \mathbf{p}_n) < 180° \ , \\ 360° - diss_H(\mathbf{p}, \mathbf{p}_n) & \text{otherwise} \ , \end{cases}$

for $\ diss_H(\mathbf{p}, \mathbf{p}_n) = |H(\mathbf{p}) - H(\mathbf{p}_n)| \ ,$

where the different criterion regarding chromaticity is used to take into account the fact that hue value (H) is meaningless when the intensity (I) is very low or very high, or when the saturation (S) is very low. For such cases only intensity is taken into account for aggregation. We use the proposal in [8,1] to define the frontier of meaningful hue, i.e., $\mathbf{p}$ is an achromatic pixel if either $I(\mathbf{p}) > 0.9I_{max}$ or $I(\mathbf{p}) < 0.1I_{max}$ or $S(\mathbf{p}) < 0.1S_{max}$, where I_{max} and S_{max} represent the maximum intensity and saturation values, respectively.

In summary, to compute Eq. (1) we use Eq. (2) for $\mathcal{I}$ with threshold $t_{agg,\mathcal{I}}$, Eq. (3) for I with threshold $t_{agg,I}$, and Eq. (4) for HSI with thresholds $t_{agg,ch}$ (chromatic case) and $t_{agg,ach}$ (achromatic case). Figure 4 shows the results obtained for examples of both asphalted and non–asphalted roads. We have manually set the $t_{agg,\mathcal{I}}$, $t_{agg,I}$, and $t_{agg,ch}, t_{agg,ach}$ parameters to obtain the best results for each feature space, but such values are not changed from image to image, i.e., all the frames of our sequences have been processed with them fixed.

These results suggest that $\mathcal{I}$ is a more suitable feature space for road segmentation than the others. Road surface is well recovered most of the times, with the segmentation stopping at road limits and vehicles[1], even with a simple

---

[1] Other on going experiments, not included here for space restrictions, also show that segmentation is quite stable regarding the chosen aggregation threshold as well as the number and position of seeds, much more stable than both I and HSI.

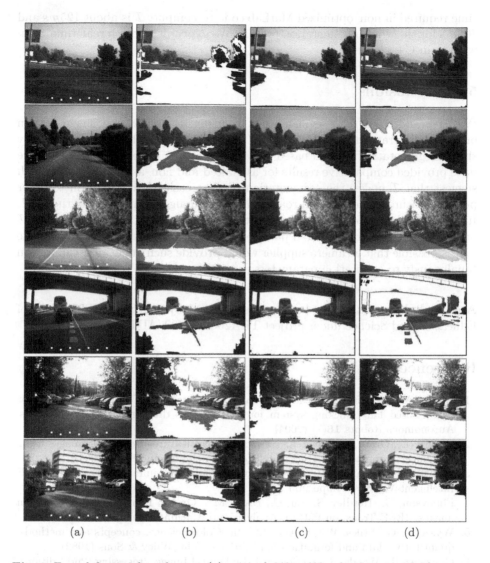

(a)   (b)   (c)   (d)

Fig. 4. From left to right columns: (a) original 640 × 480 color image with the seven used seeds marked in white; (b) segmentation using I with $t_{agg,I} = 0,008$; (c) segmentation using $\mathcal{I}$ with $t_{agg,\mathcal{I}} = 0,003$; (d) segmentation using HSI with $t_{agg,ch} = 0,08$, and $t_{agg,ach} = 0,008$. The white pixels over the original image correspond to the segmentation results. The top four rows correspond to asphalted roads and the rest to non–asphalted areas of a parking.

segmentation method. Now, such segmentation can be augmented with road shape models like in [9,10] with the aim of estimating the not seen road in case of many vehicles in the scene. As a result, road limits and road curvature obtained will be useful for applications as road departure warning. The processing time required in non–optimized MatLab code to compute $\mathcal{I}$ is about $125ms$ and $700ms$ for the whole segmentation process. We expect it to reach real–time when written in C++ code.

5 Conclusions

We have addressed road segmentation by using a shadow–free image $(\mathcal{I})$. In order to illustrate the suitability of $\mathcal{I}$ for such task we have devised a very simple segmentation method based on region growing. By using this method we have provided comparative results for asphalted and non–asphalted roads which suggest that $\mathcal{I}$ makes the segmentation process easier in comparison to other popular feature space found in road segmentation algorithms, namely the HSI. In addition, the process can run in real–time. In fact, since the computation of $\mathcal{I}$ only depends on a precalculated parameter, i.e., the camera characteristic angle θ, it is possible that a camera supplier would provide such angle after calibration (analogously to calibration parameters provided with stereo rigs).

Acknowledgments. This work was supported by the Spanish Ministry of Education and Science under project TRA2004-06702/AUT.

References

1. Sotelo, M., Rodriguez, F., Magdalena, L., Bergasa, L., Boquete, L.: A color vision-based lane tracking system for autonomous driving in unmarked roads. Autonomous Robots **16**(1) (2004)
2. Rotaru, C., Graf, T., Zhang, J.: Extracting road features from color images using a cognitive approach. In: IEEE Intelligent Vehicles Symposium. (2004)
3. Ramstrom, O., Christensen, H.: A method for following unmarked roads. In: IEEE Intelligent Vehicles Symposium. (2005)
4. Finlayson, G., Hordley, S., Lu, C., Drew, M.: On the removal of shadows from images. IEEE Trans. on Pattern Analysis and Machine Intelligence **28**(1) (2006)
5. Wyszecki, G., Stiles, W.: Section 1.2. In: Color science: concepts and methods, quantitative data and formulae (2nd Edition). John Wiley & Sons (1982)
6. Gonzalez, R., Woods, R.: Section 10.4. In: Digital Image Processing (2nd Edition). Prentice Hall (2002)
7. Finlayson, G., Hordley, S., Drew, M.: Removing shadows from images. In: European Conference on Computer Vision. (2002)
8. Ikonomakis, N., Plataniotis, K., Venetsanopoulos, A.: Color image segmentation for multimedia applications. Journal of Intelligent Robotics Systems **28**(1-2) (2000)
9. He, Y., Wang, H., Zhang, B.: Color–based road detection in urban traffic scenes. IEEE Transactions on Intelligent Transportation Systems **5**(24) (2004)
10. Lombardi, P., Zanin, M., Messelodi, S.: Switching models for vision-based on–board road detection. In: International IEEE Conference on Intelligent Transportation Systems. (2005)

Mosaicking Cluttered Ground Planes Based on Stereo Vision

José Gaspar[1], Miguel Realpe[2], Boris Vintimilla[2], and José Santos-Victor[1]

[1] Computer Vision Laboratory Inst. for Systems and Robotics Instituto Superior
Técnico Lisboa, Portugal
{jag,jasv}@isr.ist.utl.pt
[2] Vision and Robotics Center Dept. of Electrical and Computer Science Eng.
Escuela Superior Politécnica del Litoral Guayaquil, Ecuador
{mrealpe,boris.vintimilla}@fiec.espol.edu.ec

Abstract. Recent stereo cameras provide reliable 3D reconstructions.
These are useful for selecting ground-plane points, register them and
building mosaics of cluttered ground planes. In this paper we propose
a 2D Iterated Closest Point (ICP) registration method, based on the
distance transform, combined with a fine-tuning-registration step using
directly the image data. Experiments with real data show that ICP is
robust to 3D reconstruction differences due to motion and the fine tuning
step minimizes the effect of the uncertainty in the 3D reconstructions.

1 Introduction

In this paper we approach the problem of building mosaics, i.e. image montages,
of cluttered ground planes, using stereo vision on-board of a wheeled mobile
robot. Mosaics are useful for the navigation of robots and for building human-
robot interfaces. One clear advantage of mosaics is the simple representation of
robot localization and motion: they are simply 2D rigid transformations.

Many advances have been made recently in vision based navigation. Flexible (and precise) tracking and reconstruction of visual features, using particle
filters, allowed real time Simultaneous Localization and Map Building (SLAM)
[1]. The introduction of scale-invariant visual features brought more robustness
and allowed very inexpensive navigation solutions [2,3]. Despite being effective,
these navigation modalities lack building dense scene representations convenient
for intuitive human-robot interfaces. Recent commercial stereo cameras came
to help by giving locally dense 3D scene reconstructions. Iterative methods for
matching points and estimation their rigid motion, allow registering the local
reconstructions and obtaining global scene representations. The Iterated Closest
Point (ICP) [4] is one such method that we explore in this work.

The ICP basic algorithm has been extended in a number of ways. Examples of
improvements are robustifying the algorithm to the influence of features lacking
correspondences or using weighted metrics to trade-off distance and feature similarity [5]. More recent improvements target real time implementations, matching
shapes with defects or mixing probabilistic matching metrics with saturations
to minimize the effect of outliers [6,7,8]. In our case, the wheeled mobile robots

J. Martí et al. (Eds.): IbPRIA 2007, Part II, LNCS 4478, pp. 17–24, 2007.

motion on the ground plane allows searching for 2D, instead of 3D, registrations. Hence we follow a 2D ICP methodology, but we take a computer vision approach, namely registering clouds of points using the distance transform [9].

Stereo cameras allow selecting ground-plane points, registering them and then building the ground plane mosaic. Stereo reconstruction is therefore an advantage, however some specific issues arise about its use. For example, the discrete nature of the imaging process, and the variable imaging of objects and occlusions due to robot motion, imply uncertainties on the 3D reconstruction. Hence, the registration of 3D data propagates also some intrinsic uncertainty. The selection of ground-plane data, is convenient for complexity reduction, however a question of the sparsity of data arises. In our work we investigate robust methodologies to deal with these issues, and in particular we investigate whether resorting to the raw image data can help minimizing error propagation.

The paper is structured as follows: Sec.2 details the mosaicking problem and introduces our approach to solve it; Sec.3 shows how we build the orthographic views of the ground plane; Sec.4 details the optimization functionals associated to mosaic construction; Sec.5 is the results section; Finally in Sec.6 we draw some conclusions and guidelines for future work.

2   Problem Description

The main objective of our work is mosaicking (mapping) the ground plane considering that it can be cluttered with objects such as furniture. The sensor is a static trinocular-stereo camera mounted on a wheeled mobile robot. The stereo camera gives 3D clouds of points in the camera coordinate system, i.e. a mobile frame changed by the robot motion. See Fig. 1

The ground plane constraint implies that the relationships between camera coordinate systems are 2D rigid motions. As in general the camera is not aligned with the floor, i.e. the camera coordinate system does not have two axis parallel to the ground plane, the relationships do not clearly show their 2D nature. In order to make clear the 2D nature of the problem, we define a new coordinate system aligned with the ground plane (three user-selected well-separated ground points are sufficient for this purpose).

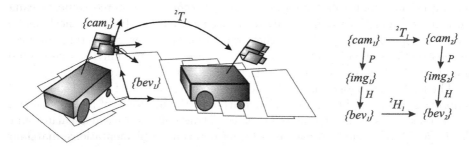

Fig. 1. Mosaicking ground planes: Stereo camera, Image and BEV coordinate systems

Commercial stereo cameras give dense reconstructions. For example, for each image feature, such as a corner or an edge point, there are usually about 20 to 30 reconstructed 3D points (the exact number depend on the size of the correlation windows). Considering standard registration methods as Iterated Closest Point (ICP, [4]), the large clouds of 3D points imply large computational costs. Hence, we choose to work with a subset of the data, namely by selecting just points of the ground plane. The 2D clouds of points can therefore be registered with a 2D ICP method.

Noting that each 3D cloud of points results from stereo images registration, the process of registering consecutive clouds of points has some error propagated from the cloud reconstruction. In order to minimize the error propagation, we add a fine tuning image-based registration process after the initial registration by a 2D ICP method. The image-based registration is a 2D rigid transformation in Bird's Eye Views (BEV), i.e. orthographic images of the ground plane. BEV images can be obtained also knowing some ground points and the projection geometry. To maintain consistent units system, despite having metric values in the 3D clouds of points, we choose to process both the 2D ICP and the image registration in the pixel metric system, i.e. the same as the raw data.

In summary our approach encompasses two main steps: (i) selection of ground points and 2D ICP, (ii) BEV image registration. Despite the 2D methodology notice that the 3D data is a principal component. The 3D sensor allows selecting the ground plane data, which is useful not only for using a faster 2D ICP method but mainly for registering the ground plane images without considering the distracting (biasing) non-ground regions.

3   Obtaining Bird's Eye Views (BEV)

The motion of the robot implies a motion of the trinocular camera which we denote as $^2T_1$. The indexes 1 and 2 indicate two consecutive times, and tag also the coordinate systems at the different times, e.g. the camera frames $\{cam_1\}$ and $\{cam_2\}$. The image plane defines new coordinate systems, $\{img_1\}$ and $\{img_2\}$, and the BEV defines another ones, $\{bev_1\}$ and $\{bev_2\}$. See Fig. 1.

The projection matrix, P relating $\{cam_i\}$ and $\{img_i\}$ is given by the camera manufacturer or by a standard calibration procedure [10]. In this section we are mainly concerned with obtaining the homography, H relating the image plane with the BEV.

The BEV dewarping, H is defined by back-projecting to the ground plane four image points (appendix A details the back-projection matrix, P^*). The four image points are chosen so to comprehend most of the field of view imaging the ground plane. The region close to the horizon line is discarded due to poor resolution. Scaling is chosen such that it preserves the largest resolution available, i.e. no image-data loss due to sub sampling.

Is interesting to note that the knowledge of the 3D camera-motion, $^2T_1$ directly gives the BEV 2D rigid transformation, $^2H_1$ (see Fig. 1):

$$^2H_1 = H.P.^2T_1.P^*.H^{-1} \tag{1}$$

The inverse transformation, i.e. obtaining $^2T_1$ from $^2H_1$, is also possible since the motion is constrained to the ground plane: a 2D frame is transformed using $^2H_1$, and the missing dimension can be recoved e.g. by the relationship of the cross products of the vectors of the frame. In other words, estimating the camera motion in the camera frame is equivalent to estimating motion in the BEV frame.

4   Mosaic Construction

The input data for mosaic creation consists of BEV images, I_t and I_{t+1}, and clouds of ground-points projected in the BEV coordinate system, $\{[u\ v]_{t,i}^T\}$ and $\{[u\ v]_{t+1,i}^T\}$. In this frame, the camera motion is a 2D rigid translation, $^2H_1$, which can be represented by three parameters $\mu = [\delta u\ \delta v\ \delta\theta]$. We want to find μ such that the clouds of points match as close as possible:

$$\mu^* = \arg_\mu \min \sum_i \left\| [u\ v]_{t+1,j}^T - Rot(\delta\theta).[u\ v]_{t,i}^T - [\delta u\ \delta v]^T \right\|^2 \qquad (2)$$

The correspondence between points of the clouds, i.e. finding the index j matching i, is based on the nearest neighbor rule, as with ICP. However in our case the matching is implemented using a distance transform. Using a distance transform allows matching 2D shapes as a 2D lookup-table reading of nearest neighbors and distances to them, instead of a combinatorial search between the clouds of points [9]. In order to smooth the cost functional and deal with the small shape differences (e.g. locally regular patterns generated by dense stereo reconstruction) we read interpolated-distance-values from the distance transform, and in order to deal with large differences (e.g. clouds leaving the field of view) we place a saturation on the distance transform (constant distances imply no influence in the optimization process).

Given the first estimation of the 2D motion and the knowledge of ground points, we can now fine tune the registration using ground plane image data:

$$\mu^* = \arg_\mu \min \sum_i \left\| I_{t+1}(Rot(\delta\theta).[u\ v]_{t,i}^T + [\delta u\ \delta v]^T) - I_t([u\ v]_{t,i}^T) \right\|^2 \qquad (3)$$

Despite the fine tuning nature of this process, there is still possible to have regions of one image that got out of the field of view in the next image. The non-matched pixels get comparison values given by the closest matchings in an initial stage. These values are updated in the optimization process only if true matchings become possible, i.e. a new hypothetical 2D rigid motion between BEV images can bring to visibility unmatched points. This allows further smoothing the optimization process for points near the border of the field of view.

Finally, given the 2D rigid motion, the mosaic composition is just an accumulation of images. A growing 2D image buffer is defined such as to hold image points of the ground plane along the robot traveled path.

5   Experimental Results

In our experiments we use the Point Grey's Digiclops trinocular camera (Fig. 2a). This stereo camera encompasses three 640 × 480 color cameras arranged in an L-shape form (top-left, bottom-left and bottom-right), with 10 cm baselines. The robot carrying the camera follows a circular path with a 9.4 meters perimeter. 215 stereo images are acquired along the path.

Figure 2 illustrates the dewarping to BEV images and the registration of the dewarped images. The BEV images are 1568 × 855. One meter measured in the ground plane is equivalent to 318 pixels the BEV (this calibration information derives directly from the stereo-camera calibration). The registration is illustrated by super-imposing consecutive BEV images after applying to the first

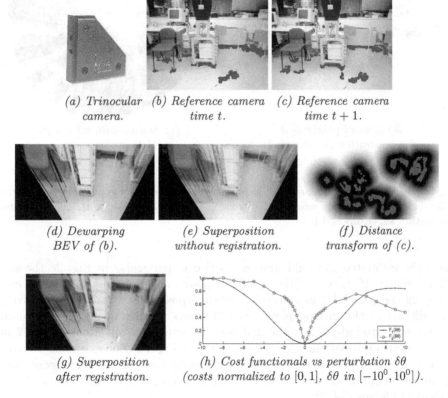

(a) Trinocular camera.   *(b) Reference camera time t.*   *(c) Reference camera time t + 1.*

(d) Dewarping BEV of (b).   *(e) Superposition without registration.*   *(f) Distance transform of (c).*

(g) Superposition after registration.   *(h) Cost functionals vs perturbation $\delta\theta$ (costs normalized to $[0,1]$, $\delta\theta$ in $[-10^0, 10^0]$).*

Fig. 2. BEV dewarping and registration. (a) Stereo camera. (b) and (c) show reconstructed ground-points (blue-points) in the reference camera of the stereo setup. (d) BEV dewarping of (b). (e) superposition of BEVs without registration (notice the blur). (f) distance transform of the ground points seen in (c). (g) correct superposition of all ground points after registration. (h) comparison of the cost functionals by perturbing $\delta\theta$ about the minimizing point: registration using Eq.2 has a larger convergence region (dots plot) but the image-based registration, Eq.3 is more precise (circles plot).

(a) View of the working space and of the robot.

*(b) Ground points used
for registration (landmarks)*

*(c) Mosaic with all imaging
data superimposed*

Fig. 3. View of the working area (a), mosaic of the ground points chosen as landmarks while registering the sequence of BEV images (b) and a mosaic with all the visual information superimposed (c).

image the estimated 2D rigid motion. Notice in particular in Fig. 2c the significant shape differences of the clouds of points as compared to Fig. 2b, and in Fig. 2g the graceful degradation of the superposition for points progressively more distant to the ground plane. Fig. 2f shows the distance transform used for matching ground-points. The matching is performed repeatedly in Eq.2 in order to obtain the optimal registration shown in Fig. 2g. The existence of local-clusters of points, instead of isolated points, motivates a wider-convergence but less precise registration which can be improved resorting to image data (Eq.3) as shown in figure Fig. 2h.

The mosaicking of BEVs shows clearly the precision of the registration process. In particular shows that the image-based registration improves significantly the 2D motion estimation. After one complete circle described by the robot, the 2D ICP registration gives about 2.7 meters localization error (28% error over path length) which is improved to about 0.23 meters (2.3% error over path length) when using image-based registration. This allows obtaining a mosaic closing almost perfectly a circular path (see Fig. 3c). Notice that only the ground points are registered in the mosaic, and thus all other points should exhibit artifacts due to parallax.

6 Conclusions

In this paper we proposed a method for creating mosaics of cluttered ground planes. Current stereo cameras provide 3D information and allow selecting ground points reliably. 3D data has been shown to be convenient as it allows selecting ground points, that can be registered and then used for building mosaics of cluttered ground planes.

The input of the mosaicking process consists mainly of many points forming local sparse clouds. This implied using robust registration methods designed for clouds instead of well separated features. We proposed using computer vision techniques such as distance transform to compare shapes and image correlation for fine tuning the registration. Results shown that the distance transform copes well with the sparse nature of the clouds. The saturation of the distance transform is useful for coping with the outliers. 3D reconstructed clouds were found to be useful for an initial registration, but fine tuning required resorting to the original image data.

Future work - The proposed mosaicking method will be used for benchmarking other registration methods based on the same input data (monocular or stereo vision). Combining reconstructed 3D information, accounting for variable local-densities of features and including color information, guaranteeing at the same time good convergence properties, is still a research topic within ICP registration.

As noted in the introduction, we plan to use the mosaics for navigation. The pairwise registration of the 2D ground features, acquired at consecutive time stamps, still suffers the error accumulation problem typical of odometry. However, from the point of view of keeping the robot localised, the image pairwise registration is enough, as the robot can always navigate on the mosaic and roll-back to its starting location by local registration over the mosaic.

Acknowledgments. This work has been partially supported by the FCT Programa Operacional Sociedade de Informação (POSI) in the frame of QCA III, and by the projects Gestinteract POSC/EEA-SRI/61911 /2004 and URUS FP6-EU-IST-045062. The second and third authors were partially supported by the AECI/CYTED Spanish Program under the RIBERO project (Red Iberoamericana de Robtica), and by the ESPOL under the VLIR project, Component 8.

References

1. Davison, A.: Real-time simultaneous localisation and mapping with a single camera. In: IEEE Int. Conf. on Computer Vision, vol. 2, pp. 1403–1410 (2003)
2. Karlsson, N., Bernardo, E.D., Ostrowski, J., Goncalves, L., Pirjanian, P., Munich, M.: The vslam algorithm for robust localization and mapping. In: Proc. IEEE Int. Conf. on Robotics and Automation, Barcelona, Spain, pp. 24–29 (2005)
3. Se, S., Lowe, D., Little, J.: Vision-based global localization and mapping for mobile robots. IEEE Trans. on Robotics 21(3), 364–375 (2005)
4. Besl, P.J., McKay, N.D.: A method for registration of 3-d shapes. IEEE Trans. on Pattern Analysis and Mach. Intel. 14(2), 239–256 (1992)
5. Fisher, R.: The iterative closest point algorithm, in cvonline: On-line compendium of computer vision http://homepages.inf.ed.ac.uk/rbf/CVonline/LOCAL_COPIES/FISHER/ICP/cvoi cp.htm (2006)
6. Rusinkiewicz, S., Levoy, M.: Efficient variants of the icp algorithm. In: Int. Conf. 3-D Digital Imaging and Modeling, pp. 145–152 (2001)
7. Chetverikov, D., Svirko, D., Stepanov, D., Krsek, P.: The trimmed iterative closest point algorithm. In: Int. Conf. on Pattern Recognition, vol. 3, pp. 545–548 (2002)
8. Biber, P., Fleck, S., Strasser, W.: A probabilistic framework for robust and accurate matching of point clouds. In: 26th Pattern Recognition Symposium (2004)
9. Gavrila, D., Philomin, V.: Real-time object detection for smart vehicles. In: IEEE, Int. Conf. on Computer Vision (ICCV). pp. 87–93 (1999)
10. Bouguet, J.: Camera calibration toolbox for matlab http://www.vision.caltech.edu/bouguetj/calib_doc/ (2006)
11. Faugeras, O.: Three-Dimensional Computer Vision - A Geometric Viewpoint. MIT Press, Cambridge (1993)
12. Hartley, R., Zisserman, A.: Multiple View Geometry in Computer Vision. Cambridge University Press, Cambridge (2000)

A   Back-Projection to the Ground Plane

Consider the projection equation in homogeneous coordinates $m \approx PM = [A\ b]M$, where $M = [x\ y\ z\ 1]^T$ is a generic 3D point, $m = [u\ v\ 1]^T$ is the image point projection of M and the sign $\approx$ denotes equality up to a scale factor [11]. We have that the camera projection center is $C = -A^{-1}b$ and the 3D direction associated to m (point at infinity) is $D = A^{-1}m$. Thus the back-projection comes $M = [C; 1] + \alpha[D; 0] = [A^{-1}(\alpha m - b); 1]$ where α is a scaling factor setting the distance from the 3D point to the camera center and ";" denotes vertical stacking of vectors [12].

Representing the ground plane by a normal vector, n and a distance to the coordinate system origin, d, the factor α in the back-projection equation can be computed by enforcing $M_{1:3}^T.n = d$. The back-projection equation can now be arranged to a single 4×3 matrix, P^* converting an image point m to a 3D point M on the ground plane:

$$M \approx P^*m = \begin{bmatrix} (d + b^T A^{-T}n)A^{-1} & -A^{-1}b \\ n^T A^{-1} & 0 \end{bmatrix} \begin{bmatrix} I_3 \\ 0\ 0\ 1 \end{bmatrix} m. \tag{4}$$

Fast Central Catadioptric Line Extraction

Jean Charles Bazin[1], Cédric Demonceaux[2], and Pascal Vasseur[2]

[1] Korea Advanced Institute of Science and Technology, Kaist
[2] CREA-EA3299- University of Picardie Jules Verne, France
JeanCharles.Bazin@gmail.com
{Cedric.Demonceaux,Pascal.Vasseur}@u-picardie.fr

Abstract. Lines are particularly important features for different tasks such as calibration, structure from motion, 3D reconstruction in computer vision. However, line detection in catadioptric images is not trivial because the projection of a 3D line is a conic eventually degenerated. If the sensor is calibrated, it has been already demonstrated that each conic can be described by two parameters. In this way, some methods based on the adaptation of conventional line detection methods have been proposed. However, most of these methods suffer from the same disadvantages than in the perspective case (computing time, accuracy, robustness, ...). In this paper, we then propose a new method for line detection in central catadioptric image comparable to the polygonal approximation approach. With this method, only two points of a chain allows to extract with a very high accuracy a catadioptric line. Moreover, this algorithm is particularly fast and is applicable in realtime. We also present experimental results with some quantitative and qualitative evaluations in order to show the quality of the results and the perspectives of this method.

1   Introduction

Catadioptric vision sensors (associations of a camera with a mirror) are now broadly used in many applications such as robot navigation, 3D scene reconstruction or video surveillance [1]. Their large field of view is indubitably the major reason of this success. Baker and Nayer classified these sensors in two respective categories [2]. First, sensors with a single viewpoint, named central catadioptric sensors are made of parabolic mirror associated to orthographic camera and hyperbolic, elliptic and plane mirrors with perspective camera. The second category with different viewpoints has geometric properties less significant and is made of the other possibilities of association between mirrors and cameras. In this paper, we are only interested in central sensors which permit a geometrically correct reconstruction of the perspective image from the original catadioptric image. However, their employment presents some drawbacks because of the deformations induced by the mirror. For example, some very useful classical treatments in perspective image processing can be no more performed on catadioptric images because they are inadequate. One of these major treatments deals with line extraction. Thus, while in the perspective case line detection is perfectly known and efficiently solved, with catadioptric images the

J. Martí et al. (Eds.): IbPRIA 2007, Part II, LNCS 4478, pp. 25–32, 2007.
© Springer-Verlag Berlin Heidelberg 2007

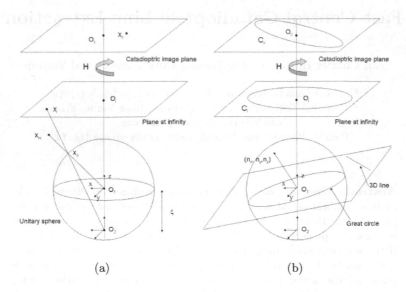

(a)   (b)

Fig. 1. (a) Image formation model. Example of projection via the unitary sphere for a 3D point. (b) Projection of a 3D line via the unitary sphere into the catadioptric image plane.

problem is absolutely not trivial. Indeed, the projection of any 3D real line is a conic eventually degenerate. Thus, in the case of an uncalibrated sensor, it is necessary to estimate five parameters for each line while only two parameters are sufficient for a calibrated sensor. If we consider the projection of a 3D point by the way of the unitary sphere (fig. 1(a)) as proposed in [3] [4] [5] with the formalism defined in [3] [4], we can define oriented projective ray P_1 passing by 3D point x_w and the center of the sphere. This ray intersects the surface of the sphere in x_s. We then consider oriented projective ray P_2 passing by x_s and a point situated on the z-axis between the center of the sphere and the north pole. This point is at distance ξ from the center of the sphere and depends only on the mirror geometric characteristics. P_2 intersects plane at infinity in point x_i. Finally, homography H defined between the plane at infinity and the catadioptric image plane projects point x_i into point x_c. H includes intrinsic parameters of the camera, possible rotations between the sphere frame and the camera frame, and finally the parameters of the mirror. According to this model, we can develop the projection of a 3D line into the catadioptric image plane (fig. 1(b)). We consider plane Π_R which contains the real 3D line and the center of the sphere. This plane intersects the sphere and then defines a great circle onto its surface. The set of oriented projective rays passing by the points of the great circle and point O_2 define then a cone which intersects plane at infinity into conic C_i. Finally, homography H transforms C_i into conic C_c in the catadioptric image plane. In plane at infinity, we know that the equation of conic C_i is equal to:

$$C_i = \begin{bmatrix} n_x^2(1 - \xi^2) - n_z^2\xi^2 & n_x n_y(1 - \xi^2) & n_x n_z \\ n_x n_y(1 - \xi^2) & n_y^2(1 - \xi^2) - n_z^2\xi^2 & n_y n_z \\ n_x n_z & n_y n_z & n_z^2 \end{bmatrix} \quad (1)$$

with $(n_x, n_y, n_z)^T$ the vector which describes the normal to plane P_w which contains the 3D line. We obtain the equation of conic C_c in image plane thanks to the following relation:

$$C_c - H^{-T} C_i H^{-1} \tag{2}$$

Finally, a pixel $x_c = (u \quad v \quad 1)^T$ belongs to the conic C_c if the equality $x_c^T C_c x_c = 0$ is verified.

In this paper, we propose a new method for calibrated catadioptric line detection which permits a very fast, robust and accurate detection. The proposed approach consists in roughly estimating the possible catadioptric lines in the image and in verifying if each possible line is a real catadioptric line. The rest of the paper is organized as follows. Section II is devoted to the related works which deal with catadioptric line detection in calibrated and uncalibrated cases. In section III, we present a complete description of the algorithm. Section IV is devoted to experimental results with quantitative and qualitative evaluations. We finally conclude in section V on different perspectives.

2 Related Works

The methods of catadioptric line detection and estimation can be divided in three categories. The first class deals with methods applicable as well in the calibrated case as in the uncalibrated case and includes the algorithms of conic fitting [6]. The second category concerns calibrated sensors and most of the proposed techniques in this category are based on adaptation of Hough transform [7] [8] [9]. Methods for uncalibrated sensors form the third category. These methods use particular geometric constraints of catadioptric sensors and are generally dedicated to paracatadioptric sensors [10] [11]. In the rest of this section, we only develop the two first categories because the third is not enough general and concerns only paracatadioptric cameras.

Conic fitting algorithms determine the curve that best fits the data points according to a certain distance metric [6]. In [10], the authors present a comparison of the normal least squares (LMS), approximate mean square (AMS), Fitzgibbon and Fisher (FF) [12], gradient weighted least square fitting (GRAD) and orthogonal distances (ORTHO) methods for the specific problem of paracatadioptric line detection. Their conclusions are that GRAD and ORTHO are the most robust to noise and that all methods perform poorly when the amplitude of the occlusion is above $240°$. Since most of the catadioptric lines have an amplitude less than $45°$, it appears clearly that these methods are unsuitable for general central catadioptric line detection and estimation. Moreover, these methods suppose that the pixels from the edges have been already classified into chains representing the different possible catadioptric lines.

In the calibrated case, homography H and parameter ξ are known. In this way, a 3D line is determined thanks to a vector $(n_x, n_y, n_z)^T$. This vector represents the normal of the great circle on the unitary sphere obtained by the intersection of the plane which contains the center of the sphere and the 3D real line (fig. 1(b)). A 3D real line can be also represented by two angles ϕ and θ which respectively are the elevation angle and the azimuth angle of the normal vector. Each catadioptric line is then represented by only two parameters and a simple adaptation of the Hough transform can solved the problem. This is this kind of approach which is proposed in [8] and [7]. The mean difference between these methods deals with the space in which the treatments are performed. In [7], the image is projected on the unitary sphere and the 3D coordinates of the pixels are then used while in [8], they apply the algorithm directly in the image. Although these two approaches present interesting results, it is worth noting that they present the classic defects of the Hough transform such as the best sampling step for ϕ and θ for example. In order to avoid these drawbacks, we can note that if two pixels of a catadioptric line are known, it is then possible to compute the normal of the great circle and then to obtain the corresponding values of ϕ and θ. In [9], the authors propose a randomized Hough transform which selects randomly two points in the image of edges in order to compute the ϕ and θ angles. These angles are then used in an accumulator for the detection of the most confident catadioptric lines.

3   Central Catadioptric Line Detection Algorithm

Our line detection algorithm for central catadioptric sensor consists first in applying a Canny edge detector (Fig 4(b)). Then, we proceed to an edge chaining which consists in extracting connected pixels from edges in order to form lists with a length superior or equal to a threshold (NbPixels) (Fig 4(c)). To detect the lines in the scene consists then in verifying if these chains are the projections of 3D lines. In this way, we apply a split and merge algorithm of the chains. First, an adaptation of the polygonal approximation of the classical perspective case is proposed in order to find which chains or parts of chains are catadioptric projections of lines. This process is performed thanks to a division criterion which cuts the chains at a particular position if the chain is not verified as a catadioptric line. Next, we use a fusion criterion in order to group the different chains in the image which represents the same central catadioptric lines. These both criteria are discussed in the following of the paper.

3.1   Division Criterion

Consider the two endpoints of a chain of N pixels with coordinates $P_1 = (X_1, Y_1, Z_1)$ and $P_2 = (X_2, Y_2, Z_2)$ on the unitary sphere S^2. These points define a single central catadioptric line in the image and then a great circle $\mathcal{C}$ on the sphere (cf fig(1(a)(b)). This circle results from the intersection of the unitary sphere and a plane which contains the sphere origin 0_1 and whose a normal vector is $\overrightarrow{n} = \overrightarrow{O_1 P_1} \times \overrightarrow{O_1 P_2} = (n_x, n_y, n_z)^T$. Then, the equation of $\mathcal{C}$ is:

$$\begin{cases} n_x X + n_y Y + n_z Z = 0 \\ (X, Y, Z) \in S^2 \end{cases}$$

We consider that a point on the sphere with coordinates (X_i, Y_i, Z_i) of the chain belongs to the great circle if the distance between this point and the plane defined by the great circle is less than a threshold:

$$|n_x X_i + n_y Y_i + n_z Z_i| \leq \text{DivThreshold}.$$

This chain is then considered as a central catadioptric line if at least 95% of its points belong to the great circle.

In the opposite case, we cut the chain into two sub-chains at the point (X_j, Y_j, Z_j) which maximizes the following error $||(X_i, Y_i, Z_i).\overrightarrow{n}||$, $i = 1 \cdots n$ (the furthest point from the plane).

This division step stops when the chain is considered as a central catadioptric line or when the length of the sub-chains is less than the threshold (NbPixels). At the end of this step, we then obtain the whole set of central catadioptric lines in the image. However this method may generate a multi-detection of the same lines. In order to compensate this drawback, we then propose to merge the similar catadioptric lines.

3.2 Fusion Criterion

Let define two catadioptric lines d_1 and d_2 detected with the previous method. These lines respectively characterized by $\overrightarrow{n_1}$ and $\overrightarrow{n_2}$ define two planes in the 3D space passing through the origin of the unitary sphere, $\Pi_1 = \{U = (X, Y, Z) \in \mathbb{R}^3, \overrightarrow{n}_1.U = 0\}$ and $\Pi_2 = \{U = (X, Y, Z) \in \mathbb{R}^3, \overrightarrow{n}_2.U = 0\}$. We consider that these detected catadioptric lines are similar if they define the same 3D plane, that is to say if:

$$1 - |\overrightarrow{n}_1.\overrightarrow{n}_2| \leq \text{FusThreshold}.$$

In this case, the two catadioptric lines are merged into a single line. The catadioptric line equation is then updated from the pixels of the chains which belong to d_1 and d_2 as follows. Let note respectively $M^1 = (X_i^1, Y_i^1, Z_i^1)_{i=1\cdots N_1}$ and $M^2 = (X_i^2, Y_i^2, Z_i^2)_{i=1\cdots N_2}$, the pixels of catadioptric line d_1 (resp. d_2). Let M, the matrix of dimension $(N_1 + N_2) \times 3$,

$$M = \begin{pmatrix} X_1^1 & Y_1^1 & Z_1^1 \\ \vdots & \vdots & \vdots \\ X_{N_1}^1 & Y_{N_1}^1 & Z_{N_1}^1 \\ X_1^2 & Y_1^2 & Z_1^2 \\ \vdots & \vdots & \vdots \\ X_{N_2}^2 & Y_{N_2}^2 & Z_{N_2}^2 \end{pmatrix},$$

The normal vector $\overrightarrow{n} = (n_x, n_y, n_z)^T$ of the great circle associated to the catadioptric line is then solution of:

$$M.\overrightarrow{n} = (0, \cdots, 0)^T. \tag{3}$$

The solution of (3) is obtained from the SVD of matrix M [13].

4   Experimentations

We have tested our central catadioptric line detector on different kinds of omnidirectional images. We first propose some results with synthesis images for
which we perfectly know the line equations in order to show the accuracy of the
approach. Then, some results on real images are also proposed. In the whole
set of experimentations except in one indicated case, the different thresholds are
fixed as follows : NbPixels =100, DivThreshold = 0.0005, FusThreshold = 1°.

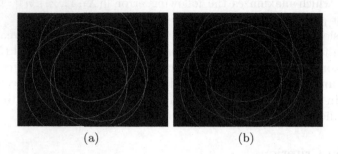

(a)   (b)

Fig. 2. (a) Original image, (b) Detected catadioptric lines

4.1   Synthesis Images

We have generated two synthesis images for which we perfectly know the calibration parameters and line equations. The first image contains five catadioptric
lines (fig 2(a)). The five lines are obviously easily detected (fig 2(b)). However,
results show a very high accuracy of the catadioptric line estimation. Indeed,
contrary to Hough based methods which require a sampling of the search space
and for which the accuracy depends on this sampling, in the proposed method
the catadioptric line estimation is performed analytically. Thus, let note H_c^i the
3×3 matrix of the conic associated to a catadioptric line i $(i = 1 \cdots 5)$ and $\widehat{H_c^i}$,

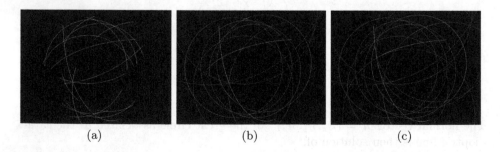

(a)   (b)   (c)

Fig. 3. (a) Original image, (b) Red catadioptric lines correspond to detected catadioptric lines, (c) False catadioptric lines when the length NbPixel is too low

the estimation of this matrix from the proposed method. For the five catadioptric lines of the first image Fig 2(a), the mean error:

$$\frac{1}{5}\sum_{i=1}^{5}\frac{||H_c^i/H_c^i(3,3) - \widehat{H_c^i}/\widehat{H_c^i}(3,3)||}{||H_c^i||} = 5.10^{-5}.$$

The second synthesis image is composed of eight catadioptric lines and two 'false' catadioptric lines (fig 3(a)). Results show that the eight catadioptric lines are correctly detected Les résultats montrent bien que les 8 droites sont correctement détectées while the two ellipses which are 'false' catadioptric lines are not detected (fig 3(b)). Nevertheless, if the minimal length NbPixel decreases (in this example, NbPixel=50), we can note that some parts of these ellipses may correspond to catadioptric lines (fig 3(c)).

4.2   Real Catadioptric Images

We present here result for a real catadioptric image. In this case, sensor has been calibrated with the method described in [4]. This image (fig 4(a)) is a paracatadioptric image issued from the calibration toolbox proposed by Barreto [4]. In figure 4(b), we present the result of Canny edge detector and consecutively the detected chains of pixels extracted for the catadioptric line verification (fig 4(c)). Figure 4(d) shows the catadioptric line detection before the fusion step

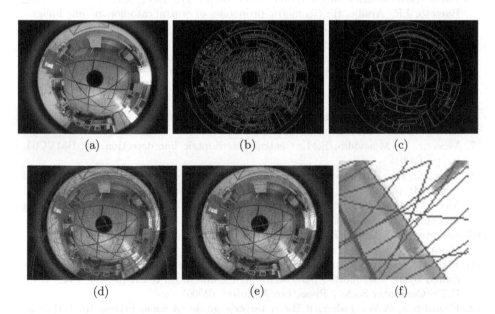

(a)   (b)   (c)

(d)   (e)   (f)

Fig. 4. (a) Original image, (b) Canny edge detector result, (c) Extracted chains, (d) Catadioptric line detection results after division step, (e) Catadioptric line detection results after fusion step, (f) Detailed view of final results

while figure 4(e) presents the final result after the fusion step. In figure 4(f), we propose a more detailed view of a part of the image in order to show the accuracy of the results. Finally, from a computational time point of view, the method takes near 3 seconds with Matlab. A real time implementation constitutes the next perspective of this work.

5   Conclusion

In this paper, we deal with the problem of line detection in central catadioptric images. Our method is valid for calibrated sensor and is comparable to the polygonal approximation algorithm. Indeed, it consists in looking for pixels in chains of edges which correspond to catadioptric lines thanks to an analytic approach contrary to previous methods based on Hough transform which depends on the sampling of the search space. Moreover, we then obtain a very fast algorithm which could be implemented for real time applications.

References

1. Benosman, R., Kang, S.B.: Panoramic Vision: Sensors, Theory, Applications. Springer, Heidelberg (2001)
2. Baker, S., Nayar, S.K.: A theory of single-viewpoint catadioptric image formation. International Journal on Computer Vision **35**(2), 175–196 (1999)
3. Barreto, J.P., Araújo, H.: Geometric properties of central catadioptric line images. In: Heyden, A., Sparr, G., Nielsen, M., Johansen, P. (eds.) ECCV 2002. LNCS, vol. 2353, pp. 237–251. Springer, Heidelberg (2002)
4. Barreto, J.P.: General Central Projection Systems: Modeling, Calibration and Visual Servoing. PhD Thesis, University of Coimbra (2003)
5. Geyer, C., Daniilidis, K.: Catadioptric projective geometry. International Journal of Computer Vision **45**(3), 223–243 (2001)
6. Zhang, Z.: Parameter estimation techniques: a tutorial with application to conic fitting. Image Vision Comput. **15**(1), 59–76 (1997)
7. Vasseur, P., Mouaddib, E.M.: Central catadioptric line detection. In: BMVC04. xx–yy (2004)
8. Ying, X., Hu, Z.: Catadioptric line features detection using hough transform. In: ICPR (4), pp. 839–842. IEEE Computer Society Press, Los Alamitos (2004)
9. Mei, C., Malis, E.: Fast central catadioptric line extraction, estimation, tracking and structure from motion. In: IROS (2006)
10. Barreto, J.P., Araújo, H.: Fitting conics to paracatadioptric projections of lines. Computer Vision and Image Understanding **101**(3), 151–165 (2006)
11. Vandeportaele, B., Cattoen, M., Marthon, P.: A fast detector of line images acquired by an uncalibrated paracatadioptric camera. In: ICPR (3), pp. 1042–1045. IEEE Computer Society Press, Los Alamitos (2006)
12. Fitzgibbon, A.W., Fisher, R.B.: A buyer's guide to conic fitting. In: BMVC95 (1995)
13. Jennings, A., McKeown, J.J.: Matrix Computation, 2nd edn. Jonh Wiley & Sons, New York (1992)

Similarity-Based Object Retrieval Using Appearance and Geometric Feature Combination

Agnés Borràs and Josep Lladós*

Computer Vision Center - Dept. Ciències de la Comunicació,
UAB Bellaterra 08193, Spain
{agnesba,josep}@cvc.uab.es
http://www.cvc.uab.es

Abstract. This work presents a content-based image retrieval system of general purpose that deals with cluttered scenes containing a given query object. The system is flexible enough to handle with a single image of an object despite its rotation, translation and scale variations. The image content is divided in parts that are described with a combination of features based on geometrical and color properties. The idea behind the feature combination is to benefit from a fuzzy similarity computation that provides robustness and tolerance to the retrieval process. The features can be independently computed and the image parts can be easily indexed by using a table structure on every feature value. Finally a process inspired in the alignment strategies is used to check the coherence of the object parts found in a scene. Our work presents a system of easy implementation that uses an open set of features and can suit a wide variety of applications.

1 Introduction

The goal of Content-Based Image Retrieval (CBIR) is to find all images in a given database that contain certain visual features specified by the user. When these features refer not to the whole image but a subpart, we deal with a problem known as Similarity-Based Object Retrieval (SBOR). Some authors consider two main approaches on the SBOR problem: data-independent and data-dependent [3]. In the data-independent approach images are coarsely divided into rectangular regions where a searched object is mean to be found. Images are indexed from the feature vectors that had been computed using the whole information of the image regions. This fact represents the main advantage on the data-independent systems because classical strategies of CBIR can then be applied to characterize the image from its parts [1] [2]. Otherwise, they involve the hard restriction of dealing with query objects that must fit a rectangular piece of the scene [4] [5]. To overcome this limitation data-dependent approaches deal directly with the particular content of each image. The strategy consists in detecting a set

---

* This work has been partially supported by the grant UABSCH2006-02.

J. Martí et al. (Eds.): IbPRIA 2007, Part II, LNCS 4478, pp. 33–39, 2007.
© Springer-Verlag Berlin Heidelberg 2007

of invariants from which to decompose the image content in a set of regions. Then, local descriptions of these regions are extracted and represented by feature vectors. Two of the most popular approaches on detecting image invariants are the use of the Harris corner detector and the use of the DoG (Difference of Gaussians) operator. Data-dependent strategies are based on the evidence that a query object is likely to be found in a scene if the feature vectors that describe its parts can be matched in the scene. Even though this criterion represents a useful filter in the retrieval solution, it is not robust enough when the target object constitutes a small portion of the whole scene. To avoid the incorporation of false positives in the query result the system has to check the structural coherence of the object parts found in a scene. This testing process can be performed with techniques as diverse as Hough-like voting strategies [8] or correspondence algorithms such as RANSAC [7]

We present a SBOR system of general purpose that given the image of an object is able to retrieve those cluttered database images that likely contain an instance of this object. The retrieval strategy is based on a data-dependent approach to be flexible enough to handle with a single instance of an object despite its rotation, translation and scale variations. Finally a process inspired in the alignment strategies is used to check the spatial disposition of the object parts. The main contribution of our work is centered in the selection and treatment of the image descriptors. The selection of the image descriptors has to be understood as a compromise between the discriminant power for the content indexing and the tolerance in the similarity matching. Some authors [9] discriminate between the descriptors based on the signal image information [8] and those based on the geometrical properties [6]. In one hand, signal-based descriptors stand out to be very precise and discriminant and, in the other hand, geometrically-based ones provide a suitable encoding of the object structure. Consequently, we propose to use a combination of simple features of both groups instead of using a sophisticated description compacted in a single feature. This way, the feature combination allows a fuzzy computation of the similarity values and provides robustness and tolerance to the retrieval process.

In the next section of this paper we describe the region extraction process and we give a general view of the database features organization. In section 3 we present the two main stages of the object detection strategy: the local matching and the global matching. Section 4 contains some results and finally, in the section 5, we expose the conclusions of this work.

2   Information Modelling

Our retrieval system consists in a data-dependent approach where the image parts are obtained from the polygonal approximation of the contour information. Let us name I an image and v a vector belonging to its polygonal approximation. Every vector has associated an influence area from which the image content is decomposed in parts. These parts are denoted p and are characterized by a set of independent features F. Thus, a set of tables, one for each feature type, provides an easy system to store and index the image parts. Let us denote T^k the table structure that stores the image information for a certain feature type F^k. The lines of a table are referred to the values comprised in its feature range and the columns are referred to the image parts. A table describes the image content using binary information: a cell $T^k(x, y)$ is set to 1 if the image part p_x has the value y for the feature F^k. Figure 2 exemplifies the extraction of the image parts and feature storage structure.

We distinguish between two kind of features used by our system: the local features F_L and the global features F_G. The local features allow to obtain an independent description of the image parts. Otherwise, the global features are used to establish the relations between these parts and describe their translation, rotation and scale with respect to the whole image. We use a total amount of 14 features distributed in 4 global features and 10 local features (6 based on the signal information and 4 based on the geometric properties). Figure 1 shows them graphically.

In the next section we expose how the features are used in the retrieval process: the local features identify the presence of the image parts and the global ones assure their structural coherence.

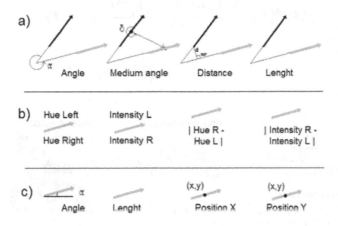

Fig. 1. Image features $F = \{F^k\}$ a) Local features based on the geometric properties of the vectors belonging to the influence area b) Local features based on the signal values sampled on the left and right side along the vector c) Global features

3   Retrieval Process

The retrieval process is divided in two main stages: the retrieval of the query object parts and the analysis of their structural distribution.

3.1   Object Part Identification

Let us name p_i^M a part of the query object and p_j^E a part of a scene. To evaluate the similarity between these two image parts we formulate a query on the database information for each value of the local features F_L. Let us name $F_i^{M,k}$ the value of the feature k belonging to the query object part p_i^M. Instead of retrieving only the scene parts that match exactly the value $F_i^{M,k}$ we use a similarity function FS that deals with a wider range of solutions. The similarity computation consists in a ramp function that evaluates de difference of the feature values respect to a given tolerance ϵ^k. The result varies in the range of 0 to 1 where 1 means maximum similarity.

$$FS(\epsilon^k, F_i^{M,k}, F_j^{E,k}) = \begin{cases} 0 & \text{if } d > \epsilon^k \\ 1 - \frac{d}{\epsilon^k} & \text{otherwise} \end{cases}$$

$$\text{where} \quad d = |F_i^{M,k} - F_j^{E,k}|$$

The matching between a part of a query object and a part of a scene is evaluated by the mean of the similarity values for all the local features $LFS_{i,j}^{M,E}$. Then, the matching of p_i^M in the whole scene is denoted $ILFS_i^{M,E}$ and it is obtained by the maximum similarity of all the possible comparisons.

$$LFS_{i,j}^{M,E} = \frac{\sum FS(\epsilon^k, F_i^{M,k}, F_j^{E,k})}{\#F_L} \quad | \quad k \in F_L$$

$$ILFS_i^{M,E} = max\{LFS_{i,j}^{M,E}\} \quad \forall j \in p_j^E$$

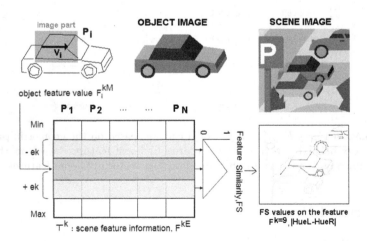

Fig. 2. The figure shows the vectorization of an object image and an image part example (shaded region) belonging to one of its vectors. A binary table contains the feature information of the scene image. An example shows the similarity results FS for every scene vector respect to the object value F_i^k (where k=9 for the feature $|HueR - HueL|$). We represent in black the scene vectors with maximum similarity.

Figure 2 shows an example of similarity computation FS for a single feature F_k. Moreover, Figure 3 illustrates the combination values $ILFS$ between the signal features and the geometric ones.

Some retrieval systems select those database images that present the highest accumulation of the local part identification similarities $ILFS$. This single criterion does not check the coherence of the spatial arrangement of the object parts. Thus, a large amount of false positives can be introduced in the retrieval solution. To solve this problem, our proposal introduces a final phase where the global structure is tested for the local matching pairs with highest score.

3.2 Checking of the Structural Arrangement of the Object Parts

Given a vector of the model object image v_q^M and a vector of the scene image v_r^E we can define an alignment of both image contents by computing the affine geometric transformations to map v_q^M on v_r^E in the orientation O (the same or opposite). These geometric transforms can consist in changes of scale, rotation, and translation. As we have introduced in the section 2 the features that describe the image content in relation to the whole image aspect are identified as global features F_G. This way, the alignment transformations only affect to the global features of the query object.

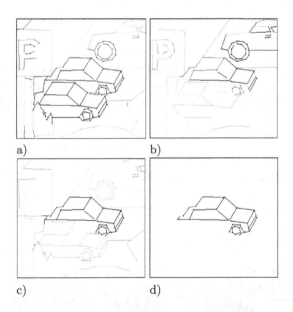

a)   b)

c)   d)

Fig. 3. a) Similarity values $ILFS$ of the object parts (black means maximum similarity) using signal-based features b) using geometrical features c) using both feature groups d) Vectors representing the best matching solution, maximum $IGFS$ value, for both feature groups. Notice the collaboration between the signal based-based features that match the cars by their color and the geometrical-based ones that match them by shape.

Let us name F' the modified global feature values of the query object according to a given vector alignment. The object similitude is computed using the same strategy as the local one but adding a hard restriction to the global feature values. To preserve the spatial disposition of the object parts is necessary the similarity of all the features values to be accomplished. The following function, GFS, describes the calculus of the similarity between an object part p_i^M and a scene part p_j^E given a fixed alignment.

$$GFS_{i,j,(q,r,O)}^{M,E} = min\{LFS_{i,j}^{M,E}, FS(\epsilon^k, F_i'^{M,k}, F_j^{E,k})\}$$

$$\forall k \in F_G$$

Then the similarity between the query object and the scene image correspond to the best result provided by the function $IGFS$ on the checked alignments.

$$IGFS_{(q,r,O)}^{M,E} = max\{GFS_{i,j,(q,r,O)}^{M,E}\}$$

$$| LFS_{i,j}^{M,E} > Thr, \quad \forall i \in p_i^M, \quad \forall j \in p_j^E$$

The computed value is used in the retrieval process to rank the solutions of given query. The example of the Figure 3 d) shows the object detection solution as the scene vectors with maximum $IGFS$ value.

4   Results

We have tested the system with 72 images belonging to two databases. The first database consists in a set of 40 images of invoices that can be identified by 4 different logos. The other database is conformed of 32 scenes where 4 objects

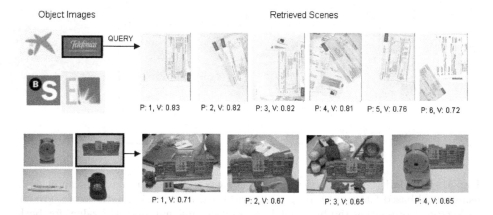

Fig. 4. Query examples on the selected objects. Every retrieved image has its position (P) and retrieval value (V).

can be found. For every query image we have computed the rate of database images that contain the searched object and that have been retrieved in the first n positions (being n the total amount of database images where the query object can be found). The obtained results for both tests are 92% of success.

We have observed that the variations that mainly affect to the retrieval measure $IGFS$ are caused by illumination changes and viewpoint distortions. Nevertheless the success on the object location is maintained due to the feature combination and the effect of the query tolerance ranges. Figure 4 illustrates the results with two examples.

5 Conclusions

We have developed a SBOR system that deals with a combination of independent image features that provides a fuzzy value on the similarity comparison of the image parts. A future research line of our work is centered in the development of a process that initially analyzes the query image and adapts the similarity tolerances according to the most characteristic features of the query object. The system has proved to be robust against effects such as noise, shades, slightly modifications of the viewpoint and partial occlusions. We have tested the system with two databases of scanned documents and images of objects taken in real environments obtaining promising results.

References

1. Huang, T., Rui, Y.: Image retrieval: Past, present, and future. International Symposium on Multimedia Information Processing (1997)
2. Forsyth, D.A., Malik, J., Fleck, M.M., Greenspan, H., Leung, T.K., Belongie, S., Carson, C., Bregler, C.: Finding Pictures of Objects in Large Collections of Images, Object Representation in Computer Vision, pp. 335–360 (1996)
3. Fodor, I.K.: Statistical Techniques to Find Similar Objects in Images. In: Proceedings of the American Statistical Association (October 2003)
4. Luo, J., Nascimento, M.A.: Content Based Sub-Image Retrieval via Hierarchical Tree Matching. In: Proceedings of ACM MMDB 2003, New Orleans, USA, pp. 63–69, (November 2003)
5. Lewis, P.H., Martinez, K., Abas, F.S., Ahmad Fauzi, M.F., Addis, M., Lahanier, C., Stevenson, J., Chan, S.C.Y., Mike, J.B., Paul, G.: An Integrated Content and Metadata based Retrieval System for Art. IEEE Trans. on Image Proc. 13(3), 302–313 (2004)
6. Huet, B., Cross, A., Hancock, E.R.: Shape Retrieval by Inexact Graph Matching. ICMCS 1, 772–776 (1999)
7. Matas, J., Chum, O., Urban, M., Pajdla, T.: Robust wide-baseline stereo from maximally stable extremal regions. Image Vision Computing 22(10), 761–767 (2004)
8. Lowe, D.G.: Object Recognition from Local Scale-Invariant Features. In: ICCV, pp. 1150–1157 (1999)
9. Lamiroy, B., Gros, P., Picard, S.: Combining Local Recognition Methods for Better Image Recognition. Vision 17(2), 1–6 (2001)

Real-Time Facial Expression Recognition for Natural Interaction

Eva Cerezo[1], Isabelle Hupont[1], Cristina Manresa-Yee[2], Javier Varona[2],
Sandra Baldassarri[1], Francisco J. Perales[2], and Francisco J. Seron[1]

[1] Departamento de Informática e Ingeniería de Sistemas, Instituto de Investigación en
Ingeniería de Aragón, Universidad de Zaragoza, Spain
{ecerezo,478953,sandra,seron}@unizar.es
[2] Departament de Matemàtiques i Informàtica, Universitat de les Illes Balears, Spain
{cristina.manresa,xavi.varona,paco.perales}@uib.es

Abstract. The recognition of emotional information is a key step toward giving computers the ability to interact more naturally and intelligently with people. This paper presents a completely automated real-time system for facial expression's recognition based on facial features' tracking and a simple emotional classification method. Facial features' tracking uses a standard webcam and requires no specific illumination or background conditions. Emotional classification is based on the variation of certain distances and angles from the neutral face and manages the six basic universal emotions of Ekman. The system has been integrated in a 3D engine for managing virtual characters, allowing the exploration of new forms of natural interaction.

Keywords: real-time features tracking, emotional classification, natural interfaces.

1 Introduction

Human computer intelligent interaction is an emerging field aimed at providing natural ways for humans to use computers as aids. It is argued that for a computer to be able to interact with humans it needs to have the communication skills of humans. One of these skills is the ability to understand the emotional state of the person, and the most expressive way humans display emotions is through facial expressions. Nevertheless, to develop a system that interprets facial expressions is difficult. Two kinds of problems have to be solved: facial expression feature extraction and facial expression classification. Related to feature extraction, and thinking in interface applications, the system must be low-cost with real-time, precise and robust feedback. Of course, no special lighting or static background conditions can be required. The face can be assumed to be always visible, however, difficulties can arise from in-plane (tilted head, upside down) and out-of-plane (frontal view, side view) rotations of the head, facial hair, glasses, lighting variations and cluttered background [1]. Besides, when using standard USB web cams, the provided CMOS image resolution has to be taken in account. Different approaches have been used for non invasive face/head-based interfaces, mainly for the control of the head's position analyzing

J. Martí et al. (Eds.): IbPRIA 2007, Part II, LNCS 4478, pp. 40–47, 2007.
© Springer-Verlag Berlin Heidelberg 2007

facial cues such as color distributions [2], head motion [3] or, recently, by means of facial features' tracking [4,5]. From the extracted facial features, emotional classification has to be performed. Three different classification methods are usually used for expression recognition: patterns, neuronal networks or rules [6]. Most of them follow the emotional classification of Ekman [7] that describes six universal basic emotions: joy, sadness, surprise, fear, disgust and anger.

The aim of this work is to show how a non-invasive robust face tracking system can feed an effective emotional classifier to build a facial expression recognition system that can be of great interest in developing new multimodal user interfaces. As it will be shown, the system developed has been successfully integrated in a character-based interface, allowing the exploration of new forms of affective interaction.

2   Real-Time Facial Feature Tracking

The computer vision algorithm is divided into two steps: initialization and tracking. The initialization step is responsible of learning the user's facial characteristics such as its skin color, its dimensions and the best face features to track. This process is totally automatic and it can also be used for system's recovering when a severe error occurs, adding the robustness necessary so that it can be used in a human-computer interface.

First of all, the algorithm automatically detects the user's face by means of a real-time face detection algorithm [8]. The face will not be considered as found until the user sits steady for a few frames and the face is detected in the image within those frames. A good detection of the features is very important for an effective performance of the whole system and the user must start the process with the so called neutral face: the mouth is closed and the gaze is directed perpendicular to the screen plane, the eyes are open and the eyelids are tangent to the iris. Then, it is possible to define the initial user's face region to start the search of the user's facial features. Based on anthropometrical measurements, the face region can be divided into three sections: eyes and eyebrows, nose, and mouth region. In the nose region, we look for those points that can be easily tracked, that is, those whose derivative energy perpendicular to the prominent direction is above a threshold [9]. This algorithm theoretically selects the nose corners or the nostrils. However, the ambient lighting can cause the selection of points that are not placed over the desired positions; this fact is clearly visible in Fig. 1 (a). Ideally, the desired selected features should be at both sides of the nose and should observe certain symmetrical conditions. Therefore, an enhancement and a re-selection of the features found is carried out taking into account symmetrical constraints. Fig. 1 (b) shows the selected features when symmetry respect to the vertical axis is considered. This reselection process achieves the best features to track and contributes to the tracking robustness. Fig. 1 (c) illustrates the final point considered, that is, the mean point of all the final selected features; due to the reselection of points it will be centered on the face.

Finally, in order to learn the user's skin color and complete the initialization step, the pixels inside the face region are used as a learning set of color samples to find the parameters of a Gaussian model in 3D RGB density using standard maximum likelihood methods.

The aim of the tracking step is to control the position of the face in order to detect and constraint the search region of the 10 face features used in the expression recognition stage. The detected and enhanced features of the initialization step are tracked by using the spatial intensity gradient information of the images in order to find the best image registration [10]. As it was mentioned before, for each frame the mean of all nose features is computed and it is defined as the *face tracking point* for that frame. The tracking algorithm is robust for handling rotation, scaling and shearing, so that the user can move in a more unrestricted way.

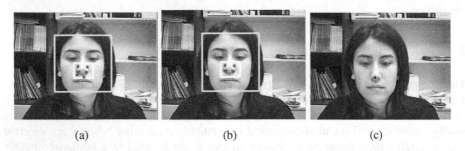

(a)   (b)   (c)

Fig. 1. (a) Automatic face detection and initial set of features. (b) Best feature selection using symmetrical constraints. (c) Mean of all features: face tracking point.

The *face tracking point* is used to constrain the image region to process and the color probability distribution, both computed in the initialization step, is used to calculate the probability of a face pixel being skin so that "skin mask" of the user's face can be created. Using this mask the system can detect, as a result of their non-skin-color property, the user's eyebrows, eyes and mouth bounding boxes and due to their position related to the *face tracking point,* the system can label the zones. One problem can appear if the user has got his eyes a little bit sunk, then due to the shadow in the eyelid, most probably the eyebrow and eye will be found as a single blob. In that case, we divide this bounding box assuming that the eyebrow has been detected together with the eye. Finally, from the bounding boxes positions, 10 face features are extracted. These 10 feature points of the face will later allow us to analyze the evolution of the face parameters (distances and angles) used for expression recognition. Fig. 2 shows the correspondence between these points and the ones defined by the MPEG-4 standard.

3   Classification of Emotions

3.1   General Method Description

Our classification method works with the emotional classification of Ekman and it is based on the work of Hammal et al [11]. They have implemented a facial classification method for static images. The originality of their work consisted, on the

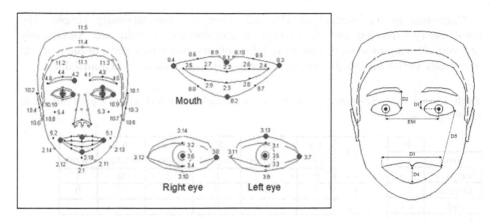

Fig. 2. Facial feature points extracted and used for expression recognition according to the MPEG-4 standard (left). Characteristic distances used in our method (right).

one hand, in the supposition that all the necessary information for the recognition of expressions is contained in the deformation of certain characteristics of the eyes, mouth and eyebrows and, on the other hand, in the use of the Belief Theory to make the classification. Our method studies the variation of a certain number of face parameters (basically distances and angles between some feature points of the face) with respect to the neutral expression. The characteristic points, shown in section 2, are used to calculate the five distances also shown in Fig. 2. All the distances are normalized with respect to the distance between the eyes, which is a distance independent of the expression. In addition to the five distances our system works with additional information about the mouth shape (from the four feature points two angles and the width/height relationship is extracted).

The objective of our method is to assign a score to each emotion, according to the state acquired by each one of the parameters in the image. The emotion (or emotions in case of draw) chosen will be the one that obtains a greater score.

Each parameters can take three different states for each of the emotions: C^+, C^- and S. State C^+ means that the value of the parameters has increased with respect to the neutral one; state C^- that its value has diminished with respect to the neutral one; and the state S that its value has not varied with respect to the neutral one. First, we build a descriptive table of emotions, according to the state of the parameters, like the one of the Table 1 (left). From this table, a set of logical rules tables can be built for each parameter (right), in which a score is assigned to each state for each emotion, depending on the degree in which this state of the parameter is characteristic of the emotion. Once the tables are defined, the implementation of the identification algorithm is simple. When a parameter takes a specific state, it is enough to select the vector of emotions (formed by the scores assigned to this state for each emotion) corresponding to this state. If we repeat the procedure for each parameter, we will obtain a matrix of as many rows as parameters we study and 6 columns, corresponding to the 6 emotions. The sum of the scores present in each column of the matrix gives the total score obtained by each emotion. If the final score does not surpass a certain threshold, the emotion is classified as "neutral".

Compared to the method of Hammal, ours is computationally simple. The combinatory explosion and the number of calculations to make are considerably reduced, allowing us to work with more information (more parameters) of the face and to evaluate the six universal emotions, and not only four of them, as Hammal does.

Table 1. Proposed table of one parameters' states for each emotion (left) and logical rules table for that parameter

	Pi
Joy	C-
Surprise	C+
Disgust	C-
Anger	C+
Sadness	C-
Fear	S/C+

Pi	E1 joy	E2 surprise	E3 disgust	E4 anger	E5 sadness	E6 fear
C+	0	3	0	2	0	1
C-	1	0	2	0	2	0
S	0	0	0	0	0	1

3.2 Tuning the Method: The FG-NET Database

In order to define the emotions in terms of the parameters states, as well as to find the thresholds that determine if a parameter is in a state or another, it is necessary to work with a wide database. In this work we have used the facial expressions and emotions database FG-NET of the University of Munich [12] that provides images of 19 different people showing the 6 universal emotions from Ekman plus the neutral one. From these data, we have built a descriptive table of the emotions according to the value of the states (Table 2).

Table 2. Proposed table of the states for the parameters used by the classification method. Some features do not provide any information of interest for certain emotions (squares in gray) and in these cases they are not considered.

	D_1	D_2	D_3	D_4	D_5	Ang 1	Ang 2	W/H
Joy	C-	S/C-	C+	C+	C-	C+	S/C+/C-	S/C-
Surprise	S/C+	S/C+	S/C-	C+	S/C+	C-	C+	C-
Disgust	C-	C-	S/C+/C-	S/C+	S/C-	S/C+/C-	S/C+	S/C-
Anger	C-	C-	S/C-	S/C-	S/C+/C-	C+	C-	C+
Sadness	C-	S	S/C-	S	S/C+	S/C+/C-	S/C-	S/C+
Fear	S/C+	S/C+/C-	C-	C+	S/C+	C-	C+	C-

3.3 Validation

Once the states that characterize each emotion and the value of the thresholds are established, the algorithm has been tested on the 399 images of the database. In the evaluation of results, the recognition is marked as "good" if the decision is coherent with the one taken by a human being. To do this, we have made surveys to 30 different people to classify the expressions shown in the most ambiguous images. Related to classification success, it is interesting to realize that human mechanisms for face detection are very robust, but this is not the case of those for face expressions interpretation. According to Bassili [13], a trained observer can correctly classify faces showing emotions with an average of 87%. The obtained results are shown in Table 3. The method has also been tested with other databases different from the one used for the threshold establishment, in order to confirm the good performance of the system.

Table 3. Classification rates of Hammal [11] (second column) and of our method with five distances (second column) and plus the information about the mouth shape (third column)

EMOTION	% SUCCESS HAMMAL METHOD	% SUCCESS FIVE DISTANCES	% SUCCES MOUTH SHAPE
Joy	87.26	36.84	100
Surprise	84.44	57.89	63.16
Disgust	51.20	84.21	100
Anger	not recognized	73.68	89.47
Sadness	not recognized	68.42	94.74
Fear	not recognized	78.95	89.47
Neutral	88	100	100

3.4 Temporal Information: Analysing Video Sequences

After having tuned and validated the classification system with the static images, the use of the automatic feature extraction has enabled us to track video sequences of user's captured by a webcam. Psychological investigations argue that the timing of the facial expressions is a critical factor in the interpretation of expressions. In order to give temporary consistency to the system, a temporary window that contains the emotion detected by the system in each one of the 9 previous frames is created. A variation in the emotional state of the user is detected if in this window the same emotion is repeated at least 6 times and is different from the detected in the last emotional change.

The parameters corresponding to the neutral face are obtained calculating the average of the first frames of the video sequence, in which the user is supposed to be in the neutral state. For the rest of the frames, a classification takes place following the method explained in the previous sections.

4   Application: New Input Data for Natural Interfaces

To demonstrate the potential of our emotional tracking system, we have added it to Maxine [14], a general engine for real-time management of virtual scenarios and characters developed by the group. Maxine is a tool that has been created with the aim of making it easy the use of character-based interfaces in different application domains. The general vision is that if a user's emotion could be recognized by computer, human interaction would become more natural, enjoyable and productive. The system presented here has been configured as a new multimodal input to the system. The system recognizes the emotion of the user and responds in an engaging way. The features extraction program captures each facial frame and extracts the 10 feature points which are sent to the emotion classifier. When an emotional change is detected, the output of the 7-emotion classifier constitutes an emotion code which is sent to Maxine's character. For the moment, the virtual character's face just mimics the emotional state of the user (Fig. 3), accommodating his/her facial animation and speech.

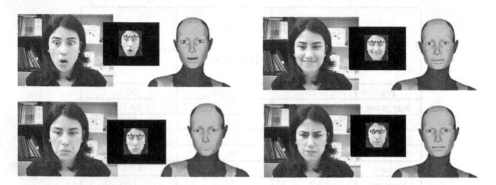

Fig. 3. Examples of the integrated real-time application: detection of surprise, joy, sadness, anger. For each example, images captured by the webcam, small images showing automatic features' tracking and synthesized facial expressions are shown. The animated character mimics the facial expression of the user.

5   Conclusions and Future Work

We have presented a simple and effective system for the real-time recognition of facial expressions. In opposition to other systems that rely on the use of wearable detectors, the system developed in non-invasive and is based on the use of a simple low cost webcam. The automatic features extraction program allows the introduction of dynamic information in the classification system, making it possible the study of the time evolution of the evaluated parameters, and the classification of user's emotions from live video.

To test its usefulness and real-time operation, the system has been added to the Maxine system, an engine developed by the group for managing 3D virtual scenarios and characters to enrich user interaction in different application domains. For the moment, and as a first step, the emotional information has been used to accommodate facial animation and speech of the virtual character to the emotional state of the user. More sophisticated adaptive behaviour is now being explored. As it has been pointed out, recognition of emotional information is a key step toward giving computers the ability to interact more naturally and intelligently with people.

Acknowledgments

We would like to thank Sergio Garcia Masip for his work in Maxine. This work has been partially financed by the Spanish "Dirección General de Investigación", contract number N° TIN2004-07926 and by the Aragon Government through the WALQA agreement (ref. 2004/04/86).

J. Varona acknowledges the support of a Ramon y Cajal fellowship from the Spanish MEC.

References

1. Turk, M., Kölsch, M.: Perceptual Interfaces. In: Medioni, G., Kang, S.B. (eds.) Emerging Topics in Computer Vision, Prentice Hall, Englewood Cliffs (2005)
2. Bradski, G.R.: Computer Vision Face Tracking as a Component of a Perceptual User Interface. In: Proceedings of the IEEE Workshop on Applications of Computer Vision, pp. 214–219 (1998)
3. Toyama, K.: "Look, Ma – No Hands!" Hands-Free Cursor Control with Real-Time 3D Face Tracking. In: Proceedings of the Workshop on Perceptual User Interfaces, pp. 49–54 (1998)
4. Gorodnichy, D.O., Malik, S., Roth, G.: Nouse 'Use Your Nose as a Mouse' – a New Technology for Hands-free Games and Interfaces. Image and Vision Computing 22, 931–942 (2004)
5. Betke, M., Gips, J., Fleming, P.: The Camera Mouse: Visual Tracking of Body Features to Provide Computer Access for People with Severe Disabilities. IEEE Transactions on neural systems and Rehabilitation Engineering, vol. 10 (2002)
6. Pantic, M., Rothkrantz, L.J.M.: Automatic Analysis of Facial Expressions: The State of the Art. Pattern Analysis and Machine Intelligence. IEEE Transactions 22(12), 1424–1445 (2000)
7. Ekman, P.: Facial Expression, the Handbook of Cognition and Emotion. John Wiley et Sons, Chichester (1999)
8. Viola, P., Jones, M.: Robust Real-Time Face Detection. International Journal of Computer Vision 57, 137–154 (2004)
9. Shi, J., Tomasi, C.: Good Features to Track. In: Proceedings of the IEEE Conference on Computer Vision and Pattern Recognition, pp. 593–600 (1994)
10. Baker, S., Matthews, I.: Lucas-Kanade 20 Years On: A Unifying Framework. International Journal of Computer Vision 56, 221–225 (2004)
11. Hammal, Z., Couvreur, L., Caplier, A., Rombaut, M.: Facial Expressions Recognition Based on the Belief Theory: Comparison with Different Classifiers. In: Proc. 13th International Conference on Image Analysis and Processing (2005)
12. http://www.mmk.ei.tum.de/~waf/fgnet/feedtum.html (Reviewed in February 2006)
13. Bassili, J.N.: Emotion recognition: The role of facial movement and the relative importance of upper and lower areas of the face. Journal of Personality and Social Psychology 37, 2049–2059 (1997)
14. Seron, F., Baldassarri, S., Cerezo, E.: MaxinePPT: Using 3D Virtual Characters for Natural Interaction. In: Proc. WUCAmI'06: 2nd International Workshop on Ubiquitous Computing and Ambient Intelligence, pp. 241–250 (2006)

A Simple But Effective Approach to Speaker Tracking in Broadcast News

Luis Javier Rodríguez, Mikel Peñagarikano, and Germán Bordel

Grupo de Trabajo en Tecnologías del Software
Departamento de Electricidad y Electrónica. Facultad de Ciencia y Tecnología.
Universidad del País Vasco. Barrio Sarriena s/n. 48940 Leioa. Spain
luisjavier.rodriguez@ehu.es

Abstract. The automatic transcription of broadcast news and meetings involves the segmentation, identification and tracking of speaker turns during each session, which is known as *speaker diarization*. This paper presents a simple but effective approach to a slightly different task, called *speaker tracking*, also involving audio segmentation and speaker identification, but with a subset of known speakers, which allows to estimate speaker models and to perform identification on a segment-by-segment basis. The proposed algorithm segments the audio signal in a fully unsupervised way, by locating the most likely change points from an purely acoustic point of view. Then the available speaker data are used to estimate single-Gaussian acoustic models. Finally, speaker models are used to classify the audio segments by choosing the most likely speaker or, alternatively, the *Other* category, if none of the speakers is likely enough. Despite its simplicity, the proposed approach yielded the best performance in the speaker tracking challenge organized in November 2006 by the Spanish Network on Speech Technology.

1 Introduction

The automatic transcription of broadcast news and meetings involves the segmentation, identification and tracking of speaker turns during each session, which is known as *speaker diarization* [1][2]. This task involves the segmentation of the input signal into speaker turns, advertising, music, noise and whatever other content is included in the audio file. Then, speech segments corresponding to the same speaker are clustered together and tagged with the same label. Non-speech segments are all tagged with the special label *Other*.

To measure the speaker diarization error, first the system and reference segmentations are aligned. Then, among those labels assigned by the system to any given speaker, that appearing most times is taken as the system choice and considered equivalent to the reference label. Finally, the speaker diarization error is computed as the fraction of time speakers are correctly identified. Consider the example shown in Figure 1, where not only segmentation errors but also clustering errors are illustrated. Note, for instance, that the last segment is erroneously assigned to a third speaker. After the alignment is done, the label *s01* is considered equivalent to *mm* and the label *s02* equivalent to *ft*. Finally, it is

J. Martí et al. (Eds.): IbPRIA 2007, Part II, LNCS 4478, pp. 48–55, 2007.

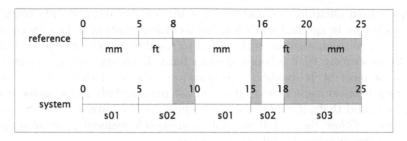

Fig. 1. An example of speaker diarization. The system provides a sequence of segments with *blind* speaker labels. After aligning the system and reference segmentations, label equivalences are set. Finally, the speaker identification error is computed as the fraction of time speakers are erroneously identified (shaded regions).

found that speakers have been erroneously identified during 10 seconds out of 25 (the shaded regions in Figure 1), which means a 40% speaker diarization error.

A slightly different task, called *speaker tracking*, is posed when speaker data are available a priori, because speaker models can be estimated and used to segment and label the audio file. Like speaker diarization, speaker tracking involves audio segmentation and speaker identification, but this latter is performed in a supervised way. In other words, the objective is to detect target speakers in a continuous audio stream. Clustering is not needed because each segment can be independently scored against speaker models and classified accordingly. Consider the example shown in Figure 2. It is close to that of Figure 1, except for the fact that the system does not provide *blind* labels, but labels of known speakers. The alignment does not determine which is the most likely mapping between reference labels and system labels. The speaker identification error is computed in a straightforward way, as the fraction of time system labels do not match reference labels. In the example of Figure 2 speakers are erroneosuly identified during 15 seconds out of 25, which means a 60% speaker identification error.

In this paper a simple approach is presented for speaker tracking in broadcast news. The segmentation step is done in a fully unsupervised way, by locating the most likely change points in the acoustic signal. Segmentation is completely

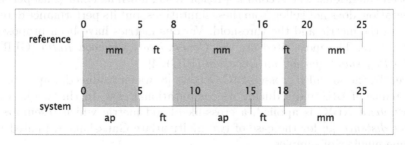

Fig. 2. An example of speaker tracking. The system provides a sequence of segments with labels of known speakers. The speaker identification error is computed as the fraction of time speakers are erroneously identified (shaded regions).

decoupled from identification and does not use speaker data. It only takes into account changes in spectral statistics. Speaker identification is done by computing the score of each segment with regard to speaker models, which are trained beforehand starting from labelled speaker data. Each segment is assigned the label of the most likely speaker or, alternatively, the label *Other*, if none of the speakers is likely enough. Note that broadcast news include music, noise, adverstising, etc. and that only a subset of the speakers is known a priori. So, under the category *Other* should fall not only non-speech segments, but also speech segments corresponding to unknown speakers.

This paper is organized as follows: in the next two sections, the audio segmentation and speaker identification algorithms are explained in detail; in section 4 the experimental setup is described, including the speech database, the audio processing and the tuning experiments; results are shown and discussed in section 5; finally, section 6 gives conclusions and tracks for future work.

2   Audio Segmentation

Audio segmentation, also known as *acoustic change detection*, consists of exploring an audio file to find acoustically homogeneous segments, or, in other words, detecting any change of speaker, background or channel conditions. It is a pattern recognition problem, since it strives to find the most likely categorization of a sequence of acoustic observations, yielding the boundaries between segments as a by-product. Audio segmentation becomes useful as a preprocessing step in order to transcribe the speech content in broadcast news and meetings, because regions of different nature can be handled in a different way.

There are two basic approaches to this problem: (1) *model-based* segmentation [3], which estimates different acoustic models for a closed set of acoustic classes (e.g. noise, music, speech, etc.) and classifies the audio stream by finding the most likely sequence of models; and (2) *metric-based* segmentation [4][5][6], which defines some metric to compare the spectral stastistics at both sides of successive points of the audio signal, and hypothesizes those boundaries whose metric values exceed a given threshold. The first approach requires the availability of enough training data to estimate the models of acoustic classes and does not generalize to unseen conditions. The second approach, also known as *blind* (unsupervised) segmentation, does not suffer from these limitations, but its performance depends highly on the metric and the threshold. Various metrics have been proposed in the literature. The most cited are the *Generalized Likelihood Ratio* (GLR) [7] and the *Bayesian Information Criterion* (BIC) [4].

Recently, the so called crossed-BIC (XBIC) [8] was introduced, improving the performance of BIC and reducing its computational cost. In this work, a kind of *normalized* XBIC is applied, a cross-likelihood metric which resembles the *Rabiner distance* [9] for the case of two multivariate Gaussians estimated from the same number of samples.

Consider two segments of speech, X and Y, of the same length, and the corresponding sequences of spectral feature vectors, $x = x_1, \ldots, x_N$ and $y = y_1, \ldots, y_N$. Assuming that the acoustic vectors are statistically independent and that can be modelled by a multivariate Gaussian distribution, we estimate the models $\lambda_x = N(O; \mu_x, \Sigma_x)$ and $\lambda_y = N(O; \mu_y, \Sigma_y)$ and define the *dissimilarity measure* between X and Y as follows:

$$d(X, Y) = - \log \left(\frac{P(x|\lambda_y)P(y|\lambda_x)}{P(x|\lambda_x)P(y|\lambda_y)} \right) \tag{1}$$

where $P(z|\lambda) = \prod_{i=1}^{N} N(z_i; \mu, \Sigma)$ is the likelihood of the acoustic sequence z given the model λ. In other words, if X and Y are acoustically close, their respective models will be quite close too, which means that $d(X, Y) \approx 0$. On the other hand, the more X and Y differ, the greater $d(X, Y)$ will become.

The audio segmentation algorithm considers a sliding window W of N acoustic vectors and computes the likelihood of change at the center of that window, then moves the window n vectors ahead and repeats the process until the end of the vector sequence. To compute the likelihood of change, each window is divided in two halfs, W_l and W_r, then a Gaussian distribution (with diagonal covariance matrix) is estimated for each half and finally the cross-likelihood ratio (Eq. 1) is computed and stored as likelihood of change. This yields a sequence of cross-likelihood ratios which must be post-processed to get the hypothesized segment boundaries. This involves applying a threshold τ and forcing a minimum segment size δ. In practice, a boundary t is validated when its cross-likelihood ratio exceeds τ and there is no candidate boundary with greater ratio in the interval $[t - \delta, t + \delta]$. An example of audio segmentation is shown in Figure 3.

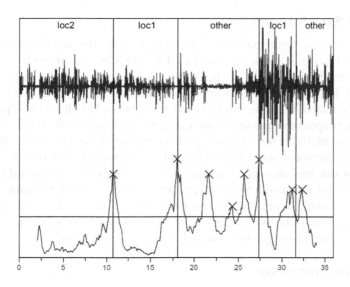

Fig. 3. An example of audio segmentation. Vertical lines represent actual boundaries, either between two speaker turns, or between a speaker turn and non-speech content. The local maxima marked with 'X' represent the boundaries hypothesized by the system.

3   Speaker Identification

Once the segmentation is done, each segment must be given a speaker label or, alternatively, the special label *Other* when no speaker is likely enough. Assuming that a certain amount of training data is available for L target speakers, speaker models can be estimated beforehand. In this work, speaker models are multivariate Gaussian distributions: $\lambda_i = N(O; \mu_i, \Sigma_i)$, for $i = 1, \ldots, L$. This is just a special case of the GMM classifiers routinely used for speaker identification [10]. To classify any given segment X, firstly the *segment model* is estimated (again as a Gaussian distribution with diagonal covariance matrix) $\lambda_X = N(O; \mu_X, \sigma_X^2)$, starting from the sequence of acoustic vectors $x = x_1, \ldots, x_N$. Note that $P(x|\lambda_X) \geq P(x|\lambda_i) \ \forall i$. The label $l(X)$ is given according to the following rule:

$$
l(X) = \begin{cases} k = \arg \max_{i=1,\ldots,L} P(X|\lambda_i) & \text{if } \frac{1}{N} \log \left(\frac{P(x|\lambda_k)}{P(x|\lambda_X)} \right) > \epsilon \\ \\ Other & \text{otherwise} \end{cases} \tag{2}
$$

where ϵ is a heuristically fixed margin which determines a threshold in the average log-likelihood ratio over which the most likely speaker k is validated as the best choice. Alternatively, if the likelihood ratio of the most likely speaker does not exceed ϵ, the label *Other* is assigned to X.

4   Experimental Setup

4.1   The Speech Database

There was a short-term motivation for this work in the challenge for speaker tracking in broadcast news proposed in July 2006 by the Spanish Network on Speech Technologies (RTH). In fact, the experiments reported here are those carried out for that challenge, under the conditions set by the RTH [11]. The database consisted of audio tracks taken from radio broadcasts in Spanish, including many speakers, music, movie excerpts, advertising, overlaps, etc. Training data were available for 5 target speakers, consisting of 5 short utterances per speaker, 4 of them distorted with echo and reverberation. The training material for each speaker had an average length of 12.8 seconds (64 seconds all together). The test corpus consisted of 20 long tracks, with an average length of nearly 4 minutes (around 77 minutes all together). One of the training tracks, including material from only two of the target speakers, was also used for developing purposes (tuning the segmentation and identification algorithms).

4.2   Audio Processing

Radio broadcasts were all sampled at 16 kHz and stored in PCM format using 16 bits per sample. The audio was analysed in frames of 25 milliseconds (400 samples) at intervals of 10 milliseconds. A Hamming window was applied and a 512-point FFT computed. The FFT amplitudes were then averaged in 24 overlapped triangular filters, with central frequencies and bandwidths defined according to the Mel scale. A Discrete Cosine Transform was finally applied to the logarithm of the filter amplitudes, obtaining 12 Mel-Frequency Cepstral Coefficients (MFCC). The choice of MFCC is based on the fact that historically there have been no features specifically designed for audio segmentation, and the MFCC are the most commonly used parameters for speaker identification.

4.3 Tuning Experiments

The tuning phase consisted on running various experiments to adjust the parameters of the audio segmentation and speaker identification algorithms. As noted above, one of the audio files included in the test set, as well as the corresponding reference labels (set by human experts), were available to make the adjustments. Parameters were set to get the best match between system labels and reference labels (see Table 1). However, some considerations were taken into account beforehand, which we summarize in the following lines.

The size of the sliding window (N) should balance the performance of the segmentation algorithm for short and long segments. If N was too short, the estimation of spectral properties would focus on instantaneous events but would be less robust. If N was too long, the estimations would be robust but less sensitive to instantaneous events, and therefore very short turns would be missed. The window step (n) should be as small as possible to allow maximum resolution. However, this would increase the computational cost of the approach. The threshold for the likelihood of change (τ) should balance false alarms and missings. If τ was too low, many false boundaries would be detected; inversely, if τ was too high, some actual boundaries would be missed. However, since our objective was not an accurate segmentation but the identification of target speakers, over-segmentation did not pose a problem as long as the segments were all assigned the right speaker label. So, τ could be skewed to low values. The minimum segment size (δ) allowed to choose the most likely segment boundary in any given interval of size 2δ. If δ was too high, short segments might be missed, so it should be as small as possible, as long as it fulfils the task of avoiding *noisy boundaries* around an actual boundary. Finally, the threshold for the speaker identification likelihood (ϵ) should balance the false alarms (segments erroneously assigned to a known speaker) and missings (segments produced by known speakers and erroneously tagged as *Other*).

Table 1. Tuned settings for the audio segmentation and speaker identification parameters: size of the sliding window (N), window step (n), threshold for the likelihood of change (τ), minimum segment size (δ) and threshold for the speaker identification likelihood (ϵ)

	Audio segmentation				Speaker identification
Parameter	N	n	τ	δ	ϵ
Tuned setting	400 (4 seconds)	10 (0.1 seconds)	1200	6 (0.6 seconds)	-1.1

5 Results

To measure the performance of the proposed approach, it was used the NIST evaluation software for speaker diarization included in the Spring 2006 Rich Transcription Meeting Recognition Evaluation Plan [12]. This software takes the system labels as if they were *blind*, applying the label mapping function that minimizes the speaker diarization error, as shown in Figure 1. But what we produce are not blind but informed labels, and the speaker identification error must be measured by comparing the system and reference labels on a frame-by-frame basis, as shown in Figure 2. To accomplish that, a little change was introduced in the NIST software, so that the score is computed as the time system labels match reference labels divided by the total audio time. Our system yields a *17.25%* speaker identification error, which is slightly better than that yielded by a more complex and computationally expensive system competing with ours.

Our score is comparable to other results reported in the literature [13], and is specially relevant due to the following issues:

- All the acoustic models are single Gaussians, which can hardly model the spectral variability of speakers and segments, but at the same time provide robust estimates (even when not many training data are available) and allow real-time operation of the speaker tracking system.
- Audio segmentation and speaker identification are independent modules, but further improvements might be obtained by using speaker information at the segmentation phase.
- Speaker models are estimated from a few utterances taken from radio broadcasts, many of them (80%) intentionally distorted.
- The system parameters are tuned almost blindly, using only one of the 20 audio files in the test set. More robust tuning may be accomplished if more development data were available. In particular, a *16.26%* speaker identification error has been obtained by tuning the parameters over the 20 audio files of the test set.

6 Conclusion

A simple approach to speaker tracking in broadcast news is presented in this paper. The audio is segmented in a fully unsupervised way, by locating the most likely change points in the acoustic signal. Speaker identification is done by computing the score of each segment with regard to speaker models, which are trained beforehand starting from labelled speaker data. All the acoustic models are single Gaussians, which provide robust estimations even when few training data are available, and allow real-time operation. The proposed system yields a *17.25%* speaker identification error, which is comparable to other results reported in the literature. Current work includes applying this system to a bigger database and extending its capabilities to perform speaker diarization in broadcast news and meetings.

Acknowledgments. This work has been partially funded by the Basque Government, under program SAIOTEK, projects S-PE05UN32 and S-PE05IK06. We thank to Rubén San Segundo, from the Technical University of Madrid, for his support in preparing the speech database and using the NIST evaluation software.

References

1. Tranter, S.E., Reynolds, D.A.: Speaker Diarisation for Broadcast News. In: Proceedings of the ISCA Speaker and Language Recognition Workshop (Odyssey 2004), pp. 337–344. Toledo, Spain. May 31 - June 3 (2004)
2. Jin, Q., Laskowsky, K., Schultz, T., Waibel, A.: Speaker Segmentation and Clustering in Meetings. In: Proceedings of Interspeech 2004 (International Conference on Spoken Language Processing, ICSLP), pp. 597–600. Jeju Island, South Korea. October (2004)
3. Gauvain, J.L., Lamel, L., Adda, G.: Partitioning and Transcription of Broadcast News Data. In: Proceedings of the International Conference on Spoken Language Processing (ICSLP'98), Sydney, Australia, pp. 1335–1338 (November-December 1998)
4. Chen, S.S., Gopalakrishnan, P.S.: Speaker, Environment and Channel Change Detection and Clustering via the Bayesian Information Criterion. Proceedings of the DARPA Broadcast News Transcription and Understanding Workshop. Lansdowne, Virginia, USA. February 8-11 (1998)
5. Delacourt, P., Wellekens, C.J.: DISTBIC: A speaker-based segmentation for audio data indexing. Speech Communication 32, 111–126 (2000)
6. Zhou, B., Hansen, J.H.L.: Efficient Audio Stream Segmentation via the Combined T^2 Statistic and Bayesian Information Criterion. IEEE Transactions on Speech and Audio Processing 13(4), 467–474 (2005)
7. Gish, H., Siu, M.H., Rohlicek, R.: Segregation of Speakers for Speech Recognition and Speaker Identification. In: Proceedings of the IEEE International Conference on Acoustics, Speech and Signal Processing (ICASSP 1991), pp. 873–876. Toronto, Canada. May 14-17 (1991)
8. Anguera, X., Hernando, J., Anguita, J.: XBIC: nueva medida para segmentación de locutor hacia el indexado automático de la señal de voz. Actas de las Terceras Jornadas en Tecnología del Habla, pp. 237–242. Valencia, España. 17-19 de noviembre de (2004)
9. Juang, B.H., Rabiner, L.R.: A Probabilistic Distance Measure for Hidden Markov Models. AT&T Technical Journal 64(2), 391–408 (1985)
10. Reynolds, D.A., Rose, R.C.: Robust Text-Independent Speaker Identification Using Gaussian Mixture Speaker Models. IEEE Transactions on Speech and Audio Processing 3(1), 72–83 (1995)
11. Red Temática de Tecnologías del Habla: Propuesta de Evaluación de Sistemas ALBAYZIN-06 (Segmentación e Identificación de hablantes). IV Jornadas en Tecnología del Habla. Zaragoza, pp. 8–10 de Noviembre de http://jth2006.unizar.es/evaluacion/albayzin06.html (2006)
12. NIST: Spring 2006 (RT-06S) Rich Transcription Meeting Recognition Evaluation Plan. http://www.nist.gov/speech/tests/rt/rt2006/spring/
13. Dunn, R.B., Reynolds, D.A., Quatieri, T.F.: Approaches to Speaker Detection and Tracking in Conversational Speech. Digital Signal Processing 10, 93–112 (2000)

Region-Based Pose Tracking*

Christian Schmaltz[1], Bodo Rosenhahn[2], Thomas Brox[3], Daniel Cremers[3],
Joachim Weickert[1], Lennart Wietzke[4], and Gerald Sommer[4]

[1] Mathematical Image Analysis Group, Faculty of Mathematics and Computer Science,
Building E1 1 Saarland University, 66041 Saarbrücken, Germany
{schmaltz,weickert}@mia.uni-saarland.de
[2] Max-Planck Institute for Informatics, 66123 Saarbrücken, Germany
rosenhahn@mpi-sb.mpg.de
[3] Department of Computer Science,University of Bonn, 53117 Bonn, Germany
{brox,dcremers}@cs.uni-bonn.de
[4] Institute of Computer Science, Christian-Albrecht-University, 24098 Kiel, Germany
{lw,gs}@ks.informatik.uni-kiel.de

Abstract. This paper introduces a technique for region-based pose tracking without the need to explicitly compute contours. We assume a surface model of a rigid
object and at least one calibrated camera view. The goal is to find the pose parameters that optimally fit the model surface to the contour of the object seen in
the image. In contrast to conventional contour-based techniques, which acquire
the contour to be extracted explicitly from the image, our approach optimizes an
energy directly defined on the pose parameters. We show experimental results for
rather challenging scenes observed with a monocular and a stereo camera system.

1 Introduction

The task to pursue the 3-D position and orientation of a known 3-D object model from a
2-D image data stream is called 2-D–3-D pose tracking [8]. The need for pose tracking
occurs in several applications, e.g. self localization and object grasping in robotics,
or camera calibration. Particularly in scenes with cluttered backgrounds, noise, partial
occlusions, or changing illumination, pose tracking is still a challenging problem even
after more than 25 years of research [10].

A lot of different approaches to pose tracking have been considered [7,12]. In [6],
an iterative algorithm for real-time pose tracking of articulated objects, which is based
on edge detection, has been proposed. Often points [1] or lines [2] are used for feature
matching, but other features such as vertices, t-junctions, cusps, three-tangent junctions,
limb and edge injections, and curvature L-junctions have also been considered [9].

Another way to approach pose estimation is to match a surface model of the object
to be tracked to the object region in the images. Thereby, the computation of this region
yields a typical segmentation problem. It has been proposed to optimize a coupled formulation of both problems and to solve simultaneously for the contours and the pose
parameters via graph cuts [3] or via iterative approaches [4]. Although the coupled estimation of contours and pose parameters is beneficial compared to the uncoupled case,
segmentation results can be inaccurate, as seen in Figure 1.

---

* We acknowledge funding by the German Research Foundation under the projects We 2602/5-1
and SO 320/4-2, and the Max-Planck Center for Visual Computing and Communication.

J. Martí et al. (Eds.): IbPRIA 2007, Part II, LNCS 4478, pp. 56–63, 2007.

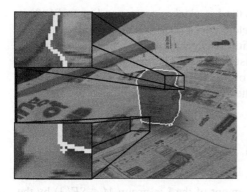

Fig. 1. Problems often occurring in variational segmentation algorithms: (a) An inaccurate segmentation. Note the split up into multiple connected components. (b) An error due to oversmoothing and another kind of undesired topological change.

In this paper, we build upon the method in [4] including its statistical representation of regions. However, instead of estimating 2-D segmentation and 3-D pose parameters separately we directly estimate 3-D pose parameters by minimizing the projection error in the respective 2-D images. Consequently, we can estimate segmentations which are by construction consistent with the 3-D pose. Moreover, the estimation of an infinite-dimensional level set function is replaced by the optimization of a small number of pose parameters. This results in a drastic speed-up and near real-time performance.

In the next section, we will briefly review pose estimation from 2-D–3-D point correspondences. We will then explain our approach in Section 3, followed by experimental results in Section 4. Section 5 concludes with a summary.

2 Pose Estimation from 2-D–3-D Point Correspondences

This section introduces basic concepts and notation and briefly describes the point-based pose estimation algorithm used in our approach [13]. Given some 3-D points x_i on the object, which are visible as 2-D points q_i in an image, the algorithm seeks a rigid body motion ξ such that each point x_i is on the line passing through q_i and the camera origin. Section 3 shows how such point correspondences are obtained with our method.

2.1 Rigid Motion and Twists

A rigid body motion in 3-D can be represented as $m(x) := Rx + t$, where $t \in \mathbb{R}^3$ is a translation vector and $R \in SO(3)$ is a rotation matrix with $SO(3) := \{R \in \mathbb{R}^{3 \times 3} : \det(R) = 1\}$. By means of homogeneous coordinates, we can write m as a matrix M:

$$m((x_1,x_2,x_3)^T) = M(x_1,x_2,x_3,1)^T = \begin{pmatrix} R_{3\times3} & t_{3\times1} \\ 0_{1\times3} & 1 \end{pmatrix} x . \tag{1}$$

The set of all matrices of this kind is called the *Lie group SE*(3). To every Lie group there is an associated Lie algebra. Its underlying vector space is the tangent space of the Lie group evaluated at the origin. The Lie algebra associated with the Lie group $SO(3)$

is $so(3) := \{A \in \mathbb{R}^{3\times3}|A^T = -A\}$, whereas the Lie algebra corresponding to $SE(3)$ is $se(3) := \{(v, \omega)|v \in \mathbb{R}^3, \omega \in so(3)\}$. Since elements of $se(3)$ can be converted to $SE(3)$ and vice versa, we can represent a rigid motion as element of $se(3)$. Such an element is called *twist*. This is advantageous since a twist has only six parameters while an element of $SE(3)$ has twelve. Both have six degrees of freedom, though.

Elements of $so(3)$ and $se(3)$ can be written both as vectors $\omega = (\omega_1, \omega_2, \omega_3)$, $\xi = (\omega_1, \omega_2, \omega_3, v_1, v_2, v_3)$ and as matrices:

$$\hat{\omega} = \begin{pmatrix} 0 & -\omega_3 & \omega_2 \\ \omega_3 & 0 & -\omega_1 \\ -\omega_2 & \omega_1 & 0 \end{pmatrix} \in so(3), \qquad \hat{\xi} = \begin{pmatrix} \hat{\omega} & v \\ 0_{3\times1} & 0 \end{pmatrix} \in se(3) . \qquad (2)$$

A twist $\hat{\xi} \in se(3)$ can be converted to an element of the Lie group $M \in SE(3)$ by the exponential function $\exp(\hat{\xi}) = M$. This exponential can be computed efficiently with the Rodriguez formula. For further details we refer to [11].

2.2 Pose Estimation with 2-D–3-D Point Correspondences

Let (q,x) be a 2-D–3-D point correspondence, i.e. $x \in \mathbb{R}^4$ is a point in homogeneous coordinates on the 3-D silhouette of the object and $q \in \mathbb{R}^2$ is its position in the image. Furthermore, let $L = (n,m)$ be the Plücker line [14] through q and the respective camera origin. The distance of any point a to the line L given in Plücker form can be computed by using the cross product: $\|a \times n - m\|$, i.e., $a \in L$ if and only if $\|a \times n - m\| = 0$.

Our goal is to find a twist ξ such that the transformed points $\exp(\hat{\xi})x_i$ are close to the corresponding lines L_i. Linearizing the exponential function $\exp(\hat{\xi}) = \sum_{k=0}^{\infty} \frac{\hat{\xi}^k}{k!} \approx I + \hat{\xi}$ (where I is the identity matrix), we like to minimize with respect to ξ:

$$\sum_i \left\| \left(\exp\left(\hat{\xi}\right) x_i \right)_{3\times1} \times n_i - m_i \right\|^2 \approx \sum_i \left\| \left(\left(I + \hat{\xi}\right) x_i \right)_{3\times1} \times n_i - m_i \right\|^2 \rightarrow \min, \qquad (3)$$

where the function $\cdot_{3\times1} : \mathbb{R}^4 \mapsto \mathbb{R}^3$ removes the last entry, which is 1. Evaluation yields three linear equations of rank two for each correspondence (q_i, x_i). Thus, to solve for the 6 twist parameters, we need at least three correspondences for a unique solution. Usually, there are far more point correspondences and one obtains a least squares problem, which can be solved efficiently with the Householder algorithm. Since the twist ξ only corresponds to the pose change it is rather "small". Thus, linearizing the exponential function does not create large errors. Moreover, we iterate this minimization process.

3   Region-Based Model Fitting

Existing contour-based pose estimation algorithms expect an explicit contour to establish correspondences between contour points and points on the model surface. This involves a matching of the projected surface and the contour. Our idea is to avoid explicit computations of contours and the contour matching. Instead, we seek to adapt the pose parameters in such a way that the projections of the surface optimally split all images into the object and the background region. For simplicity, we will describe this setting for a single camera, but the concept is trivially extended to multiple views.

Fig. 2. From left to right: (a) Input image. The puncher is to be tracked. (b) Projection of the model in an inaccurate pose onto the image (magnified). The two marked points are the points referenced to in Section 3.2 (c) The 2-D contour of the projection (magnified). The arrows show into which directions these points should move in our algorithm.

3.1 Energy Model

Like in a segmentation task, we seek an optimal partitioning of the image domain Ω. This can be expressed as minimization of the energy function

$$E(\xi) = -\int_{\Omega} (P(\xi, q) \log p_1 + (1 - P(\xi, q)) \log p_2) \, dq, \qquad (4)$$

where the function $P(\xi, q) \in (\mathbb{R}^6 \times \Omega \mapsto \{0, 1\})$ is 1 if and only if the surface of the 3-D model with pose ξ projects to the point q in the image plane. P splits the image domain into two parts, in each of which different feature distributions are expected. These distributions are modeled by probability density functions p_1 and p_2.

Note the similarity of (4) to variational segmentation methods [4]. The important difference is that the partitioning is not represented by a contour, i.e. a function, but by only six parameters. Moreover, there is no constraint on the length of the boundary in (4).

The probability densities are modeled by local Gaussian distributions [4] of the color in CIELAB color space, and texture in the texture feature space proposed in [5]. Since there is only a limited amount of data available to estimate the density functions, we consider the separate feature channels to be independent. Thus, the total probability density function is the product of the single channel densities.

The densities are adapted when the estimated pose has changed. Given the projection of the model, and hence a partitioning of the image into object and background region, p_1 and p_2 can be computed from the local mean and variance in these regions.

3.2 Minimization

We minimize (4) by computing force vectors along the contour implicitly given by the projected surface. These force vectors indicate the direction to which the projection of the model should move to minimize $E(\xi)$. Using the framework from Section 2, we can transfer this force to the 3-D points and estimate the corresponding rigid body motion.

To this end, we create 2-D–3-D point correspondences (q_i, x_i) by projecting silhouette points x_i, given the current pose ξ, to the image plane where they yield q_i. If the function value $p_1(q_i)$ is greater than $p_2(q_i)$, it is likely that q_i belongs to the interior of the object region. Thus, q_i will be shifted in inward normal direction to a new point q_i'.

For each frame:
Extrapolate new pose from previous poses and compute image features
<div style="writing-mode:vertical">Iterate</div> − Project 3D objet model onto image plane − Generate prob. density functions for inside/outside the proj. model (Section 3.1) − Adapt 2D–3D point correspondences (q_i, x_i) to (q_i', x_i) (Section 3.2) − Construct projection rays from (q_i', x_i) − Generate and solve system of equations to get a new pose (Section 2.2)

Fig. 3. Summary of the region-based pose tracking algorithm

Vice versa, points q_i where the inequality $p_1(q_i) < p_2(q_i)$ holds will be shifted in outward normal direction. The normal direction is given by ∇P approximated with Sobel operators. The length $l := \|q' - q\|$ of the shift vector is a parameter. More advanced methods how to choose l - including scaling l by $|\log p_1 - \log p_2|$, i.e. performing a gradient decent on E - have been tested but results were worse for our sequences.

This concept is illustrated in Figure 2. Figure 2b shows a white puncher, onto which the surface model has been projected. Figure 2c depicts the boundary between the interior and exterior of the projected model. Most of the points in the interior are white. So is the point marked by the right circle. Thus, it better fits to the statistical model of the object region than to the background and is moved away from the object. Vice-versa, the marked cyan point on the left side is moved inwards as it better fits to the background.

We iterate this process. At some point, the pose changes induced by the force vectors mutually cancel out. We stop iterating when the average pose change after up to three iterations is smaller than a given threshold. Before changing frames in an image sequence, we predict the object's pose in the new frame by linearly extrapolating the results from the two previous frames. Figure 3 shows an overview of the algorithm.

4 Experiments

Figure 4 shows two frames of a monocular sequence, in which a wooden toy giraffe has been tracked with our method. The estimated pose fits well to the object in the image.

Figure 5 depicts tracking results of a stereo sequence. First, a wooden beam moves between the cameras and the static object. Then the tea box is picked up and rotated several times. In the most challenging part of this sequence, the tea box is rotated around two different axis simultaneously while the bottom of the box reflects the background and moving specular highlights are visible. Nevertheless, our algorithm can track the tea box accurately over all 395 frames of this sequence.

For this sequence, an average of 12.03 iterations were necessary to reach the requested threshold (0.1mm for translation, 0.001 for rotations), with a maximum of 72 iterations. Approximately 28.75 minutes of processor time were needed on an Intel Pentium 4 with 3.2GHz ($\approx$ 12 frames per minute), about 86% of which was used for preprocessing (loading the images, computing texture features, etc.) while the rest was spent in the iteration steps. The parameters (i.e. the threshold and l) have been optimized to yield good poses. Faster but less accurate computations are possible, as explained below.

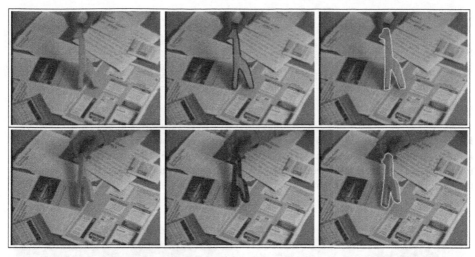

Fig. 4. From left to right: Input image, estimated pose and extracted contour for two frames of a color sequence with a wooden giraffe. **Top**: Frame 52. **Bottom**: Frame 68. The surface model consists of a single closed point grid. Thus, it is possible to look through the projected pose. Note that this is irrelevant for contour-based pose estimation, where only silhouette points are needed.

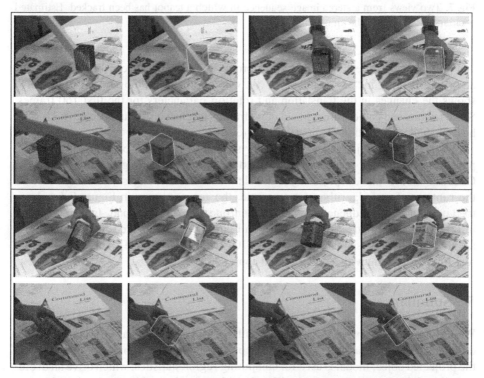

Fig. 5. Pose results for a tea box. Each block shows the computed pose (blue) and the contour (yellow) in the two views. The scene contains partial occlusions (frame 97, top left), the tea box is turned upside down (frame 230, top right), there are specular reflections (frame 269, bottom left) and the box is turned around different axes simultaneously (frame 277, bottom right).

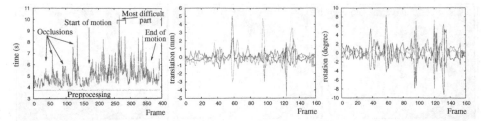

Fig. 6. Left: Time needed for preprocessing (straight green line) and the total time used per frame (red line) for the stereo image sequence shown in Figure 5. **Middle:** Changes in the three translation parameters in millimeters for the first 160 frames of this sequence. **Right:** Changes of the three Euler angles for the same frames, in degrees.

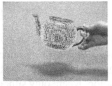

Fig. 7. Two views from a stereo image sequence in which a teapot has been tracked. Estimated contours and poses are shown in yellow.

Figure 6 shows the time used by our program per frame. It can be seen that our algorithm is faster in "easy" situations, e.g. when nothing has moved. This figure also shows the changes in the translation and rotation parameters for the first 160 frames. Since tea box and camera are static in these frames no changes should occur. Our results have a standard deviation of about 1.79 degrees and 0.83mm.

When tracking objects that are clearly separated from the background (e.g. the puncher in Figure 2), features from the texture space can be neglected and the local Gaussian model can be replaced by a global model. These changes noticeably decrease the runtime of our algorithm. For example, the teapot shown in Figure 7 has been tracked in a stereo sequence with more than one frame per second. Ignoring texture information, the tea box sequence shown in Figure 5 can be tracked (with slightly less accurate results) in less than 4 minutes ($\approx$ 104 frames per minute). This indicates that real-time processing with a region-based approach is feasible.

5 Summary

We have presented an pose tracking algorithm from 2-D regional information which does not require a separate segmentation step. The implicit partitioning of the image by the projected object model is used for computing region statistics, which drive an evolution directly in the pose parameters. The algorithm can deal with illumination changes, cluttered background, partial occlusions, specular highlights and arbitrary rigid 3-D models. Experiments show that the results compare well to methods based on explicit contour representations. However, our approach is considerably faster and close to real-time performance.

References

1. Abidi, M.A., Chandra, T.: Pose estimation for camera calibration and landmark tracking. In: Proc. International Conf. Robotics and Automation, Cincinnati, vol. 1, pp. 420–426 (1990)
2. Beveridge, J.: Local Search Algorithms for Geometric Object Recognition: Optimal Correspondence and Pose. PhD thesis, Department of Computer Science, University of Massachusetts, Amherst (May 1993)
3. Bray, M., Kohli, P., Torr, P.: PoseCut: Simultaneous segmentation and 3D pose estimation of humans using dynamic graph-cuts. In: Leonardis, A., Bischof, H., Pinz, A. (eds.) ECCV 2006. LNCS, vol. 3952, pp. 642–655. Springer, Heidelberg (2006)
4. Brox, T., Rosenhahn, B., Weickert, J.: Three-dimensional shape knowledge for joint image segmentation and pose estimation. In: Kropatsch, W.G., Sablatnig, R., Hanbury, A. (eds.) Pattern Recognition. LNCS, vol. 3663, pp. 109–116. Springer, Heidelberg (2005)
5. Brox, T., Weickert, J.: A TV flow based local scale estimate and its application to texture discrimination. Journal of Visual Communication and Image Representation, 17(5), 1053–1073 (2006)
6. Drummond, T., Cipolla, R.: Real-time tracking of multiple articulated structures in multiple views. In: Vernon, D. (ed.) ECCV 2000. LNCS, vol. 1843, pp. 20–36. Springer, Heidelberg (2000)
7. Goddard, J.: Pose And Motion Estimation From Vision Using Dual Quaternion-Based Extended Kalman Filtering. PhD thesis, Imaging, Robotics, and Intelligent Systems Laboratory, The University of Tennessee, Knoxville-College of Engineering, Tennessee (1997)
8. Grimson, W., Lozano–Perez, T., Huttenlocher, D.: Object Recognition by Computer: The Role of Geometric Constraints. MIT Press, Cambridge (1990)
9. Kriegman, D., Vijayakumar, B., Ponce, J.: Constraints for recognizing and locating curved 3D objects from monocular image features. In: Sandini, G. (ed.) ECCV 1992. LNCS, vol. 588, pp. 829–833. Springer, Heidelberg (1992)
10. Lowe, D.: Solving for the parameters of object models from image descriptions. In: Proc. ARPA Image Understanding Workshop, pp. 121–127, College Park (April 1980)
11. Murray, R.M., Li, Z., Sastry, S.S.: A Mathematical Introduction to Robotic Manipulation. CRC Press, Boca Raton (1994)
12. Rosenhahn, B.: Pose Estimation Revisited. PhD thesis, Institute of Computer Science, Chair of Cognitive Systems, University of Kiel, Germany (2003)
13. Rosenhahn, B., Sommer, G.: Adaptive pose estimation for different corresponding entities. In: Van Gool, L. (ed.) Pattern Recognition. LNCS, vol. 2449, pp. 265–273. Springer, Heidelberg (2002)
14. Shevlin, F.: Analysis of orientation problems using Plucker lines. In: Proc. 14th International Conference on Pattern Recognition. 1, pp. 685–689. IEEE Computer Society Press, Washington, DC, USA (1998)

Testing Geodesic Active Contours

A. Caro[1], T. Alonso[2], P.G. Rodríguez[1], M.L. Durán[1], and M.M. Ávila[1]

[1] Departamento de Informática, Escuela Politécnica, Universidad de Extremadura,
E-10071 Cáceres, Spain
{andresc,pablogr,mlduran,mmavila}@unex.es
[2] Sicubo S.L.[TM], Spain
talonso@sicubo.com

Abstract. Active Contours are a widely used Pattern Recognition technique. Classical Active Contours are curves evolutionate by minimizing an energy function. However, they can detect only one object within an image with several objects, and the solution is highly dependent on parameters in its formulation. A solution can be found in Geodesic Active Contours (GAC). We have developed a version of this technique and improved some aspects to apply on real and practical cases. The algorithm has been tested with both synthetic and real images.

1 Introduction

Techniques known as Deformable Models introduce interesting image segmentation methods. Active Contours, being one of these models, work with evolutive curves that depend on image features. The goal is to detect objects in an image [5, 2, 15].

The classical modeling of Active Contours achieves object recognition by means of the minimization of the energy function value at all curve points, which reach a position where the gradient is maximum (where the image energy is minimum) [5]. These models provide solutions with some degree of strength; however, they also yield noteworthy drawbacks. Some of them are the detection of just one object within the image, resistance to topological changes in the curve, or parametric dependence.

Aiming to cope with previous difficulties, an alternative is provided by our research, based on Active Contours. This model has evolved over time according to intrinsic geometric characteristics of the image itself. This technique is called Geodesic Active Contours (GAC) [4], due to the fact that its mathematical model is related to the calculation of geodesic minimal distance curves (very similar to level curves in topographic maps) in a Riemann´s space [6].

GAC can detect several objects separately or join in only one, thereby allowing the simultaneous detection of several objects within the same image. In addition, they are non-parametric models (their formulation is independent of external parameters to the image). Also, stable borders are detected when image gradients vary highly in different areas or even when they have discontinuities, cuts or gaps. Their formulation allows topological changes in the curve (the Active Contour).

J. Martí et al. (Eds.): IbPRIA 2007, Part II, LNCS 4478, pp. 64–71, 2007.
© Springer-Verlag Berlin Heidelberg 2007

2 Data Set

The current experiment is based on a data set of synthetic images and on a second group with real images. More than one hundred synthetic images have been designed for testing the validation of the GAC technique. Another image group (third in the study) includes several objects as synthetic items and real objects. Figure 1 shows some examples of the four types of images on our database.

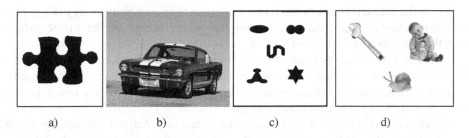

a)   b)   c)   d)

Fig. 1. Some examples of our test image database: a) Synthetic image; b) Real color image; c) A group of synthetic objects in the image; d) A group of real objects in the image

3 Methodology

GAC are geometric models whose curvature is based on Active Contour evolution. These algorithms apply Level Set methods both to allow automatic topological changes in the curve and to surround several objects simultaneously.

3.1 What Is a Riemannian Space?

It is an extension of a curved space with any number of dimensions. This kind of space does not comply with the basic theorems of classic geometry (parallel lines do not keep the same distance between them, the sum of angles in a triangle does not equal 180°, etc.). Riemann proved that the basic properties of a curved space are exclusively determined by its formula to measure distances. The choice of the way to measure this distance is equivalent to the definition of the Riemannian space [6].

3.2 Level Set Methods and PDEs

Partial Differential Equations (PDEs), on which Level Set methods are based, are used in GACs to describe the movement of a boundary. The goal is to track the evolution of the boundary, and these methods provide powerful techniques to perform this tracking. These methods are introduced in 1987 [9, 10]. The Level Set equation given by Osher and Sethian [8, 12] is used to describe their evolution over time.

3.3 From Classical Methodology to Geodesic Active Contours

Deformable Models (Active Contours, or Snakes), are curves that evolutionate according to the influence of internal and external forces [3]. These forces are defined in such a manner that the snake can detect the image objects of interest. Classical Active Contours are defined by an energy function. By minimizing this energy function, the contour converges, and the solution is reached.

$$E = \int \left[E_{int}(v(s)) + E_{image}(v(s)) \right] ds =$$

$$= \int \left[\alpha(s)E_{cont}(v(s)) + \beta(s)E_{curv}(v(s)) + \gamma(s)E_{image}(v(s)) \right] ds \qquad (1)$$

E_{int} is the internal energy of the contour. It consists of continuity energy (E_{cont}) plus curvature energy (E_{curv}). E_{image} represents the proper energy of the image, which greatly varies from one image to another.

α, β and γ are values that can be chosen to control the influence of the three terms [7, 10]. For example, a large value of γ means that the energy image is more significant than the rest. When a discontinuity occurs at a point, α is zero. β is zero at certain corners of the image (null curvature energy).

Caselles et al. [4] consider a particular case of classical Active Contours, for which the rigidity coefficient β is set to zero. This selection allows us to derive the relationship between these energy based Active Contours and geometric curve evolution contours. Maupertius' and Fermat's principles are applied to show that a geodesic curve is equivalent to a local minimal distance path between given points. In order to achieve object detection, these authors embed the geodesic curve flow equation into the Level Set formulation.

3.4 Geodesic Flows with Level Sets: Derivation and Boundary Detection

Caselles et al. [4] rely their formulation on the fact that the curvature equals the divergence of the normal vector on each point of the contour. The authors compute the Euler-Lagrange differential equation in the minimization problem via the steepest-descent method to deform the initial curve towards a local minimum [13]. This formulation can then be interpreted geometrically and applied to the image segmentation enabled by GAC, thus achieving the general model (equation 2).

$$\frac{\partial u}{\partial t} = |\nabla u| div\left(g(I)\frac{\nabla u}{|\nabla u|} \right) + c\nabla g(I)|\nabla u| \qquad (2)$$

where u is the Level Set function; c is a constant; I represents the color intensity level of the input image (previously processed with a smoothing filter); and $g(I)$ is the boundary detector function that leads the curve to stop where the gradient values are maximum.

4 Adaptation and Improvement of Methodology

The GAC general formula is always the same [1, 8, 12]. What makes some implementations to work better than others is the way of calculating each component separately (e.g., different smoothing filters, boundary detector functions based on the gradient, the speed function, the curvature treatment, etc.).

4.1 Drawbacks of the Basic Geodesic Formulation

Major GAC advantages have been discussed; however this methodology implies some noteworthy drawbacks:

- The initial contour has a natural high tendency to contract. The contour only expands when there are points placed in the exterior of the object. For this reason, the Active Contour searching area also tends to decrease over time.
- The so-called "rubber band" effect tends to occur; whenever there may be parts of the objects in the image which present noticeable hollows or concavities, the contour tends to place straight lines over them and to stop the algorithm.
- The algorithm evolves too slowly.

4.2 Improving Geodesic Active Contours

Some solutions can be proposed, given the previous drawbacks:

A positive curvature value corresponds to convex areas, and a negative value to concave ones. Adding or subtracting small quantities (*f*) to the curvature value, we achieve to avoid the so-called "rubber band" effect. The solution stays stable with values of *f* from -0.5 to +0.5. We call *f* "expanding force" when positive and "contracting force" when negative. By using *f*, we achieve that when the algorithm can decide towards where to move the Active Contour, *f* remains ignored. But when the algorithm would decide to stop, *f* will make the Active Contour slightly evolutionate towards the direction of its sign. In equation 3,

$$\frac{\partial u}{\partial t} = |\nabla u|g(I)\left(div\left(\frac{\nabla u}{|\nabla u|}\right) + f \right) + c\nabla g(I)|\nabla u| \tag{3}$$

f represents the curvature increase or decrease (expanding or contracting force). Some examples of the results obtained using *f* can be found in Figure 2.

Regarding the slowness of the algorithm, a solution consists of the increase in the size of the step (*∂t*). This growth represents the maximum color intensity change allowed for each pixel in the current Level Set. We obtain the best results combining the size of the step with the use of *f*.

Figure 2 shows the most general case in which it is necessary to apply *f* with a certain sign and, afterwards (and just in order to increase the stability of the solution) apply again *f* with the opposite sign, given that when the Active Contour has reached the objects edges, *f* is never strong enough to take it out of there.

In order to get a stable numerical implementation, we compute *∂t* as shown in equation 4,

$$\partial t = \frac{velocity}{1 + \frac{1}{2}\max(\nabla g(I))} \tag{4}$$

where velocity can take values from +0.5 to +0.9 and $_{max}(\nabla g(I))$ is the maximum gradient value obtained from the boundary detector function.

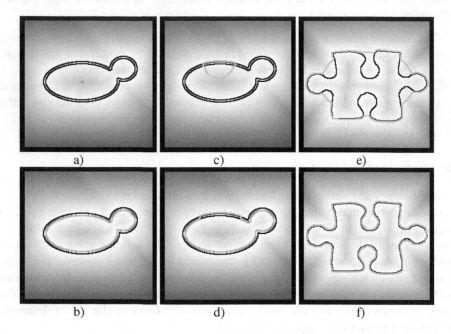

Fig. 2. Energy images from the synthetic image database: a) Collapsed contour; b) With an expanding force; c) Deteriorating the contour; d) With contracting and expanding forces; e) Rubber band; f) With a contracting force

Another improvement is the reduction of the GAC searching area or portion of the original image in which the initial contour is enclosed (figure 3). If the contour decreases, different parts of the image will not need be examined outside the initial searching area. If the opposite occurs, the searching area will expand as needed.

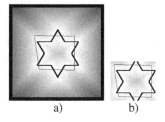

Fig. 3. Energy image: a) Original image; b) The algorithm searching area

Figure 4 shows an example of the coincidence percentage implementation. It consists of the regular (every ten iterations, for example) comparison between the actual contour and these same pixels in the image that represents the gradient values computed by the boundary detector function g(I). As we are working with pixel values inthe range 0...255, a gradient value < 125 corresponds to a probable object contour. If the actual Active Contour is placed on pixels whose corresponding gradient image value is less than 125, we can compute a percentage of coincidence to take into account in order to know how is the algorithm evolutionating.

Fig. 4. An application with a coincidence percentage: a) Initial contour; b) 75% of coincidence; c) Gradient image

Some other minor modifications to take into account are:

- The limitation of the iteration number by the user. The advantage of his improvement is the saving of time.
- The possibility to stop the algorithm depending on the coincidence percentage. For instance, we can control if the coincidence percentage starts to decrease and stop the algorithm before it get worse.
- The application of the algorithm to different color bands of the image separately. In general, we obtain more accurate contours when we process the image in the band of the color predominant in the image background.
- The implementation of different gradient functions. Sobel and Álvarez-Mazorra gradient functions produce good results.
- The application of different smoothing filters. Gaussian filters provide the best results.

5 Results

The evaluation of our algorithm has been performed by measuring three parameters: Recall, Precision, and Fallout [14]. The major improvements are related to the contour accuracy. Figure 5 shows different individual synthetic images processed with the GAC basic formula and the same images processed with the improved one. Precision, Recall and Fallout of the resulting contours are also shown in both cases (Table 1).

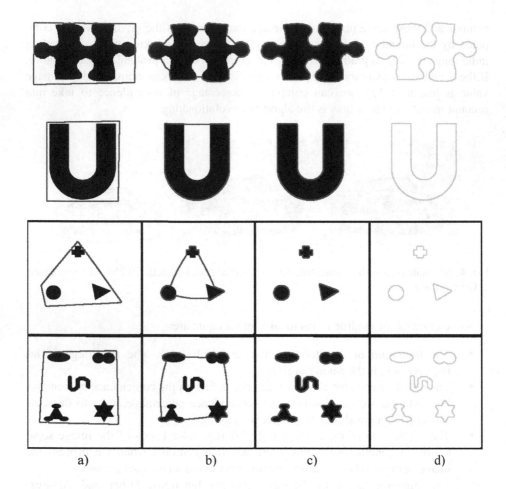

Fig. 5. Accuracy of the GAC basic formula and the improved one: a) The original contour of four example images. b) The final GAC with the basic formula. c) The final contour with the improved GAC. d) The final contour, in detail.

Table 1. Precision, Recall and Fallout percentages for each final GAC

Images	1b	2b	3b	4b	1c	2c	3c	4c
Precision	81.23	67.80	22.19	22.00	100.00	96.73	93.49	94.03
Recall	99.99	100.00	99.90	99.94	99.99	100.00	99.90	0.22
Fallout	7.74	14.61	10.86	26.99	0.00	1.04	0.22	0.48

6 Conclusions

As observed, Precision and Fallout are the two main parameters being improved. Accuracy is reached optimally according to our proposal. One other advantage has to do with the accessibility and display of useful information during contour evolution. In this line of work, we have been able to apply and adapt the GAC technique by customizing it according to our specific needs. It can thus be found that results can be reached in a more effective manner when this technique is personalized.

References

1. Angelini, E., Jin, Y., Laine, A.: State of the Art of Level Set Methods in Segmentation and Registration of Medical Imaging Modalities. Handbook of Biomedical Image Analysis-Registration Models, Kluwer Academic/ Plenum Publishers, pp. 47–102 (2005)
2. Amini, A.A., Weymouth, T.E., Jain, R.: Using Dynamic Programming for Solving Variational Problems in Vision. IEEE Transactions on Pattern Analysis and Machine Intelligence 12, 855–867 (1990)
3. Blake, A., e Isard, M.: Active Contours. edn. Springer, Heidelberg (1998)
4. Caselles, V., Kimmel, R., Sapiro, G.: Geodesic Active Contours. International Journal of Computer Vision 22(1), 61–79 (1997)
5. Kass, M., Witkin, A., Terzopoulos, D.: Snakes: Active Contour models. In: Proceedings of First International Conference on Computer Vision, pp. 259–269 (1987)
6. Kichenassamy, S., Kumar, A., Olver, P., Tannenbaum, A., Yezzi, A.: Gradient Flows and Geometric Active Contour Models. In: Proc. Int. Conf. on Computer Vision, Cambridge (1995)
7. Larsen, O.V., Radeva, P., Martí, E.: Guidelines for Choosing Optimal Parameters of Elasticity for Snakes. In: Proc. Int. Conf. Computer Analysis and Image Process, pp. 106–113 (1995)
8. Osher, S., Fedkiw, R.: Level Set Methods and Dynamic Implicit Surfaces. edn. Springer, Heidelberg (2002)
9. Osher, S., Sethian, J.A.: Fronts Propagating with Curvature Dependent Speed: Algorithms Based on Hamilton-Jacobi Formulations. Journal of Computational Physics 79, 12–49 (1988)
10. Ranganath, S.: Analysis of the effects of Snake Parameters on Contour Extraction. In: Proc. Int. Conference on Automation, Robotics, and Computer Vision, pp. 451–455(1992)
11. Sethian, J.A.: Numerical methods for propagating fronts. In: Concus, P., Finn, R. (eds.) Variational Methods for Free Surface Interfaces, Springer, Heidelberg (1987)
12. Sethian, J.A.: Level Set Methods and Fast Marching Methods: Evolving Interfaces in Geometry, Fluid Mechanics, Computer Vision, and Materials Sciences. Cambridge University Press, Cambridge (1999)
13. Strang, G.: Introduction to applied mathematics. Wellesley Cambridge University Press, Cambridge (1986)
14. Van Rijsbergen, C.J.: Information Retrieval. Butterworths, London (1979)
15. Williams, D.J., Shah, M.: A Fast Algorithm for Active Contours and Curvature Estimation, Computer Vision, Graphics and Image. Processing: Image Understanding 55, 14–26 (1992)

Rate Control Algorithm for MPEG-2 to H.264/AVC Transcoding

Gao Chen, Shouxun Lin, and Yongdong Zhang

Institute of Computing Technology, Chinese Academy of Sciences
Beijing, 100080, P.R. China
{chengao,sxlin,zhyd}@ict.ac.cn

Abstract. There is strong need for research in transcoding technologies to enable smooth displacement from MPEG-2 to H.264/AVC since H.264/AVC has been standardized as international standard. In this paper, a novel rate control algorithm for MPEG-2 to H.264/AVC transcoding, which adopting a new block activity measurement, is proposed. Specifically, the standard deviation of the residual error is introduced into the quadratic rate distortion (R-D) model adopted in JVT-G012 instead of the mean of absolute difference (MAD) to measure macroblock (MB) complexity. Meanwhile, based on the fact that the mean square of AC coefficients in an 8×8 DCT block is equal to the variance of an 8×8 block before DCT, we derive a close-form formulation to calculate the variance of a residual MB using the DCT coefficients rather the pixel values. Obviously, this rate control method can be used for MPEG-2 to H.264/AVC transcoder in both pixel domain and transform domain. Experiments show that our proposed algorithm can meet the target bit-rate accurately and achieves a better performance than the JVT-G012.

1 Introduction

H.264/AVC is the latest international video coding standard, developed and standardized collaboratively by ISO/IEC and ITU-T as International Standard 14496-10 (MPEG-4 part 10) Advanced Video Coding (AVC) or as Recommendation H.264 [1]. H.264/AVC achieves high coding efficiency by adopting a variety of state-of-the-art tools and is expected to replace the existing standards such as H.263 and MPEG-1/2/4. Given its outstanding coding efficiency, H.264/AVC is expected to have a wide range of applications, including mobile broadcasting and storage. However, MPEG-2 video has been widely used in many existing systems, such as digital TV, DVD, and HDTV applications etc. To solve the standard incompatibility problems for Universal Multimedia Access (UMA) [2], there is a big demand for converting video in the MPEG-2 format to the one in H.264/AVC format.

Several issues on rate control for H.264/AVC transcoding have been addressed recently in [3]-[5]. An algorithm of adopting the rate control model TM5 in MPEG-2 to compute the values of quantization parameters (QP) for I and B frames based on the side information from the pre-coded MPEG-2 video is presented in [3]. In [4], a fast macroblock (MB) mode decision approach has been proposed to reduce the

J. Martí et al. (Eds.): IbPRIA 2007, Part II, LNCS 4478, pp. 72–79, 2007.

complexity of Rate Distortion Optimization (RDO) and an improved rate control method depending on statistics of input MPEG-2, which is effective in transcoding the input steams into low bit rate streams, has been proposed. In [5], an idea that we should reuse information extracted from the input MPEG-2 video stream as efficiently as possible is proposed. The experiment results demonstrate that the proposed rate control algorithm is very efficient. However, all of the aforementioned works mainly focus on the MPEG-2 to H.264/AVC transcoder in pixel domain and can not be used in the transform domain simultaneously. Recently, transcoding MPEG-2 into H.264/AVC in transform domain has been an actively studied topic in academia and industry community. In [6], an efficient method has been proposed to convert DCT coefficients to H.264/AVC integer transform coefficients completely in the transform domain. A transform domain MPEG-2 to H.264/AVC intra video transcoder is proposed in [7] and the proposed transcoder is equivalent to the conventional one in pixel domain in terms of functionality and achieves complexity saving more than 20%. Specially, a comprehensive solution to transcode MPEG-2 into H.264/AVC in transform domain is proposed in [8]. To perform the rate control for transform domain MPEG-2 to H.264 transcoding, we propose a novel rate control algorithm which can be used in both pixel domain and transform domain. To our best knowledge, no works in this respect has been reported before in this literature.

The rest of the paper is organized as follows. In Section 2 we propose a new quadratic rate distortion (R-D) model. In Section 3 we present a way to calculate the variance of MB using only the DCT coefficients. Section 4 describes our proposed rate control method for MPEG-2 to H.264 transcoding in summary. Experimental results will be presented in Section 5, and conclusion is shown in Section 6.

2 New Rate Distortion Model

According to the rate control algorithm based on the R-D theory, the quantization step size of a MB is selected according to its activity, which is usually measured by variance, mean of absolute differences (MAD), sum of absolute differences (SAD), etc. H.264/AVC rate control proposal JVT-G012 adopts the MAD as the MB activity [9]. At the same time, the R-D model adopted in JVT-G012 is the well known quadratic R-D model, which is shown in equation (1).

$$T - H = c_1 \frac{MAD^2}{QP^2} + c_2 \frac{MAD}{QP} \tag{1}$$

Where c_1 and c_2 are the model parameter.

Replacing MAD with standard deviation to measure the MB activity, we can get a new R-D model. The new R-D model is formulated in the equation as follows:

$$T - H = c_1 \frac{\sigma^2}{QP^2} + c_2 \frac{\sigma}{QP} \tag{2}$$

Where σ represents the standard deviation of the residue error.

In order to improve the accuracy of the new R-D model, we verify this new R-D model in the context of encoding system. That is, we first implement the new R-D model in the H.264 encoder of the H.264/AVC reference software JM 8.2 [10]. Then, we compare the encoding results with the one using JVT-G012. Sequences with different amounts of motion and spatial details are used in our experiments. Due to the limit of pages, only the results of six sequences are provided there and the results of other sequences are similar. As shown in Fig. 1(a) and Fig. 1(b), we can see that that using standard deviation in quadratic R-D model can obtain the same or better coding efficiency compared to using MAD, which prove the accuracy of our proposed new R-D model.

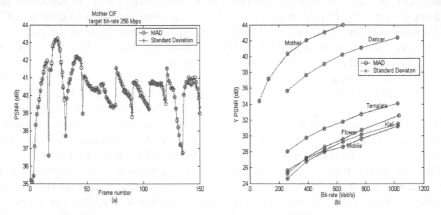

Fig. 1. (a) The PSNR (dB) of Mother (CIF) obtained by quadratic R-D model using MAD and standard deviation. (b) R-D curves of six different sequences with quadratic R-D model using MAD and standard deviation.

3 Variance Calculation in Transform Domain

Due to the reconstruction of picture in pixel domain is not needed in the context of transform domain transcoder, the MAD of residue error can not be achieved in the process of transcoding. So, the R-D model in equation (1) can not be used in transform domain transcoder. In the following, we derive a close-form formulation to calculate the variance of a MB only using the DCT coefficients. So, we can use that the R-D model in equation (2) in transform domain and pixel domain transcoder simultaneously.

In what follows, we describe the process of how to calculate the variance of a MB in transform domain. The 8×8 two dimension Discrete Cosine Transform (DCT) [6] is given by

$$F(u,v) = \frac{1}{4} C(u) C(v) \sum_{x=0}^{7} \sum_{y=0}^{7} f(x,y) \cos\left(\frac{(2x+1)u\pi}{16}\right) \cos\left(\frac{(2y+1)v\pi}{16}\right) \quad (3)$$

Where u, v, x, y =0, 1, 2, ……, 7, $\begin{cases} C(u), C(v) = \sqrt{1/2}, & u,v = 0. \\ C(u), C(v) = 1, & u,v = other \end{cases}$

For an 8×8 DCT block, we define $\overline{AC^2}$ as the mean square of AC coefficients in DCT, which is showed in equation (4).

$$\overline{AC^2} = \frac{1}{8 \times 8}\left(\sum_{u=0}^{7}\sum_{v=0}^{7} F^2(u,v) - F^2(0,0)\right) \tag{4}$$

Where $F(0,0)$ is the DC coefficient of this 8×8 DCT block.

According to the Parseval's theorem [11], we have:

$$\sum_{u=0}^{7}\sum_{v=0}^{7} F^2(u,v) = \sum_{x=0}^{7}\sum_{y=0}^{7} f^2(x,y) \tag{5}$$

Furthermore, let $\overline{f(x,y)}$ be the mean pixel value of an 8×8 block before DCT, then $F(0,0) = 8 \times \overline{f(x,y)}$.

As described in [12], we can compute $\overline{AC^2}$ as follows.

$$\begin{aligned}
\overline{AC^2} &= \frac{1}{8 \times 8}\left(\sum_{u=0}^{7}\sum_{v=0}^{7} F^2(u,v) - F^2(0,0)\right) \\
&= \frac{1}{8 \times 8}\left(\sum_{x=0}^{7}\sum_{y=0}^{7} f^2(x,y) - \left(8 \times \overline{f(x,y)}\right)^2\right) \\
&= \frac{1}{8 \times 8}\sum_{x=0}^{7}\sum_{y=0}^{7} f^2(x,y) - \overline{f(x,y)}^2 \\
&= \frac{1}{8 \times 8}\sum_{x=0}^{7}\sum_{y=0}^{7}\left(f(x,y) - \overline{f(x,y)}\right)^2 = \sigma^2
\end{aligned} \tag{6}$$

Where σ^2 is the variance of an 8×8 block before DCT.

The above equations show that the mean pixel value and the variance of an 8×8 block can be computed directly using its corresponding DCT coefficients. That is:

$$\begin{aligned}
\overline{f(x,y)} &= F(0,0)/8 \\
\sigma^2 &= \overline{AC^2}
\end{aligned} \tag{7}$$

It is well known that in typically block-based video coding standard, the block size used for transform is corresponded to the dimension of the transform. Such as in MPEG-2, 8×8 block is used for transform corresponding to 8×8 DCT and Inverse DCT operations. However, the basic unit of rate control in video encoder is 16×16 MB usually. We need to deduce an approach to compute the variance of a 16×16 MB using the DCT coefficients of 8×8 blocks. Because that only the DCT coefficients of 8×8 DCT transform exist in MPEG-2 video stream.

Let b_i, $\overline{f_i(x,y)}$ and σ_i^2, $i = 1,2,3,4$ denote the four 8×8 blocks of a 16×16 MB, the mean values and the variances of the four 8×8 blocks, respectively. From aforementioned conclusion, we have:

$$\begin{aligned}
\overline{f_i(x,y)} &= F_i(0,0)/8 \\
\sigma_i^2 &= \overline{AC_i^2}
\end{aligned} \tag{8}$$

Fig. 2 shows the demonstration of a MB containing four 8×8 blocks.

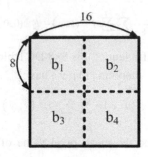

Fig. 2. Four 8×8 blocks in a MB

Let $\overline{f_{MB}(x,y)}$ and σ^2_{MB} denote the mean value and the variance of a MB, respectively. Firstly, we can compute $\overline{f_{MB}(x,y)}$ and σ^2_{MB} in pixel domain as follows.

$$\overline{f_{MB}(x,y)} = \frac{1}{16 \times 16} \sum_{x=0}^{15} \sum_{y=0}^{15} f(x,y)$$

$$\sigma^2_{MB} = \frac{1}{16 \times 16} \sum_{x=0}^{15} \sum_{y=0}^{15} \left(f(x,y) - \overline{f_{MB}(x,y)} \right)^2 \tag{9}$$

$$= \frac{1}{16 \times 16} \sum_{x=0}^{15} \sum_{y=0}^{15} f^2(x,y) - \overline{f_{MB}(x,y)}^2$$

Secondly, we can use $\overline{f_i(x,y)}$ and σ_i^2, $i = 1,2,3,4$ to compute σ^2_{MB} as follows:

$$\overline{f_{MB}(x,y)} = \frac{1}{16 \times 16} \sum_{x=0}^{15} \sum_{y=0}^{15} f(x,y)$$

$$= \frac{1}{4} \left(\overline{f_1(x,y)} + \overline{f_2(x,y)} + \overline{f_3(x,y)} + \overline{f_4(x,y)} \right) \tag{10}$$

$$\frac{1}{16 \times 16} \sum_{x=0}^{15} \sum_{y=0}^{15} f^2(x,y)$$

$$= \frac{1}{4} \left(\frac{1}{8 \times 8} \sum_{x=0}^{7} \sum_{y=0}^{7} f^2(x,y) - \overline{f_1(x,y)}^2 + \frac{1}{8 \times 8} \sum_{x=7}^{15} \sum_{y=0}^{7} f^2(x,y) - \overline{f_2(x,y)}^2 \right.$$

$$\left. + \frac{1}{8 \times 8} \sum_{x=0}^{7} \sum_{y=7}^{15} f^2(x,y) - \overline{f_3(x,y)}^2 + \frac{1}{8 \times 8} \sum_{x=7}^{15} \sum_{y=7}^{15} f^2(x,y) - \overline{f_4(x,y)}^2 \right) \tag{11}$$

$$+ \frac{1}{4} \left(\overline{f_1(x,y)}^2 + \overline{f_2(x,y)}^2 + \overline{f_3(x,y)}^2 + \overline{f_4(x,y)}^2 \right)$$

$$= \frac{1}{4} \left(\sigma_1^2 + \sigma_2^2 + \sigma_3^2 + \sigma_4^2 \right) + \frac{1}{4} \left(\overline{f_1(x,y)}^2 + \overline{f_2(x,y)}^2 + \overline{f_3(x,y)}^2 + \overline{f_4(x,y)}^2 \right)$$

Substituting equation (8), equation (10) and equation (11) into (9), we have:

$$\sigma^2_{MB} = \frac{1}{4} \left(\overline{AC_1^2} + \overline{AC_2^2} + \overline{AC_3^2} + \overline{AC_4^2} \right)$$

$$+ \frac{1}{16 \times 16} \left\{ F^2_1(0,0) + F^2_2(0,0) + F^2_3(0,0) + F^2_4(0,0) \right. \tag{12}$$

$$\left. - \left((F_1(0,0) + F_2(0,0) + F_3(0,0) + F_4(0,0))/2 \right)^2 \right\}$$

Where the $\overline{AC}_i^2$ and $F_i(0,0), i = 1,2,3,4$ denote mean square of AC coefficients in DCT and the DC coefficients of the four 8×8 blocks, respectively.

4 Rate Control Algorithm

From equation (12), we can say that the variance of MB can be calculated directly using the DCT coefficients of 8×8 blocks in the case of transform domain transcoding. Combing the R-D model in equation (2), we propose a novel rate control for transform domain MPEG-2 to H.264 transcoder. Because of that most parts of our proposed algorithm inherits JVT-G012, we only present the different part there. The full procedure can refer to [13] for details.

Step 1: Using the equation (12) to calculate MPEG-2 MB activity.

Step 2: To solve the well known chicken-and-egg problem in the context of transcoding, the final standard deviation for current MB is adjusted with that gotten in Step 1 as follows:

$$\sigma_{final} = \alpha \times \sigma_{mpeg-2} + (1-\alpha) \times \sigma_{pred} \qquad (13)$$

Where σ_{mpeg-2} is the standard deviation obtained from the incoming MPEG-2 DCT coefficients using the equation (12), and the σ_{pred} is the one predicted with the linear model using the actual standard deviation of encoded MB in the same spatial position of the previous frame. The constant α serves as weighting factor and its typical value is 0.5 in our experiments.

Step 3: Adopting the new R-D model in equation (2) to calculate the QP.

5 Experimental Results

Our proposed rate control method is implemented in our MPEG-2 to H.264 transcoder to verify its performance. Our MPEG-2 to H.264 transcoder utilizes a decoder provided by the MPEG Software Simulation Group [14] to decode the incoming MPEG-2 test video streams into images in pixel domain and cascades an encoder based on the reference software H.264/AVC JM 8.2 (hereafter referred to as the JM 8.2) [10] to compress the images into H.264 format bit stream with the same coding structure and resolution. In our experiments, for each test sequence, the first 150 frames are firstly encoded to MPEG-2 streams at bit-rate of 1 or 2 Mbps and a frame rate of 30 fps with the structure of group of picture (GOP) as the first frame is I frame and 14 P frames are followed (i.e., IPP......PPP).

The average peak signal-to-noise ratio (PSNR) and the actual bit-rate obtained for transcoding the pre-coded Dancer and Kiel sequences to six different target bit-rates are show in Table 1. The results show that the proposed method can provide a better performance than JVT-G012 in terms of both average PSNR and achieved bit-rate.

Table 1. PSNR and actual bit-rate botained for the Dancer and Kiel sequences at six different target bit-rates

Target bit-rate (kbps)	Dancer				Kiel			
	My proposed method		JVT-G012		My proposed method		JVT-G012	
	Actual bit-rate (kbps)	PSNR (dB)	Actual bit-rate (kbps)	PSNR (dB)	Actual bit-rate (kbps)	PSNR (dB)	Actual bit-rate (kbps)	PSNR (dB)
256	256.67	35.38	256.69	35.36	256.69	24.82	256.57	24.81
384	385.03	37.08	385.03	37.05	385.85	25.79	384.79	25.79
512	512.95	38.15	513.08	38.12	513.25	26.48	513.23	26.47
640	640.86	38.92	641.04	38.90	641.59	26.82	641.75	26.82
768	769.39	39.42	769.00	39.41	769.78	27.35	770.07	27.34
1024	1024.87	40.05	1025.22	40.04	1025.60	28.00	1025.89	28.00

Fig. 3 (a) shows the frame-to-frame PSNR results of the Dancer sequence obtained by the proposed and JVT-G012 rate control methods. No surprisingly, the fluctuation of PSNR obtained by the proposed method is less than that of the JVT-G012 method.

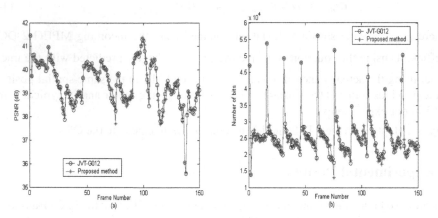

Fig. 3. (a) The PSNR (dB) of the Dancer sequence obtained by the proposed method and JVT-G012 methods. (b) The number of actual coding bits obtained by using the QP determined by the proposed method and JVT-G012.

Fig. 3 (b) shows the distribution of the number of bits over the entire sequence when the FOREMAN sequence was transcoded at the target bit-rate 768 Kbps by using the proposed rate control method and JVT-G012. It can be seen that the fluctuation of bits of the transcoded video obtained by the proposed method is a little better than that of JVT-G012.

6   Conclusion

In this paper, a new rate control algorithm, which adopting standard deviation as MB activity measurement is presented. The variance can be directly calculated in transform domain makes it suitable for the transform domain transcoder where the MAD of residue error can not obtained. The experimental results show the accuracy of the model and the effectiveness of the proposed rate control algorithm. So we can say that this algorithm will be popularized in DCT based video transcoding. In the further, we will focus on improving the efficiency of our method by reusing the motion information in MPEG-2 inputting bit-stream.

Acknowledgments. This work is supported by national nature science foundation of China under grant number 60302028.

References

1. Wiegand, T., Sullivan, G.: Draft ITU-T recommendation and final draft international standard of joint video specification (ITUT Rec. H.264 – ISO/IEC 14496-10 AVC)JVT-G050, Pattaya, Thailand (March 2003)
2. Mohan, R., Smith, J.R., Li, C.S.: Adapting Multimedia Internet Content for Universal Access. IEEE Transactions on Multimedia 1, 104–114 (1999)
3. Xiao, Y.-N., Lu, H., Xue, X., Nguyen, V.-A., Tan, Y.-P.: Efficient Rate Control For Mpeg-2 To H.264/AVC Transcoding, IEEE International Symposium on Circuits and Systems (ISCAS), pp. 1238–1241 (May 2005)
4. Zhang, P., Huang, Q.-M., Gao, W.: Key Techniques of Bit Rate Reduction for H.264 Streams, Advances in Multimedia Information Processing - PCM 2004: 5th Pacific Rim Conference on Multimedia, Tokyo, Japan, pp. 985–992 (November 30–December 3 2004)
5. Yang, J., Dai, Q., Xu, W., Ding, R.: A Rate Control Algorithm for MPEG-2 to H.264 Real-time Transcoding. In: Proc. Visual Communication and Image Processing VCIP-2005, pp.1995-2003, Beijing, China (2005)
6. Xin, J., Vetro, A., Sun, H.F.: Converting DCT Coefficients to H.264/AVC Transform coefficients. Pacific-rim Conference on Multimedia (PCM) 2, 939–946 (2004)
7. Su, Y., Xin, J., Vetro, A., Sun, H.: Efficient MPEG-2 to H.264/AVC intra transcoding in transform-domain. In: Proceedings of the IEEE International Symposium on Circuits and Systems (ISCAS '05), vol. 2, pp. 1234–1237, Kobe, Japan (May 2005)
8. Qian, T., Sun, J., Li, D., Yang, X., Wang, J.: Transform domain transcoding from MPEG-2 to H.264 with interpolation drift-error compensation. IEEE Transaction on Circuits and Systems for Video Technology 16(4), 523–534 (2006)
9. Chiang, T., Zhang, Y.: A New Rate Control Scheme Using Quadratic Rate Distortion Model. IEEE Trans. Circuits Syst. Video Technol. 7, 287–311 (1997)
10. H.264/AVC reference software JM8.2, available online at http://bs.hhi.de/~suehring/tml/download
11. Oppenheim, A.V., Schafer, R.W.: Discrete-Time Signal Processing, 2nd (edn.). p. 60. Prentice Hall, UpperSaddle River, NJ (1999)
12. Bo, Z., Cheng-Ke, W.: A Novel Rate Control Algorithm in Video Coding for Low-delay Communications. Chinese Journal of Computers 28(1), 53–59 (2005)
13. Zh. Li, F., Pan, K., Lim, G., Feng, X.: Lin, Rahardja, S.: Adaptive Basic Unit Layer Rate Control for JVT, JVT-G012, 7th Meeting: Pattaya II, Thailand (March 2003)
14. MPEG-2 video encodec/decodec v12, available online at http://www.mpeg.org/MPEG/MSSG

3-D Motion Estimation for Positioning from 2-D Acoustic Video Imagery

H. Sekkati and S. Negahdaripour

University of Miami, FL, USA

Abstract. We address the problem of estimating 3-D motion from acoustic images acquired by high-frequency 2-D imaging sonars deployed in underwater. Utilizing a planar approximation to scene surfaces, two-view homography is the basis of a nonlinear optimization method for estimating the motion parameters. There is no scale factor ambiguity, unlike the case of monocular motion vision for optical images. Experiments with real images demonstrate the potential in a range of applications, including target-based positioning in search and inspection operations.

1 Introduction

Autonomous navigation is a critical capability in the deployment of submersible platforms for a range of applications in underwater [1,2]. Utilizing various navigational sensors, e.g., INS and velocity doppler, current generation of autonomous underwater vehicles (AUV) can carry out certain tasks, such as sea floor imaging and mapping, in long-duration operations, say from a few hours to over a day. In particular, the main bottleneck in length of the operation is power that is provided by onboard batteries.

A certain class of underwater operations, such as search and inspection, rely more heavily on target-based positioning, that is, the ability to establish position relative to a target of interest, to station keep, etc. Extensive worldwide research over the last decade and half have concentrated on the use of optical cameras for target-based positioning and local navigation, resulting in the realization of machine vision-based technologies by various research groups [9,12,16,17,19,21,23,25]. Unfortunately, optical cameras are constrained by limited visibility range, and in particular become totally ineffective in turbid waters.

In recent years, *2-D high-frequency acoustic cameras* – e.g., 1.1/1.8MHz *D*ual-Frequency *ID*entification *SON*ar (DIDSON)and 450/900KHz BlueView[1] – have become commercially available. These cameras provide video imagery with high enough details that allows visual target recognition by human operators. Unlike traditional acoustic imaging systems operating in 10's to low 100's KHz with ranges as far as several kilometers, these high-frequency 2-D imaging sonars have a range of no more than 10's of meters, which is more than adequate for many search and inspection missions that they are targeted for [5]. While useful when deployed by human operators or divers, more extended utility comes from the development of computer vision methods that provide 3-D interpretation of the sonar imagery.

---

[1] Trademarks of Sound Metrics and BlueView Technologies, respectively [4,3].

J. Martí et al. (Eds.): IbPRIA 2007, Part II, LNCS 4478, pp. 80–88, 2007.

Recent work has explored the application of homography-based registration methods for the construction of acoustic photo-mosaics as a target mapping product [11,7]. In [6], a novel paradigm in 3-D reconstruction based on the deployment of an acoustic and optical cameras in stereo configuration has been proposed. In [8], we have proposed various 3-D reconstruction algorithms, comparing their performances with traditional binocular stereo imaging through computer simulations. This paper deals with the realization of critical target-based 3-D positioning capability based on recovery of 3-D motion from a monocular sonar video imaging system. Unlike optical cameras that utilize the epipolar geometry of optical rays from two or more views, 3-D interpretation of 2-D sonar video involves the exploitation of range and azimuth information of target features in multiple views. Utilizing the mathematical models of sonar projection, we give the equations of correspondences for sonar images, and present an algorithm for 3-D motion estimation. Performance of the algorithm is tested through experiments with 2 real data sets, in order to demonstrate the potential in automatic 3-D motion interpretation from acoustic video.

2 Preliminaries

2.1 Projection Model

In the sonar-based Cartesian system, a 3-D scene point is represented by $\mathbf{P}=(X,Y,Z)^T$. Spherical coordinates $(\Re,\theta,\phi)^T$ – $\Re$ is range, and θ and ϕ denote azimuth and elevation angles – is a more suitable coordinate system in analyzing sonar video, since a 2-D sonar image $I(\Re,\theta)$ represents acoustic reflections from 3-D points at ranges $\Re$ (within a down-range window $[\Re_{min}:\Re_{max}]$) and azimuth direction θ (within cross-range filed of view $[-\theta_o:\theta_o]^2$). While the elevation angle ϕ is typically unknown, it is constrained by the vertical width of each transmitted beam; see fig. 1. Relationship between the Cartesian and spherical coordinates is useful in analyzing the sonar data:

$$\mathbf{P}=\begin{pmatrix} X \\ Y \\ Z \end{pmatrix} = \Re \begin{pmatrix} \cos\phi\sin\theta \\ \cos\phi\cos\theta \\ \sin\phi \end{pmatrix}, \begin{pmatrix} \Re \\ \theta \\ \phi \end{pmatrix} = \begin{pmatrix} \sqrt{X^2+Y^2+Z^2} \\ \tan^{-1}(X/Y) \\ \tan^{-1}\left(\frac{Z}{X^2+Y^2}\right) \end{pmatrix}. \quad (1)$$

2.2 Preprocessing

Sonar data, in contrast to optical images, are corrupted by a much higher noise level. To improve performance of 3-D interpretation algorithms, some preprocessing is necessary to remove noise, and account for non-uniform insonification. Also, the noisy nature of sonar images often prohibits the application of gradient-based optical flow methods for image registration and motion estimation, favoring the use of feature-based methods. While it is desired to develop feature detection and matching methods that are specifically suited to the physical and geometrical characteristics of sonar imaging, this work employs traditional methods based on Harris corner detector and Lucas-Kanade tracking algorithms [13,18,24].

---

[2] $\theta_o \approx 15$ [deg] for DIDSON, and $\theta_o \approx 25$ [deg] for BlueView sonar.

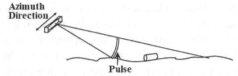

Fig. 1. Sonar beams have a relatively narrow width in the elevation direction, 14 [deg] for a DIDSON. Insonifying at small grazing angles provides a larger scene surface coverage.

Certain sonar systems, e.g., DIDSON, do image forming by scene insonification at different times to minimize cross talk between neighboring receivers. More precisely, scan lines in the azimuth direction are filled by returns from several fields (in analogy to interlaced video). Therefore, some beam realignment becomes necessary in order to rectify an image. DIDSON software provides the capability to exploit navigation data for sonar motion estimation and beam realignment. In practice, the motion information may be derived directly from temporal correlation across successive raw frames.

2.3 Sonar Homography Model

We assume a stationary target viewed by a mobile sensor platform. This assumption is not a serious limitation in many applications, e.g., search and inspection, since we are often interested in the relative motion between the target and sensor platform for target-based positioning. The relative rigid body motion may be represented by a 3-D translation vector $\mathbf{t}$ and a 3-parameter rotation vector ω or 3×3 rotation matrix $\mathbf{R}$. Accordingly, coordinates $\mathbf{P}$ and $\mathbf{P}'$ of a 3-D scene point in sensor coordinate systems at two views are related by:

$$\mathbf{P}' = \mathbf{R}\mathbf{P} + \mathbf{t}$$

The general 3-D reconstruction problem involved determining the scene structure – say the 3-D positions of features on the scene surfaces – and the relative motion $\{\mathbf{R},\mathbf{t}\}$ of the sonar between the two views based on the projections into the two views. Here, we are primarily concerned about the recover of the sonar motion. This establishes the epipolar geometry of the two views, and once can readily reconstruct each 3-D feature from its two projections (triangulation in the context of sonar projections).

Given the operation range of high-resolution sonars, as far as 10's of meters, increasing target distance enables imaging a larger potion of the scene in each view. This is desirable from the point that existing 2-D imaging sonars have a relatively small cross-range field of view (roughly 30 [deg] for DIDSON and 50 [deg] for BlueView). While this comes at the expense of lower spatial resolution of the scene targets, coverage-vs-resolution tradeoff is application dependent issue. Generally speaking, reasonable resolution can still be achieved at lower ranges of say 2-5 [m]. At such distances, one can typically identify scene features that approximately lie on a plane. Alternatively, we may target identifying and utilization those features that roughly lie on a single plane, given by the equation $\mathbf{n} \cdot \mathbf{P} = 1$, where $\mathbf{n} = [n_x, n_y, n_z]^T$ is the scaled normal vector derived from the plane equation $Z = Z_o + \zeta_x X + \zeta_y Y$.

For features lying on the plane with normal $\mathbf{n}$, the rigid body motion model takes the form

$$\mathbf{P}' = (\mathbf{R} + \mathbf{tn}^T)\mathbf{P} = \mathbf{QP} \tag{2}$$

Constructing a rectangular $x_s y_s$ sonar image from $(x_s, y_s) = \Re(\cos\theta, \sin\theta)$, it can be readily shown that [7]

$$\mathbf{p}' = \mathbf{Hp}; \quad \mathbf{H} = \begin{bmatrix} \alpha q_{11} & \alpha q_{12} & \beta q_{13} \\ \alpha q_{21} & \alpha q_{22} & \beta q_{23} \\ 0 & 0 & 1 \end{bmatrix} \tag{3}$$

where q_{ij} denotes i-j element of $\mathbf{Q}$, $\alpha = \frac{\cos\phi}{\cos\phi'}$, $\beta = \Re\frac{\sin\phi}{\cos\phi'}$, and $\mathbf{p} = [x_s, y_s, 1]^T$ and $\mathbf{p}' = [x'_s, y'_s, 1]^T$ denote correspondences in two views. While this suggests an affine homography at first glance, the dependency on elevation angles ϕ and ϕ' of each feature relative to the two sonar views suggests a more complicated homography. Matrix $\mathbf{Q}$ in (2) is the up-to-scale homography that describes the transformation between the two optical views of the plane, and can be decomposed in closed-form to compute the underlying motion $\{\mathbf{R}, \mathbf{t}\}$ and surface normal $\mathbf{n}$ up to the well-known scale-factor ambiguity of motion vision [26,27]. In contrast, the homography $\mathbf{H}$ of two acoustic views is a complex trigonometric function of the surface normal, and a closed-form decomposition to motion and surface normal has not been derived. In section 3.1, we propose a recursive method based on MLE formulation.

3   3-D Motion Estimation

A general analogy with classical motion vision of two optical views can be established by noting that the elevation angle ϕ can be expressed in terms of the surface normal, and two coordinate measurements $\{\Re, \theta\}$. More precisely, we can first express the surface equation in the form

$$(n_x \sin\theta + n_y \cos\theta)\cos\phi + n_z \sin\phi = 1/\Re \tag{4}$$

enabling us to solve for the elevation angle ϕ in terms of the surface normal:

$$\phi = -\gamma + \sin^{-1}\left(\frac{-1}{\Re\sqrt{(n_x \sin\theta + n_y \cos\theta)^2 + n_z^2}} \right) \tag{5}$$

where

$$\gamma = \tan^{-1}\left(\frac{n_x \sin\theta + n_y \cos\theta}{n_z} \right) \tag{6}$$

It trivially follows that the homography in (3), while a complex nonlinear constraint, can be expressed in terms of the 9 motion and surface parameters.

A distinct difference with traditional two-frame motion problem is the fact that no scale factor ambiguity exists with two sonar views. In other words, projections into two views of a small number of features allows us to determine the unknown motion and plane parameters. Simple count reveals that a minimum of 5 points is necessary, providing us with 10 constraints in terms of 9 unknowns. If the motion is modeled by pure translation, a minimum of 3 points is necessary for a solution.

While such issues as ambiguous configurations, number of possible solutions, etc., are intriguing theoretical problems that also provide insight into solution degeneracies, we are interested with devising a motion estimating method, here.

3.1 Minimization Problem

Various minimization problems can be formulated based on the Mahalanobis distance between the measurements and reprojected points, say vectors $\mathbf{p}' = (x'_s, y'_s, 1)$ and $\hat{\mathbf{p}}' = \mathbf{H}\mathbf{p}$. A symmetric formulation incorporates both distance measures $\|\mathbf{p}' - \mathbf{H}\mathbf{p}\|$ and $\|\mathbf{p} - \mathbf{H}^{-1}\mathbf{p}'\|$ [14]:

$$\mathscr{E}(\mathbf{R},\mathbf{T},\mathbf{n}) = \sum_k (\mathbf{p}_k - \hat{\mathbf{p}}_k)^T \Sigma^{-1} (\mathbf{p}_k - \hat{\mathbf{p}}_k) + \sum_k (\mathbf{p}'_k - \hat{\mathbf{p}}'_k)^T \Sigma'^{-1} (\mathbf{p}'_k - \hat{\mathbf{p}}'_k) \tag{7}$$

where $\Sigma = E[(\mathbf{p}_k - \hat{\mathbf{p}}_k)(\mathbf{p}_k - \hat{\mathbf{p}}_k)^T]$ and $\Sigma' = E[(\mathbf{p}'_k - \hat{\mathbf{p}}'_k)(\mathbf{p}'_k - \hat{\mathbf{p}}'_k)^T]$. Note abuse of notation, here: We are only concerned with the first two components of $\mathbf{p}$ and $\mathbf{p}'$. The rotation matrix $\mathbf{R}$ can be parameterized by a sequence of 3 rotations of the form $\mathbf{R}_u(\alpha_u)$ about the 3 axes of the coordinate system; $\mathbf{R}_u(\alpha_u)$ denotes rotation by angle α_u about axis u. This allows to minimize the function in (7) with respect to $(\alpha, \mathbf{t}, \mathbf{n})$, where $\alpha = (\alpha_x, \alpha_y, \alpha_z)$. Without loss of generality, further simplification can be made by assuming independency among noises in the components of various image measurements, allowing us to write Σ (and Σ') as a diagonal matrix with elements (σ_x, σ_y).

$$\mathscr{E}(\mathbf{R},\mathbf{T},\mathbf{n}) = \sum_k \frac{(x_k - \hat{x}_k)^2}{\sigma_x^2} + \frac{(y_k - \hat{y}_k)^2}{\sigma_y^2} + \sum_k \frac{(x'_k - \hat{x'}_k)^2}{\sigma_x^2} + \frac{(y'_k - \hat{y'}_k)^2}{\sigma_y^2} \tag{8}$$

This nonlinear optimization problem has been solved by applying the Levenberg-Marquardt algorithm.

4   Experiments

Results from two experiments with real image sequences are presented to assess the application of the proposed 3-D motion estimation method for sonar imagery. We have applied standard feature detection and matching method commonly applied for optical images [28,29].

The first experiment deals with 10 frames of a video, where sonar moves approximately laterally relative to the hull surface of a ship. The first two frames are shown in fig. 2 (a). In the left, detected features in the first view have been superimposed (yellow crosses). The right image is the second view with initial matches (yellow crosses) and the reprojections based on the estimated motion and surface parameters (red crosses); see Eq. (3). Only the inlier matches with a reprojection error of less than 2 [pix] have

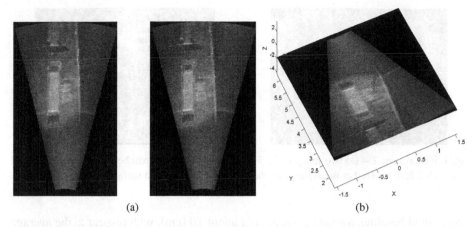

(a)   (b)

Fig. 2. Experiment 1 – (a) First two views from a sequence of 10 images with initial matches (yellow crosses) and reprojected inliers (red crosses) based on the estimated motion and surface parameters. (b) Estimated sonar trajectory.

been shown; see below. As the motion is dominantly translational, a translation motion model has been applied in estimating the 6 motion and surface parameters. The trajectory between frames 1 to 10 is shown in figure 2(b). The first frame is wrapped on the bottom surface utilizing the estimated normal vector for rendering. In the absence of ground truth, reprojection errors provide one measure of accuracy, as given in fig. 3(a). These errors are not unreasonable, considering that compared to typical high-resolution optical image: 1) Sonar images are much noisier; 2) Sonar features are rather sparse, often less by 1-2 orders of magnitude; 3) Features are typically localized within a smaller region from the entire field of view. Furthermore, these results have been derived for a

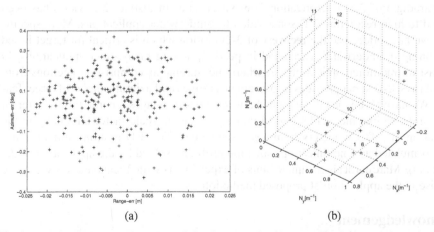

(a)   (b)

Fig. 3. Experiment 1 – (a) Histogram of absolute reprojection errors for 9 consecutive pairs in the 10-frame sequence, and the estimated surface normal vector as a 3-D point for each of these 9 consecutive pairs. see text for details.

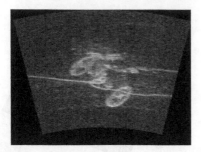

Fig. 4. Experiment 2 – (a) two images of a 3-D target with initial matches (yellow crosses) and reprojected features (red crosses) based on the estimated motion and surface parameters

rather small baseline, average translation of about 10 [cm], with respect to the average target distance of 2 [m]. As another measure, we have plotted in (b) the estimated surface normals over the entire sequence as 3-D points. These form a relatively compact cluster, suggesting that we have computed the ship hull surface orientation in the sonar coordinate system with reasonable accuracy.

In another experiment, we have tested the sensitivity of the proposed method to the planarity assumption. The data has been collected in an indoor pool by moving a 3-D target, an AUV towing cradle, across the sonar field of view; see fig. 4. The motion estimation has been applied to these two target views. Here, the images have been superimposed with the original matches, and the reprojections in the second view. For the most part, the results show insensitivity of the motion estimation algorithm to the simplified planar surface model.

5   Summary and Conclusion

The paradigm of 3-D interpretation from visual cues in distinct 2-D views has been applied to high-resolution 2-D sonar video for underwater applications. More specifically, we have addressed the recovery of 3-D motion which is critical for target-based positioning in underwater search and inspection, among many other applications. In contrast to traditional optical images where measurements comprise projections from optical rays, 2-D sonar provides measurements ranges and azimuth angles of target features. We have given the homography between pairs of images recorded from different viewpoints. Unlike monocular optical video, there is no scale-factor ambiguity in the estimation of 3-D parameters from sonar sequences. The 3-D motion estimation has been formulated as a nonlinear optimization problem, solved by the application of the Levenberg-Marquardt algorithm. Results of experiments with 2 real data sets verify the promise in the application of proposed methodology.

Acknowledgement

This work is based on research supported in part by ONR under grant N000140510717 and in part by NSF under SGER grant IIS0513989. Views and conclusions expressed in this paper are those of the authors, and are not to be interpreted as opinions shared and endorsements by either ONR or NSF. We are grateful to our friends at Teledyne Benthos, N. Falmouth, MA, who assisted us in the collection of the data in the second experiment in their pool facility.

References

1. http://www.bluefinrobotics.com
2. http://www.underwater.com/archives/arch/034.07.shtml
3. http://www.blueviewtech.com
4. http://www.soundmetrics.com
5. http://www.videoray.com/ftp/HULSFest/spawar_incoming/HF_Conf_Granger.pdf
6. Negahdaripour, S.: Epipolar geometry of optic-acoustic stereo imaging, in print. On IEEE PAMI (also appeared in Proc. IEEE Oceans 05)
7. Negahdaripour, S., Firoozfam, P., Sabzmeydani, P.: On Processing and registration of forward-scan acoustic video imagery. In: Proc, Canadian Conf. Computer & Robot Vision, Victoria, BC, Canada (May 2005)
8. Sekkati, H., Negahdaripour, S.: Direct and Indirect 3-D Reconstruction from Opti-Acoustic Stereo Imaging. In: Third International Symposium on 3D Data Processing, Visualization and Transmission, Chapel Hill, USA (June 14-16, 2006)
9. Balasuriya, A., Ura, T.: Underwater cable following by Twin-Burger 2. In: Proc. IEEE Robotics Automation (2001)
10. Belcher, E.O., Gallagher, D.G., Barone, J.R., Honaker, R.E.: Acoustic lens camera and underwater display combine to provide efficient and effective hull and berth inspections. In: Proc. Oceans'03, San Diego, CA (September 2003)
11. Kim, K., Neretti, N., Intrator, N.: Non-iterative construction of super-resolution image from an acoustic camera video sequence. In: Proc. CIHSPS (2005)
12. Garcia, R., Nicosevici, T., Ridao, P., Ribas, D.: Towards a real-time vision-based navigation system for a small-class UUV. IEEE IROS, Las Vegas (2003)
13. Harris, C., Stephens, M.: A combined corner and edge detector. In: Proc. Alvey Vision Conference (1988)
14. Hartley, R., Zisserman, A.: Multiple View Geometry in Computer Vision. Cambridge Univ. Press, Cambridge (2001)
15. Kullback, S.: Information theory and statistics. Dover publications, Mineola, NY (edition 1968)
16. Marks, R., Wang, H.H., Lee, M., Rock, S.: Automatic visual station keeping of an underwater robot. In: Proc. Oceans'94, Brest, France (September 1994)
17. Lots, J-F., Lane, D.M., Trucco, E., Chaumette, F.: A 2-D visual servoing for underwater vehicle station keeping. In: Proceedings IEEE Conference Robotics and Automation, Seoul, Korea (2001)
18. Lucas, B., Kanade, T.: An iterative image registration technique with an application to stereo vision. In: Proc. Int. Joint Conference on Artificial Intelligence, Vancouver, Canada (August 1981)
19. Majumder, S., Scheding, S., Durrant-Whyte, H.F.: Multi sensor data fusion for underwater navigation, Robotics and Autonomous Systems, vol. 35(1) (2001)
20. Marquardt, D.: An algorithm for least-squares estimation of nonlinear parameters, J. Society for Industrial and Applied Mathematics, vol. 11(2) (1963)
21. Ortiz, A., Oliver, G., Frau, J.: A vision system for underwater real-time control tasks. In: Proc. Oceans'97, Halifax, CA, pp. 1425–1430 (1997)

22. Rosenblum, L.J., Kamgar-Parsi, B., Belcher, E.O., Engelsen, O.: Acoustic imaging: The reconstruction of underwater objects. IEEE Visualization (1991)
23. Gracias, N., Santos-Victor, J.: Underwater video mosaics as visual navigation maps, Computer Vision Image Understanding, vol. 79 (July 2000)
24. Shi, J., Tomasi, C.: Good features to track. In: Proc. IEEE CVPR, Seattle, WA (June 1994)
25. Silpa-Anan, C., Brinsmead, T., Abdallah, S., Zelinsky A.: Preliminary experiments in visual servo control for autonomous underwater vehicle In: Proc. IEEE Int. Conf. Intelligent Robots and Systems, Maui, Hawaii (October/ November 2001)
26. Longuet-Higgins, H.: A computer algorithm for reconstructing a scene from two projections. Nature 293, 133–135 (1981)
27. Tsai, R., Huang, T.: Uniqueness and estimation of three-dimensional motion parameters of rigid objects with curved surfaces. IEEE Transactions on Pattern Analysis and Machine Intelligence 6, 13–27 (1984)
28. Shi, J., Tomasi, C.: Good features to track. In: Proc. IEEE Conference on Computer Vision & Pattern Recognition, Seattle, WA, pp. 593–600 (June 1994)
29. Bouguet, J.: Pyramidal implementation of the Lucas Kanade feature tracker. Microprocessor Research Labs, Intel Corporation, Tech. Rep (2000)

Progressive Compression of Geometry Information with Smooth Intermediate Meshes

Taejung Park[1], Haeyoung Lee[2], and Chang-hun Kim[1]

[1] Computer Graphics Lab.
Dept. Of Computer Science and Engineering,
Korea University, Seoul, Korea 136-701
Tel.: +82-2-3290-3574; Fax: +82-2-953-0771
{unox,chkim}@korea.ac.kr
[2] Hongik University
72-1 Sangsudong, Mapogu, Seoul, Korea 121-719
Tel.: +82-2-320-3049; Fax: +82-2-332-1653
leeh@cs.hongik.ac.kr

Abstract. We present a new geometry compression algorithm for manifold 3D meshes based on octree coding. For a given mesh, regular volume grids are built with an adaptive octree. For each grid point, a binary sign, which indicates inside or outside of the mesh, is generated based on the distance to the mesh. In each leaf cell having a vertex, a least square fitting plane is created for a localized geometry range with signs. Finally, quantized geometry information is locally encoded. We demonstrate that the octree with signs can be used to predict the vertex positions. As a result, the proposed method generates competitive bitrates compared to the current state-of-art progressive geometry coder. Our method also shows better rate-distortion performance during decompression or transmission with improved smoothness.

1 Introduction

3D mesh has been a robust medium for various applications such as animation, virtual reality, game, scientific visualization, and medical imaging. Thanks to those various applications, mesh compression also has been an active area of research in order to reduce storage space and transmission time for last 10 years. Most compression techniques published[1-4] focus on connectivity compression with single compression rate. Recently, some progressive techniques using space-partitioning schemes(called *geometry-driven*) are presented with improved compression rates[5, 6]. Compared with the single-rate methods, the progressive compression techniques have advantages during decoding or transmission process because the meshes are decoded and appear in a progressive way so that users can interact with those decoded meshes even during the process.

Meshes typically consist of geometry information, connectivity information, and extra attributes such as colors or textures. Since the geometry information takes the most part of compressed data(up to 90%), it is still required to reduce the bitrates for geometry coding.

J. Martí et al. (Eds.): IbPRIA 2007, Part II, LNCS 4478, pp. 89–96, 2007.

Previous geometry compression techniques usually adopt global coordinate system. On the contrary, our scheme introduces local coordinate systems built on the least square fitting planes to improve predictability for geometry information.

Our prediction technique provides with better rate-distortion performance during transmission or decompression as shown in Fig. 3. Though we did not implement connectivity coding yet, the final geometry results are compared based on the Dual Contouring polygonization method[7] to ensure the same connectivity structures. As shown in Table 1, our new octree compression method generates better geometry compression rates in the final level(generally level 12) than the kd-tree based method[6], being competitive to the current state-of-art method[5].

2 Previous Work

In early progressive compression researches, progressivity in mesh compression is implemented naturally based on the edge decimation or the mesh simplification techniques[8]. Because those methods code connectivity changes progressively, they are called *connectivity-driven*. After that, a kd-tree-based method[6] and an octree-based method[5] are proposed with better compression rates. Because those two methods code mesh information by partitioning space (with kd-tree and octree, respectively), they are called *geometry-driven*. Since the compression performances reported for the geometry-driven techniques are better than those of connectivity driven ones in general, we focus on the geometry-driven approach.

In [5], octree is coded with number of non-empty child nodes and their combinations (tuples). Also sophisticated pseudo probability models are applied to enhance compression rates. For each subdivision, subdivision priorities are determined according to the probability models. As a result, a sequence of symbols with low entropy is created. In a similar way, the connectivity is coded based on other pseudo probability models. While the kd-tree-based method[6] does not use connectivity information in compressing geometry, the octree-based method[5] utilizes the connectivity information to improve compression rates further. However, both the two methods produce stair-like appearances in the intermediate meshes during decoding process. In our proposed method, those artifacts are eliminated for the same compression rates (Fig. 2). In other words, removal of those artifacts means better distortion rates. Therefore, our method provides with better rate-distortion performance, i.e., lower distortion in the intermediate meshes during decoding as shown in Fig. 1 and 2. Our method is inspired by the isosurface compression technique by Lee et al. [9]. Volume data are transformed to binary signs, i.e. inside or outside of the isosurface. Octree is also binarized based on the number of child nodes that one parent node has. [9] applies a simple context-modeling with signs. In this study, some of the techniques used in [9] are applied to compress sign information.

3 Proposed Progressive Geometry Compression

Our geometry coding is a two-pass algorithm; during the 1st pass, a localized range for quantization is calculated; in the 2nd pass, localized range for each vertex is quantized.

The first pass also consists of two parts: compression of octree with binarized volume data and localized prediction. The pseudo code for our progressive geometry encoding is as follows:

For a given mesh,

1. Build an adaptive octree.
2. Classify each grid point of the octree as inside or outside of the mesh.
3. Encode the octree with binarized volume data progressively (2nd pass only).
4. For each leaf cell having a vertex,
    4-1. Build a localized coordinates on the least-square fitting plane(Fig 1).
    4-2. Quantize and generate symbols to encode(2nd pass only).

Geometry decoding begins with restoring the adaptive octree along with volume data level by level. In intermediate levels, predicted vertex positions in localized coordinate systems are used and no explicit geometry decoding is required. Only at the leaf node having a vertex of the mesh, explicit full geometry decoding is processed.

3.1 Adaptive Octree and Binarized Volume Data

For a given manifold mesh, an adaptive octree is constructed based on the nearest bounding box of the mesh in the first step. The nearest bounding box is regularly subdivided until every leaf node has only one vertex. One bit information is measured at each grid point of the octree to classify whether it is inside or outside of the mesh(*sign information* or *binarized volume data*). Once the adaptive octree and binarized volume data are created, they are encoded from the root node to the leaf nodes in the breath-first traversal order. The octree is perfectly encoded with 3 symbols, namely, STOP, GO, and ONE_VERT. During the encoding process, the encoder generates STOP symbols for leaf nodes without vertices, GO symbols for internal nodes, and ONE_VERT symbols for leaf nodes with only one vertex.

Those generated symbols are coded with an arithmetic coder [10]. To find appropriate context, several context models have been tested. The best results are achieved by applying *octree level* and *number of inside signs at the node*. This context is determined from the observation that 1) the nodes at lower levels (i.e. closer to the leaf nodes) tend to have ONE_VERT and 2) the octree symbol at any node tends to be STOP when the eight corner signs of the node are all empty (outside) or all non-empty (inside). In the example of figure 1(*left*), the generated code sequence is ONE_VERT-STOP-GO-GO according to the fixed space indices (numbers shown in the nodes).

3.2 New Geometry Prediction Method

When the octree coding process is finished, the vertex positions are not yet fully described. However, at this step, each vertex should be confined within a specific leaf node where the size and location are already revealed in the previous step. This means, in the viewpoint of the decoder, the uncertainty for the vertex position has

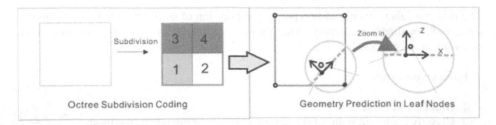

Fig. 1. *Left* – When an octree node is to be subdivided, this subdivision produces code sequence. In this example, the darker grey child nodes have more than one vertex, the lighter grey node has only one vertex, and the white node has no vertices. The numbers shown in the nodes are fixed indices. *Right* - Least square fitting plane in a leaf node for geometry prediction. The square shown is the leaf node; the three hollow dots at the corners are empty signs and the other black dot is non-empty sign; the hollow dot in the gray circle means mesh vertex; the connected thin lines are the mesh edges; the dotted gray line indicates the least square plane. The bigger circle zooms out the local coordinates configured.

decreased to a certain extent. To get more specified information, the vertex positions are further refined using a prediction method based on the sign and neighbor connectivity information.

We note that the sign information represents the contour of the mesh model. Based on this observation, we can guess an approximate surface normal vector from the position where the sign information changes. With this, we setup a local coordinate system whose z axis is configured to be approximately close to the surface normal vector. Other components of the local coordinates are setup by calculating a least square fitting plane for the leaf node (See the *right* column of figure 1). The origin of the local coordinates is set to be the predicted position and the error between the prediction and the actual vertex position is transformed into the local coordinates for each leaf node. [9] predicts the vertex positions, which are generated by the Dual Contouring method[7] in a similar fashion. However, it only calculates the local z coordinate component based on the mentioned technique. In [9], the vertex positions are generated to visualize the isosurface models so that the positions within the leaf nodes are quite regular. As a result, [9] does not need to predict vertex positions in local x and y directions and the origin of the local coordinates(i.e. the predicted position) is just set to be the barycenter position of the least square fitting plane.

Unlike the case in [9], the vertex positions of general meshes are rather randomly distributed within each leaf nodes. To improve the prediction in general meshes, we utilize the neighbor information; the predicted positions in the x and y directions are guessed by averaging the barycenter origins of neighbor connected vertex positions. This approach is based on the observation that the neighbor edges of one vertex tend to have similar lengths. This method seems similar to the parallelogram prediction method [3] but our approach is more comprehensive in that [3] uses only one triangle information for prediction, neglecting other neighbor connectivity information. Fig. 4 illustrates the proposed prediction scheme.

After all vertex positions have been transformed into the local coordinates, a *spanning range* is defined with the maximum and minimum values of x, y, and z.

This spanning range is quantized and arithmetic-coded in x, y, and z coordinates respectively. In arithmetic-coding the quantized positions, sign information is also used as context to further improve compression rate.

3.3 Smoothing Intermediate Meshes

Most previous progressive compression methods based on space partitioning produce stairs-like intermediate meshes in decoding process as shown in the left columns of Fig. 2. The reason is that no smoothing information is available during the transmission so that the vertex positions are set to centroids of the leaf nodes. Unlike this, our method utilizes the sign information to produce better appearances in the intermediate meshes. Though the connectivity coding scheme is still under progress, we find that the sign information itself also works fine as an intermediate visualization tool. Since the sign information represents the contour of meshes, the intermediate meshes can be produced using the Dual Contouring connectivity information which is generated purely with the sign information. Also, the intermediate vertex positions can be set to be closer to the surface, which means better distortion rates for the intermediate meshes.

4 Result

Fig. 2 and 3 demonstrate better rate-distortion performance by our method for intermediate meshes during mesh transmission. For comparison purpose, both use the Dual Contouring [7] connectivity information for the intermediate meshes and the final level models use uncompressed connectivity information. As shown, our method produces smoother appearance and less distortion for intermediate meshes.

Fig. 4 illustrates the improvement in quantum number distribution achieved by our method in the quantum compression process explained in section 3.2. The X coordinates of the graphs represent the symbols required to cover the spanning range, and the Y coordinates indicate the number of symbols. The scales of Y coordinates in each column are set to be identical for comparison. From these graphs, we conclude that the proposed method generates excellent distributions for better compression rates (i.e. lower entropy). Table 1 compares the compression rates with recently reported results. The results are measured when distortion rates are set to be equivalent to those of [3] for 12 bit quantization (for fandisk model, 10 bits). The results are quite competitive considering our scheme produces better intermediate distortion rates than the listed two methods. We adopt "binarized octree" which requires only one bit for each octree node. Contouring information is captured by sign data generated by building the BSP tree during the encoding process, which consumes the largest part of total encoding time. The process for encoding takes around one minute for the test meshes in Intel Duo2Core 1.83 GHz, RAM 1GB machine. Because the decoding process does not need the BSP tree, the decoding process is $O(n)$ where n is the number of octree nodes.

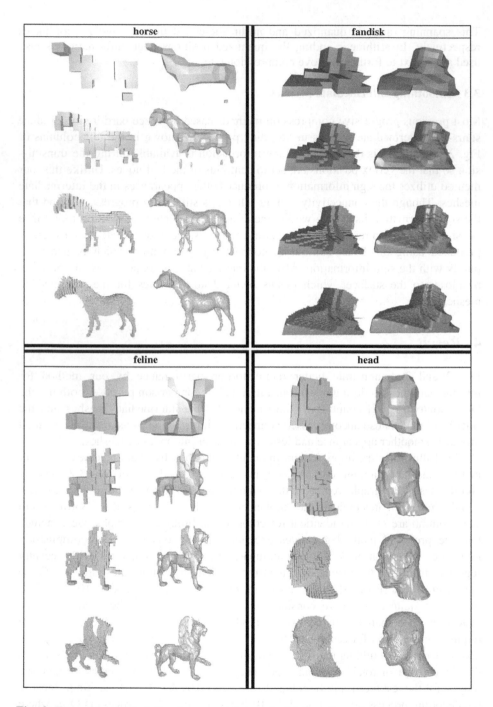

Fig. 2. For each model, left columns - stair-case looking surfaces for intermediate meshes decoded in the previous methods [5,6]; right columns - enhanced smooth surfaces in the proposed method

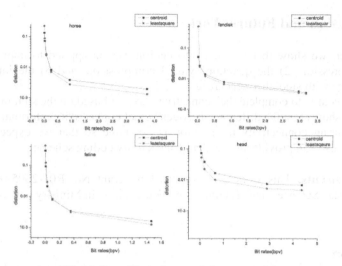

Fig. 3. Rate-Distortion graph for test models

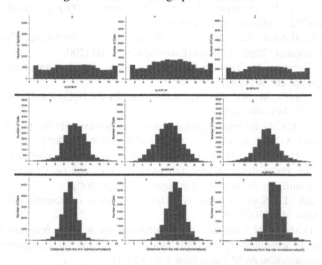

Fig. 4. Geometry symbol distributions for the horse model. *Upper row* - Distributions aligned with the global coordinates. *Middle row* - Distributions based on [9] without predictions for x and y coordinates. *Lower row* - Distributions based on the proposed method. The proposed method improves the entropy.

Table 1.

Model name	Kd-tree based[11]		Octree based[5]		Proposed method	
	Geo	Con	Geo	Con	Geo	Sign
horse	16.4	3.9	13.7	2.9	13.3	2.5
fandisk	12.1	2.9	10.7	2.6	10.8	1.0
feline	15.4	-	13.1	3.6	13.3	2.8
tore high	16.9	-	8.9	2.9	12.0	2.5
Head	-	-	-	-	14.0	2.3

5 Conclusion and Future Work

In this paper, we show that the sign information can be applied to improve 1) the octree compression, 2) the quantum symbol compression, and 3) the intermediate distortion rate with smoother appearance.

Our next goal is to complete the connectivity coding based on the sign information. Experiment shows that the difference between actual connectivity information and the Dual Contouring connectivity information is not huge so that we expect the sign information also can provide an excellent connectivity coding scheme.

Acknowledgments. This work was supported by grant No. R01-2005-000-10120-0 from Korea Science and Engineering Foundation in Ministry of Science & Technology.

References

1. Lee, H., Alliez, P., Desbrun, M.: Angle-Analyzer: A Triangle-Quad Mesh Codec. Eurographics'02 Conference Proceedings (2002)
2. Kaelberer, F., Polthier, K., Reitebuch, U., Wardetzky, M.: FreeLence - Coding with Free Valences Computer Graphics Forum (Eurographics 2005) (2005)
3. Touma, C., Gotsman, C.: Triangle Mesh Compression. Graphics Interface 98 Conference Proceedings, pp. 26–34 (1998)
4. Alliez, P., Desbrun, M.: Valence-Driven Connectivity Encoding for 3D Meshes. EG 2001 Proceedings 20, 480–489 (2001)
5. Peng, J., Kuo, C.C.J.: Geometry-guided progressive lossless 3D mesh coding with octree decomposition. ACM Transactions on Graphics 24, 609–616 (2005)
6. Pierre-Marie, G., Olivier, D.: Progressive lossless compression of arbitrary simplicial complexes. In: Proceedings of the 29th annual conference on Computer graphics and interactive techniques, ACM Press, San Antonio, Texas (2002)
7. Tao, J., Frank, L., Scott, S., Joe, W.: Dual contouring of hermite data. ACM Trans. Graph 21, 339–346 (2002)
8. Alliez, P., Desbrun, M.: Progressive compression for lossless transmission of triangle meshes. In: Proceedings of the 28th annual conference on Computer graphics and interactive techniques, ACM Press, New York (2001)
9. Lee, H., Desbrun, M., Schroeder, P.: Progressive Encoding of Complex Isosurfaces. ACM Transactions on Graphics 22, 471–476 (2003)
10. Wheeler, F.W.: Adaptive Arithmetic Coding Source Code
11. Gandoin, P.-M., Devillers, O.: Progressive lossless compression of arbitrary simplicial complexes. In: Proceedings of the 29th annual conference on Computer graphics and interactive techniques, ACM Press, San Antonio, Texas (2002)

Rejection Strategies Involving Classifier Combination for Handwriting Recognition

Jose A. Rodríguez, Gemma Sánchez, and Josep Lladós

Computer Vision Center Computer Science Department
Edifici O, Campus Bellaterra, 08913 Bellaterra, Spain
{jrodriguez,gemma,josep}@cvc.uab.es

Abstract. This paper introduces a general methodology for detecting and reducing the errors in a handwriting recognition task. The methodology is based on confidence modeling and its main difference is the use of two parallel classifiers for error assessment. The experimental benchmark associated with this approach is described as well as exhaustive results are provided for two real world recognizers on a large database.

1 Introduction

Handwriting recognition is still an unsolved problem for totally unconstrained input, as the state-of-the-art recognition rates (from 50% to 80%) show [1]. For many applications, more robust recognition is required.

Some methods exist for making recognizers robust. Classifier combination [2] is an example. The rationale is to increase the recognition rate by using more than one classifier, in such a configuration that the errors that one single classifier would made are compensated by the others. This approach has been employed for many years but usually more than two or three classifiers are required.

A newly formulated approach is confidence modeling. It stands for all the methodologies that are carried out once the classification is done and a confidence value estimate for correct classification exists. An exhaustive formalization and survey can be read in [3]. One type of confidence modeling is what is known under recognition verification. Its aim is to try to predict classification failures to increase the robustness of classifiers. Contrary to classifier combination, recognition verification does not increase the recognition rate but at least reduces the number of errors and suggests an alternative treatment of the rejected samples.

We propose a general methodology for detection of classification errors in handwriting recognition. The main difference with respect to the state-of-the-art in confidence modeling is that it makes use of two parallel classifiers. In other words, we import the idea of classifier combination into recognition verification.

In section 2 confidence modeling and its application to rejection are reviewed. In section 3 the proposed methodology is described with exactitude. In section 4 possible configurations are presented. In section 5 the performed experiments are described and their results commented. Conclusions and future work are discussed in section 6.

J. Martí et al. (Eds.): IbPRIA 2007, Part II, LNCS 4478, pp. 97–104, 2007.

2   Confidence Modeling

In a confidence modeling framework, one starts from the following assumptions. For each sample of handwritten text the output of a classifier is a ranked set of labels $\{l_i\}_{i=1}^{N_C}$ called candidates, corresponding to the recognition guesses. Each candidate has an associated confidence score C_i, interpreted as the amount of trust that the classifier gives to that candidate. In a confidence modeling framework, the internal architecture of the classifier is not of interest. In other words, they behave as black boxes.

One recent, popular use of confidence modeling is recognition verification [4], often referred to as rejection strategies. They are applied when the recognition rate is insufficient and it is of great value at least to predict an error in the output.

In its most general version, outputs with an associated confidence measure below a threshold are labeled as rejected. This does not increase the recognition rate; however, it reduces the number of classification mistakes and therefore suggests an alternative treatment of these samples. A scheme of such a system is presented in Fig. 1(a).

Fig. 1. Schemes of an ordinary rejection strategy (a) and the proposed combination-based rejection strategy (b)

One can study the fraction of still non-detected errors and the detected errors for different threshold values. This fractions are known as error and rejection rates and their concurrent plot is called error-reject characteristic. From this measure, one can select the threshold that leads to the desired error rate for a given affordable rejection rate. The typical form of the error-reject characteristic is depicted as a solid line in Fig. 2.

How to assign a confidence measure to each output is one of the decisive steps. Several proposals for rejection measures can be read in [5]. In this kind of works, most measurements highly depend on the underlying algorithm, usually involving some posterior probability from the employed model. In [1] a rejection strategy for discarding suspicious words in sentence candidates is used. Arlandis et al. [6] assume there are two causes for rejecting samples- doubt and outliers- and associate a different confidence measurement to each cause. In [7] multiple classifiers are used to compute a measure for rejecting samples.

On the contrary, the approach proposed in this paper uses measures that can be computed for any classifier, thus resulting in a general methodology for recognition verification.

3   Methodology Using Two Classifiers

We modified the "classical" recognition verification approach explained in section 2 by using two classifiers in parallel. For each classifier, we apply a threshold to label rejected samples. But the objective is not to minimize the error rate of each classifier. Instead, we want to minimize the error rate of a subsequent classifier combination where only the non-rejected samples from each classifier participate. Our idea is represented in Fig. 1(b).

The first significant difference appears when interpreting the error-reject curves. With two degrees of freedom, the error-reject points obtained when varying both thresholds do not lie on a curve. Instead, they are spread over the error-rejection space. This situation is depicted in Fig. 2.

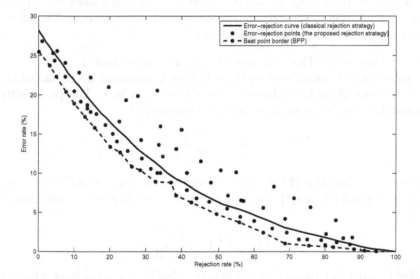

Fig. 2. Typical error-reject characteristic obtained by an ordinary rejection strategy (dotted line) and the proposed rejection strategy (single points). The border where the best single points lie is plotted (dashed line).

Given such a cloud of points in the error-rejection space, we are only interested in those for which there is no other point with less rejection and less error rate. They do stay on a line, which we have called "Best point border" (BPB). Formally, BPB is defined as

$$(r, e) \in BPB \Leftrightarrow (\{(r_i, e_i)|r_i \leq r, e_i \leq e\} = \emptyset), \tag{1}$$

where (r, e) represents a point of the error-reject characteristic. From now the realizations of the explained 2-classifier recognition verification scheme will be characterized by their BPB.

4   Combination Methods and Rejection Measures

An implementation of the previous idea requires the specification of a particular combination method and a particular rejection strategy. The ensemble of a combination method and a rejection measure will be called *configuration* from now on. The performance of different configurations can be tested and compared with respect to each other, and also with respect to the error-reject curves of single classifiers.

To generalize the methodology, we will employ combination methods that do not depend on the internal classifier design. Majority voting[1] [2] and Borda count [8] are chosen for this purpose. For review of other combination methods please refer to [9].

In contrast to the referred works on rejection strategies, where there is knowledge about the underlying classifiers available, when using black-box classifiers there is a limitation in the information we can obtain from them. Therefore the measures proposed for rejection are simple:

- Confidence score: The value directly given by the classifier.
- Probability: A rough probability estimate is obtained by normalizing the confidences of each candidate so that their sum is 1. The probability of candidate i to be correct can be then expressed as:

$$p_i = \frac{C_i}{\sum_{k=1}^{N} C_k}. \tag{2}$$

- First candidate bias (FCB): The difference between the confidence score of the first candidate and the mean confidence score of all candidates. Expressed as

$$FCB = C_1 - \frac{1}{N} \sum_{k=1}^{N} C_k. \tag{3}$$

Higher values of this measure indicate reliable top candidates while lower values show up for doubtful ones.

With each of the two combination methods and each of the rejection measures proposed, we obtain six different configurations that will be tested in experiments.

We additionally introduce another rejection strategy that makes use of two parallel classifiers which is a variation of the one represented in Fig. 1(b). In this new approach, samples are first processed with one classifier. The non-rejected samples go directly to the output and the rejected samples undergo a Borda count combination involving the first classifier and a second classifier. This situation is depicted in Fig. 3.

---

[1] In the majority voting scheme, each classifier assigns one vote to the output label. If the sample is rejected, no vote is given. Hence in practice, for two classifiers majority voting chooses the output from the non-rejected classifier (or from a default classifier if there is a tie).

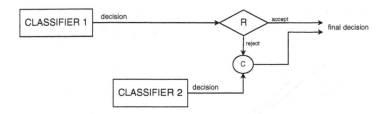

Fig. 3. The cascading Borda rejection approach

This scheme is very suitable for being used with rejection measures such as the FCB. A high value of FCB stands for confident candidates and these are directly sent to the output. A low value of FCB can mean that maybe the first candidate is not the correct one. The subsequent Borda count combination stands for resolving the doubt by comparing with the candidate list of another classifier, like "a second opinion".

5   Experiments

The proposed rejection scheme is applied for improving the results of two commercial handwritten text classifiers on unconstrained handwritten words. The classifiers will be called M and V from now on.

Experiments are conducted on public and self-acquired datasets. On the one hand, the methodology is tested for the most populated datasets of the UNIPEN [10] database (category 6: isolated words). These datasets are *cee, cec, hpp2, lex0, nic* and *sta0* and contain, respectively, a number of 4880, 3977, 5383, 5660, 6813 and 13907. On the other hand, the own dataset (CVC) consists of 1878 samples from a 43-word lexicon acquired by more than 40 writers. Samples were obtained with a digital pen and Anoto paper system. Examples are plotted in Fig. 4.

For each of the rejection measures proposed in section 3 we test ordinary rejection strategies. Recall the consideration about majority voting of section 4. We compare the resulting error-reject curves with the best point borders (BPB)

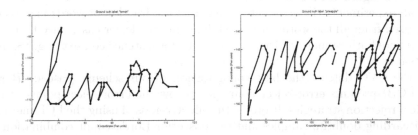

Fig. 4. Rendered samples from the CVC on-line database corresponding to the words "lemon" and "pineapple", respectively

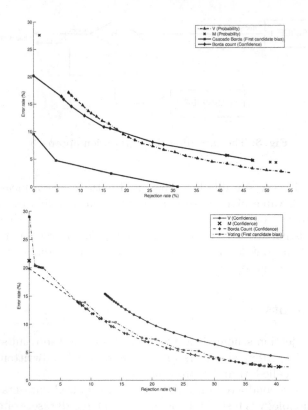

Fig. 5. Error-reject plot for different rejection strategies on the dataset collected at the CVC(left) and on the *nic* dataset of the UNIPEN database (right)

obtained by different configurations of our proposed rejection strategy. Borda count methods use $N = 5$ and in cascade Borda the first classifier is V.

Some of these results for the CVC and *nic* dataset are plotted in Fig. 5, showing: the curves for the best classical rejection strategy for M and V, the BPB of the proposed rejection strategy leading to best results and the BPB of another configuration for comparison.

In all experiments the error rate is taken as the fraction of words incorrectly recognized from all the words processed, ignoring the letter case, since there are cases where both cannot be distinguished out of a sentence context (e.g. "Same" and "same").

In the CVC dataset the best configuration of our scheme (cascade Borda with FCB) presents error-reject points far below the error-reject points of the classical rejection strategies. It proves the effectiveness of using the FCB measure for discarding doubtful samples and the posterior Borda count combination to resolve this doubt. In the UNIPEN datasets we are also able to outperform the classical rejection strategies at least for rejection values under about 40%. This is sufficient as rejections of 40% are too high for most applications. For the M classifier few error-reject points are available because it only gives three different confidence values indicating *strong*, *intermediate* or *poor* guesses.

For appreciating the results of every configuration in all datasets, we have built Table 1. It shows, for every configuration, the error rate improvement of each configuration with respect to using the best classifier alone. This point is obtained by considering that recognition, error and rejection rate sum 1.

Table 1. Error rates (in %) achievable by the different configurations of our scheme for the same recognition rate of the best classifier working stand-alone. This recognition value is indicated in the last column (in %). In bold, the lowest error rate achieved for each dataset. A dash indicates that the corresponding error rate was not achievable by the configuration.

Datasets →	CVC	cec	cee	hpp2	lex0	nic	sta0
Best classifier	V	M	M	M	M	M	M
Error rate of best classifier	17.15	9.88	21.40	23.76	9.47	21.25	12.89
Voting (Confidence)	13.63	9.88	21.40	23.76	5.74	-	10.29
Voting (Probability)	17.41	9.88	21.40	23.76	6.80	-	11.32
Voting (FCB)	11.50	-	-	-	5.62	-	11.27
Borda Count (Confidence)	12.89	8.55	**21.05**	22.24	**5.44**	19.86	**9.33**
Borda Count (Probability)	17.41	8.55	21.25	22.96	6.68	19.90	10.43
Borda Count (FCB)	10.92	8.50	-	**21.90**	5.49	**18.96**	10.39
Cascade Borda (Confidence)	4.762	**8.16**	21.40	23.76	7.69	-	9.71
CascadeBorda (Probability)	17.41	8.22	20.72	23.17	7.67	19.87	-
Cascade Borda (FCB)	**2.38**	8.22	-	-	7.79	-	9.87
Recognition rate	75.40	90.12	78.60	76.24	90.53	78.75	87.11

For the CVC dataset the best configuration (cascade Borda with FCB) is able to sink the error rate from 17.15% to 2.38%. This good result may be due to the small size of the CVC dataset and its lexicon. For the UNIPEN database, the best result is obtained for the *lex0* dataset where the error can be lowered from 9.47% to 5.44%. Error rate differences from 0.35% to 3.56% are achieved in the other datasets.

6   Conclusions and Future Work

A recognition verification methodology to detect errors in a handwriting recognition task using two classifiers has been proposed. The experiments show that the use of a second classifier allows reducing the error rate with respect to the first one, and without a loss in recognition rate. The generality of the method has been assessed by working with commercial classifiers, which from our point of view are black boxes.

The methodology could be extended to work with more classifiers if results should be further improved. However, the success using only two classifiers makes it useful as a fast and resource-cheap solution.

An interesting further work would be trying to identify the rejected samples as doubts or outliers, as other authors do. This semantic information would allow a more precise post-processing of the rejected samples. We are working in embedding this idea into the proposed cascade Borda rejection approach.

References

1. Zimmermann, M., Bertolami, R., Bunke, H.: Rejection strategies for off-line handwritten sentence recognition. In: Proceedings of the 17th international conference on pattern recognition (ICPR'04), pp. 550–553 (2004)
2. Kittler, J., Hatef, M., Duin, R.P., Matas, J.: On combining classifiers. IEEE Transactions on Pattern Analysis and Machine Intelligence 20, 226–239 (1998)
3. Pitrelli, J.F., Subrahmonia, J., Perrone, M.P.: Confidence modeling for handwriting recognition: algorithms and applications. International Journal on Document Analysis and Recognition 8(1), 35–46 (2006)
4. Pitrelli, J., Perrone, M.: Confidence modelling for verification post-processing for handwriting recognition. In: Proceedings of the Eighth International Workshop on Frontiers in Handwriting Recognition (IWFHR'02), p. 30 (2002)
5. Brakensiek, A., Rottland, J., Rigoll, G.: Confidence measures for an address reading system. In: Proceedings of the seventh international conference on document analysis and recognition (ICDAR'03), p. 294 (2003)
6. Arlandis, J., Perez-Cortes, J., Cano, J.: Rejection strategies and confidence measures for a k-NN classifier in an OCR task. In: Proceedings of the 16th International Conference on Pattern Recognition, pp. 576–579 (2002)
7. Aksela, M., Laaksonen, J., Oja, E., Kangas, J.: Rejection methods for an adaptive commitee classifier. In: Proceedings of the Sixth International Conference on Document Analysis and Recognition (ICDAR'01), pp. 982–986 (2001)
8. Gader, P.D., Mohamed, M.A., Keller, J.M.: Fusion of handwritten word classifiers. Pattern Recognition Letters 17, 577–584 (1996)
9. Rahman, A.F.R., Fairhurst, M.C.: Introducing new multiple expert decision combination topologies: A case study using recognition of handwritten characters. In: Proceedings of the 4th International Conference on Document Analysis and Recognition (ICDAR'97), p. 886 (1997)
10. Guyon, I., Schomaker, L., Plamondon, R., Liberman, M., Janet, S.M.: Unipen project of on-line data exchange and recognizer benchmarks. In: Proceedings of the 12th International Conference on Pattern Recognition (ICPR'94), pp. 29–33 (1994)

Summarizing Image/Surface Registration for 6DOF Robot/Camera Pose Estimation

Elisabet Batlle, Carles Matabosch, and Joaquim Salvi

Institut d'Informàtica i Aplicacions, University of Girona
Campus Montilivi, 17071 Girona, Spain

Abstract. In recent years, 6 Degrees Of Freedom (DOF) Pose Estimation and 3D Mapping is becoming more important not only in the robotics community for applications such as robot navigation but also in computer vision for the registration of large surfaces such as buildings and statues. In both situations, the robot/camera position and orientation must be estimated in order to be used for further alignment of the 3D map/surface. Although the techniques differ slightly depending on the application, both communities tend to solve similar problems by means of different approaches. This article is a guide for any scientist interested in the field since the surveyed techniques have been compared pointing out their pros and cons and their potential applications.

1 Introduction

Thus far, robot navigation has been focused on 2D mapping in flat terrains and usually restricted to indoor structured scenarios [34]. Recently, the need to explore complex and unstructured environments has increased [27]. The complexity of this sort of environments requires 6DOF movement due to the unevenness of natural terrains. Besides, the growing interest in 3D modeling of large objects such as buildings and statues has forced the scientific community to face new challenges with the aim of reducing the propagation error present in registration [33]. In both situations, the robot/camera pose is estimated in order to be used in a further alignment of the 3D map/surface. Although the techniques differ slightly depending on the application, both communities tend to solve similar problems by means of different approaches [11] [31].

In general, a good estimation of the initial position is always required independently of the approach or technique used. Hence, section 2 provides a classification of the most important methods used to obtain a coarse pose estimation, including inertial navigation, visual odometry and surface-to-surface matching, among others. Then, pair-wise registration approaches such as the Iterative Closest Point are used to refine the alignment between two clouds of points, see section 3. Finally, any error accumulated between correlated views is minimized by means of cycles and overlapping regions common among the acquired views. Hence, section 4 discusses a new classification of these techniques including analytic methods such as bundle adjustment and the well known ICP

J. Martí et al. (Eds.): IbPRIA 2007, Part II, LNCS 4478, pp. 105–112, 2007.
© Springer-Verlag Berlin Heidelberg 2007

Table 1. Coarse one-to-one pose estimation techniques. R: Restricted (some DOF are constrained in a limited range); TOF: Time-of-flight; LT: Laser Triangulation; DLP: Digital Light Projector.

Technique				author	DOF	sensor	scene
Coarse one-to-one pose estimation	mechanical devices	sensors		Nüchter, 2004 [27]	6	TOF	outdoor
				Folkesson, 2003 [11]	6R	TOF	outdoor
		mechanisms		Pulli, 1999 [31]	6	LT	object
				Bernardini, 2002 [2]	6	LT	object
	Computer vision	Image to image	Feature to point	Huang, 1989 [18]	6	monocular	indoor
				Shang, 1998 [39]	6	binocular	indoor
				Davison, 2003 [9]	6	monocular	indoor
			Point to feature	Lowe, 1999 [23]	6	binocular	indoor
		Surface to surface	Point to feature	Chen, 1998 [6]	6	DLP	object
				Johnson, 1999 [20]	6	DLP	object
				Carmichael, 1999 [5]	6	DLP	object
				Chua, 1997 [8]	6	database	object
				Huber, 2003 [19]	6	LT	object
			Feature to point	Nister, 2004 [28]	6	monocular	outdoor
				Stamos, 2003 [33]	6	TOF	outdoor
				Wyngaerd, 2003 [38]	6	DLP	object
				Triebel, 2005 [36]	6R	TOF	outdoor

multi-view approach, and statistical methods such as Simultaneous Localization And Mapping (SLAM), among others. These techniques are compared and discussed analyzing their pros and cons and potential applications. The article ends with conclusions.

2   Coarse One-to-One Pose Estimation

The initial position is always required independently of the approach or technique used. The initial pose can be obtained using two well-known approaches: 1) Initial pose estimation by mechanical devices and 2) Initial Pose estimation by computer vision. The first technique is based on benefiting by using some sort of device: a) sensors, such as odometers, compasses or inertial systems [11]; or b) mechanisms, such as rotating tables, robot arms or conveyors [31] [2].When sensors or mechanical devices can not be used or when their measure is rough or inaccurate, an estimation of the initial position by means of computer vision may be a good choice. Therefore, the second technique is based on directly analyzing the visual images (given by cameras) or the surface views (given by scanners) looking for correspondences which are used to solve the alignment and consequently the pose. Although in this paper the final registration concerns 3D objects, the initial pose estimation can be achieved using both 2D or 3D views. Therefore, two main groups of pose estimation techniques using computer vision are proposed: a) Image-to-image correspondences and b) Surface-to-surface correspondences. Image-to-image techniques are based on 2D image-to-image matching using both discrete and differential epipolar constraint dealing with 2D images directly acquired by a stereo-head [18] or a moving camera [9]. Note that in the calibrated case the 3D is computed by triangulation. Besides, in uncalibrated systems the motion up to a scale factor is estimated by solving the well-known Kruppa equations computing a perspective reconstruction. The

Table 2. Fine one-to-one pose estimation techniques. R: Restricted (some DOF are constrained in a limited range); TOF: Time-of-flight; LT: Laser Triangulation; DLP: Digital Light Projector.

Technique		author	DOF	sensor	scene
Fine one-to-one pose estimation (Pair-wise)	Point to point	Besl, 1992 [3]	6	LT	outdoor
		Greenspan, 2001 [14]	6	DLP	object
		Jost, 2002 [21]	6	database	object
		Guidi, 2004 [15]	6	DLP	object
		Triebel, 2005 [36]	6R	TOF	outdoor
		Trucco, 1999 [37]	6	synthetic data	object
	Point to plane	Chen, 1991 [7]	6	DLP	object
		Gagnon, 1994 [13]	6	monocular	object
		Park, 2003 [29]	6	database	object

Euclidean reconstruction is obtained by taking any metric measure from the scene that allows the determination of the scale factor, usually a distance between two 3D features [9]. On the other hand surface-to-surface techniques deal with 3D features or clouds of points acquired by any 3D acquisition technique such as stereo [28], laser triangulation or time-of-flight lasers [33], among others. Here, the main difference is in the way of selecting the matching points.

All these methods process the 2D/3D points of the given images/surfaces to extract significant points which are used in the matching process. Hence, the techniques are classified according to: a) feature-to-point approach when the significant points are only those that satisfy a given feature [17] [33]; and b) point-to-feature approach when an arbitrary group of points are characterized obtaining a set of features that differ one to another depending on point neighborhood [23] [8] [5].

In summary, although coarse pose estimation methods based on mechanical devices provide good results in flat terrains, a combination of both mechanical and computer vision methods is usually required in the presence of rough and unstructured environments. Techniques based on the discrete epipolar geometry have been widely studied and nowadays robust solutions are available even in 6DOF. Besides, the differential movement estimators are quite sensitive to noise. Hence, these methods are, in general, adapted to the application constraining the number of DOF with the aim of reducing the error in the estimation. Therefore, surface-to-surface alignment is more adequate for complex 3D scenarios, but then we have to avoid symmetries in the views to obtain accurate registrations.

3 Fine One-to-One Pose Estimation

Once an initial 3D pose is estimated by any coarse registration technique, an iterative minimization should be applied to obtain a refined pose and hence a better alignment between both views. Herein, the methods are classified according to the minimization function, which is usually the distance between corresponding points (point-to-point) or the distance between points and their corresponding plane (point-to-plane). For instance, Point-to-point alignment, such as the Iterative Closest Point (ICP) [3], focus on finding the distance between point correspondences. ICP is the most common point-to-point fine registration method and the results provided by authors are good [14] [36]. However, the method can not cope with non-overlapping regions because outliers are barely removed. In addition, this method usually presents problems of convergence, many iterations are required and, in some cases, the algorithm converges to local minima. The algorithm proposed by Chen [7] (Point-to-plane) is an alternative to ICP. Given a point in the first image, the intersection of the normal vector at this point with the second surface determines a second point in which the tangent plane is computed. The distance between this plane and the initial point is the function to minimize. Despite the difficulty of determining the cross point between a line and a plane in a cloud of points, some techniques such as the fast variant of ICP proposed by Park [29] and the method of Gagnon [13] are presented to speed this process up. Compared to ICP, this method is more robust to local minima and, in general, better results are obtained. Moreover, the method is less influenced by the presence of non-overlapping regions and usually requires less iterations compared to ICP.

4   Cycle Minimization

One-to-one alignment of views in a sequence causes a drift that is propagated throughout the sequence. Hence, some techniques have been proposed to reduce the propagating error benefiting from the existence of cycles and re-visited regions and considering the uncertainty in the alignment. This sort of techniques is classified into analytic and statistic, as shown in Table 3 and explained in the following paragraphs.

Analytic minimization: In order to minimize the propagating error, some authors have improved their algorithms by adding a final step that aligns all the acquired views at the same time. These approaches spread one-to-one pair-wise registration errors throughout the sequence of views. Early approaches proposed the aggregation of subsequent views in a single metaview, which is progressively enlarged each time another view is registered [7]. Here, the main constraint is the lack of flexibility to re-register views already merged in the metaview. Some modifications of metaview approach have been presented to improve the efficiency of the algorithm [31] [27]. A different multi-view approach proposes a multi-view registration technique based on the graph theory: views are associated to nodes and transformations to edges. Authors consider all views as a whole and align all them simultaneously [19] [32]. Analytic methods based on the metaview approaches present good results when initial guesses are accurate and the surface to be registered does not have a large scale. Otherwise, the method suffers a large propagation error producing drift and misalignments and its greedy approach usually falls in local minima. The use of methods based on graphs has the advantage of minimizing the error in all the views simultaneously but they usually require a previous pairwise registration step, which accuracy can be determinant in the global minimization process. Besides, closing the loop

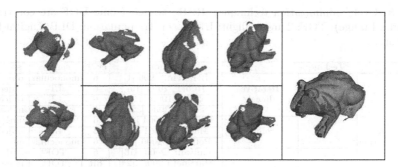

Fig. 1. Multi-view registration of multiple 3D views of a ceramic frog out in our lab

strategies provide trustworthy constraints for error minimization but require a huge amount of memory and usually involve a high computational cost.

Statistic minimization: The same problem of registering 3D views in a sequence has been also faced by means of a probabilistic approach (statistic techniques), especially in mobile robot navigation. The technique receives the name of Simultaneous Localization and Mapping (SLAM) since both the pose and the structure of the environment are estimated simultaneously. The main difference compared to analytic multi-view is that the uncertainty in the measure is not neglected. Hence, two main groups of techniques have been considered depending on the way of representing such uncertainty: a) Gaussian filters and b) non-parametric filters. Both Kalman Filter (KF) for linear systems and Extended Kalman Filter (EKF) for non-linear systems are undoubtedly the most well-known Gaussian filters. Both consist in two main steps: a) Prediction, which estimates the current state by using the temporal information of previous states; and b) Update, which uses the current information provided by robot on-board sensors to refine prediction. Whenever a landmark is observed by the on-board sensors of the robot, the system determines whether it has been already registered and updates the filter. Hence, when part of the scene is revisited, all the gathered information from past observations is used by the system to reduce the uncertainty in the whole mapping, strategy known as closing the loop. Besides, mobile robot localization and mapping has also been tackled by using non-parametric filters such as histogram filter or particle filter. The main advantage compared to Gaussian filters is the possibility of dealing with multimodal data distribution, so that multiple values (particles) are used to represent the belief [35] [9]. Nevertheless, note that Gaussian filters have a polynomic computational cost whereas the computational cost of a non-parametric filter may be exponential. In the presence of large environments in which tons of data are gathered, Gaussian filters state vectors increase considerably leading to inefficiency in terms of computational cost. Similar problems appear using non-parametric filters such as the particle filter. Hence, some authors have proposed different techniques to cope with computational cost and memory size [16] [22]. This drawback can be solved by using methods based on building submaps [4] which present more robustness against uncertainty compared to methods based

Table 3. Cycle minimization techniques. R: Restricted (some DOF are constrained in a limited range); TOF: Time-of-flight; LT: Laser Triangulation; DLP: Digital Light Projector.

Technique			author	DOF	sensor	scene
Cycle minimization	Analytic (Multiview)	Iterative lineal	Bergevin, 1996 [1]	6	monocular	object
			Huber, 2003 [19]	6	LT	object
			Pulli, 1999 [31]	6	LT	object
			Sharp, 2004 [32]	6	DLP	indoor
		robust	Nüchter, 2004 [27]	6	TOF	outdoor
			Masuda, 2001 [25]	6	LT	object
			Pollefeys, 2000 [30]	6	monocular	outdoor
	Statistic	Gaussian	Guivant, 2000 [16]	6	TOF	outdoor
			Martinelli, 2005 [24]	6R	TOF	indoor
			Liu, 2003 [22]	6R	TOF	outdoor
			Bosse, 2003 [4]	6	TOF	outdoor
			Estrada, 2003 [10]	6R	TOF	outdoor
		Non Parametric	Davison, 2003 [9]	6	monocular	indoor
			Montemerlo, 2002 [26]	6R	TOF	outdoor

on a unique global map. Some methods impose global restrictions for global map joining, providing accurate solutions in the presence of short loops [12]. However, loop consistency constraints used in methods such as Hierarchical SLAM [10] can be essential in order handle larger loops and prevent inconsistency and misalignments in the final map.

In summary analytic methods are the most common in high-resolution object reconstruction by means of multi-view registration techniques. Although multi-view registration methods have demonstrated to provide accurate solutions, misalignments can appear in the presence of featureless environments, symmetries and smooth objects. Besides, statistical methods are the most used in 3D mapping in mobile robot navigation. The advantage of statistical methods is in their performance in the presence of less reliable sensors, complex environments and unstructured scenes with few features and landmarks. However, they are not recommended for handling tons of data since the manipulation of large state vectors derives to an inefficient computation.

5   Conclusion

This paper presents a state of the art of the most representative techniques for 6DOF pose estimation and 3D registration of large objects and maps. The most referenced articles over the last few decades have been discussed analyzing their pros and cons and potential applications.

The article is intended to be a guide for any researcher interested in the field. To the best of our knowledge, this article is the first that compares the techniques present in both robotics and computer vision communities, providing new classification criteria, discussing the existing techniques, and pointing out their pros and cons and potential applications.

Acknowledgments. This research has been supported by Spanish Project TIC2003-08106-C02-02.

References

1. Bergevin, R., Soucy, M., Gagnon, H., Laurendeau, D.: Towards a general multi-view registration technique. IEEE Transactions on Pattern Analysis and Machine Intelligence 18(5), 540–547 (1996)
2. Bernardini, F., Martin, I., Mittleman, J., Rushmeier, H., Taubin, G.: Building a digital model of michelangelo's florentine pietà. IEEE Computer Graphics and Applications 22, 59–67 (2002)
3. Besl, P.J., McKay, N.D.: A method for registration of 3-d shapes. Trans. on Pattern Analysis and Machine Intelligence 14, 239–256 (1992)
4. Bosse, M., Newman, P., Leonard, J., Soika, M., Feiten, W., Teller, S.: An atlas framework for scalable mapping. In: IEEE International Conference on Robotics and Automation, Amherst, MA, USA, vol. 2, pp. 1899–1906 (2003)
5. Carmichael, O., Huber, D., Hebert, M.: Large data sets and confusing scenes in 3-d surface matching and recognition. In: International Conference on 3-D Digital Imaging and Modeling, pp. 258–367, Ottawa, Ont. Canada (October 1999)
6. Chen, C.-S., Hung, Y.-P., Cheng, J.-B.: A fast automatic method for registration of partially overlapping range images. In: International Conference on Computer Vision, pp. 242–248, Bombay (January 1998)
7. Chen, G., ad Medioni, Y.: Object modeling by registration of multiple range images. Int. Conf. on Robotics and Automation 3, 2724–2729 (1991)
8. Chua, C.S., Jarvis, R.: Point signatures: A new representation for 3d object recognition. International Journal of Computer Vision 25(1), 63–85 (1997)
9. Davison, A.J., Mayol, W.W., Murray, D.W.: Real-time localization and mapping with wearable active vision. In: Proceedings of the Second IEEE and ACM International Symposium on Mixed and Augmented Reallity, pp. 18–27 (2003)
10. Estrada, C., Neira, J., Tardos, J.D.: Hierarchical slam: real-time accurate mapping of large environments. IEEE Transactions on Robotics 21(4), 588–596 (2005)
11. Folkesson, J., Christensen, H.: Outdoor exploration and slam using a compressed filter. Int. Conf. on Robotics and Automation 1, 419–426 (2003)
12. Folkesson, J., Jensfelt, P., Christensen, H.I.: Graphical slam using vision and the measurement subspace. In: IEEE/RSJ International Conference on Intelligent Robots and Systems, pp. 3383–3390, Edmundton, Canada (August 2005)
13. Gagnon, H., Soucy, M., Bergevin, R., Laurendeau, D.: Registration of multiple range views for automatic 3-d model building. In: Computer Vision and Pattern Recognition, pp. 581–586 (June 1994)
14. Greenspan, M., Godin, G.: A nearest neighbor method for efficient icp. In: Third International Conference on 3-D Digital Imaging and Modeling, pp. 161–168, Quebec, Canada, May-June (2001)
15. Guidi, G., Beraldin, J.-A., Atzeni, C.: High-accuracy 3-d modeling of cultural heritage: The digitizing of donatello's "maddalena". IEEE Transactions on Image Processing 3, 370–380 (2004)
16. Guivant, J.E., Nebot, E.M.: Optimization of the simultaneous localization and map building algorithm for real time implementation. IEEE Transactions on Robotics 3(17), 242–257 (2000)
17. Harris, C.J., Stephens, M.: A combined corner and edge detector. In: Fourth Alvey Vision Conferences, pp. 147–151 (1988)
18. Huang, T.S., Faugeras, O.D.: Some properties of the e matrix in two-view motion estimation. Pattern Analysis and Machine Intelligence 11(12), 1310–1312 (1989)

19. Huber, D., Hebert, M.: Fully automatic registration of multiple 3d data sets. Image and Vision Computing 21(7), 637–650 (2003)
20. Johnson, A.E., Hebert, M.: Using spin images for efficient object recognition in cluttered 3d scenes. PAMI 21(5), 433–449 (1999)
21. Jost, T., Hugli, H.: A multi-resolution scheme icp algorithm for fast shape registration. In: First International Symposium on 3D Data Processing Visualization and Transmission, pp. 540–543 (2002)
22. Liu, Y., Thrun, S.: Results for outdoorslam using sparse extended information filters. ICRA, USA 1, 1227–1233 (2003)
23. Lowe, D.G.: Object recognition from local scale-invariant features. In: Int. Conf. on Computer Vision ICCV, pp. 1150–1157, Corfu, Greece (September 1999)
24. Martinelli, A., Tomatis, N., Siegwart, R.: Some results on slam and the closing the loop problem. In: IROS, pp. 2917–2922, Lausanne, Switzerland (August 2005)
25. Masuda, T.: Generation of geometric model by registration and integration of multiple range images. In: Third International Conference on 3-D Digital Imaging and Modeling, pp. 254–261 (May 2001)
26. Montemerlo, M., Thrun, S., Koller, D., Wegbreit, B.: Fastslam: A factored solution to the simultaneous localization and mapping problem. In: National Conference on Artificial Intelligence, pp. 593–598, Vancouver, BC (July 2002)
27. Nüchter, A., Surmann, H., Lingemann, K., Hertzberg, J., Thrun, S.: 6d slam with an application in autonomous mine mapping. IEEE International Conference on Robotics and Automation 2, 1998–2003 (2004)
28. Nister, D., Naroditsky, O., Bergen, J.: Visual odometry. Computer Vision and Pattern Recognition 1, 652–659 (2004)
29. Park, S.-Y., Subbarao, M.: A fast point-to-tangent plane technique for multi-view registration. In: 3-D Digital Imaging and Modeling, pp. 276–283 (2003)
30. Pollefeys, M., Koch, M.R., Vergauwen, M., Van Gool, L.: Automated reconstruction of 3d scenes from sequences of images. Photogrammetry and Remote Sensing 55, 251–267 (2000)
31. Pulli, K.: Multiview registration for large data sets. In: International Conference on 3-D Digital Imaging and Modeling, pp. 160–168 (October 1999)
32. Sharp, G., Lee, S., Wehe, D.: Multiview registration of 3d scenes by minimizing error between coordinate frames. In: PAMI, pp. 1037–1050 (2004)
33. Stamos, I., Leordeanu, M.: Automated feature-based range registration of urban scenes of large scale. IEEE Computer Society Conference on Computer Vision and Pattern Recognition 2, 555–561 (2003)
34. Tardos, D., Neira, J., Newman, P., Leonard, J.: Robust mapping and localization in indoor environments using sonar data. The International Journal of Robotics Research 21(4), 311–330 (2002)
35. Fox D Thrun, W., Burgard, S.: Probabilistic Robotics (2005)
36. Triebel, R., Burgard, W.: Improving simultaneous mapping and localization in 3d using global constraints. National Conference on Artificial Intelligence 3, 1330–1335 (2005)
37. Trucco, E., Fusiello, A., Roberto, V.: Robust motion and correspondences of noisy 3-d point sets with missing data. Pattern Recognition Letters 20(9), 889–898 (1999)
38. Wyngaerd, J.V.: Combining texture and shape for automatic crude patch registration. In: Int. Conf. on3-D Digital Imaging and Modeling, pp. 179–186 (2003)
39. Zhang, Z., Luong, Q.-T., Faugcras, O.: Motion of an uncalibrated stereo ring: Self-calibration and metric reconstruction. In: IEEE Transactions on Robotics and Automation, pp. 103–113 (1996)

Robust Complex Salient Regions

Sergio Escalera[1], Oriol Pujol[2], and Petia Radeva[1]

[1] Computer Vision Center, Dept. Computer Science, UAB, 08193 Bellaterra, Spain
[2] Dept. Matemàtica Aplicada i Anàlisi, UB, Gran Via 585, 08007, Barcelona, Spain

Abstract. The challenge of interest point detectors is to find, in an un-supervised way, keypoints easy to extract and at the same time robust to image transformations. In this paper, we present a novel set of saliency features that takes into account the region inhomogeneity in terms of intensity and shape. The region complexity is estimated at real-time by means of the entropy of the grey-level information. On the other hand, shape information is obtained by measuring the entropy of normalized orientations. The normalization step is a key point in this process. We compare the novel complex salient regions with the state-of-the-art key-point detectors. The new set of interest points shows robustness to a wide set of transformations and high repeatability. Besides, we show the tem-poral robustness of the novel salient regions in two real video sequences.

1 Introduction

Visual saliency [1] is a broad term that refers to the idea that certain parts of a scene are pre-attentively distinctive and create some form of immediate significant visual arousal within the early stages of the Human Vision System. The term 'salient feature' has previously been used by many other researchers [12][1]. Although definitions vary, intuitively, saliency corresponds to the 'rarity' of a feature [2]. In the framework of keypoint detectors, special attention has been paid to biologically inspired landmarks. One of the main models for early vision in humans, attributed to Neisser [6], is that it consists of pre-attentive and attentive stages. In the pre-attentive stage, 'pop-out' features are only detected. These are the salient local regions of the image which present some form of spatial discontinuity. In the attentive stages, relationships between these features are found, and grouping takes place in order to model object classes.

Region detectors have been used in several applications: baseline matching for stereo pairs, image retrieval from large databases, object retrieval in video, shot location, and object categorization [9][8], to mention just a few. One of the most well-known keypoint detector is the Harris detector [3]. The method is based on searching for edges at different scales to detect interest image points. Several variants and application based on the Harris point detector have been used in the literature, such as Harris-Laplacian [5], Affine variants [3], DoG [4], etc. In [11], the authors proposed a novel region detector based on the stability of the parts of the image. Nevertheless, the homogeneity of the detected regions makes the description of the parts ambiguous when considered in object recognition

J. Martí et al. (Eds.): IbPRIA 2007, Part II, LNCS 4478, pp. 113–121, 2007.

frameworks. Schmid and Mohr [3] proposed the use of corners as interest points in image retrieval. They compared different corner detectors and showed that the best results were provided by the Harris corner detector [5]. Kadir et al. [1] estimate the entropy of the grey levels of a region to measure its magnitude and scale of saliency. The detected regions are shown to be highly discriminable, avoiding the exponential temporal cost of analyzing dictionaries when used in object recognition models, as in [12]. Nevertheless, using the grey level information, one can obtain regions with different complexity and with the same entropy values. In [10], a method for introducing the cornerness of the Harris detector in the method of [1] is proposed. Nevertheless, the robustness of the method is directly dependent on the cornerness performance.

In this paper, we propose a model that allows to detect the most relevant image features based on their saliency complexity. We use the entropy measure based on the color or grey level information and shape complexity (defined by means of a novel normalized pseudo-histogram of orientations) to categorize the saliency levels. This new Complex Salient Regions can be related to the pre-attentive stage of the HVS. In this sense, they are biologically inspired since it is known that some neural circuits are specialized or sensitive to a restrictive set of visual shapes, as edge, contour and motion detectors as others related to color and spatial frequencies [7]. Although orientations have been previously used in the literature with very few success[1], our approach defines a normalized procedure that makes this measure very relevant and robust.

The paper is organized as follows: chapter 2 explains our Complex Salient Regions, section 3 shows experimental results, and section 4 concludes the paper.

2 Complex Salient Regions

In [1], Kadir et al. introduce the grey-level saliency regions. The key principle is that salient image regions exhibit unpredictability in their local attributes and over spatial scale. This section is divided in two parts: firstly, we describe the background formulation, inspired in [1]. And, secondly, we introduce the new metrics to estimate the saliency complexity.

2.1 Detection of Salient Regions

The framework to detect the position and scale of the saliency regions uses a saliency estimation (defined by the Shannon entropy) at different scales of a given point. In this way, we obtain a function of the entropy in the space of scales. We consider significant saliency regions those that correspond to maxima of that function, where the maxim entropy value is used to estimate the complex salient magnitude. Now we define the notation and description of the stages of the process.

Let H_D be the entropy of a given descriptor D, S_p the space of significant scales, and W_D the relevance factor (weight). In the continuous case, the saliency measure γ_D, a function of scale s and position x, are defined as:

$$\gamma_D(S_p, x) = W_D(S_p, x)H_D(S_p, x) \tag{1}$$

for each point x and the set of scales S_p at which entropy peaks are obtained. Then, the saliency is determined by weighting the entropy at those scales by W_D. The entropy H_D is defined as $H_D(s,x) = -\int p(I,s,x)\log_2 p(I,s,x)dI$, where $p(I,s,x)$ is the probability density of the intensity I as a function of scale s and position x. In the discrete case, for a region R_x of n pixels, the Shannon entropy is defined as

$$H_D(R_x) = -\sum_{i=1}^{n} P_{D,R_x}(i)log_2 P_{D,R_x}(i) \tag{2}$$

where $P_{D,R_x}(i)$ is the probability of descriptor D taking the value i in the local region R_x, for n grey levels. The set of scales S_p is defined by the maxima of the function H_D in the space of scales $S_p = \{s : \frac{\partial H_D(s,x)}{\partial s} = 0, \quad \frac{\partial^2 H_D(s,x)}{\partial s^2} < 0\}$

These equations are illustrated by the detected local maxima in fig. 1. In the figure, a point x is evaluated in the space of scales, obtaining two local maxima. These peaks of the entropy estimation correspond to the representative scales for the analyzed image point.

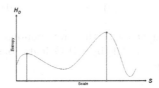

Fig. 1. Local maxima of function H_D in the scale space S

The relevance of each position of the saliency at its representative scales is defined by the inter-scale saliency measure $W_D(s,x) = s\frac{\partial}{\partial s}H_D(s,x)$.

Considering each scale s of S_p and the pixel x, we estimate W_D in the discrete case as,

$$W_D(s,x) = s\frac{|H_D(s-1,x) - H_D(s,x)| + |H_D(s+1,x) - H_D(s,x)|}{2} \tag{3}$$

where $s \in [1, ..., S]$, for S the total number of scales. Using the previous weighting factor, we assume that the significant salient regions correspond to that locations with high distortion in terms of the Shannon entropy and its peak magnitude.

2.2 Traditional Grey-Level and Orientation Saliency

Kadir et al. [1] used the grey-level entropy to define the saliency complexity of a given region. However, this approach falls short in front of clear cases of different complexities. In fig. 2 one can observe different regions with the same amount of pixels for each grey level and different visual complexity. Note that the approach proposed by [1] gives the same entropy value for all of them.

A natural and well founded measure to solve this pathology is the use of complementary orientation information. In the same work [1], Kadir et al. considered the

Fig. 2. Regions of different complexity with the same grey level entropy

use of orientations with very limited and inconclusive results. The use of orientations as a measure of complexity involves several problems. In order to exemplify those problems, suppose that we have the regions (a) and (b) of fig. 3. Both regions have the same pdf (fig. 3(c)), although contain different number of significant orientations with the same proportion (histograms of fig. 3(d) and (e)).

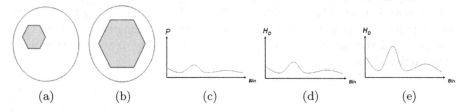

Fig. 3. (a)(b) Two circular regions with the same content at different resolutions. (c) Coincident pdf for the regions (a) and (b). (d) Orientations histogram for (a), and (e) orientations histogram for (b).

To solve the commented problems, we propose a design of the normalized orientation.

2.3 Normalized Orientation Entropy Measure

The normalized orientation entropy measure is based on computing the entropy using a pseudo-histogram of orientations. The usual way to estimate the histogram of orientations of a region is to use a range from 0 to 2π radians. However, a very important information related to the orientation is omitted, the lack of orientation, referred from now on as '*non-orientation*'. Our proposed orientation metric consists of computing the saliency including this *non-orientations* in the modified orientation pdf.

Considering the $k \leq K$ most significant orientations using an experimental threshold, where K is the total orientation magnitudes from a given region, we compute the histogram h_O. The normalization bin is then added as $h_O(n+1) = K - k$. In this way, the modified orientation pdf for the histogram h_O is obtained by means of:

$$PDF_O(i) = \frac{h_O(i)}{\sum_{j=1}^{n+1} h_O(j)}, \forall i \in [1, .., n+1] \tag{4}$$

In order to obtain the orientation entropy value, we consider the first n values of the normalized histogram. Note that the $n + 1$ position is not included in the entropy evaluation since its goal is to normalize the first n positions, as shown in eq. (4).

2.4   Combining the Saliency

In our particular case, the grey-level histogram is combined with the pseudo-histogram of orientations. In this way, once estimated the two corresponding pdf, we apply equations (1), (2), and (3) to each one, and the final measure combination is obtained by means of the simple addition[1] $\gamma = \gamma_G + \gamma_O$, where γ_G and γ_O are estimated by equation (1) for the grey and orientation saliency, and γ is the result, where the final significant saliency positions, magnitudes (level of complexity), and scales are defined. This new saliency measure gives a high complexity value when the region contains different grey levels information (non-homogeneous region), and the shape complexity is high (high number of gradient magnitudes at multiple orientations). The complexity order to detect the salient regions is $O(dl)$, where d is the number of image pixels, and l is the number of scales searched for each pixel.

3   Results

We compare the presented CSR with the Harris-Laplacian, Hessian-Laplacian, and the grey-level saliency in terms of repeatability and false alarm rate. The parameters used for the region detectors are the default parameters given by the authors [11][1][3]. The number of regions obtained by each method strongly depends on the image type since each one responds to different type of features. Nevertheless, we use the 20% maximum responses of each detector to analyze the robustness of the most significant salient regions.

Fig. 4. Caltech database samples used to test the keypoint detectors

In order to validate our results, we selected the samples of fig. 4 from the public Caltech repository database. In this set of samples, we applied a set of transformations: rotation (10 degrees per step up to 100), white noise addition (0.1 of the variance per step up to 1.0), scale changes (15% per step up to 150), and affine distortions (5 pixels x-axis distortion per step up to 50). The mean results for the repeatability and false alarm ratios are shown in fig. 5. We consider the repeatability defined as the percentage of the initial detected regions that is maintained

---

[1] We have experimentally observed that this simple combination obtains the most relevant results in comparison with other kinds of combinations.

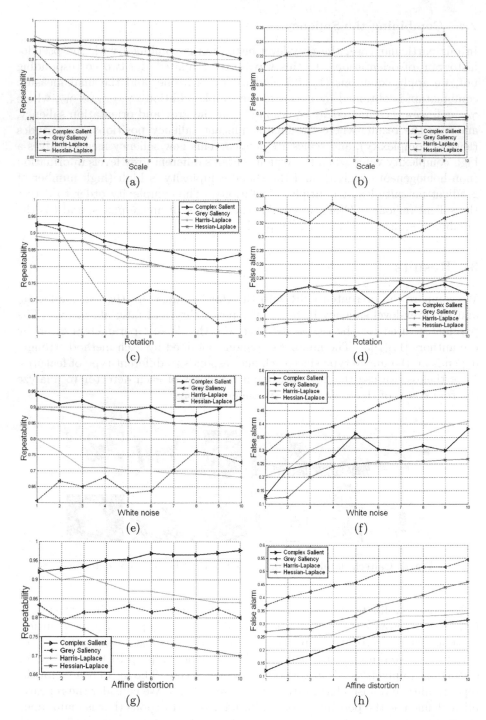

Fig. 5. (a)(b) Hit rate (H) and false alarm rate (FA) for scale, (c)(d) rotation, (e)(f) white noise, and (g)(h) affine invariants in the space of transformations

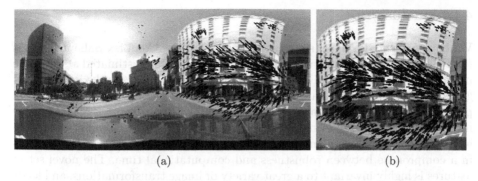

Fig. 6. (a) Smoothed oriented CSR matches, (b) Zoomed right region

(a)   (b)   (c)   (d)

Fig. 7. (a)(b) Samples, (c) Smoothed oriented CSR matches, (d) Zoomed right region

in the space of transformations, and the false alarm rate as the percentage of detected regions that do not have a correspondence in the initial image. Observing the figures, one can see that the CSR regions obtain better performance in terms of repeatability, obtaining the highest percentage of intersected regions for all types of image distortions. For the case of false alarm rate, the CSR and the Hessian Laplace methods are the best, obtaining similar results.

The next experiment is to apply the CSR regions to video sequences to show its temporal robustness. We have used the video images from the Ladybug2 spherical digital camera from Point Grey Research group [13]. The car system has six cameras that enable the system to collect video from more than 75% of the full sphere [13]. Besides, we have tested road video sequences from the Geovan Mobile Mapping process from the Institut Cartogràfic de Catalunya [14]. For both experiments we have analyzed 100 frames, using the SIFT descriptor [4] to describe the regions. The matching is done by similar regions descriptors in a neighborhood of the detected CSRs. The smoothed oriented maps from CSR matchings are shown in fig. 6 and fig. 7. Fig. 6(a) shows the oriented map in the first analyzed frame of [13]. Fig. 6(b) focuses on the right region of (a). One can see that the matched complex regions correspond to singularities in the video sequence and approximates roughly the video movement. From the road experiment of fig. 6, where appear cars and traffic signs (fig. 6(a) and (b)), the oriented map is shown in fig. 6(c), where the amplified right region shown in fig. 6(d) shows the correct temporal behavior of the road video sequences.

4   Conclusion

We have presented a novel set of salient features, the Complex Salient Regions (CSR). These features are based on complex image regions estimated at real-time using an entropy measure. The presented CSR analyzes the complexity of the regions using the grey-level, and orientations information. We introduced a novel procedure to consider the anisotropic features of image pixels that makes the image orientations useful and highly discriminable in object recognition frameworks. One can use the complexity criteria to adjust the detector requirements in a compromise between robustness and computational time. The novel set of features is highly invariant to a great variety of image transformations, and leads to a better repeatability and lower false alarm rate than the state-of-the-art keypoint detectors. These novel salient regions show robust temporal behavior on real video sequences, and can be potentially applied to real-time matching and image retrieval problems (less than 1 second in 800×640 medium resolution images), avoiding the exponential number of features and time complexity of the exhaustive methods.

Acknowledgements

This work was supported in part by the projects, FIS-G03/1085, FIS-PI031488, MI-1509/2005, and TIN2006-15308-C02-01.

References

1. Kadir, T., Brady, M.: Saliency, Scale and Image Description. Intl. J. of Computer Vision 45(2), 83–105 (2001)
2. Hall, D., Leibe, B., Schiele, B.: Saliency of Interest Points under Scale Changes. In: Proc. of the British Machine Vision Conference (2002)
3. Mikolajczyk, K., Schmid, C.: Scale & Affine Invariant Interest Point Detectors. International Journal of Computer Vision 60, 63–86 (2004)
4. Lowe, D.: Distinctive image features from scale-invariant keypoints. International Journal of Computer Vision 20, 91–110 (2003)
5. Harris, C., Stephens, M.: A combined corner and edge detector. Alvey Vision Conference, pp. 147–151 (1999)
6. Neisser, U.: Visual Search. Scientific American 210(6), 94–102 (1964)
7. Grimson, W.E.L.: From Images To Surfaces: A Computational Study of the Early Human Visual System. MIT Press, Cambridge, MA (1981)
8. Schmid, C., Mohr, R.: Local grayvalue invariants for image retrieval. IEEE Transactions on Pattern Analysis and Machine Intelligence 19(5), 530–535 (1997)
9. Fergus, R., Perona, P., Zisserman, A.: Object class recognition by unsupervised scale-invariant learning. In: Proceedings IEEE Conference on Computer Vision and Pattern Recognition, Madison, Wisconsin, USA (2003)
10. Fraundorfer, F., Bischof, H.: Detecting Distinguished Regions by Saliency. In: Bigun, J., Gustavsson, T. (eds.) SCIA 2003. LNCS, vol. 2749, pp. 208–215. Springer, Heidelberg (2003)

11. Matas, J., Chum, O., Urban, M., Pajdla, T.: Robust Wide baseline Stereo from Maximally Stable Extremal Regions. In: Proc. of the British Machine Vision Conference, vol. 1, pp. 384–393 (2002)
12. Serre, T., Kouh, M., Cadieu, C., Knoblich, U., Kreiman, G., Poggio, T.: A Theory of Object Recognition: Computations and Circuits in the Feedforward Path of the Ventral Stream in Primate Visual Cortex, AIM. vol. 36 (2005)
13. http://ptgrey.com/products/ladybug2/samples.asp
14. http://www.icc.es

Improving Piecewise-Linear Registration Through Mesh Optimization

Vicente Arévalo and Javier González

Dept. of System Engineering and Automation,
University of Málaga, Campus Teatinos, 29071, Málaga, Spain
varevalo@ctima.uma.es, jgonzalez@ctima.uma.es

Abstract. Piecewise-linear methods accomplish the registration by dividing the images in corresponding triangular patches, which are individually mapped through affine transformations. For this process to be successful, every pair of corresponding patches must lie on projections of a 3D plane surface; otherwise, the registration may generate undesirable artifacts, such as broken lines, which diminish the registration quality. This paper presents a new technique for improving the registration consistency by automatically refining the topology of the corresponding triangular meshes used by this method. Our approach iteratively modifies the connectivity of the meshes by swapping edges. For detecting the edges to be swapped, we analyze the local registration consistency before and after applying the action, employing for that the mutual information (MI), a metric for registration consistency significantly more robust than other well-known metrics such as normalized cross correlation (NCC) or sum of square differences (SSD). The proposed method has been successfully tested with different sets of test images, both synthetic and real.

1 Introduction

Image registration is the process of overlapping two images of the same scene acquired on different dates, from differences point of views and/or using different sensors. In this process, one image remains fixed (*fixed* image) whereas the other (*moving* image) is spatially transformed until fitting with the first one. Image registration is a crucial step in many image analysis applications like image fusion, change detection, 3D scene reconstruction, etc. Traditionally, the registration process is dealt with in two stages. In the first one, the positions of a set of pairs of corresponding points (so-called correspondences) are identified in the images, and in the second stage, this set of correspondence pairs is exploited to robustly estimate a mapping function which is then used to transform all the pixels of the moving image onto the fixed one (some kind of interpolation is required in this step).

Different mapping functions have been reported in the literature for image registration, such as polynomial, radial basis, piecewise (linear or cubic), splines, etc. [1]. For registering images of polyhedral scenes (typical in indoor and urban environments), piecewise-linear functions are especially suitable, since they

J. Martí et al. (Eds.): IbPRIA 2007, Part II, LNCS 4478, pp. 122–129, 2007.
© Springer-Verlag Berlin Heidelberg 2007

divide the images into triangles which are individually registered through linear transformations that preserve the topology of the triangular mesh [2]. Of particular significance is the case where the perspective deformation of the images can be simplified by an affine transformation, since a triangle in the moving image must perfectly overlap onto the fixed one provided that it comes from the projection of a planar patch of the scene [3].

Given a set of corresponding point pairs in the images, isomorphic triangular meshes are typically generated onto them by using the Delaunay's triangulation method [4], which produces triangles of balanced size and shape, but which does not guarantee that the created topology is the best possible one for registering the images through a piecewise-linear method. For that purpose, it is clear that we should minimize the number of triangles covering on projections of different planar 3D patches, that is, those whose vertices are projections of 3D points of different planar patches (see fig. 1). This is the aim of this work: to improve the accuracy of piecewise-linear image registration by only applying edge swapping modifications to the mesh. This process can be seen as an optimization procedure that modifies the mesh connectivity, that is, without varying the number of vertices neither their coordinates. It is remarkable also that, the resulting optimized mesh is in compliance with the 3D scene structure up to the level that the mesh geometrical realization allows. To our knowledge, this is a novel approach for the image registration problem, since previous methods reported in the literature focus on optimization/simplification of 3D triangular meshes, requiring a complete knowledge of the scene geometry derived, for example, from a laser range finder [5][6] or calibrated images [7][8].

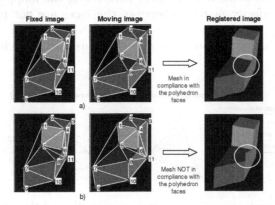

Fig. 1. For a piecewise-linear registration process to be successful, the triangles must be projections of one single polyhedral face of the scene as in (a), otherwise broken lines are produced and the registration of that triangle shows a clear inconsistency (b)

A key aspect in the proposed optimization method is that of determining when an edge swapping operation is necessary. Our solution consists of checking the local registration consistency of the two triangles involved (those that share the analyzed edge) before and after performing the swap. In this process, no threshold needs to be considered. Another novelty of this work is the usage of the mutual information (MI) as a measurement of registration consistency [9] which, unlike other well-known metrics such as normalized cross correlation (NCC) or sum of square differences (SSD), is less sensitive to changes in lighting conditions or noise. The overall registration method has been successfully tested with a broad variety of test images (both synthetic and real) acquired under different lighting conditions and viewpoints.

The remainder of this paper is organized as follows. Section 2 contains several assumptions and definitions, as well as, the formulation used in subsequent sections. In section 3, we describe our method, the inconsistency estimation function and the optimization process. In section 4, we present and discuss some experimental results. Finally, some conclusions and future work are outlined.

2   Assumptions and Definitions

In this work we assume that the 3D-to-2D camera projection can be modelled by a paraperspective transformation which basically means that parallel lines in space keep their parallelism in the image. This simplification is assumable in most computer vision setups and leads to a great reduction in complexity in many vision problems [10]. For image registration, this assumption implies that 3 correspondences (instead of the 4 correspondences required for its general form) suffice to estimate the affinity which transfers points from one image patch to another [3]. In other words, if a pair of corresponding faces are projections of a plane surface, the geometric transformation which maps the pixels of one to another is an affinity. Thus, after performing the mapping, both image patches should perfectly match; otherwise, the faces are not projections of a planar surface.

Next, we introduce the notation employed in this work as well as some useful definitions.

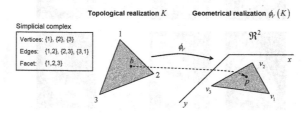

Fig. 2. Example of mesh representation: a mesh consisting of one face

A mesh is a piecewise-linear surface, consisting of triangular faces put together along their edges. Formally, a mesh is a pair $M = (K, V)$, where K is a structure, called simplicial complex [11], which determines the connectivity of the vertices, edges and faces (its *topological realization*), and $V = \{v_i | i = 1, \ldots, m\}$, $v_i \in \Re^2$ is a set of vertex positions which defines the shape of the mesh in $\Re^2$ (its *geometrical realization*) [6] (see fig. 2). To refer to any point within the mesh, we employ the notation $p \in \phi_V(s)$, where $s \subseteq K$, thus, we use $p \in \phi_V(t)$ to refer to one point within a triangular face $t = \{i, j, k\} \in K$; $p \in \phi_V(q)$ to refer to one point within a quadrilateral of M consisting of two adjacent triangles $q = [\{i, j, k\}, \{i, j, l\}] \in K$, and so on.

In addition to the above general definition, we introduce the following ones, of interest for describing our method in the next section:

- An edge $\{i, j\} \in K$ is *external* or *boundary* if it is a subset of only one face, and *internal* or *shared* otherwise.
- An edge $\{i, j\} \in K$ is *3D-compatible* if it lies on a projection of a 3D plane surface, and *3D-incompatible* otherwise.
- Given a set of point correspondences $\{(v_i, v_i')|i = 1, \ldots, n\}$, $v_i \in V$ and $v_i' \in V'$ identified in two images, two isomorphic triangular meshes $M = (K, V)$ and $M' = (K, V')$, and a simplicial complex $s \subseteq K$, we define the piecewise-linear function $\boldsymbol{f}$ which geometrically maps a point $p \in \phi_V(s)$ to another $p' \in \phi_{V'}(s)$ as follows:

$$p' = \boldsymbol{f}_{\phi_V(s)}(p) = \begin{cases} f_1(p) \ if \ p \in \phi_V(t_1) \\ \vdots \\ f_m(p) \ if \ p \in \phi_V(t_m) \end{cases} \tag{1}$$

where $t_i = \{j, k, l\} \in s$; f_i is an affinity estimated from the geometrical realization of the vertices of t_i in both meshes, namely the point pairs (v_j, v_j'), (v_k, v_k'), and (v_l, v_l'); and m is the number of triangular faces.

Notice that once the transformation has been applied $\phi_V(s) = \phi_{V'}(s)$, that is, the corresponding faces of both meshes must perfectly overlap.

3 Description of the Proposed Method

The method presented in this paper is aimed to improve the accuracy of piecewise-linear registration, especially when applied to images of polyhedral scenes. For this purpose, we iteratively modify the connectivity of the triangular meshes by swapping 3D-incompatible edges (see fig. 3(a)). To detect such edges our algorithm checks, before and after applying the swap, the registration consistency of the two triangles that share the analyzed edge: the edge is swapped if that operation leads to a registration improvement. Notice that this procedure only modifies the mesh connectivity, since the number of vertices and their coordinates remain without modification.

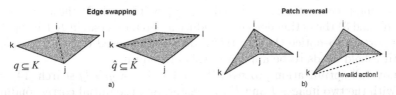

Fig. 3. The topological action of swapping an edge when a) all preconditions are verified and b) the action produces a patch reversal

The employed metric for measuring the registration consistency is the mutual information (MI) [12]. From a statistical viewpoint, the MI measures the statistical dependency or information redundancy of two random variables. Unlike other consistency measures such as the sum of square differences (SSD) or the normalized cross correlation (NCC) which assume a priori functional relationship between both image patches, the MI postulates a statistical relationship which can be estimated from the joint entropy. The advantage of this metric is that it is more robust to image changes caused by different lighting conditions, observation angles, noise, etc. [13]. Mathematically, the MI of two image patches A and B can be written as follows:

$$MI(A, B) = \sum_i \sum_j P_{A,B}(i,j) \log \left(\frac{P_{A,B}(i,j)}{P_A(i)\, P_B(j)} \right) \tag{2}$$

where $P_A(i)$, $P_B(j)$ and $P_{A,B}(i,j)$ are the probability functions estimated from the intensity joint histogram of A and B ($h_{A,B}$), that is:

$$P_A(i) = \sum_j h_{A,B}(i,j)/N,$$
$$P_B(j) = \sum_i h_{A,B}(i,j)/N, \text{ and}$$
$$P_{A,B}(i,j) = \sum_i \sum_j h_{A,B}(i,j)/N$$

being N is the number of pixels.

We take advantage of the robustness of the MI for effectively detecting 3D-incompatible edges. Thus, given two images I and I' to register and their corresponding meshes defined as $M = (K, V)$ and $M' = (K, V')$, we determine the 3D-compatibility of an edge $\{i,j\} \in K$ by measuring the improvement in consistency, before and after being swapped, through the following expression:

$$\omega(\{i,j\}) = MI\left(I(r), I'\left(\boldsymbol{f}_{\phi_V(\hat{q})}(r) \right) \right) - MI\left(I(r), I'\left(\boldsymbol{f}_{\phi_V(q)}(r) \right) \right) \tag{3}$$

where $r = \phi_V(q) \equiv \phi_V(\hat{q})$ are the pixels contained in $\phi_V(q)$ or $\phi_V(\hat{q})$, being $q = [\{i,j,k\}, \{i,j,l\}]$ and $\hat{q} = [\{l,k,j\}, \{l,k,i\}]$ the two adjacent faces, before and after the swapping, respectively. Thus, $I(r)$ represents the patch of the fixed image defined by q, and $I'(\boldsymbol{f}_{\phi_V(q)}(r))$ and $I'(\boldsymbol{f}_{\phi_V(\hat{q})}(r))$ the transformations of its moving counter parts according to the two possible topological configurations.

An edge is considered for swapping only if $\omega > 0$, otherwise, the topological realization of the meshes remains without modification. Also, before evaluating the 3D-compatibility of any edge $\{i,j\} \in K$, the edge should be checked to verify the following preconditions: 1) the edge $\{i,j\}$ is internal, 2) the resultant edge $\{k,l\} \notin K$, and 3) the action does not produce a patch reversal in $\hat{K}$ (see fig. 3(b)). It is important to notice that, in this process, (3) is used only for comparison, so no threshold needs to be applied in this procedure.

The overall optimization process is formulated as a *greedy* search [14], which starts with the two images I and I' to register, and the initial corresponding triangular meshes M and M' resulting of triangulating (by means of the Delaunay's method) a set of point pairs identified in both images. The process finishes when the topological realization can not be longer improved by the greedy algorithm.

4   Experimental Tests

In this section we show some experimental results which illustrate the performance of our approach. Most of the images considered in our experiments belongs to the ALOI library [15], which includes images of 1000 objects acquired under different viewpoints and lighting conditions. We have also evaluated our implementation with scenes more complex, where several different objects are put together.

Fig. 4 graphically illustrates the process described in section 3 when applied to two image pairs of polyhedral scenes. This figure shows the isomorphic meshes automatically generated from sets of corresponding points previously identified in each of the image pairs (see fig. 4(a)), and the optimized ones once the refinements have been accomplished (see fig. 4(b)). With the aim of showing the benefits of using the *MI*, we have repeated the experiments twice: firstly, employing (3), and secondly, replacing the *MI* by the *NCC*. The results of these experiments are summarized in table 1. They reveal the advantage of the *MI* against *NCC* for driving the optimization process, concretely: an improvement in the accuracy of the piecewise-linear registration process (see also fig. 4(c)) and a reduction in the computational time.

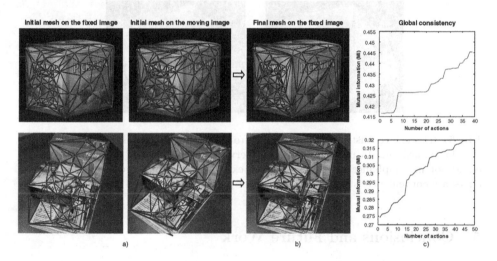

Fig. 4. (a) Real images of polyhedron scenes and their corresponding Delaunay triangular meshes. (b) Optimized triangular meshes provided by our method. Observe how the process swaps edges which go from one plane surface of the scene to another. (c) Overall registration consistency during the optimization process. The flat intervals mean that the actions performed there do not lead to significant improvements, though they carry out suitable topological changes that are exploited in subsequent iterations, as shown in the evolution of the curves.

Finally, with the purpose of showing that the optimization process ends up with meshes in compliance with the 3D scene structure (obviously, limited by

Table 1. Experiment results

	MI		NCC	
Scene (# of edges)	Correctness[1] (%)	CPU time[2] (sec.)	Correctness	CPU time
Cube (275)	100	23.89	98.88	29.39
Stacked boxes (140)	99.28	18.56	93.23	21.34

the initial set of corresponding points), in figure 5, we have re-projected them into 3D space employing the factorization algorithm for affine reconstruction proposed in [3] (pag. 437). It can be clearly observed the undesirable artifacts which appear when the mesh contains 3D-incompatible edges.

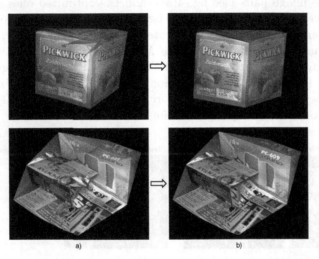

Fig. 5. 3D scene reconstructions generated from two meshes: (a) the initial mesh and (b) the refined one. In plots (a) we can observe some artifacts in those places where edges not in compliance with the 3D scene exist. These artifacts disappear when all edges are conveniently swapped, as showed in plots (b).

5   Conclusions and Future Work

In this paper we have proposed a new technique for automatically optimizing the triangular mesh employed by piecewise-linear registration process in order to improve the registration consistency. To achieve that, we iteratively modify the connectivity of both meshes through edge swapping actions. The function employed for evaluating the edge to be swapped is based on the *MI*, which is significantly more robust than other well-known metric such as *NCC*, since it is less sensitive to changes in lighting conditions or noise. The optimization procedure is formulated as a greedy search which finishes when all mesh edges

---

[1] Percentage of 3D-compatible edges, which are not boundary edges.

[2] We have employed Matlab on a Pentium 4 HT 2.6GHz for implementing the tests.

have been swapped. The proposed method has been successfully tested with different sets of test images acquired under different conditions (from different angles and lighting conditions) and sensors.

In spite of the achieved results, we have detected mesh configurations where the registration consistency can not be improved. Such configurations occur when the vertices of the mesh are not well-localized (i.e. in the central part of the faces). In these cases, additional actions should be considered, for example, edge splitting. Unlike edge swapping, it involves changes in both, the topological and geometrical realizations of the meshes, making the optimization process significantly more complex and time demanding, and generating new challenges such as, where the new vertices should be located or what is the best way of splitting an edge. This is one of our concerns for future work.

References

1. Zitová, B., Flusser, J.: Image registration methods: A survey. Image and Vision Computing 21(11), 977–1000 (2003)
2. Goshtasby, A.: Piecewise linear mapping functions for image registration. Pattern Recognition 19(6), 459–466 (1986)
3. Hartley, R.I., Zisserman, A.: Multiple View Geometry in Computer Vision, 2nd edn. Cambridge University Press, Cambridge, UK (2004)
4. Shewchuk, J.R.: Lecture notes on Delaunay mesh generation. Technical Report 3, University of California at Berkeley (1999)
5. Hoppe, H.: Progressive meshes. Computer Graphics (Annual Conference Series) 30, 99–108 (1996)
6. Hoppe, H., DeRose, T., Duchamp, T., McDonald, J., Stuetzle, W.: Mesh optimization. Computer Graphics (Annual Conference Series) 27, 19–26 (1993)
7. Morris, D.D., Kanade, T.: Image-consistent surface triangulation. In: Computer Vision and Pattern Recognition (CVPR 2000) pp. 332–338 (2000)
8. Vogiatzis, G., Torr, P., Cipolla, R.: Bayesian stochastic mesh optimisation for 3D reconstruction. In: British Machine Vision Conference (BMVC 2003) pp. 711–718 (2003)
9. Viola, P., Wells, W.M.: Alignment by maximization of mutual information. Computer Vision, International Journal 24(2) 137–154 (1997)
10. Xu, G., Zhang, Z.: Epipolar Geometry in Stereo, Motion, and Object Recognition: A Unified Approach, 1st edn. Kluwer Academic Publishers, Norwell, MA, USA (1996)
11. Spanier, E.H.: Algebraic Topology, 1st edn. McGraw-Hill, New York, NY, USA (1966)
12. Cover, T.M., Thomas, J.A.: Elements of Information Theory, 1st edn. John Wiley & Sons, Inc. New York, NY, USA (1991)
13. Chen, H., Varshney, P., Arora, M.: Performance of mutual information similarity measure for registration of multitemporal remote sensing images. Geoscience and Remote Sensing, IEEE Transactions 41(11), 2445–2454 (2003)
14. Strang, G.: Introduction to Applied Mathematics, 1st edn. Wellesley-Cambridge Press, Wellesley, MA, USA (1986)
15. Geusebroek, J.M., Burghouts, G.J., Smeulders, A.W.M.: The Amsterdam library of object images. Computer Vision, International Journal 61(1), 103–112 (2005)

Registration-Based Segmentation Using the Information Bottleneck Method

Anton Bardera, Miquel Feixas, Imma Boada, Jaume Rigau, and Mateu Sbert

Institut d'Informàtica i Aplicacions, Universitat de Girona
abardera@ima.udg.edu

Abstract. We present two new clustering algorithms for medical image segmentation based on the multimodal image registration and the information bottleneck method. In these algorithms, the histogram bins of two registered multimodal 3D-images are clustered by minimizing the loss of mutual information between them. Thus, the clustering of histogram bins is driven by the preservation of the shared information between the images, extracting from each image the structures that are more relevant to the other one. In the first algorithm, we segment only one image at a time, while in the second both images are simultaneously segmented. Experiments show the good behavior of the presented algorithms, especially the simultaneous clustering.

1 Introduction

Medical image segmentation plays a crucial role in clinical practice, mainly for diagnosis and disease treatment. It consists in subdividing an image into its constituent parts, a significant step towards image understanding [1]. Registration is also a fundamental task in a medical scenario since it allows to combine different image models in a single one in order to enhance data interpretation. In [2] the influence of intensity clustering on mutual information based image registration is studied. On the contrary, the main purpose of this paper is analyze how the segmentation process can benefit from image registration. With this aim, we introduce two clustering algorithms for image segmentation based on the registration of the images to be segmented. These algorithms apply the information bottleneck method [3,4], which compresses a variable X with minimal loss of mutual information with respect to another variable Y.

Given two registered 3D-images, our algorithms work by merging neighbor histogram bins driven by the minimization of the loss of mutual information between the two images. The first algorithm segments just one image at a time, while the second segments both simultaneously. These algorithms provide us with a completely automatic global segmentation method. The intuition behind them is to segment an image A by extracting the structures that are most relevant for another image B, i.e., the segmentation of A attempts to preserve the maximum dependence with B. Thus, image B controls the segmentation of A and viceversa. Our techniques have been tested on several MR-CT datasets, which have been previously registered using the normalized mutual information [5]. The obtained

J. Martí et al. (Eds.): IbPRIA 2007, Part II, LNCS 4478, pp. 130–137, 2007.
© Springer-Verlag Berlin Heidelberg 2007

results show the good behaviour of both segmentation algorithms, especially the simultaneous clustering. This approach can be considered as a first step towards multimodal image visualization.

This paper is organized as follows. In Section 2, some information-theoretic definitions and the information bottleneck method are presented. In Section 3, two new registration-based segmentation algorithms are introduced. In Section 4, experimental results show the suitability of the presented algorithms. Finally, our conclusions are given in Section 5.

2 Information Theoretic Tools

We review some basic concepts of information theory [6], the information bottleneck method [3,4], and the application of mutual information to image registration [7,8].

Entropy. The *Shannon entropy* $H(X)$ of a discrete random variable X with values in the set $\mathcal{X} = \{x_1, x_2, \ldots, x_n\}$ is defined as $H(X) = -\sum_{i=1}^{n} p_i \log p_i$, where $n = |\mathcal{X}|$, $p_i = Pr[X = x_i]$. The logarithms are taken in base 2 and therefore entropy is expressed in bits.

Mutual information. Given two discrete random variables, X and Y, with values in $\mathcal{X} = \{x_1, \ldots, x_n\}$ and $\mathcal{Y} = \{y_1, \ldots, y_m\}$, respectively, the *mutual information* (MI) between X and Y is defined as

$$I(X,Y) = \sum_{i=1}^{n} \sum_{j=1}^{m} p_{ij} \log \frac{p_{ij}}{p_i q_j} \qquad (1)$$

where $n = |\mathcal{X}|$, $m = |\mathcal{Y}|$, $p_i = Pr[X = x_i]$ and $q_j = Pr[Y = y_j]$ are the marginal probabilities, and $p_{ij} = Pr[X = x_i, Y = y_j]$ is the joint probability. MI is a measure of the shared information between X and Y [6]. A fundamental property of MI is the *data processing inequality* which can be expressed in the following way: if $X \rightarrow Y \rightarrow Z$ is a Markov chain, i.e., $p(x, y, z) = p(x)p(y|x)p(z|y)$, then

$$I(X,Y) \geq I(X,Z). \qquad (2)$$

This result demonstrates that no processing of Y can increase the information that Y contains about X [6].

Jensen-Shannon divergence. A convex function on the interval $[a, b]$, fulfils that $\sum_{i=1}^{n} \lambda_i f(x_i) - f\left(\sum_{i=1}^{n} \lambda_i x_i\right) \geq 0$, where $0 \leq \lambda \leq 1$, $\sum_{i=1}^{n} \lambda_i = 1$, and $x_i \in [a, b]$. For a concave function, the inequality is reversed. If f is substituted by the Shannon entropy, which is a concave function, we obtain the *Jensen-Shannon inequality* [9]:

$$JS(\Pi_1, \ldots, \Pi_n) = H\left(\sum_{i=1}^{n} \pi_i \Pi_i\right) - \sum_{i=1}^{n} \pi_i H(\Pi_i) \geq 0, \qquad (3)$$

where $JS(\Pi_1, \ldots, \Pi_n)$ is the *Jensen-Shanon divergence* of probability distributions $\Pi_1, \Pi_2, \ldots, \Pi_n$ with prior probabilities or weights $\pi_1, \pi_2, \ldots, \pi_n$, fulfilling $\sum_{i=1}^{n} \pi_i = 1$. The Jensen-Shannon divergence is identical to $I(X,Y)$ when

$\{\pi_i\}$ is the marginal probability distribution $\{p_i\}$ of X and $\{\Pi_i\}$ are the rows $\{p(Y|i)\}$ of the conditional probability matrix of the information channel, i.e., $p(Y|i) = \{p_{1|i}, p_{2|i}, \ldots, p_{m|i}\}$.

Information bottleneck method. The objective of the *information bottleneck method*, introduced by Tishby et al. [3], is to extract a compact representation of the variable X, denoted by $\widehat{X}$, with minimal loss of MI with respect to another variable Y, i.e., $\widehat{X}$ preserves as much information as possible about the relevant variable Y. Soft [3] and hard [4] partitions of X can be adopted. In the first case, every cluster $x \in X$ can be assigned to every cluster $\widehat{x} \in \widehat{X}$ with some conditional probability $p(\widehat{x}|x)$ (soft clustering). In the second case, every cluster $x \in X$ is assigned to only one cluster $\widehat{x} \in \widehat{X}$ (hard clustering). Our approach is based on this case, also called *agglomerative information bottleneck method* [4].

MI-based image registration. Successful image registration methods are based on the maximization of mutual information between two images [7,8]. The registration of two images can be represented by an information channel $X \rightarrow Y$, where the random variables X and Y represent the images. Their marginal probability distributions, $\{p_i\}$ and $\{q_j\}$, and the joint probability distribution, $\{p_{ij}\}$, are obtained by simple normalization of the marginal and joint intensity histograms of the overlapping areas of both images [7]. The registration method based on the maximization of MI [7,8] is based on the conjecture that the correct registration corresponds to the maximum MI between the overlapping areas of the two images. Later, Studholme et al. [5] proposed a normalization of mutual information defined by

$$NMI(X,Y) = \frac{I(X,Y)}{H(X,Y)}, \tag{4}$$

where $H(X,Y)$ is the joint entropy. NMI is more robust than MI, due to its greater independence of the overlap area.

3   Clustering Algorithms

In this section, two clustering algorithms based on the registration of images A and B are introduced. First, we present a greedy hierarchical clustering algorithm [4] that clusters the histogram bins of image A by preserving the maximum MI between A and B. Second, we present a similar algorithm which simultaneously clusters the two images.

3.1   One-Sided Clustering Algorithm

In a preprocessing step, images A and B are registered, establishing a discrete information channel $X \rightarrow Y$, where X and Y denote, respectively, the histograms of A and B. From the data processing inequality (2), we know that any clustering over X (for instance, merging neighbour histogram bins x_i and x_{i+1}), denoted by $\widehat{X}$, will reduce $I(X,Y)$. Thus, $I(\widehat{X},Y) \leq I(X,Y)$.

At the initial stage of our algorithm, only one intensity value is assigned to each cluster $\widehat{x}$ (or bin) of X. Then, the algorithm proceeds greedily by merging two neighbour clusters so that the loss of MI be minimum. This procedure merges the two clusters which are more similar from the perspective of B. Note the constraint that only neighbour bins or clusters can be merged. The cardinality $|\widehat{X}|$ of $\widehat{X}$ goes from $|X|$ to 1.

The efficiency of this algorithm can be greatly improved if the reduction of MI due to the merging of clusters $\widehat{x}_i$ and $\widehat{x}_{i+1}$ [4] is computed by

$$\delta I_{\widehat{X}} = (p(\widehat{x}_i) + p(\widehat{x}_{i+1}))\ JS(p(Y|\widehat{x}_i), p(Y|\widehat{x}_{i+1})), \tag{5}$$

where $JS(p(Y|\widehat{x}_i), p(Y|\widehat{x}_{i+1}))$ is the Jensen-Shannon divergence (3) and $p(Y|\widehat{x}_i)$ denotes the row i of the conditional probability matrix of the information channel. The evaluation of $\delta I_{\widehat{X}}$ for each pair of clusters is done in $O(|Y|)$ operations and, at each iteration of the algorithm, it is only necessary to compute the $\delta I_{\widehat{X}}$ of the new cluster with its two corresponding neighbors [4]. All the other precomputed $\delta I_{\widehat{X}}$ remain unchanged.

Similarly to [10], clustering can be stopped using several criteria: a fixed number of clusters, a given ratio $MIR = I(\widehat{X}, Y)/I(X, Y)$ or a variation $\delta I_{\widehat{X}}$ greater than a given ϵ. The MIR ratio can be considered as a quality measure of the clustering. In the next section, we analyze the behavior of the normalized mutual information, $NMI = I(\widehat{X}, Y)/H(\widehat{X}, Y)$, which provides us with an efficiency coefficient [11] of the segmentation process, and $-\delta I_{\widehat{X}}/I(X, Y)$, which indicates the relative loss of information of a given clustering [3].

3.2   Co-clustering Algorithm

It is of interest now to consider a simultaneous clustering of images A and B. Unlike the algorithm presented by Dhillon [12] for word-document clustering, which alternatively clusters the variables $\widehat{X}$ and $\widehat{Y}$, our algorithm (see Fig. 1) chooses at each step the best merging of one of the two images, i.e., the one that entails a minimum reduction of MI. The similarity between the two images is being symmetrically exploited. Thus, each clustering step benefits from the progressive simplification of the images. One of the main advantages of this algorithm is the great reduction of sparseness and noise of the joint probability matrix. As we will see in the next section, the simultaneous merging over the images A and B obtain better results than with the one-sided algorithm.

From the data processing inequality (2), $I(\widehat{X}, \widehat{Y})$ is a decreasing function with respect to the reduction of the total number of clusters $|\widehat{X}| + |\widehat{Y}|$. Thus, $I(\widehat{X}, \widehat{Y}) \leq I(X, Y)$. Like the one-sided algorithm, the stopping criterion can be given by a predefined number of bins, a given ratio $MIR = I(\widehat{X}, \widehat{Y})/I(X, Y)$ or a variation $\delta I_{\widehat{X}}$ (or $\delta I_{\widehat{Y}}$) greater than a given ϵ. Similarly to the above one-sided algorithm, the reduction of MI can be computed from the Jensen-Shannon divergence (5). But in the co-clustering algorithm, for each clustering of $\widehat{X}$ (or $\widehat{Y}$), it is necessary to recompute all the $\delta I_{\widehat{Y}}$ (or $\delta I_{\widehat{X}}$). Figure 1 shows the co-clustering algorithm where the stopping criterion is given by the total number of clusters.

Input
    Join probability distribution: $p(x, y)$
    Number of clusters: $m \in \{1..|X| + |Y|\}$
Ouput
    A partition of (X, Y) into m clusters
Computation
    Let $(\widehat{X}, \widehat{Y}) \leftarrow (X, Y)$
    $\forall i \in \{1..|X| - 1\}.\delta I_{\widehat{X}}(i) \leftarrow (p(\widehat{x}_i) + p(\widehat{x}_{i+1}))JS(p(Y|\widehat{x}_i), p(Y|\widehat{x}_{i+1}))$
    $\forall j \in \{1..|Y| - 1\}.\delta I_{\widehat{Y}}(j) \leftarrow (p(\widehat{y}_j) + p(\widehat{y}_{j+1}))JS(p(X|\widehat{y}_j), p(X|\widehat{y}_{j+1}))$
    while $|\widehat{X}| + |\widehat{Y}| > m$ do
        $k \leftarrow \min_{i,j}(\delta I_{\widehat{X}}(i), \delta I_{\widehat{Y}}(j))$
        if k indexes $\widehat{X}$ then associate $(Z, \bar{Z})$ to $(\widehat{X}, \widehat{Y})$ else associate $(Z, \bar{Z})$ to $(\widehat{Y}, \widehat{X})$
        Let $z_{\cup} \leftarrow \text{merge}(z_k, z_{k+1})$
        Let $Z \leftarrow (Z - \{z_k, z_{k+1}\}) \bigcup \{z_{\cup}\}$
        Update δI_Z corresponding to $z_{\cup}$ and its neighbours
        Update all $\delta I_{\bar{Z}}$
    end while

Fig. 1. Co-clustering algorithm

4   Results and Discussion

To evaluate the performance of the proposed algorithms, the results of two different patients from the Vanderbilt database are shown. Both datasets are composed of MR and CT image modalities. The resolution of the MR and CT is $256 \times 256 \times 26$ and $512 \times 512 \times 28$, respectively. For each patient, MR and CT images have been registered using the NMI measure [5].

In Fig. 2, we show the results obtained with the one-sided and co-clustering algorithms applied on the CT (Fig. 2($ii.a$)) and MR (Fig. 2($iii.a$)) original images of the first dataset. Columns (b-d) show the segmented images with 2, 4, and 6 clusters, respectively. The results obtained with the one-sided algorithm applied on the CT and MR images are shown in Fig. 2($i.b$-d) and Fig. 2($iv.b$-d), respectively. The results obtained with the co-clustering algorithm are shown for the CT image in Fig. 2($ii.b$-d) and for the MR in Fig. 2($iii.b$-d).

If we compare the original unsegmented images with the resulting segmented images, the following is observed. First, we can see that the best results are obtained with the co-clustering algorithm (Fig. 2(ii-$iii.b$-d)). There is clear evidence that hidden structures of the image are more precisely recovered. Compare, for instance, the images for an equal number of clusters of Fig. 2($i.c$) and Fig. 2($ii.c$). This better behaviour can be explained because in the co-clustering case we make use of all bidirectional information obtained with the progressive simplification of both images. Second, for both algorithms, results appear much better segmenting the CT images than the MR ones. This is due to the fact that the segmentation of the CT images benefits a lot from the precise information contained in the MR histogram.

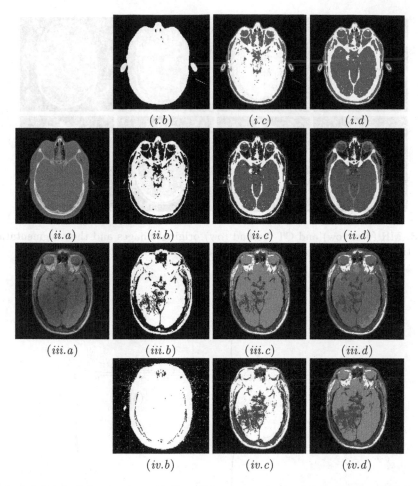

Fig. 2. (*a*) Original dataset images. (*b, c, d*) Images segmented using 2, 4, and 6 bins, respectively. (*i, iv*) Images obtained with the one-sided algorithm. (*ii, iii*) Images obtained with the co-clustering algorithm.

Results of the application of the co-clustering algorithm on the second dataset are illustrated in Fig. 3. MR and CT images, corresponding to two different slices, are shown with 3, 4 and 5 clusters. Observe the quality of the resulting images, where anatomical structures are progressively segmented. For instance, in the MR case with 5 clusters, we observe the correct separation of gray matter, white matter, cerebro spinal fluid, skin and background.

Fig. 4(*a*) and Fig. 4(*c*), corresponding to the dataset of Fig. 2, plot the *MIR* vs the number of clusters for the one-sided and co-clustering algorithms, respectively. We can clearly observe the high quality of the resulting images with a low number of clusters. If the number of clusters decreases below a critical value, MI falls dramatically. On the contrary, to the left of this critical value, MI does

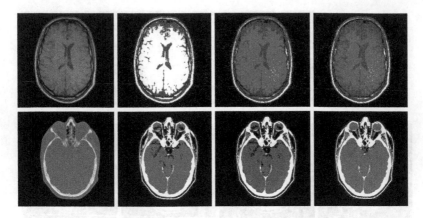

Fig. 3. MR (first row) and CT (second row) original images and their segmentations using the co-clustering algorithm with 3, 4 and 5 bins, respectively

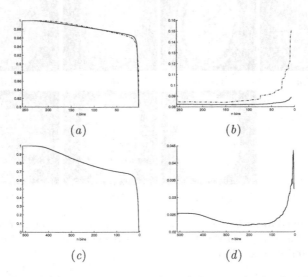

Fig. 4. (*a*) *MIR* and (*b*) *NMI* vs the number of clusters obtained with the one-sided algorithm applied on CT (solid line) and MR (dashed line) images of Fig. 2. (*c*) *MIR* and (*d*) *NMI* vs the number of clusters obtained with the co-clustering algorithm.

not increase significantly with the number of clusters. This critical point can be detected by the stopping criterion given by the variation of MI (see Sec. 3).

On Fig. 4(*b*) and Fig. 4(*d*), the efficiency coefficient *NMI* against the number of clusters for the one-sided and co-clustering algorithms is plotted, respectively. Notice that the efficiency is maximum when the number of bins is low. Comparing both plots, we can see that, while the one-sided algorithm always increases monotonically, in the co-clustering there are fluctuations. This is due to the different decreasing rate of MI and joint-entropy for the co-clustering algorithm.

5 Conclusion

In this paper, we have presented a new image segmentation approach based on the registration of the images and the information bottleneck method. Two algorithms have been presented and analyzed. The first one is a one-sided algorithm which clusters the neighbor bins of only one image based on the minimization of the loss of mutual information between the two images. The second one is a co-clustering algorithm which chooses at each step the best clustering of one of the two images by minimizing the loss of mutual information. Experiments have shown the good behaviour of the presented algorithms. However, it has been shown that the co-clustering algorithm performs better than the one-sided one. In our future work, we will develop a multimodal data visualization framework based on the proposed algorithms.

Acknowledgments. This project has been funded in part with grant numbers TIN2004-08065-C02-02, TIN2004-07451-C03-01 and 2001-SGR-00296.

References

1. Gonzalez, R.C., Woods, R.E.: Digital Image Processing. Prentice Hall, Upper Saddle River (NJ), USA (2002)
2. Knops, Z., Maintz, J., Viergever, M., Pluim, J.: Normalized mutual information based registration using k-means clustering and shading correction. Medical image analysis 10(3), 432–439 (2006)
3. Tishby, N., Pereira, F.C., Bialek, W.: The information bottleneck method. In: Proceedings of the 37th Annual Allerton Conference on Communication, Control and Computing, pp. 368–377 (1999)
4. Slonim, N., Tishby, N.: Agglomerative information bottleneck. In: Proceedings of NIPS-12 (Neural Information Processing Systems), pp. 617–623. MIT Press, Cambridge, MA (2000)
5. Studholme, C.: Measures of 3D Medical Image Alignment. PhD thesis, University of London, London, UK (1997)
6. Cover, T.M., Thomas, J.A.: Elements of Information Theory. Wiley Series in Telecommunications (1991)
7. Maes, F., Collignon, A., Vandermeulen, D., Marchal, G., Suetens, P.: Multimodality image registration by maximization of mutual information. IEEE Trans. on Medical Imaging 16(2), 187–198 (1997)
8. Viola, P.A.: Alignment by Maximization of Mutual Information. PhD thesis, Massachusetts Institute of Technology, Massachusetts (MA), USA (1995)
9. Burbea, J., Rao, C.: On the convexity of some divergence measures based on entropy functions. IEEE Trans. on Information Theory 28(3), 489–495 (1982)
10. Rigau, J., Feixas, M., Sbert, M., Bardera, A., Boada, I.: Medical image segmentation based on mutual information maximization. In: Barillot, C., Haynor, D.R., Hellier, P. (eds.) MICCAI 2004. LNCS, vol. 3216, Springer, Heidelberg (2004)
11. Butz, T., Cuisenaire, O., Thiran, J.P.: Multi-modal medical image registration: from information theory to optimization objective. In: Proceeding of 14th International Conference on Digital Signal Processing (DSP'02) (2002)
12. Dhillon, I.S., Mallela, S., Modha, D.S.: Information-theoretic co-clustering. In: Proceedings of the 9th ACM SIGKDD 2003, pp. 89–98. ACM Press, NY, USA (2003)

Dominant Points Detection Using Phase Congruence

Francisco José Madrid-Cuevas, Rafel Medina-Carnicer,
Ángel Carmona-Poyato, and Nicolás Luis Fernández-García

Dpto. de Informática y Análisis Numérico. Universidad de Córdoba, Campus de
Rabanales, s/n, 14071 Córdoba, Spain
ma1macuf@uco.es

Abstract. This paper proposes a new method for simplifying a 2d shape
boundary based on its phase congruence and the optimisation of a function criterion. The phase congruence is a dimensionless feature that
stands out boundary salient structures over different scales allowing a
hierarchical fast optimisation process over the detected structures. The
proposed method has been compared with other two well-known methods
using an objective measure of the quality of the generated approximation. The experimental results have shown that the the proposed method
is superior in performance to those reviewed in our study.

1 Introduction

A very interesting subject in contour matching is contour simplification that preserves the original characteristics of shape features. This simplification process
can be described as the partition of a contour into meaningful parts [3]. Contour
partition can be divided into two generic phases. The first phase determines
the segmentation points along the contour, while the second phase represents
each segment in terms of instances of a predefined geometric primitive. Since
the simplest and most commonly adopted primitives are straight segment lines,
the output of such a process is a polygonal approximation of the original contour. The segmentation points of the original contour that define the polygonal
approximation are commonly called Dominant Points.

Dominant points detection is an important research area in contour approximation methods. Many algorithms are used to detect dominant points. These
methods can be classified into three categories [5]:

- Methods which search for dominant points using some significant measure
  other than curvature from the original contour scale or from a multi-scale/
  multi-resolution contour representation.
- Methods which evaluate the curvature by transforming the contour to the
  Gaussian scale space.
- Methods which search for dominant points by directly estimating the curvature in the original picture space.

J. Martí et al. (Eds.): IbPRIA 2007, Part II, LNCS 4478, pp. 138–145, 2007.

In this paper a new boundary simplification method using a polygonal approximation of the contour is proposed. The vertexes of the approximation will be dominant points of the contour. The dominant points are an optimum sub-set, regarding a criterion function to be maximised using a scale-hierarchical optimisation process over the all maxima phase congruence points of the contour. The criterion function provides the best trade-off between minimum distortion and minimum number of dominant points that define the approximation.

In Section 2 the phase congruence feature is described. The proposed method for dominant points detection and the procedure to obtain the sub-set of them, which define the best polygonal approximation, are shown in Section 3. In Section 4 the result of a comparative study with a representative number of proposed methods are shown. Lastly, the main conclusions are summarised in Section 5.

2   Phase Congruence Feature

The information provided by the local phase of a signal serves as the basis of our method for two reasons:

- The phase is a dimensionless quantity that allows invariant characteristics to be developed.
- The phase of a signal has been shown to be crucial in shape perception [11].

The Local Energy Model was initially proposed by Morrone *et al.* [10,9]. This model explains the perception of signal features and postulates that these features are perceived at points where the Fourier components are maximally in phase. This model has been developed in subsequent studies [8,12,15,7] to detect borders in digital images.

Given a point $C(t)$ of a signal, the phase congruence at this point can be obtained from the Fourier series expansion of the signal as follows [9]:

$$PC(t) = \arg \max_{\bar{\phi}(t) \in [0,2\pi]} \frac{\sum_N A_n \cos(\phi_n(t) - \bar{\phi}(t))}{\sum_N A_n} , \tag{1}$$

where A_n and $\phi_n(t)$ represent the amplitude and the local phase of the n-th Fourier term respectively. The value $\bar{\phi}(t)$ that maximises $PC(t)$ is the amplitude weighted mean local phase of all the Fourier terms at the point being considered.

Calculating the phase consistency using (1) is an awkward task. Venkatesh *et al.* [15] propose an easier alternative to obtain the phase congruence which consists of looking for local maxima in the Local Energy function $E(t)$ since

$$E(t) = PC(t) \sum_N A_n , \tag{2}$$

that is to say, $E(t)$ is directly proportional to the phase congruence. Therefore the local maxima of local energy are correspondent with the local maxima of phase congruence.

The Local Energy of a unidimensional signal can be obtained as

$$E(t) = \sqrt{F^2(t) + H^2(t)}, \tag{3}$$

where $F(t)$ is the zero DC version of the original signal and $H(t)$ is its Hilbert transform.

An initial approach to calculate the Local Energy could be to use the Fourier transform of the signal. However, this approach has two main drawbacks:

– The importance of a signal feature is compared to the complete signal (great scale) without taking into account the signal feature's importance regarding its most immediate environment (small scale).
– The number of congruent terms at a point is not taken into account. The larger the number of congruent terms at a signal point, the more outstanding the signal feature will be.

One way to address these problems is to use a multi-scale analysis of the local phase. Kovesi [7] proposes to use banks of even/odd filters to obtain the local energy of a signal with spatially localised frequency.

2.1   Calculation of the Phase Congruence Using Wavelets

The wavelet analysis of a signal allows spatially localised frequency information to be obtained in a very precise way. The wavelet analysis uses a filters bank that is created from re-scalings of a wave shape. Each scaling is designed to analyse a given range of signal frequencies. In order to preserve phase information, lineal phase filters should be used, that is to say, quadrature filters.

Let $M : \{(M_n^e, M_n^o)\}$, $n = \{0, 1, \ldots, N\}$ the bank of quadrature filters where n represents the scale parameter and N is the number of analysed scales. The phase congruence of a signal $C(t)$ can be obtained from (2) and (3) where

$$e_n(t) = C(t) * M_n^e, \ o_n(t) = C(t) * M_n^o, \tag{4}$$

$$F(t) = \sum_N e_n(t), \tag{5}$$

$$H(t) = \sum_N o_n(t) \text{ and} \tag{6}$$

$$\sum_N A_n(t) = \sum_N \sqrt{e_n(t)^2 + o_n(t)^2}. \tag{7}$$

Here $*$ represents the digital convolution operation.

As stated above, a signal feature will be more important if it is present in a larger number of analysed scales. To make these points stand out, Kovesi proposes weighting the term that approximates the local energy by means of the following sigmoid function:

$$W(t) = \frac{1}{1 + e^{10(0.4 - s(t))}}, \tag{8}$$

where $s(t)$ is a measure of the the range of congruent frequencies at a point t of the signal and is defined as:

$$s(t) = \frac{1}{N} \left(\frac{\sum\limits_{N} A_n(t)}{A_{\max}(t) + \epsilon} \right), \tag{9}$$

Where N is the number of analysed scales, $A_{\max}$ is the maximum filter bank response obtained and ϵ is a small quantity used to avoid division by zero.

Hence, a first alternative to obtain the phase congruence using wavelet analysis of the local phase is:

$$PC_1(t) = \frac{W(t)E(t)}{\sum\limits_{N} A_n(t) + \epsilon}, \tag{10}$$

where $E(t)$ and $\sum_N A_n(t)$ are obtained from (5, 6 and 7).

One of the drawbacks to compute the phase consistency by means of (10) is that $E(t)$ is proportional to the cosine of the phase angle deviation $\phi_n(t)$ from the overall scales mean phase angle $\bar{\phi}(t)$. The cosine function is not very sensitive to small variations, for example $\cos(25°) \approx 0.9$. This implies that a poor localisation of the signal features can be provided by the phase congruence measure PC_1. To improve localisation, Kovesi proposes using a measure of the deviation from the phase angle which is more sensitive to small variations:

$$\Delta\Phi(t) = \cos\left(\phi_n(t) - \bar{\phi}(t)\right) - \left|\sin\left(\phi_n(t) - \bar{\phi}(t)\right)\right|, \tag{11}$$

providing a second approach to calculate the phase congruence:

$$PC_2(t) = \frac{W(t) \sum\limits_{N} A_n(t)\Delta\Phi(t)}{\sum\limits_{N} A_n(t) + \epsilon}. \tag{12}$$

Equation (12) can be calculated from the quadrature filter responses. For each scale n, the filter response can be considered as a vector $(e_n(t), o_n(t))$ whose magnitude is $A_n(t)$. The unitary vector that provides the direction of the overall mean phase angle is given by:

$$(\bar{\phi}_e(t), \bar{\phi}_o(t)) = \frac{1}{\sqrt{F(t)^2 + H(t)^2}}(F(t), H(t)), \tag{13}$$

where $F(t)$ and $H(t)$ are calculated as (5) and (6).

2.2 Filters Bank Design

Given that lineal phase filters should be used to preserve the phase information of the analysed signal, even/odd filters will be used. This restriction avoids to use orthogonal filters, that is to say, the perfect reconstruction of the signal will not be possible.

In this work LogGabor filters have been used because they present some advantages [4] over traditional Gabor filters. By definition, they do not have a DC component and a bandwidth of up to three octaves is allowed, thus making a better spatial localisation possible.

The definition of the LogGabor filter in a lineal frequency scale is:

$$\text{LogG}^s(\omega) = \exp\left(\frac{-(\log(\omega/\omega_0^s))^2}{2\log(\sigma)^2}\right),$$

where $\omega_0^s = \omega_{\min} m^{s-1}$ represents the central frequency of the filter in the scale s, m is a scale factor among the successive wavelets and σ defines the filter's bandwidth ($\sigma = 0.75 \approx 1$ octave while $\sigma = 0.55 \approx 2$ octaves).

3   Proposed Method

A contour will be a sequence of points in $\mathbb{R}^2$ and defined as a finite and non-empty ordered set of coordinates pairs $C(t) = \{(C_x(t), C_y(t))\}$, with $t = \{1, 2, \ldots, N\}$ and $N \geq 2$.

A polygonal approximation V on C is an increasing sequence of indexes specifying which points of C are the vertexes of V.

The proposed method has two stages:

- The first stage consists of detecting the dominant points of the contour C which correspond to local extrema of the phase congruence, symmetry and asymmetry features obtained from $C_x(t)$ and $C_y(t)$.
- The second stage consists of looking for a polygonal approximation V^* of C whose vertexes are a sub-set of the dominant points obtained in the first stage and which provides the best trade-off between minimum distortion and smaller number of points.

3.1   Detection of the Dominant Points of the Contour

A multi-scale analysis of the phase congruence, symmetry and asymmetry features associated to the signals $C_x(t)$ and $C_y(t)$ is performed as specified in Section 2. Therefore, for each contour point the features obtained will be $\{\text{PC}_2(C_x(t)), \text{PC}_2(C_y(t))\}$.

A contour point will be a dominant point if it is a local maximum in at least one of the features above described, and for at least one interval of the contour points centred in it (called support region) with size $r = 2i + 1$, $i = \{1, 2, \ldots, \lfloor (N-1)/2 \rfloor\}$, where $\lfloor x \rfloor$ represents the largest integer q, $q \leq x$. Let $V^i \subset C$ be the set of dominant points defined in this way for a given value of i. Notice that $V^{i+1} \subset V^i$.

3.2   Search for the Optimum Sub-set of Dominant Points

A procedure is proposed for finding the polygonal approach V^* of C whose vertexes are a sub-group of the dominant points of the contour (defined above) that provides the best trade-off between minimum distortion and smaller number of points.

Carmona et $al.$ [2] have recently shown that this can be obtained by means of an optimisation procedure (minimisation) using the following expression as the objective function $E2 = e^2/CR^2$, where $e^2 = \sum_N e_t^2$, e_t is the normal distance of a point t to the approximation and $CR = N/|V^*|$. The e^2 factor measures the distortion due to the approximation, while the CR factor measures the obtained compression rate. Here $|\,|$ means the number of elements of a set.

A sub-optimum hierarchical search method is designed to optimise the E2 criterion. The aim of this method is to add dominant points to the approximation by giving higher priority to the dominant points defined in a larger support region since these points are present in a larger number of analysed scales. A dominant point will be added to the approximation if it minimises the E2 criterion.

Algorithm

Let s the greatest integer such that $1 \le s \le \lfloor \frac{N-1}{2} \rfloor$ and $|V^s| > 1$.
$V^* \leftarrow V^s$.
FOR $i \leftarrow (s-1), \ldots, 1$, DO
    $Q \leftarrow \{V^i - V^*\}$
    exit $\leftarrow$ *false*
    REPEAT
        $v^* \leftarrow \arg\min_{v \in Q} \{E2(V^* + \{v\})\}$.
        IF $E2(V^* + \{v^*\}) < E2(V^*)$ THEN
            $V^* \leftarrow V^* + \{v^*\}$
            $Q \leftarrow Q - \{v^*\}$
        ELSE
            exit $\leftarrow$ *true*.
        END–IF
    UNTIL exit.
END–FOR

4   Performance Evaluation

A experiment has been designed to evaluate the performance of the method proposed in this work compared with other two methods. The selected methods are due to Garrido et $al.$ [6] that uses a multi-scale approach for computing the contour curvature, and Arrebola et $al.$ [1] that uses a multi-resolution pyramid for representing the contour's chain-code.

Several measures to evaluate the quality of a polygonal approximation to a contour have been proposed. In this work, the Merit measure developed by Rosin [14] was used because we consider it to be the most impartial measure. The Merit measure is a geometric mean between two values: Fidelity and Efficiency. Fidelity measures the distortion caused by the generated approximation relative to the distortion obtained by the optimum approximation with the same number of points. Efficiency measures the obtained compression rate relative to the compression rate of the optimum approximation that causes the same distortion. To obtain the optimum approximations, the dynamic programming method of optimisation developed by Pérez *et al.* [13] has been used.

We have used four classic contours shown in Figure 1. This contours are used a lot in the literature on contour approximation.

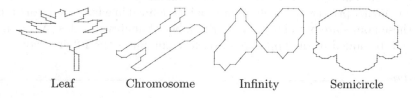

Leaf   Chromosome   Infinity   Semicircle

Fig. 1. Contours used in the comparative study

Table 1 shows the results obtained by the compared methods for each contour and the average Merit value obtained. From the data shown in this table, it can be concluded that the quality of the approximation provided by our method, regarding the Merit measure, is significantly better than the provided by the other two compared methods.

Table 1. Comparison of the results obtained by the proposed method and other methods using the Merit measure

Method	Chrom.	Leaf	Semic.	Inf.	Average
Garrido *et al.*	38.74	66.66	47.57	62.70	53.8
Arrebola *et al.*	45.44	46.93	19.64	45.59	39.4
Proposed	85.74	70.05	59.38	56.27	67.97

5   Conclusion

This work has shown how phase congruence can be used to detect dominant points of a contour. The phase congruence extracted from a multi-scale analysis of the contour is used by the proposed novel method to find the polygonal approximation that optimises the objective function E2 (Carmona *et al.* [2]).

Our method was compared to other two well-known proposals (Garrido *et al.* [6] and Arrebola *et al.* [1]) to generate a contour approximation. The objective Merit measure proposed by Rosin [14] has been used to measure the performance provided by each method. The comparative study has shown, regarding the Merit measure, the performance provided by our method is significantly better than the provided by the other compared methods.

6 Future Work

We are interested in extending our method to address the noise effect to make a robust method. Other research line will be to study how an affine transform affects to the dominant point detection algorithm.

References

1. Arrebola, F., Sandoval, F.: Coner detection and curve segmentation by multiresolution chain-code linking. Pattern Recognition 38, 1596–1614 (2005)
2. Carmona-Poyato, A., Fernández-García, N.L., Medina-Carnicer, R., Madrid-Cuevas, F.J.: Dominant point detection: a new proposal. Image and Vision Computing 23, 1226–1236 (2005)
3. Fontoura Costa, L., Marcondes Cesar, R.: Shape Analysis and Classification. In: Theory and Practice, CRC Press, Boca Raton, FL (2001)
4. Field, D.J.: Relations between the statistics of natural images and the response properties of cortical cells. Journal of the Optical Society of America 4(12), 2379–2394 (1987)
5. Fu, A.M.N., Yan, H.: Effective classification of planar shapes based on curve segment properties. Pattern Recognition Letters 18, 55–61 (1997)
6. Garrido, A., Pérez, N., García-Silvente, M.: Boundary simplification using amultiescale dominant-point detection algorithm. Pattern Recognition 31, 791–804 (1998)
7. Kovesi, P.D.: Image features from phase congruency. Videre: Journal of Computer Vision 1(3), 1–26 (1999)
8. Morrone, M.C., Burr, D.C.: Feature detection in human vision: A phase–dependent energy model. R. Sod. Lond. B. 235, 221–245 (1988)
9. Morrone, M.C., Owens, R.A.: Feature detection from local energy. Pattern Recognition Letters 6, 303–313 (1987)
10. Morrone, M.C., Ross, J.R., Owens, R.A.: Mach bands are phase dependent. Nature 324(6094), 250–253 (1986)
11. Oppenheim, A.V., Lim, J.S.: The importance of phase in signals. IEEE 69, 529–541 (1981)
12. Owens, R.A., Venkatesh, S., Ross, J.: Edge detection is a projection. Pattern Recognition Letters 9, 223–244 (1989)
13. Pérez, J.C., Vidal, E.: Optymum polygonal approximation of digitized curves. Pattern Recognition Letters 15, 743–750 (1994)
14. Rosin, P.L.: Techniques for assesing polygonal approximation of curves. IEEE Transactions on Pattern Analysis and Machine Intelligence 19, 659–666 (1997)
15. Venkatesh, S., Owens, R.A.: On the classification of image features. Pattern Recognition Letters 11, 339–349 (1990)

Exploiting Information Theory for Filtering the Kadir Scale-Saliency Detector

Pablo Suau and Francisco Escolano

Departamento de Ciencia de la Computación e Inteligencia Artificial
Universidad de Alicante, Ap. de correos 99, 03080, Alicante, Spain
{pablo,sco}@dccia.ua.es

Abstract. In this paper we propose a Bayesian filter for the Kadir Scale Saliency Detector. Such filter is addressed to deal with the main bottleneck of the Kadir detector, which is the scale space search for all pixels in the image. Given some statistical knowledge about images considered, we show that it is possible to discard some points before applying the Kadir detector by using Information Theory and Bayesian Analysis, increasing efficiency with low error. Our method is based on the intuitive idea that homogeneous (not salient) image regions at high scales probably will be also homogeneous at lower scales of scale space.

1 Introduction

Low-level vision in general, and affine feature extraction in particular, is a basic step in many computer vision tasks. Reliability and efficiency of these tasks strongly depend on the quality of extracted features. Thus, interest point detection remains as an important topic in computer vision research, resulting in a wide variety of different approaches being proposed and improved during last years. Recent surveys [1] declare that in the domain of state of the art detectors there does not exist any detector that outperforms the other ones for all scene types and all type of transformations. In fact, feature extractors are complementary: they extract regions with different properties.

Kadir-Brady scale saliency filter [2] is widely used [3][4] due to its invariance to planar rotation, scaling, intensity shift and translation. However, its application usually introduces a computational bottleneck, due to the fact that computation must be performed for each image pixel at each scale. Reducing such overload is an interesting objective, since it can help to improve computational efficiency of vision tasks relying on this kind of low level vision algorithms.

In this paper we are focused on optimizing Kadir scale saliency detector from a Bayesian perspective, which has been successfully applied to edge detection [5]. This approach is quite interesting but assumes a learning step preceding filter application. Consequently, environmental (categorical) statistics must be available. Such analysis has been recently applied to compare the effectiveness of different detectors [6], but here we consider how to get statistics and exploit Information Theory measures for reducing the search through scale space, which

J. Martí et al. (Eds.): IbPRIA 2007, Part II, LNCS 4478, pp. 146–153, 2007.

is the bottleneck of the Kadir algorithm. We propose a training step where a log-likelihood threshold from saliency at highest scale for an image category set is computed. This threshold can then be used to discard pixels from an image belonging to the same image category, in order to discard not interesting points, that is, pixels that probably will not be part of the most salient features of that image. Experimental results show promising results on how efficiency can be notably improved having low error.

This paper is organized as follows: section 2 summarizes the Kadir scale saliency detection process. Formal basis of our method is explained in section 3; Section 4 describes our approach to improve the performance of the Kadir scale saliency detector. In section 5 several experimental results are shown. Finally, in section 6, we present our conclusions and future work.

2   Kadir Scale Saliency Detector

Visual saliency may be defined as a measure of local complexity or unpredictability [2]. Salient features are distinctive, due to this local unpredictability, and have proved useful in the context of image registration. Using Shannon entropy, Gilles formulated local saliency in terms of local intensity histograms [7]. Given a point x, a local neighbourhood R_x, and a descriptor D that takes values $\{d_1, ..., d_r\}$ (e.g. in an 8 bit grey level image D would range from 0 to 255), local entropy is defined as:

$$H_{D,R_x} = -\sum_i P_{D,R_x}(d_i) \log_2 P_{D,R_x}(d_i) \tag{1}$$

where $P_{D,R_x}(d_i)$ is the probability of descriptor D taking the value d_i in the local region R_x.

However, this approach may be improved in many ways. The main drawback is that scale ($|R_x|$ in the latter equation) is a pre-selected parameter, so this model is only proper for images that contain features existing over a small range of scales. In order to solve this problem and others, Kadir and Brady proposed their scale-saliency algorithm [2], extending saliency to work through scale space as well as through feature space; their approach is based on detecting salient features that exist over a narrow range of scales. This method can be summarized as follows: for each pixel x, local entropy H_D (Eq. 2) is calculated for each scale s between s_{min} and s_{max}; the scales S_p (Eq. 3) at which the entropy is a local maximum (is peaked) are chosen, and then the entropy is weighted (W_D, Eq. 4) at such scales by some measure of the self-dissimilarity in scale-space of the feature. The algorithm yields a sparse three dimensional array of scalar values Y_D (Eq. 5), containing weighted local entropies for all pixels at those scales where entropy is peaked.

$$H_D(s, x) = -\sum_{d \in D} P_{d,s,x} \log_2 P_{d,s,x} \tag{2}$$

$$S_p = \{s : H_D(s-1, x) < H_D(s, x) > H_D(s+1, x)\} \tag{3}$$

$$W_D(s,x) = \frac{s^2}{2s-1} \sum_{d \in D} |P_{d,s,x} - P_{d,s-1,x}| \qquad (4)$$

$$Y_D(s_p,x) = H_D(s_p,x)W_D(s_p,x) \qquad (5)$$

The main constraint of this approach is that scale is isotropic. This isotropic requirement may be relaxed [8], but the dimensionality of the salient space increases and, as a consequence, the computational cost is higher, and it is not admissible for real-time applications (e.g. robotics). Anyway, although only isotropic salient features are detected, the algorithm is still slow: entropy must be calculated for every pixel at every scale.

3   Chernoff Information and Optimal Filtering

Our method is based on the intuitive idea that image regions that are homogeneous (not salient) at higher scales will probably be also homogeneous at lower scales. As a consequence, an entropy threshold could be learnt from a set of images belonging to a same environment or category. All these images have similar intensity distributions and textures, so entropy values of the most salient features will be approximately in the same range. Following supervised learning, the range of entropy values of the most salient features from a training set of images is obtained, and then a likelihood threshold value T is calculated through statistical analysis. This learnt threshold can then be used with the rest of the images from the same environment or category, with low detection and localization error.

The proper identification of such threshold given a set of images involves the learning of the distribution probabilities $P(\theta|on)$ and $P(\theta|off)$ for the entropy value θ at s_{max} of a point conditioned on wether this point is one of the most salient features (on) or not (off) [5]. As can be seen in the example of Fig. 1, the most salient features have the closest entropies to H_{max}. Other points that are not part of the most salient features can also have high entropy values, but as entropy value decreases, the probability that a point having that entropy value becomes part of the most salient features also decreases.

A preliminary process to extract a threshold could be to choose the minimum θ value with $P(\theta|on) > 0$. In this case, all points from an image belonging to the same image class having $h/H_{max} < \theta$ could be filtered before applying the complete Kadir process, as explained above. However, we propose a more precise method to extract a valid threshold that allows filtering more image points knowing how the error will increase, by means of Chernoff Information and Kullback-Leibler divergence. This additional computation takes place offline during learning and does not affect final performance.

Chernoff Information [9] gives a measure of the easiness to discriminate between two probability distributions. As can be seen in the experimental results section, a low Chernoff Information value between $P(\theta|on)$ and $P(\theta|off)$ means that these probability distributions are similar and, consequently, it is difficult to find an adequate threshold [5]. The closer $P(\theta|on)$ and $P(\theta|off)$ are, the

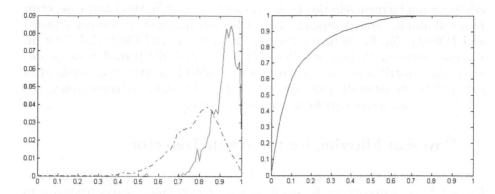

Fig. 1. Example of $P(\theta|on)$ (solid line) and $P(\theta|off)$ (dashed line) distributions for the same image. The vertical axis labels the probability density and the horizontal axis labels $\frac{h}{H_{max}}$, being h the entropy value for a given pixel and H_{max} the maximum entropy value for any pixel, both at s_{max}. Most salient features will have entropy values closest to H_{max}. At the right, the corresponding ROC curve.

higher error rate the extracted threshold produces. Thus, this measure must be obtained during learning in order to know whether our image classes are homogeneous enough for applying our filtering method. If any image class results in a too low Chernoff Information value, then splitting this image class into more homogeneous classes will be needed. The Chernoff Information $C(p, q)$ between two probability distributions p and q is defined as follows:

$$C(p, q) = - \min_{0 \leq \lambda \leq 1} log(\sum_{j=1}^{J} p^{\lambda}(y_j) q^{1-\lambda}(y_j)) \qquad (6)$$

where $\{y_j : j = 1, ..., J\}$ are the variables for which the distributions are defined (in this case, the probability values of each relative threshold between 0 and 1).

For a given $\theta = h/H_{max}$, the log-likelihood ratio $log(P(\theta|on)/P(\theta|off))$ is zero when $P(\theta|on) = P(\theta|off)$. Positive values correspond to entropy of the most salient features displayed at the end of Kadir algorithm. Therefore, log-likelihood ratio is used in our approach to filter points before Kadir algorithm. A threshold T is chosen for each image category, so all points from images belonging to that category with $log(P(\theta|on)/P(\theta|off)) < T$ can be discarded.

Kullback-Leibler divergence $D(p||q) = \sum_{j=1}^{J} p(y_j) log(p(y_j)/q(y_j))$ or relative entropy, as Chernoff Information, estimates the dissimilarity between two distributions [9]. The range of valid values of threshold T for an image class is given by [10]:

$$- D(P_{off}||P_{on}) < T < D(P_{on}||P_{off}) \qquad (7)$$

Selecting the minimum T value from this range results in a conservative filter that provides a correct trade-off between low error rate and high efficiency. This efficiency can increase selecting higher values of T. But, in this latter case, error rate will also increase depending of the Chernoff Information between $P(\theta|on)$ and $P(\theta|off)$ [5]. Furthermore, Chernoff Information and Kullback-Leibler divergence between $P(\theta|on)$ and $P(\theta|off)$ are related: if Chernoff value is low, probability distributions are similar and it is difficult to extract a threshold to split points into interesting and not interesting categories; as a consequence, the value of T must be selected from a narrower range.

4   Bayesian Filtering for the Kadir Detector

Assuming that the input images are divided into classes or categories, a threshold for each image category can be learnt from a set of training images belonging to that image class:

1. Calculate $P(\theta|on)$ and $P(\theta|off)$ probability distributions from all points in the set of training images.
2. Evaluate Chernoff Information between these two probability distributions. If $C(P(\theta|on), P(\theta|off))$ is too low[1], split the image class into new subclasses and repeat the learning process for each of them.
3. Calculate Kullback-Leibler divergences $D(P_{off}||P_{on})$ and $D(P_{on}||P_{off})$.
4. Select a threshold from the range $-D(P_{off}||P_{on}) < T < D(P_{on}||P_{off})$.

Then, learned thresholds can be used to discard points, that probably are not part of final displayed most salient features, of the images belonging to the same classes before applying Kadir algorithm, decreasing computation time with low error.

1. Calculate the local relative entropy $\theta_x = \frac{H_{Dx}}{H_{max}}$ at scale s_{max} for each pixel x, where H_{max} is the maximum entropy value for any pixel at s_{max}.
2. $X = \{x \,|\, \log \frac{P(\theta_x|on)}{P(\theta_x|off)} > T\}$, where T is the learnt threshold for the class the input image belongs to.
3. Apply Kadir algorithm only to pixels $x \in X$.

5   Experiments and Discussion

In order to test our algorithm a test set obtained from the Visual Geometry Group was used: the VGG database[2]. This test set is composed of several image categories (planes, faces, cars, and so on) with different number of images, and also different sizes. In this case, we used the original partition of image classes, although subsequent experiments showed that Chernoff Information was too low for some of them. This fact means that these classes are not homogeneous enough, and learning algorithm would improve its accuracy by subdividing them. In all cases a 10% of the images from each image category was

---

[1] In this paper we don't address the point of selecting an optimal threshold for image class partition.
[2] http://www.robots.ox.ac.uk/~vgg/

randomly selected for learning the corresponding threshold, and the rest for testing. The range of scales was between $s_{min} = 5$ and $s_{max} = 20$. Initially, only the 50 most salient features were displayed. Input images were scaled before the process. As a result, all images had a maximum width or height of 320 pixels.

Table 1. Results for the Visual Geometry Group database

Test set	Chernoff	T	% Points	% Time	ϵ
airplanes_side	0.415	-4.98	30.79%	42.12%	0.0943
		0	60,11%	72.61%	2.9271
background	0.208	-2.33	15.89%	24.00%	0.6438
		0	43.91%	54.39%	5.0290
bottles	0.184	-2.80	9.50%	20.50%	0.4447
		0	23.56%	35.47%	1.9482
camel	0.138	-2.06	10.06%	20.94%	0.2556
		0	40.10%	52.43%	4.2110
cars_brad	0.236	-2.63	24.84%	36.57%	0.4293
		0	48.26%	61.14%	3.4547
cars_brad_bg	0.327	-3.24	22.90%	34.06%	0.2091
		0	57.18%	70.02%	4.1999
faces	0.278	-3.37	25.31%	37.21%	0.9057
		0	54.76%	67.92%	8.3791
google_things	0.160	-2.15	14.58%	25.48%	0.7444
		0	40.49%	52.81%	5.7128
guitars	0.252	-3.11	15.34%	26.35%	0.2339
		0	37.94%	50.11%	2.3745
houses	0.218	-2.62	16.09%	27.16%	0.2511
		0	44.51%	56.88%	3.4209
leaves	0.470	-6.08	29.43%	41.44%	0.8699
		0	46.60%	59.28%	3.0674
motorbikes_side	0.181	-2.34	15.63%	27.64%	0.2947
		0	38.62%	51.64%	3.7305

Table 1 shows results for the latter test set. For each image class, two different thresholds were used; a very conservative one corresponding to the minimum value of T in the range $-D(P_{off}||P_{on}) < T < D(P_{on}||P_{off})$, and an average threshold $T = 0$ [10]. The % Points column shows the mean amount of points discarded for each image before Kadir feature extraction, and % Time column indicates the mean saved time comparing the filtered Kadir algorithm to the not filtered original method. Finally, Mean error column shows the mean localization error rate for each image category. This error is calculated using the following equation:

$$\epsilon = \frac{1}{n} \sum_{i=1}^{n} \frac{d(A_i, B_i) + d(B_i, A_i)}{2}, \quad d(X, Y) = \sum_{x \in X} \min_{y \in Y} ||x - y|| \quad (8)$$

where n is the number of images of the test set, A_i represents the clustered most salient regions [2] obtained from original Kadir algorithm for image i, B_i

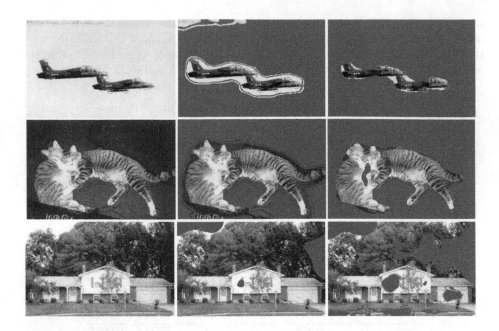

Fig. 2. Examples of filtering for three images from different image categories (*airplanes_side*, *google_things* and *houses*). Red regions represent discarded points. From left to right: results of the original Kadir algorithm, results using the minimum T value for each image and results using $T = 0$.

represents the clustered most salient regions obtained from our filtered scale saliency algorithm for image i, being $d(X, Y)$ a Euclidean based measure between most salient clustered regions belonging to both clustering results. Best results are obtained when Chernoff Information is high, resulting in more discarded points or a lower mean error value. Although using $T = 0$ generally yields noticeable improved results with low error rate, another threshold T in the valid range may be used depending on the requirements of the problem. Fig. 2 shows examples of filtering.

6   Conclusions and Future Work

Kadir scale saliency detector may be slow when extracting multiple size landmarks from an image, due to the calculation of entropy values for each pixel at each scale. In order to speed up Kadir algorithm, a simple Bayesian learning algorithm that yields a threshold for a set of images in order to discard points when applying Kadir algorithm to images belonging to that category is proposed. Experimental results showed that such approach makes Kadir detector to extract salient features faster with low error.

Our present work is addressed to design new filters, in order to discard more points. Our working hypothesis is that these new filters should be organized in cascade, so that each filter processes the output from the previous one, testing not discarded points rather than the whole image. For instance, calculating entropy at s_{max} for the whole image takes too much time, so a faster first filter could be applied before filtering using the approach described in this section.

Acknowledgements. This work was funded by project DPI2005-01280 from Ministerio de Educación y Ciencia (Spain).

References

1. Mikolajczyk, K., Tuytelaars, T., Schmid, C., Zisserman, A., Matas, J., Schaffalitzky, F., Kadir, T., Van Gool, L.A.: A Comparison of Affine Region Detectors. International Journal of Computer Vision 65(1–2), 43–72 (2005)
2. Kadir, T., Brady, M.: Saliency, Scale and Image Description. International Journal of Computer Vision 45(2), 83–105 (2001)
3. Fergus, R., Perona, P., Zisserman, A.: Object Class Recognition by Unsupervised Scale-Invariant Learning, 2003 IEEE Computer Society Conference on Computer Vision and Pattern Recognition (CVPR 2003), Madison, WI, USA, pp. 264–271 (2003)
4. Oikonomopoulos, A., Patras, I., Pantic, M.: Kernel-based recognition of human actions using spatiotemporal salient points, 2006 IEEE Computer Society Conference on Computer Vision and Pattern Recognition (CVPR 2006), New York, NY, USA, pp. 151–151 (2006)
5. Konishi, S., Yuille, A.L., Coughlan, J.M., Zhu, S.C.: Statistical Edge Detection: Learning and Evaluating Edge Cues. IEEE Trans. Pattern Anal. Mach. Intell. 25(1), 57–74 (2003)
6. Carneiro, G., Jepson, A.D.: The Distinctiveness, Detectability, and Robustness of Local Image Features, 2005 IEEE Computer Society Conference on Computer Vision and Pattern Recognition (CVPR 2005), San Diego, CA, USA, pp. 296–301 (2005)
7. Guilles, S.: Robust Description and Matching of Images, Ph. D. Thesis, University of Oxford (1998)
8. Kadir, T., Zisserman, A., Brady, M.: An Affine Invariant Salient Region Detector, 8th European Conference on Computer Vision (EVVC 2004), Prague, Czech Republic, pp. 228–241 (2004)
9. Cover, T.M., Thomas, J.S.: Elements of Information Theory. Wiley-Interscience, New York, NY, USA (1991)
10. Cazorla, M., Escolano, F.: Two Bayesian methods for junction classification. IEEE Transactions on Image Processing 12(3), 317–327 (2003)

False Positive Reduction in Breast Mass Detection Using Two-Dimensional PCA

Arnau Oliver, Xavier Lladó, Joan Martí, Robert Martí, and Jordi Freixenet

Institute of Informatics and Applications
University of Girona
Campus Montilivi, Ed. P-IV, 17071, Girona, Catalunya, Spain
{aoliver,llado,joanm,marly,jordif}@eia.udg.es

Abstract. In this paper we present a novel method for reducing false positives in breast mass detection. Our approach is based on using the Two-Dimensional Principal Component Analysis (2DPCA) algorithm, recently proposed in the field of face recognition, in order to extract breast mass image features. In mammography, it is well known that the breast density measure is highly related to the risk of breast cancer development. Hence, we also propose to take advantage of a previous breast density classification in order to increase the overall breast mass detection performance. We test our approach using a set of 1792 RoIs manually extracted from the DDSM database. Moreover, we compare our results with several existing methods. The obtained results demonstrate the validity of our approach, not only in terms of improving the performance but being a generalizable, simple, and cost-effective approach.

1 Introduction

Breast cancer is a major health problem in western countries. A study developed in the United States by the American Cancer Society estimates that between one in eight and one in twelve women will develop breast cancer during their lifetime [1]. The most used method to detect breast cancer is mammography, because it allows the detection of the cancer at early stages, a crucial issue for a high survival rate [2].

A breast mass is a localized swelling, protuberance, or lump in the breast, and usually is one of the clearest signs of breast cancer. Recently, several algorithms have been proposed for the automatic detection of masses [3,4]. Most of these algorithms are based on solving two different steps: firstly, the detection of regions with high probability of being mass (Regions of Interest, RoIs); and secondly, a validation step to ensure that the detected RoIs really depict true masses. Note the second step, which is the main interest of this paper, deals with the well-known problem called *false positive reduction*.

Yang et al. [5], in the framework of face detection and face recognition, have recently proposed the Two-Dimensional Principal Component Analysis algorithm (2DPCA) with the goal of improving the eigenfaces method [6]. Both approaches are based on finding (by means of the Karhunen-Loeve transform) the sub-space

J. Martí et al. (Eds.): IbPRIA 2007, Part II, LNCS 4478, pp. 154–161, 2007.

which contains the principal variations of the original face image database. Afterwards, the projection of an unknown face sample into the sub-space provides an efficient image representation which is used for face classification purposes. As Yang et al. stated, the use of 2DPCA has important advantages over PCA: firstly, it is simpler and more straightforward to use for image feature extraction since 2DPCA is directly based on the image matrix; secondly, it is easier to evaluate the covariance matrix accurately; and thirdly, it is computationally more efficient.

In this work we present a novel method for reducing false positives in breast mass detection. Our approach is inspired by the 2DPCA algorithm initially proposed for face recognition purposes. While the face recognition framework deals with a large number of different people, including images of different viewpoints and illuminant conditions, in the image mass detection we are dealing with a two-class problem. Note that although several mammographic databases are available with a large number of cases, from the mass detection point of view, they only contain two different types of RoIs: the ones containing masses and the ones containing normal tissue. Therefore, the intra class variability is mainly due to grey-level and texture differences of the breast, and also to the shape and size of the mass or other structures present in the RoIs.

Recent studies have also shown [7] that the sensitivity of most of the mass detection algorithms is decreasing as the density of the breast increases. Therefore, it is difficult to achieve the desired constant sensitivity which is required at a given specificity of these systems. Moreover, the breast density measure is highly related to the risk of breast cancer development [8]. Hence, taking those issues into account, one could argue that the knowledge of the breast tissue prior to the detection could improve the breast mass detection performance. Although in this paper this classification is manually done by an expert, recent works have shown the feasibility of using automatic systems for this purpose [9].

The rest of the paper is structured as follows: Section 2 introduces the 2DPCA algorithm. In Section 3 we describe our proposal of false positive reduction in breast mass detection, while Section 4 describes how to introduce the breast density information into the system. Section 5 shows the obtained results, comparing them with the classical PCA approach and also with different existing methods. Finally, conclusions and further work are discussed in Section 6.

2   The 2DPCA Approach

Both eigenfaces and 2DPCA algorithms were initially designed for face recognition purposes, where an unknown face image is assigned to a known person. These algorithms start with a database of M face images corresponding to I known individuals, where usually $I << M$ because the database contains a set of images for each person, including variations on pose and light.

In the original eigenfaces approach each image – of width w and height h – is represented by a 1D vector x_k of length $N = w \times h$ which contains all the grey-level values. Given the database of 1D face images, the Karhunen-Loeve transform is used in order to find the vectors that best account for the distribution of face images within the entire image space (the eigenvectors). However, the transformation of 2D images to 1D image vectors seems an unnatural trick, as actually the algorithm is dealing with images. This fact was discussed by Yang et al. [5] and originated the main motivation for their 2DPCA proposal. Opposed to conventional PCA, 2DPCA is based on 2D matrices rather than 1D vectors. Therefore, using 2DPCA the image covariance matrix G_t is defined as:

$$G_t = \frac{1}{M} \sum_{j=1}^{M} (A_j - A_\mu)^t (A_j - A_\mu) \tag{1}$$

where A_μ is the mean image of all training samples. Then, using the Karhunen-Loeve transform it is possible to obtain the corresponding face space, which is the subspace defined as:

$$\begin{cases} \{X_1, ...X_d\} = arg \max |X^t G_t X| \\ X_i^t X_j = 0, \quad i \neq j, \quad i, j = 1, ...d \end{cases} \tag{2}$$

where X is a unitary column vector. The first equation looks for the set of d unitary vectors where the total scatter of the projecting samples is maximized (the orthonormal eigenvectors of G_t corresponding to the first d largest eigenvalues). On the other hand, the second equation is needed to ensure orthonormality.

With the selected set of eigenvectors is possible to construct a family of feature vectors for each image. Thus, for an image sample A, the projected feature vectors (the principal components) $Y_1, ..., Y_d$ are found by:

$$Y_k = AX^k, k = 1...d \tag{3}$$

It is important to note that while for PCA each principal component is a scalar, for 2DPCA each principal component is a vector. It is this set of vectors for image that is used to construct the feature image (a matrix of size $m \times d$) as $B = [Y_1, ...Y_d]$.

In a similar way to the eigenfaces approach, comparing images means to compare the constructed features. As the dimension of the feature space has increased in one dimension, now the comparison of images is done by comparing matrices:

$$d(A_1, A_2) = \sum_{k=1}^{d} ||Y_k^i - Y_k^j|| \tag{4}$$

where $||Y_k^i - Y_k^j||$ denotes the Euclidean distance between the two principal components (vectors) Y_k^i and Y_k^j.

3   Mass Detection Using 2DPCA

The transition from face recognition to mass detection is not an easy task, basically due to the variance of the grey-level range of the images and the multiple sizes of the RoIs. Note that this size is depending on the detected mass, and there is a huge range of mass sizes [2].

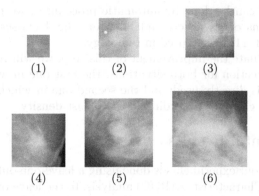

(1)   (2)   (3)

(4)   (5)   (6)

Fig. 1. One RoI with clear mass (the brightest region) belonging to each size group. Note that the relation between the mass lesion and the RoI is maintained.

Grey-level and texture variation of RoIs are mainly related to the variation of the acquisition parameters (exposure time, x-ray energy) of mammograms obtained at different time intervals and also to the nature of the breast (breast density, thickness). Assuming a commonly used simplification, these parameters are considered to affect only the range of the grey-level values of each RoI. Thus, a solution which takes those variations into account is computed by equalizing the images. In this sense, a uniform distribution model is used for equalization.

On the other hand, and in contrast with the face recognition framework where a database of faces of the same size is available, the size of the RoIs is not always the same. In order to deal with this problem of the size, different proposals were analyzed in [10]. The authors concluded that better performances were obtained when the database was clustered in different groups according to their size. Note that in this situation, the mass sizes variability is reduced for each cluster. Thus, when a new RoI has to be analyzed, the corresponding cluster in terms of its size is used. In our work, we also adopt this strategy to solve the problem of the mass size. Figure 1 shows one image sample belonging to each size group (6 different sizes are considered). Each of those groups is then used to apply the 2DPCA algorithm described in Section 2. Thus, the 2DPCA is used to extract breast mass image features according to its size.

4   Including Breast Density Information

As described in Section 1, the sensitivity of most of the mass detection algorithms decreases as the density of the breast increases. In order to take advantage of such information, we introduce a previous step of breast density classification with the goal of increasing the overall breast mass detection. This step consists on a first classification of the database of RoIs according to the breast density parameter. Therefore, we can divide our database of images based on their breast density. Although recent works [9] have demonstrated that this breast density classification task can be done by automatic procedures, we perform this step manually by means of an expert and following the 4 classes specified in the BIRADS standard [11] widely used in radiology.

In order to evaluate the improvement of this step, we will repeat our experiments of mass detection for both situations: the first one in which the original database of RoIs is directly used; and the second one in which the database of RoIs is previously classified according to the breast density.

5   Experimental Results

The evaluation of our experiments is done using a leave-one-out scheme and Receiver Operating Characteristics (ROC) analysis. In the leave-one-out methodology, we are using for each RoI the set of features extracted by 2DPCA approach. Subsequently, these features are compared with the features obtained with the model, classifying the RoIs according to our two-class problem: RoIs depicting a mass or RoIs depicting normal tissue. This procedure is repeated until all the RoIs have been used as a query image. The classifier used, is a combination of the C4.5 decision tree [12] and the k-Nearest Neighbour algorithm. This classifier provides a numerical value related to the membership of each class. Thus, varying the threshold of this membership it is possible to generate the ROC analysis [13], widely used in the medical field. In such analysis, the graphical curve represents the true positive rate as a function of the false positives rate. Moreover, the percentage value under the curve (known as A_z) is an indication for the overall performance of the observer, and is typically used to analyze the performance of the algorithms.

However, in order to perform a more global evaluation of our results we propose to compute the Az value for different ratios of number of RoIs depicting masses and number of RoIs depicting normal tissue (from ratio $1/1$ to ratio $1/6$). The idea of analyzing these different ratios is twofold: firstly, to evaluate the performance of our method on different levels of difficulty; and secondly, to compare our proposal with existing methods (Section 5.3). It is important to notice that previous works only provide results for specific ratios. Hence, analyzing all these ratios will enable the comparison with them. On the other hand, and for showing the improvement of the 2DPCA, we include a previous developed algorithm directly based on the classical eigenfaces approach (from now on, we will refer to it as PCA approach).

The algorithm was evaluated using a database of 1792 RoIs extracted from the DDSM mammographic database [14]. From this set, 256 depicted a true mass, while the rest 1536 were normal, but suspicious tissue. According to the size of the lesion, we used six different groups of RoIs. In order to evaluate in more detail our proposal in terms of using 2DPCA and considering breast density information, we will focus on the experiments with the ratio $1/3$ although we include a plot showing the results of all the ratios. Each group of RoIs corresponded to the following mass sizes intervals: $< 10\ mm^2, (10 - 60)\ mm^2$, $(60 - 120)\ mm^2, (120 - 190)\ mm^2, (190 - 270)\ mm^2, > 270\ mm^2$, and the number of masses en each interval were respectively, 28, 32, 37, 57, 69, and 33 masses.

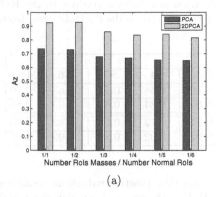
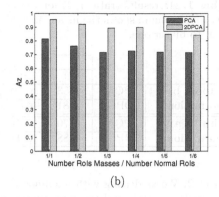

(a)   (b)

Fig. 2. Performance of our approach using the DDSM database. (a) without including breast density information and (b) considering this information.

5.1 Results Without Considering Breast Density Information

For obtaining the results of this experiment all the RoIs of the database were used, classifying them only according to their size. Figure 2(a) shows the mean Az value obtained using the leave-one-out strategy and varying the ratio between both kind of RoIs. Note the performance of both PCA and 2DPCA approaches decreases as the ratio of RoIs depicting masses decrease. For the PCA approach we obtained $Az = 0.73$ for the ratio 1/1 and $Az = 0.60$ for the ratio 1/6, while using the 2DPCA approach we obtained $Az = 0.92$ and $Az = 0.81$ respectively. Thus, the 2DPCA approach obtained better performances than the PCA.

The Az values for the ratio 1/3 are detailed in the first row of Table 1. The overall performance of the system at this relation is 0.70 for PCA and 0.86 for the 2DPCA. Note that both approaches are more suitable for false positive reduction of larger masses than smaller ones. This is due to the fact that larger masses have a larger variation in grey-level contrast with respect to their surrounding tissue than smaller masses, which are usually more subtle, even for an expert.

5.2 Results Considering Breast Density Information

Figure 2(b) shows the obtained mean Az values considering the breast density information. We classified the RoIs database not only according to the RoIs size, but also to the density of the breast. Using this added knowledge, the performance of both PCA and 2DPCA approaches increased compared with the previous experiment. In particular, for the PCA approach we obtained $Az = 0.81$ for the ratio 1/1 and $Az = 0.71$ for the ratio 1/6, while for the 2DPCA we obtained $Az = 0.96$ and $Az = 0.85$ respectively.

The last two rows of Table 1 show the Az values for the ratio 1/3 according to the size of the mass. Clearly, the overall performance of the approaches increased. For instance, the mean performance of PCA improved up to 0.75 while the 2DPCA performance was 0.91, obtaining an improvement of 5%.

Table 1. Az results (ratio 1/3) for the classification of masses according to the RoI size. Final column shows the mean Az value. S1 to S6 refers to the six RoIs sizes, from small to bigger one.

		Az						
		$S1$	$S2$	$S3$	$S4$	$S5$	$S6$	Mean
Without breast information	PCA	0.53	0.70	0.70	0.68	0.72	0.83	0.70
	2DPCA	0.81	0.83	0.87	0.84	0.89	0.93	0.86
With breast information	PCA	0.70	0.71	0.71	0.72	0.77	0.89	0.75
	2DPCA	0.88	0.93	0.91	0.92	0.89	0.92	0.91

Table 2. Works dealing with mammographic mass false positive reduction, detailing the number of RoIs and the ratio (number of RoIs with masses / number of normal tissue RoIs) used. Further, we include the results obtained with the proposed approach at the same ratio (where BDI means including breast density information).

	Az of Other Works			Az of Presented approaches			
	$RoIs$	$Ratio$	Az	PCA	$2DPCA$	$PCA+BDI$	$2DPCA+BDI$
Sahiner [15]	672	1/3	0.90	0.70	0.86	0.75	0.91
Qian [3]	800	1/3	0.86	0.70	0.86	0.75	0.91
Chang [16]	600	1/1	0.83	0.73	0.92	0.81	0.96
Tourassi [4]	1465	$\cong$ 1/1	0.87	0.73	0.92	0.81	0.96

5.3 Discussion

We include in Table 2 a comparison of our method with the performance of various existing methods. Note that our efforts have concentrated on obtaining the same ratio of masses used in their experiments. However, we want to clarify that not all methods used the same databases and therefore our aim is only to provide a general view of the performance of our approach with respect to different strategies. For instance, the works of Sahiner et al. [15] and Qian et al. [3], which used a ratio 1/3, obtained Az values of 0.90 and 0.83 respectively. Note that using the 2DPCA approach with specific density learning, we obtain better performances. Similar behaviour is observed with the proposals which used a ratio of 1/1.

6   Conclusions and Further Work

In this paper, we have presented a new strategy which is a generic, simple and cost-effective method for mass segmentation. The strategy consists on training a classifier with RoIs representing masses and normal tissue, but using different training sets according to the internal breast density category. The classification algorithm is based on the use of 2DPCA for extracting RoIs features.

The performance of the system was evaluated using a leave-one-out methodology and ROC analysis, and calculated at different ratios of RoIs with masses and RoIs depicting normal tissue. The obtained results demonstrate the validity of our proposal. Further work will be focused in expanding the training database with the aim to detect other kind of mammographic lesions, such as microcalcifications or architectural distortions.

Acknowledgments

This work was partially supported by MEC grant nb. TIN2006-08035.

References

1. American Cancer Society: Breast cancer: facts and figures. 2003-04. ACS (2003)
2. Kopans, D.: Breast Imaging. Lippincott-Raven, Philadelphia (1998)
3. Qian, W., Sun, X., Song, D., Clarke, R.A.: Digital mammography - wavelet transform and kalman-filtering neural network in mass segmentation and detection. Acad. Radiol. 8, 1074–1082 (2001)
4. Tourassi, G.D., Vargas-Vorecek, R., Catarious, D.M., Floyd, C.E.: Computer-assisted detection of mammographic masses: A template matching scheme based on mutual information. Med. Phys. 30, 2123–2130 (2003)
5. Yang, J., Zhang, D., Frangi, A.F., Yang, J.: Two-dimensional PCA: a new approach to appearance-based face representation and recognition. IEEE Trans. Pattern Anal. Machine Intell. 26, 131–137 (2004)
6. Turk, M.A., Pentland, A.P.: Eigenfaces for recognition. J. Cogn. Neuro. vol. 3 (1991)
7. Ho, W.T., Lam, P.W.T.: Clinical performance of computer-assisted detection (CAD) system in detecting carcinoma in breasts of different densities. Clinical Radiology 58, 133–136 (2003)
8. Wolfe, J.N.: Risk for breast cancer development determined by mammographic parenchymal pattern. Cancer 37, 2486–2492 (1976)
9. Oliver, A., Freixenet, J., Martí, R., Zwiggelaar, R.: A comparison of breast tissue classification techniques. In: Larsen, R., Nielsen, M., Sporring, J. (eds.) MICCAI 2006. LNCS, vol. 4191, pp. 872–879. Springer, Heidelberg (2006)
10. Oliver, A., Martí, J., Martí, R., Bosch, A., Freixenet, J.: A new approach to the classification of mammographic masses and normal breast tissue. IAPR Int. Conf. on Patt. Rec. 4, 707–710 (2006)
11. American College of Radiology: Illustrated Breast Imaging Reporting and Data System BIRADS. 3rd edn. American College of Radiology (1998)
12. Quinlan, J.: C4.5: Programs for Machine Learning. Morgan Kaufmann, New York (1993)
13. Metz, C.: Evaluation of digital mammography by ROC analysis. In: Int. Work. on Dig. Mammography, pp. 61–68 (1996)
14. Heath, M., Bowyer, K., et al.: The Digital Database for Screening Mammography. In: Int. Work. on Dig. Mammography, pp. 212–218 (2000)
15. Sahiner, B., Chan, H.P., et al.: Image feature selection by a genetic algorithm: Application to classification of mass and normal breast tissue. Med. Phys. 23, 1671–1684 (1996)
16. Chang, Y.H., Hardesty, L.A., et al.: Knowledge-based computer-aided detection of masses on digitized mammograms: A preliminary assessment. Med. Phys. 28, 455–461 (2001)

A Fast and Robust Iris Segmentation Method

Noé Otero-Mateo, Miguel Ángel Vega-Rodríguez, Juan Antonio Gómez-Pulido, and Juan Manuel Sánchez-Pérez

Dept. of Computer Science, University of Extremadura
Escuela Politécnica. Campus Universitario s/n. 10071, Cáceres, Spain
{noe,mavega,jangomez,sanperez}@unex.es

Abstract. Image preprocessing stage (also known as iris segmentation) is the first step of the iris recognition process and determines its accuracy. In this paper, we propose a method for iris segmentation. In order to get a robust method we combine several well-know techniques to achieve final result. As some of these techniques are based on intensive searching, therefore slow, we apply our knowledge of the problem (iris image features and iris morphology) to speed up the algorithms by reducing search spaces and discarding information. We present a fast and robust iris segmentation method that successfully works on CASIA 1.0 dataset.

1 Introduction

Iris recognition technology has proved to be a highly reliable choice for biometric identification. It is fast, non intrusive, cheap and very reliable. Some of these features would not be possible without a proper preprocessing stage, since this stage can be quite slow in searching the iris in the image or, if fast, not accurate enough. This is especially remarkable when working on non ideal images, where irises are sometimes highly occluded by eyelids and eyelashes and are therefore hard to find.

Several stages can be included in image preprocessing, such as iris location, eyelid and eyelash detection and some quality test aimed to check if image features (brightness, focus, iris occlusion, etc) are appropriate for the rest of the process. In this paper, we propose a method for iris region location.

The proposed method employs several well known techniques. It is based on the classical schema of Canny edge detector followed by Hough transform [6]. Such method has proved to be accurate but slow. For that reason, we introduce other techniques to reduce computational demands. Pyramidal image scaling is used to perform a coarse to fine search. In each processing stage, we also discard as much information as possible from the search space, without losing accuracy. We employ some image and iris morphology features for that purpose. We also use that information to guide the method to a correct solution and, in the case of failure, to minimize failure seriousness. We consider a failure everything but a perfect location, so segmentation failures not necessarily lead to recognition failures (they do not invalidate the whole process) but may decrease accuracy.

Our system works on the CASIA 1.0 database. This is a well known iris database and makes our results comparable to those of other systems. Images in CASIA

J. Martí et al. (Eds.): IbPRIA 2007, Part II, LNCS 4478, pp. 162–169, 2007.

database are suitable for iris recognition but, in a number of them the iris is occluded by eyelids and, more frequently, eyelashes. This makes the segmentation process harder because these elements introduce edges in the computed edge map, similar to those produced by the iris-sclera edge and the subsequent shape detection process can get confused by these edges. Moreover, it also reduces system accuracy since the iris region is partially covered by eyelids and eyelashes, inserting noise in the final description if they are not properly isolated.

Finally, we have developed a method that suits a specific dataset. Our algorithms may not work properly on images different than CASIA 1.0 ones, but we have shown how classical techniques can be modified and successfully employed to solve a particular problem. Although they may not be suitable for a different input, we believe a modification of our method can successfully work on different datasets.

The contents of this paper are as follows: In section 2 we briefly introduce our previous work, it being the motivation for our actual researching. In section 3 we present our segmentation method in fine detail. Section 4 is about the experimental results. Conclusions and future work are provided in section 5.

2   Our Previous Work

In our previous work [7], we developed a complete iris recognition system as our first approach to iris recognition, based on [6]. The system was accurate enough to keep working on it. But it also was significantly slow. We applied several processing stages to an image to segment it. The most intensive searching was in the circular Hough transform stage, as shown in Figure 1.

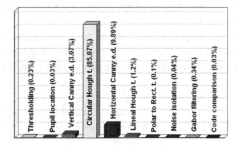

Fig. 1. Time distribution in our previous system. The whole recognition process is considered. Segmentation covers the first six stages *(first six bars in the graph)* and more than 99% of the overall time.

Therefore, more work should be done on improving segmentation algorithms. In particular, the Hough transform stage must be significantly improved. Our main effort is therefore aimed at this algorithm (Hough transform). In this paper we describe in depth how we modified our algorithms to get the iris image segmented in a few second tenths, without losing of precision.

3 Proposed Segmentation Method

In the proposed method, iris segmentation is achieved in three stages. First, we calculate several scaled representations of the image in order to perform subsequent coarse to fine iris searching. Then, for each scaled image as well as for the original image itself, we compute a modified Canny edge map. Finally, we choose the appropriate scale to start searching roughly and we gradually increase searching space, up to per pixel precision that provides a fine location of the iris region. Between one stage and another we also perform some image processing.

3.1 Pupil Location

Pupil location is easy and fast on CASIA images because every CASIA image shows a uniform colour circle that covers the pupil. Since the pupil area is big enough, its colour is clearly emphasized in the image histogram. Due to this distinctive feature, first step to iris location is to isolate this group of pixels by means of histogram-based thresholding. Nearly every pixel the thresholding outputs belongs to the pupil circle.

There may be pixels in the image that, having the same value as pupil pixels, do not belong to it. They appear as noisy pixels after thresholding. These pixels are easily detected and removed by a subsequent process. These pixels are identified because they have few neighbour pixels (usually zero). As they do not belong to the pupil circle, they are not grouped. On the other hand, pupil pixels, as being grouped into a circle, always present three or more neighbour pixels. A 3 x 3 median filter is very appropriate for this task. Eliminating noisy pixels with this procedure is valid for every CASIA image.

Last step in pupil location, once isolated, is to calculate the parameters of the pupil circle, its centre and radius. The gravity centre of every circle fits its geometrical centre and diameter is any of its diameters.

Let $C = (x_c, y_c)$ be the pupil centre, where x_c is the mean of the x coordinates of every point in the isolated region and y_c the average of the y coordinates. Considering a region formed by n pixels, we can calculate the region centre as done in (1).

$$C = (x_c, y_c) = (\frac{\sum_{i=1}^{n} x_i}{n}, \frac{\sum_{i=1}^{n} y_i}{n}) \tag{1}$$

Being (x_i, y_i) the coordinates of the i-th pixel in the region. The diameter d of the region can be calculated as the maximum distances between each two pixels belonging to it (eq. 2).

$$d = \max_{i,j} \left(\sqrt{(x_i - x_j)^2 + (y_i - y_j)^2} \right) \quad i, j \in [1..n] \tag{2}$$

In practice, the diameter calculation can be optimized by considering only region edge pixels. If the region is a circle, further optimization can be done by calculating the diameter as the difference between the maximum and minimum values of the x (or y) coordinate (eq. 3).

$$d = \max(x_i) - \min(x_i) = \max(y_i) - \min(y_i) \qquad (3)$$

This is the algorithm we use to locate the pupil since it is fast, simple and has proved to be successful for every CASIA image.

3.2 Histogram Equalization

One of the problems we identified in CASIA images is that some irises are clearly darker than sclera (background) and present a sharp edge while some others are nearly as light as the background and present a very smooth edge.

Such variation on iris tone between images makes the edge map computation harder. It is known that classical Canny edge detector is controlled by two threshold values which are used to find initial segments of strong edges and to perform edge linking. Thus, we can configure Canny edge detector to find only strong edges in those images where irises are clearly isolated from sclera. But we need to detect more edges in images with light iris tones because iris-sclera edges are diffuse and may be overlooked. By doing that, other edges than the iris ones are detected. These edges increase Hough transform computation time and can even make it fail.

To solve this problem, we perform histogram equalization on the original image before edge detection. This normalizes brightness and increases contrast of the image, in particular, the iris-sclera contrast. Let I be an iris image. Let S be the resulting image after equalization. This is how histogram equalization is performed:

o   Calculate histogram H for I.
o   Normalize H, so that the sum of histogram bins is 255.

o   Compute the integral of the histogram: $H'(i) = \sum_{j=0}^{i} H(j)$

o   Transform the image using H' as a look-up table: $S(x, y) = H'(I(x, y))$

After that histogram equalization, images are much more suitable for optimal edge extraction by using Canny edge detector.

3.3 Scaled Representations of the Iris Image

Image scaling has been widely used in computer vision as a way to reduce search space or minimize the amount of information to deal with [3]. Some authors works over downscaled images [6]. Though they do not get per pixel precision in their location algorithms, they achieve good balance between speed and accuracy.

Some others, as we do, successively downscale iris image in order to take the smallest image as starting point for coarse to fine iris searching [2].

CASIA 1.0 images are 320 × 240 pixels each. We perform scaling to obtain a 160 pixel × 140 pixel and 80 pixel × 70 pixel representations. Initially we also obtained a 40 pixel × 35 pixel representation, but it proved to be useless for our purposes. Each representation is half as height, half as wide as the preceding, that is, four times smaller. We interpose Gaussian smoothing before each scaling so the smaller the image, the more smoothed it becomes. We obtain a three smoothed images pyramid.

3.4   Edge Detection and Reduction

The next step is to perform Canny edge detection in every image of the pyramid. We employ different parameters for different images and therefore we obtain different edge maps for each resolution. For the smallest, only strong edges are detected so we detect iris inner and outer border, eyelids and some eyelash borders and few more. For bigger ones, we allow the edge detector to detect much more borders. There are two main reasons for that differentiation:

- We establish coarse iris localization in the smallest image, but we need it to be right, or the rest of the process will fail.
- As we have previous knowledge about iris position when processing bigger images, we can perform an aggressive edge cleaning on the image so remaining edges are true iris boundary edges [5]. Moreover, we look for accurate iris location in bigger images so, after edge reduction, the most edge points we have, the more precise the location is.

Once Canny edge maps are computed, we try to reduce edge points as much as possible. To do so, we employ several techniques, depending on the pyramid image we are dealing with and the item we are looking for in this image.

For the first image (the smallest one) we eliminate every edge pixel in a column that covers the pupil. If the pupil is centred at *(px, py)* and has a radius of pr, let point A be *A(px-pr,0)* and point B be *B(px+pr,h)* -being h the height of the image- then we force every pixel in the a rectangle with the upper left corner in A and the bottom right corner in B to be same colour as the background. This is how we discard pupil-iris edges. Meanwhile, some useless eyelid edges over and under the pupil are erased.

Next, we also paint a background colour circle over the pupil. This circle is centred on the pupil but its radius is bigger in order to erase edges inside iris region. The radius of this circle is also slightly inferior to the minimum iris radius (which is known by analysing each image in the dataset) to prevent the iris border to be erased.

Finally, every odd line in the image is turned to be background colour. As only vertical edges are taken into consideration at this point, erasing horizontal lines does not damage useful edges. Furthermore, this process can unintentionally erase useless near-horizontal edges. This whole process, illustrated in Figure 2, eliminates about 60% edge pixels in each image. By doing that, the subsequently Hough transform performance is greatly increased.

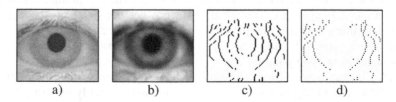

a)   b)   c)   d)

Fig. 2. How edge map is calculated and simplified. a) is the original image (not to scale). b is the image in a) after scaling, smoothing and histogram equalization. c) is the output of the Canny edge detector when fed with image b). d) is the edge map after reduction. The image in c has 386 edge pixels while d has only 124. 68% of the edge pixels have been removed.

From the obtained image, we can roughly compute the iris location and size. This is very useful to perform further edge reduction on subsequent images. How iris is located from edge map is explained in the next section of this paper. For now, let us consider that we have a rough iris location and size estimation. Consider also the centre of the iris to be $C(ix, iy)$ and its radius to be ir for this first approximation.

With these data, we can compute and simplify the other two edge maps. For bigger images, more edges are obtained from edge detector, but more edges are also deleted after edge cleaning. As we roughly know the iris position, every edge pixel but iris-sclera ones are removed. To do so, the following procedure is employed:

- Draw a white (all ones colour) circle on a black (all zeroes colour) background with same radius as iris and some thickness. The image is as big as the image currently being processing.
- Use the obtained image as a mask to perform bitwise and operation with the edge map and store this result.

After that every pixel that is not in the iris edge is removed. The final effect can be seen in Figure 3.

As shown in Figure 3, the horizontal line erase process is also performed on these images. In the last one (the biggest), four of each five lines are erased, drastically reducing the number of edge points to compute in Hough transform.

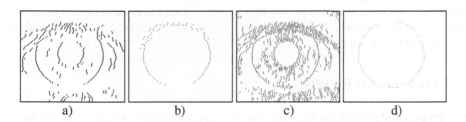

| a) | b) | c) | d) |

Fig. 3. Edge maps from bigger images and the result of simplifying them. a) is the edge map from the 160 x 140 image and b) its simplified version. c) is the edge map from the 320 x 280 image (full size) and d) its simplified version. The images have 827, 89, 4975 and 101 edge pixels respectively. From a) to b) 89% of the edges are removed. From c) to d) 98% of them.

Now, let D be the rough iris descriptor calculated from previous image and employed in mask calculation for the current one. The circle mask thickness must be enough to compensate the iris and pupil eccentricity and the supposed errors in calculation of C from smaller images. In practice we use 10 pixels for the 160 x 140 image and 5 pixels for the 320 x 240 image. A bigger value is employed in smaller image because many errors in D calculation can be recovered at that point with less effort. When processing the final image we do not intend to recover from any error, only to precisely calculate the final version of D. That is why a thinner circle is employed and why edges are reduced more than 95% at this last stage.

3.5 Iris Location

The iris circle is computed from the obtained edge maps using Hough transform. The key to make Hough transform faster is the low number of edge pixels in images, the use of integer arithmetic and optimized circle drawing primitives. To obtain the final (fine) location of the iris, the followed process is:

- Perform Hough transform in the smallest image and get the iris circle descriptor we called D in 3.4.
- Properly scale D (multiply its coordinates and radius by two) so it fits the next image, four times bigger. Use D to perform edge reduction on next image.
- Perform Hough transform in next image and actualize D with a more accurate value.

This process is carried for the three images in the pyramid. As the image to process grows in size, the approximation of the iris circle by D becomes more accurate.

To further improve Hough transform speed, the search space is restricted. As know, the iris and pupil are not concentric, but in the smallest image, the distance between centres is never bigger than a few pixels -in practice we use 5 pixels-. So, in the Hough accumulator, we look for the centre only in the 5 x 5 window surrounding the pupil centre, which is a known point. For bigger images we use 5 x 5 and 7 x 7 windows. If D were accurate enough from the beginning, a 3 x 3 window should be enough, but making the search window a bit bigger can make out for some slight errors in D calculation and does not significantly increased computation time as the number of edge points to compute is the same in every case (it does not depend on how big the search window is).

4 Experimental Results

The proposed algorithm for iris detection has experimentally proved to be far more accurate and fast than the one we used before. It works over CASIA images detecting irises in 0.15 seconds (average time), these times being fairly competent among modern systems (see table 1). Furthermore, the location is perfect in 95% cases (manually checked) and, when an error is made, it does not compromise the whole process as it is a small error, usually missing only one side edge but not both. Our algorithm works even on highly occluded images, due to the special searching process described in 3.5.

Table 1. Comparisons of some recent segmentation algorithms over CASIA 1.0 (Results supplied by respective authors)

Reference	Avg time	Accuracy	Year / Machine
[8]	0.227 s.	99.45 %	2005 / ???
[1]	0.2426 s.	99.34 %	2004 / P4@2.4GHz, 256 Mb RAM
Proposed	0.15 s.	95 %	2006 / P4@3GHz, 1024 Mb RAM

5   Conclusions and Future Work

We recently started to work on iris recognition and we are developing a fully featured system. Even in early stages the system has proved to be valid for research purposes. Now that the segmentation method is accurate and fast enough, our future work is to further test and improve our algorithms and start researching on and improving other stages than image preprocessing, specially feature extraction to get a real iris recognition system working.

Acknowledgments. The work in this paper has been partially supported by the research project TIN2005-08818-C04-03.

References

1. Cui, J., Wang, Y., Tan, T., Ma, L., Sun, Z.: A Fast and Robust Iris Localization Method Based on Texture Segmentation. In: Proceedings of the SPIE 5404, 401–408 (2004)
2. Daugman, J.G.: How Iris Recognition Works. IEEE Transactions on Circuits and Systems for Video Technology 14(1), 21–30 (2004)
3. Forsyth, D., Ponce, J.: Computer Vision: A Modern Approach. Prentice-Hall, Englewood Cliffs (2002)
4. Institute of Automation (IA), Chinese Academy of Sciences (CAS): CASIA Iris Image Database. At http://www.sinobiometrics.com (2006)
5. Liu, X., Bowyer, K., Flynn, P.: Experiments with An Improved Iris Segmentation Algorithm. 4th. IEEE Workshop on Automatic Identification Advanced Technologies, pp. 118–123 (2005)
6. Masek, L.: Recognition of Human Iris Patterns for Biometric Identification. Internal Report, The University of Western Australia, Australia (2003)
7. Otero, N., Vega, M.A., Gómez, J.A., Sánchez, J.M.: Irisrec: A Biometric Identification System by Means of Iris Recognition. In: 6th IASTED International Conference on Visualization, Imaging, and Image Processing, vol. 1, pp. 243–248 (2006)
8. Yuan, W., Lin, Z., Xu, L.: A Rapid Iris Location Method Based on the Structure of Human Eyes. Engineering in Medicine and Biology 27th Annual Conference, pp. 3020–3023 (2005)

Detection of Lung Nodule Candidates in Chest Radiographs

Carlos S. Pereira[1,2], Hugo Fernandes[1], Ana Maria Mendonça[1,2],
and Aurélio Campilho[1,2]

[1] INEB - Instituto de Engenharia Biomédica
Laboratório de Sinal e Imagem; Campus FEUP (Faculdade de Engenharia da
Universidade do Porto), Rua Roberto Frias, s/n, 4200-465 Porto, Portugal
[2] Universidade do Porto, Faculdade de Engenharia, DEEC
{cmsp,amendon,campilho}@fe.up.pt

Abstract. This paper presents an automated method for the selection
of a set of lung nodule candidates, which is the first stage of a computer-
aided diagnosis system for the detection of pulmonary nodules. An innovative operator, called sliding band filter (SBF), is used for enhancing
the lung field areas. In order to reduce the influence of the blood vessels
near the mediastinum, this filtered image is multiplied by a mask that
assigns to each lung field point an *a priori* probability of belonging to
a nodule. The result is further processed with a watershed segmentation
method that divides each lung field into a set of non-overlapping areas.
Suspicious nodule locations are associated with the regions containing
the highest regional maximum values. The proposed method, whose result is an ordered set of lung nodule candidate regions, was evaluated on
the 247 images of the JSRT database with very promising results.

1 Introduction

The detection of pulmonary nodules in chest radiography is one of most studied
problems in X-ray image analysis, and many computerized schemes have been
developed aiming at obtaining a solution for this important problem. Most of the
proposed computer-aided diagnosis (CAD) systems adopt a two-stage approach,
with an initial selection of nodule candidates, followed by the reduction of false
positives, frequently based on the extraction of features and classification of the
pre-selected areas.

In the system proposed by Wei *et al.* [1], the location of tumor candidates is
performed by an adaptive ring filter, and afterwards 210 features are evaluated
to look for the optimum feature set for discriminating between normal and abnormal regions. Keserci *et al.* [2] describes an approach for the detection of lung
nodules based on a combination of morphological features with an edge-guided
wavelet snake model. With this combination, the authors are able to largely reduce the number of false positives. Yoshida [3] complemented this system with a
method for the reduction of false positives exploring the symmetry between the
two lungs and assuming that a nodule candidate region in one lung would correspond to a normal region in the other. In [4], Suzuki *et al.* reported a reduction of

J. Martí et al. (Eds.): IbPRIA 2007, Part II, LNCS 4478, pp. 170–177, 2007.
© Springer-Verlag Berlin Heidelberg 2007

false-positives, by using the so-called multiple massive-training neural network; in this system, the scheme for obtaining the initial set of candidates is based on a difference-image technique and linear-discriminant analysis. The computer algorithm presented by Schilham *et al.* in [5] uses multi-scale approaches for both nodule candidate selection and classification; candidates are found by looking for intensity maxima in Gaussian scale space and some features for classification are taken from a multi-scale Gaussian filterbank. In a recent work [6], the same authors proposed two optional extensions to this scheme, namely candidate selection and candidate segmentation.

This paper presents an automated method for the selection of a set of lung nodule candidates, which can constitute the first stage of a CAD system for the detection of pulmonary nodules. The two lung field areas are initially enhanced with an innovative operator, the sliding band filter (SBF), which belongs to the class of convergence index (CI) filters [7]. The result is further processed with a watershed segmentation method that divides each lung field into a set of non-overlapping areas. Suspicious nodules locations are associated with the regions containing the highest regional maximum values. In order to reduce the influence of the blood vessels near the mediastinum, the filtered image is multiplied by a mask that assigns to each lung field point an *a priori* probability of belonging to a nodule. The proposed method, whose result is an ordered set of lung nodule candidate regions, is just the initial phase of a complete computer-aided diagnosis system for the detection of lung nodules in chest radiographs.

The structure of the paper is as follows. The next section gives a brief description of the new convergence index filter. Section 3 describes the candidate region selection procedure, including the implementation of the probability mask and the morphological segmentation process. The results obtained with our method for the JSRT database [8] are shown in section 4, and section 5 contains some conclusions and guidelines for future work.

2   Sliding Band Filter

The contrast in chest radiograph images is usually low and the noisy environment is frequently high, primarily due to the limitations placed on X-ray dose. These characteristics are naturally intrinsic to all the structures that can be found in these images, and in particular to lung nodules, which normally appear as local low-density rounded areas exhibiting very weak contrast against their background. As the lack of contrast was found to be a serious drawback for the effective use of image detection methods based on the magnitude of spatial differences, Kobatake and Murakami [9] proposed an adaptive filter to detect rounded convex regions, the iris filter, which evaluates the degree of convergence of gradient vectors in the neighbourhood of the pixel of interest. This concept was further extended to generate a class of new filters, the convergence index filters [7,10,11], mainly differing on the region of support used for calculating the convergence degree of the gradient vectors.

2.1   Convergence Index Filters

The convergence index filter is based on the concept of convergence degree of a gradient vector, which is calculated from the angle $\theta_i(k, l)$ of the orientation of the gradient vector at point (k, l) with respect to a reference line with direction i. If we consider a pixel of interest P with spatial coordinates (x, y), the convergence index calculated in the neighbourhood of P that is the region of support of the filter, denoted by R, is defined as the average of the convergence indices at all M points in R, as in equation (1)

$$C(x, y) = \frac{1}{M} \sum_{(k,l) \in R} \cos \theta_i(k, l) . \tag{1}$$

In [10], a set of filters belonging to the convergence index class was proposed for detecting lung nodules candidates on chest X-ray images. In this work, the region used for evaluating the convergence degree consists of N half-lines radiating from the pixel of interest, which are defined over a circular convex region that was established based on the expected rounded shape of the lung nodules. When different criteria are established for selecting the points on the ith half-line that are used for calculating the convergence index for direction i, distinct types of filters can be obtained. The coin filter (CF) has a fixed region of support formed by all the points in the complete set of half-lines, while the iris filter (IF) is an adaptive coin filter whose region of support can change in each direction. The adaptive ring filter (ARF) uses a ring-shaped region whose radius changes adaptively.

The iris filter automatically adjusts the length of each radial line used for measuring the averaged convergence index for direction i along the n pixels ($R_{min} \leq n \leq R_{max}$) away from $P(x, y)$, as defined by equation (2), aiming at the maximization of this value. The output of the iris filter, $IF(x, y)$, is the average of the maximal convergence indices for the N half radial directions. A slightly different implementation of the iris filter is presented in [2], where the parameter R_{min} also establishes the inner limit of the filter support region.

$$IF(x, y) = \frac{1}{N} \sum_{i=0}^{N-1} \left(\max_{R_{min} \leq n \leq R_{max}} \left(\frac{1}{n} \sum_{m=1}^{n} \cos \theta_{i,m} \right) \right) \tag{2}$$

2.2   Sliding Band Filter

The new enhancement filter proposed in this paper, called sliding band filter (SBF), is also a member of the CI filter class as its output is also a measure of the degree of convergence of gradient vectors. The main difference between this new filter and the iris filter is that the SBF searches in each radial direction the band of fixed width that corresponds to the maximum degree of convergence, while in the IF the radial line always begins in the point of interest P and the number of pixels can vary from a minimum to a maximal value. As in the ARF, the width of the band used for calculating the convergence index is equal in

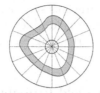

Fig. 1. Region of support of the sliding band filter

each half-line, but its position is variable in the SBF. An example of a region of support for the proposed filter is represented in Fig. 1.

The output of the SBF at a pixel of interest P is defined by equation (3),

$$SBF(x,y) = \frac{1}{N} \sum_{i=0}^{N-1} \left(\max_{R_{min} \leq n \leq R_{max}} \left(\frac{1}{d} \sum_{m=n}^{n+d} \cos \theta_{i,m} \right) \right) \tag{3}$$

where N is the number of radial directions leading out from P, d represents the fixed width of the band, $\theta_{i,m}$ is the angle of the gradient vector at the point m pixels away from P with direction i, and R_{min} and R_{max} represent, respectively, the inner and outer sliding limits of the band, as illustrated in Fig. 1.

When compared with the IF, this new approach has a more selective response for those nodules whose central region has a more random degree of convergence, because only the band of the nodule with the highest convergence indices is considered. Our proposal also has the advantage of being more flexible than the ARF when the shape of nodule differs from the expected rounded area. An original image of one lung field and enhanced images obtained with the IF, ARF and SBF are shown in Fig. 2.

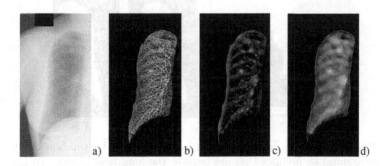

Fig. 2. a) Original lung field image; Enhanced images using: b) IF; c) ARF; d) SBF

3   Detection of Lung Nodule Candidate Regions

Our approach for detecting suspicious nodular regions consists of two main phases. The first phase aims at delineating and enhancing the lung field regions using the SBF described in the previous section. In the second stage, a probability value is assigned to each lung field pixel, and afterwards these two areas are subdivided into smaller non-overlapping regions, with the goal of identifying probable locations of nodules.

3.1 Estimation of the Lung Field Probability Mask

The enhanced image resulting from the sliding band filter is strongly influenced by the blood vessels and bronchi that are located near the mediastinum. The analysis of the distribution of the nodules in the images of the JSRT database, represented in the histogram of Fig. 3a, also supports the idea that some lung field locations can have a higher probability of allocating nodules. Based on this assumption, a probability value is assigned to each lung field pixel according to equation (4),

$$P(x) = 1 - e^{-ax^n}(1 - p_0). \qquad (4)$$

where x is the normalized distance of the pixel to the line parallel to the orientation axis of the lung field mask that limits the lung on the mediastinum side. In this equation a, n and p_0 are parameters, whose values of $a = 10$, $n = 4$ and $p_0 = 0.68$ were estimated from a set of randomly selected images of the JSRT database, and validated on the remaining images. These parameter values were chosen with the goal of minimizing the number of non detected nodules. The pixel distances are normalized by the width of the lung field, which is calculated as the distance between the two lines parallel to the lung field mask orientation axis, as depicted in Fig. 3b. The probability mask calculated for this particular lung field is shown in Fig. 3c.

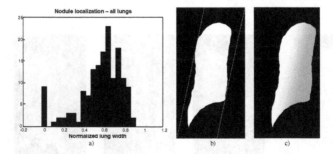

Fig. 3. a) Histogram of the nodules localization normalized by the lungs width (null distances correspond to nodules that are outside the lung field masks); b) Lung field mask with limiting lines parallel to the orientation axis; c) Probability mask

3.2 Detection of Suspicious Nodular Regions

The original radiographic image is automatically delineated aiming at obtaining two binary masks for limiting the lung field regions. Afterwards, the sliding band filter is applied thus producing enhanced images similar to the one presented

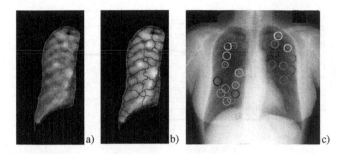

Fig. 4. a) Output of the SBF; b) Watershed segmentation result; c) Output of the algorithm showing the set of selected candidate nodules

in Fig. 2d. Each of these images is further multiplied by the corresponding probability mask described in the previous subsection.

In this new image, suspicious nodular regions are associated with local intensity maxima. However, because the number of detected points is excessive, the image is processed with a morphological watershed segmentation operator aiming at dividing each lung field into a set of non-overlapping regions, each one considered as a potential lung nodule candidate. For each of these areas, all the local maximum values are discarded except the highest one, which is regarded as a tentative center of one potential nodule. The output of the *SBF* for this particular point is used for candidate nodule characterization as it can be understood as the probability of being a lung nodule, while the actual filter support region gives some indication concerning probable nodule size. The output of the filter and the result of the watershed segmentation are presented in Fig. 4a and Fig. 4b, respectively.

The output of our algorithm is an ordered set of candidate image areas, corresponding to the highest filter responses. The location of each lung nodule candidate is coded using a color circumference, where the color identifies the rank of the candidate in the ordered set, and the radius of the circumference is related with the estimated size of the candidate nodule, as shown in Fig. 4c.

4 Results

The algorithm proposed in this paper was evaluated on a publicly available database, the JSRT database [8], which is a well-known dataset that has already been used by several other researchers. This database contains a total number of 247 radiographs, 154 with nodules and 93 without nodules. In our experiences, from the total set of 154 nodules, 14 are excluded as they lie outside the lung fields. From the remaining 140 radiographs with nodules, we were not able to detect other 7 nodules, thus achieving a maximum detection rate of 86.4%. These results were obtained with the *SBF* parameter values $N = 256$, $d = 5$, $R_{min} = 2$ and $R_{max} = 21$, which were established empirically to maximize the nodule detection rate. The *IF* and *ARF* outputs, as well as combinations of the *SBF*

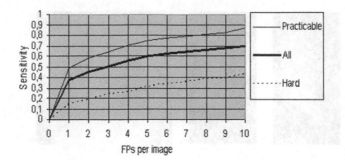

Fig. 5. FROC curves for the complete JSRT database, showing the sensitivity of our method for all nodules, for the practicable nodules (subtlety levels 3, 4 and 5 as defined in [8]) and for the hard nodules (subtlety levels 1 and 2 as defined in [8])

and ARF outputs using the arithmetic and geometric means, were also evaluated but the obtained detection rates were always lower than those achieved with the SBF alone.

In order to facilitate the comparison of our results with those recently reported by Schilham et al. [6], the performance of our method is presented using Free Response Receiver Operating Characteristics (FROC) curves, measuring sensitivity as a function of the average number of false positives per image, as shown in Fig. 5.

The results obtained with our algorithm are quite similar to those reported by Schilham in [6] for their basic and segmentation schemes. Despite this fact, it is worth mentioning that the values represented in Fig. 5 are essentially a consequence of the enhancement ability of the new filter in combination with the a priori probability assignment, which greatly facilitates the subsequent segmentation task used for detecting potential nodular areas. Actually, the output of the proposed algorithm is a just set of nodule candidate regions that are intended to be the input for a false positive reduction stage that will validate or reject each element of this set, thus reducing the number of final probable nodular regions to be presented to the specialist.

5   Conclusion

We have presented a method for the detection of suspicious regions that is just the initial phase of a more complete computer-aided diagnosis system for the detection of pulmonary nodules. The new member of the convergence index filter class proposed in this paper, the sliding band filter, has proved to be more selective than reported alternatives for the enhancement of nodular structures in pulmonary images, as the filtered image can be easily segmented to produce a reduced set of non-overlapping regions which can be associated with probable nodule candidates. The previous assignment of a probability value to each lung field pixel was also an important achievement to reduce the number of false positives associated with blood vessels and other round-shaped structures.

The algorithm was evaluated on a publicly available database, the JSRT database, which has already been used by other researchers for the assessment of lung nodules detection schemes. With an average of two false positives per image, our method achieved a sensitivity of 0.45, while this value is increased to 0.55 when four false positives are accepted. These results can be considered very promising, because we intend to use this initial set of candidates as input for a final stage of classification that will further validate or reject each one of these candidates as a probable lung nodule.

References

1. Wei, J., Hagihara, Y., Shimizu, A., Kobatake, H.: Optimal image feature set for detecting lung nodules on chest X-ray images, CARS 2002 (2002)
2. Keserci, B., Yoshida, H.: Computerized detection of pulmonary nodules in chest radiographs based on morphological features and wavelet snake model. Medical Image Analysis 6, 431–447 (2002)
3. Yoshida, H.: Local contralateral subtraction based on bilateral symmetry of lung for reduction of false positives in computerized detection of pulmonary nodules, Biomedical Engineering. IEEE Transactions 51, 778–789 (2004)
4. Suzuki, K., Shiraishi, J., Abe, H., MacMahon, H., Doi, K.: False-positive reduction in computer-aided diagnostic scheme for detecting nodules in chest radiographs by means of massive training artificial neural network. Academic Radiology 12, 191–201 (2005)
5. Schilham, A., van Ginneken, B., Loog, M.: Multi-scale Nodule Detection in Chest Radiographs. In: Ellis, R.E., Peters, T.M. (eds.) MICCAI 2003. LNCS, vol. 2878, pp. 602–609. Springer, Heidelberg (2003)
6. Schilham, A., van Ginneken, B., Loog, M.: A computer-aided diagnosis system for detection of lung nodules in chest radiographs with an evaluation on a public database. Medical Image Analysis 10, 247–258 (2006)
7. Kobatake, H., Hashimoto, S.: Convergence index filter for vector fields, IEEE Transactions on Image Processing, vol. 8(8) (1999)
8. Shiraishi, J., Katsuragawa, S., Kezoe, S., Matsumoto, T., Kobayashi, T., Komatsu, K., Matsui, M., Fujita, M., Kodera, Y., Doi, K.: Development of a Digital Image Database for Chest Radiographs With and Without a Lung Nodule: Receiver Operating Characteristic Analysis of Radiologists' Detection of Pulmonary Nodules. American Journal of Roentgenology 174, 71–74 (2000)
9. Kobatake, H., Murakami, M.: Adaptive filter to detect rounded convex regions: Iris filter. Int. Conf. Pattern Recognition ll, 340–344 (1996)
10. Wei, J., Hagihara, Y., Kobatake, H.: Detection of cancerous tumors on chest X-ray images - Candidate detection filter and its evaluation, ICIP99, no. 27AP4.2 (1999)
11. Kobatake, H., Wei, J., Yoshinaga, Y., Hagihara, Y., Shimizo, A.: Nonlinear Adaptine Convergence Index Filters and Their Characteristics, Int. Conf. Pattern Recognition, pp. 522–525 (2000)

A Snake for Retinal Vessel Segmentation

L. Espona[1], M.J. Carreira[1], M. Ortega[2], and M.G. Penedo[2]

[1] Computer Vision Group. Dpto. Electrónica e Computación. Universidade de
Santiago de Compostela. Spain
luciaep@usc.es, mjose@dec.usc.es
[2] Grupo VARPA. Dpto. de Computación. Universidade da Coruña. Spain
mgpenedo@udc.es

Abstract. This paper presents an innovative methodology to detect the vessel
tree in retinal angiographies. The automatic analysis of retinal vessel tree facilitates the computation of the arteriovenous index, which is essential for the diagnosis of a wide range of eye diseases. We have developed a system inspired in
the classical snake but incorporating domain specific knowledge, such as blood
vessels topological properties. It profites mainly from the automatic localization
of the optic disc and from the extraction and enhancement of the vascular tree
centerlines. Encouraging results in the detection of arteriovenous structures are
efficiently achieved, as shown by the systems performance evaluation on the publicy available DRIVE database.

1 Introduction

The automatic analysis of blood vessels is becoming more and more important in many
clinical investigations and scientific researches related to vascular features. The early diagnosis of several pathologies, such as arterial hypertension, arteriosclerosis or diabetic
retinophaty could be achieved analysing the vascular structures. The Digital Colour
Fundus Photographs here used are a non invasive and innocuous technique to obtain the
retinal vascular tree. Moreover, a specific CAD system is also necessary in large-scale
ocular screening programs to make the ophthalmologist diagnosis process more efficient and accurate [1]. The retina arteriovenous index (AV index) indicates the relation
between afferent and efferent blood vessels, that is arteries and veins of the retina. This
index takes a vital priority in order to diagnose these illnesses and evaluate their consequences. This paper deals with the research of a vascular tree detection system, which
would constitute the first step to allow the precise and robust AV index measuring [2].

The retinal angiographies are 2-D medical images quite problematic. The main difficulties in them are the inadequate contrast, lighting variations and remarkable noise
influence mainly due to its complex acquisition. Another drawback is the anatomic variability depending on the particular patient, affecting both the retinal background texture
and the blood vessels structure. Blood vessels particular features make them complex
structures to detect as the color of vascular structures is not constant even along the same
vessel. Their tree-like geometry is often strange and complicated, including bifurcations
and overlaps that may mix up the detection system. Nevertheless, other characteristics,
like the linearity or the tubular shape, could make the contour detection easier.

J. Martí et al. (Eds.): IbPRIA 2007, Part II, LNCS 4478, pp. 178–185, 2007.

As blood vessels segmentation becomes essential for several medical diagnostic systems, numerous research efforts have been done in this field. The vascular detection has been tackled from different approaches and techniques including pattern recognition, pixel-based approaches [3] or classification methods [4]. The contour deformable models are widely followed in vessel tracking, even combined with other techniques [6]. Even though many promising techniques and algorithms have been developed, vessel segmentation is still an open area for more research. For further reading on retinal fundus image segmentation, we refer to comparative studies as [5].

This work presents an innovative methodology, which incorporates domain specific knowledge into the generic contour deformable model. The snake model is specialised with the blood vessels topological properties, which determine the detection system behaviour. We have taken a great advantage of the vascular tree graph, composed by the vessels centerlines obtained from a creases extraction system developed previously by a research group [7]. The system initialisation includes grayscale conversion of the original image and re-sampling with bi-cubic interpolation to work at subpixel level in a three dimensional space. This is very important for the arteriovenous index calculus, where accurate and fast measures of vessel diameters are needed, as it will be shown in the results section.

Next we will explain our vessel tree detection system, beginning with crease extraction in order to perform the deformable contour evolution.

2 Vessel Tree Detection System

Our model for the detection of the vessel tree is based on a deformable contour guided by a vessel crease. This section will begin explaining the creases extraction process,then the classical deformable contour model will be described. Once the theorical fundamentals have been presented, our particular snake model will be analysed in depth, presenting the innovative specific features and their resulting behaviour.

2.1 Creases Extraction

A crease is a continuous area of points on the image, shaping a highest or a lowest level in its environment. In this way, blood vessels can be considered as regions which form an extreme and tubular level on their neighbourhood. This fact allows to locate the vessels by using the creases position (see Fig. 1(a)). The creases extraction is essential for the detection process, since it will determine the initial snake and act as external energy guiding the contour expansion.

The creases image is obtained using the MLSEC-ST operator(Multilevel Set Extrinsic Curvature based on the Structure Tensor) as explained in [7]. The parameters wich control the crease expansion are: confidence degree (Confidence), minimum grey level (MinGrey), deviation of a Gaussian smoothing, and the minimum length (MinLenght). These parameters must be fine-tuned to obtain high-quality results.

The creases extraction is a crucial and irreversible step in the snake evolution. If a crease is not detected, the corresponding vessel will remain unsegmented. Thus, we have enhanced the creases image by exploiting an existent tool, part of a biometric authentication system from our research group [8]. The feature points (ridge endings and

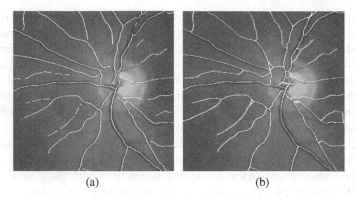

(a)   (b)

Fig. 1. Creases image: (a) A retinal image with its creases overlapped in white, corresponding to the vessel centerlines. (b) Creases image enhanced in terms of continuity.

bifurcations) obtained with this system are adequately connected to get rid of disconinuites along the centerline that guides the snake advance properly(see Fig. 1(b)).

Once the creases were introduced, we will see how they will be used in our snake model.

2.2 Deformable Contour Model

Our approach is based on the deformable contour model, also called snake model, proposed by Kass et al. [9] to segment objects in 2-D images. A snake is a parametric curve which can evolve to fit the shape of the desired structure and it may be represented by $v(s) = (x(s), y(s))$, where s is the arc length. Once placed on the image, this curve performs an iterative contour adaptation in order to minimise its global energy defined as the sum of the internal and the external energy. The internal energy controls to the snake flexibility and elasticity and the external energy corresponds to the forces that drive the snake towards the edges of the shape to locate. The contour deforms under the influence of internal and external forces until it reaches the minimum of its global energy function.

This deformable contour can be seen as a polynomial closed contour composed by linked nodes. This particular snake model will not consider the internal energy as the vessel shape may be very tortuous. Based on the external energy, three possible node states are defined : *normal, crease and edge*. The nodes in the *crease* state are located in the vessel crease and they make the snake to advance along the vessel center line. The positions close to vessel boundaries are occupied by nodes in the *edge* state that tend to become stable when reaching the vessel edge. The rest of nodes are in the *normal* state and they contribute to the snake expansion in an intermediate direction. Thus, the **external energy** affecting the snake will be defined as a set of energies and weighting factors:

$$\varepsilon_{ext} = \gamma\varepsilon_{edge} + \delta\varepsilon_{cres} + \nu\varepsilon_{dir} + \sigma\varepsilon_{mark} + \omega\varepsilon_{dif} \tag{1}$$

The first term ε_{edge} corresponds to the edge distance energy calculated by assigning to each point its euclidean distance to the nearest edge obtained with the Canny Filter [10].

This energy helps the snake advance of nodes close to vessel boundaries but it also stops them when they reach an edge point . The second term ε_{cres} corresponds to the creases distance energy obtained from the crease image just in the same way as for the edges. This energy drives the snake along the arteriovenous structure and blocks it if a maximum distance threshold is reached. The inflate pressure ε_{dir} is the strongest expansion force of the snake. Each node has one assigned direction that determines the three adjacent possible positions to choose the one with the lowest energy. The fourth term ε_{mark} is the marker energy to ensure that self overlapping or turning back never happens. The difference energy ε_{dif} reinforces the precision of the snake expansion as it hints the nodes to occupy positions different from its neighbours situations.

2.3   Contour Evolution

Once introduced the energy functions influencing the snake, we have to deal with the snake initialisation.

Firstly, the creases and edge images and energy maps are calculated on the original re-sampled image. Next, a circumference surrounding optical nerve is traced either automatically by an integrated tool developed by a research team [11] or manually, and then the intersections of creases and this circumference are directly obtained (see Fig. 2). A unique snake is created, which corresponds exactly with the previously traced circumference and it is composed by inactive nodes, except those placed close enough to the intersection with creases, called *seed nodes*.

After its initialisation, the snake evolves following a deterministic and iterative algorithm to minimise these energy functions locally (see Fig. 2). Each active node tries to move towards a lower energy position until it becomes irreversibly inactive when arriving to an edge or due to the control operations that will be described below. The system execution automatically ends when all nodes are inactive, that is, when the snake reaches the stability. To completely segment the vascular structure, the snake grows by new active nodes insertion considering an euclidean distance threshold.

At a given moment, the snake nodes have a position in the image space and an assigned **node state**: edge, normal or crease. The nodes in the *edge* state are near vessel boundaries, so they are supposed to be soon stabilised when arriving to an edge point. Naturally, the most significant energy term for *edge* nodes is the edge distance ε_{edge}. These weights are similar for *normal* state nodes, as they are expected to become *edge* nodes, except in situations such as bifurcations. The *crease* state is assigned to central nodes, that are in charge of the snake advance along the vessel centerline. Therefore, they are strongly influenced by the inflate pressure and the crease distance energy terms. These behaviour is modeled by sets of energy term weights associated to each node state. The energy for each possible node movement is calculated considering the energy terms values associated to the position and the weights associated to the node. Iteratively, each vertex is moved according to forces that work on it, that is towards the local minimum energy situation. Consequently, the whole contour expands and the snake flows inside the vessel covering the vascular branch.

In addition, we perform control operations derived from vessel structural features(see Fig. 3). These control operations work considering the snake as composed by sequences of consecutive active nodes, called *forward fronts*. Each front is forced to have exactly

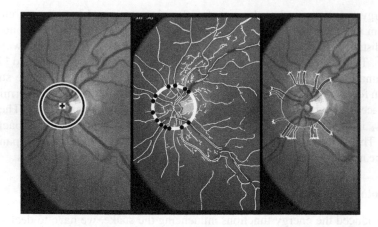

Fig. 2. Snake Evolution: Selection of centre and radius to trace a circumference around the optical nerve (left). Calculation of intersection points of the vessel creases and the selected circumference (center). A circular snake is created whose seed nodes begin to adapt the contour to the vessels (right).

one crease node and the total number of nodes is also periodically checked. When a front becomes too large, all its nodes are inactivated and the snake contour slightly shrinks, since it is considered as a flood (see Fig. 3(a)). The nodes of very small fronts are also inactivated, as this situation corresponds to an small edge discontinuity (see Fig. 3(c)). At this point, we have to estimate two critical parameters as references to evaluate the front size : the maximum and the minimum vessel width(see Fig. 3). A too high maximum vessel width may increase the floods (see Fig. 3(a)), but a too little one could block the snake in a bifurcation (see Fig. 3(b)). The minimum width is also critical: if it is too big, thin vessels are not detected (see Fig. 3(c)), but if it is extremely small, it lets the nodes to get through to every edge discontinuity (see Fig. 3(d)).

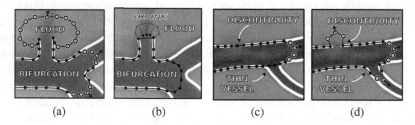

(a)	(b)	(c)	(d)

Fig. 3. Influence of Vessel Width Parameters: The snake contour (in black) presents active nodes (as circles) and inactive nodes (as black squares). A large maximum vessel width may cause huge floods (a), but a small one, could stop the snake at vessel bifurcations (b). If the minimum vessel width is too high, the snake will not go into thin vessels (c). Nevertheless if it is too small, the snake will go through every edge discontinuity (d).

3   Results

This paper ends reporting results of vessel segmentation obtained by our snake model on medical images from the publicy available DRIVE database [12]. The test set here used contains 20 JPEG compressed images acquired using a Canon CR5 non-mydriatic 3CCD camera with a 45 degree field of view (FOV). Originally, the images were of size 768x584 and 8 bits per color plane but we converted them into bigger grayscale images (256 gray levels) of 1064x1100 pixels. The manual segmentation results and the FOV mask images for computating the performance measures (see Table 1) were provided toghether with the DRIVE database.

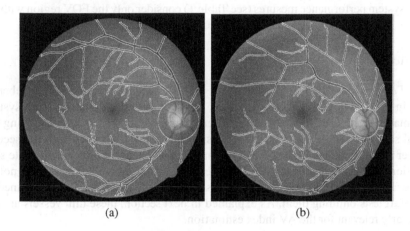

(a)   (b)

Fig. 4. Vessel detection results

In the initialisation, the centre and the radius to get the intersection points have been defined on each image. The creases extractor parameters have been selected considering the characteristics of these images and the indications found in [7]. The snake parameters have been empirically adjusted to be quite suitable for all images.

Regarding to the efficiency, we just intend to show rough time need estimations of the detection system as no exhaustive optimization effort has been done. The model has been implemented in C++ and executed on a PC with two Pentium4 processors (1GHz) and 1Gb memory. The optic disc automatic detection has been excluded from time costs because it is still being improved and optimized.

After perform time measurements in three executions for each image, the average value obtained for the whole vessel detection process (T_{total}) is 32.2 seconds (see Table 1). Almost half of this time (41.5%) is spent in resampling the image to double size using bicubic interpolation ($Tres$). The creases extraction and enhancement(T_{cr}) is the second step in duration, as it roughly represents the 28.4% of the whole process. Another critical step is obtaining the edges (T_{ed}) since it needs approximately the 14.9%. Calculating the energy images takes a time directly proportional to the distance limit selected, a value of 5 pixels was used. The snake evolution itself (T_{snk}) is here completed in just 4.9 seconds (15.2%), after an average of 2040 iterations. Although this

Table 1. Left: Average execution times in seconds for the proposed vessel detecion model. T_{res} corresponds to double size resampling. The extraction is T_{cr} for creases and T_{ed} for edges. The snake evolution is represented by T_{snk}. T_{total} is the whole segmentation process time. Right: Average performance of our snake model (Snake) and an independent observer (2^{nd}Ob.), with the same human segmentation as ground truth.

Time Costs						Accuracy	Sensitivity	Specifity
T_{res}	T_{cr}	T_{ed}	T_{snk}	T_{tot}	Snake	**0.9316**	0.6634	0.9682
13.3	9.1	4.8	4.9	**32.1**	2^{nd}Ob.	0.9486	0.7732	0.9726

step now presents an even shorter duration, the snake parameters still have a significant incidence on it as they affect the number of nodes, hence the calculations per iteration.

The system performance mesures (see Table 1) consider only the FOV region without the optic disc. They are defined as follows:

$$Accuracy = \frac{TP+TN}{\#pixels}; \quad Sensitivity = \frac{TP}{TP+FN}; \quad Specifity = \frac{TN}{TN+FP}; \quad (2)$$

where TP represents the true positives, TN the true negatives, $\#pixels$ the number of pixels in the image, FP the false positives and FN the false negatives. The system performance results are very satisfying in terms of accuracy and specificity, using the manual segmentation of the first observer as ground truth. Compared with the second observer results needing 2 hours for each image, this system achieves an accurate segmentation in a very short time (about 32 seconds). The sensitivity values are not so high because of very thin vessels, in fact a sensitivity increment has been obtained in some draft tests omitting them. As explained in next section, these thin vessels are not particularly relevant for the AV index estimation.

4   Conclusions and Discussion

In conclusion, we have developed an innovative methodology to segment the vessel tree on retinal angiographies. The classical snake model is here redefined with the incorporation of domain specific knowledge and information from the vascular tree graph obtained from a creases extraction system.

The reported performance results are very encouraging (see Table 1), as the remarkable accuracy and specifity shows. Just the sensitivity of the system is not so high due to unsegmented very thin vessels. This drawback could be partially solved by a dynamical tuning of the vessel width parameter. Actually, thin vessels are not very important in the detection process since the accuracy required for ophthalmologists is quite low. In fact, they are only interested on main vessels detection to calculate the AV index.

A extreme efficiency in terms of execution time cost has been already achieved even resampling the images (see Table 1), compared with the tedious and long manual detection (about two hours each image). Other state-of-the-art segmentation methods obtain better accuracy values but the time costs are much higher. Even the performance is not exactly equally calculated Soares et al. [4] achieved an accuracy of 0.9466 but spending more than 3 minutes for each image, appart from the training time. Mendoça et al. [3] results need about 2.5 minutes considering just the algorithm for an accuracy of 0.9463 and Staal et al. [12] get an accuracy of 0.9441 in 15 minutes for image. Our system reaches an average accuracy of 0.9316 in just 30 seconds, because it does not need to perform any complicated image preprocessing and it only handles one snake instance for the whole vascular tree. This short execution time for image, makes it suitable for real-time applications.

Our researching efforts are now mainly focused on automatically tuning the parameters depending on the image and on enhancing and optimising the energy minimisation. This system can be used in other applications related to retinal or vascular pathologies. To set an example, removing the vessel tree detected could make easier the location of retinal background lessions.

Acknowledgements. This paper has been partly funded by the Xunta de Galicia and the Ministerio de Ciencia y Tecnología through grant contracts TIC2003-04649-C02 and PGIDIT04PXIC20602PN. We also would like to thank the authors of the DRIVE database for making their data publicy available [12].

References

1. Niemeijer, M., van Ginneken, B., Staal, J., Suttorp-Schulten, M.S.A., Abràmoff, M.D.: Automatic Detection of Red Lesions in Digital Color Fundus Photographs. IEEE Transactions on Medical Imaging 24(5), 584–592 (2005)
2. Aurell, E., col.: A Note of Signs in the Fundus Oculi Hypertension Conventional Assessment and Significance. Bull. World Health Organ. 34, 95–960 (1967)
3. Mendoça, A.M., Campilho, A.: Segmentation of Retinal Blood Vessels by Combining the Detection of Centerlines and Morphological Reconstruction. IEEE Transactions on Medical Imaging 25(9), 1200–1213 (2006)
4. Soares, J.V.B., Leandro, J.J.G., Cesar Jr., R.M.C., Jelinek, Cree, M.J.: Retinal Vessel Segmentation Using the 2-D Gabor Wavelet and Supervised Classification. IEEE Transactions on Medical Imaging 25(9), 1214–1222 (2006)
5. Niemeijer, M., Staal, J., van Ginneken, B., Loog, M., Abràmoff, M.D.: Comparative Study of Retinal Vessel Segmentation Methods on a new Publicy Avaliable Database. In: Proceedings of the SPIE. Medical Imaging 2004: Image Processing, vol. 5370, pp. 648–656 (2004)
6. Toledo, R., Orriols, X., Binefa, X., Redeva, P., Vitri, J., Villanueva, J.J.: Tracking elongated structures using statistical snakes. In: Proceedings IEEE Conference on Computer Vision and Pattern Recognition, vol. 1(1), pp. 157–162 (2000)
7. Caderno, I.G., Penedo, M.G., Mariño, C., Carreira, M.J., Gómez-Ulla, F., González, F.: Automatic Extraction of the Retina AV Index. LNCS 3212, vol. 2, pp. 132–140, (2004)
8. Ortega, M., Mariño, C., Penedo, M.G., Blanco, M., González, F.: Personal Authentication based on Feature Extraction and Optic Nerve Location in Digital Retinal Images Wseas Transactions on Computers, vol. 5(6), pp. 1169–1176 (2006)
9. Kass, M., Witkin, A., Terzopoulos, D.: Active Contour Models. International Journal of Computer Vision 1(2), 321–331 (1998)
10. Canny, J.A: Computational Approach to Edge-Detection. IEEE Transactions on Pattern Analysis and Machine Inteligence 8(6), 679–689 (1986)
11. Blanco, M., Penedo, M.G., Barreira, N., Penas, M., Carreira, M.J.: Localization and Extraction of the Optic Disc using th Fuzzy Circular Hough Transform Artificial Intelligence and Soft Computing. In: Rutkowski, L., Tadeusiewicz, R., Zadeh, L.A., Zurada, J.M. (eds.) ICAISC 2006. LNCS (LNAI), vol. 4029, pp. 713–721. Springer, Heidelberg (2006)
12. Staal, J.J., Abràmoff, M.D., Niemeijer, M., Viergever, M.A., van Ginneken, B.: Ridge based vessel segmentation in color images of the retina. IEEE Transactions on Medical Imaging 23, 501–509 (2004)

Risk Classification of Mammograms Using Anatomical Linear Structure and Density Information

Edward M. Hadley[1], Erika R.E. Denton[2], Josep Pont[3], Elsa Pérez[3], and Reyer Zwiggelaar[1]

[1] Department of Computer Science, University of Wales, Aberystwyth, UK
emh05@aber.ac.uk, rrz@aber.ac.uk
[2] Department of Radiology, Norfolk and Norwich University Hospital, UK
[3] University Hospital Dr Josep Trueta, Girona, Spain

Abstract. Mammographic risk assessment is concerned with the probability of a woman developing breast cancer. Recently, it has been suggested that the density of linear structures is related to risk. For 321 images from the MIAS database, the images were segmented in to dense and non-dense tissue using a method described by Sivaramakrishna, *et al.* In addition, a measure of line strength was obtained for each pixel using the Line Operator method. The above-threshold linearity was calculated in dense and non-dense tissue for each image and the images were then classified by BIRADS class using linear discriminant analysis. The results show a marked improvement when both density and linear structure information is used in classification over density information alone.

1 Background

Mammographic risk assessment is concerned with estimating the probability of women developing breast cancer. Risk assessment is a rapidly developing area of research and can provide an indication of when to recommend more frequent screening, which has been shown to improve the likelihood of the early detection of breast cancer [1]. Breast density is an important indicator of mammographic risk [2] and the best predictor of mammographic sensitivity [3]. However, more recently, it has been suggested that the distribution of linear structures is also correlated with mammographic risk [4,5,6]. So far it is not entirely clear if it is just the density of linear structures (either by percentage area or volume) or if the distribution of the linear structures plays a role as well.

Tabár et al. have proposed a mammographic risk assessment model based on four structural components, where the relative proportions of each component is linked to the risk of developing breast cancer [4,5,6]. One of the four structural components is linear density. The main purpose of this work is to investigate if automatic methods can be used to correlate the density of linear structures to mammographic risk classification metrics.

J. Martí et al. (Eds.): IbPRIA 2007, Part II, LNCS 4478, pp. 186–193, 2007.
© Springer-Verlag Berlin Heidelberg 2007

2   Method

Three hundred and twenty-one mammographic images from the Mammographic Image Analysis Society (MIAS) database [7] were classified according to BIRADS classes [8] by three expert radiologists. Example images of low, moderate and high risk mammograms are shown in Fig. 1 (a).

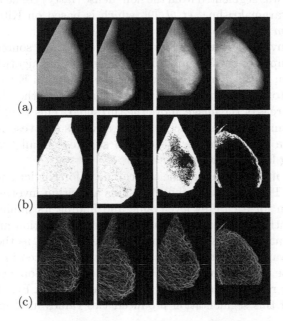

Fig. 1. Some typical mammograms of various BIRADS classes. The left column shows a mammogram of BIRADS class 1 (low risk), the second column shows a mammogram of BIRADS class 2 (low–moderate risk) and the third column shows a mammogram of BIRADS class 3 (moderate–high risk), and the final column shows a mammogram of BIRADS class 4 (high risk). The images in row (a) show the original mammograms, row (b) shows the results of density segmentation (non-dense tissue is shown in white), and row (c) shows the results after processing with the line operator. The images have had a mask applied to remove everything outside the breast area. The lines in (c) have been enhanced for viewing.

All 321 images were initially segmented using a method described by Sivaramakrishna, *et al.* [9], which is based on Kittler and Illingworth's *Minimum Error Thresholding* [10] (see Sec. 2.1). This produced masks identifying the dense tissue in the image and allowed for the consideration of linear structures in each tissue type independently. Examples of density masks produced are shown in Fig. 1 (b).

In addition, the images were processed using Dixon and Taylor's line operator method [11,12] (see Sec. 2.2), producing a measurement of line strength at each pixel. Fig. 1 (c) shows examples of low, moderate and high risk mammograms following processing with the line operator.

Finally, the images were classified in BIRADS classes using linear discriminant analysis (see Sec. 2.3) based on the features extracted from the processed images and the results analysed.

2.1 Density Segmentation

The dense tissue was segmented from the non–dense (fatty) tissue using a method described by Sivaramakrishna, *et al.* [9], which is based on Kittler and Illingworth's *Minimum Error Thresholding* [10].

The method involves creating a variation image from the source image, which is then used as input to the Minimum Error Thresholding algorithm to produce an approximation of the dense tissue area. If the Minimum Error Thresholding algorithm were to be performed over the original image, the algorithm would place all bright areas of the image above the threshold. This would include dense tissue, but also smaller bright structures such as ducts and vessels. The purpose of the conversion to a variation image is to suppress small bright structures whilst enhancing large bright areas.

The variation image is used as the source image for Kittler and Illingworth's Minimum Error Threshold algorithm [10]. This algorithm involves calculating a criterion function for each grey level value and finding its minimum. This is a relatively straightforward computation. The criterion function minimum J was found for each image and its corresponding value was used as the threshold for segmenting the variation image. A tissue mask was produced in order to easily identify the dense tissue areas in subsequent calculations. Some examples of the images and their resultant dense tissue masks are shown in Fig. 1(b).

The results of this segmentation produced two values used in later calculations:

– the total number of pixels in dense tissue: A_d,
– the total number of pixels in fatty tissue: A_f.

2.2 Line Detection

The method of line detection is based on that used in previous work [13]. A study of various methods for detecting linear structures in mammograms showed that Dixon and Taylor's line operator [11] is more accurate than other methods [12]. As such, the line operator was used in our experiments. The method produces a measure of line strength and orientation for each pixel in an image.

A multi-scale approach was used in order to detect lines of a range of thicknesses and the resultant images were combined to produce line strength values for pixels at the original scale. Scaling of the images was achieved firstly by blurring the image using a 3x3 Gaussian kernel and subsequently by subsampling to provide a resultant image of half the width and height of the original. Our approach comprised processing with the line operator at three scales, since this appeared to produce the most reasonable output for the images under examination.

Finally, the pixel line strengths were thresholded to remove background texture. Using a line length of 5, the measures of line strength fall in the theoretical range of $0 - 204$, however the results showed that most (if not all) pixels had line strength values in the range $0 - 30$. A range of threshold values were chosen experimentally, and $4/204$ was finally selected for our analysis as it removed most background noise whilst maintaining most of the linear structure information.

When considered alongside the density mask produced by the density segmentation method described in Sec. 2.1 two further values were produced for use in further calculations:

– the number of pixels with above-threshold linearity in dense tissue: L_d,
– the number of pixels with above-threshold linearity in fatty tissue: L_f.

2.3   Classification

The BIRADS [8] metric uses a scale of four classes, where class 1 represents a low risk and class 4 represents a high risk.

Classification was conducted using linear discriminant analysis, which takes several factors as predictors and attempts to classify each mammogram in to BIRADS classes. Classification was conducted three times – firstly using density information only, secondly using linear structure information only, and a third time using both density and linear structure information.

Linear discriminant analysis uses one or more predictors, which are used to attempt to distinguish between objects of the various classes. In the classification based on density information, the following values were used as predictors:

$$\frac{A_d}{A_d + A_f}, \log \frac{A_d}{A_d + A_f}. \tag{1}$$

During experimentation it was found that adding the log of the value as an additional predictor increased the performance of the classifier. It can be assumed that the log function accentuates the lower parts of the scale where most of the mammograms lie, producing greater separation between classes. The classification based on linear structure information used the following values as predictors:

$$\frac{L_d}{A_d}, \frac{L_f}{A_f}, \log \frac{L_d}{A_d}, \log \frac{L_f}{A_f}. \tag{2}$$

The classification based on both linear structure and density information uses a single classifier which incorporates all of the above six values as predictors (i.e. the predictors from both the density classification and linear structure classification are used in the third classification).

Results of each classification are shown in table form, including the proportion of correct classifications and the kappa (κ) coefficient [14,15]. The κ coefficient is a means of estimating agreement in categorical data, and is given by

$$\kappa = \frac{P(D) - P(E)}{1 - P(E)} \tag{3}$$

where $P(D)$ is the proportion of correct classifications and $P(E)$ is the proportion expected by chance. Since the κ coefficient is a means of estimating agreement in categorical data, and can be used to assess the performance of the classification. A list of common interpretations of κ values is shown in Table 1 [15].

Table 1. Common interpretations of κ values [15]

κ	Agreement
< 0	Poor
$0 - 0.20$	Slight
$0.21 - 0.40$	Fair
$0.41 - 0.60$	Moderate
$0.61 - 0.80$	Substantial
$0.81 - 1.00$	Almost Perfect

3 Data

The method was applied to 321 mammograms from the Mammographic Image Analysis Society (MIAS) database [7]. This database is composed of left and right mammograms from 161 women digitised into $50\mu m \times 50\mu m$ pixels.

The 321 mammograms were annotated by three expert radiologists according to the BIRADS risk classification metric. Consensus between the annotations of the three individual radiologists was used, as is common in screening mammography, in order to improve the reliability of the annotations.

Where disagreement occurred between the experts, the consensus was determined using the following strategy: where two out of three radiologists agree, the majority value was used, and where all three experts disagreed, the median value was used. Of the 321 mammograms, all three experts agreed in 138 cases, two experts agreed whilst a third disagreed in 171 cases, and in 12 cases all three experts disagreed.

4 Results

4.1 Classification Based on Density

Results of linear discriminant analysis by BIRADS class based on density information are shown in Table 2. The results indicate a 66% accuracy in classifying the mammograms. The κ coefficient indicates moderate agreement between the classified results and the true classes.

4.2 Classification Based on Linear Structures

Results of linear discriminant analysis by BIRADS class based on linear structure information are shown in Table 3. The results indicate a 67% accuracy in classifying the mammograms. The κ coefficient indicates moderate agreement between the classified results and the true classes.

Table 2. Classification results by BIRADS class based on density information

		True Class			
		1	2	3	4
Placed Class	1	**62**	14	2	0
	2	18	**57**	19	4
	3	4	28	**68**	9
	4	3	4	5	**24**
Proportion correct		0.713	0.553	0.728	0.649
Total prop. correct		0.657			
κ coefficient		0.54			

Table 3. Classification results by BIRADS class based on linear structure information

		True Class			
		1	2	3	4
Placed Class	1	**68**	10	7	1
	2	9	**71**	27	0
	3	9	19	**50**	9
	4	1	3	10	**27**
Proportion correct		0.782	0.689	0.532	0.730
Total prop. correct		0.673			
κ coefficient		0.56			

4.3   Classification Based on Linear Structures and Density

Results of linear discriminant analysis by BIRADS class based on a combination
of density and linear structure information are shown in Table 4. The results indicate a 72% accuracy in classifying the mammograms. The κ coefficient indicates
a substantial agreement between the true classes and the placed classes. These
results show that a combined approach is superior to using a single component.

Table 4. Classification results by BIRADS class based on density and linear structure
information

		True Class			
		1	2	3	4
Placed Class	1	**70**	12	2	1
	2	12	**73**	25	0
	3	2	15	**60**	9
	4	3	3	7	**27**
Proportion correct		0.805	0.709	0.638	0.730
Total prop. correct		0.717			
κ coefficient		0.62			

5   Discussion and Conclusions

The results are promising and show a substantial improvement between classification using density information and classification using combined information,
leading to the conclusion that linear structure information is valuable in the
automatic risk classification of mammograms.

An alternative approach to the analysis might be to look at whether the
mammograms are correctly classified in to high/low risk groups. Results of this

analysis for combined density and linear structure information are shown in Table 5. We can see that the classifier provides 84% correct high/low classification ($\kappa = 0.79$) based on both density and linear structure information.

Table 5. Classification results by BIRADS class based on density and linear stucture information summarised as low (classes 1-2)/high (classes 3-4) groups

		True Class	
		Low	High
Placed Class	Low	167	28
	High	23	103
Proportion correct		0.879	0.786
Total prop. correct		0.841	
κ coefficient		0.79	

A comparison with with other methods described in literature shows that the proposed method performs well, achieving 72% correct classification. Oliver, *et al.* [16] performed texture–based classification by BIRADS class on the MIAS images used in this analysis. This classification achieved 66% accuracy when classifying the images without prior segmentation. Results were improved significantly to between 79% and 82% correct classification when the images were segmented in to regions prior to the texture analysis as first suggested by Karssemeijer [17].

The alternative classifications described in literature suggest that texture–based classification with prior segmentation performs better that density–based segmentation. As such, it is intended for future work to investigate classification based on this approach combined with linear structure information. The combination technique used was a straightforward one, however optimisation techniques exist which may provide improved results for the combined classification.

A number of problems were found with the density segmentation method. Some images produced criterion function graphs that were not bimodal, having either zero or multiple minima. In addition, spurious values at the edges of the criterion function curves (caused by, for example, an image having no pixels with a greyscale value of 255) leading to false minima were initially a problem. This was overcome by selecting the lowest minimum where multiple minima occurred, and as a result of observations, by classifying the whole area as non-dense tissue where no minima occurred.

The segmentation was also found to be heavily dependent on the area used for segmentation, since if too much background area was included, in many non-dense breasts the threshold was placed between the background tissue and the breast tissue, resulting in the whole of the breast area being classified as dense tissue. To overcome this, a threshold was set and all pixels with greyscale values below this threshold were ignored. This effectively removed any surrounding background tissue from the analysis.

For the purposes of a comparison between density, linear structure and combined information the methods used were adequate, however more accurate methods for the segmentation of dense tissue and classification have been demonstrated [16]. The results shown demonstrate that the inclusion of linear structure information improves automatic risk classification.

References

1. van Gils, C.H., Otten, J.D., Hendriks, J.H., Holland, R., Straatman, H., Verbeek, A.L.: High mammographic breast density and its implications for the early detection of breast cancer. Journal of Medical Screening 6, 200–204 (1999)
2. Wolfe, J.N.: Risk for breast cancer development determined by mammographic parenchymal pattern. Cancer 37(5), 2486–2492 (1976)
3. Kolb, T.M., Lichy, J., Newhouse, J.H.: Comparison of the performance of screening mammography, physical examination, and breast us and evaluation of factors that influence them: An analysis of 27, 825 patient evaluations. Radiology 225(1), 165–175 (2002)
4. Tabár, L., Dean, P.B.: Mammographic parenchymal patterns. risk indicator for breast cancer? Journal of the American Medical Association 247(2), 185–189 (1982)
5. Gram, I.T., Funkhouser, E., Tabár, L.: The Tabár classification of mammographic parenchymal patterns. European Journal of Radiology 24(2), 131–136 (1997)
6. Tabár, L., Tot, T., Dean, P.B.: Breast Cancer - The Art and Science of Early Detection with Mammography. Georg Thieme Verlag, Stuttgart (2005)
7. Suckling, J., Parker, J., Dance, D., Astley, S., Hutt, I., Boggis, C., Ricketts, I., Stamatakis, E., Cerneaz, N., Kok, S., Taylor, P., Betal, D., Savage, J.: The mammographic images analysis society digital mammogram database. Exerpta Medica. International Congress Series 1069, 375–378 (1994)
8. American College of Radiology: Illustrated Breast Imaging Reporting and Data System. 3rd edn. American College of Radiology (1998)
9. Sivaramakrishna, R., Obuchowski, N.A., Chilcote, W.A., Powell, K.A.: Automatic segmentation of mammographic density. Academic Radiology 8(3), 250–256 (1998)
10. Kittler, J., Illingworth, J.: Minimum error thresholding. Pattern Recognition 19(1), 41–47 (1986)
11. Dixon, R.N., Taylor, C.J.: Automated asbestos fibre counting. Institute of Physics Conference Series 44, 178–185 (1979)
12. Zwiggelaar, R., Astley, S.M., Boggis, C.R.M., Taylor, C.J.: Linear structures in mammographic images: Detection and classification. IEEE Transactions on Medical Imaging 23(9), 1077–1086 (2004)
13. Hadley, E.M., Denton, E.R.E., Zwiggelaar, R.: Mammographic risk assessment based on anatomical linear structures. In: Astley, S.M., Brady, M., Rose, C., Zwiggelaar, R. (eds.) IWDM 2006. LNCS, vol. 4046, pp. 626–633. Springer, Heidelberg (2006)
14. Cohen, J.: A coefficient of agreement for nominal scales. Educ. Psychol. Meas. 20, 27–46 (1960)
15. Landis, J., Koch, G.: The measurement of observer agreement for categorical data. Biometrics 33(3), 159–174 (1977)
16. Oliver, A., Freixenet, J., Martí, R., Zwiggelaar, R.: A comparison of breast tissue classification techniques. In: Larsen, R., Nielsen, M., Sporring, J. (eds.) MICCAI 2006. LNCS, vol. 4191, pp. 872–879. Springer, Heidelberg (2006)
17. Karssemeijer, N.: Automated classification of mammographic parenchymal pattern. Physics in Medicine and Biology 28, 365–378 (1998)

A New Method for Robust and Efficient Occupancy Grid-Map Matching

Jose-Luis Blanco, Javier Gonzalez, and Juan-Antonio Fernandez-Madrigal

Department of System Engineering and Automation
University of Malaga
Malaga 29071, Spain

Abstract. In this paper we propose a new matching method for occupancy grid-maps under the perspective of image registration. Our approach is based on extracting feature descriptors by means of a polar coordinate transformation around highly distinctive points. The proposed method presents a modest computation complexity, although it can find matchings between features reliably and regardless their orientation. Experimental results show the robustness of the estimates even for dynamic environments. Our proposal has important applications into the field of mobile robotics.

1 Introduction

Occupancy grid-maps, introduced into the robotics community two decades ago [1], are a very valuable representation for map building applications of planar environments [2]. In this representation, the space is arranged in a metric grid of cells that store the probability of that area being occupied by some obstacle. A recent trend in map-building research is to consider hierarchical models, where each node within a topological graph represents a local metric map [3]. A critical issue for this paradigm is to detect when two local maps correspond to the same physical place, and, in that case, to compute the relative transformation between those maps. Solving this problem is crucial for the consistency of the mapping process. The aim of the present work is to provide a solution to this problem from an image registration viewpoint when local maps are occupancy grid-maps.

Occupancy grids can be naturally interpreted as grayscale images (called here *map images*), where cells in the grid correspond to pixels in the image, thus by registering the images we obtain the spatial transformation between the maps. Image registration techniques can be straightforwardly grouped into intensity-based ones, and those based on feature extraction (see [4] for a review). Although the former approach has been already applied to grid-map matching [2], an approach based on feature extraction, as the one presented here, is less computationally expensive, becoming more appropriate for being integrated into a real-time mapping framework.

Our overall approach consists of the following three steps: (i) feature-point detection in the map images and extraction of their descriptors, (ii) estimation

J. Martí et al. (Eds.): IbPRIA 2007, Part II, LNCS 4478, pp. 194–201, 2007.
© Springer-Verlag Berlin Heidelberg 2007

of the likely correspondences between features, and (iii) robust estimation of the rigid transformation between the maps. Since the cell size of all the maps can be set to any fixed value, there are not differences in scale in this problem. Taking this into account, in this paper we propose a new descriptor and an associated method for finding correspondences that are able to efficiently and robustly solve correspondences between feature points in map images of arbitrary orientation. Other previously proposed descriptors in the literature, in spite of being very useful for dealing with real images taken from cameras, become unpractical here due to different reasons:

- The Scale Invariant Feature Transform (SIFT) descriptor, introduced in [5], implies much more computation effort than required for the problem addressed here, since it achieves scale invariance by constructing a pyramid of auxiliary sub-sampled images.
- In [6] it is presented a descriptor that, although based on polar coordinate transformation like ours, proposes an additional step for extracting moments from the Fourier transform. However, we have experimentally verified that this method is not as well suited as ours to effectively discriminate between features typically found in map images.
- In [7] it is proposed to take Gaussian derivatives as descriptors, in the context of developing an affine invariant descriptor. We believe that the low dimensionality of the descriptor proposed there is not appropriate for the highly ambiguous features in map images.

In the next section we describe our proposal for a feature point descriptor in map images. Next, section 3 describes the associated methods for measuring the degree of matching between a pair of features and how to robustly estimate the map displacement from those matchings. Finally, in section 4 we provide experimental results for different map matching situations, all of them employing real data.

2   The Cylindrical Descriptor

We assume that a set of N feature points $\varphi = \{p_1, ..., p_N\}$ has been extracted from a map image using any appropriate method with a good repeatability. In this work we employ the method proposed by Shi and Tomasi [8], although using other methods, like the Harris corner detector [9], leads to similar results.

Once a feature point $p_a = [x_a \ y_a]^T$ has been localized, we define its associated descriptor f_a as a mapping of the annular area around the feature point into the two-dimensional space of polar coordinates r and θ (refer to Fig. 1). Notice that the cylindrical topology of this transformed space can be interpreted as a "panoramic image" of the neighborhood of the feature point, as shown with an example in Fig. 1(c)–(d). Hence it is clear that a rotation in the grid-map becomes a rotation of the cylindrical image around the θ axis. Here we consider radial distances only within the range $[R_{min}, R_{max}]$, e.g. from 0.10 to 1.50 meters, and implement the descriptor as a $N_r \times N_\theta$ matrix with dimensions $N_r = (R_{max} - R_{min})/\Delta_r$ and

$N_\theta = 2\pi/\Delta_\theta$, provided the desired spatial and angular resolutions Δr and $\Delta \theta$, respectively. The value of the descriptor for each pair (i, j) in the range $[0, N_r - 1] \times [0, N_\theta - 1]$ is given by integration over the corresponding annular sector (please, refer to Fig. 1(a)–(b)):

$$f_a[i, j] = \int_{\phi_j}^{\phi_{j+1}} \int_{r_i}^{r_{i+1}} m\left(\begin{bmatrix} x_a + r\cos\theta \\ y_a + r\sin\theta \end{bmatrix} \right) dr d\theta \tag{1}$$

$$r_i = R_{min} + i\Delta r$$
$$\phi_j = j\Delta\phi$$

where $m(\mathbf{x})$ represents the contents of the map at the 2D point $\mathbf{x}$. Notice that, in practice, the above integration can be computed through a Monte-Carlo ap-
ŗ
v

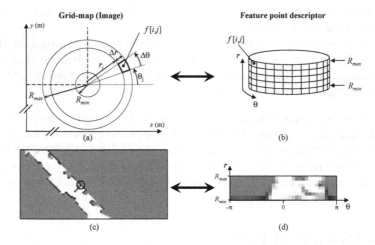

Fig. 1. (a)-(b) The geometry of the descriptor proposed in the text, which maps the circle around the feature into a cylindric space. An example is shown in (c)-(d).

3   Map Matching

3.1   Measuring the Degree of Matching Between a Pair of Descriptors

As a motivating example, please consider the pair of features detected in the maps of Fig. 2(a)–(b), which correspond to the same physical point. The associated descriptors are shown in Fig. 2(c). It is clear that their cylindrical descriptors will be very similar for some shift in θ if the features represent a valid correspondence. In this particular example that shift is 214°, and the similarity between the conveniently rotated descriptors is patent in Fig. 2(d). Hence we propose to measure the degree of matching $d(f_a, f_b)$ for a pair of descriptors f_a and f_b through the minimum Euclidean distance between the descriptors, taken over all possible rotations:

$$d(f_a, f_b) = \min_{j_0 \in [0, N_\theta - 1]} \sum_{i=0}^{N_r - 1} \sum_{j=0}^{N_\theta - 1} (f_a[i,j] - f_b[i, (j - j_0) \bmod N_\theta])^2 \qquad (2)$$

Once a matching measure is defined for pairs of features, it must be addressed how to obtain the whole set of correspondences $\mathcal{C} = \{\mathcal{C}_1, ..., \mathcal{C}_k\}$, where each correspondence $\mathcal{C}_i = \langle a_i, b_i \rangle$ consists of a pair of feature indexes a_i and b_i, one from each map. When (2) is evaluated for a fixed feature in the first map and all the features in the other, we expect to obtain a low distance (a good matching) only for a few (ideally only one) of the possible correspondences. An example is shown i
the rest
next, it
for eacl
the set
First
tiated f
to be b

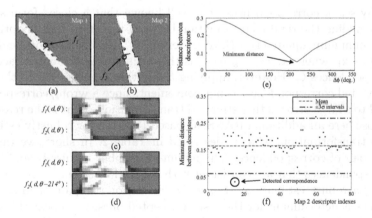

(a)   (b)

$f_1(d,\theta):$

$f_2(d,\theta):$

(c)

$f_1(d,\theta):$

$f_2(d,\theta-214°):$

(d)

Distance between descriptors

0.3

0.2

0.1 Minimum distance

0

0   50   100   150   200   250   300   350
$\Delta\theta$ (deg.)

(e)

Minimum distance between descriptors

0.35

0.25

0.15 Mean
±3σ intervals

0.05

0 Detected correspondence

0   20   40   60   80
Map 2 descriptor indexes

(f)

Fig. 2. Two maps of the same environment are shown in (a)–(b), while the descriptors corresponding to the highlighted features are shown in (c) and (d), for a shift in θ of 0° and 214°, respectively. The matching distance between those features is plotted in (e) for all the possible rotation angles, and in (f) it is shown the minimum distance between the feature f_1 and all the features in the second map, from where the right correspondence is clearly revealed.

standard deviation, respectively, of the evaluation of $d(f_a, f_j)$ for all the possible values of j. The selectivity of this threshold is controlled by the parameter κ. Any value in the range 1.5-3.0 is appropriate for most situations, although the higher its value, the more demanding we are in accepting a correspondence, at the cost of finding less of them. Secondly, to cope with features without a valid correspondence, we must set a fixed threshold τ_f for the maximum distance between descriptors to be accepted as a correspondence. This parameter, determined heuristically, has been set to 0.07 for all the experiments in this paper. This algorithm is summarized in Table 1.

Table 1. The algorithm for finding compatible correspondences between maps

---

algorithm findCorrespondences$(m_1, m_2) \mapsto \mathcal{C}$
   $\mathcal{C} = \emptyset$
   for each $f_i \in m_1$
      $\mu = \mathrm{E}_j\{d(f_i, f_j)\}$; Mean and standard deviation, where
      $\sigma = \sqrt{\mathrm{E}_j\{(d(f_i, f_j) - \mu)^2\}}$; j spans over all features in m_2
      $\tau_d = \mu - \kappa\sigma$; Compute the dynamic threshold
      for each $f_j \in m_2$
         if $d(f_i, f_j) < \min(\tau_d, \tau_f)$; Compatibility test
            $\mathcal{C} = \mathcal{C} \cup \langle i, j \rangle$; Accept the correspondence
  end

3.2 Robust Estimation of the Rigid Transformation Between Maps

Given any set of correspondences, it is well known that a closed-form solution exists for finding the rigid transformation between the maps that is optimal, in the least-minimum-square-error (LMSE) sense [10]. Let this method be denoted by $T(\mathcal{C}_i) \mapsto \mathbf{x_i}$, where $\mathbf{x_i} = [x_i \ y_i \ \phi_i]^T$ is the optimal transformation according to correspondences $\mathcal{C}_i$. However, applying this estimation directly to the whole set of detected correspondences is not convenient, since a wrong correspondence may lead to a large error in the estimated transformation. That is the reason why we propose here an additional RANSAC-based [11] step for robustly estimating the map transformation, what is described in Table 2. In short, we randomly choose a pair of correspondences (the minimum number required), and then all the correspondences that are consistent with the initial estimation are included, providing a robust estimate $\mathbf{x}_i$. Since the choice for the pair of initial correspondences is determinant for the rest of accepted ones, we repeat this process a number of times M, each time with a randomly chosen initial pair of correspondences. Additionally, only those sets of correspondences of a minimum size C_{min} (e.g. 8 correspondences) are considered, achieving improved consistency in the results. In this way, we obtain a set of robust estimates $\mathbf{X} = \{\mathbf{x}_i\}_{i=1}^{L}$. If we assume the correspondence between features to be an unknown random variable, this set $\mathbf{X}$ can be interpreted as a sample-based (Monte-Carlo) approximation to the probability density of the map transformation, which can be used, for example, for fitting a Gaussian distribution for the maps transformation.

Table 2. The method for robustly estimating the transformation

---

algorithm robustEstimation($\mathcal{C}$) $\mapsto$ **X**
  X $= \emptyset$
  for $i = 1..M$ do   ; Repeat the simulation M times.
    randomly choose $\mathcal{C}_i = \{c_1, c_2\} \subset \mathcal{C}$, such as $c_1 \neq c_2$
    $\mathbf{x}_i = T(\mathcal{C}_i)$
    for each $c_j \in \mathcal{C} - \mathcal{C}_i$
      if $\|T(\mathcal{C}_i \cup c_j) - \mathbf{x}_i\| < \tau$; If the new estimation is consistent
        $\mathcal{C}_i = \mathcal{C}_i \cup c_j$; according to a given threshold τ,
        $\mathbf{x}_i = T(\mathcal{C}_i)$; accept the correspondence c_j.
    if $|\mathcal{C}_i| \geq C_{min}$
      X $=$ **X** $\cup \mathbf{x}_i$
  end

---

4   Experimental Results and Conclusions

We have applied our method to two pairs of maps obtained from real data gathered by a mobile robot in the same physical places, but at different times. As shown in Fig. 3, the pairs of image maps contain some differences, especially the pair in Fig. 3(a) where several pieces of furniture were moved within the room. The computed map transformations are shown in Fig. 3(c)–(f). It is noticeable the high robustness when establishing correspondences, what is reflected in the low uncertainty of the estimations: below 15 cm. for the translation, and less than 2 degrees for the orientation. The estimation process takes 600ms and 807ms for the two pair of maps, respectively, for a number of simulations $M = 5000$. We have also intensively tested the performance of our approach against two kinds of realistic errors that can appear in occupancy grids built from range scans [2]: errors in the ranges themselves, and in the localization of the sensor within the map. Both errors have been simulated by additive Gaussian noise, characterized by σ_{range} and σ_{pose}, respectively. In this experiment we have arbitrarily chosen a map as reference and synthetically generated a test map with a known transformation of $(\Delta x, \Delta y, \Delta \phi) = (1m, 2m, 45°)$ to compute the mean errors achieved by our method, both in translation ϵ_{XY} and in orientation ϵ_ϕ. Errors have been computed for a set of different error levels σ_{range} and σ_{pose}. We have also contrasted our estimation with that from the LMSE method applied on the whole set of correspondences. All these results are summarized in Fig. 4, where it should be highlighted the small absolute errors achieved over the wide range of noise levels and for both kind of errors, in the range values, Fig. 4(d)-(f), and in the poses, Fig. 4(g)-(i). In all the cases the mean errors are below 10 cm. and 0.5 degrees. In comparison with the LMSE estimate, our method achieves an improvement of above one order of magnitude, clearly justifying the integration of the robust step in the process.

We have also computed the estimation based on the normalized cross correlation (NCC) for comparison purposes (see Fig. 4(j)), where it is clear that the maximum value of the NCC reveals the transformation between the maps,

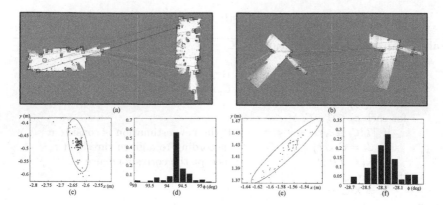

Fig. 3. Matching results from our method for two pairs of real maps, shown in (a)–(b). The samples obtained from the estimation process are shown in (c)–(f), where the estimated translations and orientations have been separated for ease of visualization. Gaussian fit is shown for the translation estimations and a 95% confidence interval.

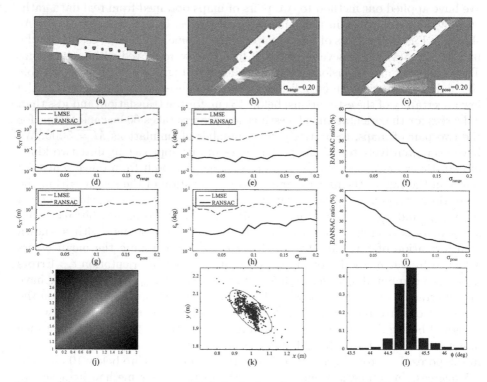

Fig. 4. (a) The reference map, which is displaced and corrupted with noise in sensor measurements (b), and in the sensor localization (c). (d)-(i) Show the performance of our method for different levels of noise. The result from NCC (for a fixed value of $\Delta\phi = 45°$) is shown in (j), whereas (k)-(l) show the samples obtained from our method, where the fitted Gaussian is represented by its 95% confidence interval. See the text for further details.

but it also assigns high values to many wrong transformations, which contrasts with the results from our approach in Fig. 4(k). Regarding computation time, it takes approximately 420 sec. to evaluate the NCC in a 3.2GHz Pentium 4 using a straightforward implementation, whereas out method takes less than 1 sec.

To summarize, in this paper we have presented a new method for robust matching of occupancy grid-maps, a technique with many potential applications in robotics. Our approach has been devised from a image-registration viewpoint, hence we introduce a new feature-point descriptor for easing the matching. Adding a robust step to the estimation process is shown to provide a significant improvement in the overall precision. Future work should be aimed to provide a more detailed comparison between the performance attainable from different feature-point detectors, and to integrate this work into robotic mapping frameworks.

Acknowledgments. This work was partly supported by the Spanish Government under research contract DPI2005-01391.

References

1. Elfes, A.: Using occupancy grids for mobile robot perception and navigation. Computer 22(6), 46–57 (1989)
2. Gutmann, J., Konolige, K.: Incremental mapping of large cyclic environments. In: Proceedings of IEEE International Symposium on Computational Intelligence in Robotics and Automation, pp. 318–325 (1999)
3. Estrada, C., Neira, J., Tardos, J.: Hierarchical SLAM: Real-Time Accurate Mapping of Large Environments. IEEE Transactions on Robotics 21(4), 588–596 (2005)
4. Zitova, B., Flusser, J.: Image registration methods: a survey. Image and Vision Computing 21(11), 977–1000 (2003)
5. Lowe, D.: Object recognition from local scale-invariant features. In: Proceedings of the Seventh IEEE International Conference on Computer Vision, vol. 2 (1999)
6. Matas, J., Bılek, P., Chum, O.: Rotational Invariants for Wide-baseline Stereo. In: Proceedings of the Computer Vision Winter Workshop, vol. 2, pp. 296–305 (2002)
7. Mikolajczyk, K., Schmid, C.: An affine invariant interest point detector. In: Proceedings of European Conference on Computer Vision, vol. 1, pp. 128–142. Springer, Heidelberg (2002)
8. Shi, J., Tomasi, C.: Good features to track. In: Proceedings of the IEEE Computer Society Conference on Computer Vision and Pattern Recognition, pp. 593–600 (1994)
9. Harris, C., Stephens, M.: A combined corner and edge detector. In: Proceedings of Alvey Vision Conference, vol. 15 (1988)
10. Besl, P., McKay, N.: A method for registration of 3-D shapes. IEEE Transactions on Pattern Analysis and Machine Intelligence 14(2), 239–256 (1992)
11. Fischler, M., Bolles, R.: Random sample consensus: a paradigm for model fitting with applications to image analysis and automated cartography. Communications of the ACM 24(6), 381–395 (1981)

Vote-Based Classifier Selection for Biomedical NER Using Genetic Algorithms

Nazife Dimililer, Ekrem Varoğlu, and Hakan Altınçay

Department of Computer Engineering, Eastern Mediterranean University,
Mağusa, Northern Cyprus, via Mersin-10, Turkey
{nazife.dimililer,ekrem.varoglu,hakan.altincay}@emu.edu.tr

Abstract. We propose a genetic algorithm for constructing a classifier ensemble using a vote-based classifier selection approach for biomedical named entity recognition task. Assuming that the reliability of the predictions of each classifier differs among classes, the proposed approach is based on dynamic selection of the classifiers by taking into account their individual votes. During testing, the classifiers whose votes are considered as being reliable are combined using weighted majority voting. The classifier ensemble formed by the proposed scheme surpasses the full object F-score of the best individual classifier and the ensemble of all classifiers by 2.5% and 1.3% respectively.

1 Introduction

Named entity recognition (NER) in the biomedical domain is a significantly challenging task due to several factors such as the use of descriptive naming conventions, conjunctions and disjunctions in biomedical entity names, non-standardized naming conventions, use of synonyms, extensive use of abbreviations, and the fact that some biomedical entity names may be cascaded [1],[2]. Moreover, new names are constantly being introduced in the domain vocabulary and yet some of these are used only for relatively short time periods. In addition, there exists ambiguity in the tokenization and tagging of biomedical text.

Recent studies in NER in the biomedical domain mainly focus on feature extraction. The wide variety of features considered for this purpose include orthographic features, morphological patterns, lexical features, semantic triggers, name alias features, gene sequences, and external resources such as gazetteers. Extensive research has been carried out for computing better feature sets so as to improve NER in this domain [3], [4]. This is generally done by trial-and-error approach where the main goal is to include discriminative features and avoid using correlated ones.

Instead of finding the best-fitting feature set, ensembling several NER systems where each member is based on a different feature representation has recently been considered as an alternative research direction. For instance, Zhou et al. combined three NER systems, each using a different modeling technique and feature set [3]. In classifier ensembles, the generalization accuracy of an ensemble depends on the *diversity* of the classifiers as well as their individual performances. This means that

J. Martí et al. (Eds.): IbPRIA 2007, Part II, LNCS 4478, pp. 202–209, 2007.

the classifiers should be different from each other using different model parameters and feature sets and hence make errors for different inputs [5]. Although it is evident that combining the same classifiers does not make any contribution, selecting a diverse subset is still a challenging problem due to the lack of a well-established diversity measure. In the case of NER, it is generally argued that diversity can be achieved with the use of classifiers providing better precision together with others providing better recall [3].

Analogous to best-fitting feature set selection in designing individual systems instead of using all available features, *classifier selection* aims at finding a diverse *subset* of available classifiers by removing similar ones to ensure an optimal combined performance for an a priori specified combination rule. In its static implementation, the classifiers that are considered to be redundant are discarded from the ensemble. In order to achieve this, although several diversity measures are proposed as candidate selection criteria, the combined performance on the training data is generally considered as the most natural choice and genetic algorithms (GA) have been successfully used for this purpose [6].

In this study, the idea of GA based static classifier selection is improved to *vote-based* form and a GA is developed accordingly for NER on the GENIA Corpus v.3.02 [7]. Assuming that the reliability of the predictions differs among classes, the proposed approach is based on dynamic selection of the classifiers by taking into account their individual votes. In particular, a subset of the predictions of each classifier is taken into account during weighted majority voting. Others are considered as unreliable and are not used during combination. In this approach, it is not the classifiers but each one of their predictions that is evaluated as being redundant or not. Although a different classifier set may be used for each test sample, since the proposed scheme does not take into account the behavior of the classifiers in the neighborhood of the corresponding sample, we preferred to name it vote-based rather than dynamic. The proposed approach is also compared to combination of all available classifiers and, GA based static classifier selection where only selected classifiers are allowed to vote, but for all its predictions. Experimental results have shown that the proposed approach improved the full object F-score achieved by the best individual classifier, the ensemble of all classifiers and GA based static classifier selection by 2.5% and 1.3% and 0.6% respectively.

2 Proposed Approach

Assume that there are totally N tags (classes) corresponding to the entities considered in the NER problem under concern including the out class. Let the total number of available classifiers be denoted by M. The solution of the selection problem encoded in the form of a chromosome has N×M entries. First N entries belong to the first classifier. The encoding of a chromosome is illustrated in Fig. 1 where details of only the first classifier are provided for N=11. The entries of each chromosome are randomly initialized to either 0, corresponding to blocking voting or 1, representing allowing voting. In the exemplar chromosome shown in Fig. 1, the first classifier is

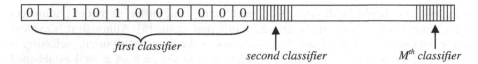

Fig. 1. Encoding of a chromosome

allowed to vote for only second, third and fifth classes. During the reproduction phase, tournament selection is used. The crossover operator is an important tool in GA that allows different chromosomes to share information. In the proposed approach, either uniform or two point crossover method is randomly selected with equal probability. The selected operator is applied with a probability $p_{cross} = 0.7$ to generate two offspring. The mutation operator is applied to each entry of the offspring chromosomes with a probability $p_{mut} = 0.02$, where the entry is randomly replaced by either 0 or 1. In addition, elitism is applied at the end of each iteration where the best 20% of the original population are used to replace those in the offspring producing the lowest fitness. The tournament size is fixed to 40. In the simulation experiments, the population size is selected as 100. This means that 100 different ensemble candidates evolved simultaneously. The algorithm is executed for 1000 iterations.

The fitness of each chromosome is defined as the full object F-score provided by the weighted majority voting type decision combination rule. In this method, the class receiving the maximum combined score is selected as the joint decision. The combined score of a particular class is defined as,

$$f(c_i) = \sum_{m=1}^{M} F_m \times I(m,i) \tag{1}$$

where M denotes the total number of classifiers and F_m denotes the full object F-score of mth classifier. $I(m,i)$ is the entry of the chromosome under concern corresponding to mth classifier and ith class. If it is equal to 1, the classifier contributes to the combined F-score of c_i. The overall algorithm is presented in the next page.

In order to compare the proposed vote-based classifier selection approach with static classifier selection where classifiers that are considered redundant are fully discarded, each chromosome is encoded as a string having M entries, one for each classifier. If the value of a gene is 1, this means that the classifier is selected for being used in the corresponding ensemble. All the design parameters of the algorithm described above including population size, number of iterations, crossover and mutation rate etc. are kept the same. The selected subset of classifiers are combined using weighted voting as before where each selected classifier is allowed to vote for all classes.

The best-fitting solution is obtained using the classifier outputs generated through three-fold cross-validation on the training data. In this method, the training data is initially partitioned into three parts. Each classifier is trained using two parts and then tested with the remaining part. This procedure is repeated three times and the whole set of training data are used for computing the best-fitting solution. During the testing phase, the classifiers are trained using all three parts.

The Genetic Algorithm used for evolving the classifier ensembles.

```
1.  Generate randomly an initial chromosome population of size
    MAX_POPULATION
2.  For each chromosome in the population
    2.1. Apply weighted majority to the selected voters
    2.2. Compute full object F-score as fitness of the chromosome
3.  For generation_index in 1 .. MAX_GENERATION
    3.1. For chromosome_index in 1 .. MAX_POPULATION
         3.1.1. Select two parents from the old population
         3.1.2. Crossover the two parents to produce two offspring
                with probability P_cross
         3.1.3. Mutate each bit of each offspring with probability
                P_mut
         3.1.4. Apply weighted majority to each of the offspring
         3.1.5. Compute full object F-score as fitness of each
                offspring
    3.2. Replace the worst ELIT_SIZE% of the offspring with the best
         chromosomes from the original population to form the new
         population
4.  Select the best chromosome as the resultant ensemble
```

3   Data Set Used and Individual Classifiers

The experiments are conducted on the training and test data set provided for Biomedical Entity Recognition in JNLPBA 2004[1] shared task. The training data used came from GENIA corpus v.3.02 [7] which is a hand annotated corpus of 2000 paper abstracts extracted using MeSH query *human, blood,* and *transcription factor* and is formed by reducing the number of entities from 36 to 5, namely Protein, DNA, RNA, Cell Line, and Cell Type.

Both training and test data sets use IOB2 representation for chunking where every word is tagged with a entity label extended with 'I', representing that the token is inside a named entity chunk, 'O' representing that the token is outside a named entity chunk and 'B', representing that the token is at the beginning of a named entity chunk. Thus for each entity, two different tags are used resulting in 10 tags for the entities and one additional tag for all non-entities. From classification perspective, this translates to a total of 11 classes.

The general purpose text chunker named YamCha[2] (Yet Another Multipurpose Chunk Annotator) that uses TinySVM[3] is used for training the classifier [8]. SVM is a powerful machine learning method that has been used successfully in NER tasks in the biomedical as well as other domains [1], [2]. As it is mentioned in Sect. 1, diversity can be achieved by using different model parameters and features in each ensemble member. Because of this, each classifier is trained using different settings of YamCha parameters such as dimensionality of the polynomial kernel, range of the

---

[1] http://research.nii.ac.jp/~collier/workshops/JNLPBA04st.htm
[2] http://chasen.org/~taku/software/yamcha
[3] http://chasen.org/~taku/software/TinySVM

Table 1. Feature Types and parameters used for training the individual classifiers. The following abbreviations are used; L: Lexical Feature O: Orthographic Feature M: Morphological Feature S: Surface Word Feature W: Context Window, D: Degree of Polynomial Kernel, P: Parse Direction.

Classifier No	L	O	M	S	W	D	P	Precision	Recall	F-score
e_1			X		-2..2	2	B	67.96	68.78	68.37
e_2			X		-2..2	2	F	64.53	66.49	65.50
e_3		X			-2..2	2	B	66.44	67.83	67.12
e_4		X	X		**-3..3**	2	B	**68.51**	**69.75**	**69.13**
e_5		X	X		**-3..3**	2	F	**67.21**	**68.59**	**67.89**
e_6	X				**-3..3**	2	F	**66.75**	**65.90**	**66.32**
e_7	X				**-4..4**	2	B	**68.62**	**66.06**	**67.31**
e_8	X	X	X	X	-2..2	2	B	68.77	70.38	69.57
e_9	X		X		**-2..2**	1	F	**65.01**	**68.69**	**66.80**
e_{10}	X		X		-2..2	3	B	69.61	67.99	68.79
e_{11}	X		X		-3..3	2	B	69.13	69.06	69.10
e_{12}	X				-3..3	2	B	68.54	66.21	67.36
e_{13}	X				-3..3	2	F	66.88	65.54	66.20
e_{14}	X				-4..4	2	B	68.63	65.64	67.10
e_{15}	X				-4..4	2	F	67.10	64.35	65.70
e_{16}	X				-2..2	2	B	66.80	66.00	66.40
e_{17}		X			-2..2	2	B	67.03	68.93	67.97
e_{18}		X			-2..2	2	B	67.16	69.59	68.36
e_{19}			X		-2..2	2	B	68.73	65.89	67.28
e_{20}			X		-2..2	2	B	67.14	67.72	67.43
e_{21}		X			-2..2	2	B	66.70	67.16	66.93
e_{22}	X	X	X	X	-2..2	2	B	67.88	70.32	69.08
e_{23}	X	X	X	X	-2..2	2	B	68.24	70.70	69.45
e_{24}				X	-2..2	2	B	68.29	64.11	66.13
e_{25}		X	X	X	-2..2	2	B	68.15	70.25	69.18
e_{26}			X	X	-2..2	2	B	68.70	68.82	68.76
e_{27}				X	-2..2	2	B	68.51	63.92	66.14
e_{28}	X		X	X	-2..2	2	B	68.65	70.02	69.33
e_{29}	X		X	X	-2..2	2	B	68.52	69.80	69.15
e_{30}				X	-2..2	2	B	68.02	63.30	65.57
e_{31}	X		X	X	-2..2	2	F	64.96	66.95	65.94
e_{32}	**X**	**X**	**X**	**X**	**-2..2**	**2**	**B**	**69.22**	**70.63**	**69.92**
e_{33}	**X**	**X**	**X**	**X**	**-2..2**	**2**	**F**	**65.52**	**68.22**	**66.84**
e_{34}	**X**	**X**	**X**	**X**	**-2..2**	**2**	**B**	**69.40**	**70.60**	**69.99**
e_{35}	**X**	**X**	**X**	**X**	**-2..2**	**2**	**B**	**68.70**	**69.95**	**69.32**
e_{36}		X			-3..3	2	B	68.63	64.11	66.29
e_{37}	X				-3..3	2	B	68.46	66.41	67.42
e_{38}	X				-4..4	2	F	67.23	65.27	66.24
e_{39}	X		X		-2..2	3	F	67.10	65.42	66.25
e_{40}	X		X		-3..3	2	F	67.96	67.70	67.83
e_{41}	X				-3..3	2	B	68.49	64.08	66.21
e_{42}	X				-4..4	2	B	68.74	63.02	65.76
e_{43}	X				-4..4	2	F	67.44	62.35	64.80
e_{44}	X				-4..4	2	B	68.61	63.30	65.85
e_{45}	X				-4..4	2	F	67.61	63.18	65.32
e_{46}	X	X	X	X	-2..2	2	B	68.17	70.55	69.34

context window and direction of parsing as used in [4]. Four different feature types which are frequently used for NER are considered in this study. Lexical features include part of speech tags (POS), base phrase classes, and base noun phrase chunks. Morphological feature used in this study corresponds to the first or last n-grams of an input token. Orthographic feature includes token properties such as the existence of an upper case character or Greek letter in the token or a combination of such properties. Surface words are constructed from training data as described in [4]. The feature types mentioned include many different variations and are used in different combinations as well as in isolation to train the classifiers as illustrated in Table 1. For example classifiers e_{28} and e_{29} use the same feature types but e_{28} uses POS tags whereas e_{29} uses base noun phrase as lexical features, all three other features remaining the same.

Context window of YamCha includes both static and dynamic content. The static content of the context window includes preceding and following tokens and the respective features to be used for classification. The dynamic component of the context window may only include the estimated tags of the preceding tokens. In all classifiers both dynamic and static components are used.

4 Experimental Results and Discussions

The full object F-score of the best individual classifier, ensemble of all classifiers and best-fitting classifier ensembles based on classifier selection are presented in Table 2.

Table 2. Full object F-score of the best individual classifier and classifier ensembles

Classification Scheme	Full Object F-score (in %)
Best Classifier	69.99
Full Ensemble	71.25
Static Classifier Selection	71.71
Vote-based Classifier Selection	72.51

It can be seen in Table 2 that best-fitting ensembles formed using static and vote-based selection schemes surpass both the best individual classifier and the ensemble of all classifiers.

The static classifier selection scheme selected the classifiers e_4, e_5, e_6, e_7, e_9, e_{32}, e_{33}, e_{34}, e_{35} presented using bold characters in Table 1. As seen in Table 1, e_{32} and e_{34} achieves the highest full object F-scores. This shows that the GA based algorithm is successful in selecting the two individually best performing classifiers. Four forward-parsed classifiers (e_5, e_6, e_9, and e_{33}) and five backward-parsed classifiers (e_4, e_7, e_{32}, e_{34}, and e_{35}) are selected. This behavior agrees with the discussion in [4] that training SVMs with different parse directions produce systems that make errors at different boundaries. The forward-parsed classifiers are selected even though their full object F-scores are lower than many backward-parsed classifiers that are not included in the ensemble. However, the selected forward-parsed classifiers are ranked among the top five forward-parsed classifiers in terms of full object F-scores. Thus, when choosing the classifiers that make mistakes at different boundaries, the genetic algorithm favors classifiers with highest full object F-score for each parse direction. It should also be noticed that the algorithm selects 3 forward parsed classifiers together with their backward parsed counterparts for each feature set. The selected classifiers provide the highest score for Precision, Recall, or F-scores for one or more classes. This is inline with the argument presented in [3] that differences in precision and recall contribute to diversity leading to better ensembles.

Four of the selected classifiers utilize all four feature types even though the exact form of the feature for each feature type may differ as explained in Sect. 3. This is reasonable since better ensembles generally include classifiers exploiting a rich set of features [3], [9]. Others that use fewer number of feature types employ a different window size or different degree of polynomial kernel from the four mentioned above. For instance, e_6 and e_7 use only the lexical feature which is successful in providing evidence about the boundaries of biomedical names [3]. However, the window size of e_6 is -3..3 whereas -4..4 is used in e_7.

Table 3. Distribution of vote counts among classifiers

Number of Votes	no vote	1	2	3	4	5	6	7	8	9	10	11
Number of Classifiers	0	3	5	3	7	8	8	6	0	2	4	0

The proposed vote-based selection scheme is shown to improve the full object F-score to 72.51%. The distribution of vote counts among the classifiers is presented in Table 3. As seen in the table, every classifier contributed to the decision of at least one of the classes whereas some classifiers contributed for almost all classes. There is no classifier which votes for all 11 classes. These observations justify the argument that vote-based selection is important for taking into account the individual strengths of the classifiers. Out of 46 classifiers, only e_6, e_7, e_{10}, e_{34}, e_{35}, and e_{36}, vote for 9 or 10 classes. There are 20 classifiers that vote for more than 5 classes. This set of classifiers includes 7 of the individual classifiers selected by the static classifier selection approach. The classifiers e_4 and e_5 that are selected by the static approach contribute to the decision of 4 and 5 classes respectively. Moreover, 3 classifiers have only one vote. These classifiers would normally be excluded when static classifier selection approach is considered.

5 Concluding Remarks and Future Work

In this study, a vote-based classifier selection scheme is proposed and tested on JNLPBA data. In this approach, instead of eliminating some classifiers permanently, each is allowed to vote for a subset of its predictions. Indeed, simulation experiments have shown that the classifiers which are removed from the ensemble by the static classifier selection approach contribute to decision making process for a subset of their predictions. As seen in Table 3, majority of the classifiers vote for approximately half of their predictions. That is, 29 classifiers vote for 4 to 7 different predictions. On the two extremes, either voting for almost all or voting for only few predictions, there are much fewer classifiers. In other words, there are much fewer classifiers that can either be considered as redundant or reliable for all of its predictions which is the fundamental assumption in static classifier selection. As a matter of fact, the improvement provided by the vote-based classifier selection approach can be attributed to its ability in using strengths and avoiding weaknesses of all ensemble members. The proposed approach can be further improved. Our future work will include modifying the vote-independent weights of each classifier. Instead of using full object F-scores, vote-specific F-scores obtained using the validation data can be utilized for weighting the contribution of each classifier.

Acknowledgements

This work is supported by the TRNC Ministry of Education and Culture.

References

1. Collier, N., Takeuchi, K.: Comparison of Character-level and Part of Speech Features for Name Recognition in Biomedical Texts. Journal of Biomedical Informatics 37, 423–435 (2004)
2. Zhou G., Zhang J., Su J., Shen D., Tan C.: Recognizing Names in biomedical texts: a machine learning approach. Bioinformatics, pp. 1178–1190 (2003)
3. Zhou, G., Shen, D., Zhang, J., Su, J., Tan, S.: Recognition of Protein/Gene Names from Text using an Ensemble of Classifiers. BMC Bioinformatics 6(Suppl. 1), S7 (2005)
4. Dimililer, N., Varoglu, E.: Recognizing Biomedical Named Entities using SVMs: Improving Recognition Performance with a Minimal Set of Features. In: Bremer, E.G., Hakenberg, J., Han, E.-H(S.), Berrar, D., Dubitzky, W. (eds.) KDLL 2006. LNCS (LNBI), vol. 3886, pp. 53–67. Springer, Heidelberg (2006)
5. Krogh, A., Vedelsby, J.: Neural network Ensembles, Cross Validation and Active Learning. In: Touretzky, D.S., Tesauro, G., Leen, T.K. (eds.) Advances in Neural Information Processing Systems, pp. 231–238. MIT Press, Cambridge, MA (1995)
6. Ruta, D., Gabrys, B.: Classifier Selection for Majority Voting. Special issue of the journal of Information Fusion on Diversity in Multiple Classifier Systems 6(1), 63–81 (2005)
7. Ohta, T., Tatishi, Y., Mima, H., Tsujii, J.: The GENIA corpus: an annotated research abstract corpus in the molecular biology domain. In: Proc. 2nd Intl. Conf. on Human Language Technology Research, San Diego, CA, pp. 82–86 (2002)
8. Kudo, T., Matsumoto, Y.: Chunking with Support Vector Machines. In: Proceedings of Second Meeting of North American Chapter of the Association for Computational Linguistics(NAACL) pp. 192–199 (2001)
9. Florian, R., Ittycheriah, A., Jing, H., Zhang, T.: Named entity recognition through classifier combination. In: Proceedings of the 7th Conference on Natural Language Learning At HLT-NAACL 2003, vol. 4 (Edmonton, Canada). Association for Computational Linguistics, Morristown, NJ, pp. 168–171 (2003)

Boundary Shape Recognition Using Accumulated Length and Angle Information

Marçal Rusiñol[1], Philippe Dosch[2], and Josep Lladós[1]

[1] Computer Vision Center, Dept. Ciències de la Computació, Edifici O, Universitat Autònoma de Barcelona, 08193 Bellaterra (Barcelona), Spain
[2] Loria UMR 7503, 615, rue du jardin botanique, B.P. 101, 54602 Villers-lès-Nancy Cedex, France

Abstract. In this paper we present a method to recognize shapes by analyzing a polygonal approximation of their boundaries. The method is independent of the used approximation method since its recognition strategy does not rely on the number of segments composing the shape. Length and turning angle information are extracted from the chain of segments. The comparison method is invariant to scale, translation and some occlusions of the extracted contour. A simple pre-processing method, also based on arc-length features, is presented to be used as a coarse fitting method to determine angle rotation and as a first filter to eliminate non pertinent candidates.

1 Introduction

Content based image retrieval is one of the topics of interest in the computer vision field which nowadays is at its very peak, due to the growth in the last years of the amount of stored graphical information. For this kind of data, underlying analysis processes mainly lie on graphics recognition, allowing then classification of the images, typically in terms of available symbols. From a general viewpoint, several kind of recognition approaches can be involved, according to data representation. Bitmap images are usually analyzed with statistical methods, which are time-consuming and quite accurate, but can also be analyzed with structural methods, faster but requiring a pre-vectorization step. In the context of content based image retrieval, the last approach is usually preferred, as the amount of considered data implies the use of efficient processes.

One of the most important visual features when classifying images is shape of the represented objects and subsequently a lot of literature deal with object recognition by shape. Zhang and Lu review in [9] shape representation and description techniques. A great part of the existing methods focus on the contour to represent the shape. Those contour-based descriptors are usually classified as statistical or structural approaches. Focusing in structural descriptors, for reasons explained above, a prior polygonal approximation of the contour is required, yielding a description of the shape in terms of segments and structural relationship between them. From these data, Stein and Medioni in [5] extract a feature vector achieving a more global viewpoint than a pairwise segment comparison.

J. Martí et al. (Eds.): IbPRIA 2007, Part II, LNCS 4478, pp. 210–217, 2007.
© Springer-Verlag Berlin Heidelberg 2007

But, since in the literature we can find many strategies to perform a raster-to-vector conversion, and by now it does not exist any "perfect" algorithm, as argue Tombre *et al.* in [6], it is interesting to define a method to discriminate shapes between them, independently of the used approximation method, robust with respect to the numbers of resulting segments and with respect to the generated artifacts.

To give an example, Rosin and West method [3], has the advantage that it does not use any parameter to compute the approximation. This generality has its negative part, since in the high curvature points, the method tend to over-segment the shape. On the other hand, Wall and Danielsson method [7], use a threshold to determine at which points the curvature of the shape is high enough to cut the pixel list into several segments. But this method has to be well tuned to provide accurate results. Even if both strategies perform good approximations, they can result in very different segment chains, in particular for the number of segments of these chains. A method which aim to be independent of the approximation strategy has to be independent of the number of segments composing the shape. Most of methods try to counteract the effect of the cardinality of the segment chain by re-sampling the polygonal approximation at extremal points, as in [2,8]. Our presented method aims to be invariant to the number of segments and consequently of the approximation method.

The key idea of the proposed method is that two shapes are similar if, starting from a reference segment, and covering a certain length, we have turned the same angle in both shapes. Thus, accumulated lengths and accumulated turning angles are used as feature vectors to describe a shape, which aims to achieve cardinality independence of the analyzed segment chains.

The remainder of this paper is organized as follows: we will introduce in the next section how we compute a coarse matching between two shapes. This first step will be used as a pre-processing method to determine angle rotations between shapes and as a first filter if the two shapes are found too different. In section 3, the matching method is presented, using accumulated length and turning angle as features to describe a given shape. We provide the experimental results in section 4. Finally a summary and discussion of extensions and future work is presented in section 5.

2   Coarse Shape Fitting: Undoing Rotation

Given a closed contour of a shape $S = \{s_1, ..., s_n\}$ polygonally approximated with n segments and total perimeter length $|S|$, we encode all the segments by a tuple of numbers (l_i, ϕ_i), where l_i denotes the length of the segment s_i and ϕ_i denotes the angle between s_i and s_{i-1} in the counterclockwise direction.

We compute a vector of accumulated lengths, normalized with the total perimeter of the shape.

$$\ell(i) = \frac{1}{|S|} \times \sum_{k=1}^{i} l_k \quad where \ 1 \leq i \leq n \tag{1}$$

We then define a mapping function f which assign the corresponding turned angle ϕ_i at each value of $\ell(i)$.

$$f(\ell(i)) = \phi_i \tag{2}$$

Sudden direction changes in the analyzed shape result in pulses in f arc-length function which act as discriminative key points to fit two shapes. As the number of segments of two shapes to compare can be completely different, we need to define a method which is independent of the number of segments. An equally sampling of $\ell(i) \in [0, 1]$ is done to compare a couple of vectors of the same size.

However, since we compute a vector of accumulated length, f values has to be shifted in the x axis depending on the reference segment choice. Given two shapes to compare, a normalized cross correlation can be used as a fast method for template matching of the two vectors, and then find the correct shift between two segment lists where the maximum correlation value has been reached. Experimentally we find that using only a 75% of the number of segments composing a shape as sample rate is enough to find correct shift between two shapes. We can find an example of shape fitting to determine angle rotation in Fig. 1.

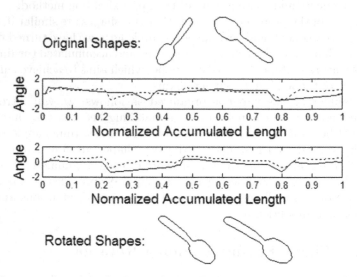

Fig. 1. Shapes and arc-length plots before and after the fitting process. A normalized cross correlation is computed between the two functions to determine the shift between them, thus normalizing the shapes to a certain rotation.

But polygonal approximation methods usually introduce some small noisy segments, which may not seem very important since they have small lengths, but may have important turned angle values. The presence of these small segments results in pulses of elevated values in the f function. Even though this possible presence of noise, the method could be used as a pre-processing step to identify a rotation parameter to correctly choice a reference starting segment, thus determining the rotation between two shapes. The method is also used as a first filter when compared shapes have completely different representations. Let us further detail in the next section how can we improve the presented method to be used for boundary shape recognition.

3   Shape Matching

Following the same idea than the presented coarse fitting method, we describe shapes in terms of accumulated length and turning angles. To avoid the influence of the noise introduced by the presence of small segments, we use accumulated turning angles instead of the mapping function to guarantee more stability.

$$\Theta(i) = \sum_{k=1}^{i} \phi_k \tag{3}$$

Now, the idea of this shape comparison is to use the ℓ values to know how many segments are necessary in both shapes to achieve a certain covered length and then look if the turned angles Θ are close or not. Let us further detail how these shape matching is performed.

Given two shapes to compare $S_1 = \{s_{11}, ..., s_{1n}\}$ and $S_2 = \{s_{21}, ..., s_{2m}\}$, having $n <= m$, we compute their ℓ and Θ feature vectors. For all the segments of S_1 we check how many segments of S_2 are necessary to achieve a similar length.

$$L(i) = arg \min_{1 \leq j \leq m} (abs(\ell_1(i) - \ell_2(j))) \tag{4}$$

Given a certain number i of segments of the shape S_1, $\ell_1(i)$ is the total covered length from the starting segment up to the ith segment, $L(i)$ is then defined as the number of segments of S_2 required to achieve the closest covered length. To be more tolerant to the presence of small segments which can distort the distance between accumulated angles in a given accumulated length, we denote as $\widetilde{L(i)}$ the segment set containing $L(i)$ and its two adjacent segments, accumulating only the minimum distance between $\Theta_1(k)$ and $\Theta_2(L(k-1))$, $\Theta_2(L(k))$ and $\Theta_2(L(k+1))$. To give a distance between the two shapes, we look if at similar lengths, we have a similar turned angle. The distance $d(S_1, S_2)$ between the two shapes S_1 and S_2 is computed as follows

$$d(S_1, S_2) = \sum_{k=1}^{n} \min \left(\delta(\Theta_1(k), \Theta_2(\widetilde{L(k)})) \right) \tag{5}$$

Being $\delta(\phi, \theta)$ the difference between two turned angles considering that angles close to 0 and 2π must have very low difference, and thus computed as a distance in the trigonometric circle

$$\delta(\phi, \theta) = \sqrt{(\cos \phi - \cos \theta)^2 + (\sin \phi - \sin \theta)^2} \tag{6}$$

We can appreciate in Fig. 2 how the turned angles plots are matched between the two shapes of different scale and number of segments. Even if the distance between the two resulting angle vectors $\Theta_1(k)$ and $\Theta_2(\widetilde{L(k)})$ is elevated, we can see that the trend of both of them is almost the same.

Better recognition results are reached when the distance is formulated more accurately. DTW (Dynamic Time Warping) is a well-known method used in speech recognition field that measures similarity between two sequences which may be shifted in time, involving the alignment between two sequences with minimum edit cost. The use of this kind of edit distances [4], can fix the remaining shifts between angles giving better results than a bin to bin comparison of sequences. But a simple analysis of the slope and variations of the resulting functions yields acceptable results.

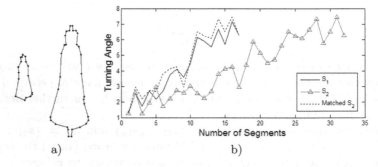

Fig. 2. Angle fitting. (a) S_1 and S_2. (b) Turning angle plots. The influence of the number of segments composing the shape has been avoided, and the resulting turning angle plots are comparable.

We can see that the presented method can find a matching between close shapes undergoing some noise, scaling and different number of segments, since the used features are based on the accumulation of lengths and angles. The invariance to rotation is not guaranteed by the matching method itself because as all the used features are accumulated metrics, the method is very dependent on the first segment choice. But the previous coarse fitting method which use almost the same computed features makes possible the use of the presented method with no significant complexity addition.

4   Experimental Results

To test the method, we use the MPEG silhouette database consisting of 1400 images grouped in 70 different shape classes. In Table 1, we show the resulting ten most similar images when querying a given shape against the whole database. As we can appreciate, the retrieved images are usually components of the queried class, or at least, for the false positives, are quite visually similar. The number of segments composing the queries and the results are also shown, and we can

Table 1. Sorted ten similar symbols. (Number of segments composing the shape approximation).

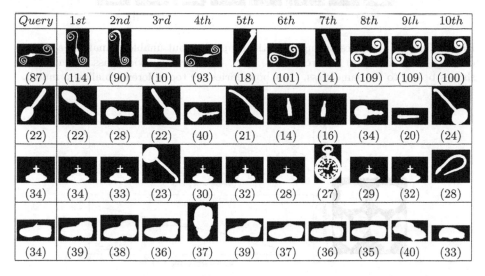

Query	1st	2nd	3rd	4th	5th	6th	7th	8th	9th	10th
(87)	(114)	(90)	(10)	(93)	(18)	(101)	(14)	(109)	(109)	(100)
(22)	(22)	(28)	(22)	(40)	(21)	(14)	(16)	(34)	(20)	(24)
(34)	(34)	(33)	(23)	(30)	(32)	(28)	(27)	(29)	(32)	(28)
(34)	(39)	(38)	(36)	(37)	(39)	(37)	(36)	(35)	(40)	(33)

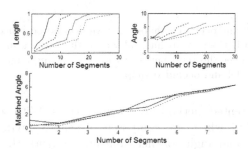

Fig. 3. Shape matching depending on the number of segments. The matched angles have the same trend independently of the number of segments composing the shape (8, 14, 20 and 28).

appreciate that similar shapes with a significant difference of segments can be matched. In [1] different shape descriptors as CSS, wavelet representations of contours, Zernike moments, etc. are tested against this database, performing good recognition tasks. All these descriptors are pixel-based, and thus can not be compared with the presented method which aims to discriminate polygonal approximations of graphical symbols by a fast and simple representation.

To see if the method is really tolerant to changes in the number of segments composing a shape, we compute polygonal approximations of a heart shape at different scales, resulting thus in a different number of segments, going from 8 to 28 segments. In Fig. 3 we can appreciate that the resulting turning angle functions are matched in an acceptable way. Notice that the shape with less segments is always the one taken as model, thus introducing some noisy results if the approximation is too rough.

Fig. 4. Couples of shapes belonging to the same class but unable to match. (a) Beetle class. (b) Deer class. (c) Squared-device class. (d) Circular-device class. Even if these shapes belong to the same class, their boundaries are too different to allow a match.

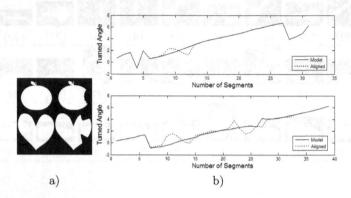

Fig. 5. Matching partially occluded shapes. (a) Model and occluded shapes. (b) Turning angle plots. Even if there is an interval where the turning angle does not fit,the method is able to recover the tend between the two turning angles giving acceptable distances between model and occluded shape.

However, the presented method has its limitations. With some classes which can seem similar, but which are composed of shapes having important local distortions of length and angles of their contour segments, the method is unable to find the similarity between objects of these classes as most of contour-based approaches. Some examples are shown in Fig. 4. But the method is still tolerant to slight changes in the contour due to occlusions, as shown in Fig. 5 were we can appreciate that the resulting turned angles are totally matched in the part of contour not affected by the occlusion.

5   Conclusion

In this paper we presented a method for shape recognition based on accumulated length and angular information. Having a polygonal approximation of the contours, two shapes are considered similar if starting from a reference segment and covering a certain length, the accumulated turned angle is also similar. A method based on a similar idea is also presented as a pre-processing step to act as a first filter when shapes are found completely different, and to determine the correct reference segment guaranteeing invariance to rotation.

Even if a lot of shape descriptors based on an approximation of the contour exist in the literature achieving great recognition rates, we consider that is very important to define description techniques able to maintain its performance in despite of the approximation method used. Most existing methods seem to be designed *ad hoc* for an approximation method in particular, or at least need a tuning of parameters depending on the number of segments which composes a shape. The use of accumulated metrics allow to be invariant of the cardinality of the segment chains encoding a shape. However, the use of accumulated length and angle has its drawback, since the method is dependent on a good reference segment choice. It would be interesting to further investigate how to provide rotation invariance without the need of a pre-processing step.

Acknowledgments

This work has been partially supported by the Spanish project TIN2006-15694-C02-02, the Integrated project HF2004-0188 and the French project SymbolREC INRIA équipe associée. We would also thank Alicia Fornés for her implementation of DTW.

References

1. Latecki, L.J., Lakamper, R., Eckhardt, T.: Shape descriptors for non-rigid shapes with a single closed contour. In: IEEE Conference on Computer Vision and Pattern Recognition, Proceedings, vol. 1, pp. 424–429 (2000)
2. Nishida, H.: Structural feature indexing for retrieval of partially visible shapes. Pattern Recognition 35(1), 55–67 (2002)
3. Rosin, P.L., West, G.A.: Segmentation of Edges into Lines and Arcs. Image and Vision Computing 7(2), 109–114 (1989)
4. Sankoff, D., Kruskal, J.B.: Time Warps, String Edits, and Macromolecules: The Theory and Practice of Sequence Comparison. Addison-Wesley, London, UK (1983)
5. Stein, F., Medioni, G.: Structural Indexing: Efficient 2D Object Recognition. IEEE Transactions on Pattern Analysis and Machine Intelligence 14(12), 1198–1204 (1992)
6. Tombre, K., Ah-Soon, C., Dosch, P., Masini, G., Tabbone, S.: Stable and Robust Vectorization: How to Make the Right Choices. In: Chhabra, A.K., Dori, D. (eds.) GREC 1999. LNCS, vol. 1941, pp. 3–18. Springer, Heidelberg (2000)
7. Wall, K., Danielsson, P.E.: A fast sequential method for polygonal approximation of digitized curves. Computer Vision, Graphics, and Image Processing 28(2), 220–227 (1984)
8. Wolfson, H.J.: On curve matching. IEEE Transactions on Pattern Analysis and Machine Intelligence 12(5), 483–489 (1990)
9. Zhang, D., Lu, G.: Review of shape representation and description techniques. Pattern recognition 37(1), 1–19 (2004)

Extracting Average Shapes from Occluded Non-rigid Motion

Alessio Del Bue

Institute for Systems and Robotics, Instituto Superior Tecnico, Lisbon, Portugal

Abstract. This paper presents a method to efficiently estimate average 3-D shapes from non-rigid motion in the case of missing data. Such a shape can be further used to accomplish full reconstruction of deformable objects and registration of non-rigid shapes. The approach is based firstly on a power method which linearly provides an initial estimate of the 3-D structure and motion components of the object shape. Secondly, non-linear optimisation is used to refine the initial linear estimation. Tests on both real and synthetic sequences show the procedure effectiveness in dealing with different degrees of occlusions in the measurements.

1 Introduction

Recently the inference of the 3-D structure of a deforming body viewed by an uncalibrated camera has attracted increasing interest. In a Structure from Motion (SfM) domain, non-rigid shapes have posed new problems since they violate the rigidity constraints on which previous SfM methods strongly rely. Most of the model-free approaches to non-rigid SfM available nowadays are based either on closed-form solutions [12], assuming pre-specified shape priors, or iterative non-linear optimisation techniques [5,1,11], requiring an appropriate initialisation in order to converge. In the latter case, average shape and motion [9] have experimentally proven to be a successful initialisation to such tasks and they can be easily computed when the full trajectory of a point lying on the deforming body is available.

However, in the case of missing data affecting the trajectories (i.e. a point being occluded for some frames) a solution for the average shape is not currently available. Estimation of structure and motion from occluded data (see [3] for a review) is an essential task for most practical applications given the difficulty to obtain complete trajectories. At this end, the solution proposed here is an iterative power method which can estimate average shapes in the case of missing data and its reliability is assessed in a full 3-D reconstruction task for deforming objects. The approach is based on the notion of average shape introduced in [9] which penalizes in a certainty-reweighted scheme the non-rigidity of trajectories. This method can be extended by reformulating power methods for SfM [7] to include the notion of non-rigidity of a trajectory and extend it to the case of missing data.

In detail, the paper firstly introduces the non-rigid factorization framework and the definition of average shape (Section 2). Then, power methods for SfM are presented in Section 3 for the case of rigidly moving objects. The new approach with missing entry is explained in Section 4 and experiments (Section 5) show its effectiveness on synthetic test and on a face modelling task.

J. Martí et al. (Eds.): IbPRIA 2007, Part II, LNCS 4478, pp. 218–225, 2007.

2 Non-rigid Structure from Motion

2.1 A Factorization Approach to Deformable Modelling

Tomasi and Kanade's factorization algorithm [10] has been reformulated to the case of non-rigid 3-D structure [2]. A linear approximation of a set of K basis shapes S_k is used to describe a 3-D time varying shape X such that:

$$X = \sum_{k=1}^{K} l_k S_k \qquad X, S_k \in \Re^{3 \times P} \quad l_k \in \Re \tag{1}$$

Each basis shapes S_k represent the mode of deformations of the deforming body and they are parameterised as a $3 \times P$ matrix which contains the 3-D locations of P object points for that particular mode of deformation. Assuming an orthographic camera model the shape is then projected onto an image frame i giving P image points:

$$W_i = \begin{bmatrix} \mathbf{w}_{i1} \dots \mathbf{w}_{iP} \end{bmatrix} = R_i \left(\sum_{k=1}^{K} l_{ik} S_k \right) \tag{2}$$

where each $\mathbf{w}_{ij} = [u_{ij} v_{ij}]^T$ with $j = 1 \dots P$ contains the horizontal and vertical image coordinates of the point – referred to the centroid of the object – and R_i encodes the first two rows of the rotation matrix for a specific frame i. If all P points are tracked in F image frames we may construct the measurement matrix W which can be expressed as:

$$W = \begin{bmatrix} \mathbf{w}_{11} \dots \mathbf{w}_{1P} \\ \vdots \qquad \vdots \\ \mathbf{w}_{F1} \dots \mathbf{w}_{FP} \end{bmatrix} = \begin{bmatrix} l_{11}R_1 \ \dots \ l_{1K}R_1 \\ \vdots \qquad \vdots \\ l_{F1}R_F \dots l_{FK}R_F \end{bmatrix} \begin{bmatrix} S_1 \\ \vdots \\ S_K \end{bmatrix} = MS. \tag{3}$$

Clearly, the rank of the measurement matrix is constrained to be at most $3K$, where K is the number of deformations. This rank constraint can be exploited to factorize the measurement matrix into a motion matrix $\tilde{M}$ and a shape matrix $\tilde{S}$ by truncating the SVD of W to rank $3K$. However, this factorization is not unique since any invertible $3K \times 3K$ matrix Q can be inserted in the decomposition leading to the alternative factorization: $W = (\tilde{M}Q)(Q^{-1}\tilde{S})$. The focal problem to solve in non-rigid factorization schemes is to find the Q that renders the appropriate replicated block structure of the motion matrix and that removes the affine ambiguity, upgrading the reconstruction to a metric one.

2.2 Extracting Average Shapes from Deformations

Based on the framework described in the previous section, Kim & Hong [9] recently introduced a measure called the Degree of Non-rigidity (*DoN*) to estimate the deviation of a deformable point from its average position. This measure can in turn be used to extract an average shape using an iterative certainty reweighted scheme. If the average 3-D shape of a time varying shape $X_i = [X_{i1} \dots X_{iP}]$ is given by $\hat{X} = [\hat{X}_1 \dots \hat{X}_P]$ the *DoN* for point j is defined as:

$$DoN_j = \sum_{i=1}^{F} (\mathbf{X}_{ij} - \hat{\mathbf{X}}_j)(\mathbf{X}_{ij} - \hat{\mathbf{X}}_j)^T. \tag{4}$$

The 2-D projection C_j of the DoN will be thus given by:

$$C_j = \sum_{i=1}^{F} R_i(\mathbf{X}_{ij} - \hat{\mathbf{X}}_j)(\mathbf{X}_{ij} - \hat{\mathbf{X}}_j)^T R_i^T = \sum_{i=1}^{F}(\mathbf{w}_{ij} - \hat{\mathbf{w}}_{ij})(\mathbf{w}_{ij} - \hat{\mathbf{w}}_{ij})^T \quad (5)$$

where $\mathbf{w}_{ij}$ are the image coordinates of point j at frame i and $\hat{\mathbf{w}}_{ij}$ are the coordinates of its projected mean shape. While the DoN cannot be computed without an estimation of the mean 3-D shape, the value of its projection can be estimated directly from image measurements.

An initial estimate of the projected 2-D mean shapes $\hat{\mathbf{w}}_{ij}$ could be given simply by the first basis shape S_1 (as in equation (3)) which could be computed with a rank-3 approximation $SVD_3(\mathbb{W}) = \hat{\mathbb{M}}\hat{\mathbb{S}}$. The projected deviation from the mean for all the points would then be defined by $\{\mathbf{w}_{ij} - \hat{\mathbf{w}}_{ij}\} = \mathbb{W} - \hat{\mathbb{M}}\hat{\mathbb{S}}$. However, a straight application of a rank-3 factorization over the first basis component does not produce an accurate measure of C_j as showed in [9]. To adjust the covariances, the average shape and C_j are iteratively estimated until convergence. However, the procedure is unable to deal with the case of missing data affecting the measurements. We will show in the next section how power methods can efficiently solve this issue.

3   Power Methods for Structure from Motion

SfM algorithms based on factorization require an initial decomposition of the motion M and structure matrix S given the data W. In this context, power methods were introduced with the name *powerfactorization* by Schaffalitzky and Hartley [7] to efficiently factorise rank-constrained image measurements. This approach is an alternation method which iteratively estimates M and S by simply executing multiplications and matrices inverse. The update rules at iteration q are given by [7]:

$$M_q = WS_{q-1}(S_{q-1}^T S_{q-1})^{-1}$$

$$S_q = (M_q^T M_q)^{-1} M_q^T W \qquad (6)$$

They are a straightforward derivation from the orthogonal power method [6] which convergence rate depends on the ratio of the dominant singular values of W. In the case of an affine camera viewing a moving rigid body, the update rules (6) can be modified to account for the geometrical properties of the measurements. For each frame $i = 1 \cdots F$, the projection of a point $j = 1 \cdots P$ can be expressed as:

$$\mathbf{w}_{ij} = A_i \mathbf{X}_j + \mathbf{a}_i \qquad (7)$$

where A_i is a 2×3 camera projection matrix, $\mathbf{X}_j$ a 3-vector of the 3-D coordinates and $\mathbf{a}_i$ a 2-vector of the affine camera translation. In a more compact form, equation (7) can be rewritten for every point at each frame as:

$$W_i = \begin{bmatrix} A_i | \mathbf{a}_i \end{bmatrix} \begin{bmatrix} \mathbf{X}_1 & \cdots & \mathbf{X}_P \\ 1 & \cdots & 1 \end{bmatrix} = M_i \begin{bmatrix} \mathbf{X} \\ \mathbf{1}^T \end{bmatrix} \qquad (8)$$

where $\mathbf{1}$ is a P-vector of ones. Finally, the global expression for each frame can be written as:

$$W = \begin{bmatrix} W_1 \\ \vdots \\ W_F \end{bmatrix} = \begin{bmatrix} [A_1|a_1] \\ \vdots \\ [A_F|a_F] \end{bmatrix} \begin{bmatrix} X \\ 1^T \end{bmatrix} = [A|a] \begin{bmatrix} X \\ 1^T \end{bmatrix} = MS \qquad (9)$$

The algorithm for extracting the affine motion and structure of a rigid object can be summarized as follows:

- Initialize X_0 with random entries.
- Compute the $2F \times 4$ update of M_q given equation (6).
- Extract the $2F \times 1$ measurements centroid a_q such that $M_q = [A_q|a_q]$.
- Compute the $3 \times P$ update of X_q such that: $X_q = (A_q^T A_q)^{-1} A_q^T (W - T_q)$ where $(W - T_q)$ are the centered coordinates and $T_q = a_q \mathbf{1}_{1 \times P}$

---

4   Average Shape Estimation with Missing Data

4.1   Power Iterations and Degree of Non-rigidity

In the case of affine estimation of average shape $\hat{S}$ and motion $\hat{M}$, strongly non-rigid trajectories (which in turn provide high covariances C_j) are penalized in the estimation of the average components. The estimation task can be recast in the minimisation of a cost function χ such that:

$$\chi = \sum_{i,j} (\mathbf{w}_{ij} - \hat{M}_i \bar{\mathbf{X}}_j)^T C_j^{-1} (\mathbf{w}_{ij} - \hat{M}_i \bar{\mathbf{X}}_j) \qquad (10)$$

where $\bar{\mathbf{X}}_j$ contains the the homogeneous coordinate for the average point such that $\bar{\mathbf{X}}_j = [\hat{\mathbf{X}}_j^T \; 1]^T$. Minimizing χ can be carried out with a minor reformulation of the power method [7]. In brief, each matrix C_j^{-1} can be factored as $C_j^{-1} = B_j^T B_j$ giving:

$$\chi = \sum_{i,j} (\mathbf{w}_{ij} - \hat{M}_i \bar{\mathbf{X}}_j)^T B_j^T B_j (\mathbf{w}_{ij} - \hat{M}_i \bar{\mathbf{X}}_j) = \sum_{i,j} \| B_j \mathbf{w}_{ij} - B_j \hat{M}_i \bar{\mathbf{X}}_j \|^2 \qquad (11)$$

Notice the similarity with equation (6) which hints to a solution of the minimization of (10) with a power approach. In order to obtain the two updates rules for motion and structure we can rewrite (11) such that:

$$\chi = \sum_{i,j} \| B_j \mathbf{w}_{ij} - B_j \tilde{X}_j \tilde{\mathbf{m}}_i \|^2 \qquad (12)$$

with:

$$\tilde{X}_j = \begin{bmatrix} \bar{\mathbf{X}}_j^T & 0 \\ 0 & \bar{\mathbf{X}}_j^T \end{bmatrix} \text{ and } \tilde{\mathbf{m}}_i = [\mathbf{m}_{1i}^T \; \mathbf{m}_{2i}^T]^T \qquad (13)$$

where $\mathbf{m}_{1i}^T$ and $\mathbf{m}_{2i}^T$ are respectively the first and second 4×1 rows of $\hat{\mathsf{M}}_i$. Given the quadratic costs (11) and (12) we can express the power updates for the motion as:

$$\tilde{\mathbf{m}}_i = (\sum_j \tilde{\mathbf{X}}_j^T \mathsf{B}_j^T \mathsf{B}_j \tilde{\mathbf{X}}_j)^{-1} \sum_j \tilde{\mathbf{X}}_j^T \mathsf{B}_j^T \mathsf{B}_j \mathbf{w}_{ij} = (\sum_j \tilde{\mathbf{X}}_j^T \mathsf{C}_j^{-1} \tilde{\mathbf{X}}_j)^{-1} \sum_j \tilde{\mathbf{X}}_j^T \mathsf{C}_j^{-1} \mathbf{w}_{ij} \quad (14)$$

After rearranging $\tilde{\mathbf{m}}_i \mapsto \hat{\mathsf{M}}_i = [\mathsf{A}_i | \mathbf{a}_i]$ we obtain:

$$\hat{\mathbf{X}}_j = (\sum_i \mathsf{A}_i^T \mathsf{C}_j^{-1} \mathsf{A}_i)^{-1} \sum_i \mathsf{A}_i^T \mathsf{C}_j^{-1} (\mathbf{w}_{ij} - \mathbf{a}_i) \quad (15)$$

where $\mathbf{a}_i$ is the overall translation component as defined in (9). Once the estimates for the average $\hat{\mathsf{M}}$ and $\hat{\mathsf{S}}$ are available, C_j is update by equation (5).

4.2   The Missing Data Case

We can now assume that some points are not visible in some frames due to occlusion. In order to include missing data, we can modify the power update equations in (14) and (15) to simply not include the equations regarding the missing entries giving:

$$\tilde{\mathbf{m}}_i = (\sum_j \tilde{\mathbf{X}}_j^T \mathsf{C}_j^{-1} \tilde{\mathbf{X}}_j)^{-1} \sum_j \tilde{\mathbf{X}}_j^T \mathsf{C}_j^{-1} Z_{ij} \mathbf{w}_{ij} \quad (16)$$

$$\hat{\mathbf{X}}_j = (\sum_i \mathsf{A}_i^T \mathsf{C}_j^{-1} \mathsf{A}_i)^{-1} \sum_i \mathsf{A}_i^T \mathsf{C}_j^{-1} Z_{ij} (\mathbf{w}_{ij} - \mathbf{a}_i) \quad (17)$$

where Z_{ij} is a scalar which is zero whenever a point is missing and one otherwise. The updates have the property of efficiently estimating the centroid at each frame $\mathbf{a}_i$ since the measurement matrix of missing data may be not mean-centered. Schematically, the algorithm can be outlined as follows[1]:

- Initialize X with random entries.
- Compute the $2F \times 4$ update of $\hat{\mathsf{M}}_i$ for $i = 1 \cdots F$ given equation (16).
- Given $\hat{\mathsf{M}}_i = [\mathsf{A}_i | \mathbf{a}_i]$, extract the measurements centroid $\mathbf{a}_i$.
- Compute the update of the average 3-D structure with (17).
- Recompute $\mathsf{C}_j = \sum_{i=1}^F Z_{ij} (\mathbf{w}_{ij} - \mathbf{a}_i - \mathsf{A}_i \hat{\mathbf{X}}_j)(\mathbf{w}_{ij} - \mathbf{a}_i - \mathsf{A}_i \hat{\mathbf{X}}_j)^T$.
- Iterate until convergence.

A metric update of the average shape can be then obtained in the case of orthographic [10] and weak or para-perspective cameras [8] by computing the correct 3×3 transformation Q for the average shape.

4.3   Non-linear Optimisation and Non-rigid SfM

A full deformable 3-D reconstruction as presented in Section 2.1 can be successfully computed linearly only when particular assumptions over the data are given and when

---

[1] For clarity we drop the iteration subscript q.

the full trajectories are available. For instance, in [12] the authors proved the existence of a unique solution and a closed form algorithm when K independent 3-D shapes can be identified in the measured data. On the other hand, a more general solution consists in performing non-linear optimisation [5,1,11] by minimizing a cost function which reflects the full deformable model as presented in equation (3) giving:

$$\min_{R_i S_{kj} l_{ik}} \sum_{i,j} Z_{ij} \parallel \mathbf{w}_{ij} - \hat{\mathbf{x}}_{ij} \parallel^2 = \min_{R_i S_{kj} l_{ik}} \sum_{i,j} Z_{ij} \parallel \mathbf{w}_{ij} - (R_i \sum_k l_{ik} S_{kj}) \parallel^2 \quad (18)$$

where $\mathbf{S}_{kj}$ is the 3×1 basis for the point j such that $S_k = [\mathbf{S}_{k1} \cdots \mathbf{S}_{kP}]$. Again, the least-squares entries for the missing data are omitted. Initialisation of the model parameters are provided by the average shape computed with our power approach.

5 Experiments

5.1 Synthetic Data

The proposed power approach was first validated using randomly generated synthetic data of a deforming shape. The 3-D bodies were generated by firstly sampling the first basis shape S_1 over the surface of a sphere. The following basis $S_2 \ldots S_K$, which represent the modes of deformation of the body, were generated randomly. In order to obtain a given deformation at frame i, the configuration weights $l_{i1} \ldots l_{iK}$ were computed by fitting 4-order polynomials to random samples, this gave more regular deformation rather then erratic motion. The computed 3-D shapes are then normalized to obtain a specific ratio of deformation defined as $\frac{\sum_{i=1}^{F} \| \sum_{k=2}^{K} l_{ik} S_k \|^2}{\sum_{i=1}^{F} \| l_{i1} S_1 \|^2}$ which is fixed to 0.25. The final measurement matrix W is obtained by projecting each 3-D non-rigid shape onto the image plane by means of random orthographic cameras Finally, points are eliminated given different ratios of missing data.

The algorithm's performances were tested in providing a meaningful initialisation to the optimisation problem as defined in Section 4.3. Firstly, the method was less likely to converge when the iterative re-weighting C_j was not included in the power steps showing that the *DON* was effectively helping the convergence. The overall results are shown in table 1 with different levels of image noise affecting the data. A decrease in the

Table 1. Left: Mean of the the absolute rotation error expressed in degrees. Right: 3-D reconstruction error expressed in percentage relative to the scene size. The variance of the added noise is expressed in terms of image pixel. The value are computed on 10 trials for each configuration of noise and missing data ratios.

Missing %	Noise				
	0	0.5	1	1.5	2
10%	1, 32	1, 47	1, 89	2, 11	2, 13
20%	2, 85	3, 69	3, 45	3, 69	4, 05
30%	3, 75	4, 74	4, 76	5, 03	5, 78
40%	3, 99	4, 64	5, 18	5, 47	6, 87

Rotation Error

Missing %	Noise				
	0	0.5	1	1.5	2
10%	0.84	1.10	1.02	1.38	1.94
20%	1.26	1.38	2.05	1.26	2.55
30%	1.41	1.62	2.19	2.21	2.18
40%	1.78	1.86	1.96	2.39	2.40

3-D Structure error

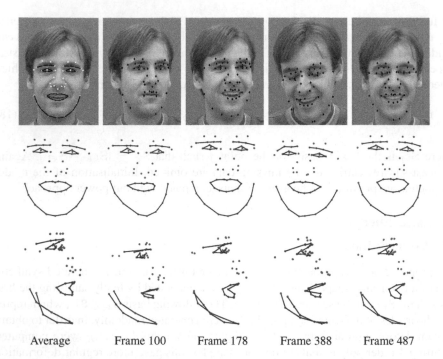

Average   Frame 100   Frame 178   Frame 388   Frame 487

Fig. 1. The first column shows the complete set of 56 points used for reconstruction (first row) and the recovered 3-D average shape (front and side views). The remaining columns present 4 key frames of the sequence with the available points at each frame. The second and third rows present respectively the front and side views of the reconstructed 3-D structure after non-linear optimisation. The number of basis shapes was fixed to $K = 6$.

algorithm's performances is given for ratios of 30% and more missing data. Regarding the mean shape computation, convergence was generally achieved after 15 iterations with 10% of missing data, higher ratios increase this number however, in the worst case, the algorithm was not performing more than 50 steps.

5.2   Real Data

The real experiments were focused on extracting a mean shape from a deforming face[2] exhibiting a light rotation and non-rigid motion especially in the mouth region We selected a 700 frames long sequence from the overall 5000 frames and 56 points were collected to form the measurement matrix W. Occluded points appeared with an overall 20% ratio of missing entries. The recovered mean shape (see figure 1) was then used to initialize a full deformable reconstruction and some frames presenting the recovered 3-D depth and deformations are presented (front and side view). The approach is able to successfully recover a reasonable estimates of the depth and deformations even if the subject was not performing strong rigid motion. The final number of iterations for the power method was of 50 followed by 40 iterations of non-linear optimisation.

---

[2] Sequence available at: www-prima.inrialpes.fr/FGnet/data/01-TalkingFace/talking_face.html

6 Conclusion

This paper presented a power approach to estimate average shapes from non-rigid motion in the case of missing data. Experimentally we have shown the effectiveness of the method in a deformable 3-D reconstruction task with affine cameras. The extracted average shape and motion have been shown to provide a reliable initialisation for SfM optimisation tasks in the tested cases. As a further study, the power method may be extended to more general camera models (i.e. full perspective), however initial results have shown increased instability in the convergence given by the difficulty in decoupling deformations from perspective distortions. In such cases, an approach using shape priors as shown in [4] may help to successfully compute a reliable average shape.

Acknowledgments. This work was supported by Fundação para a Ciência e a Tecnologia (ISR/IST plurianual funding) through the POS-Conhecimento Program (include FEDER funds). Thanks to João Paulo Costeira for support and for a careful reading of this paper.

References

1. Brand, M.: A direct method for 3d factorization of nonrigid motion observed in 2d. In: Proc. IEEE Conference on Computer Vision and Pattern Recognition, San Diego, California, pp. 122–128 (2005)
2. Bregler, C., Hertzmann, A., Biermann, H.: Recovering non-rigid 3d shape from image streams. In: Proc. IEEE Conference on Computer Vision and Pattern Recognition, Hilton Head, South Carolina, pp. 690–696 (June 2000)
3. Buchanan, A.M., Fitzgibbon, A.: Damped newton algorithms for matrix factorization with missing data. In: Proc. IEEE Conference on Computer Vision and Pattern Recognition, San Diego, California, vol. 2, pp. 316–322 (2005)
4. Del Bue, A., Lladó, X., Agapito, L.: Non-rigid face modelling using shape priors. In: Proc. IEEE Conference on Computer Vision and Pattern Recognition, New York, NY (2006)
5. Del Bue, A., Smeraldi, F., Agapito, L.: Non-rigid structure from motion using ranklet–based tracking and non-linear optimization. Image and Vision Computing 25(3), 297–310 (2007)
6. Golub, G.H., Van Loan, C.F.: Matrix computations. Johns Hopkins, Baltimore, MD (1989)
7. Hartley, R.I., Schaffalitzky, F.: Powerfactorization: an approach to affine reconstruction with missing and uncertain data. In: Australia-Japan Advanced Workshop on Computer Vision, Adelaide, Australia (September 2003)
8. Kanatani, K., Sugaya, Y.: Factorization without factorization: complete recipe. Memories of the Faculty of Engineering, Okayama University 38(1–2), 61–72 (2004)
9. Kim, T., Hong, K.-S.: Estimating approximate average shape and motion of deforming objects with a monocular view. International Journal of Pattern Recognition and Artificial Intelligence 19(4), 585–601 (2005)
10. Tomasi, C., Kanade, T.: Shape and motion from image streams under orthography: A factorization approach. International Journal of Computer Vision 9(2), 137–154 (1992)
11. Torresani, L., Yang, D., Alexander, E., Bregler, C.: Tracking and modeling non-rigid objects with rank constraints. In: Proc. IEEE Conference on Computer Vision and Pattern Recognition, Kauai, Hawaii (2001)
12. Xiao, J., Chai, J., Kanade, T.: A closed-form solution to non-rigid shape and motion recovery. International Journal of Computer Vision 67(2), 233–246 (2006)

Automatic Topological Active Net Division in a Genetic-Greedy Hybrid Approach

N. Barreira, M.G. Penedo, O. Ibáñez, and J. Santos

Computer Science Department, University of A Coruña, Spain
{nbarreira,mgpenedo,oibanez,santos}@udc.es

Abstract. In this paper we propose an automatic division procedure for the Topological Active Net model in a hybrid combination of a genetic and a greedy algorithm. This procedure allows the division of the active net in subnets with the aim of segmenting several objects in the same image. The combination of the greedy algorithm and the global search improves the results in both synthetic and real images.

Keywords: Topological Active Nets, Genetic Algorithms, Hybrid Optimization Algorithms, Lamarckian Strategy.

1 Introduction

Deformable models, proposed by Kass et al. [8] in 1988, are well-known tools for image segmentation. The active nets model was proposed by Tsumiyama and Yamamoto [10] as a variant of the deformable models that integrates features of region–based and boundary–based segmentation techniques. The Topological Active Net (TAN) model [1] was developed as an extension of the original active net model that solves some intrinsic problems to the deformable models such as the initialization problem.

In the field of deformable models, the Genetic Algorithms (GA) [6] have mainly been used for edge or surface extraction [2,5,9]. Also, Tohka [9] have developed a hybrid approach since he has used a greedy algorithm to strengthen the minimum obtained by a global GA minimization process.

GAs have some advantages in the active model adjustment. They are less sensitive to noise than other minimization approaches and do not depend on the parameter set or the mesh size [7]. However, the biggest limitation of the GA relates to perform changes in the mesh structure in order to achieve a fine adjustment, detect concavities, or divide the net to segment several objects in the same image. Last issue is the aim of this paper.

Regarding to the net division, Yoshino et al. [11] and Bro-Nielsen [3] have developed several works about automatic net division. The first one has modelled the links as springs, whose strengths correspond to their lengths. This way, the net arcs are dynamically unlinked when their strength value exceeds a threshold. However, this method fails when two neighboring nodes are well placed but too far and, moreover, it does not take into account any dependence between

J. Martí et al. (Eds.): IbPRIA 2007, Part II, LNCS 4478, pp. 226–233, 2007.

consecutive link cuts. In this sense, Bro-Nielsen [3] has developed a link cutting process that allows the division of the net following a specific route based on cutting priorities. Nevertheless, the main problem of this approach is the selection of an appropriate threshold for the badly placed nodes.

This paper proposes an automatic net division procedure in a hybrid approach that overcomes the difficulties of previous division methods and takes advantage of both local and global search techniques provided by the greedy and the genetic algorithms, respectively.

It is organized as follows. Section 2 introduces the basis of the TAN model. Section 3 explains the combination between the GA and the greedy algorithm, with emphasis in the net division procedure and its combination with a GA. Section 4 shows some results of the new method and, finally, section 5 expounds the conclusions of this work.

2   Topological Active Nets in Brief

A Topological Active Net (TAN) is a discrete implementation of an elastic 2D mesh with interrelated nodes [1]. The model has two kinds of nodes: internal, related to the inside of the objects, and external, related to contours.

A Topological Active Net is defined parametrically as $v(r, s) = (x(r, s), y(r, s))$ where $(r, s) \in ([0, 1] \times [0, 1])$. The mesh deformations are controlled by an energy function defined as follows:

$$E(v(r,s)) = \int_0^1 \int_0^1 (E_{int}(v(r,s)) + E_{ext}(v(r,s))) dr ds \qquad (1)$$

where E_{int} and E_{ext} are the internal and the external energy of the TAN, respectively. The internal energy controls the shape and the structure of the mesh whereas the external energy represents the external forces which govern the adjustment process.

The internal energy depends on first and second order derivatives which control contraction and bending, respectively. It is defined as follows:

$$E_{int}(v(r,s)) = \alpha(|v_r(r,s)|^2 + |v_s(r,s)|^2) + \\ \beta(|v_{rr}(r,s)|^2 + |v_{rs}(r,s)|^2 + |v_{ss}(r,s)|^2) \qquad (2)$$

where subscripts represents partial derivatives. α and β are coefficients that control the first and second order smoothness of the net. In order to calculate the energy, the parameter domain $[0, 1] \times [0, 1]$ is discretized as a regular grid defined by the internode spacing (k, l) and the first and second derivatives are estimated using the finite differences technique.

The external energy represents the features of the scene that guide the adjustment process. It is defined by the following equation:

$$E_{ext}(v(r,s)) = \omega f[I(v(r,s))] + \frac{\rho}{|\aleph(r,s)|} \sum_{p \in \aleph(r,s)} \frac{1}{\|v(r,s) - v(p)\|} f[I(v(p))] \qquad (3)$$

where ω and ρ are weights, $I(v(r,s))$ is the intensity value of the original image in the position $v(r,s)$, $\aleph(r,s)$ is the neighborhood of the node (r,s) and f is a function, which is different for both types of nodes since the external nodes fit the edges whereas the internal nodes model the inner features of the objects.

If the target objects are dark and the background is bright, the energy of an internal node energy will be minimum on a point with a low grey level. On the other hand, the energy of an external node will be minimum on a contour and on a light point outside the object. In this case, function f is defined as:

$$f[I(v(r,s))] = \begin{cases} h[\overline{I(v(r,s))_n}] & \text{for internal nodes} \\ \\ h[I_{max} - \overline{I(v(r,s))_n} + \xi(G_{max} - G(v(r,s)))] & \text{for external} \\ + \delta GD(v(r,s)) & \text{nodes} \end{cases} \quad (4)$$

where ξ and δ are weighting terms, I_{max} and G_{max} are the maximum intensity values of image I and the gradient image G, respectively, $I(v(r,s))$ and $G(v(r,s))$ are the intensity values of the original image and the gradient image in node position $v(r,s)$, $\overline{I(v(r,s))}_n$ is the mean intensity in a $n \times n$ square and h is an scaling function. The external energy also includes the gradient distance term, $GD(v(r,s))$, this is, the distance from the position $v(r,s)$ to the nearest edge. This term introduces a continuous range in the external energy since its value diminishes as the node gets closer to an edge. This way, the gradient distance facilitates the adjustment of the external nodes to the object contours.

The minimization of these energy functions adjusts the net to the objects. In the case of the greedy algorithm, the mesh is placed over the whole image and, in each step, the energy of each node is computed in its current position and in its nearest neighborhood. The position with the lowest energy value is selected as the new position of the node. The algorithm stops if no node can move to a position with lower energy.

3   Hybridization of the Evolutionary and Greedy Algorithms

The greedy algorithm gets good results in most cases since it takes the best local adjustment. However, this local adjustment may not be the best global one. This way, if the model reaches a wrong segmentation, it gets stuck in it. The global search provided by the GA reduces the probability of falling in local energy minima [7]. In this approach, the genotypes coded the Cartesian coordinates of the TAN nodes, the classic GA operators were adapted to the TAN features, and new *ad hoc* operators were developed to improve the results.

The main drawback of the GA approach is related to changes in the mesh structure since there is no way to conclude if a topological change is the best minimization step in an individual (except for the best one). This way, the topological changes could only be performed when the GA reaches a minimum.

As a consequence, next generations of individuals would have the same topology and the population heterogeneity would be reduced.

To avoid these limitations, a local greedy search stage is included in the evolutionary process. The main idea is to perform a given number of steps of the greedy algorithm in each individual of the genetic population in some generations of the evolutionary process. This way, the variability of TAN structures is maintained since each individual performs different topological changes in the minimization process. The search begins with high exploration (a greedy stage every 15 GA generations) and turns progressively to higher exploitation (a greedy stage every 1-5 generations). Additionally, a Lamarckian strategy is followed so all the changes made by the greedy procedure are reverted in the original genotypes.

Regarding to local search depth, the number of greedy algorithm steps is between 0 and 6 (depending on the kind of image) to minimize the probability to deeply fall in local minima and, at the same time, maintain an adequate heterogeneity in the population, that can be reduced using the Lamarckian strategy.

3.1 Link Cutting Procedure

The greedy algorithm can perform topological changes, this is, cuts of links between adjacent external nodes after the minimization process. First, external nodes that are more distant to the object edges are identified using the Tchebycheff's theorem. This way, an external node n is badly placed if its gradient distance, $GD_{v_{ext}}(n)$, fulfills that:

$$GD_{v_{ext}}(n) > \mu GD_{v_{ext}} + 3\sigma GD_{v_{ext}} \tag{5}$$

where $\mu GD_{v_{ext}}$ and $\sigma GD_{v_{ext}}$ represent the average and the standard deviation of the gradient distance of the external nodes.

Once the outlier set is identified, the link to remove is selected. It is the node with the highest gradient distance and its worst neighbor in the outlier set.

After the cutting, some internal nodes become external since they are on the boundaries of the net as figure 1 shows. The increase of external nodes allows a better adjustment to object boundaries.

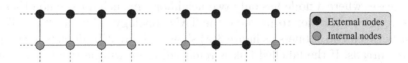

Fig. 1. Link cutting procedure. The figures show the TAN before and after the link cutting. After the cut, the neighboring internal nodes become external nodes.

In the hybrid approach proposed, the greedy method uses the link cutting to improve the results of the pure GA approach. Figure 2 shows several steps (best

Fig. 2. Four steps in the link cutting process

individual in several generations) in the link cutting process in areas where the GA alone cannot obtain an optimal segmentation.

As we follow a Lamarckian strategy, the modified topologies have to be transferred to the genotypes, so the genotype features need to be redefined. This way, for each node, the genotype must include not only the x and y coordinates, but also the directions where the node has neighbors, the kind of node (internal or external), and, as next section explains, the priority for a link cut in the node.

Additionally, to maintain fitness coherence in the population individuals, a node that turns from internal to external after a link cut is only considered as external for fitness computation when it is over the object edges. Also, a balloon pressure is used in order to move these nodes towards the contours [4].

The topological changes force the crossover between nets with the same topology in order to avoid crossings in the connections of the resulting nets. This fact implies a population categorization. Each population group with identical topology can be associated with the "niche" concept, this is, a group based on common features [6]. Only crossover between individuals of the same niche is allowed.

3.2   Automatic Net Division

Since the link cutting process breaks the net topology to improve the adjustment, when the image has several objects, the net should be divided to segment them. To this end, a net reconfiguration mechanism must be developed in order to perform multiple object detection and segmentation.

The net division is performed by the link cutting algorithm. However, this algorithm cannot be applied directly to the automatic division. The problems arise in cases where a node has only two neighbors. In such a case, no other link can be removed in order to preserve the TAN topology. Thus, a "thread" will appear between two subnets as figure 3(a) shows. Figure 3(b) depicts a case that leads to threads. If the labelled link is removed, there will be two threads since no other link can be cut.

However, this problem can be overcome if a direction in the cutting process is considered [3]. This way, a cutting priority is associated to each node whose connections are removed. A higher priority is assigned to the nodes in cut direction whereas a lower priority is assigned to the nodes involved in the cut. Figure 3(c) shows the recomputation of the node priorities after several cuts.

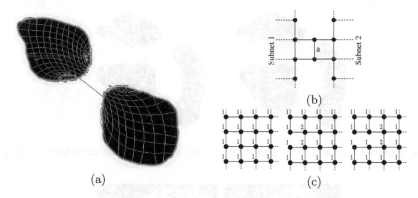

Fig. 3. Threads and cutting priorities. (a) Image segmentation with threads. (b) If link "a" is removed, no other link can be removed in order to preserve the TAN topology. (c) Recomputation of cutting priorities. When a link is broken in a direction, the neighborhood in this direction increases its priorities.

The cutting priority weights the gradient distance of each node. Thus, once the set of badly placed external nodes is obtained using equation 5, the link to remove consist of two neighboring nodes within this set, n_1 and n_2, that fulfill:

$$
\begin{aligned}
GD_{v_{ext}}(n_1) \times P_{cut}(n_1) &> GD(n) \times P_{cut}(n), \ \forall n \neq n_1 \\
GD_{v_{ext}}(n_2) \times P_{cut}(n_2) &> GD_{v_{ext}}(m) \times P_{cut}(m), \ \forall m \neq n_2, m \in \aleph(n_1),
\end{aligned}
\tag{6}
$$

where $P_{cut}(x)$ is the cutting priority of node x, $GD_{v_{ext}}(x)$ is the distance from the position of the external node x to the nearest edge, and $\aleph(n_1)$ is the set of neighboring nodes of n_1.

4   Results

We have tested the methodology with synthetic and CT images and we have compared the results with the greedy alternative. Both synthetic and CT images are 256 grey level images. The real ones are slices of the knee bones. They have been chosen from a set of CT images of body bones and represent the advantages of the hybrid approach. In all the examples, the same image was used as the

Table 1. TAN parameters used in the segmentation examples of figures 4 and 5 for both approaches. The gradient distance parameter is only used in the hybrid approach.

Image	Size	α	β	ω	ρ	ξ	δ
Fig. 4	22×22	2	0.0001	2	4	2	4
Fig. 5 (first row)	14×18	1.8	0.01	2	2	4	6
Fig. 5 (second row)	13×16	2	0.01	4	2	4	6

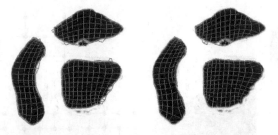

Fig. 4. Results on synthetic images. Left: greedy algorithm. Right: hybrid approach.

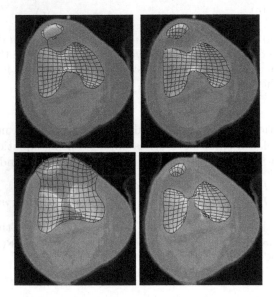

Fig. 5. Results on CT images. Left: greedy algorithm. Right: hybrid approach.

external energy for the internal and external nodes. The GA parameters used in the hybrid approach are the same as in [7]. Table 1 shows the TAN parameter sets used.

Figure 4 shows a synthetic example of a successful automatic division. The initial net is divided in three subnets. The segmentation results are similar in both methods, but the hybrid approach gets a better adjustment to the contours.

Figure 5 shows images of the knee. In the hybrid approach, the genetic population was 600 in the case of figure 5 (first row, right) and 700 in the case of figure 5 (second row, right). In these examples, the greedy method does not achieve a good adjustment due to the similar gray levels of the bones and the background. On the contrary, the hybrid approach overcomes the gray level similarity and gets good results. The gradual transition between the two bigger bones difficults the segmentation of both examples, even the hybrid one.

Regarding the computing times, the greedy method is faster (5 seconds for a simple image and 30-60 seconds for a complex one in an AMD Athlon at 1.2

GHz). The computing times of the hybrid approach depend on the number of generations and the number of iterations of the greedy search. Usually, it requires 10-20 minutes of computation. The advantages of the hybrid approach justify the higher computation times.

5 Conclusion

In this paper we have presented an automatic methodology for the Topological Active Net division in a hybrid genetic-greedy energy minimization approach. The hybrid method achieves a better adjustment to the objects due to the global search method and it also allows topological changes (link cuts) in the net structure as the greedy approach. The link cutting procedure is improved using cutting priorities that allow an automatic net division in order to segment several objects in the scene.

The greedy and hybrid approaches have been tested with synthetic and real images. The results have shown that the hybrid method achieved better results in the detection of several objects in the scene and the adjustment to the contours. Future work in this field includes the extension of this methodology to 3D.

Acknowledgements. This paper has been partly funded by the Xunta de Galicia through the grant contracts PGIDT04PXIC10501PN and PGIDIT06TIC10502PR.

References

1. Ansia, F.M., Penedo, M.G., Mariñno, C., Mosquera, A.: A new approach to active nets. Pattern Recognition and Image Analysis 2, 76–77 (1999)
2. Ballerini, L.: Medical image segmentation using genetic snakes. In: Proceedings of SPIE, vol. 3812, pp. 13–23 (1999)
3. Bro-Nielsen, M.: Active nets and cubes. IMM Tech. Rep. pp. 94–13 (1994)
4. Cohen, L.D.: On active contour models and ballons. Computer Vision, Graphics and Image Processing: Image Understanding 53(2), 211–218 (1991)
5. Fan, Y., Jiang, T.Z., Evans, D.J.: Volumetric segmentation of brain images using parallel genetic algorithms. IEEE Tran. on Medical Imaging 21(8), 904–909 (2002)
6. Goldberg, D.E.: Genetic Algorithms in Search, Optimization and Machine Learning. Addison-Wesley Longman Publishing Co., Inc, Boston, MA, USA (1989)
7. Ibáñez, O., Barreira, N., Santos, J., Penedo, M.G.: Topological active nets optimization using genetic algorithms. In: Campilho, A., Kamel, M. (eds.) ICIAR 2006. LNCS, vol. 4141, pp. 272–282. Springer, Heidelberg (2006)
8. Kass, M., Witkin, A., Terzopoulos, D.: Snakes: Active contour models. International Journal of Computer Vision 1(2), 321–323 (1988)
9. Tohka, J.: Global optimization of deformable surface meshes based on genetic algorithms. In: Proceedings ICIAP, pp. 459–464. IEEE Computer Society, Los Alamitos, CA, USA (2001)
10. Tsumiyama, K.S.Y., Yamamoto, K.: Active net: Active net model for region extraction. IPSJ SIG notes 89(96), 1–8 (1989)
11. Yoshino, K., Morita, S., Kawashima, T., Aoki, Y.: Dynamic reconfiguration of active net structure for region extraction. IEICE Transactions on Information and Systems 10, 1288–1294 (1995)

Using Graphics Hardware for Enhancing Edge and Circle Detection

Antonio Ruiz, Manuel Ujaldón, and Nicolás Guil

Computer Architecture Department, University of Malaga, 29071 Málaga, Spain

Abstract. A broad family of problems in computer vision and image analysis require edge and circle detection. This paper explores the properties of the Hough transform for such tasks, improving them under a novel implementation on commodity graphics hardware. We demonstrate both a faster execution and a more reliable detection under different scenarios and a range of parameters selection. Overall, a consistent 3-6 acceleration factor and beyond is achieved for a 500 MHz GeForce 7950 GX2 graphics card versus a typical 3 GHz Pentium 4 dual-core CPU.

1 Introduction

Edge and circle detection is a popular task in computer vision and image analysis. What it is a naive achievement for the human eye, has been proven tough and costly for computers, essentially because without prior knowledge, an extensive search has to be perfomed on the entire image to identify the desired feature.

The Hough transform [4] performs this search by discretizing all possible transformations between object and image space, where matches between object and image features count as votes which are interpreted as the likelihood for the object to be present in the image. Computational complexity comes from the fact that a huge number of potential candidates have to be considered for voting, leading to a vast memory use.

The homogeneity of the operations involved in the Hough transform and its computational cost have revealed it like an ideal target for parallelization. In this respect, a number of efforts were carried out within the last decade, including distributed memory multiprocessors [7], pyramid computers [2], SIMD machines [8], special purpose hardware and reconfigurable architectures [11].

After setting its basic principles in the 80's and improving its performance in multiprocessors during the 90's, this decade it is the time for graphics platforms to accelerate the execution of the Hough transform. The increasing flexibility and programmability of graphics processing units (GPUs) have allowed them to be used as target platforms in a wide spectrum of applications beyond graphics [1], mostly with an outstanding performance [10]. Throughout this paper, we show that the Hough transform is not an exception to this trend.

This paper is organized as follows. We start summarizing related work in section 2. Section 3 describes the Hough transform along with some preprocessing steps. Section 4 deals with the implementation within the GPU, section 5 describes the input data set and hardware platforms and section 6 analyzes the experimental results both from performance and quality prospectives.

J. Martí et al. (Eds.): IbPRIA 2007, Part II, LNCS 4478, pp. 234–241, 2007.

2 Related Work

The use of GPUs for general-purpose computing is steadily gaining popularity. Shader programming has transformed its vertex and pixel processors into configurable units willing to compute problems as diverse as sparse linear algebra, differential equations, database operations, physically-based simulations, signal and image processing, among many others [10]. Following this trend, the Hough transform has recently been ported to graphics platforms, both in its basic form for detecting lines [6] and its generalized version for arbitrary shapes [15].

The generalized version (Strzodka et al, 2003) relies on textures as the main resource for the input data set, enabling blending functions for accumulating votes on the image space. This represents an improvement in old platforms where fill-rate was higher on textures than on pixels, but not in current GPUs where pixel units are around 50. Our implementation relies on vertex processor for registering the votes and pixel processors for accumulating and counting them.

The basic version is more recent (Fung et al, 2005) and also takes advantage of the rasterizer, which is used for creating a contiguous mapping between the object and the image space after discretization of the angle variable within the $(0,2\pi)$ range. Unfortunately, such strategy doubles the number of input vertices, overloading the vertex processor, which becomes the major bottleneck. Instead, we try to balance the workload among all the functional units in the GPU.

3 The Algorithm

The very first step in pattern recognition is to isolate the points of interest on an image. To perform this, a filtering operation is implemented followed by another filter for removing noise and improve the input, after which the Hough transform is computed.

3.1 Edge Detection: The Canny Filter

Edge detection filters try to identify edges based on gradient magnitudes. Among all existing filters [12], we choose Canny [5] as one of the most successfully applied to a grayscale or single-color component image; for the cases where the input image covers the whole RGB color space, the luminance operator is computed beforehand to convert to grayscale (see equation 2).

The Canny operator works in a multi-stage process.

1. First convolution: The image is smoothed by a Gaussian operator acting as a noise removal stage while controlling the amount of detail which appears in the edge image.
2. Second convolution: A simple 2-D first derivative Sobel operator is applied to the smoothed image to highlight regions of the image with high first spatial derivatives. Edges give rise to ridges in the gradient magnitude image.
3. Non-maximal suppression: Ridges are tracked at the top to reset all pixels that are not actually on the ridge top so as to give a thin line in the output.

4. Double threshold hysteresis: T1 and T2 are two thresholds with T1 > T2. Tracking can only begin at a point on a ridge higher than T1, and continues from that point until the height of the ridge falls below T2. Hysteresis helps to ensure that noisy edges are not broken up into multiple edge fragments.

3.2 Pattern Recognition: The Hough Transform

In its more basic form, the Hough transform can be used for detecting lines on an image, where each image edge point generates a curve in a 2D parameter space. Curves from all edge points are accumulated in the parameter space, in such a way that the problem of object detection becomes the calculation of the maximum in that parameter space.

The Hough transform can also be used to more complex contours [13]. Such is the case of the Circle Hough Transform (CHT) [3], where each edge point generates a surface in a 3D parameter space with an equation as follows:

$$(x - a)^2 + (y - b)^2 = r^2 \qquad (1)$$

where (x, y) represents the coordinates for each edge point, and (a, b) and r stand for the circle center and radius, respectively. Simple extensions can also be applied to detect more complex shapes like ellipses.

4 Implementation on the GPU

In order to detect circular patterns on an image, the Hough transform takes as input a set of points which have been considered as the borders of the objects within an image after luminance and Canny filter are applied.

4.1 Preliminary Renderings

Luminance, or pixel intensity, converts a RGB-color image into a grayscale by applying the following expression:

$$L = 0.299 \cdot R + 0.587 \cdot G + 0.114 \cdot B \qquad (2)$$

This expression is computed directly on a pixel shader, taking the original image as an input texture with three color channels per pixel and returning as output another texture reduced to a single channel per pixel.

4.2 Vertex Processor

After luminance, convolutions and hysteresis are computed in the pixel processor, the final result is written into a texture, which has to be transformed into a list of vertices representing the set of points detected as borders.

Border points are finally accepted by the vertex processor, with its location mapped into the (x, y) position attribute. Now image space has to be converted into a parameter space, which considers all the circles that can be drawn passing through each point. Every circle is characterized by its center (a, b) and radius r, resulting into a 3D parameters space fulfilling the following pair of equations:

$$a = x - r \cdot cos(t) t \in [0, 2\pi] \qquad b = y - r \cdot sin(t) t \in [0, 2\pi] \qquad (3)$$

The goal now is to compute a vote for all (x,y) points on the image, the values of discretized values for t, and the list of candidates radius. As the discretization for t decreases, the workload for the vertex processor and the accuracy for the votes both increase, having a simultaneous impact on the execution time and quality for the final cicle detection (see section 6).

4.3   Pixel Processor

The total number of votes are stored on 3D textures whose dimensions depend on the discretization of the parameter space, where circle center as the first two dimensions and t steps being the third. The accumulation for the votes is performed on the pixel shader by projecting the 3D texture into a 2D texture.

The final circle detection corresponds to the maximum values taken within the parameters space, given a chosen threshold as sensitivity. The process is then repeated for each radius within a range selected according to image features.

5   Experimental Setup

To demonstrate the effectiveness of our techniques, we have conducted a number of experiments on regular PCs.

On the GPU side, we use OpenGL and the Cg language for programming the shaders. GL_POINTS was selected as drawing primitive to keep computations strictly over the input list of vertices. The GPU is a 500 MHz GeForce 7950 GX2 with 8 vertex processors and 24 pixel processors and endowed with 512 MB of GDDR3 video memory at 2x600 MHz. This results in a peak processing power exceeding 190 GFLOPS and a memory bandwidth of 38.4 GB/s.

For programming the CPU, we use Visual C++ 7.0 running under Windows XP. Multimedia extensions (SSE3 on Pentium 4) were enabled relying directly on HAL layer without any specific library in between. The CPU is a Pentium D 930 model, a dual-core architecture running at 3 GHz and endowed with 1 GB of DDR memory at 2x266 MHz, which delivers peak 12 GFLOPS and 8.5 GB/s.

The input data set consisted of four different images as far as circle properties are concerned: radius size, number of objects and irregularities, overall noise and resolution - see Table 1 for image features and Figure 1.(a-d) for pictures.

Table 1. Our input data set for circle detection (radius and resolution given in pixels)

Image name	Number of circles to be detected	Radius used for searching	Image resolution	Challenging issues
Golf ball	1	37	300x300	Background noise
Pebbles	117	9	256x300	Irregular shapes
Grapefruits	12	50	500x400	Thick contour (r varies)
Water drops	42 big, 140 med, 140 small, approx.	4,12,20,28, 36,44,52	400x400	Diversity, population, plenty of tiny radius

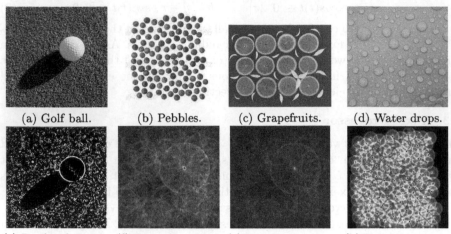

(a) Golf ball.   (b) Pebbles.   (c) Grapefruits.   (d) Water drops.

(e) Border detection (f) Parameter space (g) Parameter space (h) Parameter space
for golf ball.   for golf ($t+ = 0.01$). for golf ($t+ = 0.1$). for pebbles ($t+ = 0.1$).

Fig. 1. (a-d) The input data set used for our experiments. (e) The output of our algorithm for the golf ball after Luminance and Canny stages. (f-g) The output of Hough (votes accumulated into the parameter space) as written by the GPU on the frame-buffer under two different angle steps for the golf ball case (brighter colors means higher voting). (h) Same as in g, but applied to the image in b (pebbles).

6   Empirical Results

This section compares CPU and GPU when performing the Hough transform both from a quantitative and qualitative assessment. We start with the latter.

6.1   Accuracy

After applying the luminance operator and the Canny filter, a canonical representation was used in both processors to compute the Hough transform using the same input (see Figure 1.e for the golf ball case). This guarantees that differences in the final results are no longer due to deficiencies in any of the preprocessing stages, which were somehow manually tuned.

Table 2 shows the overall number of circles detected by each implementation. The number of votes to compute depends widely on the image resolution and the discretization step used for traversing the t variable within the $[0, 2\pi]$ interval. We run two versions with t increments of 0.01 and 0.1, which respectively produces more than 56 and 5.6 million votes for a 300x300 image like *golf ball*.

As the number of votes increases, so does it workload and accuracy, but also the negative influence of noise like the background grass behind the golf ball. This effect is noticeable in Figure 1.(f-g), where we depict the output from the GPU code for the two *golf ball* executions, that is, the frame buffer contents displayed

Table 2. (left) Number of circles detected on each Hough implementation for each sample image and contrast against its correct value, revealed in the last column. (right) Accumulative process for the votes performed on graphics textures.

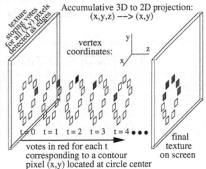

Image name	$t+=0.01$ CPU	$t+=0.01$ GPU	$t+=0.1$ CPU	$t+=0.1$ GPU	Correct number
Golf ball	1	1	1	1	1
Pebbles	117	116	115	117	117
Grapefruit	14	12	17	20	12
Water drops	300	356	339	324	≈322

on screen using the RGB color channels for accumulating votes (brighter color means higher voting).

Pebbles is a different experiment with a better foreground segmentation and more than 100 circles to work on. The skills of each processor are quite similar here, despite the circle irregularities and the overwhelming number of votes due to circle density (see Figure 1.h for the output from the GPU, much brighter as compared to the golf ball case under the same angle step in Figure 1.g).

Grapefruits pose two challenges to the GPU. First, thicker circle contour in the image space may lead to consider several circles where a single one exists; this is something that also affects to the CPU, as we see it counting 14 and 17 units instead of 12. Second, higher radius size makes votes to draw circles of higher radius in the parameter space as well (compare *golf ball* with *pebbles* in the image space and Figure 1.g with 1.h in the parameter space). Those votes are likely to produce side-effects in neighbour circles, an effect which amplifies with the angle step where the weight of each real vote diminishes. In fact, the 20 circles detected by the GPU under $t = 0.1$ were very close to each other, also as a consequence of the thicker circle contour in the image space. All those effects were corrected when increasing the workload on the GPU up to $t = 0.01$.

Finally, *water drops* is the most demanding picture, containing plenty of tiny circles and some oddities. However, the GPU here performs really well, as we see the two undesirable effects described above to fade away.

Overall, slight differences between the results obtained by the CPU and the GPU lie in the way that votes following equation 3 are rounded due to discretization in parameter space. When the (a,b) candidates for circle center coordinates are very close to each other for consecutive angle steps, they accumulate votes on the CPU; those are not repeatedly counted by the GPU because all vertices matching on the same screen location on a single rendering pass overwrite the same pixel and count as a single vote when mapped onto the texture for storing the final results. Though we expected duplicated votes to penalize results on the CPU, we have seen scenarios here where they are beneficial as well.

Table 3. Computational weight in milliseconds for each task involved in our pattern recognition algorithm and overall improvement factor achieved by the GPU implementation against its CPU counterpart. Times for the Hough transform are shown for two angle steps, $t = 0.01$ and $t = 0.1$, and the times in the last row are given for each radius value, being nearly the same in all the seven cases executed.

| Image name | CPU | | | | GPU (and GPU vs CPU factor improvement) | | | |
	Luminance	Canny filter	Hough (t+=.01)	Hough (t+=.1)	Luminance	Canny filter	Hough (t+=0.01)	Hough (t+=0.1)
Golf ball	7.18	168.54	798.58	84.25	2.31 (**3.1x**)	4.49 (**37.5x**)	324.03 (**2.4x**)	37.50 (**2.2x**)
Pebbles	5.46	120.85	1817.01	188.18	2.04 (**2.6x**)	5.42 (**22.2x**)	482.71 (**3.7x**)	51.32 (**3.6x**)
Grapefruits	15.90	365.10	1907.32	187.17	2.52 (**6.3x**)	10.32 (**35.3x**)	508.36 (**3.7x**)	57.54 (**3.2x**)
Water drops	13.74	292.16	3955.76	395.63	2.80 (**4.9x**)	7.60 (**38.4x**)	856.98 (**4.6x**)	93.30 (**4.2x**)

6.2   Performance

The speed of algorithms running on GPUs highly depends on how well they can be arranged to fit and exploit its inherent parallelism and high memory bandwidth. Persistent use of textures becomes paramount for a code to benefit from video memory, so as arithmetic intensity does it from parallelism. The implementation of the Hough transform that we have presented here combines well both features to reach significant improvement factors (see Table 3): We extensively use shaders with homogeneous operations which can be evenly distributed among all existing processors; in addition, main data structures involved in the computation are all defined in terms of 2D and 3D arrays, finding a natural mapping onto graphics textures.

Finally, the Canny filter is our most remarkable achievement, with a 40x reduction factor versus the CPU code. This stage is defined as a set of convolution operators where arithmetic and memory participate at high rates. Moreover, pixel processors traverse images organized in 2x2 groups, which is ideal for access patterns used by convolution masks where neighbour data are always coupled.

7   Conclusion

We have mapped well-known methods for border extraction and subsequent circle detection onto graphics processors. The algorithms were tested against an assorted set of images to demonstrate better skills and much faster processing on the GPU side as compared to a CPU of similar cost in the PC marketplace.

As time goes on, we are seeing the graphics pipeline evolving towards a general-purpose architecture and assisted by compilers to benefit the scientific community from its extraordinary scalability, with a performance growing rate doubling the Moore's Law in present CPUs and for years to come. As a low-cost platform for accelerating a wide variety of problems within this transition process, we envision image processing as one of the most natural fields to benefit from dozens of GB/s in memory bandwidth and hundreds of GFLOPS in peak processing power.

8   A Look to the Future

The new generation of GPU architects face the challenge of balancing flexibility and performance concerning general-purpose applications (GPGPU) [1]. Performance has played a primary role in GPGPU, but researchers are required to understand about vertices, pixels and textures, as well as DirectX/OpenGL prior to any general-purpose implementation on the GPU. At the time of writing this article, Nvidia has released the CUDA architecture [9] in conjunction with a C compiler that allows to write regular C code for its graphics platforms G80 and beyond; a similar corporate initiative, RapidMind [14], emerges as a tool for automatically adapting C code into multicore CPUs, GPUs and the Cell processor. It remains to be seen the performance hit that these tools will have when running on a GPU an automatically transformed code as compared to the somehow manual and scientific implementation described throughout this paper.

References

1. A Web page dedicated to the latest developments in general-purpose on the GPU: http://www.gpgpu.org (accessed November 2006)
2. Atiquzzaman, M.: Pipelined implementation of the multiresolution Hough transform in a pyramid multiprocessor. Pattern Recogn. Let. 15(9), 841–851 (1994)
3. Atiquzzaman, M.: Coarse-to-fine search technique to detect circles in images. The Int'l Journal of Advanced Manufacturing Technology, vol. 15(2) (February 1999)
4. Ballard, D.: Generalized Hough transform to detect arbitrary patterns. IEEE Trans. on Pattern Analysis and Machine Intelligence 13(2), 111–122 (1981)
5. Canny, J.: A computational approach to edge detection. IEEE Transactions on Pattern Analysis and Machine Intelligence. 8(6), 679–698 (1986)
6. Fung, J., Mann, S., Aimone, C.: OpenVIDIA: Parallel GPU Computer Vision. In: Proceedings of the 13th ACM Intl. Conf. on Multimedia, Singapore, pp.849–852 (2005)
7. Guil, N., Zapata, E.L.: A parallel pipelined Hough transform. In: Proceedings Europar., vol. 2, pp. 131–138 (1996)
8. Kumar, S., Ranganathan, N., Goldgof, D.: Parallel algorithms for circle detection in images. J. Pattern Recognition 27(4), 1019–1028 (1994)
9. CUDA: http://developer.nvidia.com/object/cuda.html (accessed November 2006)
10. Owens, J., Luebke, D., Govindaraju, Harris, M., Kruger, J., Lefohn, A., Purcell, T.: A survey of general-purpose computation on graphics hardware. In: Proceedings Eurographics 2005, Trinity College, Dublin (Ireland) (2005)
11. Pan, Y., Li, K., Hamdi, M.: An improved constant-time algorithm for computing the Radon and Hough transforms on a reconfigurable mesh. IEEE Transactions on Systems, Man, and Cybernetics, Part A. 29(4), 417–421 (1999)
12. Pratt, W.K.: Digital Image Processing. John Wiley & Sons,Inc, New York (1978)
13. Princen, J., Yuen, H.K., Illingworth, J., Kittler, J.: A Comparison of Hough Transform Methods. I. Conf. on Image Processing and its Applications, pp. 73–77 (1989)
14. RapidMind Homepage: http://www.rapidmind.net (accessed November 2006)
15. Strzodka, R. Ihrke, I., Magnor, M.: A Graphics Hardware Implementation of the Generalized Hough Transform for fast Object Recognition, Scale and 3D Pose Detection. In: Procs. Int'l Conf. on Image Analysis and Processing, pp. 188–193, (2003)

Optimally Discriminant Moments for Speckle Detection in Real B-Scan Images

Robert Martí[1], Joan Martí[1], Jordi Freixenet[1], Joan Carles Vilanova[2], and Joaquim Barceló[2]

[1] Computer Vision and Robotics Group. University of Girona, Spain
{marly,joanm,jordif}@eia.udg.es
[2] Girona Magnetic Resonance Center. Girona, Spain
{kvilanova,rmgirona}@comg.es

Abstract. Detection of speckle in ultrasound (US) images has been regarded as an important research topic in US imaging, mainly focusing on two specific applications: improving signal to noise ratio by removing speckle noise and, secondly, for detecting speckle patches in order to perform a 3D reconstruction based on speckle decorrelation measures.

A novel speckle detection proposal is presented here showing that detection can be improved based on finding optimally discriminant low order speckle statistics. We describe a fully automatic method for speckle detection and propose and validate a framework to be efficiently applied to real B-scan data, not being published to date. Quantitative and qualitative results are provided, both for real and simulated data.

1 Background

US imaging captures the difference of sound scattering and reflection in tissues. Taking into account spatially randomly distributed sub-resolution scatterers, one can talk about incoherent scattering which gives rise to **speckle noise** or fully developed speckle. However, if this distribution follows a given pattern, a **coherent** component is introduced. The main aim of this work is to provide an automatic method for the detection of fully developed speckle patterns in B-scans. A common approach is to describe speckle using a known statistical model. Various models have been proposed for speckle characterisation, Rayleigh and Rician models were originally used but more general models such as the Nakagami [1], K [2], Generalised K and Homodyned K distributions [3,4] have shown to account for better speckle description at the expense of a more complex formulation. An alternative approach, adopted here, is to describe speckle based on statistical features extracted from the amplitude moments of the B-scan. The work presented here is based on an earlier work [5] but incorporates relevant novel aspects such as the optimally discriminant computation of speckle statistics and the methodology for its fully automatic application to real B-scan data. The paper is structured as follows: Sect. 2 presents the formulation for obtaining optimally discriminant speckle statistics; Section 3 proposes a method for speckle detection in B-scans, while Sect. 4 shows evaluation results using simulated and real data. The paper finishes with conclusions and future work.

J. Martí et al. (Eds.): IbPRIA 2007, Part II, LNCS 4478, pp. 242–249, 2007.

2   Speckle Characterisation

Speckle in ultrasound images is commonly characterised by three parameters: the coherent signal energy s^2, the diffuse signal energy $2 * \sigma^2$ and the number of scatters per resolution cell μ. The coherent and diffuse signals are also commonly expressed as the ratio $k = s/\sigma$, the proportion of coherent to diffuse signal. As demonstrated by different authors [5,6], speckle can be characterised by two low order moments: the ratio between the mean and the standard deviation (R) and the skewness (S), defined as follows,

$$R = \frac{E\{A^v\}}{\sqrt{E\{A^{2v}\} - E^2\{A^v\}}} \quad S = \frac{E\{(A^v - E\{A^v\})^3\}}{(E\{A^{2v}\} - E^2\{A^v\})^{3/2}} \quad (1)$$

where A is the signal amplitude, and v the power of the statistical moment. Effectively, R and S can be computed using v values different from one. This issue is important as the use of an specific value of v could lead to a better discrimination between speckle and non-speckle signals. For instance, in all experiments described by Prager et al. [5] a fixed v value was used ($v = 1.8$ for simulated and $v = 1$ for real US images). As noted in [7], this assertion may not be always valid. Authors show that an analysis of the discriminant power of the R-S features should be carried out in order to determine the optimal order of the statistics. Nevertheless, their experiments are based on simulated data and do not discuss how this optimal v value affects the final speckle detection algorithm, nor how this criteria can be applied to real B-scan data.

2.1   Discriminant Power Analysis

The R-S statistics can be regarded as features for a classic pattern recognition problem [8]: given a set of feature values classify them as being speckle or non-speckle. As a set of R-S is obtained for each sampled v value, one could think that the most appropriate R-S features are those which maximise a certain measure of discriminating power. One of the most commonly used methods is the analysis of the *within class* (S_w) and the *between class* (S_b) scatter matrices [8]. Defining the matrix S_m as the sum of the S_w and S_b, different measures of discrimination power can be computed. In order to follow a consistent notation with [7], those measures are referred to as J_1, J_2 and J_3 and are defined as follows.

$$J_1 = trace(S_m)/trace(S_w) \quad J_2 = det(S_m)/det(S_w) \quad J_3 = trace(S_w^{-1} * S_b) \quad (2)$$

For all cases a higher value denotes higher class separability, although this criteria does not always coincide for all measures, which, excerpted from the experiments, is specially true for J_1 measures. Back to the problem of speckle detection, having those measures of class separability one can conduct different experiments in order to obtain the value of v which maximises class separability, we will refer to this value as v_{opt}. Nevertheless, the problem of developing a method for detecting speckle in real B-scan images using those discriminant features has not been addressed yet. This is presented in the next section.

3   Speckle Detection in Real B-Scans

This section adapts the speckle detection methodology in order to be applied to real B-scan ultrasound images. An added difficulty is that intensity data in B-scan images is log compressed by the ultrasound machine in order to account for the full dynamic range. If the original non-compressed signal is unavailable, intensity information needs to be decompressed in order to correctly characterise speckle. Several authors suggest a compression of the form $p = Dln(I)+G$, where p is the final B-scan intensity, D the compression factor, G an offset value and I the original intensity signal. The offset value is often disregarded as it does not affect the statistics of the speckle. It is then D the important factor to be determined in order to obtain a good speckle detection.

3.1   Speckle Detection

As previously stated, our work builds up on the speckle detection methodology proposed by Prager et al. [5], but incorporates novel aspects such as the optimal selection of the statistics applied to real B-scans and removing the need of manual intervention, aspects which we believe make the method more robust. Prager et al. proposal is based on a simultaneous method for estimating B-scan decompression parameters and subsequently detect speckle regions based on the ellipsoid discriminant function obtained from simulated speckle data. The ellipsoid function is used to classify a patch as being speckle if its $R - S$ features lie within the ellipse. The original approach presents some drawbacks. A first issue is the need of manually detecting initial speckle regions in order to extract sample statistics, prone to errors due to human variability and to the fact that in some images it is difficult to obtain those regions. Manual intervention is also needed in order to obtain the ellipse parameters for the speckle discriminant function. This is solved in this work by using eigenanalysis of the covariance matrix obtained from the R-S simulated data. Another important drawback is the fact that $R - S$ features are computed using an arbitrarily value. The power of the statistics can play an important role in discriminating speckle regions as it is shown in the results section. The steps of our proposal are described below,

1. Obtain an **ellipse discriminant function** from speckle simulated data for different v values ranging from 0 to 3 (i.e. with increments of 0.1).
2. Automatically detect **core speckle** and **core non-speckle** regions and estimate decompression factor D_v from the real B-scan data (see Sect. 3.2).
3. Using speckle and non-speckle, compute $R - S$ statistics and find v_{opt}, the v value where those statistics are optimally discriminant.
4. Adapt the ellipse centre parameters using the mean $R - S$ features from the speckle patches, similarly to the original method.
5. For all patches in the image, decompress it using the $D_{v_{opt}}$ value, obtain $R - S$ features and use the ellipse discriminant function to assert if it is a speckle patch (is inside the ellipse), also similarly to the original method.

The following section describes the core speckle and decompression estimation method (step 2 of the proposal).

3.2   Core Speckle and Decompression Estimation

In order to estimate the decompression factor, a number of speckle patches needs to be detected. However, speckle patches can not be detected if no decompression estimation is obtained. This is clearly an optimisation problem where decompression and speckle patches need to be simultaneously estimated. In the original work [5] this was approached by manually detecting fully developed speckle patches. Here, this is solved using a RANSAC based approach, which automatically detects representative speckle and non-speckle patches from randomly sampled patches in the B-scan data.

The detection of speckle and non-speckle patches is based on the assumption that the estimated decompression values D found after an optimisation process (see [5]) are stable as a function of v for speckle patches. In the case of non-speckle patches those values will present high variability for different v values, explained by the fact that optimisation will be unable to find a meaningful D value. This assumption is corroborated by different experiments on both simulated and real data, some of them shown in Sect. 4.2. The method for core speckle and simultaneous decompression estimation is described using the following steps:

1. Choose an initial compression value D.
2. Extract a N random patches from the B-scan data.
3. For each patch p
   (a) **Decompress** the patch intensity using $I_p = exp(p/D)$
   (b) Compute $R - S$ from I_p, for a range of v values from 0 to 3, (F_{pv}).
   (c) For each F_{pv} use an optimisation algorithm to estimate the decompression value, D_{pv}.
4. Extract the most stable (smallest standard deviation) D_{pv} values as a function of v, D'_{pv}.
5. Compute the median of the D'_{pv} obtaining a final estimation of the compression factor as a function of v, D_v (see Sect. 4.2).
6. Core **speckle** patches are defined as the N_{sp} patches with D_{pv} values closest to D_v, while core **non-speckle** patches will be randomly sampled (N_{nsp}) from the patches with the largest difference to D_v.

In addition to the log compressed image, some modern ultrasound machines already provide the uncompressed echo amplitude signal. In that case, the method would not need to estimate the decrompression parameter, making the core speckle and non-speckle step less computationally costly, avoiding the use of the optimisation algorithm in order to obtain the estimation of the decompression factor D. However, if this information is unavailable, for instance due to the limitations of the ultrasound scanner or to the fact that images are from retrospective studies (where non-compressed images are not available), the presented method provides an estimation of this compression.

4   Evaluation and Results

4.1   Discriminant Analysis

Other works have already justified the need of finding discriminant statistics for speckle detection [7]. Nevertheless this needs to be investigated as a different detection approach is adopted here and moreover, the discriminant analysis applied to real B-scan data conforms one of the novel aspects of our approach.

As an initial evaluation, different experiments are presented using simulated data. A total of four different speckle and non-speckle patterns have been simulated using different k and μ parameters, namely $I_a = (0, 50)$ as fully developed speckle and $I_b = (1, 50)$, $I_c = (0, 2)$, $I_d = (1, 2)$ as non-speckle patterns. For each pattern a total of 1000 different sets of 1000 samples have been simulated, subsequently $R - S$ features have been computed as a function of v. Fig. 1(a) shows class separability for the 2-class problem as a function of v. The maximum value for J_1 is around 1.3, whereas J_2 and J_3 seem slightly consistent in finding the $v_{opt} = 0.9$. As pointed out previously J_2 and J_3 values correspond to similar discrimination criteria. Therefore, and similarly to [7], J_3 will be used as discriminant criteria (J_2 could also be used). Those results, and other simulated experiments not shown here, suggest that class separability is not close to a fixed value as suggested in [5]. For the v_{opt} value, Fig. 1(b) shows the scatter plot of the R-S features where a clear discrimination can be seen between the data except for I_a and I_b. This overlap is explained by the similar parameters used, related to fully developed speckle and speckle with an small amount of coherent scattering.

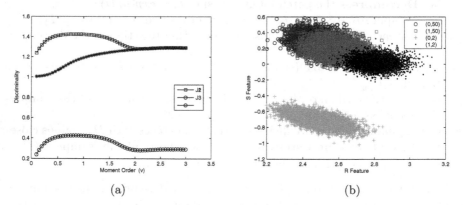

(a)   (b)

Fig. 1. 2-class problem: (a) Class separability as a function of v and (b) the scatter plot of the R-S features for the case where J_3 is maximal ($v_{opt} = 0.9$)

Another experiment is presented in order to asses if the use of the discriminant criteria for v value corresponds to a better speckle detection rate. Speckle and non-speckle data characterised by different parameters has been simulated.

An ellipsoid discriminant function has been fitted using the $R - S$ features from speckle data for different v values. The experiment is based on selecting a number of random samples from the simulated data and test if they belong to speckle using the ellipsoid function. The aim is to evaluate if the optimally discriminant v value (v_{opt}) improves speckle detection results. Table 1 summarises the results in two different simulations (600 and 4000 sample sizes) in terms of correct classification rate (CCR), sensitivity ($Sens$) and specificity ($Spec$). For the experiment with 4000 samples, sensitivity and CCR using v_{opt} are increased, while specificity does not significatively change compared to other v values. When a smaller number of data is used, this difference is not that significative, although the v_{opt} does not degrade the results and is in line with the best detection rates. Results with different simulated data (not included here) also corroborates those findings. In conclusion, the use of v_{opt} obtains the optimal v statistic for speckle detection in our approach.

Table 1. Speckle detection for simulated data using different sample sizes: 600 (left) and 4000 (right) samples. For both tables the last row corresponds to the v_{opt} value.

v	CCR	Sens	Spec	v	CCR	Sens	Spec
3	0.844	0.975	0.676	3	0.893	0.983	0.779
2	0.853	0.969	0.704	2	0.895	0.981	0.785
1.8	0.846	0.979	0.678	1.8	0.891	0.980	0.778
1.1	0.852	0.980	0.685	1.2	0.900	0.991	0.783

4.2 Decompression Estimation

The assumption that the decompression values found after optimisation are stable as a function of v for speckle patches, compared to non-speckle patches is evaluated. A set of speckle and non-speckle patches have been manually labeled, subsequently, step 3 described in Sect. 3.2 is applied in order to obtain the behaviour of a D estimation for both speckle and non-speckle patches as a function of v. Figure 2(a) shows these estimations for speckle and non-speckle, it is clear that non-speckle regions obtain a highly variable D estimation, whereas speckle patches are fairly stable. In our method, a decompression estimation as a function of the v values is obtained by computing the median of these stable values. This estimation, D_v, is shown in Fig. 2(b).

4.3 Detection of Core Speckle and Non-speckle

Figure 3 shows the core speckle and non-speckle detection results using the described approach in real B-scan data from a prostatic phantom. The N_{sp} and N_{nsp} values are set to 20, a non particularly critical value. Core speckle clearly shows typical low intensity fully developed speckle patches, whereas core non-speckle are characterised by the high contrast regions with important coherent signal components.

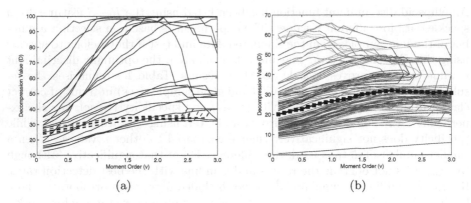

(a)   (b)

Fig. 2. Decompression estimation: (a) D estimation as a function of v using manually labeled speckle (dotted) and non-speckle (solid) patches; (b) final D_v estimation from the median of the most stable estimations

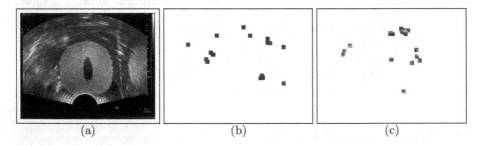

(a)   (b)   (c)

Fig. 3. Results for the proposed core speckle detection in prostatic phantom images. (a) original B-scan, (b) core speckle, (c) core non-speckle patches.

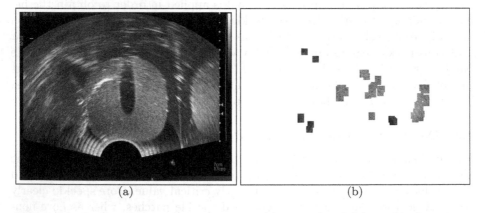

(a)   (b)

Fig. 4. Results in prostatic phantom images. (a) original and (b) speckle detection.

4.4 Speckle Detection

Speckle detection results are shown in this section. The algorithm was tested using US images from a prostatic phantom. Although a single image was used for the core speckle detection (more images could be used), detection results are qualitatively satisfactory as shown in Fig. 4. Interestingly, the method detects regions not only with dark speckle patches (similar to the core speckle) but also lighter speckle areas inside the prostate area.

5 Conclusion

A novel approach for the detection of speckle in real B-scan images has been presented. We have shown that optimally discriminant speckle statistics can be used for obtaining a better speckle characterisation. In addition, an automatic method for detecting core speckle and non-speckle areas has been presented, which eliminates the need of manual intervention. Quantitative and qualitative results have been given which prove the validity of our approach. Future work will be focused on applying the speckle detection algorithm to particular applications such as 3D reconstruction from sensorless freehand images or increasing signal to noise ratio in US images.

Acknowledgments. Work partially supported by MEC grant nbs. TIN2005-08792-C03-01 and TIN2006-08035 and grants from the SERAM and ACMCB.

References

1. Ghofrani, S., Jahed-Motlagh, M., Ayatollahi, A.: An adaptive speckle suppression filter based on Nakagami distribution. In: IEEE EUROCON'2001, International Conference onTrends in Communications, vol. 1 (2001)
2. Wachowiak, M., Smolikova, R., Zuranda, J., Elmaghraby, A.: Estimation of K distribution parameters using neural networks. IEEE Transactions on Biomedical Engineering 49(6), 617–620 (2002)
3. Wagner, R., Smith, S.W., Sandrik, J., Lopez, H.: Statistics of speckle in ultrasound B-scans. IEEE Transactions on Sonics and Ultrasonics 30(3), 156–163 (1983)
4. Dutt, V., Greenleaf, J.: Adaptative speckle reduction filter for Log-compressed B-scan images. IEEE Transactions on Medical Imaging 15(6), 802–813 (1996)
5. Prager, R., Gee, A., Treece, G., Berman, L.: Speckle Detection in ultrasound images using first order statistics. Technical Report TR 415, University of Cambridge (2001)
6. Dutt, V.: Statistical Analysis of Ultrasound Echo Envelope. PhD thesis, Mayo Graduate School (1995)
7. Martín-Fernández, M., Alberola-López, C.: On low order moments of the Homodyned-K distribution. Ultrasonics 43, 283–290 (2005)
8. Webb, A.: Statistical Pattern Recognition, 2nd edn. John Wiley and Sons, New York (2003)

Influence of Resampling and Weighting on Diversity and Accuracy of Classifier Ensembles

R.M. Valdovinos[1], J.S. Sánchez[2], and E. Gasca[1]

[1] Lab. Reconocimiento de Patrones, Instituto Tecnológico de Toluca
Av. Tecnológico s/n, 52140 Metepec. México
[2] Dept. Llenguatges i Sistemes Informàtics, Universitat Jaume I
Av. Sos Baynat s/n, E-12071 Castelló de la Plana. Spain

Abstract. Diversity in the decisions of a classifier ensemble appears as one of the main issues to take into account for its construction and operation. However, the potential relationship between diversity and accuracy, with respect to the resampling method and/or the classifier fusion technique has not been clearly proved. The present paper analyzes the influence of different resampling methods and dynamic weighting schemes on diversity and how this can affect to the accuracy of the classifier ensemble. This is specifically studied in the framework of the Nearest Neighbor classification algorithm.

1 Introduction

Many researchers have investigated the technique of combining the predictions of multiple classifiers to produce a single decision. The basic idea considers a number of advantages when compared to the use of an individual classifier [10], the most important argues that the resulting classifier (typically called *ensemble*) is generally more accurate than any of the single classifiers making up the ensemble.

It is widely accepted that the major factor for a better accuracy is the diversity among the classifiers to be combined, that is, they must differ in their decisions to complement each other [2, 13, 15]. To obtain diversity, there exist many distinct techniques for constructing classifier ensembles. One consists of using different classifiers over a unique training set; in this case, the classifiers themselves must be different enough to produce diverse decisions. Another consists of manipulating (or resampling) the data set on which the classifiers are trained. Under this scenario, classifiers may be all based upon the same technique, e.g., a k-Nearest Neighbor (k-NN) classifier.

Another issue of interest in the framework of combining classifiers refers to the different methods to obtain the output of an ensemble. Two main strategies are discussed in the literature: classifier selection and classifier fusion. The idea in classifier selection is that each individual classifier has expertise in some local area of the feature space and therefore, only one expert is responsible to label a new input pattern. Conversely, classifier fusion assumes that all classifiers have equal knowledge of the whole feature space and the decisions of all of them are taken into account for any input pattern.

Within the fusion context, the most popular method for combining the decisions corresponds to the majority voting [12]; however when the performance of the ensemble

J. Martí et al. (Eds.): IbPRIA 2007, Part II, LNCS 4478, pp. 250–257, 2007.

components is not uniform, the efficiency of this type of voting results affected negatively. More elaborated schemes employ weighted voting rules, in which each individual classifier is associated with a different weight [14, 18]. Importance of this comes from the fact that a choice of an appropriate fusion strategy can improve further on the performance of the ensemble.

This study mainly concentrates on establishing the relationship, if any, between diversity and the techniques used for constructing the classifier ensemble, that is, how is diversity affected by the resampling method and/or the fusion strategy? Also, we are interested in knowing the empirical effects of diversity on accuracy, that is, does lower (higher) diversity really imply lower (higher) overall accuracy performance?

In order to address these questions, we here use different resampling methods existing in the literature: selection without replacement [3], Bagging [4], Boosting [8], and Arc-x4 [5]. With respect to the fusion strategies, we introduce a number of techniques to weight the individual decisions dynamically. Finally, we use four measures of diversity: Q-statistics, correlation coefficient, disagreement measure, and variability measure. While the first three correspond to well-known measures properly adopted from the Statistics literature, the latter is a new measure proposed in this paper.

2   Measures of Diversity

Let $\mathcal{D} = \{D_1, \ldots, D_L\}$ be a set of L classifiers, and $\Omega = \{\omega_1, \ldots, \omega_c\}$ be a set of c classes. Each classifier D_i $(i = 1, \ldots, L)$ gets as input a feature vector $\mathbf{x} \in \Re^d$, and assigns it to one of the c problem classes. The output of an ensemble of classifiers is an L-dimensional vector $r = [D_1(\mathbf{x}), \ldots, D_L(\mathbf{x})]^{\mathrm{T}}$ containing the decisions of each classifier.

In the last years, numerous measures of diversity have been proposed in the literature, most of them being adapted from existing statistical measures. In practice, these measures can be categorized into two groups [13]: pairwise measures and non-pairwise measures. The pairwise measures are computed for each pair of classifiers in $\mathcal{D}$ and then averaged. The non-pairwise measures ether use the concept of entropy or correlation of individual outputs with the averaged output of $\mathcal{D}$ or are based on the distribution of "difficulty" of the data points. In this work, we concentrate on three pairwise measures taken from the literature, Q-statistics, correlation coefficient and disagreement measure. Moreover, a new non-pairwise measure, here called *variability measure*, will be proposed in the present section.

2.1   The Q-Statistics

Let $Y = \{y_1, y_2, \ldots, y_N\}$ be a set of labelled data. For two classifiers D_i and D_j, the Q-statistics is defined as

$$Q_{i,j} = \frac{ad - bc}{ad + bc} \tag{1}$$

where a is the number of elements in Y correctly classified by D_i and D_j, b is the number of elements correctly classified by D_i but not by D_j, c is the number of elements wrongly classified by D_i and correctly classified by D_j, and d is the number of elements wrongly classified by D_i and D_j. Then, $N = a + b + c + d$.

For a set of L classifiers, the averaged Q-statistics over all pairs of classifiers can be expressed as [13]

$$Q_{ave} = \frac{2}{L(L-1)} \sum_{i=1}^{L-1} \sum_{j=i+1}^{L} Q_{i,j} \tag{2}$$

For statistically independent classifiers (and $N \to \infty$), $Q_{i,j} = 0$. Q varies between -1 and $+1$. Classifiers that tend to classify the same objects correctly will have positive values of Q, while those which err on different objects will obtain negative values.

2.2 The Correlation Coefficient

This measure allows to quantify the relation between a pair of classifiers D_i and D_j.

$$\rho_{i,j} = \frac{ad - bc}{\sqrt{(a+b)(c+d)(a+c)(b+d)}} \tag{3}$$

For any two classifiers, ρ is between -1 and $+1$. Both -1 and $+1$ represent a total correlation between D_i and D_j, while $\rho_{i,j} = 0$ means that the pair of classifiers are not correlated at all. On the other hand, Q and ρ have the same sign, and it can be proved that $|\rho| \le |Q|$.

2.3 The Disagreement Measure

This measure is the ratio between the number of elements correctly classified by one classifier and wrongly by the other to the total number of elements [17, 13]. For two classifiers D_i and D_j, the disagreement measure varies between 0 and $+1$.

$$Dis_{i,j} = \frac{b+c}{a+b+c+d} \tag{4}$$

2.4 The Variability Measure

This corresponds to a new diversity measure proposed in this paper. Unlike the previous measures, this makes use of a decision matrix to store the class labels given by the L classifiers to each object. The measure can be defined as the proportion of the cases that have received different decisions, that is, at least one classifier disagrees with the rest of classifiers.

$$v = \frac{\sum_{i=1}^{N} \lambda}{N} \tag{5}$$

where $\lambda = 0$ if $D_1(\mathbf{y}) = D_2(\mathbf{y}) = \cdots = D_L(\mathbf{y})$, and $\lambda = 1$ otherwise.

The variability measure varies between 0 and $+1$. For $L = 2$ and $c = 2$, the variability measure matches the disagreement measure, that is, $v = Dis_{i,j}$.

3 Some Classifier Fusion Techniques

The simplest way to combine multiple classifiers is by *voting*, which corresponds to take a linear combination of the classifiers. Let w_j be the weight of the j classifier D_j, then the final output of the ensemble is computed as

$$r = \sum_{j=1}^{L} w_j D_j(\mathbf{x}) \tag{6}$$

where $\forall j, w_j \geq 0$ and $\sum_{j=1}^{L} w_j = 1$.

If each classifier just provides the class of the input pattern $\mathbf{x}$, then one can only have the *simple majority voting* where all classifiers have equal weight $w_j = 1/L$. If the classifiers can also supply additional information, then their votes can be weighted [14, 18], for example by a function of their distance to the input pattern. In this section, we introduce several weighting functions for classifier ensembles; some of them are taken from the Pattern Recognition literature and conveniently adapted to combine multiple classifiers, while others are now proposed for the first time.

A voting rule for the k-NN classifier, in which the votes of different neighbors are weighted by a function of their distance to the input pattern $\mathbf{x}$, was first proposed by Dudani [7]. A neighbor with smaller distance is weighted more heavily than one with a greater distance: the nearest neighbor gets a weight of 1, the furthest neighbor a weight of 0, and the other weights are scaled linearly to the interval in between.

$$w_j = \begin{cases} \frac{d_k - d_j}{d_k - d_1} & \text{if } d_k \neq d_1 \\ 1 & \text{if } d_k = d_1 \end{cases} \tag{7}$$

where d_j denotes the distance of the j'th nearest neighbor, d_1 is the distance of the nearest neighbor, and d_k indicates the distance of the furthest (k'th) neighbor.

In order to employ this weighting function in the context of classifier fusion, the value of k (i.e., the number of neighbors in Dudani's rule) can be here replaced by the number of classifiers L that constitute the ensemble. Moreover, the L distances of $\mathbf{x}$ to its nearest neighbor in each individual classifier have to be sorted in increasing order $(d_1, d_2, \ldots, d_L)$. Thus, the original Dudani's weight (Eq. 7) can be now rewritten as:

$$w(D_j) = \begin{cases} \frac{d_L - d_j}{d_L - d_1} & \text{if } d_L \neq d_1 \\ 1 & \text{if } d_L = d_1 \end{cases} \tag{8}$$

where d_1 denotes the shortest of the L distances of $\mathbf{x}$ to the nearest neighbor, and correspondingly d_L is the longest of those distances.

Dudani further proposed the *inverse distance weight* [7], which can be expressed as follows:

$$w(D_j) = \frac{1}{d_j} \quad \text{if } d_j \neq 0 \tag{9}$$

Another weighting function proposed here is based on the work of Shepard [16], who argues for a universal perceptual law which states that the relevance of a previous stimulus for the generalization to a new stimulus is an exponentially decreasing function of its distance in psychological space. This gives the weighted voting function of Eq. 10, where α and β are constants and determine the slope and the power of the exponential decay function.

$$w(D_j) = \exp^{-\alpha d_j^\beta} \tag{10}$$

A modification to Shepard's weight function consists of using a different value of α for each input pattern. Firstly, the L distances of $\mathbf{x}$ to its nearest neighbor in each individual classifier have to be sorted in decreasing order. Then, the value of α for each input pattern is computed according to $\alpha = L - j + 1$. By this, the higher the distance given by a classifier, the higher the value of α and thereby, the lower the weight assigned to such a classifier.

Finally, we propose another weighting function, which corresponds to the *average distance weight*. In summary, the aim is to reward (by assigning the highest weight) the individual classifier with the nearest neighbor to the input pattern. The rationale behind this function is that the classifier with the nearest neighbor to $\mathbf{x}$ will probably correspond to that with the highest accuracy in its classification.

$$w(D_j) = \frac{\sum_{i=1}^{L} d_i}{d_j} \tag{11}$$

4   Experimental Results

In this section, we present the results corresponding to the experiments carried out over seven data sets taken from the UCI Machine Learning Database Repository (http://www.ics.uci.edu/~mlearn). We adopted a 5-fold cross-validation process: each data set was divided into five equal parts, using four folds as the training set and the remaining block as an independent test set.

All classifier ensembles consist of nine individual classifiers ($L = 9$). The ensembles have been constructed through a class-dependent (stratified) resampling method by using four different techniques: selection without replacement (SWR), Bagging, Boosting, and Arc-x4. The unique classifier used for training all subsets corresponds to a 1-NN decision rule. Table 1 reports the averaged diversity computed over the different ensembles of classifiers, thus making possible to determine which resampling method produces the highest diversity, according to the measures introduced in Sect. 2.

It has to be noted that small values of the Q-statistics and the correlation coefficient indicate high diversity. Conversely, high values of the disagreement and the variability measures point to high diversity. This has been represented in Table 1 by including in brackets the relative position of each resampling method in a ranking of diversity (1 – highest; 4 – lowest). From this, one can see that while Arc-x4 clearly produces the highest diversity (except in the case of using the variability measure), the other resampling strategies give very similar levels of diversity (despite Boosting could be viewed as the method with the second highest diversity).

Theoretically, from these results, it is expected that the highest overall accuracies will be achieved when using Arc-x4, followed by Boosting. This will be checked in the next section, where we analyze the possible relation between diversity and accuracy, with respect to the resampling technique and/or the fusion scheme applied.

Table 1. Diversity by using different resampling techniques

	Heart	Pima	Vehicle	German	Phoneme	Waveform	Liver
Q-statistics							
SWR	0,27 (2)	0,45 (4)	0,48 (3)	0,40 (3)	0,68 (3)	0,49 (1)	0,17 (4)
Bagging	0,32 (3)	0,41 (3)	0,47 (2)	0,46 (4)	0,70 (4)	0,50 (2)	0,16 (3)
Boosting	0,39 (4)	0,39 (2)	0,48 (3)	0,38 (2)	0,67 (2)	0,57 (4)	0,12(2)
Arc-x4	0,13 (1)	0,22 (1)	0,41 (1)	0,34 (1)	0,61 (1)	0,54 (3)	0,04 (1)
Correlation coefficient							
SWR	0,16 (2)	0,26 (4)	0,30 (3)	0,23 (3)	0,44 (4)	0,29 (3)	0,13 (3)
Bagging	0,20 (3)	0,23 (3)	0,30 (3)	0,23 (3)	0,43 (3)	0,29 (3)	0,12 (2)
Boosting	0,22 (4)	0,22 (2)	0,26 (2)	0,19 (2)	0,36 (2)	0,28 (2)	0,55 (4)
Arc-x4	0,07 (1)	0,10 (1)	0,22 (1)	0,17 (1)	0,32 (1)	0,26 (1)	0,02(1)
Disagreement measure (%)							
SWR	0,41 (2)	0,33 (4)	0,34 (4)	0,36 (4)	0,22 (3)	0,26 (2)	0,42 (4)
Bagging	0,39 (3)	0,34 (3)	0,35 (3)	0,36 (3)	0,22 (3)	0,25 (3)	0,43 (3)
Boosting	0,38 (4)	0,36 (2)	0,37 (2)	0,38 (2)	0,26 (2)	0,28 (1)	0,47 (2)
Arc-x4	0,46 (1)	0,42 (1)	0,39 (1)	0,39 (1)	0,28 (1)	0,28 (1)	0,48 (1)
Variability measure							
SWR	0,92 (1)	0,80 (3)	0,84 (2)	0,88 (2)	0,55 (3)	0,62 (2)	0,95 (3)
Bagging	0,87 (2)	0,81 (2)	0,85 (1)	0,86 (3)	0,55 (3)	0,62 (2)	0,97 (1)
Boosting	0,82 (3)	0,84 (1)	0,83 (3)	0,89 (1)	0,61 (1)	0,67 (1)	0,96 (2)
Arc-x4	0,80 (4)	0,71 (4)	0,58 (4)	0,62 (4)	0,59 (2)	0,55 (4)	0,97 (1)

4.1 On the Relation Between Accuracy and Diversity

Importance of considering the possible relationship between accuracy and diversity of different resampling and/or fusion strategies comes from the fact that by this, it would be feasible to establish an appropriate policy to select the most suitable method for constructing classifier ensembles. The experimental results in Table 2 correspond to the average accuracy (and standard deviations) over the five folds when using the different resampling strategies (SWR, Bagging, Boosting, Arc-x4) together with the simple majority voting and the dynamic weighting methods described in Sect. 3.

From results in Table 2, we can sketch some comments. First, all ensembles provide similar performances, showing a slight improvement over the average accuracy of the single classifier. Second, application of some weighting function outperforms the simple majority voting on 6 out of 7 databases. Comparing the different weighting strategies, the best results correspond to the average distance and the inverse distance. Third, when focusing on the resampling strategies, although Boosting seems to be the method with the highest performance, in general differences are not statistical significant. Taking into account these preliminary results, it is possible to conclude that the fusion technique has a more important influence on accuracy than the resampling scheme.

When relating the diversity levels given in Table 1 with the accuracy rates reported in Table 2, one can observe that in most cases the highest diversity does not produce the highest performance, thus not fulfilling the theoretical expectations. It is worth pointing out that the variability measure is the one reflecting better the behavior of the ensembles, in the sense that those methods with the smallest values correspond to the lowest

Table 2. Average accuracies (and standard deviations) with different resampling and fusion methods. Values in bold type denote the highest accuracy for each database.

	Heart	Pima	Vehicle	German	Phoneme	Waveform	Liver
Single	58,2(6.2)	65,9(5.2)	64,2(1.8)	65,2(2.6)	76,1(8.4)	78,0(2.9)	65.2(4.8)
Simple voting							
SWR	62.2(2.1)	**72.8(5.0)**	61.4(1.9)	68.8(3.4)	75.0(10.0)	82.7(1.8)	63.8(7.2)
Bagging	62.6(5.0)	72.7(1.2)	60.6(2.3)	70.2(3.0)	75.0(9.4)	83.2(1.4)	63.2(5.2)
Boosting	63.0(5.5)	71.0(2.6)	62.3(4.7)	68.5(2.1)	71.9(13.7)	80.0(1.9)	65.2(4.7)
Arc-x4	59.3(3.9)	69.7(2.9)	54.8(4.3)	68.7(2.5)	74.4(11.1)	78.8(2.3)	63.8(6.9)
Average distance weight							
SWR	62.2(4.8)	72.0(4.5)	63.1(3.0)	69.3(3.3)	75.4(9.6)	82.7(1.7)	65.2(7.7)
Bagging	62.6(5.1)	72.7(1.7)	60.7(2.4)	**70.8(3.1)**	75.2(9.2)	83.2(1.4)	64.9(7.2)
Boosting	**63.4(3.5)**	69.7(3.2)	63.9(3.9)	68.8(2.2)	72.9(11.8)	80.0(1.9)	62.9(5.1)
Arc-x4	60.0(5.9)	69.5(3.1)	58.4(2.7)	67.6(2.8)	74.5(11.4)	79.5(1.9)	**66.1(4.8)**
Inverse distance weight							
SWR	62.2(4.8)	72.0(4.5)	63.1(3.0)	69.3(3.3)	75.4(9.6)	**83.5(0.8)**	64.6(7.9)
Bagging	62.6(5.1)	72.7(1.7)	60.7(2.4)	**70.8(3.1)**	75.2(9.2)	83.2(1.4)	64.4(6.7)
Boosting	**63.4(3.5)**	69.7(3.2)	63.9(3.9)	68.8(2.2)	72.9(11.8)	80.0(1.9)	62.6(5.0)
Arc-x4	60.0(5.9)	69.5(3.1)	58.4(2.7)	67.6(2.8)	74.5(11.4)	79.5(1.9)	64.9(5.0)
Shepard's weight							
SWR	58.2(3.4)	66.9(5.6)	63.7(2.2)	67.3(2.1)	75.0(9.9)	82.1(1.9)	65.8(4.1)
Bagging	59.6(10.2)	66.1(4.7)	61.5(2.9)	67.1(2.7)	74.8(9.4)	83.1(1.7)	62.6(5.6)
Boosting	61.1(4.0)	65.0(4.7)	65.6(1.5)	68.1(2.8)	72.9(12.2)	79.5(2.3)	57.4(8.6)
Arc-x4	58.5(8.1)	65.6(5.5)	59.2(3.4)	65.7(1.3)	74.4(11.0)	79.3(1.7)	63.8(3.4)
Modified Shepard's weight							
SWR	58.9(3.8)	66.8(5.4)	63.2(2.5)	64.3(1.9)	**75.7(10.0)**	77.7(2.5)	64.4(4.2)
Bagging	59.6(9.3)	66.0(4.8)	61.1(2.8)	64.4(2.7)	75.5(8.7)	78.1(2.1)	61.5(5.0)
Boosting	60.7(3.2)	65.8(5.0)	**65.7(0.8)**	66.1(1.7)	73.2(10.9)	76.3(3.1)	56.8(5.6)
Arc-x4	58.9(7.9)	65.1(5.4)	59.2(3.4)	65.8(1.1)	73.9(11.2)	76.2(1.6)	62.0(4.3)

accuracies. For example, Arc-x4 appears as the scheme with the lowest variability and also with the lowest accuracy.

5   Concluding Remarks

The present paper has analyzed the relationship between four diversity measures and the overall accuracy obtained with an ensemble of nine individual classifiers constructed by means of different resampling methods and various weighting functions for classifier fusion.

From the experiments, it seems that in general, diversity has low influence on the overall accuracy. In this sense, we found that not always the best results correspond to those situations with a higher diversity; analogously, small values of diversity do not directly imply low accuracy. With regards to resampling, we found that Arc-x4 appears as the scheme that produces ensembles with the highest diversity levels, although other methods, such as randomization [6], should be tested in a further research.

Acknowledgments. Partially supported by grants 10007-2006-01 (51626) and SEP-2003-C02-44225 from Mexican CONACyT, and DPI2006-15542 from Spanish CICYT.

References

1. Bahler, D., Navarro, L.: Methods for combining heterogeneous sets of classifier. In: Proc. 17th Natl. Conf. on Artificial Intelligence, Workshop on New Research Problems for Machine Learning (2000)
2. Banfield, B.E., Hall, L.O., Bowyer, K.W., Kegelmeyer, Jr., W.P.: A new Ensemble diversity measure applied to thinning ensembles. In: Proc. 4th Intl. Workshop on Multiple Classifier Systems, Guildford, UK, pp. 306–316 (2003)
3. Barandela, R., Valdovinos, R.M., Sánchez, J.S.: New applications of ensembles of classifiers. Pattern Analysis and Applications 6, 245–256 (2003)
4. Breiman, L.: Bagging predictors: Machine Learning. vol. 26, pp. 123–140 (1996)
5. Breiman, L.: Arcing classifiers: Annals of Statistics. vol. 26, pp. 801–823 (1998)
6. Dietterich, G.T.: An experimental comparison of three methods for constructing ensembles of decision trees: bagging, boosting, and randomization. Machine Learning 40, 139–157 (2000)
7. Dudani, S.A.: The distance weighted k-nearest neighbor rule. IEEE Trans. on Systems, Man and Cybernetics 6, 325–327 (1976)
8. Freund, Y., Schapire, R.E.: Experiments with a new boosting algorithm. In: Proc. 13th Intl. Conference on Machine Learning, pp. 148–156. Morgan Kaufmann, San Francisco (1996)
9. Ho, T.K.: Complexity of classification problems and comparative advantages of combined classifiers, In: Proc. 1st. Intl. Workshop on Multiple Classifier Systems, Cagliari, Italy, pp. 97–106 (2000)
10. Kuncheva, L.I.: Using measures of similarity and inclusion for multiple classifier fusion by decision templates. Fuzzy Sets and Systems 122, 401–407 (2001)
11. Kuncheva, L.I., Bezdek, J.C., Duin, R.P.W.: Decision templates for multiple classifier fusion. Pattern Recognition 34, 299–314 (2001)
12. Kuncheva, L.I., Kountchev, K.R.: Generating classifier outputs of fixed accuracy and diversity. Pattern Recognition Letters 23, 593–600 (2002)
13. Kuncheva, L.I., Whitaker, C.J.: Measures of diversity in classifier ensembles. Machine Learning 51, 181–207 (2003)
14. Littlestone, N., Warmuth, M.: Weighted majority algorithm. Information and Computation 108, 212–261 (1994)
15. Narasimhamurthy, A.: Evaluation of diversity measures for binary classifier ensembles. In: Proc. 6th Intl. Workshop on Multiple Classifier Systems, Seaside, CA, pp. 13–15 (2005)
16. Shepard, R.N.: Toward a universal law of generalization for psychological science. Science 237, 1317–1323 (1987)
17. Shipp, C.A., Kuncheva, L.I.: Relationships between combination methods and measures of diversity in combining classifier. Information Fusion 3, 135–148 (2002)
18. Wanas, N., Kamel, M.: Weighted combining of neural network ensembles. In: Proc. Intl. Joint Conf. on Neural Networks, vol. 2, pp. 1748–1752 (2002)

A Hierarchical Approach for Multi-task Logistic Regression

Àgata Lapedriza[1], David Masip[2], and Jordi Vitrià[1]

[1] Computer Vision Center-Dept. Informàtica
Universitat Autònoma de Barcelona, 08193 Bellaterra, Spain
{agata,jordi}@cvc.uab.es
[2] Universitat de Barcelona (UB), 08007 Barcelona, Spain
davidm@maia.ub.es

Abstract. In the statistical pattern recognition field the number of samples to train a classifier is usually insufficient. Nevertheless, it has been shown that some learning domains can be divided in a set of related tasks, that can be simultaneously trained sharing information among the different tasks. This methodology is known as the multi-task learning paradigm. In this paper we propose a multi-task probabilistic logistic regression model and develop a learning algorithm based in this framework, which can deal with the small sample size problem. Our experiments performed in two independent databases from the UCI and a multi-task face classification experiment show the improved accuracies of the multi-task learning approach with respect to the single task approach when using the same probabilistic model.

1 Introduction

Automatic pattern classification is one of the most active research topics in the machine learning field. This problem consists in assigning a given instance to a predefined group or class after observing different samples of this group. Examples of these frameworks in scientific areas are medical diagnosis, speech recognition or image categorization.

Statistical procedures have been shown to be a powerful tool to treat these classification problems, where an underlying probability model is assumed in order to calculate the posterior probability upon which the classification decision is made. Nevertheless, in these classical approaches a considerable number of training examples is needed to correctly learn the parameters of the model. For this reason, their application can be not appropriate when the obtention of training samples is difficult.

There are some situations where the estimation of a predictive model can take benefit from the estimation of other related ones. For instance, in a multiple speech recognition problem, we can share information from modelling the speech of different subjects, in handwritten text classification from different writers we could also take benefit from the several related classification tasks. Other examples in the computer vision field are identity verification problems, or related

J. Martí et al. (Eds.): IbPRIA 2007, Part II, LNCS 4478, pp. 258–265, 2007.

tasks in automatic drive guiding problems such as road lane tracking, broken or solid line classification, or direction marks identification. In these examples, each of the considered tasks belong to different problems. Nevertheless it seems clear that they belong to a related domain, where they share common information that can be used to improve the classification accuracies obtained in the single task learning framework.

One of the most important open problems in the statistical classification approach, is the lack of learning samples necessary to properly estimate the parameters of the classifier. Usually, in classification problems the data lays on high dimensional subspaces, being the theoretical number of samples needed exponential in terms of the data dimensionality (known as the curse of dimensionality problem [1]). Recently, it has been proposed a new learning paradigm, the multi-task learning (MTL) [2], that has been shown to mitigate this small sample size problem [3,4]. The MTL approach is based on simultaneously learning a set of related tasks, sharing the hypothesis space of classifiers or assuming some common generative process in the data from each tasks [5,6]. The advantages of MTL have been proved in the recent theory, and can be summarized in: (i) the bias learned in a multiple related task environment is less specific than in a single task problem, resulting in classifiers with less generalization error; (ii) the number of samples needed to simultaneously learn several related tasks sub-linearly decreases as a function of the number of tasks [4]. More recently the idea of multi-task learning has been extended to some of the state of the art classifiers: Evgeniou et al. applied MTL to the SVM [7] and Torralba et al. extended the Adaboost algorithm to the MTL case by sharing the feature space where each weak learned is trained [8].

In this work we propose a hierarchical Multi-task learning approach for the logistic regression model and also extend this idea to the multinomial logistic regression case. Once the model is presented we develop a learning algorithm according to this framework. The paper is organized as follows: in the next section the hierarchical multi-task logistic regression approach is explained in detail as well as the corresponding algorithm and its extension to the multinomial logistic regression case, section 3 describes the performed experiments and section 4 includes the discussion of the results. Finally, section 5 concludes this work.

2   A Hierarchical Learning Approach for Multi-task Logistic Regression

Let be $T_1, ..., T_M$ a set of related binary tasks and $D = \{S_1, ..., S_M\}$ the set of corresponding training data, $S_i = \{(x_n^i, y_n^i)\}_{n=1,..,N(i)}$ such that $x_n^i \in \mathbb{R}^d$, $y_n^i \in \{-1, 1\}$. Consider for each task a logistic regression model, that is, for each T_i we learn a classifier f_i, that will give the probability of the output $y = 1$ according to the i-th task for the input x,

$$f_i(x) = P(y = 1 | x, T_i) = \frac{1}{1 + exp(-\mathbf{w}^{(i)} x^T)} \tag{1}$$

where $\mathbf{w}^{(i)} = (w_1^i, ..., w_d^i)$ is the parameters vector of the i-th task. Let be W the parameters matrix, considering all the tasks,

$$W = \begin{pmatrix} w_1^{(1)} & \cdots & w_1^{(M)} \\ \vdots & \vdots & \vdots \\ w_d^{(1)} & \cdots & w_d^{(M)} \end{pmatrix}$$

To learn the parameters of the model we can apply a negated log-likelihood estimator $L(D, W)$ and impose a prior distribution on the elements of W as a regularization therm, $R(W)$. In that case, the negated log-likelihood estimator for all the tasks T_i is

$$L(D, W) = -log[\prod_{i=1}^{M}[\prod_{n=1}^{N(i)} P(y_i^n | x_i^n, W)]] = -[\sum_{i=1}^{M}[\sum_{n=1}^{N(i)} log(P(y_i^n | x_i^n, W))] \quad (2)$$

and regarding to the regularization therm, most of the current methods use centered Gaussian priors. Then, the elements of the matrix W are obtained by the minimization of the following loss function

$$H(W) = L(D, W) + \frac{1}{\sigma^2}\|W\|_2 \quad (3)$$

where $\sigma \in \mathbb{R}^+$ is the variance of the imposed regularization distribution. This optimization problem can be solved applying any appropriated method, for example a gradient descent algorithm [9].

This method has shown to be efficient in many situations. However, observe that in this presented framework there is no transit of information between the models of the different tasks. Suppose that we want to learn the parameters of the logistic regression for this classification scenario enforcing the different classes to share information, following the principles of MTL. For this purpose, we can impose prior distributions on each row of W in a hierarchical way as follows. Consider the mean vector $\bar{\mathbf{w}} = (\bar{w}_1, ..., \bar{w}_d)$ where

$$\bar{w}_j = \frac{\sum_{i=1}^{M} w_j^{(i)}}{M} \quad (4)$$

First, we can impose a Gaussian centered prior to the mean vector $\bar{\mathbf{w}}$ and after that we can enforce that each row of W follows a Gaussian distribution with $\bar{w}_d$ mean. In short, this can be obtained by the minimization of the loss function

$$G(W) = L(D, W) + \frac{1}{\sigma_1^2}\|\bar{\mathbf{w}}\|_2 + \frac{1}{\sigma_2^2}\sum_{i=1}^{M} \|\mathbf{w}^{(i)} - \bar{\mathbf{w}}\|_2 = L(D, W) + R(W) \quad (5)$$

where $L(D, W)$ is again the negated log-likelihood estimator and σ_r^2 are the corresponding variances of the imposed priors, $r = 1, 2$.

2.1   Training Algorithm

Any optimization method that allows to minimize G will yield a training algorithm for our purpose. In this case we can apply a gradient descent algorithm to optimize it given that the loss function in equation 5 is differentiable. More concretely, we have used the BFGS gradient descent method. The principal idea of the method is to construct an approximate Hessian matrix of second derivatives of the function to be minimized, by analyzing successive gradient vectors. This approximation of the function's derivatives allows the application of a quasi-Newton fitting method in order to move towards the minimum in the parameter space.

Thus, we need to compute the partial derivatives

$$\frac{\partial G(W)}{\partial w_k^{(s)}} = \frac{\partial L(W, D)}{\partial w_k^{(s)}} + \frac{\partial R(W)}{\partial w_k^{(s)}} \tag{6}$$

Observe that $R(W)$ can rewritten as follows

$$R(W) = \sum_{j=1}^{d} [\frac{\bar{\mathbf{w}}_j^2}{\sigma_1^2} + \frac{1}{\sigma_2^2} \sum_{i=1}^{M} (w_j^i - \bar{\mathbf{w}}_j)^2] \tag{7}$$

and this is the only part of $G(W)$ that depends on $\bar{\mathbf{w}}$. Thus, given that we want to minimize this function, we can get an expression for $\bar{w}_j$ depending on W by

$$\bar{w}_j = \arg \min_w (\frac{w^2}{\sigma_1^2} + \frac{1}{\sigma_2^2} \sum_{i=1}^{M} (w_j^i - w)^2) \tag{8}$$

that yields

$$\bar{\mathbf{w}}_j(W) = \frac{\sigma_1^2 \sum_{i=1}^{M} w_j^i}{\sigma_2^2 + M\sigma_1^2} \tag{9}$$

and consequently

$$\frac{\partial \bar{\mathbf{w}}_j(W)}{\partial w_k^{(s)}} = \begin{cases} \frac{\sigma_1^2}{\sigma_2^2 + M\sigma_1^2} & \text{if } j = k \\ 0 & \text{if } j \neq k \end{cases}$$

Moreover,

$$\frac{\partial R(W)}{\partial w_k^{(s)}} = \frac{2\bar{w}_k}{\sigma_1^2} \frac{\partial \bar{\mathbf{w}}_k}{\partial w_k^{(s)}} + \frac{2}{\sigma_2^2} \sum_{i=1}^{M} [(w_k^{(i)} - \bar{\mathbf{w}}_k) \frac{\partial \bar{\mathbf{w}}_k}{\partial w_k^{(s)}}) \tag{10}$$

and substituting by the functions in equations 9 and the corresponding derivatives we obtain the final expression for the partial derivatives of $R(W)$.

2.2   Extension to the Multinomial Logistic Regression Model

Multinomial Logistic Regression model is a statistical model suitable for probabilistic multi-class classification problems. Formally, given M classes $C_1, ..., C_M$, any element x in the input space $\mathbb{R}^d$ is categorized according to the criterion

$$class(x) = \arg \max_{C_i, i=1..M} \frac{P(x \in C_i)}{\sum_{k=1}^{M} P(x \in C_k)} \tag{11}$$

where

$$P(x \in C_i) = \frac{1}{1 + exp(-\mathbf{w}^{(i)} x^T)} \tag{12}$$

and each $\mathbf{w}^{(i)}$ is the parameters vector corresponding to the ith-class, that is the ith-column of the parameters matrix

$$W = \begin{pmatrix} w_1^{(1)} & \cdots & w_1^{(M)} \\ \vdots & \vdots & \vdots \\ w_d^{(1)} & \cdots & w_d^{(M)} \end{pmatrix}$$

Assuming that we have a training set of samples $D = \{(x_n, y_n)\}_{n=1,..,N}$, where each $x_n \in \mathbb{R}^d$ and $y_n \in \{C_1, ..., C_M\}$, we can consider the loss function described above (see 5) to fix the parameters supposing that $L(W, D)$ is now the negated log-likelihood estimator for this new situation, according to equation 11 and 12.

3 Experiments

To test the presented model for both multi-task and multi-class problems we have performed different experiments. For the multi-task case we have learned different face verification tasks and have used images from the public ARFace Database [10]. For the multi-class case, we have performed classification experiments in two databases from the UCI Machine Learning Repository [11].

3.1 Multi-task Experiments

To test the algorithm in the case of multiple binary related tasks we have performed a set of face verification experiments using the public database AR Face (*http://rvl.www.ecn.purdue.edu/RVL/*). Here we consider that a verification task is a binary problem consisting on decide whether a new unseen face image belongs to the learned subject or not.

The AR Face database contains 26 frontal face images from 126 different subjects. The data set has from each person 1 sample of neutral frontal images, 3 samples with strong changes in the illumination, 2 samples with occlusions (scarf and glasses), 4 images combining occlusions and illumination changes, and 3 samples with gesture effects. Images where taken in two separately periods of time (two samples from each type). Some examples of images in the AR Face database are shown in figure 1.

We have performed the experiments considering from 2 to 10 verification problems. In this experiments we have used 2 positive samples and 4 negative samples to train the system, and the test set includes 20 positive images and 40 negatives. We have performed 10 experiments for each case, and both train and test samples have been randomly selected. The parameters of the method that we have used in multi-task case are $\sigma_1 = 2$ and $\sigma_2 = 6$. In single task case we used $\sigma = 2$.

Table 1 includes the mean error obtained in each case and the corresponding confidence intervals.

Fig. 1. Some samples of images in the AR Face database

Table 1. Obtained error and 95% confidence intervals for the logistic regression method trained separately (first row) and for our shared logistic approach (second row). When more than 4 verification tasks are simultaneously trained, the error rates of the shared approach become lower. No mean error is shown in the case of multi-task logistic regression when only one task is considered.

	1	2	3	4	5
Logistic	32.9 ± 8.2	34.5 ± 6.4	30.5 ± 5.3	31.8 ± 4.2	30.2 ± 3.9
Multi-task Logistic	-	41.6 ± 4.2	35.8 ± 5.4	32.1 ± 5.2	28.7 ± 5.2
	6	7	8	9	10
Logistic	31.8 ± 3.6	31.4 ± 3.3	29.6 ± 3.3	30.2 ± 3.0	29.6 ± 2.9
Multi-task Logistic	27.2 ± 4.2	23.6 ± 3.1	21.8 ± 2.8	17.5 ± 2.4	15.4 ± 2.3

3.2 Multi-class Classification Experiments

We have used Balance and Iris databases from the UCI Machine Learning Repository to perform multi-class classification experiments. In table 2 are detailed the characteristics of these databases.

The parameters of the method have been adjusted by cross validation. The values were $\sigma_1 = 2$ and $\sigma_2 = 6$ for the multi-task case, and $\sigma = 2$ for the single task training.

Table 2. Balance and Iris databases details

Database	Number of elements	Number of features	Number of classes
Balance	625	4	3
Iris	150	4	3

Given that multi-task learning frameworks are specially appropriated when there are few elements in the training set, we have used 10% of the data in

Table 3. Error and confidence interval in the classification experiments using Balance and Iris databases using single-task and multi-task training processes

Database	Single-Task	Multi-Task
Balance	$36.76\% \pm 1.48\%$	$31.48\% \pm 1.29\%$
Iris	$14.45\% \pm 1.85\%$	$7.04\% \pm 0.65\%$

the training step and 90% in the test step. We have performed 10 10-fold cross validation experiments and the results are detailed in table 3.

3.3   Discussion

In the multi-task learning experiments we observe a considerable improvement of the accuracy when using the proposed multi-task logistic regression approach. On the one hand, when the single task model is used, the accuracy does not variate when we consider more tasks. However, when we use the proposed MTL approach we can observe that the accuracy increases when we consider more tasks, and this improvement is specially significant when more than 7 tasks are considered, where we do not have overlapping between the obtained results with the corresponding confidence intervals in both cases. To justify this evolution of the results, it should be taken into account that with the presented model the method can detect in a more general way features that are relevant for any subject verification task. In these experiments, the task relatedness is clear: the features that can be relevant to determine whether a face belongs to a given subject or not can be as well interesting to verify another subject.

In the multi-class learning experiments performed with Balance and Iris databases from the UCI data sets, there is also a significant improvement of the results when we use the MTL approach, although the statistical relationship of the features among the different classes is not as clear as in the face verification case.

4   Conclusion

In this paper we propose a multi-task learning approach based on sharing knowledge from the parameter space of the probabilistic model. The contribution of the information sharing among the related classification tasks is specially noticeable when only a few samples per class are available.

The experiments performed using two data sets from the UCI database, and a face classification problem using the AR Face data base suggest that the multi-task approach fares better than a single task learning of the same tasks using the same probabilistic logistic regression model. Notice that the MTL restrictions that the model assumes are strong, for this reason it can not be appropriated in general data sets. However, there are cases where these restrictions do hold and in these cases the improvement of our MTL approach is notably. Therefore we plan as a future work to develop a less restrictive version of this MTL modelling.

The probabilistic model presented in this paper suggests new lines of future research. In this formulation, we impose the knowledge sharing property by constraining the parameter space of the classifiers along the multiple tasks. However, more complex approaches based on hidden distributions on the parameters space can be considered.

Moreover, in MTL topic there are still open lines of research, for example to define formally the task relatedness concept. In our model, we impose statistical priors on the task distribution, assuming certain feature information share among the tasks. Given that this assumption is quite restrictive, the method will be appropriated only when the data distribution is agree with this considerations.

Acknowledgments. This work is supported by MEC grant TIN2006-15308-C02-01, Ministerio de Ciencia y Tecnologia, Spain.

References

1. Bellman, R.: Adaptive Control Process: A Guided Tour. Princeton University Press, New Jersey (1961)
2. Caruana, R.: Multitask learning. Machine Learning 28(1), 41–75 (1997)
3. Thrun, S., Pratt, L.: Learning to Learn. Kluwer Academic Publishers, Dordrecht (1997)
4. Baxter, J.: A model of inductive bias learning. Journal of Machine Learning Research 12, 149–198 (2000)
5. Intrator, N., Edelman, S.: Making a low-dimensional representation suitable for diverse tasks. Connection Science 8, 205–224 (1997)
6. Zhang, J., Ghahramani, Z., Yang, Y.: Learning multiple related tasks using latent independent component analysis. In: Weiss, Y., Schölkopf, B., Platt, J. (eds.) Advances in Neural Information Processing Systems 18, MIT Press, Cambridge, MA (2006)
7. Evgeniou, T., Micchelli, C., Pontil, M.: Learning multiple tasks with kernel methods. Journal of Machine Learning Research 6, 615–637 (2005)
8. Torralba, A., Murphy, K., Freeman, W.: Sharing features: efficient boosting procedures for multiclass object detection. In: Proceedings of the IEEE Conference on Computer Vision and Pattern Recognition (2004)
9. Madigan, D., Genkin, A., Lewis, D.D., Fradkin, D.: Bayesian multinomial logistic regression for author identification
10. Martinez, A., Benavente, R.: The AR Face database. Technical Report 24, Computer Vision Center (1998)
11. Blake, C., Merz, C.: UCI repository of machine learning databases (1998)

Modelling of Magnetic Resonance Spectra Using Mixtures for Binned and Truncated Data

Juan M. Garcia-Gomez[1], Montserrat Robles[1], Sabine Van Huffel[2], and Alfons Juan-Císcar[3]

[1] BET-IBM, Polytechnical University of Valencia
[2] Katholieke Universiteit Leuven, Dept. of Electrical Engineering, ESAT-SCD(SISTA)
[3] DSIC, Polytechnical University of Valencia

Abstract. Magnetic Resonance Spectroscopy (MRS) provides the bio-chemical composition of a tissue under study. This information is useful for the in-vivo diagnosis of brain tumours. Prior knowledge of the relative position of the organic compound contributions in the MRS suggests the development of a probabilistic mixture model and its EM-based Maximum Likelihood Estimation for binned and truncated data. Experiments for characterizing and classifying Short Time Echo (STE) spectra from brain tumours are reported.

Keywords: Expectation-Maximization, Binned data, ^{1}H magnetic resonance spectroscopy (MRS), automatic classification, brain tumour.

1 Introduction

Magnetic Resonance Spectroscopy (MRS) exploits the magnetic properties of ^{1}H nuclei to provide information about the concentration of the compounds of materials. This makes MRS useful as non-invasive technique for brain tumour diagnosis. The MRS signals are typically interpreted in the frequency domain by visual or automatic procedures to characterize the contribution of the biological compound in the tissue. The amplitude of a compound is proportional to its concentration. This motivates the fitting of MRS spectra by mixture density models.

MRS spectra are typically analyzed by two different approaches. The first approach estimates the underlying model composed by mixtures of components to quantify the concentration of the metabolites. Frequency-domain [1] or time-domain [2] fitting methods based on signal processing are applied to the signals. The second approach extracts features from the spectra using univariate-, multivariate-statistics or pattern recognition methods [3] based on their usefulness on discrimination or regression.

This work proposes the definition and estimation of a probabilistic model based on binned and truncated data to fit ^{1}H magnetic resonance spectra using prior knowledge about the relative position of the components of the organic compounds observed in the tumoral masses of the brain. The estimated parameters for each

J. Martí et al. (Eds.): IbPRIA 2007, Part II, LNCS 4478, pp. 266–273, 2007.

spectrum summarize the information from the biological compounds and they are used as features in classification problems of brain tumour diagnosis.

Mixture modelling has been applied in some applications where data are available only in bins and may not be provided along the whole the range [4,5,6]. In [4], red blood cells were collected as volume distributions from a Coulter counter to study the disease status of animals exposed to *Anaplasma marginale*. The problem in MRS is similar to the previous problems in the sense that contributions of a mixture of biological compounds are assumed to be observed as counts of bins in a range of the ppm-axis. We present an adaptation of the EM for fitting MR spectra, qualitative results in the characterization of spectra and quantitative results in the classification of brain tumours by the use of the estimated parameters.

The rest of the paper is organized as follows. In sections 2 and 3, the probabilistic model and its EM-based Maximum Likelihood Estimation are presented. Then, results using MRS spectra of brain tumours are reported in section 4.

2 Probabilistic Model

Let $\mathcal{X}$ be a sample space partitioned into B bins, $\mathcal{X}_1, \ldots, \mathcal{X}_B$, of which only the counts on the first B' bins can be recorded, while the counts on the last $B - B'$ can not. For instance, in the univariate case, the first B' bins may be delimited by $B' + 1$ points, $p_0, p_1, \ldots, p_{B'}$, such that $p_0 < p_1 < \cdots < p_{B'}$ and $X_b = (p_{b-1}, p_b]$, $b = 1, \ldots, B'$. N independent samples (draws) from $\mathcal{X}$ are made, but our measuring instrument reports only the number of samples falling in each of these first, *observable* B' bins, but fails to report similar counts for samples out of them, in the $B - B'$ *truncated* regions (e.g. $(-\infty, p_0]$ and $(p_{B'}, \infty)$).

Let $N' = (N_1, \ldots, N_{B'})$ be the vector of observed counts and let $N' = \sum_{b=1}^{B'} N_b$. Clearly, the probability of N' can be computed by marginalisation of the joint probability of both, observed and truncated counts,

$$p(N') = \sum_{N_{B'+1}, \ldots, N_B} p(N) \tag{1}$$

where $N = (N_1, \ldots, N_{B'}, N_{B'+1}, \ldots, N_B)$ is the complete vector of counts. We do not know the truncated counts, nor even the total number of samples N, but we know that N has a multinomial distribution defined by N samples from B categories,

$$p(N) = \frac{N!}{\prod_{b=1}^{B} N_b!} \prod_{b=1}^{B} p(b)^{N_b} \tag{2}$$

where $p(b)$ is the probability for a sample to fall in bin $\mathcal{X}_b$, $b = 1, \ldots, B$.

We assume that (2) can also be computed by marginalisation of the joint density for counts and (missing) samples,

$$p(N) = \int d\boldsymbol{X}\, p(N, \boldsymbol{X}) \tag{3}$$

where $X = (X_1, \ldots, X_B)$ is the whole collection of N independent samples, $X_b = (x_{b1}, \ldots, x_{bN_b})$ is the collection of those N_b from bin $\mathcal{X}_b$ ($b = 1, \ldots, B$), and

$$p(N, X) = \frac{N!}{\prod_{b=1}^{B} N_b!} \prod_{b=1}^{B} \prod_{n=1}^{N_b} p(x_{bn}) \tag{4}$$

where $p(x_{bn})$ is the (unknown) probability density for a sample from bin $\mathcal{X}_b$.

At this point, we assume that samples come from a common probability density function, irrespective of their originating bins. This density function is a parametric, C-component mixture,

$$p_\Theta(x) = \sum_{c=1}^{C} \pi_c \, p_{\Theta'}(x \mid c) \tag{5}$$

where $\Theta = (\pi, \Theta')$ is the parameter vector of the mixture; $\pi = (\pi_1, \ldots, \pi_C)$ is the vector of mixture coefficients, subject to $\sum_c \pi_c = 1$, and Θ' includes the parameters required to define each mixture component $p_{\Theta'}(x \mid c)$, $c = 1, \ldots, C$. As usual with finite mixtures, we may think of x as an incomplete component-labelled sample which may be completed by addition of an indicator variable (component label) $z \in \{0, 1\}^C$ with 1 in the position of the indicated component and zeros elsewhere. Therefore, we can rewrite (5) as

$$p_\Theta(x) = \sum_z p_\Theta(x, z) \tag{6}$$

with

$$p_\Theta(x, z) = \prod_{c=1}^{C} (\pi_c \, p_{\Theta'}(x \mid c))^{z_c} \tag{7}$$

By substitution of (7) in (6), (6) in (4) and some straightforward manipulations, we can rewrite (4) as

$$p_\Theta(N, X) = \sum_Z p_\Theta(N, X, Z) \tag{8}$$

where Z is the collection of component labels for X, that is, $Z = (Z_1, \ldots, Z_B)$, with $Z_b = (z_{b1}, \ldots, z_{bN_b})$ and $z_{bn} \in \{0, 1\}^C$ ($b = 1, \ldots, B$; $n = 1, \ldots, N_b$); and

$$p_\Theta(N, X, Z) = \frac{N!}{\prod_{b=1}^{B} N_b!} \prod_{b=1}^{B} \prod_{n=1}^{N_b} \prod_{c=1}^{C} (\pi_c \, p_{\Theta'}(x_{bn} \mid c))^{z_{bnc}} \tag{9}$$

Note that we have added the parameter vector Θ as a subscript to the joint densities $p_\Theta(N, X)$ and $p_\Theta(N, X, Z)$ to emphasize their dependence on the parameters governing the hidden mixture (5).

Now, by substitution of (8) in (3), and (3) in (1), we can write our probabilistic model as

$$p_\Theta(N') = \sum_{N_{B'+1}, \ldots, N_B} \int dX \sum_Z p_\Theta(N, X, Z) \tag{10}$$

Note that $p_{\Theta}(N')$ can be seen as an *incomplete* model which results from marginalisation (many-to-one mapping) of the *complete* model $p_{\Theta}(N, X, Z)$.

Obviously, model (10) still needs adoption of a particular parametric form for the mixture components. Taking into account the specific application considered in this work, we will assume that samples are drawn from a C-component mixture of univariate normal densities, of means known up to a *global shift* μ_0, and independent variances $\sigma_1^2, \ldots, \sigma_C^2$; that is, for all $c = 1, \ldots, C$,

$$p_{\Theta'}(x \mid c) \sim N(\mu_0 + \delta_c, \sigma_c^2) \tag{11}$$

where δ_c is the known displacement from μ_0 of the cth component mean. Thus, the vector of parameters governing the mixture components is $\Theta' = (\mu_0, \sigma_1^2, \ldots, \sigma_C^2)$.

3   EM-Based Maximum Likelihood Estimation

Maximum likelihood estimation of Θ using the EM algorithm has been previously considered in [4] and [5] for the univariate and multivariate normal cases, respectively. Our case is similar to, but slightly different from the general, parameter-independent univariate case. More precisely, the general univariate model assumes that component means are independent, while in our model all of them are known up to a global shift. This makes our estimation problem simpler, but the EM algorithm is almost identical. In what follows, we briefly review the EM algorithm for the general model and then we provide the neccessary modifications for our modelling variation. The reader is referred to [4] for more details.

The log-likelihood function of Θ w.r.t. a given N' is

$$L(\Theta; N') = \log \sum_{N_{B'+1}, \ldots, N_B} \int dX \sum_{Z} p_{\Theta}(N, X, Z) \tag{12}$$

which is exactly the logarithm of $p_{\Theta}(N')$ as defined in (10), but interpreted as a function of Θ only, and assuming that mixture components are univariate normals. The EM algorithm maximises (12) iteratively, through the application of two basic steps in each iteration: the E(xpectation) step and the M(aximisation) step. On the one hand, the E step computes a lower bound of (12) for all Θ; the so-called Q function,

$$Q(\Theta \mid \Theta^{(k)}) = E[\log p_{\Theta}(N, X, Z) \mid N', \Theta^{(k)}] \tag{13}$$

that is, the expectation of the logarithm of the complete model, conditional to the incomplete data, N', and a current estimation of the model parameters, $\Theta^{(k)}$. On the other hand, the M step obtains a new estimate for Θ, $\Theta^{(k+1)}$, by maximisation of the Q function,

$$\Theta^{(k+1)} = \arg\max_{\Theta} Q(\Theta \mid \Theta^{(k)}) \qquad \text{s.t.} \sum_{c} \pi_c = 1 \tag{14}$$

Given an initial value of the parameters, $\Theta^{(0)}$, these two steps are repeated until convergence to a local maximum of the likelihood function.

Ignoring an additive term not involving Θ, the Q function can be written as

$$Q(\Theta \mid \Theta^{(k)}) = \sum_{c=1}^{C} \sum_{b=1}^{B} N_b^{(k)} \, E_b[z_c^{(k)}(x_b)(\log \pi_c + \log p_{\Theta'}(x_b \mid c)) \mid N', \Theta^{(k)}] \quad (15)$$

where $N_b^{(k)}$ is the expected number of samples drawn from bin $\mathcal{X}_b$,

$$N_b^{(k)} = \begin{cases} N_b & \text{if } b \leq B' \\ N' \, \dfrac{p(b)^{(k)}}{\sum_{b'=1}^{B'} p(b')^{(k)}} & \text{otherwise} \end{cases} \quad (16)$$

with $p(b)^{(k)}$ being the probability for a sample to fall in bin $\mathcal{X}_b$,

$$p(b)^{(k)} = \int_{\mathcal{X}_b} dx \, p_{\Theta^{(k)}}(x) \quad (17)$$

The expectation in (15) is with respect to a sample x_b from bin $\mathcal{X}_b$; i.e., with respect to the truncated density of the bin $\mathcal{X}_b$

$$p_{\Theta^{(k)}}^{\text{trunc}}(x_b) = \frac{p_{\Theta^{(k)}}(x_b)}{p(b)^{(k)}} \quad (18)$$

and involves the posterior probability for x_b to belong to component c of the mixture, given a current parameter estimate $\Theta^{(k)}$,

$$z_c^{(k)}(x_b) = \frac{\pi_c^{(k)} \, p_{\Theta'^{(k)}}(x_b \mid c)}{p_{\Theta^{(k)}}(x_b)} \quad (19)$$

Maximisation of (15), as indicated in (14), leads to the following re-estimates for each component c ($c = 1, \ldots, C$)

$$\pi_c^{(k+1)} = \frac{\sum_{b=1}^{B} N_b^{(k)} \, E_b[z_c^{(k)}(x_b) \mid N', \Theta^{(k)}]}{\sum_{b=1}^{B} N_b^{(k)}} \quad (20)$$

$$\mu_c^{(k+1)} = \frac{\sum_{b=1}^{B} N_b^{(k)} \, E_b[x_b \, z_c^{(k)}(x_b) \mid N', \Theta^{(k)}]}{\sum_{b=1}^{B} N_b^{(k)} \, E[z_c^{(k)}(x_b) \mid N', \Theta^{(k)}]} \quad (21)$$

$$\sigma_c^{2(k+1)} = \frac{\sum_{b=1}^{B} N_b^{(k)} \, E_b[(x_b - \mu_c^{(k+1)})^2 \, z_c^{(k)}(x_b) \mid N', \Theta^{(k)}]}{\sum_{b=1}^{B} N_b^{(k)} \, E[z_c^{(k)}(x_b) \mid N', \Theta^{(k)}]} \quad (22)$$

where, as in (15), all expectations are with respect to the truncated density (18). Their derivations were shown by McLachlan and Jones in [4,7].

Equations (20), (21) and (22) are the basic equations of an EM iteration in the general, parameter-independent univariate case (EMBTD). In our case

(EM4BTDr), with means known up to shift μ_0, the basic equations are (20), (22) and $\mu_c^{(k+1)} = \mu_0^{(k+1)} + \delta_c, c = 1, \ldots, C$, where

$$\mu_0^{(k+1)} = \frac{\sum_{c=1}^{C} \sum_{b=1}^{B} N_b^{(k)} E_b[(x_b - \delta_c) z_c^{(k)}(x_b) \mid \boldsymbol{N'}, \boldsymbol{\Theta}^{(k)}]}{\sum_{c=1}^{C} \sum_{b=1}^{B} N_b^{(k)} E_b[z_c^{(k)}(x_b) \mid \boldsymbol{N'}, \boldsymbol{\Theta}^{(k)}]}, \qquad (23)$$

4   Experimental Results

The mixture models presented in the previous sections were applied to 147 multicenter signals acquired during the Interpret project [8]. The brain tumour diagnosis and quality of signals were validated by two committees of experts [3]. The number of cases per diagnosis are 77 Glioblastoma Multiforme (GM), 50 Meningioma (MM) and 20 Astrocytoma grade II (A2). STE, (TE $\in$ [20,30]ms) Single Voxel (SV) spectra were used in the study [3]. The reference point for each spectra was set and validated visually by a spectroscopist, then little or null shifting is expected in the components.

The a priori information from biochemical knowledge used in the experiments was the chemical shift (in ppm units) of metabolites L2 (0.92), Glx (2.04), L1 (1.25), Glx2 (2.46), LAC (1.31), Glx3 (3.76), ALA (1.48, 1.46), mI (3.26), NAc (2.02, 2.00), mI2 (3.53), Cr (3.03), mI3 (3.61), Cr2 (3.92), Tau (3.25), Cho (3.19), Tau2 (3.42), Gly (3.55), ALA2 (3.78). The initial models for both algorithms was exactly the same, equal prior probability and variance for each component were established.

Figure 1 summarizes the main behaviour of the EMBTD (EM for Binned and Truncated data in general form) and EMBTDr (EM for Binned and Truncated data with means known up to shift μ_0) estimates. In the first example (top-left), the parameters estimated by both EMBTD and EMBTDr are quite similar, hence the spectrum is fitted in a similar way. In the second example (top-right), the related means restriction incorporated in the EMBTDr model keeps the position of the compounds better than the EMBTD model according to the underlying biological mixture. In the third example (bottom), the EMBTD model fits a lipid contribution at 2.75ppm not specified in the prior knowledge, but the meaning of the initial components based on biological knowledge is lost.

Two studies were carried out to characterize the behaviour of the models on average. In the first study, we measure the mean of the differences between the estimated shifting ($\hat{\mu}_c$) of the components with respect to the typical chemical shift (μ_c). None or small shifting is assumed in the spectra of the database. Therefore, the smaller difference, the closer the estimated component is to the organic compound. Table 1 shows the results obtained by EMBTD and EMBTDr on the MRS database. The differences obtained by both models are small, considering that the range is 3.6ppm and the frequency resolution 0.02ppm. However, the difference obtained on average by EMBTD is 3.6 times the difference obtained by EMBTDr. Hence, EMBTDr keeps better the position of the biological compound in the estimated model.

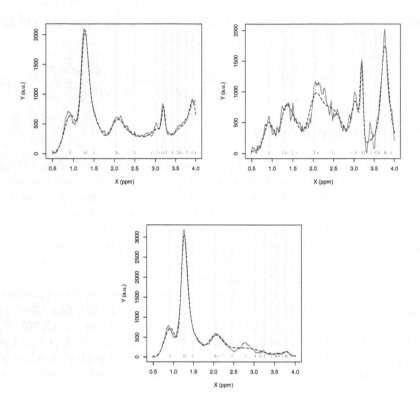

Fig. 1. Three spectra showing the behaviour of the EMBTD and EMBTDr models. Real spectra are drawn in solid lines, EMBTD models in dashed lines and EMBTDr in double-dashed lines. μ_c are marked with vertical lines, $\hat{\mu}_c$ of each model are marked with a small vertical line for EMBTD and two dots for EMBTDr.

Table 1. Mean of the difference between the estimated shifting of the components by the EM algorithms with respect to the typical chemical shift

	EMBTD	EMBTDr
$\mu_c - \hat{\mu}_c$	0.0079	0.0022

Table 2. Results in classification. Cells are composed by ϵ [95%-CI], where ϵ is the error estimation and [95%-CI] the 95% credibility intervals [9].

classes	PCA+LDA	EMBTD+LDA	EMBTDr+LDA
MM GM	17.32 [11.50,24.54]	**10.24 [5.86 16.31]**	14.17 [8.93,20.94]
MM A2	**7.14 [2.84 14.70]**	14.29 [7.59,23.70]	**7.14 [2.84,14.70]**
GM A2	8.25 [4.00,14.81]	9.28 [4.71,16.11]	**5.15 [2.05,10.74]**

In the second study, the $(\hat{\pi})$ parameters estimated by the EMBTD and EM-BTDr were the input variables of binary classifiers based on Linear Discriminant Analysis (LDA). The performace of these classifiers where compared with similar LDA classifiers based on PCA (Principal Component Analysis). Table 2 shows the estimation of the error, carried out by Cross Validation with 10 stratified partitions. EMBTDr achieves the best performance when classifing A2 from GM and A2 from MM (equal to PCA). In the discrimination of MM from GM, both EMBTDr and EMBTD estimates are considerable better than the PCA model.

5   Conclusions and Further Work

A probabilistic mixture model for binned and truncated data with univariate mixture densities of means known up to a global shift has been proposed for Magnetic Resonance Spectroscopy data characterization. The model can be efficiently estimated by means of the E(xpectation)-M(aximisation) algorithm. The new version of the algorithm keeps the biological information in the model and fits properly STE MR Spectra. The incorporation of the classifier in a Decision Support System (DSS) could be of interest for clinicians to decide the diagnosis of routine or special patients. In further work, more applications of the proposed mixture model will be considered in MRS analysis.

Acknowledgments. This work was partially funded by the EU projects eTumour (FP6-2002-LH 503094) and HealthAgents (IST-2004-27214). We thank INTERPRET partners, C. Arús (UAB), C. Majós (IDI), A. Moreno (CDP), J. Griffiths(SGUL), A.Heerschap(RU), W.Gajewicz(MUL), and J.Calvar(FLENI), for providing data.

References

1. Mierisova, S., Ala-Korpela, M.: MR spectroscopy quantitation: a review of frequency domain methods. NMR Biomed. 14(4), 247–259 (2001)
2. Vanhamme, L., Sundin, T., Hecke, P.V., Huffel, S.V.: MR spectroscopy quantitation: a review of time-domain methods. NMR Biomed. 14(4), 233–246 (2001)
3. Tate, A., et al.: Development of a DSS for diagnosis and grading of brain tumours using in vivo magnetic resonance SV spectra. NMR Biomed. 19(4), 411–434 (2006)
4. McLachlan, G.J., Jones, P.N.: Fitting mixture models to grouped and truncated data via the EM algorithm. Biometrics 44, 571–578 (1988)
5. Cadez IV, et al.: Maximum likelihood estimation of mixture densities for binned and truncated multivariate data. Mach. Learn. 47(1), 7–34 (2002)
6. Same, A., Ambroise, C., Govaert, G.: A classification EM algorithm for binned data. Computational Statistics and Data Analysis (2005)
7. Jones, P.N., McLachlan, G.J.: Statistical algorithms: Algorithm AS 254. Applied Statistics 39(2), 273–282 (1990)
8. Julia-Sape, M., et al.: A multicentre, web-accessible and quality control-checked database of in vivo MRS of brain tumour patients. MAGMA 19(1), 22–33 (2006)
9. Martin, J.K., Hirschberg, D.S.: Small sample statistics for classification error rates II. Technical Report ICS-TR-96-22 (1996)

Atmospheric Turbulence Effects Removal on Infrared Sequences Degraded by Local Isoplanatism

Magali Lemaitre[1], Olivier Laligant[1], Jacques Blanc-Talon[2],
and Fabrice Mériaudeau[1]

[1] Le2i Laboratory, University of Burgundy, France
[2] DGA/D4S/MRIS, Defence Department, France

Abstract. When observing an object horizontally at a long distance, degradations due to atmospheric turbulence often occur. Different methods have already been tested to get rid of this kind of degradation, especially on infrared sequences. It has been shown that the Wiener filter applied locally on each frame of a sequence allows to obtain good results in terms of edges, while the regularization by the Laplacian operator applied in the same way provides good results in terms of noise removal in uniform areas. In this article, we present hybrid methods which take advantages of both Wiener filter and Laplacian regularization.

1 Introduction

The main perturbation occuring in long distance ground-to-ground video acquisition is due to atmospheric turbulence. The turbulence nature essentially depends on climatic conditions and on the distance between the scene and the camera. The sequence we tested our algorithms on has been provided by *DRDC Valcartier*, Canada, and it was acquired during the NATO RTG40 campaign in New Mexico in 2005. In our sequence acquisition conditions (horizontal observation in the troposphere, at a distance of 1 km), atmospheric perturbation can be efficiently simulated by local blurring and warping and possibly additive noise. Each frame can then be split into mostly regular areas degraded by the same perturbation (*local isoplanatism*).

In our previous work [1], classical restoration methods were adapted for local processing of sequences perturbed by local isoplanatism. We analyzed and compared our results with different criteria, and showed that the Wiener filter allows to obtain good results in terms of visualization (clear edges), while the regularization by the Laplacian operator provides good results for a post-processing (noise removal in uniform areas). In this article, we try to combine the results of these two methods in order to obtain a still better restoration image.

First we briefly recall what local isoplanatism is. Then we explain the general algorithm used to process sequences locally, we show some restoration results and we analyse them. Therefore two new Wiener and Laplacian mixing algorithms are explained and mixing restoration results are shown and analyzed. Finally, a conclusion and perspectives are given.

J. Martí et al. (Eds.): IbPRIA 2007, Part II, LNCS 4478, pp. 274–281, 2007.

2   Local Isoplanatism Theory

Atmospheric turbulence induce varying perturbations on optical beams, according to beams propagation directions. On Fig. 1 is given an example where two beams coming from the same object cross a thin turbulent layer.

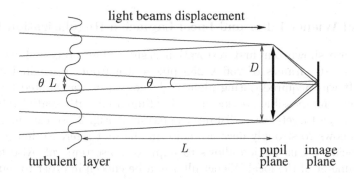

Fig. 1. Origin of different atmospheric perturbations (θ *is the angle between the two beams, L is the distance between the turbulent layer and the pupil, and D is the pupil diameter*)

Three degradation types can occur:

- Anisoplanatism: If $|\theta L| > D$, the turbulent layer areas met by the two beams have no common part. The beams are perturbed by two completely different degradations.
- Local isoplanatism: If the observed object has sufficiently small angular dimensions θ, beams originating from any point on the object and arriving on the pupil can be considered to have encountered almost identical regions of the perturbing layer [2]. That will be translated on the related image by areas with the same degradation.
- Total isoplanatism: When $\theta \approx 0$, the two beams suffer from exactly the same perturbation.

According to [1] and [3], our sequence is degraded by local isoplanatism.

3   Sequence Processing Algorithm and First Restoration Results

3.1   General Sequence Processing Algorithm

To process a sequence a generalization to different restoration methods of Fraser's and Lambert's algorithm [4] was used. This algorithm was previously tested on simulated images [5]. Its principle is to detect a local space-varying PSF describing the atmospheric turbulence. The PSF is found by using a Wiener filter acting on regions-of-interest of a reference image and each frame of the sequence. The reference image is initially the sequence average and is updated after each deconvolution pass of the complete sequence. The process is repeated until the absolute difference between the two last average images is minimized. In practice, one or two deconvolutions of the complete sequence are sufficient. This algorithm was easily adapted to the case of regularization by the Laplacian [6].

3.2　Local Wiener Filter and Local Laplacien Regularization Results

On Fig. 2 are shown our first restoration results. The processed sequence is compound of 100 frames of 256 x 256 pixels size from an original degraded sequence. It was acquired during night and the object was lighted by a laser. We consider that possible speckle noise is eliminated with spatial integration due to the large target-sensor distance. Looking at Fig. 2, we can observe that averaging allows to strongly decrease noise in the first reference image but the local Laplacian regularization allows to improve noise removal. Also the most suited parameter of the local Wiener filter can be chosen in order to remove the maximum of the remaining blur so as to obtain clearer edges.

We made our processing on MATLAB. Local restoration computing time is from few minutes to about one hour depending essentially on the frame number in the processed sequence, on their size and on regions-of-interest size used to process each frame. 32 x 32 pixels windows were used for local restorations, but the best size to choose is under investigation.

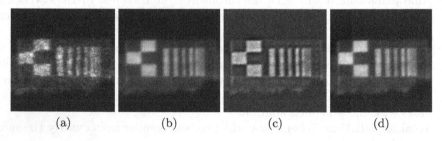

(a) (b) (c) (d)

Fig. 2. First local restoration results on the processed sequence: *(a) Degraded frame, (b) First reference image, (c) Local Wiener result and (d) Local Laplacian result*

3.3　Results Analysis

Like in [1], several criteria have been used to appreciate our restoration results. First mean variances in the three white squares and in the three black squares on the checkerwork were calculated. The best result was obtained with the local Laplacian regularization. Mean slopes of horizontal and vertical transitions between black and white squares were compared: the steepest mean slope was obtained with the local Wiener filter. The modulation transfert function (MTF) of each mean transition between black and white squares was also computed, which provides a quantified and graphic representation of simultaneous qualities of contrast and clearness. The mean transition MTF is the modulus of the Fourier transform of its derivative, and is then normalized to range between 0 and 1. According to Fig. 3(a), the local Wiener filter gives the best MTF. Furthermore for each result, correlations of each mean transition with the ideal one were compared. According to Fig. 3(b), the local Laplacian regularization gives a slightly better result than the local Wiener filter, but this is due to the fact that oscillations are present around each edge on the Wiener result.

To summarize, the local Laplacian regularization allows to improve noise removal on uniform areas whereas the local Wiener filter allows to get rid of a large part of the remaining blur on edges. An hybrid method which will take advantages of these two methods is thereafter presented.

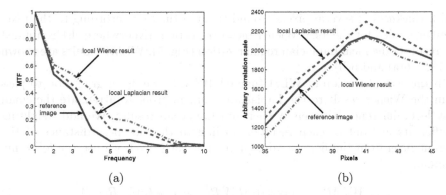

(a)   (b)

Fig. 3. First restoration results analysis. *(a) Mean transitions MTFs for the reference image, the local Wiener result and the local Laplacian result. (b) Correlation peaks of the same images mean transitions with the ideal one.*

4   Wiener and Laplacian Mixing Algorithms and Results

4.1   Segmentation Image

We first need a segmentation image to determine areas where the Wiener result will be kept. It will be obtained with the Canny-Deriche filter. To limit false edge detection, we use the three images we have in input: the reference image, the local Wiener result and the local Laplacian result. On the final segmentation image, an edge point is kept only if it's present on at least two of the three used segmentation images.

Two segmentation thresholds (*thr*) have been chosen: the first one allows to detect small white circles above and on the right of vertical bars (Fig. 4(b)), while the second one allows to obtain a "clean" segmentation (Fig. 4(c)).

4.2   Wiener and Laplacian Mixing (WLM) Algorithms

In the first version of Wiener and Laplacian Mixing (called *WLM1*), the area where we apply the result of the local Wiener filter is compound of edge points

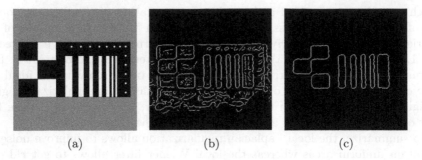

(a)   (b)   (c)

Fig. 4. Observed objet *(a)* and the 2 used segmentation images: *(b) thr=0.04 and (c) thr=0.35*

and a thickness of several pixels around them, estimated according to the pixel number needed for the local Wiener mean transition. Everywhere else is applied the result of the local Laplacian regularization (Fig. 5). WLM1 results are shown on Figs. 6(a) and 6(b).

In the second version of WLM (named *WLM2*), we use a gradation to pass from the Wiener result to the Laplacian result in order to attenuate the small gray level difference between Wiener and Laplacian results. We add weighting coefficients in front of each result according to the closeness/distance of the current pixel from the nearest edge point. For each pixel, we use the following formula:

$$\forall i,j, WLM2(i,j) = \alpha_1(c)LWR(i,j) + \alpha_2(c)LLR(i,j) \,, \tag{1}$$

where *WLM2* is the WLM2 result, *LWR* is the local Wiener result, *LLR* is the local Laplacian result, c is the distance card obtained from the segmentation image and representing the distance between each pixel and the nearest edge point, and α_1 and α_2 are defined using the three following conditions:

$$\alpha_1(c) + \alpha_2(c) = 1 \,, \ 0 \le \alpha_1(c) \le 1 \,, \ 0 \le \alpha_2(c) \le 1 \,. \tag{2}$$

The closer to an edge point, the higher α_1 and the lower α_2, and conversely. Once again, the gradation is made on several pixels from the center of the local Wiener mean transition, according to the pixel number needed for this mean transition (Fig. 5). WLM2 results are shown on Figs. 6(c) and 6(d).

4.3   Results Analysis

Analysis of our results have been realized with the same criteria than those previously used, and similar results to previous ones have been found (Fig. 7): WLM results mean transitions provide MTFs almost as good as those obtained with the local Wiener result, and correlation peak with the ideal transition has been improved compared with the local Wiener result. Moreover the Canny-Deriche filter has been tried on our restoration results, which allows us to conclude that

WITHOUT GRADATION

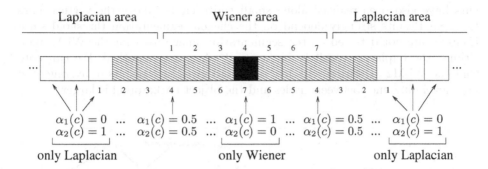

Fig. 5. Processing areas determination. *Top: division (without gradation). Bottom: overlaying (with gradation).*

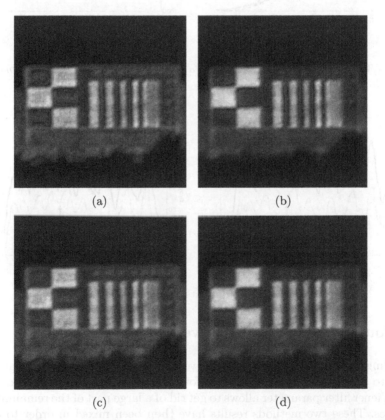

Fig. 6. WLM1 results with *thr=0.04 (a)* and *thr=0.35 (b)*. WLM2 results with *thr=0.04 (c)* and *thr=0.35 (d)*.

gradation use allows to slightly decrease false edges detection, and that white circles are better detected on the WLM2 result with low threshold. Horizontal cuts have also been realized along small white circles above the vertical bars (Fig. 8). Results strongly depend on the chosen segmentation threshold since if circles are not detected on the segmentation image used for the WLM algorithms, the Laplacian result is applied and edges are smoothed. We can note that the WLM2 algorithm with low threshold gives best results in average: the gray level difference between circles and the object background is larger.

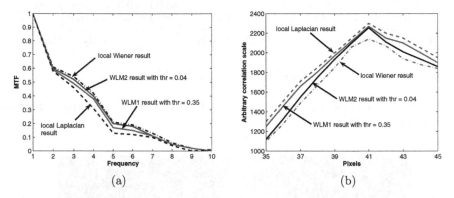

(a)   (b)

Fig. 7. WLM restoration results analysis. *(a) Mean transitions MTFs. (b) Correlation peaks with the ideal transition.*

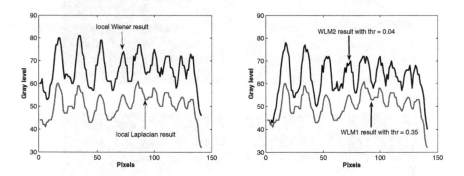

Fig. 8. Horizontal cuts along white circles

5   Conclusion and Perspectives

According to our previous restoration work, the local Laplacian regularization allows to improve noise removal on uniform areas, and a judicious choice of the local Wiener filter parameter allows to get rid of a large part of the remaining blur on edges. These two methods results have then been mixed in order to obtain a still better restoration result. The new algorithms results strongly depend on the segmentation image. The smaller the segmentation threshold, the more detected false edges and the more noisy uniform areas. Nevertheless with a small segmentation threshold and in spite of a certain noise, we managed to better detect white circles than previously. Furthermore gradation between Laplacian and Wiener areas allows to decrease gray level difference, and then to improve the result for both vizualisation and post-processing.

We are currently studying regions-of-interest size influence on restoration results quality. Automatic selection of segmentation threshold is also under investigation, with a method based on detected edge points number study, which could improve our restoration methods especially on textured areas.

References

1. Lemaitre, M., Blanc-Talon, J., Mériaudeau, F., Laligant, O.: Evaluation of Infrared Restoration Techniques. In: Driggers, R.G., Huckridge, D.A. (eds.) Proceedings of SPIE Conference in Optics / Photonics in Defence and Security, Electro-Optical and Infrared Systems: Technology and Applications III, vol. 6395, Sweden (2006)
2. Roddier, F.: Effects of Atmospheric Turbulence in Optical Astronomy. In: Wolf, E., (eds.) Progress in Optics, North-Holland, vol. 19, pp. 281–376 (1981)
3. Fried, D.L.: Anisoplanatism in Adaptive Optics. Journal of the Optical Society of America 72(1), 52–61 (1982)
4. Fraser, D., Lambert, A.: Information Retrieval from a Position-Varying Point Spread Function. In: Proceedings of Conference on Advanced Concepts for Intelligent Vision Systems (ACIVS), Belgium (2004)
5. Lemaitre, M., Mériaudeau, F., Laligant, O., Blanc-Talon, J.: Distant Horizontal Ground Observation: Atmospheric Perturbation Simulation and Image Restoration. In: Proceedings of Conference on Signal-Image Technology and Internet-based Systems (SITIS), Cameroon, pp. 77–84 (2005)
6. Tikhonov, A.N., Arsenin, V.Y.: Solutions of Ill-Posed Problems. Winston and Sons (eds.) Washington (1977)

Inference of Stochastic Finite-State Transducers Using N-Gram Mixtures*

Vicente Alabau, Francisco Casacuberta, Enrique Vidal, and Alfons Juan

Departament de Sistemes Informàtics i Computació
Universitat Politècnica de València
{valabau,fcn,evidal,ajuan}@dsic.upv.es

Abstract. Statistical pattern recognition has proved to be an interesting framework for machine translation, and stochastic finite-state transducers are adequate models in many language processing areas such as speech translation, computer-assisted translations, etc. The well-known n-gram language models are widely used in this framework for machine translation. One of the application of these n-gram models is to infer stochastic finite-state transducers. However, only simple dependencies can be modelled, but many translations require to take into account strong context and style dependencies. Mixtures of parametric models allow to increase the description power of the statistical models by modelling subclasses of objects. In this work, we propose the use of n-gram mixtures in GIATI, a procedure to infer stochastic finite-state transducers. N-gram mixtures are expected to model topics or writing styles. We present experimental results showing that translation performance can be improved if enough training data is available.

1 Introduction

In recent years, new pattern recognition approaches have been proposed to solve the machine translation (MT) problem with increasing performance ([1,2,3]). However, the problem is far from being solved and there are still numerous drawbacks in these models.

For instance, the GIATI (Grammatical inference and alignments for transducer inference) [1] technique exploits several well-known n-gram inference and smoothing techniques in order to build n-grams of bilingual phrases. N-grams have the advantage that the inference process is fairly easy and the smoothing techniques have shown to be very appropriate in other areas such as speech recognition.

However, n-grams are unable to model dependencies at distances longer than n in a sentence, but real data often involve long term constrains that would be interesting to capture. Commonly, these constrains are associated with topics. For example, the topic determines the vocabulary, expressions and even collocations

---

* Work supported by the "Agència Valenciana de Ciència i Tecnologia" under grant GRUPOS03/031, the Spanish project TIC2003-08681-C02-02 and the "Programa d'Incentiu a la Investigació 2004 UPV".

J. Martí et al. (Eds.): IbPRIA 2007, Part II, LNCS 4478, pp. 282–289, 2007.

that might be used in a sentence. Furthermore, it also implies certain grammar structure and use of language. Therefore, GIATI could benefit from taking into account topic information and achieve translations with a higher degree of quality. Previous work [4] has already shown that n-gram mixture modelling for speech recognition outperforms the traditional n-gram modelling.

The rest of the paper is structured as follows. Section 2 describes the GIATI method for n-gram transducer inference. Section 3 explains the approximation followed to create the mixtures. Next, a series of experiments that show the potential of GIATI mixtures will be presented in Section 4. Finally, Section 5 will conclude and outline future research.

2 Inference of Stochastic Finite-State Transducers

MT essentially consists in building a device that, given a sentence in a source language, obtain a sentence in a target language, both sentences holding the same meaning. The traditional statistical machine translation (SMT) approach is described as follows.

Let x be a sentence of the source language Σ^*, and y a sentence of the target language Δ^* and $p(y|x)$ the probability of y being a translation of x. The best translation of x is a sentence $\hat{y}$ that maximises the posterior probability:

$$\hat{y} = \underset{y}{\operatorname{argmax}}\, p(\boldsymbol{y}|\boldsymbol{x}) = \underset{y}{\operatorname{argmax}}\, p(\boldsymbol{x}, \boldsymbol{y}) \,. \tag{1}$$

The joint probability can be modelled as a statistical finite-state transducer (SFST). SFSTs have been thoroughly studied [5,6] and several attempts of modelling SMTs with SFSTs have already been proposed [1,7,8].

GIATI is a technique that provides a framework for SFST inference based on the stochastic morphism theorem [6] and a set of alignments [9]. A possible way of inferring SFSTs by means of GIATI is described next.

Given a finite set A of sentence pairs $(\boldsymbol{s}, \boldsymbol{t}) \in \Sigma^* \times \Delta^*$ (parallel corpus), it works in three steps:

- *Step 1. Building training strings:* Each pair of training sentences $(\boldsymbol{s}, \boldsymbol{t})$ of A is transformed into a single string $\boldsymbol{z}$ from an *extended alphabet* Γ giving a new set of strings S, $S \in \Gamma^*$. The *extended alphabet* consists of symbols that are constructed by putting together words or phrases from the source and target language that are aligned according to an alignment matrix provided by GIZA++ [10].
- *Step 2. Inferring a (stochastic) regular grammar:* A SFST $\mathcal{A}$ is inferred from S. Typically, a back-off smoothed n-gram is inferred.
- *Step 3. Transforming the inferred grammar into a SFST:* The symbols z in $\mathcal{A}$ are inversely transformed into pairs of source and target symbols $(s, t) \in \Sigma^* \times \Delta^*$ that correspond to the transducer's inputs and outputs, respectively.

It should be noticed that a n-gram language model is inferred in the *step 2*. As it has been told, some shortcomings of n-gram models could be overcome by means of mixture modelling. The next section is devoted to explain the mixture modelling approach that has been considered in this work.

3 Mixtures of Models

A finite mixture model consists of a number C of *mixture components*. In order to generate a *sample* $x = (x_1, \ldots, x_{|x|})^t$, it first selects a cth component with prior probability $p(c)$, and then generates x according to the cth *component-conditional probability (density) function* $p(x \mid c)$. The *(unconditional) mixture probability (density) function* is of the form:

$$p(x) = \sum_{c=1}^{C} p(c) \, p(x \mid c) \,. \tag{2}$$

A model of n-gram mixtures is a particular case of (2) in which

$$p(x \mid c) = \prod_{i}^{|x|} p(x_i \mid x_{i-n+1}^{i-1}, c) \,, \tag{3}$$

where $x = x_1 x_2 \ldots x_{|x|}$ is a string of symbols of an alphabet Γ such that $x \in \Gamma^*$.

Maximum Likelihood estimation of the mixture parameters is carried out by the *EM algorithm* [11].

3.1 Maximum Likelihood Estimation

Let $X = \{x_1, \ldots, x_M\}$ be a set of samples available for learning the n-gram mixture model. This is a statistical parameter estimation problem since the mixture is a probability function of known functional form, and all that is unknown is a parameter vector including the priors and component parameters.

The vector of unknown parameters for the model is:

$$\Theta = (p(1), \ldots, p(C), p_1, \ldots, p_C)^t \,, \tag{4}$$

with

$$p_c = \left\{ p(w_j \mid h_l, c) \mid \forall w_j \in \Gamma, \forall h_l \in \Gamma^{(n-1)} \right\} \quad \forall c, \tag{5}$$

where w_j is a symbol of Γ, and $h_l = (h_1 h_2 \ldots h_{n-1})$ is a history of $n-1$ symbols of Γ that precede w_j.

The number of components is excluded from the estimation problem, as it is a crucial parameter to control the model complexity and receives special attention in Section 4.

Following the maximum likelihood principle, the best parameter values maximise the log-likelihood function

$$\mathcal{L}(\Theta \mid X) = \sum_{m=1}^{M} \log \left(\sum_{c=1}^{C} p(c) \, p(x_m \mid c) \right). \tag{6}$$

In order to find these optimal values, it is useful to think of each sample x_m as an *incomplete* component-labelled sample, which can be completed by an indicator vector $\boldsymbol{z}_m = (z_{m1}, \dots, z_{mC})^t$ with 1 in the position corresponding to the component generating $\boldsymbol{x}_m$ and 0 elsewhere. In doing so, a complete version of the log-likelihood function (6) can be stated as

$$\mathcal{L}_C(\boldsymbol{\Theta}|X, Z) = \sum_{m=1}^{M} \sum_{c=1}^{C} z_{mc} \left(\log p(c) + \log p(\boldsymbol{x}_m | c) \right) , \tag{7}$$

where $Z = \{\boldsymbol{z}_1, \dots, \boldsymbol{z}_M\}$ is the so-called *missing* data.

The form of the log-likelihood function given in (7) is generally preferred because it makes available the well-known *EM* optimisation algorithm (for finite mixtures)[11]. This algorithm proceeds iteratively in two steps. The E (xpectation) step computes the expected value of the missing data given the incomplete data and the current parameters. The M(aximisation) step finds the parameter values which maximise (7), on the basis of the missing data estimated in the E step. In our case, the E step replaces each z_{mc} by the posterior probability of $\boldsymbol{x}_m$ being actually generated by the cth component,

$$z_{mc} = \frac{p(c)\, p(\boldsymbol{x}_m \mid c)}{\sum_{c'=1}^{C} p(c')\, p(\boldsymbol{x}_m \mid c')} \qquad \forall c\, \forall m . \tag{8}$$

On the other hand, the M step finds the maximum likelihood estimates for the priors,

$$p(c)^{(k+1)} = \frac{1}{M} \sum_{m=1}^{M} z_{mc} \qquad \forall c , \tag{9}$$

and the component parameters,

$$p(w_j | \boldsymbol{h}_l, c)^{(k+1)} = \frac{\displaystyle\sum_m z_{mc}{}^{(k)} \sum_{i}^{|\boldsymbol{x}_m|} \delta(x_{m,i-n+1}^i, w_j \boldsymbol{h}_l)}{\displaystyle\sum_{w_{j'} \in \Gamma} \sum_m z_{mc}{}^{(k)} \sum_{i}^{|\boldsymbol{x}_m|} \delta(x_{m,i-n+1}^i, w_{j'} \boldsymbol{h}_l)} \qquad \begin{array}{l} \forall c,\ \forall w_j \in \Gamma, \\ \forall \boldsymbol{h}_l \in \Gamma^{(n-1)} , \end{array}$$

$$\tag{10}$$

where δ is the Kronecker's delta.

3.2   GIATI Mixtures

As it was mentioned in Section 2, the second step of the training process GIATI needs some finite-state automaton inference algorithms to model the joint probability. Commonly, n-grams have been used in this step for its simplicity, extreme efficiency, and well-known smoothing techniques.

In this work, the use of n-gram mixtures in the second step of the GIATI technique is proposed. The EM algorithm is expected to identify different topics or writing styles and distribute them among the mixture components, which are GIATI transducers by themselves. Consequently, each of the GIATI transducers share the same structure. Therefore, a GIATI mixture may be represented as a single SFST in which the transition probabilities are constituted by an array of probabilities of size C. With this representation in mind, the search problem simply lies in a Viterbi search through the SFST with a slight modification. Taking advantage of the structure's parallelism, the cost of being at a given state may be calculated as the sum of all the components of the mixture. Therefore, the best path at the end of the search is obtained taking into account all the components at the same time.

One difficulty when dealing with theoretical models is that they often behave unexpectedly when they are put into practice. Specially, n-gram inference have to tackle with the sparseness of the training data. To make things worse, n-gram mixtures split the data among its components. The more components the mixture has, the more sparse the data is, so that the sparseness proportionally boosts with the complexity of the model and thereby with the n-gram order.

If we look carefully at the z_{mc} variable, it characterizes the posterior probability of the sentence x_m belonging to the class c. Informally speaking, the E step in the EM algorithm may be seen as a fuzzy clustering algorithm that assigns sentences x_m to groups and z_{mc} indicates the degree to which the sentence x_m belongs to the cluster c. Under this point of view, any fuzzy approach might be used to estimate the z parameters. Component parameters in step M would be consequently estimated using these z values. For instance, lower orders of n-grams may be used to smooth the mixtures. The following steps illustrate this process:

- 1-gram, 2-gram and 3-gram mixtures are trained until convergence.
- For each of these mixtures, the z variables corresponding to the last iteration of the EM algorithm are stored. We will refer to them as 1-gram, 2-gram and 3-gram z-values.
- Next, three 3-gram mixtures are created. The component parameters for each mixture were estimated using 1-gram, 2-gram and 3-gram z-values, respectively.
- Every component of these mixtures is smoothed. Firstly, 3-gram counts under 3 are cut off. Secondly, back-off and Witten-Bell smoothing are applied.

4 Experimental Results

In order to assess the GIATI mixture model, a series of experiments were conducted using different corpora of increasing complexity. For each corpus three 3-gram mixtures were created and smoothed as it is explained in the previous section. The component parameters for each mixture were estimated using 1-gram, 2-gram and 3-gram z-values, respectively. As stated in Section 3, the number of components C is a crucial parameter. Therefore, the experiments were run for a set of preselected values of C between 1 and 500. Finally, all the experiments were run several times in order to calculate the confidence intervals.

4.1 Corpora Description

The GIATI mixture models were evaluated using three corpora of increasing complexity. The simplest task is the MLA which define a simple language whose sentences describe a series of images. The sentences were randomly generated by means of an automaton, and hence, they are very simple.

The Eutrans-I [12] corpus is composed of pairs of sentences that describe sixteen different communication scenarios in the hall of a hotel. The sentences were semi-automatically generated from a series of travel booklets.

Finally, the simplified Xerox corpus [13] is a collection of technical manuals in English, Spanish, French, and German. The English version is the original one, while the others are translations made by a professional translator. Although it is still a restricted domain corpus, it is written in natural language. Therefore the language is more complex, which is reflected by the perplexity. Statistics of these corpora may be seen in the Figure 1.

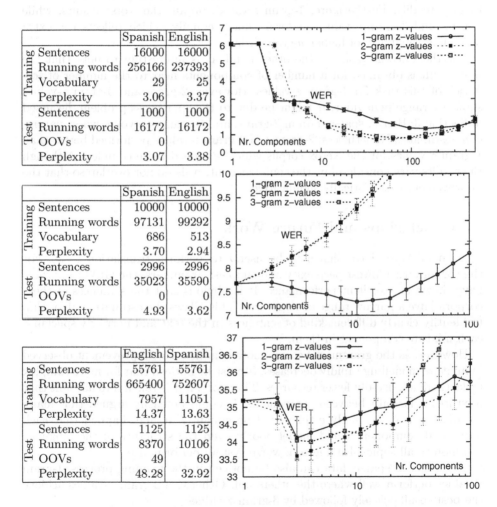

		Spanish	English
Training	Sentences	16000	16000
	Running words	256166	237393
	Vocabulary	29	25
	Perplexity	3.06	3.37
Test	Sentences	1000	1000
	Running words	16172	16172
	OOVs	0	0
	Perplexity	3.07	3.38

		Spanish	English
Training	Sentences	10000	10000
	Running words	97131	99292
	Vocabulary	686	513
	Perplexity	3.70	2.94
Test	Sentences	2996	2996
	Running words	35023	35590
	OOVs	0	0
	Perplexity	4.93	3.62

		English	Spanish
Training	Sentences	55761	55761
	Running words	665400	752607
	Vocabulary	7957	11051
	Perplexity	14.37	13.63
Test	Sentences	1125	1125
	Running words	8370	10106
	OOVs	49	69
	Perplexity	48.28	32.92

Fig. 1. MLA, Eutrans and Xerox statistics and result

4.2   Experimental Results

Performance was evaluated using the *word error rate* (WER) measure (number of deletions, insertions and substitutions needed to transform a translation hypothesis into a single target reference). Figure 1 shows the experimental results for the three tasks. Three different curves are shown in the plots corresponding to the different z-values used for parameter estimation. The bars show the 95% confidence intervals.

The MLA task exemplifies clearly what is expected from a mixture model. First, as the number of components increases, the WER rapidly decreases with a minimum WER at 41 components. However, after that point the system overtrains the parameters and loses generality. Then, the system performance begins to fall steadily. Furthermore, 1-gram z-values obtain the worst results, while 2-gram and 3-gram z-values perform almost equally, which reflects the extra modelling capability of higher n-gram orders.

For the Eutrans task, on the other hand, it is interesting to note that the best result is obtained for a number of components near to the number of scenarios of this task for 1-gram z-values. However, 2-gram and 3-gram z-values show a strange behaviour. It might be due to the sparseness problem discussed in Section 3. Hence, sparse data in 2-grams and 3-grams provokes worse parameters estimates. Nonetheless, 2-gram and 3-gram z-values performed better than 1-gram z-values for the Xerox corpus which is indeed more complex. Although the results vary considerably, the confidence intervals do not overlap so that the improvement is statistically significant.

5   Conclusions and Future Work

N-gram mixtures have shown to be useful to perform translation tasks. For the corpora with lowest perplexity and simplest grammars, the GIATI mixtures have shown an excellent performance. It is obvious that the sentences of these corpora have a narrow range of structures. This allows the estimation algorithm to identify clearly different kind of sentences in the text and narrowly specialise each mixture component in them.

However, as the grammars become more complex, the improvement observed in mixture modelling rapidly decreases. It must be noticed that for more complex tasks there are usually fewer resources. Therefore, if it is taken into account that mixtures split data between components, it could be easily argued that many parameters may be badly estimated. Consequently, it may happen that each individual component could model poorly even the structure of the language common to all topics, leading to a worse system performance.

The effect of sparse data can also be noticed in the training process. 1-gram z-values perform well where the others fail. Otherwise 2-gram z-values achieve the best results closely followed by 3-gram z-values.

There are many issues still to investigate in order to obtain the best from GIATI mixtures. First, smarter smoothing techniques should be developed. For instance, a general GIATI model could be interpolated with the GIATI mixture, or the smoothing might be embedded into the training process. Second, to avoid the sparseness problem in training, z-values might be estimated using any fuzzy clustering algorithm that gives good results in text classification. It should be also possible to use word categorization to estimate the z-value, and doing so reduce the number of parameters in the training process.

However, it should be priority to test the model against larger corpora, specially those that are naturally categorized in topics or contain texts from different sources, such as *EUROPARL*, *Acquis communautaire* or the OPUS corpus.

References

1. Picó, D.: Combining Statistical and Finite-State Methods for Machine Translation. Tesis doctoral en informática, Departamento de Sistemas Informáticos y Computación, Universidad Politécnica de Valencia (2005)
2. Bender, O., Zens, R., Matusov, E., Ney, H.: Alignment templates: the rwth smt system. In: Proceedings of the International Workshop on Spoken Language Translation (IWSLT 2004), pp. 79–84, Kyoto, Japan (September 2004)
3. Koehn, P., Och, F., Marcu, D.: Statistical phrase-based translation. In: Proceedings of NAACL/HLT, Proceedings of the Human Language Technology and North American Association for Computational Linguistics Conference, Edmonton, Canada (2003)
4. Iyer, R.M., Ostendorf, M.: Modeling long distance dependence in language: Topic mixtures versus dynamic cache models. IEEE Transactions on Speech and Audio Processing, vol. 7(1) (January 1999)
5. Vidal, E., Thollard, F., Casacuberta, F., de la Higuera, C., Carrasco, R.: Probabilistic finite-state machines - part I. IEEE Transactions on Pattern Analysis and Machine Intelligence 27(7), 1013–1025 (2005)
6. Vidal, E., Thollard, F., Casacuberta, F., de la Higuera, C., Carrasco, R.: Probabilistic finite-state machines - part II. IEEE Transactions on Pattern Analysis and Machine Intelligence 27(7), 1025–1039 (2005)
7. Casacuberta, F., Vidal, E.: Machine translation with inferred stochastic finite-state transducers. Computational Linguistics 30(2), 205–225 (2004)
8. Kumar, S., Deng, Y., Byrne, W.: A weighted finite state transducer translation template model for statistical machine translation. Journal of Natural Language Engineering 12(1), 35–75 (December 2005)
9. Brown, P., Cocke, J., Della Pietra, V., Della Pietra, S., Jelinek, F., Lafferty, J., Mercer, R., Roossin, P.: A statistical approach to machine translation. Computational Linguistics 16(2), 79–85 (1990)
10. Och, F.J., Ney, H.: A systematic comparison of various statistical alignment models. Computational Linguistics 29(1), 19–51 (2003)
11. Dempster, A.P., Laird, N.M., Rubin, D.B.: Maximum likelihood from incomplete data via the em algorithm (with discussion). Journal of the Royal Statistical Society B. 39, 1–38 (1977)
12. Juan, A., Vidal, E.: On the use of Bernoulli mixture models for text classification. Pattern Recognition 35(12), 2705–2710 (2002)
13. SchulmbergerSema S.A., Instituto Técnico de Informática, R.W.T.H. Aachen − Lehrstuhl für Informatik VI, R.A.L.I. Laboratory − University of Montreal, Celer Soluciones, Société Gamma, and Xerox Research Centre Europe. X.r.c.: Tt2. transtype2 - computer assisted translation. Project technical annex (2001)

Word Spotting in Archive Documents Using Shape Contexts*

Josep Lladós, Partha Pratim-Roy, José A. Rodríguez, and Gemma Sánchez

Computer Vision Center - Computer Science Department
Universitat Autònoma de Barcelona
08193 Bellaterra (Barcelona), Spain
{josep,partha,jrodriguez,gemma}@cvc.uab.es

Abstract. The analysis of historical document images is not only interesting for the preservation of historical heritage but also for the extraction of semantic knowledge. In this paper we present a word spotting approach to find keyword images in digital archives. Detected words allow to construct metadata on document contents for indexing and retrieval purposes. Instead of using OCR based approches that would require accurate segmentation and high image quality, we propose a shape recognition method based on the well-known shape context descriptor. Our method is proven to be robust under hightly distorted and noisy document images, a usual drawback in old document analysis. It has been used in a real application scenario, the Collection of Border Records of the Girona Archive. In particular, spotted keywords are used to extract knowledge on personal data of people referred in the documents.

1 Introduction

In the last years there is an increasing interest among the Document Image Analysis (DIA) community to focus the research on old document images. The main goal is to digitally preserve and provide access to historical document collections residing in libraries, museums and archives. Ancient documents have a historical value not only for their physical appearance but also for their contents. Thus, the convesion to digital libraries allow this heritage not only to be preserved but make it available wordlwide. But Digital Libraries do not only contain digitized documents but semantically enriched ones. Enriched documents mean to add semantical annotations to digital images of the scanned documents. Such metadata is intended to describe, classify and indexing documents by their content.

Currently, despite the presence of historical libraries, most of them available on the web, the presence of advanced features is still scarce [1]. We rarely find the possibility to do semantic search other than some of the basic typical metadata (author, date, institution). The research on digital libraries for historical documents has experienced a growing interest among the DIA community. In

---

* This work has been partially supported by the Spanish project TIN2006-15694-C02-02 and the *Subdirecció General d'Arxius de la Generalitat de Catalunya*.

J. Martí et al. (Eds.): IbPRIA 2007, Part II, LNCS 4478, pp. 290–297, 2007.

a recent survey, Baird et al. [2] stated the DIA challenges in historical digital libraries collections. First, image capture from historical artefacts needs special handling to counter the defects of document aging and the physical constraints of digitization. Second, layout analysis and metadata extraction was presented as a crucial step in creation an information base for historical digital libraries. Some outstanding contributions on the analysis of historical document images and conversion to digital libraries are the work from some UK labs [3,4], or the work within the French project ACI MADONNE [5,6,7,8].

The process of extracting keywords to generate indices for archiving and retrieval purposes depends on the document image quality and the type of collection. In document images with enough quality and structured layout, it can be easily done by first using an OCR process and afterwards a standard string search procedure. However, in images with different levels of degradation (noise, geometric deformations, complex layouts, low resolution, unnacurate binarization, etc.) this strategy might not succeed. Handwritten document images or old documents are examples of that. Since OCR methods require an accurate word segmentation and recognition, their performance can drastically decrease in this type of documents. Several authors have developed approaches based on modeling signatures of query keywords from image features. Thus, the detection of the word in the image database is done by a crosscorrelation approach between a prototype signature and the target image. This process is called *word spotting*. A number of contributions exist in the literature on word spotting methods for old documents, in particular for handwritten old documents [9,10].

The main contribution of this work is the proposal of a shape recognition approach applied to word spotting. Thus, if a word image represents a shape class described by a shape signature, its recognition in a document image involves a shape classification approach formulated in terms of the shape signature model. Shape representation and recognition is a broad domain. Good surveys may be found in the literature [11,12]. Generally speaking, shape descriptors can be classified in three categories. First, a shape can be represented as a set of points in a 2D image (silhouettes, contours, skeletons). Histograms of geometric invariants among points or shape contexts are examples of descriptors of this class. Second, a shape can be represented by a spatial configuration of a small number of key points. Examples of that are curvature points (Curvature Scale Space descriptor), or singularities in the boundary curve evolution (Shocks). Finally, a third class of shape descriptors consist in appearance-based representations, i.e. the correspondence using geometry and photometry.

In this paper we propose a word spotting strategy to retrieve keywords from a particular historical document archive. Our method is based on the *shape context* descriptor proposed by Belongie in [13]. A shape context of a feature point captures the spatial distribution of other points relative to it in polar coordinates. Thus, it can be seen as combined statistical-structural descriptor. In our case, skeletons of keyword images are taken as feature points. Thus, the set of shape context of a given keyword image is taken as a prototype descriptor. Given a document image, it is roughly segmented into words by a process that combines horizontal run length smearing and connected component labeling. Shape contexts are also extracted from candidate subimages. Finally, the segmented candidate word images of the input document are ranked in terms of a shape context distance. The first n candidate word images in the ranking are labeled as document zones likely to contain the query keyword.

The target collection of study is the archive of border records from the Civil Government of Girona. In consists of 93 linear meters of printed and handwritten documents from 1940 till 1976. This set of documents is related to people going through the Spanish-French border. Documents are organized in personal bundles. For each one, there is an index page with the names of people whose information is contained in this record. The bundles are arranged by year and record number. In each bundle there is very diverse documentation, so we can find safe-conduct to cross the border, arrest reports, information of professional activities, documents of prisoners transfer to labor camps, medical reports, correspondence with consulates, telegrams, etc. This documentation has a great importance in the studies about historical issues related with the Spanish Civil War and the Second World War. Figure 1 shows some sample images. The collection is being scanned and stored in binary raw image files. From the digital archive it is interesting to extract information regarding people (names, nationality, age, civil status, dates, etc.) that can be used for indexing purposes. Our word spotting method have been applied for a number of keywords. Keyword images are people names automatically segmented from the cover page, and some other keyword images segmented by a human operator like "year", "married", "years old", etc. After the spotting process, and applying some semantical rules to near words, the metadata can be extracted.

(a)   (b)   (c)

Fig. 1. Sample images of the target collection: (a) Cover page of one record (b)(c) Some contained documents

The structure of this paper is as follows. In Section 2 we describe the segmentation process to get name-keywords from the cover pages. In Section 3 the word spoting method based on shape contexts is presented. Section 4 presents the experimental evaluation. Finally, Section 5 is devoted to conclusions.

2   Key Word Segmentation

This process is applied to each cover page of the collection. Figure 1(a) shows an example. This kind of pages present a regular layout. A list of names and nationalities, appears in a form-like region in the bottom part of the document. The aim of this process is to segment these names automatically to spot them in the rest of the pages of the record, or even in the rest of the collection. Documents present some problems. First, the collection was scanned in binary raw images using a global binarization process. Second some words are partially deleted or present stains. Finally, words are printed on dotted underlines.

The first step is to detect where the names appear. As they are underlined, a preprocess to detect horizontal lines is done using the classical Hough Transform (HT). Once the long lines are found, the zones near them are cropped from the original image and a median filter is applied to remove the noise. Finally the connected component segmentation is performed. This would provide us the words segmented but with possible underline effect. As the words in the rest of the document will appear without underlines, first of all we need to filter the characters to extract this underline pixels. This process is done in two steps. First, the upper and lower profiles are compared and if the lower one is longer then the extra pixels are removed. Then the width of the areas in the remaining lower profiles are analyzed and thinner ones are also deleted, as they are just lines under characters with a kind of umbrella as F, T or P. Then words are segmented and ready to be used as keywords to spot the rest of the document.

3   Word Similarity in Terms of Shape Contexts

Shape Contexts were defined by Belongie in [13]. Summarizing the formulation given in the original reference, this shape descriptor can be defined as follows. Let $\mathcal{P} = \{p_1, \ldots, p_n\}$ be a set of n feature points extrated from a shape. The *shape context* of a point p_i is defined as a histogram h_i of the relative coordinates of other points around p_i,

$$h_i(k) = \#\{q \neq p_i : (q - p_i) \in \text{bin}(k)\}. \tag{1}$$

The space around p_i is therefore partitioned into regular zones (bin(k)) in terms of polar coordinates. Thus, $h_i(k)$ represents the density of points in the kth bin. A graphical illustration of the idea of shape contexts is given in Fig. 2. Since shape contexts represent distribution histograms, usually the distance between two shape contexts $d(h, h')$ is defined in terms of the χ^2 test statistic.

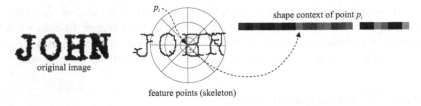

Fig. 2. Formulation of Shape Contexts

Given a shape S, it is described in terms of the set of shape contexts of its feature points $S = \{h_1, \ldots h_n\}$. Let us denote $\delta(S, S')$ the distance function between two shapes S and S'. $\delta(S, S')$ is defined in terms of the mapping distances $d(h_i, h'_j)$. In our case, since keywords are processed as shapes, word spotting is performed by looking image words that minimize the distance δ to a given prototype keyword. Belongie et al. formulated the distance between two shapes as a labeling problem, i.e. finding the best mapping between feature points of S to the feature points of S' such that the distance between the corresponding shape contexts is minimized.

In our approach, prototpype word images $\{P_1, \ldots, P_r\}$ are spotted in document images of an archive record. Prototype images may be name-keywords segmented from the front page, as explained in section 2, or keyword images manually segmented from sample images. Document images are roughtly segmented into candidate words, i.e. subimages $\{W_1, \ldots, W_s\}$ by a run-lenth smearing process combined with a connected component segmentation. Thus, prototype word images and segmented subimages of target documents are encoded with the set of shape contexts of their skeleton points. Both prototype words and candidate words are seen as shapes and then compared in terms of their shape context encoding. A candidate word W_i is labeled as a valid instance of the prototype word P_j if $\delta(W_i, P_j) \leq T$ where T is a predefined threshold experimentally set. To avoid the computational complexity of computing a mapping between shape features in each word comparison, we define a simplified distance.

Given two shapes $S = \{h_1, \ldots, h_n\}$ and $S' = \{h'_1, \ldots, h'_m\}$, the distance between them is defined as follows:

$$\delta(S, S') = \sum_{i=1}^{K} \Delta_{\sigma(i)}(S, S')$$

where Δ_i is the minimum distance between the ith shape context of S and the shape contexts of S', defined as follows:

$$\Delta_i(S, S') = \min_{j=1,\ldots.m} d(h_i, h'_j),$$

and $\sigma(i)$ is a ranking function that returns the ith element of an ordered list of values. Therefore, the intuitive idea of the distance between two shapes represented by the shape contexts of their feature points is the sum of the distances

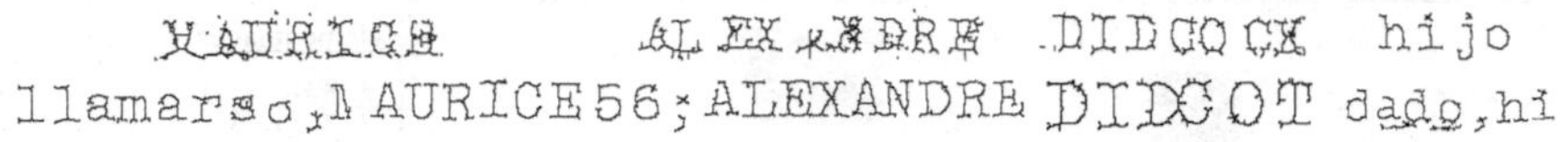

MAURICE   ALEXANDRE DIDCOCX   hijo
llamarso,MAURICE56;ALEXANDRE DIDOT dado,hi
(a)   (b)   (c)   (d)

Fig. 3. Spotting results with inexact matching: (a)(b) The word is found although hightly distorted skeletons and unnacurate word segmentation (c) Inexact word (d) Due to a fragmented segmentation, a subword is found

between the K most similar pairs of shape contexts. The advantage of this formulation is twofold. First, it can be computed with quadratic complexity in terms of the number of feature points. Second, it is very robust to noise and distortion. It is illustrated in Fig. 3 with four cases. In each one the skeletons of the indexing word image and the best detected subimage under distance δ are shown. In Figs. 3(a)(b) the prototype word is found although hightly distorted skeletons and unnacurate word segmentation (different words in the same subimage). In Fig. 3(c) a similar word is found but not the exact one. Finally, Fig. 3(d) illustrates a case where the segmentation of the document image has broken a word in two subimages. However, the best matching is one of such subimages.

4 Experimental Results

Our work is still in a preliminary stage, but the results are promising. To benchmark it, we have used one of the records (number 2 of 1940). It consists of 32 pages of different types (some of them handwritten). Names have been segmented in the first page (it results in a total of 21 names). In addition, seven keyword images have been added to the set of indexing prototype shapes. The strategy was to spot all the prototype words in the documents and consider as zones likely to contain them the first 5 images in the distance ranking. In addition, keywords found nearby names can be taken as information related to the corresponding person. An example is given in Fig. 4. Look at the detection of the name "MAURICE" "MENRIE", and the keywords "años", "soltero", "hijo", and "domicilio". With a posteriori relational rules, and an OCR process of some nearby words, it would allow to associate to this document the name of the person, the age, the civil status, the name of the parents and the address.

Quantitatively, the rate of correct detection of words (in the top five of the ranking) is 81%. If we consider the top ten of the ranking, this detection rate increases up to 92%. Undetected words are due to a very high noisy original image. We should notice that the interest in creating metadata associated to digitized documents is not only in individual words but in the combination of different keywords associated to the same knowledge item. Thus, the use of semantical rules associated to the relational associations among detected words can improve the above results.

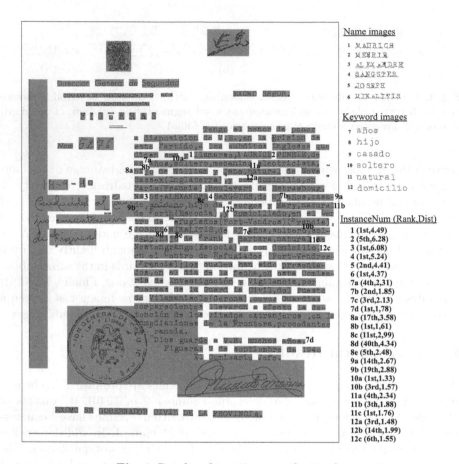

Fig. 4. Results of spotting some keywords

5   Conclusion

In this paper we have presented a shape recognition approach based on the well-known shape context descriptor applied to a problem of word spotting in documents of historical archives. The method is part of a larger project for the extraction of metadata from a real collection. Image archives present several distortions due to physical factors (aging, paper degradation overtime, speckles ...) or technical one in the scanning process (unnacurate binarisation). Because of that, the use of OCR techniques has resulted in insufficient performance rates. The use of our approach consists in the detection of shape context signatures from a set of image keywords that were compared with signatures extracted from the document images. The advantage of using such shape recognition approach for textual processing is twofold. First, it is stable under different degradation conditions, as it has been shown in the experiments where keywords are generally detected in the first positions in the ranking. Second, the use of a simple distance formulated in terms of the K nearest shape contexts between two shapes allows to detect words in a reasonable quadratic time. The work is still in a preliminary stage. The next steps in the future are a more exhaustive evaluation of the performance and the formulation of a rule-based system to find semantical relation among detected keywords to construct metadata associated to documents.

References

1. Meyyappan, N., Chowdhury, G., Foo, S.: A review of the status of twenty digital libraries. Journal of Information Science 26(5), 337–355 (2000)
2. Baird, H., Govindaraju, V., Lopresti, D.: Document analysis systems architectures for digital libraries. In: Marinai, S., Dengel, A. (eds.) DAS 2004. LNCS, vol. 3163, pp. 1–16. Springer, Heidelberg (2004)
3. Antonacopoulos, A., Karatzas, D.: A complete approach to the conversion of typewritten historical documents for digital archives. In: Marinai, S., Dengel, A. (eds.) DAS 2004. LNCS, vol. 3163, pp. 90–101. Springer, Heidelberg (2004)
4. He, J., Downton, A.: Evaluation of a user assisted archive construction system for online natural history archives. In: Proceedings of 8th Int. Conf. on Document Analysis and Recognition. Seoul, Korea, pp. 42–446 (2005)
5. Le Bourgeois, F., Kaileh, H.: Automatic metadata retrieval from ancient manuscripts. In: Marinai, S., Dengel, A. (eds.) DAS 2004. LNCS, vol. 3163, pp. 75–89. Springer, Heidelberg (2004)
6. Couasnon, B., Camillerapp, J., Leplumey, I.: Making handwritten archives documents accessible to public with a generic system of document image analysis. In: Proceedings of First International Workshop on Document Image Analysis for Libraries (DIAL04). Palo Alto, California, pp. 270–277 (2004)
7. Journet, N., Eglin, V., Ramel, J., Mullot, R.: Text/graphic labelling of ancient printed documents. In: Proceedings of 8th Int. Conf. on Document Analysis and Recognition. Seoul, Korea, pp. 1010–1014 (2005)
8. Surapong, U., Hammound, M., Garrido, C., Franco, P., Ogier, J.: Ancient graphic documents characterization. In: Proceedings of Sixth IAPR Workshop on Graphics Recognition. Hong Kong, China, pp. 97–105 (2005)
9. Tomai, C., Zhang, B., Govindaraju, V.: Transcript mapping for historic handwritten document images. In: Proc. of 8th International Workshop on Frontiers in Handwriting Recognition. Ontario, Canada, pp. 413–418 (2002)
10. Rath, T., Manmatha, R.: Word image matching using dynamic time warping. In: Proc. of the Conf. on Computer Vision and Pattern Recognition (CVPR), vol. 2, pp. 521–527 Madison, WI (2003)
11. Loncaric, S.: A survey of shape analysis techniques. Pattern Recognition 31(8), 983–1001 (1998)
12. Zhang, D., Lu, G.: Review of shape representation and description techniques. Pattern Recognition 37(1), 1–19 (2004)
13. Belongie, S., Malik, J., Puzicha, J.: Shape matching and object recognition using shape contexts. IEEE Transactions on Pattern Analysis and Machine Intelligence 24(24), 509–522 (2002)

Fuzzy Rule Based Edge-Sensitive Line Average Algorithm in Interlaced HDTV Sequences

Gwanggil Jeon, Jungjun Kim, Jongmin You, and Jechang Jeong

Department of Electronics and Computer Engineering, Hanyang University,
17 Haengdang-dong, Seongdong-gu, Seoul, Korea
{windcap315,kimjj79,rjm1214,jjeong}@ece.hanyang.ac.kr

Abstract. This paper proposes a spatial domain deinterlacing method which is based on fuzzy rule and edge-sensitive line average algorithm. The proposed algorithm consists two parts: edge direction detection part and fuzzy rule based edge-sensitive interpolation part. Once the edge direction is determined, in order to accurately reconstruct boundary of edges and peaks, edge-sensitive interpolation is utilized. Detection and interpolation results are presented. Experimental results show that the proposed algorithm provides a significant improvement over other existing deinterlacing methods.

Keywords: Deinterlacing, edge-sensitive interpolation, HDTV, fuzzy technique.

1 Introduction

The interlaced scan format, such as NTSC, PAL, and SECAM, has been widely used in various TV broadcasting standards, since it provides an efficient usage of limited bandwidth. With an interlaced scan, the frame rate is doubled while using the same bandwidth occupation [1]. Furthermore, recent HDTV systems support progressive scan in order to provide an improved picture quality. In order to provide compatibility with existing TV and camera systems, deinterlacing is used to convert interlaced video sequences to the progressive scan format.

Numerous deinterlacing techniques have been proposed for the interlaced to progressive scan conversion. Conventional works on deinterlacing can be roughly classified into three groups: methods using purely spatial interpolation techniques [2-6], temporal interpolation technique [7], and methods utilizing spatio-temporal interpolation techniques [8-10]. In general, temporal domain methods are more efficient than spatial domain methods. However, they are more complex than that of spatial domain methods. If sequences have lots of motion or scene changes, the spatial domain methods become superior to temporal domain methods. In this paper, the interest is primarily spatial domain methods. The methods in the spatial domain are the simplest among the various deinterlacing algorithms since they use only pixel values that are available from the current field. The methods in this category include line averaging and directional spatial interpolation. Intra-field linear interpolation algorithm is called as Bob [2]. Directional interpolation techniques such as the edge-based line average (ELA) [3], perform interpolation in the direction of the highest

J. Martí et al. (Eds.): IbPRIA 2007, Part II, LNCS 4478, pp. 298–305, 2007.

sample correction. In [4], the algorithm introduces an upper spatial direction vector and a lower spatial direction vector, in order to obtain a more accurate direction. In [5], an edge dependent interpolation algorithm that is based on a horizontal edge pattern is proposed. Recently, many different approaches that adopt fuzzy reasoning have been proposed in the engineering domain. Fuzzy reasoning methods have proved effective in image processing (e.g., filtering, interpolation, edge detection, and morphology), and have numerous practical applications. In [6], a line interpolation method using an intra-field edge-direction detector was proposed to obtain the correct edge information. In [8], a deinterlacing method based on Takagi-Sugeno fuzzy model was proposed. The conventional fuzzy rule based deinterlacing algorithms designed to find the exact edge direction.

In this paper, we propose a new deinterlacing method using edge-sensitive interpolation algorithm. In the literature, edge-sensitive interpolation method has been studied [11]. These methods were proposed for resampling algorithm. However, the studies involving video deinterlacing systems that are based on fuzzy edge-sensitive algorithm have not been proposed yet. The proposed algorithm is specific for deinterlacing domain, especially for the sequence with high motion region. The rest of the paper is structured as follows. In Section 2, the detail of the edge direction detector, fuzzy rule based edge-sensitive line average algorithm, and the interpolation strategy will be described. Experimental results and conclusions are finally presented in Section 3 and Section 4.

2 Fuzzy Rule Based Edge-Sensitive Line Average Algorithm

2.1 Edge Direction (ED) Detector

As we described, the proposed algorithm is intra field interpolation method that uses the current field to interpolate the missing field and to reconstruct one progressive frame at a time. Let $x(i,j-1)$ and $x(i,j+1)$ denote the upper reference line and the lower reference line, respectively. The variable i refers to the column number, and j to the line number. Consider the pixel $x(i,j)$, which will be interpolated in this work.

The edge direction (ED) detector utilizes directional correlations among pixels, in order to linearly interpolate a missing line. A 5-by-2 localized window is used to calculate directional correlations and to interpolate the current pixel, as shown in Fig. 1. $C(k)$ denotes a directional correlation measurement, i.e.,

$$C(k) = | x(i+k, j-1) - x(i-k, j+1) |, \ -2 \le k \le 2 \tag{1}$$

The measurement $C(k)$ is the intensity change in the direction, represented by k. $C(k)$ is used to determine the direction of the highest spatial correlation. The edge direction θ is determined as (2).

$$ED = \arg \min_{-2 \le k \le 2} (C(k)) \tag{2}$$

2.2 Edge-Sensitive Interpolation and Interpolation Strategy

The fuzzy rule based edge-sensitive linear average (FESA) algorithm uses fuzzy gradient values to determine if a certain missing pixel is located with a strong edge or not. It is assumed that the pixel with $(j-3)^{th}$ row is assigned to t, the pixel with $(j-1)^{th}$ row is assigned to u, the pixel with $(j+1)^{th}$ row is assigned to v, and the pixel with $(j+3)^{th}$ row is assigned to w. For each pixel (i,j) of the image (that is not a border pixel), a neighborhood window is used, as illustrated in Fig. 2. Each neighbor with respect to (i,j) corresponds to one direction {UL=up left, U=up, UR=up right, DL=down left, D=down, and DR=down right}.

The gradients $\Gamma_{(ED)}x(i,j)$, $\Gamma'_{(ED)}x(i,j)$ and $\Gamma''_{(ED)}x(i,j)$ are defined as the difference, as shown in Table 1. Table 1 provides an overview of the involved gradient values: each direction ED (column one) corresponds to a position (Fig. 2) with respect to a center position. Column two gives the basic gradient for each direction, while column three and four give the both of upper and lower gradients. It is assumed that four-tap filters are not suitable for $63°$ and $-63°$, since the window becomes too large, and it provides incorrect results. Finally, three fuzzy gradient values are defined for each of the three directions.

The five parameters ($\Gamma_{63}x(i,j)$, $\Gamma_{45}x(i,j)$, $\Gamma_{0}x(i,j)$, $\Gamma_{-45}x(i,j)$, and $\Gamma_{-63}x(i,j)$) are called the basic gradient values, the following three parameters ($\Gamma'_{45}x(i,j)$, $\Gamma'_{0}x(i,j)$, and $\Gamma'_{-45}x(i,j)$) are called the upper gradient values, and the following three parameters ($\Gamma''_{45}x(i,j)$, $\Gamma''_{0}x(i,j)$, and $\Gamma''_{-45}x(i,j)$) are called the lower gradient values. The both of the upper and the lower gradient values in the same direction are determined by the centers making a right angle with the direction of the basic gradient (ED). In general, Bob (intra-field linear interpolation) method exhibits no motion artifacts and has minimal computational requirements. However, the input vertical resolution is halved before the image is interpolated, thus reducing the detail in the progressive image. To handle the above problems, we use not only three basic gradient values, but also each

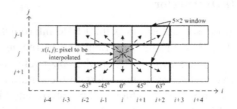

Fig. 1. 5-by-2 window for ED detector

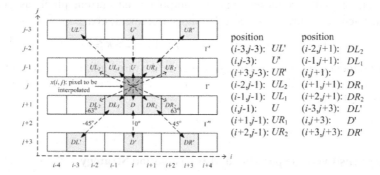

Fig. 2. Neighborhood of a central pixel

Table 1. Involved Gradient Values to Calculate the Fuzzy Gradient

ED	Basic gradient	Upper gradient	Lower gradient
63°	$\Gamma_{63}x(i,j)=UL_2-DR_2$	-	-
45°	$\Gamma_{45}x(i,j)=UL-DR$	$\Gamma'_{45}x(i,j)=UL'-UL$	$\Gamma''_{45}x(i,j)=DR-DR'$
0°	$\Gamma_0x(i,j)=U-D$	$\Gamma'_0x(i,j)=U'-U$	$\Gamma''_0x(i,j)=D-D'$
-45°	$\Gamma_{-45}x(i,j)=UR-DL$	$\Gamma'_{-45}x(i,j)=UR'-UR$	$\Gamma''_{-45}x(i,j)=DL-DL'$
-63°	$\Gamma_{-63}x(i,j)=UR_2-DL_2$	-	-

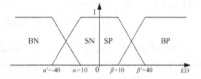

Fig. 3. Membership functions BN, SN, SP, and BP, respectively

three upper and three lower gradient values to make a conclusion. And we use not only one basic gradient for each direction, but upper and lower gradient values for each direction. The pixel $x_{FESA}(i,j)$ which should be interpolated using FESA method is expressed by the pixel values t, u, v, and w ($t=\{UL', U', UR'\}$, $u=\{UL, U, UR\}$, $v=\{DL, D, DR\}$, $w=\{DL', D', DR'\}$).

Table 2. Rule table of the proposed method

Γ'	Γ"	Γ BN	Γ SN	Γ SP	Γ BP
BN	BN	av_{uv}			
	SN	v			
	SP	v			
	BP	$av_{uv}+ad_{tu}/4$	$av_{uv}+ad_{tu}/2$	$av_{uv}+ad_{vw}/2$	$av_{uv}+ad_{vw}/4$
SN	BN	u			
	SN	au_{uv}			
	SP	$av_{uv}+ad_{tu}/2$	$av_{uv}+ad_{tu}$	$av_{uv}+ad_{vw}$	$av_{uv}+ad_{vw}/2$
	BP	u			
SP	BN	u			
	SN	$av_{uv}-ad_{vw}/2$	$av_{uv}-ad_{vw}$	$av_{uv}-ad_{tu}$	$av_{uv}-ad_{tu}/2$
	SP	au_{uv}			
	BP	u			
BP	BN	$av_{uv}-ad_{vw}/4$	$av_{uv}-ad_{vw}/2$	$av_{uv}-ad_{tu}/2$	$av_{uv}-ad_{tu}/4$
	SN	v			
	SP	v			
	BP	av_{uv}			

Employed fuzzy sets are shown in Fig. 3. Because *"big," "small," "negative,"* and *"positive"* are nondeterministic features, these terms can be represented as fuzzy sets. Fuzzy sets can be represented by a membership function. Examples of the membership function BN (for the fuzzy set *big negative*), SN (for the fuzzy set *small negative*), SP (for the fuzzy set *small positive*), and BP (for the fuzzy set *big positive*) are shown in Fig. 3. The horizontal axis of these functions represents all the possible gradient values (the universe [-255,255]) and the vertical axis represents a membership degree

($\in [0,1]$). A membership degree indicates the degree in which a certain gradient value matches the predicate (e.g., BP). If a gradient value has membership degree of one, for the fuzzy set BP, it means that it is definitely a *big positive*. The parameter set is chosen as follows, $\alpha=\beta=10$, $\alpha'=-40$, $\beta'=40$, where α is the negative lower bound, β is the positive lower bound, α' is the negative upper bound, and β' is the positive upper bound. The parameters α, α', β, and β' are determined empirically. The final utilized rule of the FESA is shown in (3) and Table 2.

$$
\begin{aligned}
&if\ ED \in \{-63°,63°\} &&x_{FESA}(i,j) = av_{uv} \\
&else &&x_{FESA}(i,j) = result\ of\ Table\ 2
\end{aligned}
\tag{3}
$$

where av_{uv} is the *average value* of u and v ($av_{uv}=(u+v)/2$). Both of ad_{tu} and ad_{vw} are the *absolute difference* between t and u, and v and w, i.e., $ad_{tu}=|t-u|$, $ad_{vw}=|v-w|$. The denominator is changed from 2 to 4 in the case of both of $\tilde{A}'$ and $\tilde{A}''$ are included in BN or BP. This is because it was found that some pixels can be overflowed or underflowed, while the difference between t and u, or the difference between v and w are quite big.

3   Simulation Results and Limitation

In this section, a comparison is made between the objective and subjective quality, and computational CPU time for the different proposed interpolation methods. Experiments were conducted to evaluate the performance of the proposed FESA method. Along with the proposed algorithm, some of the existing deinterlacing algorithms were also tested for comparison, which included spatial domain methods (Bob, ELA, DOI, NEDI), temporal domain methods (Weave), and spatio-temporal domain methods (VTMF, STELA, EDT). The experiments were run on four "real-world" HDTV sequences with a field size of 1920*1080i: Mobcal, Parkrun, Shields, and Stockholm, as shown in Fig. 4. Followings are the test image characteristics.

1) Mobcal: High spatial detail and medium amount of motion. The camera pans vertically (top to bottom). The word 'Februari' is moving from bottom to top.
2) Parkrun: High spatial detail and medium amount of motion. The camera pans horizontally (left to right). A man is running from the left to right.
3) Shields: Medium spatial detail and medium amount of motion. Firstly, the camera pans horizontally (right to left), and then it zooms in. The standard of the shields become larger, while the sequences continue.
4) Stockholm: High spatial detail and medium amount of motion. The camera pans horizontally (left to right). The sign 'DAGENS WHATER' of the building moves from right to left.

| (a) | (b) | (c) | (d) |

Fig. 4. Four 1920*1080i test sequence that are used: (a) Mobcal, (b) Parkrun, (c) Shields, and (d) Stockholm

Table 3 shows the PSNR and computational CPU time results of different deinterlacing methods for various sequences. The results show that the proposed FESA demonstrates the best objective performance compared to the other conventional methods in terms of PSNR except that Mobcal sequence. Moreover, the proposed FESA only requires 1.603 times of computational CPU time than that of Bob, and 1.127 times of computational CPU time than that of STELA. In particular, it shows slightly better (for Parkrun, Shields, and Stockholm) objective performance compared to the DOI method in terms of PSNR, even though it requires only about 7.071% of computation CPU time. Although FESA does not employ temporal information, it shows better performance than the methods with temporal domain information in these experiments.

For a subjective performance evaluation, the 100th frame of the Mobcal sequence was adopted. Fig. 5 compares the visual performance of the FESA with several major conventional methods. It is assumed that ELA, NEDI, DOI, STELA, EDT algorithms are enough to be compared, since these methods is considered to be good methods among conventional methods for comparison. It can be observed that these methods have the following main shortcomings in contrast to the proposed FESA method.

(a, b) Both of ELA and NEDI do not use temporal information, and they show no motion artifacts in motion region. However, they do not work properly with complex structures, and the edges are degraded severely. Because the edge detector may find the incorrect edge direction out, it causes artifacts and deteriorates visual quality. The artifacts are shown in the edges of the word 'Февраль' in Figs. 5(a) and 5(b).

(c) Since DOI uses spatial information only, it shows no motion artifacts as well. DOI provides the best results among all of the other conventional methods, as shown in Fig. 5(c). However, DOI requires tremendous computational CPU time. In particular, it requires about fourteen times computational CPU time than that of FESA. It makes the system less feasible.

(d) STELA can estimate the motion vector to be zero in the static region, so that it can reconstruct the missing pixel perfectly, and results in no degradation. However, it gradually reduces the vertical detail as the temporal frequencies increase. The vertical detail from the previous field is combined with the temporally shifted current field, indicating that some motion blur occurred. From Fig. 5(d), we found that flickering occurs only where there is edge motion.

(e) EDT evaluates the validity of the zero motion vectors, so that it can provide performance similar to the STELA, and results in no degradation of the static region. However, it shows edge flicker artifacts in motion region. Moreover, this method is quite sensitive to the threshold T (20 is given in [10]). See Figs. 5(e), as the word moves, the degradation is perceived as a flicker. After the EDT method, there are still many feathering defects in the word. The feathering effect appears on the boundaries of the words "Февраль," and "如月".

Fig. 5(f) shows the FESA method utilized image. FESA gives the best quality out of all methods. This FESA emphasizes edge preservation and edge sharpness after deinterlacing. From the experiment results, it is observed that the proposed FESA method has good objective and subjective qualities for different sequences, especially requires low computational CPU time to achieve the real-time processing.

Table 3. Average PSNR and CPU time (seconds/frame) results of different interpolation methods for four HDTV sequences (for the 1st to 126th sequences)

Method	Mobcal		Parkrun		Shields		Stockholm	
Spatial domain methods								
Bob	28.463	0.3414	21.131	0.4162	24.369	0.3762	26.586	0.3653
ELA	27.977	0.5070	21.296	0.5104	24.436	0.5052	26.762	0.5092
DOI	28.402	7.6688	21.120	12.7407	24.365	6.4883	26.578	7.0935
NEDI	28.088	0.7120	21.059	0.7003	24.269	0.7101	26.548	0.7266
Temporal domain methods								
Weave	25.624	0.2744	19.031	0.3644	21.743	0.3196	24.223	0.3248
VTMF	27.013	0.3117	20.783	0.3114	24.051	0.3105	26.180	0.3211
STELA	28.472	0.5234	21.268	0.5230	24.499	0.5228	26.774	0.5621
EDT	27.249	0.5672	20.154	0.8117	23.020	0.6741	25.438	0.5525
Proposed methods								
FESA	28.241	0.6181	21.324	0.5496	24.513	0.6738	26.778	0.5623

(unit: dB, ms)

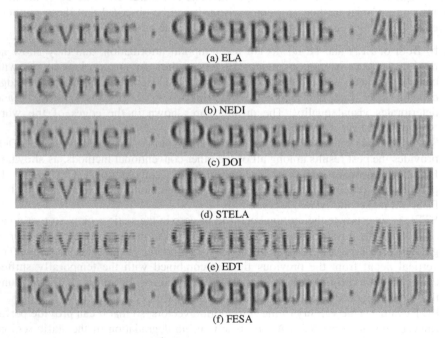

(a) ELA

(b) NEDI

(c) DOI

(d) STELA

(e) EDT

(f) FESA

Fig. 5. 100th 1920*1080i grayscale Mobcal image

However, it was found that some problems exist in the results from the FESA method. As can be seen in Table 3, the FESA method does not outperform the ELA method for Mobcal sequence. Nevertheless, the idea behind this method can be used to develop a subjective quality very well (as shown in Fig. 5). FESA method is specific for the sequence with high motion region. Thus, this method should be used with a motion adaptive or a motion compensated method that utilizes temporal domain information. Future research will be concentrated on this issue and on the construction of a fuzzy rule based interpolation algorithm for a motion adaptive and a motion compensated deinterlacing system.

4   Conclusion

In this paper, a new fuzzy rule based edge preserving deinterlacing algorithm was proposed. The proposed FESA method consists of edge detection part and fuzzy rule based edge-sensitive interpolation part. Once the edge direction is determined, in order to accurately reconstruct boundary of edges and peaks, edge-sensitive interpolation is utilized. Detection and interpolation results were presented. Experimental results of computer simulations show that the proposed method was able to outperform a number of methods in the literature in objective and subjective qualities in a feasible amount of CPU time.

Acknowledgment

"This work was supported by the Korea Research Foundation Grant funded by the Korean Government (MOEHRD) (KRF-2006-005-J04101)."

References

1. Renxiang, L., Zeng, B., Liou, L.: Reliable motion detection/compensation for interlaced sequences and its applications to deinterlacing. IEEE Trans. Circuits and Systems for Video Technology 10(1), 23–29 (2000)
2. Bellers, E.B., de Haan, G.: Advanced de-interlacing techniques. In: Proc. ProRisc/IEEE Workshop on Circuits, Systems and Signal Processing, Mierlo, The Netherlands, pp. 7–17 (November 1996)
3. Doyle, T.: Interlaced to sequential conversion for EDTV applications. In: Proc. 2nd Int. Workshop Signal Processing of HDTV, pp. 412–430 (February 1990)
4. Yoo, H., Jeong, J.: Direction-oriented interpolation and its application to de-interlacing. IEEE Trans. Consumer Electronics 8(4), 954–962 (2002)
5. Park, M.K., Kang, M.G., Nam, K., Oh, S.G.: New edge dependent deinterlacing algorithm based on horizontal edge pattern. IEEE Trans. Consumer Electronics 49(4), 1508–1512 (2003)
6. Fan, Y.-C., Lin, H.-S., Tsao, H.-W., Kuo, C.-C.: Intelligent intra-field interpolation for motion compensated deinterlacing. In: Proc. ITRE 2005, vol. 3, pp. 200–203 (2005)
7. de Haan, G., Bellers, E.B.: Deinterlacing – An overview. In: Proceedings of the IEEE, vol. 86(9), pp. 1839–1857 (September 1998)
8. Jeon, G., Jeong, J.: Designing Takagi-Sugeno fuzzy model-based motion adaptive deinterlacing system. IEEE Trans. Consumer Electronics 52(3), 1013–1020 (2006)
9. Oh, H.-S., Kim, Y., Jung, Y.-Y., Morales, A.W., Ko, S.-J.: Spatio-temporal edge-based median filtering for deinterlacing. IEEE International Conference on Consumer Electronics, pp. 52–53 (2000)
10. Chen, M.-J., Huang, C.-H., Hsu, C.-T.: Efficient de-interlacing technique by inter-field information. IEEE Trans. Consumer Electronics 50(4), 1202–1208 (2004)
11. Carrato, S., Ramponi, G., Marsi, S.: A simple edge-sensitive image interpolation filter. Proc. of IEEE ICIP, pp. 711–714, Lausanne (September 1996)

A Tabular Pruning Rule in Tree-Based Fast Nearest Neighbor Search Algorithms

Jose Oncina[1], Franck Thollard[2], Eva Gómez-Ballester[1], Luisa Micó[1],
and Francisco Moreno-Seco[1]

[1] Dept. Lenguajes y Sistemas Informáticos
Universidad de Alicante, E-03071 Alicante, Spain
{oncina,eva,mico,paco}@dlsi.ua.es
[2] Laboratoire Hubert Curien (ex EURISE) - UMR CNRS 5516
18 rue du Prof. Lauras - 42000 Saint-Étienne Cedex 2, France
thollard@univ-st-etienne.fr

Abstract. Some fast nearest neighbor search (NNS) algorithms using
metric properties have appeared in the last years for reducing computational cost. Depending on the structure used to store the training set,
different strategies to speed up the search have been defined. For instance, pruning rules avoid the search of some branches of a tree in a
tree-based search algorithm. In this paper, we propose a new and simple
pruning rule that can be used in most of the tree-based search algorithms.
All the information needed by the rule can be stored in a table (at pre-
processing time). Moreover, the rule can be computed in constant time.
This approach is evaluated through real and artificial data experiments.
In order to test its performance, the rule is compared to and combined
with other previously defined rules.

1 Introduction

Nearest Neighbor Search (NNS) techniques aim at finding the nearest point of
a set to a given test point using a distance function [4]. The naïve approach is
some times a bottleneck due to the large number of distances to be computed.
Many methods have been developped in order to avoid the exhaustive search
(see [3] and [2] for a survey). Tree-based structures are very popular in most
of the proposed algorithms [6,5,10,1,9], as this structure provides a simple way
to avoid the exploration of some subsets of points. Among these methods, only
some of them are suitable for general metric spaces, i.e., spaces where the objects
(prototypes) need not to be represented as a point, and only require a properly
defined distance function. The most popular and refereed algorithm of such a
type was proposed by Fukunaga and Narendra (FNA) [6]. This algorithm is very
suitable for studying new tree building strategies and new pruning rules [7,8] as
a previous step for extending the new ideas to other tree-based algorithms.

In this paper a new pruning rule is presented. The two keypoints in favor of
this rule are its simplicity (only a table of "distances" is stored) and its efficiency
(it allows a constant time pruning). The new rule may be used with the FNA

J. Martí et al. (Eds.): IbPRIA 2007, Part II, LNCS 4478, pp. 306–313, 2007.

algorithm in any metric space (even in a vector space with an appropiate distance metric). In a classical way, the FNA algorithm will serve as a baseline for the comparison with other techniques.

The paper is organized as follow: we will first introduce the basic algorithm (section 2). We introduce the different pruning rules that were used in the experiment in section 3 and 4. We will provide a comparative experiment on either artificial and real world data (section 5). We then conclude suggesting some future works (section 6).

2   The Basic Algorithm

The FNA is a fast search method that uses a binary tree structure. Each leaf stores a point of the search space. At each node t is associated S_t, the set of the points stored in the leaves of t sub-tree. Each node stores M_t (the representative of S_t) and the radius of S_t, $R_t = \max_{x \in S_t} d(M_t, x)$.

The tree is generally built using recursive calls to a clustering algorithm. In the original FNA the c-means algorithm was used. In [7] some other strategies were explored: in the best method, namely the *Most Distant from the Father tree* (MDF), the representative of the left node was the same than the representative of its father. Thus, each time an expansion of the node is necessary, only one new distance must be computed (instead of two), reducing the number of distances computed. As the pruning rules apply on any tree, in the following, the tree will be built using the MDF method.

In algorithm 1, a simplified version of FNA is presented; only the `Prune_FNR` function call must be changed when considering another pruning rule. In order to make the pseudo-code simpler, the $d_{\min}$ and nn are considered global variable. Also, only binary trees with one point on the leaves are considered.

The use of the Fukunaga and Narendra Rule (FNR) for pruning internal nodes is detailed in [6].

When a new sample point x is given, its nearest neighbor nn is searched in the tree using a depth-first strategy. At a given level, the node t with a smaller distance $d(x, M_t)$ is explored first. In order to avoid the exploration of some branches of the tree the FNA uses the FNR rule.

3   A Review of Pruning Rules

Fukunaga and Narendra Rule (FNR)
The pruning rule defined by Fukunaga and Narendra for internal nodes only makes use of the information in the node t to be pruned (with representant M_t and radius R_t) and the hyperspherical volume centered in the sample point x with radius $d(x, nn)$, where nn is the nearest prototype considered up to the moment.

Rule: No $y \in S_t$ can be the nearest neighbor to x if $d(x, nn) + R_t < d(x, M_t)$.

Algorithm 1: search(t,x)

Data: t: a node tree ; x: a sample point;
Result: nn: the nearest neighbor prototype; $d_{\min}$: the distance to nn;
if t *is not a leaf* then
  $r = right\_child(t); \ell = left\_child(t);$
  $d_r = d(x, M_r) ; \qquad d_\ell = d(x, M_\ell);$
  update $d_{\min}$ and nn;
  if $d_\ell < d_r$ then
    if *not Prune_FNR(ℓ)* then
      $\lfloor$ search(ℓ, x);
    if *not Prune_FNR(r)* then
      $\lfloor$ search(r, x);
  else
    if *not Prune_FNR(r)* then
      $\lfloor$ search(r, x);
    if *not Prune_FNR(ℓ)* then
      $\lfloor$ search(ℓ, x);

The Sibling Based Rule (SBR)
Given two sibling nodes r and ℓ, this rule requires that each node r stores the distance between the representative of the node, M_r, and the nearest point, e_ℓ, in the sibling node ℓ (S_ℓ).

Rule: No $y \in S_\ell$ can be the nearest neighbor to x if $d(M_r, e_\ell) > d(M_r, x) + d(x, nn)$

Unlike the FNR, SBR can be applied to eliminate node ℓ without computing $d(M_\ell, x)$, avoiding some extra distance computations at search time.

Generalized Rule (GR)
This rule is an iterated combination of the FNR and the SBR (see [8] for more details). Given a node ℓ, a set of prototypes $\{e_i\}$ is defined in the following way:

$$G_1 = S_\ell$$
$$e_i = \text{argmax}_{p \in G_i} d(p, M_\ell)$$
$$G_{i+1} = \{p \in G_i : d(p, M_r) < d(e_i, M_r)\}$$

where M_r is the representative of the sibling node r, and G_i are auxiliary sets of prototypes.

At preprocessing time, the distances $d(M_r, e_i)$ are stored in each node ℓ. This process is repeated similarly for the sibling node.

Rule: No $y \in S_\ell$ can be the nearest neighbor if there is an integer i such that:

$$d(M_r, e_i) \geq d(M_r, x) + d(x, nn) \qquad (1)$$

$$d(M_\ell, e_{i+1}) \le d(M_\ell, x) - d(x, nn) \tag{2}$$

Cases $i = 0$ and $i = s$ are also included not considering equations (1) or (2) respectively. Note that condition (1) is equivalent to SBR rule when $i = s$ and condition (2) is equivalent to FNR rule when $i = 0$.

4   The Table Rule (TR)

This rule prunes by taking the current nearest neighbor as a reference. In order to do so the distance from a prototype p to a set of prototypes S is defined as $d(p, S) = \min_{y \in S} d(p, y)$. At preprocess time, the distances from each prototype to each node set S_t in the tree are computed and stored in a table, allowing a constant time pruning. Note that the size of this table grows with the square of the number of prototypes since, as the tree is binary, the number of nodes is two times the number of prototypes.

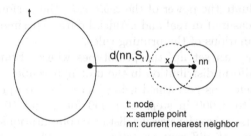

t: node
x: sample point
nn: current nearest neighbor

Fig. 1. Application of the table rule

Rule: Figure 1, Present a graphical view of the table rule.

Proposition 1 (Table Rule). *Given the table rule* $(2d(x, nn) < d(t, nn))$, *no prototype* e_i *in node* t *can be nearest to the test sample* x *than* nn, *i. e.*

$$\forall e_i \in t, \quad d(x, e_i) \ge d(x, nn)$$

Proof:
Let $e_i \in S_t$. By the definition of the distance between a point and a node

$$d(nn, S_t) = \min_{e_i \in S_t} d(e_i, nn)$$

and thus

$$d(nn, S_t) \le d(e_i, nn)$$

Moreover, by the triangle inequality, we have:

$$d(e_i, nn) \le d(e_i, x) + d(x, nn)$$

Combining these inequalities, we have:

$$d(nn, S_t) \leq d(e_i, nn) \leq d(e_i, x) + d(x, nn)$$
$$\Rightarrow \ d(e_i, x) \ \geq d(nn, S_t) - d(x, nn)$$

using the table rule, we finally have:

$$d(e_i, x) \geq 2d(x, nn) - d(x, nn) = d(x, nn)$$

which completes the proof.

5   Experiments

As seen in the proof of the correctness of the table rule, it is only required that d is a true distance. In particular, on the contrary to other techniques such as the well known kd-tree algorithm, a vector space is not needed in order to apply the table rule.

In order to evaluate the power of the *table rule*, the performance of the algorithm has been measured in real and artificial data experiments using the most significative combinations of the pruning rules.

In the artificial data set up, the prototypes where obtained from a 5 and 10-dimensional uniform distribution in the unit hypercube.

A first experiment was performed using increasing size prototypes sets from $1,000$ prototypes to $8,000$ in steps of $1,000$ for 5 and 10 dimensional data. Each experiment measures the average distance computations of $16,000$ searches ($1,000$ searches over 16 different prototypes sets). The samples were obtained from the same distribution.

Figures 2 and 3 show the results for some combinations of the pruning rules where "f", "s", "g" and "t" stand for the "Fukunaga", "sibling", "generalized" and "table" pruning rules respectively. Standard deviation of measures is also included (though with value almost negligible).

As it can be observed, the table pruning rule, when applied alone, can achieve $\sim 50\%$ distance computations reduction, although additional reduction (up to $\sim 70\%$) can be achieved when combined with "f", "fs" or "g" pruning rules. In these three cases the differences are not noticeable. Obviously, as the time complexity of the generalized pruning rule is not constant, the combinations with "f" or "fs" are more appealing.

To show the performance of the algorithm with real data, some tests were carried out on a spelling task. A database of $38,000$ words of a Spanish dictionary was used.

The input test of the speller was simulated distorting the words by means of random insertion, deletion and substitution operations over the words in the original dictionary. The edit distance was used to compare the words. In these experiments, the values of the weighting operations costs of the edit distance (insertion, deletion and substitution) were fixed to 1. This makes the edit distance a mathematical distance which makes the table rule applicable. Please note that

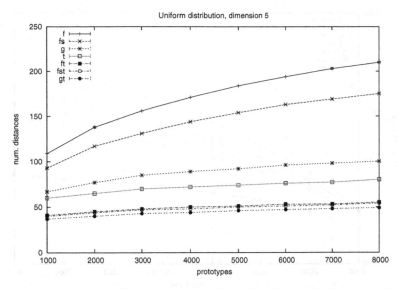

Fig. 2. Pruning rules combinations in a uniform distribution 5-dimensional space

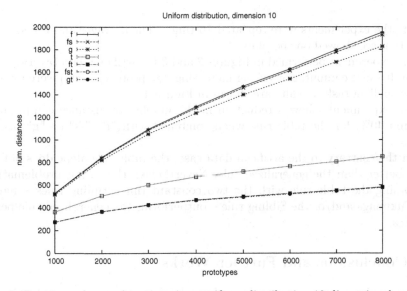

Fig. 3. Pruning rules combinations in a uniform distribution 10-dimensional space

some fast NN search techniques (i.e. kd-tree) could not be applied here as the data could hardly be represented in a vector space.

Dictionaries of increasing size (from 1,000 to 8,000) were obtained extracting randomly words of the whole dictionary. The test points were 1,000 distorted words obtained from randomly selected dictionary words. To obtain reliable

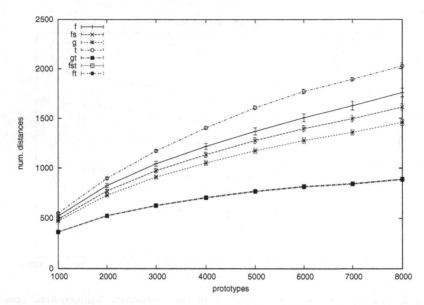

Fig. 4. Pruning rules combined in a spelling task

results the experiments were repeated 16 times. The averages and the standard deviation are showed on the plots.

The experiment performed in Figures 2 and 3 for artificial data (average number of distance computations using increasing size prototype sets) were repeated in the spelling task. Results are shown in Figure 4.

The experiments show a reduction in the number of distance computations (around 40%) for the table rule when combined with "f", "fs" or "g" pruning rules.

On the contrary to the artificial data case, the table rule alone does not perform better than the generalized rule. Nevertheless, this is not problematic as combining the table rule with the two constant time pruning rules – namely the Fukunaga and/or the Sibling rule – outperforms the generalized rule performances.

6   Conclusions and Further Works

To summarize, a new pruning rule has been defined that can been applied in tree-based search algorithms. To apply the rule, a distance table should be computed and stored in preprocess time. This table rule stores the distances between each prototype in the training set and every node of the tree; its space complexity is therefore quadratic in the size of the training set.

As the experiments suggest, this rule save the computation of 70% of distances in the case of 10-dimensional data and 40% in the case of strings with training set around 8,000 points when compared with the generalized rule.

In future works, a more exhaustive study of the rule will be performed. In particular, the idea is to study on the one hand which is the better combination of rules (with the minor cost), and on the other hand, what is the condition and order where each rule can be applied.

Other problem that should be explored is how to reduce the space complexity of the table rule.

Acknowledgments

The authors thank the Spanish CICyT for partial support of this work through projects DPI2006-15542-C04-01, TIN2006-14932-C02, GV06/166, the IST Programme of the European Community, under the PASCAL Network of Excellence, IST–2002-506778.

References

1. Brin, S.: Near neighbor search in large metric spaces. In: Proceedings of the 21st VLDB Conference, pp. 574–584 (1995)
2. Chávez, E., Navarro, G., Baeza-Yates, R., Marroquin, J.L.: Searching in metric spaces. ACM Computing Surveys 33(3), 273–321 (2001)
3. Dasarathy, B.V.: Nearest Neighbor (NN) Norms: NN Pattern Classification Techniques. IEEE Computer Society Press, Los Alamitos (1991)
4. Duda, R.O., Hart, P.E., Stork, D.G.: Pattern Classification, 2nd edn. Wiley, Chichester (2000)
5. Friedman, J.H., Bentley, J.L., Finkel, R.A.: An algorithm for finding best matches in logarithmic expected time. ACM Transactions on Mathematical Software 3, 209–226 (1977)
6. Fukunaga, K., Narendra, P.M.: A branch and bound algorithm for computing k-nearest neighbors. IEEE Transactions on Computers, IEC 24, 750–753 (1975)
7. Gómez-Ballester, E., Micó, L., Oncina, J.: Some improvements in tree based nearest neighbour search algorithms. In: Sanfeliu, A., Ruiz-Shulcloper, J. (eds.) CIARP 2003. LNCS, vol. 2905, pp. 456–463. Springer, Heidelberg (2003)
8. Gómez-Ballester, E., Micó, L., Oncina, J.: Some approaches to improve tree-based nearest neighbour search algorithms. Pattern Recognition 39(2), 171–179 (2006)
9. McNames, J.: A fast nearest neighbor algorithm based on a principal axis tree. IEEE Transactions on Pattern Analysis and Machine Intelligence 23(9), 964–976 (2001)
10. Yianilos, P.N.: Data structures and algorithms for nearest neighbor search in general metric spaces. In: Proceedings of the ACM-SIAM Symposium on Discrete Algorithms, pp. 311–321 (1993)

A General Framework to Deal with the Scaling Problem in Phrase-Based Statistical Machine Translation

Daniel Ortiz[1], Ismael García Varea[1], and Francisco Casacuberta[2]

[1] Dpto. de Inf., Univ. de Castilla-La Mancha, 02071 Albacete, Spain
ivarea@info-ab.uclm.es
[2] Dpto. de Sist Inf. y Comp., Univ. Politécnica de Valencia, 46071 Valencia, Spain
dortiz@dsic.upv.es, fcn@dsic.upv.es

Abstract. In this paper, we address the topic of how to estimate phrase-based models from very large corpora and apply them in statistical machine translation. The great number of sentence pairs contained in recent corpora like the well-known *Europarl* corpus have enormously increased the memory requirements to train phrase-based models and to apply them within a decoding process. We propose a general framework that deals with this problem without introducing significant time overhead by means of the combination of different scaling techniques. This new framework is based on the use of counts instead of probabilities, and on the concept of cache memory.

1 Introduction

The daily increase in the availability of multilingual parallel corpora during the last two decades has turned the statistical approach to machine translation (SMT) into one of the disciplines of major study within the area of natural language processing. The translation process, from a statistical point of view, can be formulated as follows: A source language string $f_1^J = f_1 \ldots f_J$ is to be translated into a target language string $e_1^I = e_1 \ldots e_I$. Every target string is regarded as a possible translation for the source language string with maximum a-posteriori probability $Pr(e_1^I|f_1^J)$. According to Bayes' theorem, the target string $\hat{e}_1^I$ that maximizes the product of both the target language model $Pr(e_1^I)$ and the string translation model $Pr(f_1^J|e_1^I)$ must be chosen. The equation that models this process is:

$$\hat{e}_1^I = \arg\max_{e_1^I}\{Pr(e_1^I) \cdot Pr(f_1^J|e_1^I)\} \tag{1}$$

In the origins of SMT, the translation models were based on structural relations at word level [1]. It is only in the last few years that statistical translation models have been extended to models that try to capture relations between groups of consecutive words (or phrases), as for example in [2,3,4].

Phrase-based models emerge as an alternative to single word-based models to overcome the limitations that they present. The main difference between single

J. Martí et al. (Eds.): IbPRIA 2007, Part II, LNCS 4478, pp. 314–322, 2007.
© Springer-Verlag Berlin Heidelberg 2007

word-based and phrase-based models is that phrase-based models work with statistical dictionaries of phrases ($Pr(\tilde{f}_k|\tilde{e}_k)$) instead of words ($Pr(f_j|e_i)$).

The translation probabilities of the phrase models are typically estimated via maximum-likelihood from a bilingual training corpus as $p(\tilde{f}|\tilde{e}) = \frac{N(\tilde{f},\tilde{e})}{N(\tilde{e})}$, where $N(\tilde{f}|\tilde{e})$ is the number of times that $\tilde{f}$ has been seen as a translation of $\tilde{e}$ in the whole training corpus.

The availability of large corpora of (multilingual) information makes phrase-based translation models much more competitive than their predecessors. In contrast, an appropriate use of such models involves great computational and memory requirements.

Most of the authors of works on phrase-based translation have shown the importance of dealing with larger corpora and longer sentences in order to build statistical machine translation systems.

However, to our knowledge, there are only two works that deal with the scaling problem in phrase-based SMT. Good solutions to the scaling problem in phrase-based SMT are presented in [5]. The authors proposed a suffix array-based data structure to store and retrieve phrases of an arbitrary length. This data structure has far less memory requirements than a standard lookup table, but has high time requirements when retrieving frequent translation pairs. To overcome this drawback, the authors proposed a faster technique to recover approximate (not exact) probabilities. Additionally, another tecnique based on suffix-arrays is proposed in in [6]. It produces exact probabilities and is even faster than the one proposed in [5]. However, even the above mentioned suffix-arrays have huge memory requirements when the models are estimated from very large corpora (up to 2 GBytes, as reported in [5]).

In this paper, we present a general framework to deal with the scaling problem in phrase-based SMT. First, we propose a fragment-based training scheme to reduce the memory requirements. This scheme consists in the use of counts instead of probabilities. Second, we propose an architecture to retrieve probabilities during the search translation process. This architecture reduces the memory requirements to a fixed quantity of memory. This architecture is inspired in the concept of cache memory and is flexible enough to be combined with existing scaling techiques like those proposed in [5] or [6]) as is shown in the following sections.

2   Model Training

Even if very efficient data structures in terms of space complexity are used, important problems arise when the phrase model is to be estimated from very large corpora. In order to overcome this limitation, we propose an algorithm which trains phrase models from corpora of an arbitrary size.

The algorithm that we propose works as follows: first, it splits the corpus into fragments of a fixed number of sentence pairs (*fragment_size*) and estimates a phrase model for each fragment. Once the *submodels* have been generated, they are merged into a single file. This file is lexicographically ordered and the phrase counts that compose the model are then merged. This process yields a phrase model that is identical to the one obtained from the whole corpus. The algorithm proposed here is similar to the algorithm that is provided with the PHARAOH decoder [7].

The proposed algorithm introduces time overhead because of the necessity of sorting and merging the phrase counts. This overhead will be empirically measured in section 5.1. However, it is important to remark that the training and sorting steps executed by the algorithm can be parallelized, resulting in a very efficient method to train phrase models.

3 Decoding with Very Long Phrase Models

The great size of phrase models is a source of problems not only during the training process as explained in the previous section, but also during the decoding process, since the whole model is to be stored in memory.

A simple solution to this problem is to extract the subset of the phrase model that is needed to translate a test set and to store it in memory. This solution is incorporated in translation systems like the PHARAOH decoder [7], but it is not a general solution since the test set must be previously known.

An approach that has been more successful consists in the use of data structures with very low memory requirements [5]. However, these tecniques may not be suitable for very large corpora unless there are machines with great memory sizes (2 GBytes or more).

We propose an alternative way to solve this problem which is strongly inspired by a classic concept of computer architecture: *cache memory*. Cache memory is based on the *principle of locality* of references: if one location is read by a program, then nearby locations are likely to be read soon afterward. In the case of machine translation, this principle manifests itself in two different ways:

1. The majority of the phrase pairs contained in a phrase model have a very low frequency. Therefore, we can predict that these phrase pairs will probably not be required during the decoding process.
2. When translating a sentence with a stack decoding algorithm or with a dynamic programming algorithm, only a small number of the entries that compose the phrase model are accessed, since these algorithms work with N-best inverse translation tables. Additionally, each entry will be accessed many times because of the iterative nature of the decoding process. Therefore, we can identify both temporal and spatial locality principles.

The locality principle explained above leads us to propose a memory hierarchy composed of two levels. The first level stores the bilingual pairs that are accessed during the translation of each sentence. This level is local to the sentence to be translated, and will be erased whenever a new translation process is started.

The second level contains a certain percentage of the most frequent phrase pairs stored within the phrase model. This level is kept in memory during the whole translation process.

Finally, the whole phrase model is stored on a hard drive and is structured to allows the retrieval of the probability of the bilingual pairs. This is done with logarithmic complexity by means of binary search.

It is important to point out that the basic information element that is handled within the memory hierarchy consists of a single target phrase f with all its source translations. This is done to favor spatial locality.

Thus, when the decoder needs to retrieve the probability of a phrase pair $(\tilde{e}\#\tilde{f})$, it searches for the pair in the first level cache. If it is present, its probability is returned. Otherwise, the translations of $\tilde{f}$ are searched for in the second level cache. If these translations exist, they are copied in the first level cache and the probability of the phrase pair is returned if $\tilde{e}$ has been stored as a possible translation of $\tilde{f}$. If there is no translation for $\tilde{f}$ in the second level cache, then the hard drive is accessed.

When the translations of $\tilde{f}$ are searched for in the hard drive, they may or may not exist. In either case, the result of the search is copied in the first level cache, and the probability of the phrase pair is returned.

When the translation process has finished, the first level cache is erased, and the decoder only keeps in memory the selected percentage of the model. The percentage of phrase pairs that are stored in the second level cache will be referred to as the α parameter. According to the first locality principle explained above, the phrase pairs stored in the second level will be those that have a greater frequency.

The parameter α takes values between 0 and 100. Both these values are particular cases with interesting features:

$\alpha=0$: second-level cache will be empty. Therefore, there is no phrase pair permanently stored in memory. This will increase the amount of cache misses. However, it allows us to translate without having to store the model in memory.

$\alpha=100$: the whole model will be stored in the second-level cache. This allows us to translate without any cache misses and can be viewed as the baseline that is implemented by common decoders such as the PHARAOH decoder. (i.e. the whole model is allocated in memory and the retrievals are cached.)

4   Selecting a Suitable Data Structure for the Phrase Model

Because of the huge size of the phrase-models, it is crucial to find a suitable data structure to represent the bilingual phrase pairs.

For the training process described in section 2, the choice of the representation for the phrase models is not an important problem, since it is possible to reduce the memory requirements by simply reducing the fragment size. The most important point here is that the data structure has to be able to work with counts instead of probabilities.

However, the data structures must be carefully chosen for the case of the decoding process. Specifically, it is important to use a fast data structure to represent the first-level cache table, and to use a low complex data structure in terms of space to represent the second-level cache table.

In our work, we have used the same representation for the first- and the second-level cache memory. Such a representation makes a tradeoff between time and space complexity and consists in an assymetrical double trie like the one shown in Figure 1, where there is a trie associated to the source language and another associated to the target language. In the upper part of the figure, a small set of English-Spanish phrases is shown. In the lower part of the figure a depiction is given of how these phrase pairs are stored by the proposed data structure.

In order to retrieve the probability of a phrase pair $(\tilde{e}\#\tilde{f})$, first, the source phrase $\tilde{e}$ is to be searched in the source trie. As a result of the search, a pointer that represents the source phrase and the count of the source phrase $c(\tilde{e})$ are obtained. Second, the target phrase $\tilde{f}$ is to be searched in the target trie. Once the search is done, we have to find the pointer to $\tilde{e}$ that was obtained in the previous step. This final step allows us to retrieve $c(\tilde{e}, \tilde{f})$. Once the two counts are retrieved, the probability of the phrase pair is given by $c(\tilde{e}, \tilde{f})/c(\tilde{e})$.

The number of comparisons that are to be done in order to retrieve the probability of the phrase pair $(\tilde{e}\#\tilde{f})$ is given by the following expression:

$$log(s) + log(t) + n,\qquad(2)$$

where s and t are the number of source words and target words respectively, that are stored by the data structure, and n is the number of source phrases that translates the target phrase $\tilde{f}$. Given that $s \approx t$ and $n \ll s$, we can conclude that the retrieval has a logarithmic complexity.

With regard to the space complexity, the proposed data structure requires only one word from the processor to express the relation between the source and target phrases. In addition, the data structure compresses source and target phrases that share the same prefix. However, more efficient implementations have been proposed, such as the suffix-arrays described in [5,6]. For this reason, we think that it might be interesting to test the performance of this data structure within the proposed cache hierarchy as a future work.

the red house # la casa roja
the green house # la casa verde

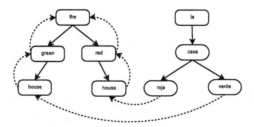

Fig. 1. Data structure for the storage of bilingual pairs

5   Experiments

In this section, we have carried out experimentation with the EUROPARL corpus (the English-Spanish version of the proceedings of the European Parliament), which includes both training and decoding experiments. All the experiments have been executed on a PC with a 2.60 Ghz Intel Pentium 4 processor with 2GB of memory. All the times are given in seconds.

As can be observed in Table 1, the EUROPARL corpus contains a great number of sentences and large vocabulary sizes. These features are common to other well-known corpora described in the literature. It is usual to impose a constraint over the length of the phrases in order to reduce the size of the model. Such a constraint does not negatively affect the translation quality if the maximum phrase length allowed is sufficiently high.

Table 1. Statistics of the EUROPARL corpus

		Spanish	English
Training	Sentences	730 740	
	Words	15 725 136	15 222 505
	Vocabulary	102 885	64 122
Test	Sentences	3 064	
	Words	91 730	85 232

5.1   Training

Table 2 shows spatial and temporal costs (in seconds) that have both the estimation from the whole corpus and the *fragment-by-fragment* estimation proposed in section 2. The experimentation has been carried out for the EUROPARL corpus, ranging from a maximum phrase size of 2 to 8.

The memory requirements for the conventional estimation are higher than 2GBytes when the maximum phrase size is equal to 8. Because of this, such an estimation may not be feasible in 32-bits machines depending on which operating system is used. In contrast, fragment-by-fragment estimation has a fixed cost that is equal to 0.12 GBytes. This value is the maximum amount of memory

Table 2. Statistics of both conventional estimation and fragment-by-fragment estimation for different values of the maximum phrase size

	conventional estimation		fragment-by-fragment estimation	
m	time	size(GB)	time	size(GB)
2	2266	0.11	2336	0.12
4	6034	0.66	5848	0.12
6	10757	1.47	10234	0.12
8	-	>2	17089	0.12

that is assigned to the sorting algorithm and can be decreased at the expense of an increase in the time needed to perform the sort.

With regard to the time cost of the algorithms, it is important to stress that fragment-by-fragment estimation can be even faster than conventional estimation for great values of the maximum phrase length. As explained in section 2, fragment-by-fragment estimation introduces time overhead because of the necessity of sorting the phrase counts. However, the time needed to store and update the counts of each phrase pair depends on the size of the model. This size is smaller if the estimation is carried out for small fragments of the corpus.

5.2 Decoding

To evaluate the performance of the technique proposed in section 3, we have carried out a series of experiments using the EUROPARL corpus. For this purpose, we have estimated a phrase model imposing a maximum phrase size of 7 words.

Table 3 shows the time in seconds required to retrieve the translations for all the phrases of the test sentences for different values of α. The table also shows the number of phrase pairs stored in memory, the number of disk accesses and the time overhead caused by these accesses. As can be observed, the retrieval of the translations from disk introduces time overhead; however, this overhead can be reduced by increasing the value of the α parameter. It is worthy of note that a great decrease in the rate of cache misses can be achieved for small values of α.

Table 3. Time in seconds required to retrieve the translations for the phrases of the test sentences ranging over the value of α

	phrases	diskAccesses	time	diskOvh
Baseline ($\alpha = 100$)	31227305	0 / 0.0%	8.6	0
$\alpha = 0$	0	559336 / 100%	651.2	649.7
$\alpha = 1$	312244	462277 / 82.6%	633.7	625.1
$\alpha = 10$	3122708	370419 / 66.2%	545.6	535.4
$\alpha = 20$	6245443	349727 / 62.5%	525.7	515.4
$\alpha = 40$	12490908	288282 / 51.5%	368.8	358.2
$\alpha = 60$	18736374	219763 / 39.2%	272.4	262.3
$\alpha = 80$	24981839	146141 / 26.1%	175.2	170.2
$\alpha = 99$	30915031	71885 / 12.8%	96.4	86.8

The access to the model during the decoding process can be viewed as a two-stage process that is repeated for each sentence to be translated. First, the translations for each phrase of the sentence are retrieved. Second, the translation probabilities for the bilingual pairs are accessed. In order to quantify the total locating time, we have translated the 3064 sentences of the EUROPARL test set by means of a monotone stack-decoding algorithm, using cache models with α equal to 100 (our baseline) and with α equal to 10. Table 4 shows the number of phrases stored in memory, the number of queries to the model (in millions),

Table 4. Time in seconds required by all model queries when translating the EUROPARL test corpus

	phrases	queries (M)	%cMisses	time	time/sent	BLEU
Baseline ($\alpha = 100$)	31227305	227	0	94.6	0.03	26.8
$\alpha = 10$	3122708	227	0.16	636.4	0.2	26.8

the percentage of cache misses, the total locating time, the locating time per sentence, and the translation quality measured in terms of BLEU. As can be observed, the low rate of cache misses allows all the queries to be fetched in only 0.2 seconds per sentence. This time cost per sentence is close to the one obtained for the baseline but only one tenth of the phrase model has to be stored in memory.

6   Concluding Remarks

In this paper, we have proposed a general framework for dealing with the scaling problem in phrase-based SMT. This framework totally or partially transforms the RAM requirements of given scaling techniques into hard disk requirements. With respect to the training process, the proposed techniques train phrase models for corpora of an arbitrary size without introducing a significant time overhead. With respect to the decoding process, the experiments have shown that it is possible to appreciably reduce the memory requirements without causing an important increase in the locating time per sentence.

The cache-inspired proposed architecture has been demonstrated to be useful when a stack-based decoding algorithm is used. We deem that this paradigm can also be applied to dynamic programming-based decoders. Moreover, we also find it useful for other phrase-based related problems such as obtaining the best segmentation at the phrase level for a given pair of sentences (i.e. the Viterbi phrase alignment), where the locality principles stated above are also applicable. The application of these techniques to language modelling can also be studied.

To the future, we plan to extend the work presented here to both in training and decoding. With regard to training, we plan to parallelize the training algorithm, which will provide a highly efficient training process. With regard to decoding, our aim is to find ways to reduce the number of disk accesses and to implement a more efficient representation of the cache hierarchy. In particular, it would be interesting to employ suffix-arrays to implement the second-level cache.

Acknowledgments. This work has been partially supported by the Spanish projects TIC2003-08681-C02-02 and TIN2006-15694-CO2-01, the *Agencia Valenciana de Ciencia y Tecnología* under contract GRUPOS03/031, the *Generalitat Valenciana*, and the project HERMES (Vicerrectorado de Investigación - UCLM-05/06).

References

1. Brown, P.F., Della Pietra, S.A., Della Pietra, V.J., Mercer, R.L.: The mathematics of statistical machine translation: Parameter estimation. Computational Linguistics 19(2), 263–311 (1993)
2. Tomás, J., Casacuberta, F.: Monotone statistical translation using word groups. In: Procs. of the MT Summit VIII, Santiago de Compostela, Spain, pp. 357–361 (2001)
3. Marcu, D., Wong, W.: A phrase-based, joint probability model for statistical machine translation. In: Proc. of the EMNLP, Philadelphia, USA, pp. 1408–1414 (2002)
4. Koehn, P., Och, F.J., Marcu, D.: Statistical phrase-based translation. In: Proceedings of the HLT/NAACL, Edmonton, Canada (2003)
5. Callison-Burch, C., Bannard, C., Schroeder, J.: Scaling phrase-based statistical machine translation to larger corpora and longer sentences. In: Proc. of the ACL, Ann Arbor, pp. 255–262 (2005)
6. Zhang, Y., Vogel, S.: An efficient phrase-to-phrase alignment model for arbitrarily long phrase and large corpora. In: Proceedings of the Tenth EAMT), Budapest, Hungary, The European Association for Machine Translation (2005)
7. Koehn, P.: Pharaoh: a beam search decoder for phrase-based statistical machine translation models. User manual and description. Technical report, USC Information Science Institute (2003)

Recognizing Individual Typing Patterns

Michał Choraś[1] and Piotr Mroczkowski[2]

[1] Image Processing Group, Institute of Telecommunications
University of Technology & Life Sciences
S. Kaliskiego 7, 85-791 Bydgoszcz
chorasm@utp.edu.pl
[2] Hewlett Packard Polska, Global Delivery Poland Center
ul. Szturmowa 2a, University Business Center, Warsaw, Poland
piotr.mroczkowski@hp.com

Abstract. In the article three methods of extracting individual typing patterns are proposed and tested. Moreover, we present satisfactory experimental results confirming that these typing patterns may be used as biometrics for human identification, especially in web-based applications (e.g. password hardening).

1 Introduction

Individual typing patterns recognition systems analyze the way a user types at a terminal by monitoring the keyboard events. In such recognition systems, several things can be analyzed: time between key-pressed and key-released events, break between two different keystrokes, duration for digraphs and trigraphs and many more. In other words not what is typed, but how it is typed is important.

These characteristics of typing patterns are considered to be a good sign of identity and therefore may be used as biometrics for human identification and for enhancing web security in client-server applications [1][2][3].

Keystroke verification techniques can be divided into two categories: static and continuous. Static verification approaches analyze keyboard dynamics only at specific times, for example during the logon process. Static techniques are considered as providing a higher level of security than a simple password-based verification system [1]. The main drawback of such an approach is the lack of continuous monitoring, which could detect a substitution of the user after the initial verification. Nevertheless, the combination of the static approach with password authentication was proposed in several papers [4] and it is considered as being able to provide a sufficient level of security for the majority of applications. Our web identification system is based on such a combination.

Continuous verification, on the contrary, monitors the user's typing behavior through the whole period of interaction [1]. It means that even after a successful login, the typing patterns of a person are constantly analyzed and when they do not mach user's profile access is blocked. This method is obviously more reliable but, on the other hand, the verification algorithms as well as the implementation process itself, are much more complex.

J. Martí et al. (Eds.): IbPRIA 2007, Part II, LNCS 4478, pp. 323–330, 2007.

One of the first studies on keyboard biometrics was carried out by Gaines et al.[5]. Seven secretaries took part in the experiment in which they were asked to retype the same three paragraphs on two different occasions in a period of four months. Keystroke latency timings were collected and analyzed for a limited number of digraphs and observations were based on those digraph values that occurred more than 10 times [6].

Similar experiments were performed by Leggett with 17 programmers [4]. In the 15 last years, much research on keystroke analysis has been done (e.g., Joyce and Gupta [7], Bleha et al. [8], Leggett et al. [4], Brown and Rogers [9], Bergadano et al. [10], and Monrose and Rubin [1][6]).

Several proposed solutions got U.S. patents (for instance Brown and Rogers [11]). Some neural network approaches (e.g., Yu and Cho [12]) have also been undertaken in the last few years. More recently, several papers where keystroke biometrics, in conjunction with the login-id password pair access control technique, were proposed (e.g., Tapiador and Sigenza [13]). Some commercial implementations are also available ('Biopassword', a software tool for Windows platform commercialized by Net Nanny Inc. [14]).

2   Typing Patterns Characteristics

In the proposed and implemented individual typing pattern recognition system three independent methods of the identity verification are performed every time a user attempts to log in.

First and second method is based on the calculation of the degree of disorder of digraphs and trigraphs respectively. The last one compares typing paths stored in the database against a typing path created at the time of logon process. Hereby we present background of our methods.

2.1   Digraphs and Trigraphs

Digraph is defined as two keys typed one after the other. In our case the duration of a digraph is measured between the press event of the first key and release event of the second key.

Trigraph is defined as three keys typed one after the other. The duration of trigraph is measured between pressing event of the first key and release of the third key.

2.2   Degree of Disorder

Having two sets of key latencies of the same $Login - Password$ pair, it is possible to measure their "similarity". One way to calculate that is the degree of disorder (do) technique [10].

Let us define vector V of N elements and vector V', which includes the same N elements, but ordered in a different way. The degree of disorder in vector V can be defined as the sum of the distances between the position of each element in V with respect to its counterpart vector V'. If all the elements in both vectors are in the same position, the disorder equals 0.

Maximum disorder occurs when elements in vector V are in the reverse order to the model vector V'. Maximum disorder (do_{max}) is given by:

$$do_{\max} = \frac{|V|^2}{2} \qquad (1)$$

where $|V|$ is the length of V and it is even or by:

$$do_{\max} = \frac{(|V|^2 - 1)}{2} \qquad (2)$$

where $|V|$ is length of V and it is odd.

In order to get the normalized degree of disorder (do_{nor}) of a vector of N elements, we divide do by the value of the maximum disorder. After normalization, the degree of disorder falls between 0 (V and V' have the same order) and 1 (V is in reverse order to V').

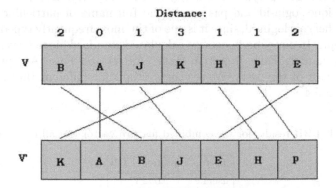

Fig. 1. The distances between the position of each element in V with respect to V'

For the vector V in Figure 1 the disorder can be calculated as:

$$do = (2 + 0 + 1 + 3 + 1 + 1 + 2) = 10 \qquad (3)$$

where do_{max} equals:

$$do_{\max} = \frac{(|V|^2 - 1)}{2} = \frac{7^2 - 1}{2} = \frac{48}{2} = 24 \qquad (4)$$

In order to normalize the disorder, we perform:

$$do_{nor} = \frac{do}{do_{\max}} = \frac{10}{24} = 0,4167 \qquad (5)$$

For a more exhaustive introduction to degree of disorder see [10].

2.3 Typing Paths

Typing paths can be described as a set of key code/key event pairs stored in order of occurrence. If some short sequence of chars is being retyped by a user several times (which is the case with the "Login - Password" mode), the analysis of such paths is likely to show some typical characteristics of a user's behavior:

- moments where keys overlap (second key is pressed before the release of the first one)
- the position of the key pressed in the case of duplicate keys (digits, SHIFT's, etc.)

3 Experimental Setup and Results

In our experiments 18 volunteers participated in testing the proposed keystroke pattern recognition methods. Typing skills varied slightly among them - the majority of the group type on PC keyboard every day. Every volunteer had assigned unique login-id and password. The full name of particular individual was used as her/his login-id, since it is one of the most frequently typed phrase for most of people. In our experiments we calculated standard biometrics recognition parameters, namely False Rejection Rate (FRR) and False Acceptance Rate (FAR) for each of the users. We set the systems for different thresholds: 0.25, 0.3, 0.35 and 0.4.

Table 1. FRR results for the combined feature vector (for all the methods)

user	Combined FRR
user1	7.6923
user2	2.5000
user3	0.0000
user4	41.3043
user5	55.5556
user6	6.2500
user7	41.6667
user8	32.0000
user9	0.0000
user10	15.0000
user11	22.7273
user12	33.3333
user13	36.8421
user14	43.7500
user15	36.3636
user16	9.5238
user17	7.6923
user18	15.7895

Table 2. FAR results for digraphs and trigraphs for the 0.25 threshold

user	Digraph FAR	Trigraph FAR
user1	0.0000	15.3846
user2	0.0000	0.0000
user6	0.0000	17.5439
user8	0.0000	0.0000
user9	0.0000	12.5000
user10	0.0000	1.9231
user14	1.2346	28.3951
user15	0.0000	9.0909
user17	0.0000	0.0000
user18	0.0000	0.0000

Table 3. FAR results for digraphs and trigraphs for the 0.3 threshold

user	Digraph FAR	Trigraph FAR
user1	1.9231	34.6154
user2	0.0000	15.3846
user6	0.0000	47.3684
user8	0.0000	1.6949
user9	0.0000	50.0000
user10	0.0000	7.6923
user14	9.8765	38.2716
user15	0.0000	45.4545
user17	0.0000	0.0000
user18	9.0909	18.1818

In the first stage every participant performed 15 attempts of log in-password authentication that were evaluated by the system in order to calculate the model vector of digraphs and trigraphs as well as to collect the typing paths.

After that users performed several another logon attempts as valid users (FRR tests) and few attempts as impostors (**trying to log on somebody's else account knowing login and password** - FAR tests).

Each user performed 20 logon attempts as valid user. The combined FRR results are presented in Table 1. Unfortunately, usually after several successful attempts most of the users wanted to find out how the system behaves in case of sudden change of typing patterns and they 'test' the system trying to type in extremely different way then they used to. This behavior of users is inevitable in real-life applications and it definitely affected the FRR performance of the system.

In the second part of experiments a participant was asked to act as impostor. She/he was trying to logon on somebody else account. In order to increase the number of logon attacks per single account, we randomly selected 10 out of 18 existing accounts to be attacked. This decision was motivated by the fact that the number of participants (and thus samples) was limited (users were not

Table 4. FAR results for digraphs and trigraphs for the 0.35 threshold

user	Digraph FAR	Trigraph FAR
user1	5.7962	48.0769
user2	7.6923	61.5385
user6	7.0175	66.6667
user8	5.0847	3.3898
user9	12.5000	68.7500
user10	9.6154	19.2308
user14	24.6914	59.2593
user15	0.0000	54.5455
user17	0.0000	0.0000
user18	27.2727	45.4545

Table 5. FAR results for digraphs and trigraphs for the 0.4 threshold

user	Digraph FAR	Trigraph FAR
user1	19.2308	50.0000
user2	46.1538	69.2308
user6	12.2807	71.9298
user8	15.2542	11.8644
user9	18.7500	81.2500
user10	26.9231	36.5385
user14	33.3333	67.9012
user15	0.0000	63.6364
user17	0.0000	10.0000
user18	54.5455	63.6364

willing to spend hours trying to hack somebody's else account). Bigger number of attacks per single account will picture more clearly the FAR, so smaller number of accounts to hack was the only reasonable solution.

The results showing FAR for each of the threshold for digraph and trigraph method are shown in the Tables 2-5. The results for typing path method and for all the methods combined together are shown in the Table 6.

In any web implementation of typing patterns recognition (e.g. password hardening), FAR is more important than FRR and therefore we think our results are satisfactory. Nevertheless some minor changes to our client-server implementation could decrease FRR, which would make the system more user-friendly. It is hard to determine which of the developed and implemented method gives the best performance for all users. The best solution is to make the logon algorithm adaptive. The algorithm should check which method gives the best performance for given user in order to give it the biggest weight while taking the access/no access decision.

In case of non-adaptive implementation the best results were observed for thresholds: 0,25 for trigraphs and 0,3 for digraphs. The threshold for digraphs

Table 6. FAR results for the typing paths method and the final FAR results for all the combined methods

user	Typing Path FAR	Combined FAR
user1	0.0000	**1.9230**
user2	7.6923	**0.0000**
user6	0.0000	**0.0000**
user8	3.3898	**0.0000**
user9	0.0000	**0.0000**
user10	1.9231	**0.0000**
user14	0.0000	**8.1649**
user15	9.0909	**0.0000**
user17	0.0000	**0.0000**
user18	0.0000	**0.0000**

and trigraphs should not be equal. It should be higher for digraphs and lower for trigraphs.

It is also noticeable that longer char sets (trigraphs) have more stable statistics for a legitimate user (the standard deviation of particular trigraph's durations is small, and thus the distance calculated from the degree of disorder is smaller), but on the other hand they are easier to forge.

Typing patterns characteristics are sensitive to the emotional and physical state of the person who is verified. Very poor typing skills are another factor which can affect the process of authentication. The good thing is that our methods of individual typing patterns extraction are very likely to achieve a high level of acceptance among ordinary users.

Moreover, unlike other biometric or security systems, which usually require additional hardware and thus are expensive to implement, typing patterns recognition system is almost for free - the only hardware required is the keyboard [1].

4   Conclusion

In the article we presented and tested methods of recognizing individual typing patterns. We also proved that biometrics system based on such extracted typing patterns is capable of identifying humans and increasing security in web applications where logging-in is the necessity for the clients (e-banking).

The combined values of FRR varied from 0% to 55% (Table 1) and the values of FAR **were equal to %0 for all but 2 users** (Table 6). For the 2 users is was possible for the impostor to logon with their password and biometrics characteristics with the probability 1.9% and 8.2%, respectively.

This means that the presented methods are effective and could be implemented to increase web security in applications where logging-in is the necessity for the clients.

References

1. Monrose, F., Rubin, A.: Keystroke Dynamics as a Biometric for Authentication. Future Generation Computer Systems 16(4), 351–359 (2000)
2. Obaidat, M.S., Sadoun, B.: Keystroke Dynamics Based Authentication. In: Jain, A.K., Bolle, R., Pankanti, S. (eds.) Biometrics: Personal Identification in Networked Society. (1998)
3. Obaidat, M.S., Sadoun, B.: Verification of Computer Users Using Keystroke Dynamics. IEEE Trans. Syst., Man, Cybern.-Part B. 24(2), 261–269 (1997)
4. Leggett, G., Williams, J., Usnick, M.: Dynamic Identity Verification via Keystroke Characteristics. International Journal of Man.-Machine Studies 35(6), 859–870 (1991)
5. Gaines, R., Lisowski, W., Press, S., Shapiro, N.: Authentication by Keystroke Timing: some preliminary results, Rand Report R-256-NSF. Rand Corporation (1980)
6. Monrose, F., Rubin, A.: Authentication via Keystroke Dynamics, Conference on Computer and Communications Security, pp. 48–56 (1997)
7. Joyce, R., Gupta, G.: User authorization based on keystroke latencies. Communications of ACM 33(2), 168–176 (1990)
8. Bleha, S., Slivinsky, C., Hussein, B.: Computer-access security systems using keystroke dynamics. IEEE Trans. on Patt. Anal. Mach. Int. 12(12), 1217–1222 (1990)
9. Brown, M., Rogers, S.J.: User identification via keystroke characteristics of typed names using neural networks. International Journal of Man.-Machine Studies 39, 999–1014 (1993)
10. Bergadano, F., Gunetti, D., Picardi, C.: User Authentication through Keystroke Dynamics. ACM Transactions on Information and System Security 5(4), 367–397 (2002)
11. Brown, M., Rogers, S.J.: Method and apparatus for verification of a computer user's identification, based on keystroke characteristics, Patent Number 5,557,686, U.S. Patent and Trademark Office, Washington, DC (September 1996)
12. Yu, E., Cho, S.: Biometrics-based Password Identity Verification: Some Practical Issues and Solutions, XVth Triennial Congress of the International Ergonomics Association (IEA), Seoul, Korea (August 24-29, 2003)
13. Tapiador, M., Sigüenza, J.A.: Fuzzy Keystroke Biometrics On Web Security. In: Proc. of AutoID (1999)
14. http://www.biopassword.com

Residual Filter for Improving Coding Performance of Noisy Video Sequences

Won Seon Song, Seong Soo Lee, and Min-Cheol Hong

School of Electronic Engineering, Soongsil University, Korea
won@vipl.ssu.ac.kr, sslee@ssu.ac.kr, mhong@ssu.ac.kr

Abstract. This paper addresses a low complexity residual filter to improve the coding performance of noisy video sequences. The additive noise decreases the coding efficiency and results in unpleasant coding artifacts due to higher frequency components. By incorporating local statistics and quantization parameter into filtering process, the spurious noise is significantly attenuated and coding efficiency is improved for given quantization step size. In addition, in order to reduce the complexity of the residual filter, the simplified local statistics and quantization parameter induced by analyzing H.264/AVC transformation and quantization processes are introduced. The simulation results show the capability of the proposed algorithm.

1 Introduction

In general, video sequence captured by imaging acquisition system represents the degraded version of an original video sequence by additive noise coming from image formation system. In such case, the reconstructed video sequence using video coding standards usually results in the loss of coding efficiency and unpleasant coding artifacts. Therefore, a filtering process is required to remove the spurious noise with preserving significant features such as edges or objects.

A number of approaches have been reported to improve the visual quality of compressed video in the literature [1,2,3,4]. Most approaches attempt to remove blocking and ringing artifacts that come from quantization process, but the removal of the additive noise for given bit rate or quantization step size is rarely investigated within video processing area. When quantization parameter is provided by a rate control algorithm, it is promising that the pre-processing is to modify the degraded video sequence so that image quality is maximized. As a general approach, a typical noise filtering approach has been employed to improve coding efficiency [5]. In Ref. [6], more sophisticated technique is introduced as a pre-processing algorithm which is operated with rate-distortion problem. The filter attempts to maximize the resulting image quality by controlling the error residual between an original image and the motion compensated frame for the given bit-rate.

H.264/AVC video coding standard has been jointly developed to obtain higher compression gain than existing video coding standard by ITU-T and

J. Martí et al. (Eds.): IbPRIA 2007, Part II, LNCS 4478, pp. 331–338, 2007.

ISO/IEC [7]. H.264/AVC is characterized by block-based integer transform, variable block- size motion estimation/compensation, context adaptive variable length coding (CAVLC), and so on. Due to the different coding strategies, the local statistics of the coded information is different to previous standards. Therefore, any algorithms for obtaining better coding efficiency or for improving visual quality should be different to other standards.

The statistics of variable length codes of almost video coding standards including H.264/AVC coder has Gaussian distribution. Therefore, it is expected that the quality can be maximized when the filtering results have the similar probability to the variable length codes. In this paper, we propose a Gaussian model based residual filter to maximize the quality by effectively removing the noise for given quantization parameter. Local statistics of the degraded image and quantization parameter are used to design the filter. Also, a simplified 3-tab filter without floating-point operations is addressed in order to reduce the complexity.

This paper is organized as follows. Section 2 describes the modified Gaussian filter model. Also, the parameters of the filter are denoted on the basis of rigorous analysis of H.264/AVC transformation and quantization. In addition, the local statistics for the simplified residual filter is presented. Finally, the experimental results and conclusions are described in Sections 3 and 4.

2   Proposed Residual Filter

When a typical image is captured by image formation system, the observed image represents the degraded version of an original image. In such case, noise reduction filtering is required to obtain the visually satisfactory results and to reduce the bit-rate for given quantization step size in video compression. HVS (Human Visual System) has been used to evaluate visual quality. According to Ref. [11], HVS can be approximated to Gaussian model and the filtering process can be written as

$$y = h_v * h_h * x,$$ (1)

where y and x represent the filtered image and the capture degraded image, respectively. In Eq. (1), h_v and h_h are one dimensional Gaussian impulse response to vertical and horizontal directions, and $*$ represents one-dimensional convolution by the separable property of two-dimensional convolution. In the rest of paper, we use H instead of h_v and h_h since both impulse responses take the same form. It is promising to take into account of local statistics and quantization noise as the parameters of Gaussian impulse response under the assumption that the statistics of the degraded image is locally different. In this paper, under the assumption that the local probability of an original image is Gaussian-distributed, the following Gaussian impulse response is defined.

$$H_i = \frac{1}{Z} exp(-\frac{i^2}{\frac{\sigma_N^2}{\sigma_B^2}k^2}),$$ (2)

where Z is the normalizing constant, and σ_N^2 and σ_B^2 represent the local variance and quantization noise of i-th filter coefficient. In addition, k denotes the parameter to reflect the visible property. In the following, we describe various parameters of Eq. (2) in more detail. First, σ_N^2, noise variance can be induced from quantization and transformation process. The previous video coding standards such as MPEG2, MPEG4, and H.263 use floating-point operational DCT (Discrete Cosine Transform), which leads to IDCT (Inverse Discrete Cosine Transform) mismatch problem. In order to resolve the problem, H.264 video coding standard uses the modified DCT and quantization mechanism. Typically, 4×4 block DCT transformation is defined as

$$Y = AXA^T = \begin{bmatrix} a & a & a & a \\ b & c & -c & -b \\ a & -a & -a & a \\ c & -b & b & -c \end{bmatrix} X \begin{bmatrix} a & b & a & c \\ a & c & -a & -b \\ a & -c & -a & b \\ a & -b & a & -c \end{bmatrix} \qquad (3)$$

where X is 4×4 block of the input image, and $a = 1/2$, $b = 1/\sqrt{2}\cos(\pi/8)$, and $c = 1/\sqrt{2}\cos(3\pi/8)$. Eq. (3) requires the floating-point operation, resulting in IDCT (Inverse Discrete Cosine Transform) mismatch. In order to avoid the problem, H.264 video coding standard defines the integer transform as

$$Y = \begin{bmatrix} 1 & 1 & 1 & 1 \\ 2 & 1 & -1 & -2 \\ 1 & -1 & -1 & 1 \\ 1 & -2 & 2 & -1 \end{bmatrix} X \begin{bmatrix} 1 & 2 & 1 & 1 \\ 1 & 1 & -1 & -2 \\ 1 & -1 & -1 & 2 \\ 1 & -2 & 1 & -1 \end{bmatrix} \otimes \begin{bmatrix} a^2 & ab/2 & a^2 & ab/2 \\ ab/2 & b^2/2 & ab/2 & b^2 \\ a^2 & ab/2 & a^2 & ab/2 \\ ab/2 & b^2/2 & ab/2 & b^2 \end{bmatrix}$$
$$= (CXC^T) \otimes S = W \otimes S \qquad (4)$$

where $\otimes$ and A^T represent the element multiplier and the transpose of matrix A, and S is utilized as a weighting matrix of quantization process, and then quantization coefficients can be written as

$$Z = [Y \otimes E]/(2^{15+QP/6}) = [(W \otimes S) \otimes E]/(2^{15+QP/6}), \qquad (5)$$

where Z, E and QP denote the quantized transform coefficient, the quantization table and the quantization index which are defined in H.264 standard, respectively. Then, the quantization noise be determined as

$$\text{Quantization Error} = (2^{15+QP/6})/E. \qquad (6)$$

In this work, Eq. (6) is used as σ_N^2 to incorporate the quantization errors into filtering process for given QP. In H.264 video coding standard, the quantization index takes a value between 0 and 51. Then, the maximum quantization error can be obtained by substituting the quantization index into Eq. (6) as shown in Table (1), where % and / represent the modulus and the divided operations.

In our algorithm, 3-tab filter is used for low complexity. For example, as shown in Fig. 1, two neighboring pixels (p_1 and q_2) are used to represent the local statistics of q_1. In Eq. (2), σ_B^2 and k are introduced to describe local properties. σ_B^2 representing the local activity should take higher value in significant

Table 1. Maximum quantization error as a function of quantization index

QP % 6 / QP/6	0	1	2	3	4	5
0	0.64	0.70	0.81	0.90	1.00	1.14
1	1.28	1.41	1.63	1.80	2.00	2.28
2	2.56	2.82	3.26	3.60	4.00	4.56
3	5.12	5.64	6.52	7.02	8.00	9.12
4	10.24	11.28	13.04	14.40	16.00	18.24
5	20.48	22.56	26.08	28.80	32.00	36.48
6	40.96	45.12	52.16	57.60	64.00	72.96
7	81.92	90.24	104.32	115.20	128.00	145.92
8	163.84	180.48	208.64	230.40		

Fig. 1. Proposed filter structure

features including edges and objects, so that they can be preserved without over-smoothness. However, calculation of variance requires compute-intensive operations. For the reduction of the complexity, the following local properties are defined. They are

$$\mu_{q_1} = \frac{p_1 + 2 \times q_1 + q_2}{4} \tag{7}$$

and

$$\sigma_B \cong \sigma'_B = \frac{|p_1 - \mu_{q_1}| + 2 \times |q_1 - \mu_{q_1}| + |q_2 - \mu_{q_1}|}{4}. \tag{8}$$

The local mean in Eq. (7) has its advantage on that it is obtained without divider. Also, the local variance can be obtained without multiplier and divider. In fact, the above is one of the most important issues in practical implementation of digital filter. The visible degree of additive noise to human viewer depends on the background as well as the local variance. In this experiments, the following equation for the parameter, k, is used to control the visibility

$$k = (|\mu_{q_1}| + 1)^{\frac{1}{4}}. \tag{9}$$

Using Eqs. (6)-(9), the filtering result of q_1 can be written as

$$Q_1 = H_0 q_1 + H_1(p_1 + p_2) \tag{10}$$

Even though it is not expressed in detail here, the complexity of the proposed algorithm can be further reduced by making the filter coefficients integer and by pre-storing the integer coefficients into Look-Up table.

3   Experimental Results

A number of experiments have been contacted with various sequences, resolutions, and quantization index. Among of them, QCIF "Foreman" and "Container" sequences, and "Test" sequence captured by a USB camera were used. The proposed algorithm was tested with JM9.0 (Joint Mode 9.0) reference code of H.264 video coding standard. For evaluating the performance of the algorithm, PSNR (Peak Signal to Noise Ratio) was utilized. For $M \times N$ dimensional 8 bits image, it is defined as

$$PSNR = 10 \log \frac{MN \times 255^2}{||f - \hat{f}||^2}, \tag{11}$$

where $|| \cdot ||$ is the Euclidean norm, and f and $\hat{f}$ represent the original image and the reconstructed image, respectively.

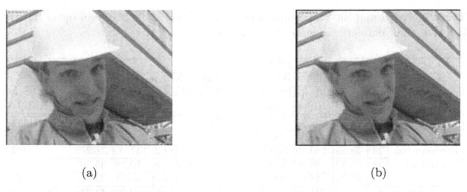

(a)   (b)

Fig. 2. (a) Reconstructed 51-st frame of Foreman sequence without filter, (b) Reconstructed 51-st frame of Foreman sequence with proposed filter (QP=20, 25 dB additive Gaussian noise)

(a)   (b)

Fig. 3. (a) Reconstructed 77-th frame of Container sequence without filter, (b) Reconstructed 77-th frame of Container sequence with proposed filter (QP=20, 25 dB additive Gaussian noise)

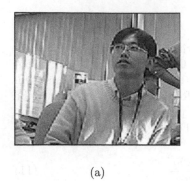

(a)

(b)

Fig. 4. (a) Reconstructed 10-th frame of Test sequence without filter, (b) Reconstructed 10-th frame of Test sequence with proposed filter (QP=20, captured frame by USB camera)

Table 2. PSNR and Bit-rate comparisons as a function of quantization index (QCIF Foreman and Container sequence, 10 frames/sec)

	QP	25 dB Noise				30 dB Noise			
		Without filter		With proposed filter		Without filter		With proposed filter	
		PSNR (dB)	Bitrate (Kbps)	PSNR (dB)	Bitrate (Kbps)	PSNR (dB)	Bitrate (Kbps)	PSNR (dB)	Bitrate (Kbps)
Foreman seq. (10 fps)	16	39.44	838.91	39.54	754.73	42.82	541.51	42.72	440.69
	20	39.11	471.30	39.24	372.69	41.24	257.72	40.80	229.56
	24	38.29	180.49	38.09	161.26	38.62	137.90	38.27	130.66
	28	35.92	86.38	35.61	81.02	35.89	79.28	35.56	75.70
	32	33.11	48.68	32.79	45.76	33.09	46.73	32.79	44.57
Container seq. (10 fps)	16	40.54	704.61	40.63	596.65	43.68	392.29	43.37	279.99
	20	40.14	340.08	40.27	211.47	41.61	143.54	40.71	107.31
	24	38.86	87.41	38.40	63.95	38.84	61.28	38.25	50.93
	28	36.25	32.80	35.86	28.32	36.13	29.10	35.76	25.95
	32	33.36	15.45	33.08	14.51	33.29	14.86	33.02	14.03

Figures 2-3 show the 51 th reconstructed frame of "Foreman" sequence and the 77 th frame of "Container" without filter and with the proposed filter. There still

Table 3. Bit-rate comparison as a function of quantization index (Test sequence, 10 frames/sec)

	QP	Without filter Bitrate (Kbps)	With proposed filter Bit rates (Kbps)
Test seq. (10 fps)	16	798.38	724.75
	20	485.02	429.88
	24	286.67	272.11
	28	179.10	174.55
	32	109.14	107.52

exists the additive noise in the reconstructed frames only by H.264/AVC video coder, which is more visible and annoying in video sequence, since the noise is randomly scattered. On the other hands, with the proposed algorithm the noise is effectively removed. However, the edge information is a little blurred, since the Gaussian impulse response represents a kind of low-pass filter. In addition, the reconstructed frames of the Test sequence are shown in Figure 4, which is more realistic case. The results verify that the proposed algorithm has the capability to remove the background noise without blurring.

PSNR and bit-rate comparisons as a function of quantization index of "Foreman", "Container" and "Test" sequences are shown in Tables 2-3. From the tables, it is observed that the proposed algorithm leads to the bit-rate saving up to 30%, and that the image quality is the similar or better than without filter, for given quantization index. The novelty of the proposed algorithm is that no prior knowledge about the noise and image is required to remove the additive noise, and to reduce the bit-rate.

4 Conclusion

In this paper, we have proposed the low complexity residual filter for improving the performance of H.264 video coding standard. The modified Gaussian impulse response is introduced, and the local activity, quantization information, and simple visibility function are incorporated into the filtering process. From the experimental results, it is observed that PSNR gain and bit-rate saving are obtained with the proposed algorithm when the noise signals are added to the original video sequence.

Acknowledgement

This research was supported by Seoul Future Contents Convergence (SFCC) Cluster established by Seoul R\BD Program and Soongsil University Research Fund.

References

1. Katsaggelos, A.K., Galatsanos, N.P. (eds.): Signal Recovery Techniques for Image and Video Compression and Transmission. Kluwer Academic Publishers, Dordrecht (1998)
2. Ramamurthi, B., Gersho, A.: Nonlinear Space-invariant Post Processing of Block Coded Images. IEEE Trans. On. ASSP ASSP-34, 1258–1268 (October 1986)
3. Rosenholtz, R., Zakhor, A.: Iterative Procedures for Reduction of Blocking Effects in Transform Image Coding. IEEE Trans. on Circuits and Systems for Video Tech. 2(1), 91–94 (March 1992)
4. Yang, Y., Galatsanos, N.P., Katsaggelos, A.K.: Regularized Reconstruction to Reduce Blocking Artifacts of Block Discrete Cosine Transform Compressed Images. IEEE Trans. on Circuits and Systems for Video Techn. 3(6), 421–432 (December 1993)

5. Brailean, J.C., Kleihorst, R.P., Efstratiadis, S.N., Katsaggelos, A.K., Lagendijk, R.L.: Noise Reduction Filters for Dynamic Image Sequences: A Review. IEEE Proceedings 83(9), 1272–1292 (September 1995)
6. Lin, L.-J., Ortega, A.: Perceptually Based Video Rate Control Using Pre-filtering and Predicted Rate-Distortion Characteristics. In: Proceedings of the IEEE International Conference on Image Processing, pp. 57–60 (October 1997)
7. Draft ITU-T Recommendation and Final Draft International Standard of Joint Video Specification (ITU-T Rec. H.264–ISO/IEC 14463-10 AVC), Geneva, Switzerland (23–27 May, 2003)
8. Richardson, I.: H.264 and MPEG-4 Video Compression. Wiley, Chichester (2003)
9. Wiegand, T., Sullivan, G., Njontegaard, G., Lutjra, A.: Overview of the H.264/AVC Video Coding Standard. IEEE Trans. On. Circuit and Systems for Video Techn. 13(9), 560–576 (2003)
10. Malvar, H.S., Hallapuro, A., Karczewicz, M., Kerofsky, L.: Low Complexity Transform and Quantization in H.264/AVC. IEEE Trans. on Circuit and Systems for Video Techn. 13(7), 598–603 (2003)
11. Watson, A.B.: DCT Quantization Matrics Visually Optimized for Individual Images. In: Proceedings of the SPIE Human Vision, Visual Processing and Display IV, vol. 1913, pp. 202–216 (1993)

Cyclic Viterbi Score for Linear Hidden Markov Models*

Vicente Palazón and Andrés Marzal

Dept. Llenguatges i Sistemes Informàtics, Universitat Jaume I de Castelló, Spain
{palazon,amarzal}@lsi.uji.es

Abstract. Hidden Markov Models (HMM) have been successfully applied to describe sequences of observable events. In some problems, objects are more appropriately described as cyclic sequences, i.e., sequences with no begin/end point. Conventional HMMs with Viterbi score cannot deal adequately with cyclic sequences. We propose a cyclic Viterbi score that can be efficiently computed for Linear HMMs. Linear HMMs model sequences that can be partitioned into contiguous segments where each state is responsible for emitting all symbols in one of the segments. Experiments show that our proposal outperforms other approaches in an isolated characters handwritten-text recognition task.

1 Introduction

A Hidden Markov Model (HMM) is a statistical description for sequences. It contains hidden parameters that can be learnt from sequences of observable events. HMMs have been successfully applied to speech recognition, on-line handwritten-text recognition, etc. In these problems, objects can be properly described as sequences of symbols, since there is a time ordering between observable events with well-defined beginning and ending instants. For instance, speech can be described as a time-ordered sequence of acoustic frames and handwritten-text can be seen as a time-ordered series of stylus location points. Other Pattern Recognition problems, such as shape retrieval or handwritten-text recognition, deal with contours of objects that can be described with cyclic sequences, i.e, sequences with no begin/end symbol. Contours of objects, for instance, can be described with cyclic sequences of primitives (points, curvature values, discretized directions, etc). Fig. 1 (a) shows some typical samples of isolated characters, handwritten-text task, and Fig. 1 (b) depicts the coding of a character contour as a cyclic string with an 8-directions code. Symbols in a cyclic string do have a relative order, but there is no beginning or ending positions in the string. Cyclic strings can be transformed into conventional strings by choosing an appropriate starting symbol. This symbol is usually chosen by means of some heuristic, error-prone procedure (taking into account extreme curvature values, extreme eccentricity values, etc.). Therefore, HMMs can result poorly trained and perform badly in recognition tasks.

* Work partially supported by the *Ministerio de Educación y Ciencia* (TIN2006-12767), the *Generalitat Valenciana* (GV06/302) and *Bancaixa* (P1 1B2006-31).

J. Martí et al. (Eds.): IbPRIA 2007, Part II, LNCS 4478, pp. 339–346, 2007.
© Springer-Verlag Berlin Heidelberg 2007

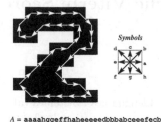

A = aaaahggeffhaheeeeedbbbabceeefecb

Fig. 1. (a) Samples from a handwritten-text recognition task. (b) A character is coded as a cyclic sequence of directions along the contour.

Arica *et al.* [2] defined an HMM topology for modeling cyclic sequences. In this paper we propose a different approach: we define a cyclic Viterbi score and a Linear HMM topology to deal with cyclic sequences. The new cyclic score can be efficiently computed for the proposed topology with an algorithm inspired in the Cyclic Edit Distance method proposed by Maes [6]. Experiments performed on a handwritten digits database show that our system outperforms the conventional HMMs and the Arica *et al.* proposal.

2   Hidden Markov Models

A Hidden Markov Model (HMM) [7] is a set of states, each one with an associated emission probability distribution. At any instant t, an observable event is produced from a particular state and only depending on that state. The transition from one state to another is a random event only depending on the departing state. Without loss of generality, in the following we will only consider discrete HMMs, i.e., the set of observable events is finite.

Given an alphabet $\Sigma = \{v_1, v_2, \ldots, v_s\}$, an HMM with n states is a triplet (A, B, π) where (1) $A = \{a_{ij}\}$, for $1 \leq i, j \leq n$, is the state transition probability matrix (a_{ij} is the probability of being in state i at time t and being at state j at time $t + 1$); (2) $B = \{b_{ik}\}$, for $1 \leq i \leq n$ and $1 \leq i \leq s$, is the observation probability matrix (b_{ik} is the probability of observing v_k while being at state i); and (3) $\pi = \{\pi_i\}$, for $1 \leq i \leq n$ is an initial state probability distribution (π_i is the probability of being at state i when $t = 1$). These conditions must be satisfied: for all i, $\sum_{1 \leq j \leq n} a_{ij} = 1$ and $\sum_{1 \leq s \leq k} b_{is} = 1$; and $\sum_{1 \leq i \leq n} \pi_i = 1$. Fig. 2 (a) depicts a state and Fig. 2 (b) shows a complete HMM (transitions with null probability are not shown). There is an alternative definition of HMMs that has been popularized by tools such as HTK [8]. It has a single, non-emitting, initial state that we will identify with the number 0. On the other hand, there is an additional non-emitting state without output arcs that we will identify with $n + 1$. These special non-emitting states eliminate the need for an explicit initial state distribution π (since a_{0i} can be interpreted as π_i), simplifies some computations and eases HMM composition. In the following, we will use this alternative definition.

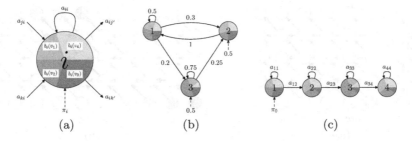

Fig. 2. (a) An HMM state that can emit any of four symbols according to the probability distribution depicted as a pie chart. (b) A complete HMM. (C) A Linear HMM.

There are efficient iterative algorithms for training the HMM parameters [3,5]. Unfortunately, there are no effective methods for estimating the number of states and the topology of the model. These are usually chosen heuristically depending on the application features. A so-called left-to-right topology imposes the restriction that $a_{ij} = 0$ for all $j < i$. Usually, $a_{01} = 1$, i.e., the first observed symbol must be emitted by the first emitting state. When the sequence of symbols can be segmented, all the symbols in a segment are emitted by the same state, and consecutive segments are associated to consecutive states, a so-called Linear HMM, i.e., a left-to-right topology like the one shown in Fig. 2 (c), can be used.

Given an HMM (A, B) and a sequence of observable symbols, $x = x_1 x_2 \ldots x_m$, there are three basic problems: (1) the evaluation problem, i.e., computing the probability that x has been generated by the HMM; (2) the decoding problem, i.e., obtaining the sequence of states that most likely produced x (the likelihood that this sequence of states produces x is the so-called Viterbi score); and (3) the learning problem, i.e., estimating (A, B) to maximize the probability of generating x. There are well-known, efficient algorithms for the two first problems. The Viterbi score can be computed by evaluating $\phi_{n+1}(m+1)$, where

$$
\phi_j(t) = \begin{cases}
1, & \text{if } t = 0 \text{ and } j = 0; \\
0, & \text{if } t = 0 \text{ and } j \neq 0; \\
\max_{1 \leq i \leq N}(\phi_i(t-1) \cdot a_{ij}) \cdot b_j(x_t), & \text{if } 1 \leq t \leq m \text{ and } 1 \leq j \leq n; \\
\max_{1 \leq i \leq N}(\phi_i(m) \cdot a_{i,n+1}), & \text{if } t = m+1 \text{ and } j = n+1.
\end{cases}
\tag{1}
$$

The Forward algorithm solves the evaluation problem by solving a similar recursive expression with summations instead of maximizations. Both recursive equations can be solved iteratively by Dynamic Programming in $O(n^2 m)$ time. The iterative algorithm for the Viterbi score computes an intermediate value at each node of the so-called trellis graph (see Figure 3 (a)). Each node (j, t) corresponds to a state (j) and a time instante (t) and stores $\phi_j(t)$. The value at $(n+1, m+1)$ is the final result. The Viterbi algorithm solves the decoding problem by recovering the optimal sequence of states in the trellis (see Figure 3 (a)).

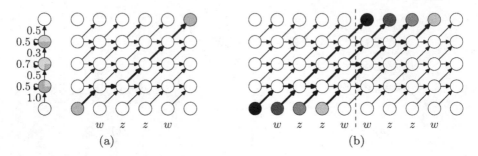

Fig. 3. (a) Trellis for a Linear HMM and a sequence of length 4. The optimal sequence of states is shown with thicker arrows. (b) Extended trellis.

There is no algorithm that optimally solves the training problem. The Baum-Welch procedure is used to iteratively improve the parameters estimation until a local maximum is found.

In classification tasks, an HMM can be trained for each class from a set of sequences labeled with their categories. The probability or the Viterbi score of unlabeled sequences can be combined with *a priori* class probabilities (Bayes rule) to classify them.

3   Hidden Markov Models for Cyclic Sequences

A cyclic sequence can be seen as the set of sequences obtained by cyclically shifting a conventional sequence. Let $x = x_1 \ldots x_m$ be a string from an alphabet Σ. The cyclic shift $\sigma(x)$ of a string x is defined as $\sigma(x_1 \ldots x_m) = x_2 \ldots x_m x_1$. Let σ^s denote the composition of s cyclic shifts and let σ^0 denote the identity. Two strings x and x' are cyclically equivalent if $x = \sigma^s(x')$, for some s. The equivalence class of x is $[x] = \{\sigma^s(x) : 0 \le s < m\}$ and it is called a *cyclic string*.

3.1   A Cyclic HMM Proposal

Since cyclic strings have no beginning/end point, Linear HMMs seem inappropriate to model them. In [2], Arica *et al.* proposed a circular HMM topology to model cyclic strings. Fig. 4 (a) shows this topology (the initial and final non-emitting states are not shown for the sake of clarity). This topology can be seen as a modification of the left-to-right one where the "last" emitting state is connected to the "first" emitting state. The proposed structure eliminates the need to define a starting point: the cyclic sequence can be segmented to associate consecutive states to consecutive segments in the cyclic sequences, but no assumption is made on which is the first state/first segment (see Fig. 4 (b)); therefore, there is an analogy with Linear HMMs. However, there is a problem that breaks this analogy: the model is ergodic (all states can be reached from any state) and the cyclic string symbols can "wrap" the model, i.e., the optimal sequence of states can contain non-consecutive, repeated states and, therefore,

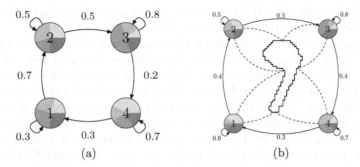

Fig. 4. (a) Cyclic HMM as proposed by Arica *et al.* (b) The contour is segmented and each segment is associated to a state of the HMM. Ideally, each state is responsible of a single segment.

a single state can be responsible for the emission of several non-consecutive segments in the cyclic string.

3.2   Cyclic Viterbi Score for Linear HMMs

To properly model cyclic sequences on Linear HMMs, the Viterbi score should take into account that any symbol of the sequence can be emitted by the first emitting state and that, once a symbol has been chosen as emitted by this state, its previous symbol must be emitted by the last state. The *cyclic Viterbi score* for a cyclic sequence $[x_1 x_2 \dots x_m]$ is defined as $\max_{0 \le s < m} P(\sigma^s(x)|\lambda)$. It can be computed by means of the conventional Viterbi score computed on m conventional strings in $O(m^2 n)$ time. We propose a more efficient algorithm to evaluate the Viterbi score. The method computes the optimal sequence of states that begins in any state, visits all the states and does not visit any state once it has been left. The algorithm is inspired in Maes' algorithm for the Cyclic Edit Distance (CED) [6] and computes the Viterbi score in $O(mn \log m)$ time for Linear HMM. The score is computed on an extended trellis where the original sequence appears concatenated with itself in the horizontal axis and sequences of states must begin and end in nodes with the same color (see Fig. 3 (b)). The efficiency of the algorithm is based on the "non-crossing paths" property [6]: Let $P(i)$ be the optimal path beginning at node $(i, 0)$ and ending at node $((m + i + 1, n + 1)$ in the extended trellis and let j, k, and l be three integers such that $0 \le j < k < l \le m$; there is an optimal path starting at node $(k, 0)$ and arriving to $(k + m + 1, n + 1)$ that lies between $P(j)$ and $P(l)$.

This property leads to a Divide and Conquer, recursive procedure: when $P(j)$ and $P(l)$ are known, $P((j + l)/2)$ is computed by only taking into account those nodes of the extended trellis lying between $P(j)$ and $P(l)$; then, optimal paths bounded by $P(j)$ and $P((j + l)/2)$ and optimal paths bounded by $P((j + l)/2)$ and $P(l)$ can be recursively computed. The recursive procedure starts after computing $P(0)$ (by means of a standard Viterbi computation) and $P(m)$, which is $P(0)$ shifted m positions to the right. Each recursive call generates up to two more recursive calls and all the calls at the same recursion depth amount to $O(mn)$ time; therefore, the algorithm runs in $O(mn \log m)$ time.

This adaptation of Maes' algorithm comes naturally after defining the cyclic Viterbi score as $\max_{0 \le s < m} P(\sigma^s(x)|\lambda)$. In principle, we could have adopted a symmetric approach defining a cyclic shift on the states of the Linear HMMs to obtain the same cyclic Viterbi score. This is appealing because $n < m$ and, therefore, "doubling" the HMM in the extended trellis instead of the string would lead to an $O(mn \log n)$ algorithm. This would be much better than $O(mn \log m)$ since $n < m$ (and, usually, $n \ll m$). But unfortunately, it cannot be done, as the next counter-example shows. Let $[x] = v_1 v_2 v_1$ be a cyclic string on the alphabet $\Sigma = \{v_1, v_2\}$. Let λ be a Linear HMM with 2 emitting states and $a_{01} = 1$, $a_{11} = 0.5$, $a_{12} = 0.5$, $a_{22} = 0.5$, $a_{23} = 0.5$, $b_{01} = 1$, and $b_{12} = 1$. Our definition of the cyclic Viterbi score leads to a value of 0.125 (for the string $\sigma^2(v_1 v_2 v_1) = v_1 v_1 v_2$). If we try to perform a cyclic shift of states in the Linear HMM, we have two possible cyclic shifts of the states and both possibilities give us 0 as the cyclic Viterbi score.

3.3 Cyclic HMMs Training

The proposed algorithm cannot be extended to Forward-value computation because there is no optimal path on the trellis on which the Maes' property holds. Since the Baum-Welch training procedure is based on the Forward (and Backward) values, we cannot use it for cyclic strings without requiring n times more time, which is too expensive. We propose to train these HMMs with non-cyclic strings obtained from the cyclic ones by splitting them at similar points. These starting points can be heuristically selected by locating points of maximum curvature, maximum eccentricity, etc., but that procedure is very sensitive to noise and error-prone. Our approach is based on a different, automatic procedure: finding an optimal starting point for all cyclic strings through comparison with a reference cyclic string via the Cyclic Edit Distance (CED) algorithm proposed by Maes [6] and improved by Marzal et al. in [1,4]. The starting point for every sequence is chosen as a subproduct of the optimal path in the extended Cyclic Edit Distance graph with respect to a reference cyclic sequence. The final results depend on the sequence chosen, but it has produced satisfactory results in the experiments. On the other hand, some strings can be improperly aligned, but they seem to be a negligible part of the whole set of strings and do not affect negatively the training procedure.

4   Experiments

In order to assess the behaviour of the algorithm in practice, we performed experiments on a handwritten digits recognition task. A test set containing 1000 digit images randomly selected from the NIST Special Database 3 were used. All the images were clipped, scaled and binarized, and their outer contours were represented by 8-directional chain-codes (the average length is 150). All the classification experiments (10 equiprobable classes, one per digit) were cross-validated (10 partitions, 100 samples for testing and 900 samples for training).

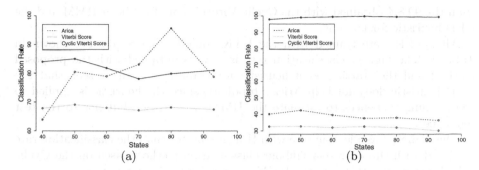

Fig. 5. (a) Classification rate for random strating point sequences as a function of the number of states. (b) Idem for the CED starting point selection heuristic.

The experiments try to show that the Cyclic Viterbi score on Linear HMMs produces better classification rates on cyclic sequences than those obtained with the conventional Viterbi score (on the same models) or with the Arica's topology [2]. Since we are interested in cyclic sequences, the contours were coded as conventional sequences with a random starting point. All HMMs were trained (1) with randomly chosen starting points for all the sequences in the training set, and (2) with starting points obtained by aligning each sequence with a reference sequence by means of the CED. Since the results can be dependent on the number of states, we have performed experiments varying this parameter. Fig. 5 (a) shows the classification rate for the three methods with random starting points as a function of the number of states. Fig. 5 (b) shows equivalent results for the CED starting point heuristic for training sequences. Table 1 shows the results obtained for 70 states (best case for our proposal) and 80 states (best case for Arica's topology). Arica's best classification rate is 95.6%, which is much lower

Table 1. Classification rate (in %) for the handwritten-text recognition task. Two different training procedure were tried and three different settings: Arica's topology with conventional Viterbi score and Linear HMM with conventional Viterbi and Cyclic Viterbi score. (a) HMMs with 70 states (best case for Linear HMM with Cyclic Viterbi score). (b) HMMs with 80 states (best case for Arica's topology).

70 states		Linear HMM	
	Arica's topology	Viterbi score	Cyclic Viterbi score
Random start-point training	83.0%	67.1%	78.0%
CED start-point training	37.6%	32.6%	99.8%

(a)

80 states		Linear HMM	
	Arica's topology	Viterbi score	Cyclic Viterbi score
Random start-point training	95.6%	68.1%	79.8%
CED start-point training	37.9%	32.0%	99.5%

(b)

than the 99.8% obtained with the Cyclic Viterbi score for Linear HMM and the CED heuristic for training.

All models were trained with the HTK toolkit. The results are shown in Table 1. The highest classification rate is always obtained with the proposed method and the starting-point heuristic for training. It can be seen that the CED heuristic does not help Arica's topology, since the heuristic is applied to the training sequences to estimate the HMM parameters, but not to the test sequences.

The highest classification rate with HMM is better than the classification rate obtained with the nearest-neighbour classification method based on the Cyclic Edit Distance (99.1%), and the HMM approach runs 7.5 times faster.

5   Conclusion

We have presented a Cyclic Viterbi score that can be efficiently computed on Linear HMMs modelling cyclic strings. The algorithm runs in $O(mn \lg m)$ time, where n is the number of states and m is the length of the cyclic sequence. Experiments performed on a digits classification task show that our approach outperforms Linear HMM with the conventional Viterbi score and the Cyclic HMM proposal of Arica *et al.*

References

1. Marzal, A., Barrachina, S.: Speeding up the computation of the edit distance for cyclic strings. Int. Conf. on Pattern Recognition, pp. 271–280 (2000)
2. Arica, N., Yarman-Vural, F.: A shape descriptor based on circular hidden markov model. In: International Conference on Pattern Recognition, vol. I, pp. 924–927 (2000)
3. Baum, L.E., Petrie, T., Soules, G., Weiss, N.: A maximization technique occurring in the statistical analysis of probabilistic functions of markov chains. Ann. Math. Stat. 41, 164–171 (1970)
4. Peris, G., Marzal, A.: Fast cyclic edit distance computation with weighted edit costs in classification. Int. Conf. on Pattern Recognition, pp. 184–187 (2002)
5. Juang, B.H., Rabiner, L.R.: The segmental K-means algorithm for estimating parameters of hidden markov models. IEEE Transactions on Acoustics, Speech, and Signal Processing 38(9), 1639 (1990)
6. Maes, M.: On a cyclic string-to-string correction problem. Information Processing Letters 35, 73–78 (1990)
7. Rabiner, L.R.: A tutorial on hidden Markov models and selected applications in speech recognition. In: Proc IEEE, vol. 77(2) (1989)
8. Young, S., Odell, J., Ollason, D., Valtchev, V., Woodland, P.: The HTK Book. Cambridge University (1996, 1995)

Non Parametric Classification of Human Interaction

Scott Blunsden, Ernesto Andrade, and Robert Fisher

Institute of Perception Action and Behaviour, School of Informatics,
University of Edinburgh, UK

Abstract. This paper presents a non parametric method for classifying interactions between two people as taken from a video camera. A nearest neighbour classifier that uses trajectory matching in feature space is introduced and shown to be superior to regular nearest neighbour classification for this problem.

1 Introduction

Many previous attempts have been made at identifying individual human activity, however only recently has the question of identification of interactions been addressed [9,3,8,5,6]. The classification of multi party interactions is necessary as there are many situations which can only be understood by considering the relationships between persons. For example the idea of 'meeting' cannot be sufficiently expressed or recognised when one only considers a single person in isolation. By considering interactions it is possible to build upon previous work on human motion understanding [4,1] to build a richer picture of what is going on in a scene.

Within this paper a non parametric approach is taken which can work with few examples of a particular interaction. The classification method is described and then results as applied to interacting pedestrians are presented. It was found that if temporal dependencies are taken into account a relatively simple classification method can improve the classification performance. First a brief review of previous work in the area is undertaken.

2 Previous Work

Previous work upon the identification of interaction has been undertaken, most notably by Oliver et al. [5] who trained coupled hidden Markov models to recognise six different types of interaction between people. The models were also capable of being 'primed' with synthetic interactions to give improved performance upon real interactions. Xiang and Gong [9] also used coupled hidden Markov models to automatically build relationship models between vehicles on an airport runway. The graphical model approach was also taken by Intille [3] who used a hand crafted Bayesian network to identify pre-defined plays within the game of American football.

J. Martí et al. (Eds.): IbPRIA 2007, Part II, LNCS 4478, pp. 347–354, 2007.

More recently Sato and Aggarwal [8] have also tackled this problem from the two person case. In order to classify interaction types only cases where people were within close proximity were considered for classification. The nearest mean method was then used for classification of the interaction with good results. Recent work by Park and Aggarwal [6] has also focused on two person interactions where the people can be segmented into parts. A hierarchical Bayesian network is then used for classification of interactions.

For multi person interactions a hidden Markov model with multiple inputs was discussed in [2]. A role variable was introduced to take account of permutations of the roles people may play in an interaction. This method was shown to work successfully with three person interactions.

3   Classification

Within this paper we take a non-parametric view of modelling and classification. Such an approach has the benefits of not requiring large amounts of data in order to obtain the parameters of a model. The sparsity of certain types of interaction along with the difficulty in obtaining and processing such video was a reason for choosing such an approach.

3.1   Feature Extraction

Throughout each video sequence every moving person was tracked and their bounding box was established. This gave the 2D position of the person in the image plane. This position was projected into ground plane co-ordinates using a homography. Ground plane coordinates were used as they help to normalise distances and speed with respect to the distance from the camera, thus enabling a fairer comparison throughout all image positions. Here $\mathbf{x}_i^t$ is the 2D vector which contains the ground plane coordinates for person i at time t.

From this point-set several features are calculated. The speed s_θ^t of each person is calculated as shown in equation 1. The reason for the w term is due to high frame rates many surveillance cameras are capable of, typically around 25 fps. This high frame rate means that there is often very little movement between subsequent frames with a high proportion of this movement being a result of noise from the tracking process. Throughout all experiments w was set to 25 (about 1 second).

The normalised direction is calculated as shown in equation 2. This measure is not used directly in the output feature vector but is used to calculate the alignment $(al_{i,j}^t)$ between person i and j, as given in equation 3. Alignment is calculated as the dot product between the two normalised directions $\hat{\mathbf{v}}_i^t$ and $\hat{\mathbf{v}}_j^t$.

$$s_\theta^t = \left\| \mathbf{x}_\theta^t - \mathbf{x}_\theta^{t-w} \right\|, \theta \in i, j \tag{1}$$

$$\hat{\mathbf{v}}_\theta^t = \frac{\mathbf{x}_\theta^t - \mathbf{x}_\theta^{t-w}}{\left\| \mathbf{x}_\theta^t - \mathbf{x}_\theta^{t-w} \right\|}, \theta \in i, j \tag{2}$$

$$al_{i,j}^t = \hat{\mathbf{v}}_i^t . \hat{\mathbf{v}}_j^t \tag{3}$$

$$d_{i,j}^t = \mathbf{x}_i^t - \mathbf{x}_j^t \qquad (4)$$

$$d\_dif_{i,j}^t = d_{i,j}^{t-w} - d_{i,j}^t \qquad (5)$$

$$d\_sp_{i,j}^t = \left\| s_i^t - s_j^t \right\| \qquad (6)$$

$$of_\theta^t = \left\| \mathbf{x}_\theta^t - \mathbf{x}_\theta^{start} \right\|, \theta \in \{i,j\} \qquad (7)$$

Difference in position ($d_{i,j}^t$, equation 4) is also used as a feature along with the change in distance at two separate time steps as given in equation 6. The offset (of_θ^t) from a starting position, given in equation 7 was calculated for both persons i and j. The difference in speed $d\_sp_{i,j}^t$ between the two persons is given by equation 6.

This gives an eight dimensional final feature vector at time t between people i and j, shown in equation 8. The features have a degree of invariance in that they do not depend upon the absolute direction or position of a person within the scene. Each feature was also scaled to have zero mean and unit variance. The mean and variance were obtained from the training set only.

$$\mathbf{f}_{i,j}^t = \left[s_i^t, s_j^t, al_{i,j}^t, d_{i,j}^t, d\_dif_{i,j}^t, d\_sp_{i,j}^t, of_i^t, of_j^t \right] \qquad (8)$$

3.2 Classifier

Once the trajectories had been obtained sequences were manually labelled as containing an interaction or non interaction. The type of interaction was also manually assigned from a restricted vocabulary (see section 4). Sequences ranged in length from a few seconds to several minutes. For every frame of these labelled interactions the features (described in section 3.1) were calculated. Using the feature vector described in the previous section a nearest neighbour classifier is used with a neighbourhood whose size was empirically set to 5. Data was partitioned into a training and testing set with a 50/50 split. The test data was not used in any way until evaluating the performance of the classifier.

It is important that these training and test sequences are complete sequences and as such are completely separate from one another. If only points are taken at random (rather than the complete sequence) then there is a high similarity between the two sets and they are in fact temporally dependent upon one another. The problem may then simply reduce to a simple interpolation procedure.

A simple strategy to classifying a point in such a sequence would be to classify a novel test point based upon its proximity to a training point as measured through some distance metric. However, as illustrated in figure 2 there is a temporal dependency between points. It is visible that the classes create a trajectory in feature space. Point by point matching such as nearest neighbour or clustering will miss this dependency. In order to take account of the trajectory 'shape' of the data the Hausdorff distance (as given in equation 10), was used to compare training and testing samples over a temporal window.

The feature vector for each person at time t is made up of the extracted features given in (8). In order to classify the activities of the tracked person at a given time a temporal window of size win around the current frame is taken. In

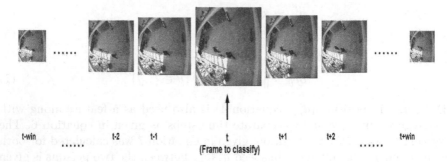

Fig. 1. Extraction of frames to be used within the classification process

these experiments the size of *win* is set to 25, meaning that the total size of each sample used for matching is 51 time steps in length. This process is illustrated in figure 1. With a video rate of 25 frames per second achievable on many surveillance cameras this is equivalent to watching one second worth of video either side of the frame. This step is taken as when comparing interactions such as two people meeting compared to simply walking past another it is necessary to watch a few seconds to determine what is happening. This is evident in figure (2) where many points are overlapping in feature space. By watching a few seconds of video it is possible to distinguish between interaction types. Results for a measure which only takes into account distance from a single point in time (and not a temporal window) are given as a comparison in the results section.

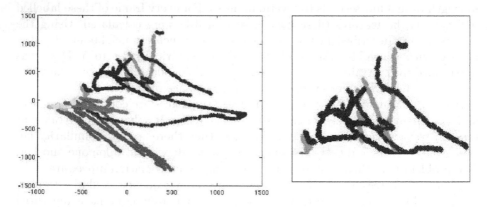

Fig. 2. Plot of first two principle components of the data. The colours refer to the class of data with walking together - red, approach - green, ignoring - blue, meeting - cyan, split - magenta and fight being yellow. The zoomed area on the right shows the ignoring and approach interactions.

For classification a k=5 nearest neighbour classifier is used. Three distance measures are compared, the standard squared distance over a window (given in equation 9), the Hausdorff distance (equation 10) and a single point distance cost function.

$$d(A, B, win) = \sum_{i=1}^{2win+1} \|A_i - B_i\|^2 \tag{9}$$

$$h(A, B) = \max_i \left\{ \min_j \left\{ \|A_i - B_j\|^2 \right\} \right\} \tag{10}$$

The matrix A is from the training database where each column contains a feature vector as given in 8, centred around the training frame. Matrix B is the novel test point and again its feature points are stored column-wise centred around the current frame. In both cases i and j refer to the whole column vector containing the calculated features as given in 8. The size of this matrix is determined by the choice of win. For instances where no window is considered then win can be set to 0.

Equation 9 is the sum of the squared distance between all points in the two matrices. The Hausdorff distance is given in equation 10.

4   Results

The results of the nearest neighbour classification scheme are now presented. The data was generated from the publicly available CAVIAR project [7]. The interaction classes along with the number of samples are given in the table below. It can be seen that the distribution of interactions is not uniform. As well as having an uneven prior distribution in a real world case such as in surveillance it is also likely that the number of ignore classes would be much higher.

We include the ignore class here as for any practical application of the method would have to distinguish when people are not interacting. For every frame in each sequence the features given in section 3 were calculated, thus giving a 9 dimensional feature vector at each time step. Sequence length ranged from a few seconds to several minutes.

For the first experiment classification of individual points was undertaken. We are in effect asking the computer to "tell me what you think is happening in every frame". In total there where 2230 test points (with a temporal window size of 51 frames). Results of classification by this method are given below. It can be seen that Hausdorff distance, which takes into account the shape of the data within the temporal window in feature space performs better than those that don't. It note that both distance measures that use a temporal window perform better than when a single point is used.

Class	Num. Samples	Dist Measure		
		$d(A, B, win)$	$d(A, B, 0)$	$h(A, B)$
Walk together	700	100	99.9	100
Approach	145	36.6	26.9	46.9
Ignore	835	80.7	73.9	85.1
Meet	382	100	61.5	100
Split	147	100	87.1	100
Fight	21	61.9	61.9	57.1
Total	2230	88.2	77.62	90.8

4.1 Complete Sequences

A second experiment was also conducted to test performance of the classifier when a contiguous video stream of pre-segmented data was given to it. The question we are asking here is "If I show you a video clip of arbitrary length tell me what the clip was about". Sequences were manually pre-segmented, continuous and contained only one type of interaction throughout their duration. The number of samples are given in the table below. In order to classify a complete sequence each point in the sequence was classified as described in the previous section. The most frequent class label was then assigned to be the class of the complete sequence. The idea of this test was to see how well the algorithm would perform in situations where longer sequences needed to be classified such as in annotating surveillance data. It is also a good test of how predictable single frame classifications are over longer sequences.

Class	Num. Samples	Dist Measure		
		$d(A, B, win)$	$d(A, B, 0)$	$h(A, B)$
Walk together	7	100	100	100
Approach	4	25	0	50
Ignore	6	83.3	100	100
Meet	1	100	100	100
Split	2	100	100	100
Fight	1	100	100	100
Total	21	80.9	80.9	90.4

4.2 Classification Summary

For classifying both complete sequences and individual points the Hausdorff method proves the best distance measure. However certain classes, such as approach which had an accuracy rate of 46.9%, prove difficult to classify and are frequently confused with ignore. This is understandable as many times when two people ignore one another they may get closer as they move through the scene but do not actually interact in any way. Situations like this could be differentiated by using longer term observations and delaying the decision until the classifier is more certian of an interaction. Situations such as these are illustrated in figure 3.

There is also the problem of obstacles within real scenes. Such obstacles can lead to misclassification as the trajectory and the resulting features can seem to veer 'off course' from what one would expect. For example in figure 3(b) the person modifies the approach of another due to an obstacle being in the way.

There are still some problems where two classes physically look like one another (such as approach and ignore) and would even fool a human observer given this limited information. Another problem is when there are very few examples, such as in the case of fighting. Even though fighting looks different to other activities there are too few examples to make accurate classifications.

(a)   (b)

Fig. 3. Plots of trajectory information for (a) Confusing ignoring with approaching. (b) Difficulties when obstacles are in the scene causing mis-classification. Here person 3 has to go round the obstacle to approach person 2. This also illustrates how you may have to watch a sequence for longer to figure out the actual intention of a person. Lines show tracked points from previous timesteps.

5   Conclusion and Future Work

The method presented here is shown to work for real interactions as captured on video cameras. The approach of interpreting a trajectory in feature space as a complete shape rather than a collection of points leads to an improvement in classification. Such an approach exploits the temporal dependencies and shape of the longer term temporal dependencies in feature space in an efficient way. By using non-parametric models of the actual data we can somewhat avoid the problem of having to generate apriori knowledge (in the form of scripts or rules) about what interactions look like. This enables new interaction classes to be incorporated within the same framework with relative ease.

For problems where it is hard to generate good parametric models to represent trajectories with a collection of cluster centres (such as a Gaussian Mixture model) matching the data shape in feature space proves a simple and effective alternative. This problem is compounded when a mixture of Gaussians is used as an observation model for something like a hidden Markov model, as much of the novel inputs generate very low input probabilities even if modelled well.

Here we do not assume that such a larger corpus of data is available to enable learning of complex parametric models such as those used by [5,9]. Neither do we assume that it it necessary to pre-define the actions which are of interest by using templates as in [3]. Template approaches may indeed be useful in real surveillance applications where explanations may be required by system operators. Future work will compare our method with theirs.

This simplicity of modelling is also an advantage when there is limited data as approaches such as hidden Markov models do not learn well when given few examples in a high dimensional space. However some of the benefits of using a probabilistic model are lost. At present there is no way to tell how certain the model is about the prediction it is giving. There is also the question of how long one should observe something before feeling confident about making a prediction which is currently left un-addressed. Both of these problems will be addressed in future work as will the identification of larger group activity.

Acknowledgments. This work was supported by the BEHAVE project funded by EPSRC, project GR/S98146.

References

1. Davis, J.W., Bobick, A.F.: The representation and recognition of action using temporal templates. In: IEEE Transactions on Pattern Analysis and Machine Intelligence, vol. 23, pp. 257–267. IEEE Computer Society Press, Los Alamitos (2001)
2. Du, Y., Chen, F., Xu, W., Li, Y.: Recognizing interaction activities using dynamic bayesian network. In: International Conference on Pattern Recognition (ICPR), p. 1 (August 2006)
3. Intille, S.S., Bobick, A.F.: A framework for recognizing multi-agent action from visual evidence. MIT Media Laboratory (1999)
4. Makris, D., Ellis, T.J.: Spatial and probabilistic modelling of pedestrian behaviour. In: British Machine Conference, vol. 1, pp. 557–566 (September 2002)
5. Oliver, N.M., Rosario, B., Pentland, A.P.: A bayesian computer vision system for modelling human interactions. IEE Transactions on Pattern Analysis and Machine Intelligence, vol. 22(8) (August 2000)
6. Park, S., Aggarwal, J.K.: A hierarchical bayesian network for event recognition of human actions and interactions. Association For Computing Machinery Multimedia Systems Journal (2004)
7. EC Funded CAVIAR project/IST 2001 37540. found at `http://homepages.inf.ed.ac.uk/rbf/caviar` (2004)
8. Sato, K., Aggarwal, J.K.: Recognizing two-person interactions in outdoor image sequences. In: 2001 IEEE Workshop on Multi-Object Tracking, IEEE, New York (2001)
9. Xiang, T., Gong, S.: Recognition of group activities using a dynamic probabilistic network. In: IEEE International Conference on Computer Vision, pp. 742–749 (October 2003)

A Density-Based Data Reduction Algorithm for Robust Estimators

L. Ferraz, R. Felip, B. Martínez, and X. Binefa

Universitat Autónoma de Barcelona,
Computer Science Department,
08193 Bellaterra, Barcelona, Spain
{luis.ferraz,rfelip,brais,xavierb}@cs.uab.es

Abstract. In this paper we present a non parametric density-based data reduction technique designed to be used in robust parameter estimation problems. Existing approaches are focused on reducing the amount of data preserving the density function. In our case the reduction is oriented to automatically remove the samples that are considered non interesting while taking into account those that are meaningful, those that have a high density associated. We use this filtering process to simplify the data sets in order to improve the performance of robust parameter estimators. We show its results when used along an existing estimator on synthetic and real LADAR data.

1 Introduction

Parametric model fitting from data samples is a topic that has had continuous contributions in the Computer Vision community along the last 25 years. This is due to the need of a simple way to represent the data to be processed in many tasks (fundamental matrix, motion estimation, LADAR and 3D data modeling, etc ...), a need that is fulfilled in a much cases by parametric models. However, describing a set of data samples with a handful of parameters turns out to be a very challenging task beacause of the error that may be present in the data that is to be analyzed.

The parameter estimation literature classifies the data samples in two groups: *inliers* and *outliers*. The first one is the subset of data samples that follows the desired model, while the second one is composed by the samples that are considered error or do not belong to the sought model.

The estimation techniques have experienced a continuous evolution. The first, basic, Least Squares (LS) approach considered all the data samples as inliers having as main issue that the existence of one single outlier could mislead the whole estimation. From that point on, many contributions focused on the retrieval of models from data overcoming the existence of outliers, differing on the quantity of outliers they could afford. While the first approaches could only handle up to 50% of data to be outliers, i.e. *Least Median of Squares* or *Least Trimmed Squares*[1], latter contributions such as Wang's MDPE[2] and ASSC[3], or our prior estimator, the HTE[4] can face much more complex scenarios, handling

J. Martí et al. (Eds.): IbPRIA 2007, Part II, LNCS 4478, pp. 355–362, 2007.

over 90% of outliers and several meaningful sample populations in datasets similar to the one depicted in figure 1a, where we can see that in the data set does not exist a single model to be retrieved but three, a fact that is often found in real cases.

Having this fact in mind, we can establish a further classification of samples: on one hand we have the *gross outliers*, samples that can be considered outliers to any existing population because they do not present any structure or pattern, and on the other hand we have the *significant samples*, elements that belong to a meaningful population but that can also be considered outliers with respect to other structured populations.

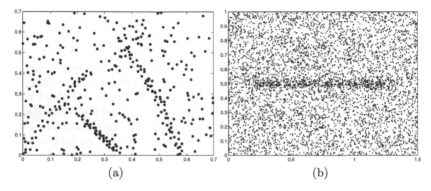

Fig. 1. Data set with 90% of outliers and three meaningful populations. (b) Complex dataset with one meaningful population and 95% of outliers.

The improvement of the parameter estimators is directly linked to the increase of their complexity and cost. Moreover, there are still cases where the existing techniques do not achieve satisfying results, mostly in scenarios where the meaningful populations hardly represent 5% or less of the total number of samples (figure 1b). However, gross outliers are discardable because they do not supply any interesting information and can be ruled out before the estimation process in order to attain more reliable results and to improve the efficiency of our methods.

In order to do so, we introduce a technique to remove non interesting samples from our dataset. The existing contributions [5,6,7,8,9,10] are too generic or focused on data mining applications. In this paper we present a density-based data reduction algorithm specially conceived to simplify automatically sample sets that are to be analyzed by parameter estimators. Our proposal does not perform only a data reduction, it preserves the dense or structured populations in front of non interesting samples by means of variable kernels. Our main objective, in other words, is to get rid of the gross outliers that may be present.

This paper is divided as follows : in section 2 we introduce our data reduction technique, the main contribution of this paper. Section 3 presents experimental results of our novel algorithm applied along our existing parameter estimator, the HTE, to synthetic and real LADAR data. Finally, section 4 closes the paper by giving a brief summary of conclusions and lines of future work.

2 Data Reduction Using Variable Kernels

Following the idea stated in the previous section, our aim is to process our source samples in order to eliminate the gross outliers that may be present. We propose a density based method to identify the gross outliers. We have the intuition that meaningful samples belong to dense clusters of information, in terms of distance with respect to other samples, while gross outliers tend to be more isolated.

Our technique can be divided in two parts. The first one retrieves a density descriptor for each point using variable bandwidth kernels and taking into account only the k nearest neighbours to the processed point. Using gaussian kernels, this yields a new probability density function that is truncated, but it has a 95% of confidence (depending on the σ parameter) with the original probability density function of our data set obtained as [11], and it also preserves the structure of the original function. Once this task has been done, the second step of our algorithm evaluates the entropy of our data and yields a threshold that is used to filter the samples.

2.1 Truncated Density Estimation

As mentioned, in order to estimate the truncated density of each point we analize its k nearest surrounding elements in terms of distance using variable kernels. The truncated density associated to a point is related to its kernel bandwidth. High densities yield small bandwidths while lower densities result in looser kernels. An example can be seen in figure 2.

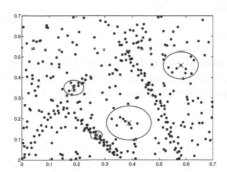

Fig. 2. Example showing the bandwidths of 4 samples assigned by means of variable kernels having $k = 10$ samples

Let $S = \{x_1...x_n\}$ our data set. We apply a Gaussian kernel centered over each element x_i with a standard deviation σ_i that depends on the k nearest samples to x_i.

$$\sigma_i = \alpha \|x_i - x_{i_k}\| \tag{1}$$

α is a smothing factor between $(0,1)$ (we use 0.5), and x_{i_k} is the kth nearest point to x_i.

The truncated density value w_i for each point x_i is defined as,

$$w_i = \frac{1}{k} \sum_{m=1}^{k} \frac{1}{\sigma_m \sqrt{2\pi}} \exp^{\frac{-d_{im}^2}{2\sigma_m^2}} \tag{2}$$

where d_{im} is the distance from x_i to the mth nearest sample.

This values w_i must be normalized to be a probability distribution. In order to improve the efficiency of this task we use a kdtree based optimization [12] in order to speed up this step.

2.2   Entropy Thresholding

Once estimated w_i to each element we need a threshold to identify the most interesting samples. Following with our initial idea, the relevant samples are those that belong to dense clusters because they provide more information.

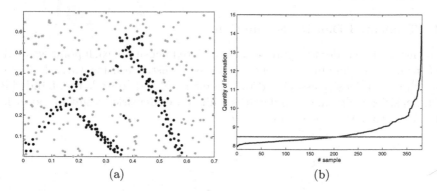

(a)   (b)

Fig. 3. Example, the application of the entropy threshold on a dataset. (a) depicts in black the subset of interesting samples. (b) we see the sorted information measure associated to each sample (blue plot) and the entropy threshold (red line) applied to obtain (a).

Let $q_i = \max(w_j) - w_i$ the complementary value of w_i with respect to the maximum concentration value. So, the probability p_i is assigned by means of the normalization of q_i:

$$p_i = \frac{q_i}{\sum_{j=1}^{n} q_j} \tag{3}$$

Using this probability we evaluate the information provided by each sample I_i by means of the measurement of the quantity of information introduced by Shannon in [13].

$$I_i = -log_2(p_i) \tag{4}$$

Once we have I_i, we calculate the entropy E:

$$E = -\sum_{i=1}^{n} p_i log_2(p_i) = \sum_{i=1}^{n} p_i I_i \qquad (5)$$

Samples with a lower quantity of information I than entropy E are rejected. Thus, our new dataset is defined as:

$$NewDataSet = \{x_i | I_i > E\} \qquad (6)$$

An example where entropy is applied to distinguish between gross outliers and significant samples is shown in figure 3a where red samples are classified as gross outliers and green samples as significant samples. In figure 3b we can see the entropy separating the samples in two datasets.

3   Experimental Results

Two types of experiments have been done. We have firstly compared the results of our data reduction technique with the ones yielded by the generic data condensation method in [9]. Secondly, we have evaluated the response of our proposal with respect to the percentage of gross outliers present in the dataset, and its application with existing parameter estimators.

As depicted in figure 4, our contribution reduces the number of samples while preserving the interesting ones (the densities). When compared with a generic approach, we can see that the dense populations are severelly diminished, provoking a possible misestimation when a fitting algorithm is applied.

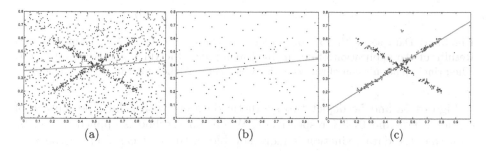

$$(a) \qquad\qquad\qquad (b) \qquad\qquad\qquad (c)$$

Fig. 4. Generic density-based data reduction technique [9] vs our proposal. a) Example dataset. b) Generic data reduction of a). c) Data reduction of a) using our proposal. The estimation of the line has been made using the LMedS algorithm.

Figure 4c also shows how a simple estimator as LMedS[1] is capable to find the desired model (a line) in conjunction with our approach in front of its performance with the generic algorithm, where it fails to retrieve the model (figure 4b).

In the following examples we evaluate the performance of our approach along with our parameter estimator, the HTE[4], in complex datasets. We stress that HTE fails in this examples to retrieve the model when applied alone, despite being capable of fitting models in scenarios with up to 90% of outliers. We have tested both algorithms running together in both synthetic and real LADAR imaging.

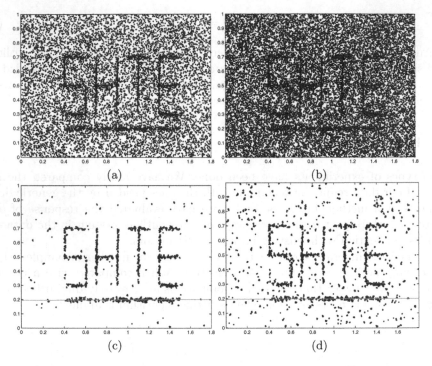

Fig. 5. a) Data set with 95% of outliers. b) Data set with 97.5% of outliers. c-d) Results of the application of our method along with the HTE parameter estimator. The principal population of the scenarios was efectively the underline below the letters.

Figures 5a and 5c depict two synthetic datasets with a high percentage of outliers, 95% and 97.5% respectivelly. When our method is applied, it can be seen that the data reduction is more notable in the first case. This is because 5b presents a higher average density in the dataset, more similar to the density of the meaningful populations than 5a. After the application of our algorithm, the percentage of significant samples in 5c is 25% while before the application was only 5%. In 5d the percentage of significant samples is 18% while before the application was only 2.5%.

Experimentally, if a priori knowledge is available, we have seen that our threshold can be modified easily to achieve a better performance using a new threshold defined as αE. We can tune our method with a value of α slightly higher that 1 (1.02) when there is a big amount of gross outliers and a value slightly lower than 1 (0.98) with a low amount of gross outliers. However, if we don't have a priori knowledge our method presents good results fixing the α value at 1.

We have also applied our data reduction technique to real LADAR images. A LADAR image contains the 3D coordinates of each pixel. We firstly preprocess the 3D LADAR image finding the ground model and then we project the data onto that plane. Once projected, it is much easier to find the sides of the objects because they have been transformed into sample densities forming lines. Using this workflow, we can see the line fitting results of our algorithm on a real dataset that contains a tank in figure 6.

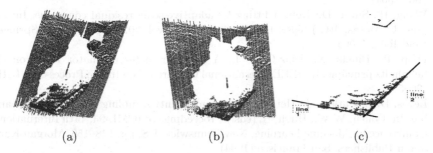

(a)   (b)   (c)

Fig. 6. a) 3D LADAR image, depicting a tank, with 21513 samples. b) 2D projection of a) onto the ground plane. c) Results of the application of our proposed algorithm and a line fitting algorithm in the dataset depicted in b), 5916 samples have been selected and 2245 are inliers of the 2 lines depicted.

4 Conclusion

We have presented a novel data reduction method to remove gross outliers from datasets designed specifically for parametric regression problems. In contrast with other existing data reduction tecniques, our approach does not perform only a condensation of data, it takes into consideration the density information associated to each sample, this value provides a significance descriptor that is used to discard the gross outliers. The threshold used to perform this classification is obtained automatically by relating the density descriptor to an information and entropy values, as detailed in section 2. Our approach preserves the dense populations of our datasets, therefore, in a parameter estimation framework, it performs an oriented data reduction task.

The main advantage of our approach is that it allows the correct estimation of parametric models in complex data set where the existing estimators failed. Moreover, in some cases we can find parametric descriptions using classical estimators in reduced datasets instead of the latter ones, much more costly. We are well aware that the complexity of the density estimation step grows exponentially with the number of samples, this is the reason why we have improved its efficiency by using kdtrees to obtain the distances between points, although it also opens lines of future work with the objective of reducing the complexity of the outlier processing step. However, in complex scenarios where multiple models are to be retrieved, the data reduction is performed only once.

Acknowledgments. This work was partially funded with Cicyt grant n TIC2003-06075 and by LADAR Laboratory Project from CIDA/SDGTECEN/DGAM.

References

1. Rosseeuw, P.J., Leroy, A.M.: Robust Regression and Outlier Detection. Wiley-Interscience, New York (1987)
2. Wang, H., Suter, D.: Mdpe: A very robust estimator for model fitting and range image segmentation. International Journal on Computer Vision (IJCV) 59(2), 139–166 (2004)
3. Wang, H., Suter, D.: Robust fitting by adaptive-scale residual consensus. In: Pajdla, T., Matas, J(G.) (eds.) ECCV 2004. LNCS, vol. 3021, pp. 107–118. Springer, Heidelberg (2004)
4. Felip, R., Binefa, X., Diaz-Caro, J.: A new parameter estimator based on the helmholtz principle. In: IEEE International Conference on Image Processing (ICIP) (2005)
5. Lewis, D.D., Catlett, J.: Heterogeneous uncertainty sampling for supervised learning. In: Cohen, W.W., Hirsh, H. (eds.) Proceedings of ICML-94, 11th International Conference on Machine Learning, New Brunswick, US, pp. 148–156. Morgan Kaufmann Publishers, San Francisco (1994)
6. Roy, N., McCallum, A.: Toward optimal active learning through sampling estimation of error reduction. In: Proc. 18th International Conf. on Machine Learning, pp. 441–448. Morgan Kaufmann, San Francisco (2001)
7. Wilson, D.R., Martinez, T.R.: Reduction tecniques for instance-based learning algorithms. Machine Learning 38(3), 257–286 (2000)
8. Leung, Y., Zhang, J.S., Xu, Z.B.: Clustering by scale-space filtering. IEEE Transactions on Pattern Analysis and Machine Intelligence (PAMI) 22(12), 1396–1410 (2000)
9. Mitra, P., Murphy, C.A., Pal, S.K.: Density-based multiscale data condensation. IEEE Transactions on Pattern Analysis and Machine Intelligence (PAMI) 24(6), 734–747 (2002)
10. Huang, D., Chow, T.W.S.: Enhancing density-based data reduction using entropy. Neural Comput. 18(2), 470–495 (2006)
11. Silverman, B.W.: Density Estimation for Statistics and Data Analysis. Chapman & Hall, Sydney, Australia (1986)
12. Deng, K., Moore, A.: Multiresolution instance-based learning. In: Proceedings of the 12th International Joint Conference on Artificial Intellingence, pp. 1233–1239. Morgan Kaufmann, San Francisco (1995)
13. Shannon, C.E., Weaver, W.: A Mathematical Theory of Communication. University of Illinois Press, Champaign, IL, USA (1963)

Robust Estimation of Reflectance Functions from Polarization

Gary A. Atkinson and Edwin R. Hancock

Department of Computer Science, University of York, York YO10 5DD, UK
{atkinson,erh}@cs.york.ac.uk

Abstract. This paper presents a new approach to image-based reflectance function estimation. The method first uses Fresnel theory for reflection and polarization analysis to estimate the surface orientation for each image pixel from a single view. The method is confined to the case where the light source and camera lie in the same direction from the target. A 2D histogram of surface zenith angles and pixel intensities is then calculated. This histogram is processed using a robust and computationally efficient statistical analysis. Histogram data are fitted to probability density functions to deduce the reflectance function. Objects of varying complexity and material are analysed and compared to ground truth.

1 Introduction

Many techniques in computer vision and graphics require a quantitative description of a material's reflectance properties. These properties are commonly described by the reflectance function of the material, or bidirectional reflectance distribution function (BRDF), which gives the ratio of reflected radiance to incident irradiance in all possible directions. The BRDF is used in graphics to render a variety of materials under different lighting conditions and in vision for surface analysis techniques. In shape-from-shading for example, Ragheb and Hancock [5] make use of the reflectance functions derived by Wolff, Nayar and Oren [10]. Approaching the problem of shape recovery from an opposite direction, Treuille et al. [8] make empirical observations of the BRDF using objects of known geometry to aid reconstruction from two views.

In this paper, we aim to estimate a "slice" of the BRDF for several different objects using polarization analysis. In the past, polarization has been used in computer vision for several tasks. Perhaps most notably, several papers have been published on shape reconstruction [9,4]. These methods are based on the premise that light undergoes a partial polarization when it is reflected from a surface. Fresnel theory [2] predicts this effect and can be used to estimate the surface orientation from measurable quantities [9]. This idea is used in this paper to obtain the relationship between surface angle and image intensity, thus acquiring a slice of the BRDF.

We focus on the retro-reflective case where the positions of the camera and a single source of illumination are almost identical. Raw data are obtained using a standard technique involving a digital camera and a linear polarizer. Our

J. Martí et al. (Eds.): IbPRIA 2007, Part II, LNCS 4478, pp. 363–371, 2007.

approach is global and uses a robust statistical analysis to account for complications caused by inter-reflections and image noise. The method uses a 2D histogram constructed from the set of pixel intensities and a set of initial zenith angle estimates. A first reflectance function estimate is then made, based on the peak frequency curve in the histogram. The result is then adjusted by fitting the data to a probability density function. The method requires just a few seconds of processing time on a typical modern computer.

Shibata et al. [7] also use polarization for BRDF estimation. They recover a more complete and accurate BRDF, but require highly specialised equipment and their method is more time consuming. Robles-Kelly and Hancock [6] devised an algorithm to estimate the retro-reflective slice of the BRDF using the cumulative distribution of intensity gradients. Their method is more reliable than our's when applied to rough surfaces, but less so for smooth, shiny objects.

2   Fresnel Theory and Polarization

Consider the reflection of a ray of light from a smooth surface. Fresnel theory provides a means to calculate the ratio of the incident light intensity to the reflected light intensity for a given angle of incidence. Further to this, if the incident light is unpolarized, the theory predicts that the reflected ray will become partially polarized, again depending on the angle of incidence.

In this paper, we study diffuse reflection, where light penetrates the surface and is scattered internally before being re-emitted (in contrast to specular reflection, where the light is reflected from the surface directly). For diffuse reflection, Fresnel theory can be applied to light as it is re-emitted from the medium into air [9]. This provides a relation between the polarization state of the reflected light and the angle of the reflection.

The standard approach to measure the polarization state of reflected light is to take a succession of images of the reflecting surface with a polarizer placed in front of a camera rotated to different angles. The measured intensity at each pixel varies sinusoidally with the polarizer angle. By performing (for example) a least squares fit on the measured pixel brightnesses as a function of the polarizer angle, the minimum and maximum intensities on the sinusoid, $I_{\min}$ and $I_{\max}$, can easily be determined.

The polarization state can then be expressed using the *degree of polarization*:

$$\rho = (I_{\max} - I_{\min}) / (I_{\max} + I_{\min}) \tag{1}$$

Fresnel theory predicts that the degree of polarization is related to the reflectance angle, θ, and the refractive index, n, by [1]

$$\rho = \frac{(n - 1/n)^2 \sin^2 \theta}{2 + 2n^2 - (n + 1/n)^2 \sin^2 \theta + 4 \cos \theta \sqrt{n^2 - \sin^2 \theta}} \tag{2}$$

We assume that the refractive index is 1.4 throughout this work, which is a typical value. Expressed slightly differently, if a surface point is observed such that the angle between its normal and the viewing direction (the zenith angle) is θ, then the observed degree of polarization is given by (2).

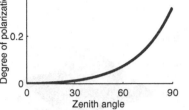

Fig. 1. Relationship between zenith angle and degree of polarization

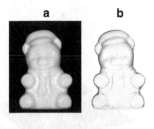

Fig. 2. (a) Greyscale image of a porcelain bear. (b) Degree of polarization (dark areas have higher values).

Figure 1 shows the relationship between the degree of polarization and the zenith angle. Figure 2 shows a greyscale image of a porcelain bear and an image where the intensity encodes the degree of polarization. This image can be converted into an estimate of the zenith angle for each pixel by numerically solving (2). However, past research [1] has shown that these estimates are highly susceptible to noise and are degraded by the presence of inter-reflections. The remainder of this paper describes a method to overcome these problems by using the pixel intensities to refine the zenith angle estimates. Results for this paper were obtained in a dark room with an small light source placed beside the camera.

The BRDF, $f\left(\theta_i, \alpha_i, \theta_r, \alpha_r\right)$, for a particular material is the ratio of reflected radiance to incident irradiance for any illumination and viewing directions. It is measured per unit solid angle per unit foreshortened area and is given by

$$f\left(\theta_i, \alpha_i, \theta_r, \alpha_r\right) = \frac{L_r\left(\theta_r, \alpha_r\right)}{L_i\left(\theta_i, \alpha_i\right)\cos\theta_i \mathrm{d}\omega} \tag{3}$$

where θ and α denote the zenith and azimuth angles, the subscripts i and r denote incidence and reflectance, and $\mathrm{d}\omega$ is the differential solid angle subtended by the light source.

In this paper we concentrate on the case where the illumination and viewing directions are identical. The intensity is then independent of the surface azimuth angle and we are estimating the BRDF where $\theta_i = \theta_r$, i.e. $f\left(\theta_i, \alpha_i, \theta_r, \alpha_r\right)$ reduces to $f\left(\theta\right)$. Technically, the BRDF is a physical quantity that needs calibration if it is to be recovered in the correct units. However, this is beyond the scope of our experimental set-up. We therefore work with normalized quantities and our recovered reflectance functions are proportional to that given in (3). For many graphics and vision applications the physical quantities are not required.

3   Statistical Analysis

Figure 3a shows a histogram of the intensities and zenith angles (*as estimated by* (2)) of the porcelain bear in Fig. 2. The footprint of the histogram is shown in Fig. 4a. Since the light source and camera directions are approximately identical, one would expect the intensity to decrease monotonically with the zenith angle. The general structure of the histogram confirms this. Note however, that

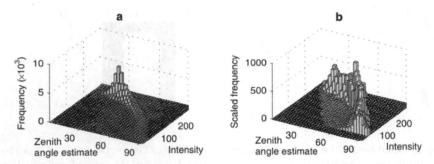

Fig. 3. (a) Histogram of intensities and zenith angle estimates for the porcelain bear shown in Fig. 2. (b) Scaled histogram.

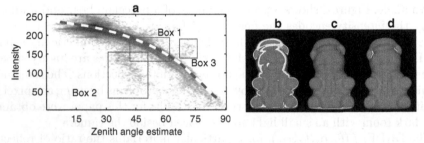

Fig. 4. (a) Footprint of the histogram in Fig. 3a. Bins of higher frequency are shown as dark patches (logarithmic scale). The exact reflectance curve is also shown. (b-d) Greyscale images where highlighted pixels fall into (b) box 1, (c) box 2 and (d) box 3.

the main curve in the histogram is broad and that a significant number of pixels fall into bins far away from this curve. Figure 4 highlights image regions corresponding to three different parts of the histogram. Unlike the pixels falling into box 1, the pixels in boxes 2 and 3 do not follow the general trend.

The main reason for the wide spread of the data in Fig. 4 (in addition to noise) is that inter-reflections are taking place. An inter-reflection occurs where light from a source is *specularly* reflected from one point on the object to another, and then toward the camera. This process therefore obeys the theory for specular reflection, although a diffuse component will be present. It can occur at the small scale between the corrugations that constitute roughness, or macroscopically between different regions of the surface or the environment.

The exact effect of an inter-reflection depends upon its strength. If it is weak, then the diffuse component still dominates. The degree of polarization, and hence the zenith angle estimate, will be reduced since the angle of polarization of specularly reflected light is perpendicular to that of diffuse reflection [9]. This process can be seen in box 2 of Fig. 4. Here, a small specular component is present due to reflections from the table on which the object rests. For strong inter-reflections, the specular component dominates, as in box 3. Since the polarizing properties of specular reflection are greater than that for diffuse reflection, we have a situation where the degree of polarization exceeds that which would be expected for purely diffuse reflection.

Notice that, apart from the cases were the strong inter-reflection limit is met (as in box 3), the degree of polarization is equal to, or less than, the expected value for a given zenith angle. This is substantiated by the fact that the exact curve (measured using an object of the same material but known shape) approximately follows the outer envelope of the histogram.

4 Proposed Method

Initial Estimate. Figure 4 suggests that we need to calculate a curve that follows the outer envelope of the histogram. However, an *initial estimate* of the reflectance function can be derived from the crest of the histogram. One difficulty is that there are too few data points at some parts of the histogram to obtain a reliable estimate.

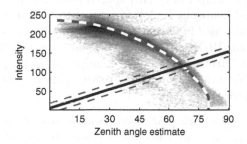

Fig. 5. Broken curve: initial BRDF estimate. Solid straight line: $I_B(\theta)$. Broken straight lines: $I_L(\theta)$ and $I_U(\theta)$.

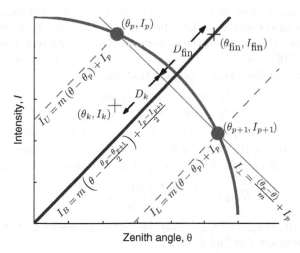

Fig. 6. Definitions used in the calculation of the reflectance curve. The bold curve is the initial estimate.

We overcome this problem by dividing the data into histogram bins of equal frequency, instead of using uniformly spaced bins. Our algorithm accomplishes this task by sorting the pixels by intensity and selecting the intensity of every $(M/N)^{\text{th}}$ pixel as a bin edge, where M is the total number of pixels and N is the desired number of intensity bins. For all pixels falling into a given intensity bin, we apply a similar process to obtain zenith angle bin edges.

The frequency for each bin is then divided by its area to give a scaled frequency at the centre points of each bin. Two-dimensional linear interpolation is then used between the bin centres to calculate a value at each point on an evenly spaced $N \times N$ grid. This interpolation results in a scaled "histogram" with identical bin positions and sizes as the original version, as shown in Fig. 3b.

Although, the resultant "histogram" has no direct physical interpretation, it makes it easier to robustly trace the peak frequency curve. The curve is first calculated in polar co-ordinates with the origin at $(\theta = 0, I = 0)$. Here, we use normalised units of bin lengths (i.e. $I \leftarrow IN/255$ and $\theta \leftarrow \theta N/90°$). Indeed, we use normalised co-ordinates for the rest of the paper.

For an arbitrary number of equally spaced polar co-ordinate angles between 0 and 90°, the scaled frequency is plotted against the distance from the origin. The distance where the scaled frequency reaches its maximum is then taken as a data point on the initial BRDF estimate. These distances are then smoothed before reverting back to Cartesian space. An example of an initial BRDF estimate is shown in Fig. 5. Note that the initial estimate is often quite reasonable by itself, without further processing.

Final Estimate. For each pair of consecutive points on the initial estimate, (θ_p, I_p) and (θ_{p+1}, I_{p+1}), we calculate a point on the refined BRDF estimate that falls on the straight line $I_B(\theta, p)$, as shown in Fig. 6. This is the line that perpendicularly bisects the second straight line $I_\perp(\theta, p)$, which connects the pair of points on the initial estimate.

The two straight lines parallel to $I_B(\theta, p)$ that pass through (θ_p, I_p) and (θ_{p+1}, I_{p+1}) are also calculated. Let these be $I_U(\theta, p)$ and $I_L(\theta, p)$ respectively. These lines define the region of the histogram that we use to estimate the point on the final BRDF curve related to point p on the initial estimate. For each p, we therefore extract data points (θ_k, I_k) that satisfy

$$I_L(\theta_k, p) < I_k < I_U(\theta_k, p)$$
$$\theta_L(I_k, p) < \theta_k < \theta_U(I_k, p) \tag{4}$$

where θ_L and θ_U are the inverse functions of I_L and I_U respectively.

We are interested in the distribution of distances $D_k(p)$ between the location of the data points k and the line $I_\perp(\theta, p)$. The distance $D_k(p)$ is given by:

$$D_k(p) = \frac{(I_k - I_p)\, m(p) + \theta_k - \theta_p}{\sqrt{m(p)^2 + 1}} \tag{5}$$

where $m(p) = (\theta_p - \theta_{p+1})/(I_{p+1} - I_p)$. Negative values of $D_k(p)$ indicate that the point lies beneath the line $I_B(\theta, p)$.

The broken straight lines in Fig. 5 indicate the region of the histogram where (4) is obeyed for a particular point on the initial BRDF estimate. In the next

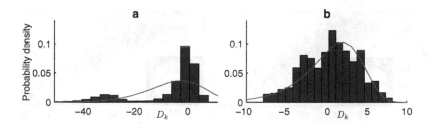

Fig. 7. (a) Histogram of the length D_k for all pixels bounded by $I_L(\theta)$ and $I_U(\theta)$ in Fig. 5. (b) Histogram after removal of pixels that do not obey (9).

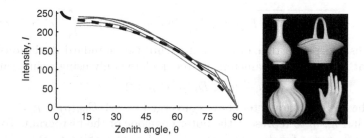

Fig. 8. Estimated reflectance functions for the four porcelain objects shown and the bear model, compared to the exact (broken) curve

stage of the algorithm, the data in this region is fitted to the Weibull probability distribution function (PDF) [3] given by

$$g\left(t|a,b,c\right) = \begin{cases} \frac{b}{a}\left(\frac{t-c}{a}\right)^{b-1}\exp\left(-\left(\frac{t-c}{a}\right)^{b}\right) & t \geq c \\ 0 & t < c \end{cases} \tag{6}$$

where a is a scale parameter, b is a shape parameter and c is a location parameter. The distribution has a shape similar to a skewed Gaussian. We use it here because we expect the majority of pixels to fall within the envelope of the peak frequency curve in the 2D histogram (i.e. to have negative $D_k(p)$) due to roughness and inter-reflections.

In Fig. 7a, the distances $D_k(p)$ bounded by (4) have been fitted to a Weibull PDF using a standard maximum likelihood approach. Clearly this is inadequate since there is an inter-reflection taking place that is resulting in a different distribution for some of the points. However, since there are generally much fewer points in the inter-reflection we can discard data that falls under the tails of the PDF and calculate a new set of parameters. We iterate this until convergence (typically only three or four iterations are necessary). The histogram in Fig. 7b shows the result. Note that we have used the same number of bins as for the first histogram, but over a smaller range.

In order to determine which points to discard, the algorithm first calculates the mean, μ, and standard deviation, σ, of the PDF, which are given by

$$\mu = a\Gamma\left(1 + 1/b\right) \tag{7}$$

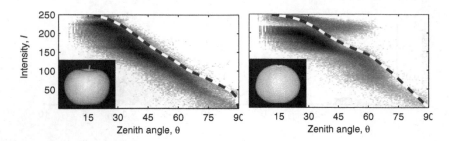

Fig. 9. Histograms and estimated reflectance functions of an apple and an orange

$$\sigma = a\sqrt{\Gamma\left(1 + 2/b\right) - \Gamma\left(1 + 1/b\right)^2} \quad \text{where} \quad \Gamma(x) = \int_0^{\infty} e^{-t} t^{x-1} dt \quad (8)$$

We then discard points that do not fall within two standard deviations of the mean. That is, the PDF parameters are recalculated only using points satisfying

$$\mu - 2\sigma < D_k(p) < \mu + 2\sigma \quad (9)$$

After the Weibull parameters have converged we set $D_{\text{fin}}(p) = \mu + 2\sigma$, which is defined in Fig. 6, to represent the outer envelope of the histogram. To ensure a smooth reflectance function we apply Gaussian smoothing to the values D_{fin} before reverting to the Cartesian pairs $(\theta_{\text{fin}}, I_{\text{fin}})$. We finally add an additional point to the BRDF at $(\theta = 90°, I = 0)$.

Recovered Reflectance Functions. The estimated reflectance functions for several porcelain objects are shown in Fig. 8. Clearly, the curves follow the general trend of the exact curve and are approximately equal. This shows that the inter-reflections have been desirably discounted from the BRDF. The algorithm appears to be most reliable at intermediate zenith angles. For retro-reflection, specularities are present for small zenith angles, often resulting in overestimates for that part of the BRDF.

In Fig. 9, we have applied the algorithm to an apple and an orange. Again, the results seem reasonable except for small zenith angles. Note that the direct specular reflections, which cover a significant part of the orange's pitted surface, have been discarded by the algorithm. This gives us an approximation of the diffuse component of the BRDF as desired.

5   Conclusion

A new method for reflectance function estimation was presented that draws data from polarization. Our method is computationally very efficient, although the additional time needed to obtain the initial polarization images is a weakness of this, and most other techniques in polarization vision. We have shown how a good initial estimate can be obtained from polarization data in just a few seconds (using Matlab and a 2.4GHz CPU). A final estimate takes about five seconds to calculate in total. Finally, we have shown how the method can be applied to several materials and object shapes.

References

1. Atkinson, G.A., Hancock, E.R.: Recovery of surface orientation from diffuse polarization. Trans. Im. Proc. 15, 1653–1664 (2006)
2. Hecht, E.: Optics, 3rd edn. Addison Wesley Longman, London, UK (1998)
3. Kotz, S., Nadarajah, S.: Extreme Value Distributions: Theory and Applications. Imperial College Press, London, UK (EU) (2000)
4. Miyazaki, D., Tan, R.T., Hara, K., Ikeuchi, K.: Polarization-based inverse rendering from a single view. In: Proc. ICCV, vol. 2, pp. 982–987 (2003)
5. Ragheb, H., Hancock, E.R.: Surface radiance correction for shape from shading. Pattern Recognition 38, 1574–1595 (2005)
6. Robles-Kelly, A., Hancock, E.R.: Estimating the surface radiance function from single images. Graphical Models 67, 518–548 (2005)
7. Shibata, T., Takahashi, T., Miyazaki, D., Sato, Y., Ikeuchi, K.: Creating photorealistic virtual model with polarization based vision system. In: Proc. SPIE, vol. 5888, pp. 25–35 (2005)
8. Treuille, A., Hertzmann, A., Seitz, S.: Example-based stereo with general BRDFs. In: Proc. ECCV, pp. 457–469 (2004)
9. Wolff, L.B., Boult, T.E.: Constraining object features using a polarisation reflectance model. Trans. Pattern Anal. Mach. Intell. 13, 635–657 (1991)
10. Wolff, L.B., Nayar, S.K., Oren, M.: Improved diffuse reflection models for computer vision. Intl. J. Comp. Vis. 30, 55–71 (1998)

Estimation of Multiple Objects at Unknown Locations with Active Contours

Margarida Silveira and Jorge S. Marques

IST - Instituto Superior Técnico, Technical University of Lisbon and ISR - Instituto de Sistemas e Robótica, Portugal

Abstract. This paper presents an algorithm for the estimation of multiple regions with unknown shapes and positions using multiple active contour models (ACM's). The algorithm organizes edge points into strokes and computes the association between those strokes and the ACM's using the component wise EM algorithm (CEM) for MAP estimation. The algorithm is randomly initialized with a high number of ACM's and performs online model selection using importance sampling. Experimental results show the effectiveness of the proposed technique.

1 Introduction

Active contour models (ACM's) or snakes [1] have been extensively used to estimate object boundaries in images. However, their difficulties with initialization and outlier rejection are still unsolved problems. In addition, most of the research done on ACM's tries to estimate a single region using one elastic model (for e.g. see [2] [3]) and little research has addressed estimation of multiple elastic models. Some examples include [4] where multiple regions are estimated but the approach is restricted to regions that have some common characteristic or property and weighting parameters are defined heuristically. In [5] several ACM's are initialized in the centers of divergence of the gradient vector flow field. Some of the centers are discarded using heuristic rules and the method is unable to deal with regions inside other regions. In [6] a single contour can break automatically to represent the contours of multiple objects. In [7] multiple level set contours are also used but they evolve independently. The initial segmentation and number of ACM's is determined by fuzzy c-means clustering. In [8] gradient vector diffusion is used for the evolution and also the initialization of multiple contours. After the contours evolution region merging reduces the number of contours.

In this paper we present a method for the automatic segmentation of multiple regions which, in simultaneous with shape estimation, deals with the problem of sensitivity to the initialization and robustness to outliers. The algorithm builds on the work proposed in [9] in which multiple ACM's compete for the boundaries of multiple regions, using the EM algorithm for MAP estimation. The algorithm proposed in this paper includes three major contributions 1) it automatically selects the number of ACM's 2) it uses a different observation model which makes it less sensitive to initialization and more robust to outliers and 3) initialization of the ACM's is fully automatic.

J. Martí et al. (Eds.): IbPRIA 2007, Part II, LNCS 4478, pp. 372–379, 2007.

This paper is organized as follows: section 2 formulates the problem, section 3 describes the proposed algorithm for multiple active contours, section 4 presents experimental results and section 5 concludes the paper.

2   Problem Formulation

Given an image with an unknown number of objects and assuming that is is possible to detect connected sets of edge points belonging to the objects boundaries, our aim is to connect segments belonging to individual object and to discard outlier segments associated with spurious edges. Let y be the set of all edge points detected in an image and let us assume that y is organized in connected components, called strokes, $y^j, j = 1, ..., N$ where $y^j = \{y_1^j, ..., y_n^j\}$ is the set of edge points belonging to the j-th stroke. We will assume for now that the number of ACM's, L is known and we add an extra model to account for outliers. We denote it the outlier model, $x^{outlier}$. Let x^k be the the k-th active contour model, $k = 1, ..., L$ defined by a sequence of 2D points $x_i^k, i = 1, ..., M^k$; the number of points for each snake is adjusted by insertion and deletion in order to keep the distance between two consecutive points constant and therefore different ACM's may have different number of points. x^k can either be an open or closed contour. We will assume that the strokes detected in the image are independent:

$$p(y|x) = \prod_j p(y^j|x) \tag{1}$$

and that the distribution of each stroke is a mixture of L+1 densities:

$$p(y^j|x) = \sum_k \alpha_k p(y^j|x^k) + \alpha_{outlier} p(y^j|x^{outlier}) \tag{2}$$

where the α_k's are the mixing proportions verifying $\alpha_k \geq 0$, $\alpha_{outlier} \geq 0$ and $\sum_k \alpha_k + \alpha_{outlier} = 1$.

Our aim is to estimate the ACM's and also their number L. We will iteratively estimate the ACM's using the MAP criterion and assuming L is fixed:

$$x^* = \arg\max_x p(x|y) = \arg\max_x [\log p(y|x) + \log p(x)] \tag{3}$$

Then a new value for L will be estimated by importance sampling. In the following we will specify each of the distributions involved in this problem.

2.1   Observation and Prior Models

We assume each stroke has i.i.d. edge points, each modelled by a mixture of M^k Gaussian densities centered in the snake elements:

$$p(y^j|x^k) = \prod_n p(y_n^j|x^k) = \prod_n \frac{1}{M^k} \sum_i N(y_n^j, x_i^k, \sigma^2 I) \tag{4}$$

where $N(y, \mu, R)$ denotes the normal density function with mean μ and covariance R. This model is closely related to the elastic net model [10] and associates every edge point with a given snake element. For the case of the outlier model, the contribution of each feature to the potential is a constant, but a different constant is used for each stroke, V^j.

$$p(y^j | x^{outlier}) = \prod_n p(y_n^j | x^{outlier}) = \prod_n N^j V^j = \left(V^j\right)^{N^j} \tag{5}$$

If V^j is set inversely proportional to the size of the corresponding stroke, N^j, then the smaller strokes will also tend to be classified as outliers, and the ACM's will be able to bridge the small outlier strokes. Therefore we used $V^j = \exp(-KN^j)$ where K is a positive constant.

We adopt the prior model proposed in [9] which is the following:

$$\log p(x) = \sum_k \left(E_{\text{int}}(x^k) + \sum_{l \neq k} E_{\text{inter}}(x^k, x^l) \right) \tag{6}$$

where $E_i(x^k)$ is a regularization energy that expresses the assumption that each contour is smooth and $E_{\text{inter}}(x^k, x^l)$ is another regularization energy that expresses the interaction between different active contours.

3   Unsupervised Multiple Active Contours Estimation

The algorithm proposed in [9] described the estimation of multiple models in which multiple ACM's compete for the boundaries of the multiple regions. The algorithm solves the association between strokes and multiple models problem and also the outlier rejection. However it does not solve the initialization problem and the estimation of the number of models. To deal with these difficulties we initiate the algorithm with an arbitrary large number of snakes, L. The initialization of these L ACM's is fully automatic; circular ACM's are randomly distributed throughout the image, inside the strokes bounding boxes. The size of the circles is defined by the average size of the bounding boxes or may be user defined. Then the algorithm iteratively performs the following two steps.

1. Update
   The ACM's are sequentially updated with the Component wise EM algorithm which is summarized in the sub-section 3.1. Convergence is achieved when all the points move less than a threshold.
2. Sampling
   The algorithm relocates the ACM's by performing Importance Sampling using the mixing proportions α_k as the importance function. The set of ACM's $x^k, k = 1, ...L$ is sampled in order to obtain a new set of L ACM's with the highest values of α_k. Obviously some ACM's will be sampled several times and other will not be sampled at all. The ACM's that are not sampled

are eliminated and the ones that were sampled several times will give rise to new ACM's that are equal. However the CEM algorithm will insure they will converge to different locations since they are updated one at a time.

The sampling step does not change the number of ACM's. Therefore, in order to reduce the number of ACM's, we add a model elimination step every P iterations. In this step we eliminate multiple copies of the models which were sampled several times and keep only one realization of such ACM. The number of different ACM's is the estimated number of models.

3.1   Component Wise EM Algorithm

In the EM algorithm it is assumed that y is incomplete data and that the complete data includes binary labels $z_j, j = 1, ..., N$ with $z_j = \{z_j^1, ..., z_j^{L+1}\}$, that indicate which model generated the stroke; $z_j^k = 1$ means that stroke y^j was generated by model x^k. The complete log likelihood is given by:

$$\log p(y, z|x) = \sum_j \sum_k z_j^k \log p(y^j|x^k) \tag{7}$$

Instead of maximizing (3), the EM algorithm alternates between two steps. In the E-step it finds the conditional expectation of the complete log likelihood with respect to the unknown x given the observed data y and the current estimate, $\hat{x}$.

$$Q(x, \hat{x}) = E\left[\log p(y, z|x)|y, \hat{x}\right] \tag{8}$$

$$= E\left[\sum_j \sum_k z_j^k \log\left[\alpha_k p(y^j|x^k)\right]\right] = \sum_j \sum_k w_k^j \log\left[\alpha_k p(y^j|x^k)\right] \tag{9}$$

where w_k^j is a set of weights summing to one assigned to each stroke. Each weight w_k^j represents the soft assignment of stroke y^j to the active contour x^k. The weights are given by:

$$w_k^j = p(z_j^k = 1|y^j, \hat{x}) = \frac{\alpha_k p(y^j|x^k)}{\sum_m \alpha_m p(y^j|x^m)} \tag{10}$$

In the M-step the estimation of the active contour is obtained by the maximization of:

$$U(x, \hat{x}) = Q(x, \hat{x}) + \log p(x) \tag{11}$$

The CEM algorithm sequentially performs one E step and one M step for each of the ACM's and iterates until convergence [11]. In our implementation the order of this estimation is predefined.

The E and M steps will be detailed in the following subsections.

The E-Step. In the E-step the weights are calculated. Substituting (4) into (10) we obtain the following expression:

$$w_k^j = \frac{\alpha_k \prod_n \frac{1}{M^k} \sum_i N(x_i^k, \sigma^2 I)}{\sum_m \alpha_m \prod_n \frac{1}{M^m} \sum_i N(x_i^m, \sigma^2 I) + \alpha^{outlier}(V^j)^{N^j}} \tag{12}$$

The mixing proportions are updated by:

$$\alpha_k = \frac{1}{N^j} \sum_j w_k^j \tag{13}$$

The M-Step. In the M-step the estimation of the active contour is obtained by the minimization of (11) performed by the gradient algorithm:

$$x_{t+1}^k = x_t^k - \gamma \nabla_x(Q(x, \widehat{x})) \tag{14}$$

where ∇_x represents the gradient. This equation can be rewritten as follows:

$$x_{t+1}^k = x_t^k - \gamma_{\text{int}} f_{\text{int}} - \gamma_{\text{ext}} f_{\text{ext}} - \gamma_{\text{inter}} f_{\text{inter}} \tag{15}$$

where $f_{\text{ext}}(x_i^k)$, $f_{\text{int}}(x_i^k)$ and $f_{\text{inter}}(x_i^k)$ are external, internal and interaction forces. External and internal forces are given by expressions (16) and (17):

$$f_{\text{ext}}(x_i^k) = -\frac{1}{\sigma^2} \sum_j w_j^k \sum_n (y_n^j - x_i^k)\phi_\sigma(|y_n^j - x_i^k|^2) \tag{16}$$

$$f_{\text{int}}(x_i^k) = -2\left(\frac{l_{i-1} - l_0}{l_{i-1}}(x_i^k - x_{i-1}^k) + \frac{l_{i+1} - l_0}{l_{i+1}}(x_i^k - x_{i+1}^k)\right) \tag{17}$$

where $l_{i-1} = \|x_i^k - x_{i-1}^k\|$ and $l_{i+1} = \|x_i^k - x_{i+1}^k\|$. The expression of the inter-action force depends on the application. For instance, if we expect each model to attract the other models, we can use $\varphi(d) = -\exp(-d/2\sigma_{\text{inter}}^2)$ leading to:

$$f_{\text{inter}}(x_i^k) = \frac{1}{\sigma_{\text{inter}}^2} \sum_{l \neq k} \sum_m (x_i^k - x_m^l)\varphi(|x_m^l - x_i^k|^2) \tag{18}$$

4   Experimental Results

This section presents examples to illustrate the performance of the proposed method. The examples were performed in the following conditions. Edges were obtained with the Canny edge detector and strokes were obtained with a connected components labelling algorithm. The external forces acting on each model unit were multiplied by independent gains to limit the maximum displacement

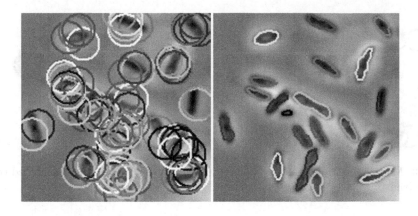

Fig. 1. Bacteria Example; 100 initial contours (left) and 21 final estimated contours (right)

of the model units in each iteration. All the experiments used $\Delta_{\max} = 2$ and the gain factors γ_{int} and γ_{inter} were chosen manually.

The first example illustrates the performance of the algorithm in the presence of multiple objects (bacteria). Fig. 1 shows the initial contours on the left and the final contours on the right. The algorithm was initialized with 100 ACM's that were overlapping and the final result was able to separate 21 different objects. All the objects were correctly associated with a different ACM.

The second example shows the performance of the proposed algorithm applied to the segmentation of pedestrians in a video sequence. In this example 10 ACM's were used to segment the image obtained from Fig. 2 a) after background subtraction. The background estimation was based on modelling the intensity of each pixel with a single gaussian. Fig. 2 shows the initial contours on the left and the final contours on the right. The algorithm successfully estimated the correct number of pedestrians, producing 4 ACM's.

The third example shows the performance of the proposed algorithm with nested regions. In this example 50 ACM's were used to segment inhibition halos

Fig. 2. Pedestrians; 10 initial contours (left) and 4 final estimated contours (right)

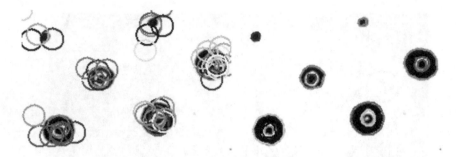

Fig. 3. Microbiologic plate assay; 50 initial contours (left) and 12 final estimated contours (right)

of antibacterial activity in microbiologic plate assays. Fig. 3 shows the initial contours on the left and the final contours on the right. The algorithm successfully estimated the correct number of objects, producing 12 ACM's and detecting no outliers.

The final example illustrates the application of the algorithm to a blood cell image using the outlier model to discard the smaller objects. The algorithm was initialized with 120 ACM's and in the final segmentation 27 contours remain. Fig. 4 shows the initial contours on the left, the final contours in the middle and the strokes classified as outliers on the right. In this example a couple of the final ACM's represent more than one object because they were overlapping in the image and originated only one stroke. The outliers that were detected correspond to the smaller strokes present in the image.

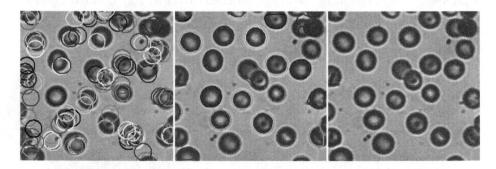

Fig. 4. Cell example; 120 initial contours (left), 27 contour estimates (middle) and outlier strokes (right)

5   Conclusion

This paper presents an algorithm for the extraction of multiple regions using multiple active contour models (ACM's). Initialization is automatic, the algorithm estimates the number of models and also accounts for outlier features detected in the image. It is shown that the proposed algorithm is able to robustly estimate all the deformable contours and to compute the association probability between strokes and multiple models.

Acknowledgments. This work was supported by Fundação para a Ciência e a Tecnologia (ISR/IST plurianual funding) through the POS_Conhecimento Program that includes FEDER funds.

References

[1] Kass, M., Witkin, A., Terzopoulos, D.: Snakes: Active contour models. International Journal of Computer Vision 1(4), 321–331 (1987)

[2] Cohen, L.: On active contour models and balloons. CVGIP: Image Understanding 53(2), 212–218 (1991)

[3] Xu, C., Prince, J.L.: Snakes, shapes, and gradient vector flow. IEEE Trans. on Image Processing 7(3), 359–369 (1998)

[4] Srinark, T., Kambhamettu, C.: A framework for multiple snakes. In: Proceedings of the 2001 IEEE Computer Society Conference on Computer Vision and Pattern Recognition, vol. II, pp. 202–209 (2001)

[5] Xingfei, G., Jie, T.: An automatic active contour model for multiple objects. In: Proceedings of the 16th International Conference on Pattern Recognition, vol. 2, pp. 881–884 (2002)

[6] Choi, W., Kin-Man, L., Siu, W.: An adaptive active contour model for highly irregular boundaries, Pattern Recognition vol. 34, pp. 323–331 (2001)

[7] Schupp, s., Elmoataz, A., Fadili, J., Herlin, P., Bloyet, D.: Image Segmentation via Multiple Active Contour Models and Fuzzy Clustering with Biomedical Applications, International Conference on Pattern Recognition (ICPR'00), vol. 1, pp. 622–625 (2000)

[8] Yu, Z., Bajaj, c.: Image Segmentation Using Gradient Vector Diffusion and Region Merging. International Conference on Pattern Recognition (ICPR'02) 2, 941–944 (2002)

[9] Silveira, M., Marques, J.: Multiple Active Contour Models based on the EM algorithm, IEEE International Conference on Image Processing, ICIP 2005, Genova, Italy (September 2005)

[10] Durbin, R., Willshaw, D.: An analogue approach to the travelling salesman problem using an elastic net method. Nature 326, 689–691 (1987)

[11] Celeux, G., Chréetien, Forbes, F., Mkhadri, A.: A component-wise EM algorithm for mixtures. Journal of Computational and Graphical Statistics 10, 699–712 (2001)

Analytic Reconstruction of Transparent and Opaque Surfaces from Texture Images

Mohamad Ivan Fanany and Itsuo Kumazawa

Imaging Science and Engineering, Tokyo Institute of Technology
fanany@isl.titech.ac.jp

Abstract. This paper addresses the problem of reconstructing non-overlapping transparent and opaque surfaces from multiple view images. The reconstruction is attained through progressive refinement of an initial 3D shape by minimizing the error between the images of the object and the initial 3D shape. The challenge is to simultaneously reconstruct both the transparent and opaque surfaces given only a limited number of images. Any refinement methods can theoretically be applied if analytic relation between pixel value in the training images and vertices position of the initial 3D shape is known. This paper investigates such analytic relations for reconstructing opaque and transparent surfaces. The analytic relation for opaque surface follows diffuse reflection model, whereas for transparent surface follows ray tracing model. However, both relations can be converged for reconstruction both surfaces into texture mapping model. To improve the reconstruction results several strategies including regularization, hierarchical learning, and simulated annealing are investigated.

1 Introduction

Many methods acquire high quality 3D shape of opaque object with a diffuse surface [3], but still not many methods acquire 3D shape of transparent object. Usually the reconstruction of transparent object is dealt exclusively from the reconstruction of opaque object, and vice versa. This is because the perception of transparent surface is a hard vision problem. Transparent surface lacks of body and surface reflections, is suffered much from inter-reflection [4], and lacks of naturally-occurring shape. The only potential sources of surface information are specular highlights, environmental reflections, and refractive distortion, whereas depth information is almost completely unavailable [5]. Only recently, some prospective techniques for modeling transparent surface have emerged. We categorize these methods into two groups as follows.

The first group elaborates as much the surface related features as possible to explicitly define the surface's shape. It includes a method to recover the shape of water surface [6], and a transparent surface, projected by a light stripe, using genetic algorithm [7]. The second group elaborates as much ways as possible to synthesize a realistic image of transparent object without using any 3D shape information. It includes a method called environment matting for capturing the optical behavior of transparent surface from known and controlled background

J. Martí et al. (Eds.): IbPRIA 2007, Part II, LNCS 4478, pp. 380–387, 2007.

for rendering and compositing purposes [2,8]. This method is extended to obtain the environment matting from uncontrolled backgrounds [9]. The Environment matte can also be obtained from multiple viewpoints to create novel views by interpolation [1]. Other method separates overlapped image of glass plates into reflected and transmitted images [10].

The first group relies heavily on real images and aimed for accurate 3D shape reconstruction. Whereas the second group relies heavily on synthesized graphical images and aimed for realistic 2D visualization. The ability to represent realistic synthetic images is beneficial, not only visually, but also for understanding the 3D shape. So for example, in medical radiation therapy for control or cure of cancer, the physician can easily locate cancerous tissue from normal tissue by modeling transparent 3D distribution of radiation dose to avoid complications [5].

In this paper, we pursue an integrated framework that enables the use of both synthesized graphical images and real images to infer the 3D shape of transparent object containing non-overlapping opaque surfaces. It is a neural network (NN) that minimizes the error between the synthesized projection and the teacher images in multiple views to approximate the true object's shape. It analytically refines the vertices position of the initial 3D model using error back-propagation learning. The main contribution of this paper is the analytic relations between the vertices position and the pixel value inside projection images of this 3D model for rendering and learning both transparent and opaque surfaces. Without such relations we have to heuristically establish a number of trial (candidate) vertex positions and choosing the positions that will maximize some objective functions [11,12]. The problem with such techniques is the appropriate trial number and positions are hard to determine, hence some additional restrictions such as texture correlation, smoothness, and silhouette restrictions are needed [13].

2   Problem Formulation

In this section, we set a relation between 3D vertices of a triangle $\mathbf{V}_k(k = 0, 1, 2)$ and the pixel value $f(x, y)$ inside projection image of this triangle. In computer graphics, this relation is called as rendering problem. But here, our genuine interest is not only to render the triangle but to actually 'learn' (modify) the triangle's vertices based on the pixel value error of its projection image compared to a given teacher image. For that purpose, we devise an analytic relation between these two variables. In our framework, the rendering problem is actually a forward mapping process that should be followed by back-propagation learning.

2.1   Learning Opaque Surface

If the triangle is opaque, the changes in vertices position give rise to different surface's normal $\mathbf{N}$, which in turn give rise to different pixel value $F(x, y)$ for a given light source pointing to $\mathbf{L}$ direction and ambient/diffuse light A spreading inside the scene. We may write this relation as:

$$\{\mathbf{V}_0, \mathbf{V}_1, \mathbf{V}_2\} \Longrightarrow \mathbf{N} \Longrightarrow \rho\lambda(\mathbf{N} \cdot \mathbf{L}) + A \Longrightarrow F(x, y). \tag{1}$$

where ρ is surface reflectance and λ is intensity of the illuminant. The $A \Longrightarrow B$ is read as changes in A give change to B. In the forward mapping process, first we give the triangle vertices position $\mathbf{V}_k$ into our NN. Then this NN uses three sigmoid gates which mimic AND gate functions to specify whether the pixel under observation is inside the triangle. If it is inside then the NN assigns a value of another sigmoid unit placed at its output, i.e., $f(x, y)$, as the value of that pixel. If the sigmoid gain is set sufficiently high, it produces near flat intensity surface, except at area closed to triangle edges. The $f(x, y)$ is then superimposed by $\rho\lambda(\mathbf{N} \cdot \mathbf{L}) + A$ to give $F(x, y)$. A smooth shaded representation (Gouraud shading) of $F(x, y)$, i.e., $S(x, y)$, is added to give more flexibility and stability during learning. Instead of explicitly compute $\rho\lambda(\mathbf{N} \cdot \mathbf{L}) + A$, we use implicit lighting, i.e., we take the average pixel values of the teacher images at corresponding projection area of the triangle. It is aimed to implicitly capture the lighting effects instead of explicitly searching the true lighting which is complicated. In the backward learning process, we measure the error $E = \|F(x, y) - G(x, y)\|^2 + \|(S(x, y) - G(x, y)\|^2$, where $G(x, y)$ is the pixel value of teacher image, to be back propagated for updating $\mathbf{V}_k$ as

$$\mathbf{V}_k^m = \mathbf{V}_k^{m-1} - \varsigma\frac{\partial E}{\partial \mathbf{V}_k} + \mu\triangle\mathbf{V}_k^{m-1} \qquad (k = 0, 1, 3), \qquad (2)$$

where ς is learning rate and μ is momentum constant. Where $\partial E / \partial \mathbf{V}_k$ is derived using a chain rule:

$$\frac{\partial E}{\partial \mathbf{V}_k} = \frac{\partial E}{\partial F}\frac{\partial F}{\partial \mathbf{N}}\frac{\partial \mathbf{N}}{\partial \mathbf{v}_k}\frac{\partial \mathbf{v}_k}{\partial \mathbf{V}_k}. \qquad (3)$$

2.2   Learning Transparent Surface

If the triangle is transparent, the changes in vertices position also give rise to different surface normal $\mathbf{N}$, which in turn gives rise to different pixel value $I(x, y)$ due to reflection $\mathbf{R}$ and transmission $\mathbf{T}$ of the light ray in that pixel. We may write this relation as:

$$\{\mathbf{V}_0, \mathbf{V}_1, \mathbf{V}_2\} \Longrightarrow \mathbf{N}_b \Longrightarrow \mathbf{R} + \mathbf{T} \Longrightarrow I(x, y). \qquad (4)$$

$$\mathbf{R} = \mathbf{u} - (2\mathbf{u} \cdot \mathbf{N}_b)\mathbf{N}_b \qquad (5)$$

$$\mathbf{T} = \frac{\eta_i}{\eta_r}\mathbf{u} - (\cos\theta_r - \frac{\eta_i}{\eta_r}\cos\theta_i)\mathbf{N}_b \qquad (6)$$

$$\cos\theta_r = \sqrt{1 - \frac{\eta_i}{\eta_r}^2(1 - \cos^2\theta_i)} \qquad (7)$$

where $\mathbf{u}$ is incoming ray direction as viewed from the center of camera, $\theta_i = -\hat{\mathbf{u}} \cdot \hat{\mathbf{N}}_b$ and $\theta_r = -\hat{\mathbf{T}} \cdot \hat{\mathbf{N}}_b$, and η_i and η_r are respectively the refraction index of incident and refracting materials [16]. Here we use $\mathbf{N}_b$, i.e., interpolated barycentric normal, instead of $\mathbf{N}$. Hence the relation in Equation 4 can also be written as:

$$\{\mathbf{V}_0, \mathbf{V}_1, \mathbf{V}_2\} \Longrightarrow \{w_0, w_1, w_2\} \Longrightarrow \mathbf{N} \Longrightarrow \mathbf{R} + \mathbf{T} \Longrightarrow I(x, y). \qquad (8)$$

The Equations (5) are analytic continuous functions. As in opaque surface reconstruction, we measure the error $E = \|I(\mathbf{R}(x,y), \mathbf{T}(x,y)) - G(x,y)\|^2$ to be back propagated for updating V_k using Equation 2. Whereas $\partial E / \partial V_k$ is computed by simple chain rule as:

$$\frac{\partial E}{\partial V_k} = \frac{\partial E}{\partial I} \frac{\partial I}{\partial (R+T)} \frac{(R+T)}{\partial N_b} \frac{\partial N_b}{\partial w} \frac{\partial w}{\partial v_k} \frac{\partial v_k}{\partial V_k}. \tag{9}$$

2.3   Learning Opaque and Transparent Surfaces

In this study, we implement the ray tracing formulation by blending the flat shaded, the smooth shaded, and the texture mapped images. We view the flat shaded (Figure 2 (c)), the smooth shaded (Figure 2 (d)), and the texture mapped (Figure 2 (f)) outputs respectively preserves the silhouette, the contour, and the transparency information. Since the texture actually applicable to both opaque and transparent surfaces, still we can simultaneously reconstruct these surfaces in a single learning shown in Figure 1 (c). The texture mapped, flat, and smooth shaded model images implicitly store the lighting information, hence, they can be safely added up to represent the object.

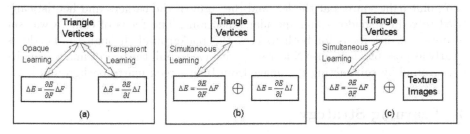

Fig. 1. Two-ways learning (a). Simultaneous learning using ray tracing (b) and texture mapping (c).

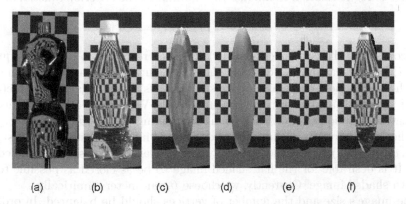

Fig. 2. The objects to reconstructed (a, b). The projection images of the initial 3D polyhedron model rendered as flat shaded (c), smooth shaded d), ray traced (e), and texture mapped (f) images.

In the forward mapping process, the process until $f(x,y)$ is produced is the same as in the opaque surface mapping. However, currently we also map the texture in addition to $(\mathbf{N} \cdot \mathbf{L}) + A$ to give $F(x,y)$. In the backward learning process, again we measure the error $E = \|T(x,y) - G(x,y)\|^2$, where $G(x,y)$ is the pixel value of teacher image, and $T(x,y) = ((G(x,y) + F(x,y) + S(x,y))/3$ is the pixel value of the blended texture image to be back propagated for updating $\mathbf{V}_k$ using Equation 2.

3   Images Acquisition

In this study, we want to reconstruct two transparent objects as shown in Figure 2 (a) and (b): one is purely transparent (woman torso model) and the other contains opaque surface (coca-cola bottle with its opaque cap). We analyze the construction of a regular pattern such as checkerboard pattern put behind that object. The refractive index of woman torso is 1.5 (acrylic) and bottle is 1.3 (plastic filled with water). For each view point, we take an image of the object with the background and also an image of the background only. We acquired eight images for woman torso and six images for bottle. The objects are put on a turn table and captured using a high resolution (HDTV) camera. We used two point light sources at the left and the right of the camera and heuristically tried to reduce shadows and specular reflections. The focus of camera was set to obtain a just focus for both to view the background through the bottle as clearly as possible. For our NN learning, we have to pull the object image from its background by subtracting the image from blue screen matte background [14].

4   Learning Strategy

Our problem to reconstruct the object from its images is surely ill-posed [15] because we rely on limited number of view images. To deal with such problem, we refer to regularization techniques that minimizes the criterion functional $\varepsilon(f)$:

$$\varepsilon(f) = c(f) + \beta s(f). \tag{10}$$

$\varepsilon(f)$ consists of the cost functional $c(f)$ which corresponds to the mean squared error (MSE) at each data point and the stabilizing functional $s(f)$ which specifies the smoothness constraint of the surface. β is a non-negative parameter to adjust the weighting between the two functionals. We can directly apply this regularization technique to our NN learning by defining $c(f) = \|T(x,y) - G(x,y)\|^2$, i.e., the MSE between the blended texture and the teacher images and $s(f) = \|F(x,y) - S(x,y)\|^2$, i.e., the MSE between the flat and the smooth shaded images. It is desirable for the flat shaded image to be as closed as possible to the smooth shaded image. Currently, we choose β parameter empirically.

The image's size and the number of vertices should be balanced. In order to achieve a well balance between them in each reconstruction stage, we perform a hierarchical reconstruction. In addition, our system is a complex system with many degrees of freedom. Its complexity sharply increases as we add the number of vertices to be trained. It is possible to get stuck in local minima or meta-stable results and to also destruct an near optimal state that has been learned in previous steps. To deal with these problems, we refer to the SA optimization method [17].

5 Experiments

In this paper, we performed three experiments that are respectively aimed to observe the 3D reconstruction results during learning, the influence of regularization, and the influence of simulated annealing optimization. These was run on a client Pentium(R) D CPU 3.00GHz PC, with 2.00 GB RAM.

The first experiment was performed at first at level-0 (200x533 pixels teacher images and 162 vertices and 320 faces initial icosahedron model) and then performed at level-1 (300x800 pixels teacher images, and 642 vertices, 1280 faces refined icosahedron model) of hierarchical learning. We set the regularization parameter $\beta = 1.0$ but no SA-optimization. At level-0, we set the learning rate $\eta = 3.0E - 9$, whereas at level-1 we set the learning rate $\eta = 5.0E - 11$. At the two levels we performed 1000 iterations. The frontal and bottom views of results at level-0 was shown in Figure 3, while the results at level-1 was shown in Figure 4.

The second experiment was performed at level-0. We compared the error profiles of the experiments without and with regularization. In the two experiments we set the learning rate $\eta = 3.0E - 9$. When using regularization, we set the regularization parameter $\beta = 1.0$. We normalized the error profile with regularization by dividing it by $(1 + \beta)$. The results of this experiment was shown in Figure 5(a). The regularization was faster and gave lower error, but slightly more unstable.

The third experiment was also performed at level-0. We compared the error profiles of experiment with and without SA-optimization. In the two experiments we use regularization ($\beta = 1.0$). We set the initial temperature $T = 3.0E11$, the

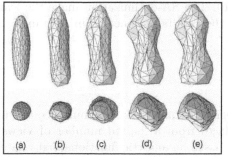 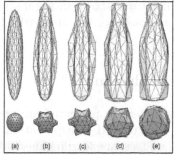

Fig. 3. The first experiment results for the woman torso (left) and cola bottle (right) at level-0 after 0 (a), 10 (b), 50 (c), 100 (d), and 1000 (e) iterations

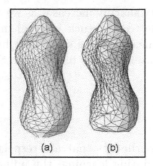 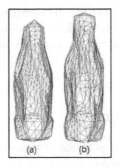

Fig. 4. The first experiment results for the woman torso (left) and cola bottle (right) at level-1 after 0 (a) and 1000 (b) iterations

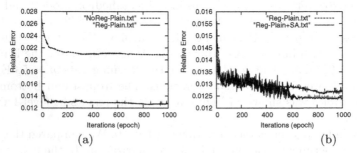

Fig. 5. The second (a) and the third (b) experiments result

Table 1. Results summary

	NoReg-Plain	Reg-Plain	Reg-Plain+SA
Lowest relative error	0.01164	0.00319	0.00315
Comp. time (1000 iterations)	34.47 mins	36.96 mins	37.13 mins.

cooling rate $\zeta = 0.99$, and the learning rate $\eta = 3.0E - 9$. The results of this experiment was shown in Figure 5(b). The SA-optimization make the learning faster to converge. We summarized the results obtained from each experiment in Table 1.

6   Conclusion

In this paper, we presented an integrated framework to simultaneously reconstruct opaque and transparent surfaces from a limited number of views. We formulated a shape learning method based on analytic functions that relates the pixel value inside training images and the vertices of an initial 3D shape. Such functions provide a way to directly refine the vertices based on images difference, instead of heuristically establish some trial vertices positions. We incorporated ray tracing formulation to ensure its generality and future use, and implemented this formulation as texture mapping to ensure its efficiency and practicality. To improve the reconstruction results we implemented some strategies including regularization, hierarchical learning and SA-optimization. We believe our method will further open ways for practical integration of computer vision and computer graphics through neural network learning.

References

1. Matusik, M., Hanspeter, P., Zieglar, R., Ngan, N., McMillan, L.: Acquisition and Rendering of Transparent and Refractive Objects, Rendering Techniques, pp. 267–278 (2002)
2. Zongker, D.E., Werner, D.M., Curless, B., Salesin, D.: Environment Matting and Compositing, SIGGRAPH, pp. 205–214 (1999)
3. Bolle, R.M., Vemuri, B.C.: On three-dimensional surface reconstruction methods. IEEE Trans. on PAMI 13(1), 1–13 (1991)
4. Saito, M., Kashiwagi, H., Sato, Y., Ikeuchi, K.: Measurement of Surface Orientations of Transparent Objects Using Polarization in Highlight, CVPR, p. 1381 (1999)
5. Interrante, V., Fuchs, H., Pizer, S.M.: Conveying the 3D Shape of Smoothly Curving Transparent Surfaces via Texture. IEEE Trans. on VCG 3, 2 (1997)
6. Murase, H.: Surface Shape Reconstruction of a Nonrigid Transport Object Using Refraction and Motion. IEEE Trans. on PAMI 14(10), 1045–1052 (1992)
7. Hata, S., Saitoh, Y., Kumamura, S., Kaida, K.: Shape Extraction of Transparent Object Using Genetic Algorithm, ICPR96, D93.6 (1996)
8. Chuang, Y., Zongker, E., Hindorff, J., Curless, B., Salesin, D., Szeliski, R.: Environment matting extensions: towards higher accuracy, SIGGRAPH, pp. 121–130 (2000)
9. Wexler, Y., Fitzgibbon, A.W., Zisserman, A.: Image-based Environment matting, Rendering Techniques, pp. 279–290 (2002)
10. Szeliski, R., Avidan, S., Anandan, P.: Layer Extraction from Multiple Images Containing Reflections and Transparency, CVPR, p. 1246 (2000)
11. Eckert, G., Wingbermuhle, J., Niem, W.: Mesh Based Shape Refinement for Reconstructing 3D-Objects from Multiple Images, CVMP04, pp. 103–110 (2004)
12. Yaguchi, S., Saito, H.: Mesh Based 3D Shape Deformation for Image Based Rendering from Uncalibrated Multiple Views, ICAT05 (2005)
13. Nobuhara, S., Matsuyama, T.: Dynamic 3D Shape from Multi-Viewpoint Images using Deformable Mesh Models. In: Proc. of 3rd Int. Symposium on Image and Signal Processing and Analysis, pp. 192–197 (2003)
14. Smith, A.R., Blinn, J.F.: Blue Screen Matting, SIGGRAPH, pp. 259–268 (1996)
15. Chen, Z., Haykin, S.: On Different Facets of Regularization Theory. Neural Computation 14(12), 2791–2846 (2002)
16. Hearn, D., Baker, M.P.: Computer Graphics: C Version, Upper Saddle River. Prentice Hall, Englewood Cliffs (1998)
17. Romeo, F., Vincentelli, A.S.: A theoretical framework for Simulated Annealing. Algorithmica 6, 302–345 (1991)

Sedimentological Analysis of Sands

Cristina Lira and Pedro Pina

CERENA, Instituto Superior Técnico, Lisboa, Portugal

Abstract. This paper presents a practical sequence to study sand grains at the macroscopical scale. The approach consists of two mains phases, the recognition of the grains and the assessment of some of its characteristics. The method is validated on the dimensional features by comparison with a sieving procedure through the analysis of eight large sand samples of different locations.

1 Introduction, Motivation and Data Sets

The understanding of sedimentary grains properties allows the acquisition of extremely useful information on their genesis and on the processes of transportation and deposition involved but also on the establishement of correlations between different types of grains and on the discovery of mineral resources [1].

The dimension or size of sand grains is one of the most important properties, since its simple measurement very often allows characterizing and distinguishing, in a roughly matter, different types of deposits. Anyhow, a more exhaustive study is naturally desirable, since the evaluation of properties related to the shape or to the mineral composition permits to better evaluate these deposits. The morphometric study of particles, *i.e.*, the study of its shape, elongation and roundness, among others, allows the additional acquisition of important information about the agents of transportation and the conditions of deposition.

Measuring size features has been performed by several approaches at laboratorial and industrial levels, being the mechanical sieving technique the most currently used. This established technique, allows the study of samples of large dimensions but requires long operational time intervals until a final result is obtained requiring, in addition, the permanent presence of human operators.

Assessing morphometric properties of sand particles is mainly performed at laboratorial level using manual techniques but with quite insignificant statistics essentially due to fastidious and time consuming measurements.

The possibility of applying digital imaging to obtain multiple features of a grain, namely granulometry, morphometry and mineralogical composition, on samples of larger dimension, is a hypothesis that naturally emerges (good overview in [2]). Quite surprisingly, the published studies related to the automation of such approaches in sedimentology at the macroscopical scale are quite restrict. The few relevant exceptions applied image analysis to consolidated sediments at the microscopical scale [3,4,5,6], to unconsolidated aggregates of different sizes [7,8,9], but none on sands.

J. Martí et al. (Eds.): IbPRIA 2007, Part II, LNCS 4478, pp. 388–395, 2007.
© Springer-Verlag Berlin Heidelberg 2007

Thus, the main objective of this paper is to show that an image analysis based mathematical morphology methodology is able to advantageously substitute the classical granulometric and morphometric methods not only in scientific terms (additional measures, more robust and reproducible results with higher statistical significance) but also in operational terms (faster evaluation and higher operator autonomy). Currently, we are only dealing with the situation where a low overlapping between grains is permitted to occur. Several types of sands from different deposits were collected and used in this investigation. Their origin in the field is quite distinct since they come from a river, a dune, a beach and a continental platform. This spatial diversity permits to better evaluate the sensibility of our approach to a larger range of characteristics presented by different types of sands. In particular, one river sample (denoted as A5), one dune sample (SCP7 Sancha), five beach samples (PFaro, F260, F263, F271 and F275) and one platform sample (9460) were used (eight in a total). These samples contained different textural and compositional characteristics (finer to coarser grains, mainly of quartz, feldspars, heavy minerals and bioclasts). The samples collected in beach environment are, in general, better calibrated (narrower granulometrical distributions) and exhibit a more uniform mineralogical composition than the samples from other locations (see examples in Fig. 1).

2 Methodology

This section describes the proposed sequence, which is constituted by image acquisition, grain recognition and measurement assessment phases.

2.1 Image Acquisition

The acquisition of images was performed using a flatbed colour scanner. Using a scanner allowed us to obtain in a simple and reliable way, large digital images of the samples of sands. The particles are facing the scanner glass with acceptable narrow size ranges, so it can be considered that all of them are correctly focused. Moreover, in order to avoid the existence of shadows a black background was used. The grains of the sands of the different samples were quartered and winnowed over the scanner glass, which was previously protected with a transparency, and placed in such a way that the contact is permitted but not the

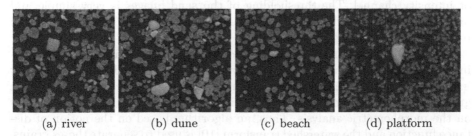

(a) river   (b) dune   (c) beach   (d) platform

Fig. 1. Close views of the sands under study (the height of each image is about 1 cm)

overlapping between them. The situation where the overlapping is permitted, like it happens in the field, is not yet addressed in this paper but is already under development and will be published in a near future.

In the particular case of the sands under study, the spatial resolution fixed to acquire the images is 1200 dpi, since the limit of the minor granulometrical sand class available and measured by other methods is 0.063 mm. This way, the chosen spatial resolution allows identifying the smallest structure in these types of sands with at least a region of 3 x 3 pixels. Digital images were acquired in true colour mode (RGB), with a spatial resolution of 1200 dpi, with sizes approximately equal to 4500 x 4500 pixels. An example of the dimension of images acquired is presented in Fig. 2.

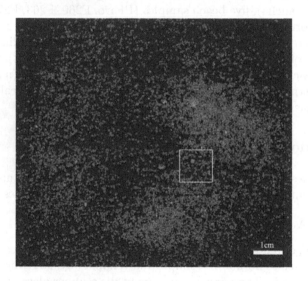

Fig. 2. Complete sand sample under stdy

2.2   Grain Recognition

At this stage of the methodology, colour information is not necessary, thus the RGB bands were converted into one single band given by their mean image or intensity channel. The thresholding of the sand images is very simple and direct, and one single threshold value is enough to correctly separate the black background from the lighter grains.

The main problem on the binary images resides in the grains that are touching each other and that need to be separated or segmented for the posterior individual analysis. This situation poses no problem for the computation of the granulometry by openings of increasing size but can produce an important bias on the morphometric analysis. Thus, an algorithm based on the notion of distance function and the watershed transform [10] is used to separate theses grains. It consists of the following main steps:

1. *Distance function*: The computation of a distance function of the grains indicates the distance that each of its pixels is from its borders (for higher distances, higher grey levels);
2. *Negative*: Computation of the negative image of the distance function;
3. *Closing*: Filtering to eliminate local extrema with low significance in order to minimize the overssegmentation effect;
4. *Watershed*: Computed on the filtered image, whose resulting catchments basins constitute the division lines between adjacent sand particles. The complementary image of those basins is subtracted to the binary image and a segmented binary image of sand particles is obtained.

The segmentation results obtained for all the studied images are highly satisfactory. This approach works correctly for grains touching each other and also in grains where the overlapping degree does not exceed about 20% of the respective surface. An example of this procedure is presented in Fig. 3.

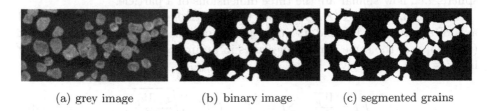

(a) grey image   (b) binary image   (c) segmented grains

Fig. 3. Segmentation of grains touching each other

2.3 Measurements Assessment

Grain size. The sand particles tend to locate themselves with their major and intermediate axis perpendicular to the plane of the scanner glass. In the sieving method, the axis that controls the passages of the particles through the sieve apertures is the intermediate axis. Thus, the particle orientation against the scanner glass permits image analysis to analyse the same fundamental axis.

In what concerns some operator to deal with this dimesnional feature, the morphological opening, $\gamma(X)$, is capable of modeling the traditional sieving processes [11], by simulating the same processes of the sieves. Particles are progressively eliminated by increasing the size of the structuring element used and their surface is reduced as in the sieving procedure whereas the size of the sieve is reduced. In this case, the initial image X is "sieved" by a squared structuring element B of size λ that eliminates the regions of the grains that do not contain it completely. By measuring the area of the remaining grains, one obtains the size distribution function, $S(X, \lambda)$, cumulative function in measure which is defined by the proportion of points x, that were eliminated by applying openings of size λ:

$$S(X, \lambda) = \frac{Area(X) - Area(\varphi^{\lambda B}(X))}{Area(X)} . \tag{1}$$

In order to compare both granulometries, the one obtained from the image analysis data and the one obtianed from sieve data, some additional calculations are necessary. In fact, the sieving technique measures the weight of the grains passing through sieves while image analysis measures the area of the grains. Thus, in order to compare both methods, the measured areas need to be transformed into weight. This transformation is made presently in a simple form by assuming that all particles are spheres and have the same density. This way, the volume V is computed with grain radius r:

$$r = \sqrt{\frac{area}{\pi}} \quad V = \frac{4}{3}\pi r^3 \; . \tag{2}$$

Grain shape. The shape of a particle is defined as the spatial geometric form of a grain [12]. The parameters more commonly used in sedimentology to describe shape are: sphericity, shape, elongation and circularity indexes. Sphericity measures the degree to which a particle shape is similar to the shape of a perfect sphere, *i.e.*, how similar are the three dimensions of a particle.

The elongation index (EI) is defined by the ratio between the minor projected axis of a particular W_p and its major projected axis L_p [13], the shape index (SI) [14] uses the same particle measures in an inverse way, and the circularity indexes (CI) [14], is given by:

$$EI = \frac{W_p}{L_p} \quad SI = \frac{L_p}{W_p} \quad CI = \sqrt{\frac{L_p.W_p}{L_p^2}} \; . \tag{3}$$

3   Results

Grain Size. The dimensions of the grains of sand of the eight samples under study were measured by the classical sieving procedure and by the application of openings of increasing size.

The sieving technique consists of using a column of sieves, which are meshes or metallic grids with different square apertures, placed from the smallest (bottom) to the largest one (top), over which is placed the sand material. The vibration of the column of sieves, permits to the grains smaller than the mesh of a certain grid to pass over the aperture and to fall into the adjacent smaller grid, whereas the grains bigger than those aperture are retained in that sieve. The size of the sieve is given as the size of the aperture measured perpendicularly to the wires through the centre of the hollow space. The results are normally presented in the form of cumulative granulometrical curves of the weight of grains between two consecutive sieve sizes. This sieving operation was performed in laboratory for each one of the eight samples. The same samples were analysed through their images and the respective granulometries were also computed. The granulometries computed by both techniques are presented for each sample in the eight graphics of Fig. 4. It can be noticed, that all size distributions obtained through the two techniques present a very similar behaviour, except in one situation: the matching is quite perfect in 5 samples (A5, PFaro,F260, F263 and F275), very good in 2 samples (SCP7 Sancha and F271) and more or less acceptable in 1 sample (9460). The discrepancy in this last case is possibly due to the characteristics of the constitutants of the sample (located in the platform), which presents a higher frequency of grains in the smaller dimension class maybe not correctly represented within the spatial resolution of the images, leading to an underestimation of the grains under 0.063 mm by the image analysis approach. We think that the acquisition of images with a sensor with a higher spatial resolution could overcome this problem in samples presenting finer grains. Anyhow, it can be concluded, from the examples studied, that both curves have the same behaviour and that image analysis distributions are extremely near the reference one given by the sieving technique.

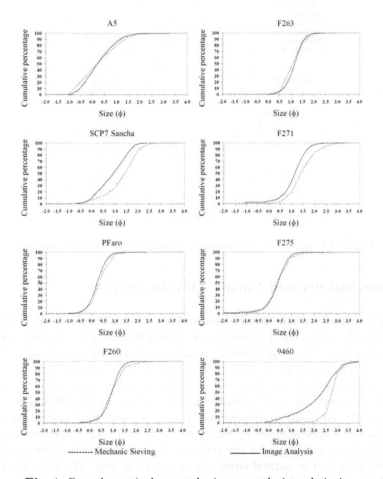

Fig. 4. Granulometrical curves by image analysis and sieving

Grain Shape. In what concerns morphometric features, we have computed for each one of the approximately 10 000 grains contained into each one of the eight samples, the parameters previosuly defined. By projecting the elongation, shape and circularity indexes into a triangular diagram we are able to identify three clusters (Fig. 5): one constituted by the river and platform samples(cluster indicated as 1), another by the dune sample and a beach sample collected closer to the dune (cluster 2) and the last one constituted by the 4 beach samples (cluster 3). This result confirms what was somehow expected, that the sand samples located in different locations should present different morphometries, but which was not possible to clearly demonstrate before due to very poor statistics given by very few grains manually analysed.

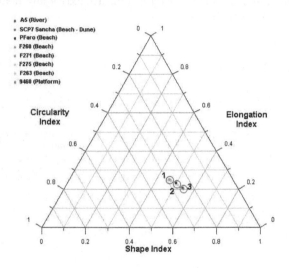

Fig. 5. Projection of morphometric features in a triangular diagram

4   Conclusions and Future Developments

We can conclude that the results obtained by the image analysis approach presented in this paper and applied to the situation were the touching and small overlapping of grains is permitted are highly satisfactory. Not only the comparison of the granulometrical curves obtained by image analysis and sieving present a high matching degree, but also, the morphometric features extracted permitted to verify on a larger population of sand grains the differences between samples collected in different locations. It can be concluded that in the present situation, the image analysis approach can substitute advantageously the classical techniques. Dealing with the real situation in the field, where overlapping between grains is the normal situation, is our next step. The possibility of being able to compute the granulometry through the images captured "in situ", avoiding the necessity of collecting the samples to posterior laboratorial analysis, is our current research objective. One possible way is to estimate the complete granulometry from the partial views of the grains using the random closed sets approach, in particular the dead leaves model, proposed by Matheron in the 1960's.

Acknowledgments. This paper was developed in the frame of the projects POCTI/ECM/37998/2001 and POCTI/ECM/46255/2002 funded by Fundação para a Ciência e a Tecnologia (Portugal).

References

1. Friedman, G.M., Sanders, J.E.: Principles of Sedimentology. Wiley, New York (1979)
2. Francus, P.: Image analysis, sediments and paleoenvironments. Kluwer Academic Publishers, Dordrecht (2004)
3. Francus, P.: An image-analysis technique to measure grain-size variation in thin section of soft clastic sediment. Sedimentary Geology 121, 289–298 (1998)
4. Heilbronner, R.: Automatic grain boundary detection and size analysis using polarization micrographs or orientation images. Jour. Struc. Geology 22, 969–981 (2000)
5. Rogen, B., Gommesen, L.E., Fabricius, I.L.: Grain size distribution of chalk from image analysis of electron micrographs. Comput. & Geosc. 27, 1071–1080 (2001)
6. Mertens, G., Elsen, J.: Use of computer assisted image analysis for the determination of the grain-size distribution of sands used in mortars. Cement and Concrete Research 36, 1453–1459 (2006)
7. Persson, A.L.: Image analysis of shape and size of fine aggregates. Engineering Geology 50, 177–186 (1998)
8. Balagurunathan, Y., Dougherty, E., Bilinski, S.F., Bilinski, H., Vdovic, N.: Morphological granulometric analysis of sediment images. Image Analysis and Stereology 20, 87–89 (2001)
9. Graham, D.J., Reid, I., Rice, S.P.: Automated sizing of coarse-grained sediments: Image processing procedures. Mathematical Geology 37(1), 1–28 (2005)
10. Beucher, S.: Lantuéjoul, Ch.: Use of watershed in contour detection. In: Proc. Int. Workshop on Image Processing: Real-Time Edge and Motion Detection/Estimation. Rennes, pp. 2.1–2.12 (1979)
11. Matheron, G.: Random sets and integral geometry. Wiley, New York (1975)
12. Carver, E.R.: Procedures in sedimentary petrology. Wiley, New York (1971)
13. Folk, R.L.: Petrology of sedimentary rocks. Hemphill Pub. Co., Austin (1965)
14. Davis, J.C.: Statistical and data analysis in geology. Wiley, New York (2002)

Catadioptric Camera Calibration by Polarization Imaging

O. Morel, R. Seulin, and D. Fofi

Laboratoire Le2i UMR-CNRS 5158, IUT Le Creusot, 12 rue de la Fonderie,
71200 Le Creusot, France

Abstract. A new efficient method of calibration for catadioptric sensors is presented in this paper. It is based on an accurate measurement of the three-dimensional parameters of the mirror by means of polarization imaging. While inserting a rotating polarizer between the camera and the mirror, the system is automatically calibrated without any calibration patterns. Moreover it permits to relax most of the constraints related to the calibration of the catadioptric systems. From the measurement of three-dimensional parameters, we apply the generic calibration concept to calibrate the catadioptric sensor. The influence of the disturbed measurement of the parameters on the reconstruction of a synthetic scene is presented. Finally, experiments prove the validity of the method with some preliminary results on three-dimensional reconstruction.

1 Introduction

Conventional perspective cameras have limited fields of view that make them restrictive in some applications such as robotics, videosurveillance and so on. A way to enhance the field of view is to place a mirror with surface of revolution in front of the camera so that the scene reflects on the mirror omnidirectionaly. Such a system, composed of both lenses (dioptric) and mirrors (catoptric) for image formation, is called catadioptric. Several configurations exist, and those statisfaying the Single View Point constraint are described in [1].

We developed a new approach of calibrating catadioptric sensor by polarization imaging. This method enables to calibrate all mirror shapes since it is based on the measurement of the three-dimensional parameters such as: height and normals orientations of the surface. The only constraint is that an orthographic camera has to be used. To calibrate the system we apply the generic calibration concept developed by Sturm and Ramalingam [2,3].

The article is structured as follows. Next section reminds previous work on paracatadioptric calibration since the measurement of the surface normals by polarization imaging induces orthographic projection. Then, after presenting some basic knowledge about polarization imaging, we detail how to calibrate the sensor with the generic calibration concept. In section 4, simulations are presented to illustrate the influence of the parameters measurement on the quality of the reconstruction. Preliminary results on a calibrated spherical mirror are also described. Finally, the paper ends with a conclusion and a few words about future work to be undertaken.

J. Martí et al. (Eds.): IbPRIA 2007, Part II, LNCS 4478, pp. 396–403, 2007.

2   Catadioptric Cameras Calibration

2.1   Previous Work

The most obvious used calibration method is an approach based on the image
of the mirror's bounding circle [4,5]. It has the main advantage of being easily
automated, but the mirror has to be constructed properly so that the mirror
boundary accurately encodes the intrinsic parameters. In the field of paracatadioptric camera calibration, more robust methods are based on the fitting of
lines projected onto the mirror [6,7,8]. This approach has also some shortcomings: lines have to be precisely detected and the optical axis of the camera is
assumed aligned with the symmetry axis of the paraboloid.

2.2   The Generic Calibration Concept

The previous calibration methods for omnidirectional catadioptric sensors assume that: *(i)* the mirror shape is perfectly known; *(ii)* the alignment of the
sensor is perfect so that the single viewpoint constraint is satisfied; *(iii)* the
projection model can be easily parametrized. Some methods relax the second
constraint and a few relax the first, but before some recent works [9,10,2] calibrating methods always underlie an explicit parametric model of projection. This
new model has the advantage of working for any type of camera (catadioptric
systems, central cameras with or without distortion, axial cameras, etc.) and to
handle heterogeneous systems [3] (for instance, a sensor composed of an omnidirectional camera and a perspective camera). By applying polarization imaging
to this method, our system enables catadioptric sensor calibration by relaxing
the three constraints listed above: *(i)*, *(ii)* and *(iii)*.

3   Polarization Imaging

Polarization imaging enables to provide three-dimensional information of the
specular objects thanks to the "Shape from polarization" method [11,12]. The
physical principle is the following: after being reflected, an unpolarized light
wave becomes partially linearly polarized, depending on the surface normal and
on the refractive index of the media it impinges on. A partially linearly polarized
light has three parameters: the light magnitude I, the degree of polarization ρ
and the angle of polarization φ.

To calibrate the mirror used in our catadioptric sensor, the polarization state
of the reflected light is measured thanks to a rotating polarizer placed between
the camera and the mirror. The complete sensor (mirror and camera) and the
polarizer are placed into a cylinder made of paper sheet (Fig. 1). Each light
intensity of pixels is linked to the angle of the polarizer and to the polarization
parameters by the following equation:

$$I_p(\alpha) = \frac{I}{2}\left(\rho \cos\left(2\alpha - 2\varphi\right) + 1\right), \tag{1}$$

where α is the polarizer angle. The purpose of polarization imaging is to compute the three parameters, I, φ, and ρ, by interpolating this formula. Fig. 2 shows the image of the degree and the angle of polarization of a spherical mirror.

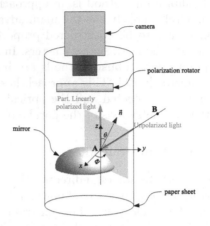

Fig. 1. Polarization imaging: after being reflected by the mirror, the light becomes partially linearly polarized

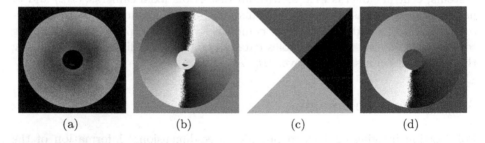

(a)   (b)   (c)   (d)

Fig. 2. Images of the polarization parameters that are needed to reconstruct the mirror shape: (a) degree of polarization ($\rho \in [0,1]$), (b) angle of polarization ($\varphi \in [0,\pi]$); and disambiguation of the azimuth angle: (c) segmented image ($I_{quad} \in \{0,1,2,3\}$), (d) image of the resulting azimuth angle ϕ ($\phi \in [-\pi/2, 3\pi/2]$).

3.1 Relationship Between the Polarization Parameters and the Normals

Wolff and Boult have demonstrated how to determine constraints on surface normals by using the Fresnel reflectance model [13]. The surface of the mirror is assumed to be continuous and described by a Cartesian expression: $z = f(x,y)$.

Therefore, each surface normal is given by the following non-normalized expression:

$$n = \begin{bmatrix} -\frac{\partial f(x,y)}{\partial x} \\ -\frac{\partial f(x,y)}{\partial y} \\ 1 \end{bmatrix} = \begin{bmatrix} p = \tan\theta\cos\phi \\ q = \tan\theta\sin\phi \\ 1 \end{bmatrix}. \tag{2}$$

The aim of "Shape from polarization" is to compute the normals from the angles θ and ϕ. By combining Fresnel formulas and the Snell-Descartes law one can find a relationship between the degree of polarization ρ and the zenith angle θ [12]. For specular metallic surfaces, the following formula can be applied [14]:

$$\rho(\theta) = \frac{2n\tan\theta\sin\theta}{\tan^2\theta\sin^2\theta + |\hat{n}|^2}, \tag{3}$$

where $\hat{n} = n(1 + i\kappa)$ is the complex refractive index of the mirror.

The reflected light becomes partially linearly polarized according to the normal of the plane of incidence. Because our imaging system uses a telecentric lens, orthographic projection is assumed and the azimuth angle ϕ can be inferred from the angle of polarization φ:

$$\phi = \varphi \pm \pi/2. \tag{4}$$

3.2   Disambiguation of the Normals

From the equations (3) and (4) the surface normals are determined with an ambiguity. Since mirrors used in catadioptric vision are of convex and revolution shape, a segmented image I_{quad} can be directly computed from the near center of the mirror (Fig. 2(c)). This image has four gray levels that represent the four quadrants oriented with an angle in $]0, \pi/2[$. The algorithm of the disambiguation process described in [15] is applied with the segmented image I_{quad} and the angle of polarization image φ:

1. $\phi = \varphi - \frac{\pi}{2}$,
2. $\phi = \phi + \pi$ if $[(I_{quad} = 0) \wedge (\phi \leq 0)] \vee [I_{quad} = 1] \vee [(I_{quad} = 3) \wedge (\phi \geq 0)]$,

where $\wedge$ and $\vee$ represent, respectively, the logical operators AND and OR. The result of the disambiguation is presented Fig. 2(d).

3.3   Calibration

To calibrate our imaging system, we use the generic calibration concept [16]. The concept considers an image as a collection of pixels, and each pixel measures the light along a particular 3D ray. Thus, calibration is the determination of all projection rays and their correspondence with pixels. A 3d-ray is represented here by a couple of points which belongs to the ray:

$$\mathbf{A} = [x_a, y_a, z_a]^T, \mathbf{B} = [x_b, y_b, z_b]^T. \tag{5}$$

To get these points, the 3D surface of the mirror has to be computed. Once the normals are given by polarization imaging, the surface shape of the mirror (z) can be computed thanks to the Frankot-Chellappa algorithm [17]. This integration process gives us the surface height of the mirror with a constant of integration. Nevertheless, this constant is not required since the orthographic projection is assumed. To calibrate the sensor, let us take the point $\mathbf{A} = [x, y, z]^T$, that both belongs to the mirror surface and the 3D-ray, be the first point of the ray (Fig. 1). The second point $\mathbf{B}$ of the ray can be written as:

$$\mathbf{B} = \mathbf{A} + k \left[\tan 2\theta \cos \phi, \tan 2\theta \sin \phi, 1 \right]^T, \tag{6}$$

where k is a non-null constant.

4   Experiments

4.1   Simulations

We have previously shown that the three-dimensional parameters of the mirror (z, θ, ϕ) are required to calibrate the catadioptric system according to the generic calibration concept. To illustrate the influence of the parameters on the reconstruction quality, the normals angles θ and ϕ were computed from a theoretical paraboloidal mirror with a 7° misalignment from the camera optical axis. The parameters are then disturbed by gaussian noise and a synthetic scene is reconstructed thanks to the generic calibration concept. Fig. 3(a) and Fig. 3(b) show respectively reconstruction error of a synthetic scene induced by noisy measurement of θ and ϕ.

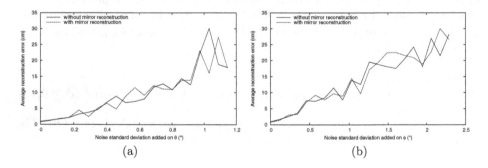

(a)   (b)

Fig. 3. Reconstruction error induced by noisy measurement of the normals parameters: (a) θ angle, (b) ϕ angle

The scene is reconstructed with or without the mirror reconstruction meaning that the integration process is carried out or not. Fig. 3 shows, on the one hand, that the scene reconstruction is quite sensitive to the measurement of the parameters θ and ϕ. On the other hand, the integration process is not required,

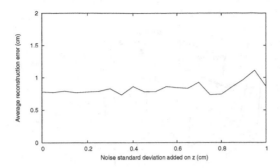

Fig. 4. Reconstruction error induced by noisy calculation of the mirror height z

and we can assume that the z parameter is negligible. In addition, Fig. 4 shows reconstruction error of the scene by only adding gaussian noise to the z mirror height. The reconstruction quality remains good even if the mirror height is very noisy (the mirror height is $1cm$ and the radius is $2cm$).

4.2 Preliminary Results

Preliminary results were carried out with a catadioptric sensor made of a camera with a telecentric lens and a calibrated spherical mirror $(radius = 1cm)$. Let us notice that our system did not satisfy the single view point constraint. Nevertheless this property is not required here for the three-dimensional reconstruction of a scene. As described in section 3, our catadioptric sensor is calibrated by measuring the three-dimensional parameters of the mirror with a liquid crystal polarization rotator placed between the camera and the mirror. To evaluate the accuracy of our system, we compare the parameters (θ, ϕ and z) obtained with our system to the theoretical parameters of the mirror (Fig. 5).

The mean quadratic errors of the angles θ and ϕ are respectively $0.49°$ and $1.02°$. Fig. 6 shows the reconstruction of the synthetic scene by taking the calibration made by polarization imaging. This scene represents a room of size $500 \times 500 \times 250cm$ with elements such as windows, doors and table. 3 images

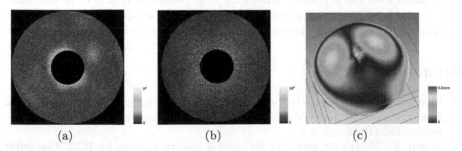

(a)   (b)   (c)

Fig. 5. Measurement errors of the three-dimensional parameters: (a) angle θ, (b) angle ϕ and (c) deviation map of the mirror z

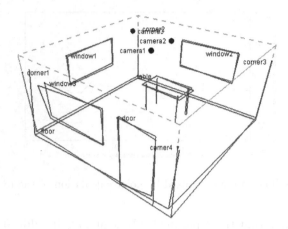

Fig. 6. Simulation of the reconstruction: theoretical scene in blue and reconstruted scene in red. Black dots depict the three locations of the sensor.

of the catadioptric sensor are used to triangulate the points of the scene. Since the mirror is spherical, slants of the surface are high and three-dimensional reconstruction errors may increase highly. Nevertheless, the synthetic scene is well reconstructed with an average error of $9.68cm$.

5   Conclusion

In this paper, a new efficient calibration method for catadioptric sensors has been presented. This method is based on the three-dimensional parameters measurement of the mirror thanks to polarization imaging. The calibration can be performed "in one click" even by a non-specialist as it only requires an optical apparatus, no image processing and no calibration pattern. Contrary to traditional methods, it deals with misalignment of the sensor and work for any shape of mirror (regular or not). Experimental results prove that the sensor is properly calibrated and a satisfactory three-dimensional reconstruction of the scene can be obtained. We have also shown that the 3D-shape of the mirror can be neglected in comparison with the normals orientations. A parabolic mirror is to be manufacturated and future work will consist in creating a paracatadioptric sensor in order to compare our method to other methods known in the litterature on real scenes.

References

1. Baker, S., Nayar, S.K.: A theory of catadioptric image formation. In: International Conference on Computer Vision, pp. 35–42. IEEE Computer Society Press, Washington, DC (1998)
2. Sturm, P.: Multi-view geometry for general camera models. In: IEEE Computer Vision and Pattern Recognition, vol. 1, pp. 206–212. IEEE Computer Society, Washington, DC (2005)

3. Ramalingam, S., Lodha, S.K., Sturm, P.: A generic structure-from-motion framework. Computer Vision and Image Understanding 103(3), 218–228 (2006)
4. Yagi, Y., Kawato, S., Tsuji, S.: Real-time omnidirectional image sensor (copis) for vision-guided navigation. IEEE Trans. Robotics and Automation 10(1), 11–22 (1994)
5. Kang, S.: Catadioptric self-calibration. In: IEEE Computer Vision and Pattern Recognition. pp. 1201–1207 (2000)
6. Geyer, C., Daniilidis, K.: Paracatadioptric camera calibration. IEEE Trans. Pattern Analysis and Machine Intelligence 24(5), 687–695 (2002)
7. Barreto, J.P., Araujo, H.: Paracatadioptric camera calibration using lines. International Conference on Computer Vision 02, 1359–1365 (2003)
8. Vanderportaele, B., Cattoen, M., Marthon, P., Gurdjos, P.: A new linear calibration method for paracatadioptric cameras. International Conference on Pattern Recognition 4, 647–651 (2006)
9. Grossberg, M.D., Nayar, S.K.: A general imaging model and a method for finding its parameters. International Conference on Computer Vision 2, 108–115 (2001)
10. Pless, R.: Using many cameras as one. IEEE Computer Vision and Pattern Recognition 2, 587–593 (2003)
11. Rahmann, S.: Reconstruction of quadrics from two polarization views. In: Perales, F.J., Campilho, A., Pérez, N., Sanfeliu, A. (eds.) IbPRIA 2003. LNCS, vol. 2652, pp. 810–820. Springer, Heidelberg (2003)
12. Miyazaki, D., Kagesawa, M., Ikeuchi, K.: Transparent surface modeling from a pair of polarization images. IEEE Trans. Pattern Analysis and Machine Intelligence 26(1), 73–82 (2004)
13. Wolff, L.B., Boult, T.E.: Constraining object features using a polarization reflectance model. IEEE Trans. Pattern Analysis and Machine Intelligence 13(7), 635–657 (1991)
14. Morel, O., Stolz, C., Meriaudeau, F., Gorria, P.: Three-dimensional inspection of highly-reflective metallic objects by polarization imaging. Electronic Imaging Newsletter 15(2), 4 (2005)
15. Morel, O., Stolz, C., Meriaudeau, F., Gorria, P.: Active lighting applied to 3d reconstruction of specular metallic surfaces by polarization imaging. Applied Optics 45(17), 4062–4068 (2006)
16. Sturm, P., Ramalingam, S.: A generic concept for camera calibration. In: European Conference on Computer Vision, Prague, Czech Republic, vol. 2, pp. 1–13. Springer, Heidelberg (2004)
17. Frankot, R., Chellappa, R.: A method for enforcing integrability in shape from shading algorithms. IEEE Trans. Pattern Analysis and Machine Intelligence 10(4), 439–451 (1988)

Stochastic Local Search for Omnidirectional Catadioptric Stereovision Design

G. Dequen, L. Devendeville, and E. Mouaddib

CREA, LaRIA, CNRS, Université de Picardie
33 rue Saint Leu
80039 Amiens Cedex 1, France
{gilles.dequen,laure.devendeville,mouaddib}@u-picardie.fr

Abstract. This paper deals with a compact catadioptric omnidirectional stereovision system based on a single camera and multi-mirrors (at least two mirrors). Many configurations were empirically designed in previous works with the aim to obtain a good 3D reconstruction accuracy. In this paper, we propose to use optimization techniques for omnidirectional catadioptric stereovision design, by using a stochastic local search method in order to find a good sensor (number, relative positions and sizes of mirrors). We explain principles of our approach and provide automatically designed sensors with a number of mirrors from two to nine. We finally simulate the 3D-reconstruction of a real environment modeled under a ray-tracing software with some of these sensors.

1 Introduction

It is very well stated that omnidirectional catadioptric vision has several advantages thanks to its wide view field. It is achieved by using convex mirrors and a conventional camera, offering a wide view field. The conventional omnidirectional stereovision systems employ either a pair of rotating cameras simultaneously [1] or two omnidirectional catadioptric cameras [7]. The first solution is better to obtain very good resolution, but it requires the rotation of the cameras and this prevents treating scenes with moving objects. The second approach avoids this problem; but it needs two cameras and two mirrors, thus increasing the weight and size of the sensor. It also has all the conventional stereovision disadvantages: synchronization problems between the cameras and their calibrations, optical response differences between cameras, and so on. Another way to recover stereovision is to exploit only one camera that observes several mirrors. This makes it possible to design sensors which have many advantages compared to the systems which use several cameras. These advantages are: single calibration, no synchronization problem, similar optical response, wide view field, rigid link between mirrors, and finally a reduced cost. Several works have dealt with a single camera and planar mirrors [2,3]. We restrict our overview to the stereo system based on a single camera (single lens) and convex mirrors. A stereo vision system based on a single conventional camera (one lens) and two specular spheres "SPHEREO" (convex mirrors) was probably used first by [9].

J. Martí et al. (Eds.): IbPRIA 2007, Part II, LNCS 4478, pp. 404–411, 2007.

In [9], the authors studied four stereo systems with a single camera looking at mirrors. They discussed the case of all single view point systems (planar, ellipsoidal, hyperboloidal and paraboloidal). A stereovision system that used two vertically aligned mirrors with different curvatures ("two-biconvex lobes") has been proposed by [12]. This approach is not suitable for small sensors; so, more recently, [11], proposed a single camera with nine spherical (they are easier to make) mirrors: a principal one with eight others around it.

Our paper aims to optimize (in the sense of the increasing of accuracy and isotropy) the design of the stereovision system using a single camera and multi-mirrors [8]. This problem can be seen as an analysis of stereovision quality ([10,13], for example can be referred to). Usually, only two mirrors are considered to design these sensors without any optimization process. In this work, we study the behavior of these sensors if we modify the number (at least two), the positions and the sizes of mirrors.

As the search-space has an exponential size depending on the number of mirrors and their coordinates, an enumerative method is prohibitive. One possible approach to avoid an exhaustive process of all possible mirrors configurations (with discrete domains values), is to use meta-heuristic techniques which will be able to provide a solution near enough the optimal configuration. Such a method has a computational cost usually lower than enumerative approaches. Some examples of these techniques: simulated annealing, genetic algorithms, ant colony, local search algorithms, etc. Such methods are incomplete, as only a small part of the search-space is visited. Thus, there is no guarantee that the optimum will be found. Within the framework of this paper, we have studied the genetic and stochastic local search approaches. The genetic algorithm needs to use a large set of individuals (candidate solutions) to evolve correctly towards good solutions. Therefore, the associated computational time was prohibitive and solutions found were very similar from stochastic local search ones. Thus, the complete study was done with a stochastic local search algorithm. The paper is organized as follows: first, the formal framework is motivated and the stochastic local search principles are briefly described. We then present the method to solve the problem of finding a sensor which has low 3D reconstruction error. Experimental results are provided to illustrate its efficiency and to compare with previous works. Finally, promising further possible paths of research are discussed.

2   Single Camera and Multiple Mirrors Systems

We can build such kind of sensor with any shape of mirror: spherical ([11]), conical, hyperboloidal, paraboloidal, ... We choose paraboloidal mirrors for this study; indeed, paraboloidal mirrors are better for a stereo single camera and for multi-mirrors, thanks to the orthographic projection (telecentric lens and a camera) and the invariance to the horizontal translations of the camera relatively to the positions of the different mirrors. We keep the single view point even if we translate mirrors.

2.1 Camera and Mirrors Model

Let $P = (X, Y, Z)$ be a three dimensional point and $p = (x, y, z)_i$ be its image on mirror i. The projection center of mirror i, is at dX, dY, dZ as shown in Fig. 1.

The general model for the not-centered mirrors, is given by (1):

$$\begin{pmatrix} x \\ y \\ z \end{pmatrix}_i = \frac{h_i}{\sqrt{\mathbf{X}^2 + \mathbf{Y}^2 + \mathbf{Z}^2} + \mathbf{Z}} \begin{pmatrix} \mathbf{X} \\ \mathbf{Y} \\ \mathbf{Z} \end{pmatrix} \tag{1}$$

where $\mathbf{X} = X - dX, \mathbf{Y} = Y - dY, \mathbf{Z} = Z - dZ$ and $4h_i$ is the latus rectum (where h is the focal length).

The orthographic projection of those points on the camera is given by (2):

$$\begin{pmatrix} u \\ v \end{pmatrix}_i = \begin{pmatrix} \alpha_u & 0 & u_0 \\ 0 & \alpha_v & v_0 \end{pmatrix} \begin{pmatrix} x + dX \\ y + dY \\ 1 \end{pmatrix}_i \tag{2}$$

where (u, v) are the image coordinates of this point and $(\alpha_u, u_0, \alpha_v, v_0)$ are intrinsic camera parameters.

To show the principle of the 3D reconstruction, we consider only two mirrors (see Fig. 1).

Equations (1) and (2) are available even if we simultaneously combine horizontal and vertical shifts. dX_i, dY_i and dZ_i represent translations between the general frame and mirror i's frame (respectively dX_j, dY_j and dZ_j for frame j).

2.2 3D Reconstruction and Error

In this section we explain how to reconstruct a real point from a sensor built with one camera and two mirrors (one image with two omnidirectional pictures).

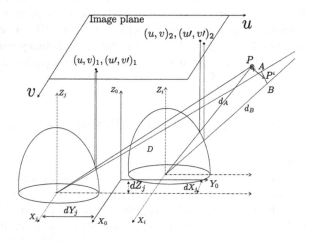

Fig. 1. Stereovision system with two mirrors and reconstruction error

Considering two images (obtained thanks to two mirrors), the main problem is to find the real point corresponding to its position in the two images. When there is no noise the problem is trivial. In the case of noise, the rays can not meet and the problem is how to find the real point that we call "back-projected point". This problem is known as "triangulation" problem which corresponds to finding the intersection of two rays in space. Let $(u', v')_1$ and $(u', v')_2$ be respectively the coordinates of the reflected points of P on the image plane thanks to the two mirrors. These points can be obtained thanks to the Harris detector [4], for example. As there is some noise, $(u', v')_1$ and $(u', v')_2$ are not the correct values. Let $(u, v)_1$ and $(u, v)_2$ be correct values that are close to $(u', v')_1$ and $(u', v')_2$ whose rays meet in P (Fig 1). As described in [5], there are many methods to find the back-projected point knowing $(u', v')_1$ and $(u', v')_2$. We used a minimization distance method between the rays from $(u', v')_1$ and $(u', v')_2$. This method can be easily adapted to any number of mirrors and is simple to implement.

The reconstruction error associated to P is the distance between P and its back-projected point P'. The shorter this distance, the better the configuration is. For any environment E (i.e. a set of points), the reconstruction error is the mean of all the reconstruction error associated to each point belonging to E. We choose this criterion among many others and we have to compute it regardless of the number of mirrors.

3   Method to Optimize Stereovision Sensor Design

Stochastic local search algorithms have been commonly used for many years to solve optimization problems. We briefly define main principles in the following (for more information you can refer to [6]).

3.1   Stochastic Local Search Algorithm

We have developed a dedicated Stochastic Local Search algorithm to solve this problem. The parameters are the number of mirrors, the size of the sensor and the surface where mirrors are places. The algorithm starts with a random feasible solution (coordinates and radius of all mirrors) and its reconstruction error is estimated. The reconstruction error of a given solution consists in the mean distance between a finite set of randomly chosen real points from a cubic environment and their associated back-projected points. The aim of this algorithm is to "walk" across (in the sense of a step-by-step movement) the search-space storing the best possible solution (the one which obtains the minimal reconstruction error). This walk is stopped when an empirical time out is reached. From a given feasible solution, the next step is computed as follows: the set of the neighborhood of this solution is computed. The neighborhood of a solution is the set of solutions from which we increment or decrement the corresponding domain value of only one mirror parameter (coordinates or radius). The solution with the lowest reconstruction error of the neighborhood is chosen for the step. To escape local extrema (i.e. solutions in the search space from which no single search step can achieve an improvement of reconstruction error), random choices are introduced in the choice of the best neighboring. At each step, a random choice occurs with a probability, 'p'(empirically set at 0.5 in this study).

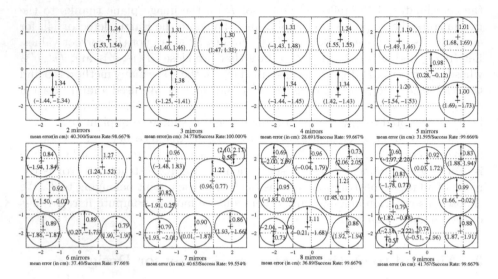

Fig. 2. Mean error, success rate and geometry of final solution for a number of mirrors from 2 to 9

3.2 Results

Let E be the environment to be reconstructed. E is a cubic volume around the sensor. A preset number of points (set at 500 in the following experiments) uniformly distributed in E are chosen to be representative of this environment. If a point is not seen by at least two mirrors, it is not considered during the reconstruction process. The mirrors are put on an $n \times n$ square below the sensor. Within the framework of this study, we define some constraints: the mirrors can't overlap each other, they can't overflow out of the sensor image and the mirrors are on the same plane ($z = 0$).

The dedicated local search algorithm has been implemented in C language and run on Power Mac G5 under 10.4 Mac OS X system. Within the experimental framework of this study, the sensor is characterized by an image plane with 1000×1000 pixels and a surface for mirrors equal to $5.6cm \times 5.6cm$[1]. Before back-projecting one given point from the image plane, we choose a random point from a distance of $\frac{1}{2}$ pixel from the initial one. The environment is a cube with edges of size 500 cm in order to simulate a realistic environment.

---

[1] Corresponding to the maximal size of telecentric lens.

The final solutions found by the our algorithm for a number of mirrors from 2 to 9 are presented in Fig. 2. Let's consider the top left solution describing a two mirror solution provided by the algorithm. The mean distance between 3D-points and their associated back-projecting points is equal to 40.3 cm and the percentage of points that could be reconstructed is 98.667%. Finally, the described solutions in Fig. 2 show that the four mirror configuration obtains the best accuracy among all the experimentations done within the framework of this study. These results confirm that the empirical sensor designed in [8] and named "TwoTwo" is within this framework also the best as possible. Moreover, we have obtained the same results with cylindrical environments (with different radius values and height). Another advantage of the four mirror solution is that the distribution error becomes more isotropic and the environment is fully 3D reconstructible.

4   Validation and Discussions

The configurations we found have been simulated under POVRAY[2] in order to validate reconstruction from realistic images. To do it, a 3D realistic environment has been modeled and targets that will be used as ground truth have been set on it. The image acquired by the configuration with four mirrors is shown on the left of Fig. 3(b). From this image, points (target corners Fig. 3(a)) are extracted by a semi automatic method: hand selection and subpixel detection of the position. Curves on Fig. 4(b) present distance (error) between detected points in images obtained by two mirror and four mirror configurations (from Fig. 2) and theoretical points. Characteristics of these detections are very closed (see table 1) because the image size obtained by two and four mirrors are quite the same (see Fig. 2).

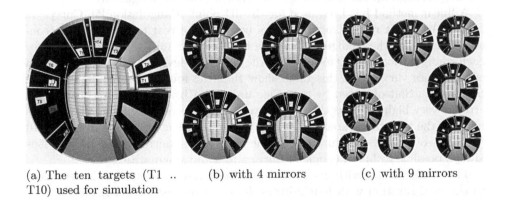

(a) The ten targets (T1 ..   (b) with 4 mirrors   (c) with 9 mirrors
T10) used for simulation

Fig. 3. Images acquired by one, four mirror and nine mirror configurations from Fig 2

---

[2] Persistence Of Vision RAY tracing software.

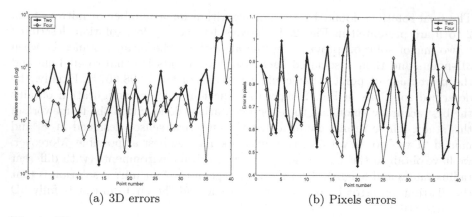

| (a) 3D errors | (b) Pixels errors |

Fig. 4. 3D errors reconstruction and pixels error for Two and Four mirrors configurations

Table 1. Image Points errors and 3D points errors

Configuration	pixels		3D points (in cm.)		
	Mean	Std	Mean	Std	Max
Two	0.74	0.16	92.95	190.80	959.32
Four	0.71	0.15	47.05	92.10	392.21

In order to compare the quality of 3D reconstruction (or triangulation), we used the mean error of the reconstructed points and the behavior of the reconstruction around the sensor. Indeed, it is easy to see that in the case of two mirror configuration, it is not possible to reconstruct points near to the axes passing through mirror centers. This is what we call the singularities.

A linear method has been used for the 3D point triangulation [5]. Curves on Fig. 4(a) present reconstruction errors between the real point and the reconstructed one for the configurations with two and four mirrors. Table 1 gives for each configuration the 3D mean error, the standard deviation and the maximum error. These curves and this table show that the four mirror configuration is better than that obtained by two. Fig. 4(a) and 4(b) show that reconstruction error is very high whereas the pixelic error is not necessarily high. The error is high for the targets situated on (or near) singularities axes (see points 37 to 40) for the two mirrors configuration. In the case of four mirror configuration, it is always possible to find a couple of mirrors to avoid singularities.

The configuration with five mirrors has been tested, because it is very close to the configuration with four mirrors. Its error reconstruction is quite higher and the mirror situated in the center did not improve the sensor because it is in the blind area of the image (camera self occlusion). For configuration with more mirrors, the point detection is very difficult due to the small size of the mirrors, for example, in Fig. 3(c) for the nine mirror configuration.

5   Conclusion and Future Works

In this paper, we have defined an automatic approach based on stochastic local search algorithms, usually used to optimize criteria of combinatorial problem solutions, to design sensors for omnidirectional catadioptric stereovision. Within the framework defined for this paper, our Stochastic Local-Search-like method, gives solutions for the design of sensors from two to nine mirrors. Thus, original configurations that have not yet been considered are provided in particular for sensors with five and nine mirrors. These configurations have been simulated thanks to the POVRAY software and the images have been treated to extract corner positions to be reconstructed. We choose this experimental conditions because the ground truth is easy to obtain in order to evaluate founded configurations. The next step of the study is to extend and improve this method to design solutions relaxing constraints of our framework such as overflow and overlap of mirrors. Another work consists in considering solutions where the mirrors aren't on the same plane (i.e. vertical shift) and can have different shapes.

References

1. Benosman, R., Maniere, T., Devars, J.: Multidirectional stereovision sensor, calibration and scene reconstruction. In: ICPR 96 (1996)
2. Gluckman, J., Nayar, S.K.: Rectified catadioptric stereo sensors. In: IEEE Conf. Computer Vision and Pattern Recognition, vol. 98, pp. 224–236 (2000)
3. Goshtasby, A., Gruver, W.: Design of a single lens stereo camera system. Pattern Recognition 26(6), 923–937 (1993)
4. Harris, C., Stephens, M.: A combined corner and edge detector. In: Proc. of the Fourth Alvey Vision Conference, Manchester University, pp. 147–152 (1988)
5. Hartley, R.I., Sturm, P.: Triangulation. Computer Vision and Image Understanding 68(2), 146–157 (1997)
6. Hoos, H.H., Stützle, T.: Stochastic Local Search Foundations and Applications. Elsevier, Amsterdam (2005)
7. Ishiguro, H., Yamamoto, M., Tsuji, S.: Omnidirectional stereo. IEEE Trans. PAMI 14(2), 257–262 (1992)
8. Mouaddib, E., Sagawa, R., Echigo, T., Yagi, Y.: Stereo vision with a single camera and multiple mirrors. In: Proc. IEEE ICRA, Barcelona, Spain, April 18-22, 2005, pp. 812–817 (2005)
9. Nene, S.A., Nayar, S.K.: Stereo with mirrors. In: ICCV98, pp. 1087–1094, (4-7 January, 1998)
10. Ollis, M., Herman, H., Singh, S.: Analysis and design of panoramic stereo vision using equi-angular pixel cameras. In: Tech. report CMU-RI-TR-99-04, Robotics Institute, Carnegie Mellon University (1999)
11. Sagawa, R., Kurita, N., Echigo, T., Yagi, Y.: Compound catadioptric stereo sensor for omnidirectional object detection. In: Proc. IEEE/RSJ IROS, vol. 2, pp. 2612–2617 Sendai, Japan (2004)
12. Southwell, D., Reyda, J., Fiala, M., Basu, A.: Panoramic stereo. In: ICPR96 (1996)
13. Stürzl, W., Dahmen, H., Mallot, H.A.: The quality of catadioptric imaging - application to omnidirectional stereo. In: ECCV (1), pp. 614–627 (2004)

Dimensionless Monocular SLAM

Javier Civera[1], Andrew J. Davison[2], and J.M.M. Montiel[1]

[1] Dpto. de Informática e Ingeniería de Sistemas, University of Zaragoza, Spain
{jcivera,josemari}@unizar.es
[2] Department of Computing, Imperial College, London, UK
ajd@doc.ic.ac.uk

Abstract. It has recently been demonstrated that the fundamental computer vision problem of structure from motion with a single camera can be tackled using the sequential, probabilistic methodology of monocular SLAM (Simultaneous Localisation and Mapping). A key part of this approach is to use the priors available on camera motion and scene structure to aid robust real-time tracking and ultimately enable metric motion and scene reconstruction. In particular, a scene object of known size is normally used to initialise tracking.

In this paper we show that real-time monocular SLAM can be initialised with no prior knowledge of scene objects within the context of a powerful new dimensionless understanding and parameterisation of the problem. When a single camera moves through a scene with no extra sensing, the scale of the whole motion and map is not observable, but we show that up-to-scale quantities can be robustly estimated.

Further we describe how the monocular SLAM state vector can be partitioned into two parts: a dimensionless part, representing up-to-scale scene and camera motion geometry, and an extra metric parameter representing scale. The dimensionless parameterisation permits tuning of the probabilistic SLAM filter in terms of image values, without any assumptions about scene scale, but scale information can be put back into the estimation if it becomes available.

Experimental results with real image sequences showing SLAM without an initialisation object, different image tuning examples and scenes with the same underlying dimensionless geometry are presented.

1 Introduction

Structure From Motion (SFM) [5], classically solved as batch process, has recently been reformulated as a sequential probabilistic estimation problem, propagating and benefitting from available priors along an image sequence. The probabilistic approach is based on SLAM techniques from the mobile robotics field, using either the Extended Kalman Filter (EKF) [3,6] or particle filtering methods such as FastSLAM [4]. This rigorous Bayesian approach is producing a significant improvement both in matching robustness and computation speed. Systems built using commodity cameras and computers have shown real-time 30 fps. robust performance in indoor or outdoors scenes with a hand-held camera.

J. Martí et al. (Eds.): IbPRIA 2007, Part II, LNCS 4478, pp. 412–419, 2007.
© Springer-Verlag Berlin Heidelberg 2007

It is a well known fact in SFM that a moving calibrated camera observing a scene can recover scene geometry and camera motion only up to a scale factor — scene scale is an non-observable magnitude if only bearing measurements are made. Unlike SFM, probabilistic SLAM methods use prior information: a camera motion model, scene depth priors and some *known structure*. These priors both aid sequential tracking (by defining search regions) and enable the computation of a *metric scene scale*. In particular, current monocular SLAM methods [3,6] have used extra information in the form of a known initialisation object to fix scene scale.

In this paper we show that this non-visual information is in fact not essential for solving the tracking problem and that no known target object needs to be added to the scene. While this means that overall scene scale cannot intrinsically be recovered, real-time tracking can still proceed — and if extra information does become available later, scale can be put back into the scene map.

This is enabled by a novel understanding of the monocular SLAM problem, based on the Extended Kalman Filter (EKF), in terms of dimensionless parameters. The new parameterisation is derived using Buckingham's Π theorem [1] which relies on the necessity for dimensional correctness in any formula and hence any estimation process. Our monocular SLAM algorithm therefore recovers dimensionless, up-to-scale geometry, and also provides benefits by allowing previous tuning parameters to be rolled up into a canonical set which give an important new understanding of the uncertainties in the system now in pixel units. These parameters in the image provide a natural way of understanding image sequences, irrespectively of the frame rate and actual scene size.

Further, we show that alongside the main dimensionless part of the SLAM state vector we can add an extra parameter representing metric scale. During tracking, vision-only measurements do not reduce the uncertainty in the scale parameter but only in the dimensionless scene geometry. However, any measurement containing metric information such as odometry, a feature at a known depth or the distance between two features can be added when available and will correctly affect both the scale and the dimensionless scene geometry.

2   Monocular SLAM Estimation Process

The state of the system in EKF SLAM is traditionally represented by a state vector $\mathbf{x}$, composed of a group of parameters referring to the camera motion, $\mathbf{x_v}$, and n others representing every feature in the map, $\mathbf{y_i}$ [7,2].

$$\mathbf{x} = (\mathbf{x_v}, \mathbf{y_1}, \mathbf{y_2}, \ldots, \mathbf{y_n})^\top \qquad (1)$$

In hand-held camera monocular SLAM, a smooth camera motion is usually supposed. The motion model in this paper is the same as in [3]: a constant velocity model with unknown acceleration inputs, a_k^W and α_k^C. These linear and angular accelerations are represented by zero mean known standard deviations

(σ_a and σ_α) Gaussian noise . The camera state vector includes camera location, rotation quaternion, and linear and angular velocities:

$$\mathbf{x_v} = \left(\mathbf{r}^{WC}, \mathbf{q}^{WC}, \mathbf{v}^W, \omega^W\right) \tag{2}$$

The equation that updates the state camera vector at every step is:

$$\mathbf{f_v} = \begin{pmatrix} \mathbf{r}^{WC}_{k+1} \\ \mathbf{q}^{WC}_{k+1} \\ \mathbf{v}^W_{k+1} \\ \omega^C_{k+1} \end{pmatrix} = \begin{pmatrix} \mathbf{r}^{WC}_k + v^W_k \Delta t + a^W_k \Delta t^2 \\ \mathbf{q}^{WC}_k \times \mathbf{q}(\omega^C_k \Delta t + \alpha^C_k \Delta t^2) \\ \mathbf{v}^W_k + a^W_k \Delta t \\ \omega^C_k + \alpha^C_k \Delta t \end{pmatrix} \tag{3}$$

Inverse depth parametrization for point features [6] is also used in this paper. This parametrization codes features by the ray extracted at first feature observation (defined by the 3D location of the optical centre of the camera and azimuth-elevation angles) and the inverse depth along this ray:

$$\mathbf{y_i} = (\mathbf{r}_i, \theta_i, \phi_i, \rho_i) = (x_i, y_i, z_i, \theta_i, \phi_i, \rho_i) \tag{4}$$

When a feature is newly initialized from a monocular camera, only information about the ray can be retrieved. As no information is available about depth, an initial inverse depth Gaussian prior on $\rho_i \sim N(\rho_0, \sigma_{\rho_0})$ is applied in order to cover with 95% probability the range of depths from the closest possible to infinity.

We propose to split the state vector into a metric parameter d — unobservable with only-vision measurements — and a dimensionless scene and camera part. Doing this, the state vector is partitioned according to observability with a monocular camera. Camera measurements will reduce scene geometry uncertainty, but not the uncertainty in the metric parameter d.

$$\mathbf{x} = \left(d, \mathbf{\Pi_r^{WC}}, \mathbf{q^{WC}}, \mathbf{\Pi_v^W}, \mathbf{\Pi_\omega^C}, \mathbf{\Pi_{y_1}}, \ldots\right)^\top \tag{5}$$

The mapping from the state vector to metric scene geometry is a non-linear computation involving the dimensionless geometry and the parameter d:

$$\mathbf{r}^{WC} = d\mathbf{\Pi_r^{WC}}, \qquad \mathbf{v}^W = d\mathbf{\Pi_v^W} \Delta t, \qquad \omega^W = d\mathbf{\Pi_\omega^W} \Delta t \tag{6}$$

$$\mathbf{y_i} = (d\Pi_{xi}, d\Pi_{yi}, d\Pi_{zi}, \theta_i, \phi_i, \Pi_{\rho i}/d) \tag{7}$$

3   Buckingham's Π Theorem Applied to Monocular SLAM

Buckingham's Π Theorem [1] is a key theorem in Dimensional Analysis. It states that physical laws are independent of units. Given a dimensionally correct equation involving n quantities of different kinds: $f(X_1, X_2, X_3, \ldots, X_n) = 0$ the existing relationship between the variables can be expressed also as: $F(\Pi_1, \Pi_2, \Pi_3, \ldots, \Pi_{n-k}) = 0$ where Π_i is a reduced set of $n - k$ independent dimensionless groups of variables, and k the number of independent dimensions that appear in the problem.

The monocular estimation process can be expressed as a function:

$$\left(\mathbf{r}^{WC}, \mathbf{q}^{WC}, \mathbf{v}^{W}, \omega^{W}, \mathbf{y}_1, \ldots, \mathbf{y}_n\right)^{\top} = \mathbf{f}(\sigma_a, \sigma_\alpha, \sigma_z, \mathbf{z}, \Delta t, \rho_0, \sigma_{\rho 0}, \sigma_{v0}, \sigma_{\omega 0}) \, , (8)$$

where vector $\mathbf{z}$ stacks all the image measurements along the image sequence. Table 1 summarizes all the variables involved in monocular SLAM estimation and and their units.

Table 1. Dimensionless parameters and the corresponding variables involved

$\mathbf{r}$	$\mathbf{q}$	$\mathbf{v}, \sigma_{v0}$	$\omega, \sigma_{\omega 0}$	$\mathbf{z},\sigma_{\mathbf{z}}$		a^W, σ_a	α^C,σ_α	x_i, y_i, z_i	θ_i, ϕ_i	$\rho_i, \sigma_{\rho 0}$
l	1	lt^{-1}	t^{-1}	l^{-1}	lt^{-1} t^{-1}	l^{-1}	1	1	lt^{-2}	t^{-2}

Based on the equation above, dimensionless groups must be chosen. The parameters ρ_0 and Δt are the parameters of the two dimensions involved (length and time) chosen to form the dimensionless groups. (Table 2).

Table 2. Dimensionless numbers and the corresponding involved variables

$\Pi_\mathbf{r}$	$\Pi_\mathbf{q}$	$\Pi_\mathbf{v}$	Π_ω	Π_{ρ_i}	$\Pi_{\sigma v0}$	$\Pi_{\sigma \omega 0}$	$\Pi_{\sigma \rho 0}$	$\Pi_\mathbf{z}$	$\Pi_{\sigma z}$	$\Pi_{\sigma a}$	$\Pi_{\sigma \alpha}$
$\mathbf{r}\rho_0$	$\mathbf{q}$	$\mathbf{v}\rho_0\Delta t$	$\omega\Delta t$	$\frac{\rho_i}{\rho_0}$	$\sigma_{v0}\rho_0\Delta t$	$\sigma_{\omega 0}\Delta t$	$\frac{\sigma_{\rho 0}}{\rho_0}$	z	σz	$\sigma_a\rho_0\Delta t^2$	$\sigma_\alpha\rho_0\Delta t^2$

4   Dimensionless Monocular SLAM Model

The state vector is composed of dimensionless parameters defining camera location, rotation and velocities, and the map features:

$$\mathbf{x}_\mathbf{v} = (\mathbf{\Pi_r}, \mathbf{q}, \mathbf{\Pi_v}, \mathbf{\Pi_\omega})^{\top} \quad \mathbf{\Pi_{y_i}} = (\mathbf{\Pi_{r_i}}, \theta_i, \phi_i, \Pi_{\rho_i})^{\top} \tag{9}$$

The dimensionless state update equation is:

$$\mathbf{f_v} = \begin{pmatrix} \mathbf{\Pi_r}_{k+1}^{WC} \\ \mathbf{q}_{k+1}^{WC} \\ \mathbf{\Pi_v}_{k+1}^{WC} \\ \mathbf{\Pi_\omega}_{k+1}^{WC} \end{pmatrix} = \begin{pmatrix} \mathbf{\Pi_r}_k^{WC} + \mathbf{\Pi_v}_k^{WC} + \mathbf{\Pi_a}_k^{WC} \\ \mathbf{q}_k^{WC} \times \mathbf{q}(\mathbf{\Pi_\omega}_k^{WC} + \mathbf{\Pi_\alpha}_k^{WC}) \\ \mathbf{\Pi_v}_k^{WC} + \mathbf{\Pi_a}_k^{WC} \\ \mathbf{\Pi_\omega}_k^{WC} + \mathbf{\Pi_\alpha}_k^{WC} \end{pmatrix} \tag{10}$$

Next the monocular camera measurement equation is detailed. First, features coded in inverse depth must be converted to 3D points in the world reference:

$$\mathbf{\Pi}_h^W = \mathbf{\Pi_{r_i}} + \Pi_{\rho_i}\mathbf{m}(\theta_i, \phi_i) \, , \tag{11}$$

where $\mathbf{m}(\theta_i, \phi_i)$ is the unit vector defined by the pair of azimuth-elevation angles. These world-referenced 3D points are converted to the camera frame:

$$\mathbf{\Pi}_h^C = \mathbf{R}^{CW}(\mathbf{\Pi}_h^W - \mathbf{\Pi_r}) \, , \tag{12}$$

and then are projected into the camera using the pinhole model:

$$v = \frac{\mathbf{\Pi}_h^C|_x}{\mathbf{\Pi}_h^C|_z} \quad \nu = \frac{\mathbf{\Pi}_h^C|_y}{\mathbf{\Pi}_h^C|_z} \tag{13}$$

Finally, camera calibration including radial distortion is applied to obtain pixel coordinates from angular coordinates.

There camera measurements clearly do not involve the size of the scene. If the metric parameter d has to be estimated, other types of measurements must be made. For instance, the equation that gives the distance between two points:

$$\mathcal{D}(\mathbf{P_1}, \mathbf{P_2}) = d\sqrt{(\mathbf{\Pi_{y_2}}|_x - \mathbf{\Pi_{y_1}}|_x)^2 + (\mathbf{\Pi_{y_2}}|_y - \mathbf{\Pi_{y_1}}|_y)^2 + (\mathbf{\Pi_{y_2}}|_z - \mathbf{\Pi_{y_1}}|_z)^2} \tag{14}$$

5   Image Interpretation of Dimensionless Parameters and Image Filter Tuning

The most representative of the dimensionless parameters can be seen in Figure 1. Their geometrical interpretation as camera angles is detailed here.

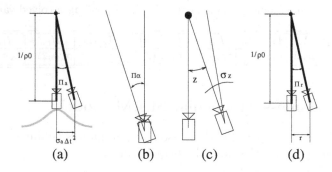

Fig. 1. Dimensionless monocular SLAM parameters

Figure 1(a) shows the dimensionless parameter $\Pi_{\sigma a}$. The product $\sigma_a \Delta t^2$ represents the effect of the acceleration noise on the camera location. This value divided by $1/\rho_0$ gives the angle represented in the figure. This angle can be seen as the parallax allowed to a feature at depth $1/\rho_0$ due to camera acceleration.

The camera angular acceleration covariance in Figure 1(b) can clearly be interpreted as an angle between frames, and can be mapped to image pixels. Image measurements and image noise, in Figure 1(c) are directly measured in the image, so they are already dimensionless angles.

The translation estimate, Π_r (in fig 1(d)), can also be seen as the angle defined by the translation between frames and the initial inverse depth.

As a consequence of this interpretation, EKF tuning is greatly simplified. Image values, observable in an image sequence, replace non-observable 3D real world values. Tuning parameters are related to image motion and no assumptions on the 3D scene are done.

6 Real Image Results

Real image experiments without adding any target to the scene has been performed. The first one shows how the scale of the scene in usual monocular SLAM depends on the prior knowledge of the scene. The second one illustrates the use of image tuning and the reduction in the number of tuning parameters. In the third experiment, the same image tuning is used in two different sequences which have different metric qualities but lead to the same image motion. All of the sequences have been recorded with a IEEE 1394 320×240 monochrome camera at 30 fps. A wide angle lens is used.

6.1 Dependence of Scene Scale on a Priori Parameters

The same sequence was processed with the dimensional EKF SLAM algorithm varying the ρ_0 parameter. Figure 2 shows the estimation for $\rho_0 = 0.5m^{-1}$ and $\rho_0 = 0.1m^{-1}$. Notice that the estimated depth of the scene (the distance between the camera and the points in the bookcase) tends to be at the depth prior ($2m$ and $10m$). The two estimated scenes have the same form, the difference is just the scale of the axis. If $\mathbf{\Pi_r^{WC}} = \rho_0 \mathbf{r^{WC}}$ and $\mathbf{\Pi_{y_i}}$ were estimated using the dimensionless monocular SLAM proposed, these two experiments would be normalized into one, in which normalized depth tends to be at *dimensionless* '1'.

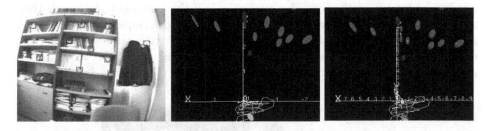

Fig. 2. Left: sample. Centre: EKF SLAM estimation result $\rho_0 = 0.5m^{-1}$. Right: EKF SLAM estimation result $\rho_0 = 0.1m^{-1}$. Feature uncertainty in red and blue, the camera uncertainty in cyan and the camera trajectory in yellow.

6.2 Image Tuning in a Pure Rotation Sequence

This sequence is a pure camera rotation in a hallway. Dimensional monocular SLAM should have been tuned with real camera accelerations and depth priors. As these values are not observable, they need to be assumed. Dimensionless monocular SLAM is tuned directly with image values.

Two experiments with the same $\Pi_{\sigma a} = 0$, $\Pi_{\sigma z} = 1pxls$ values but different tuning in $\Pi_{\sigma \alpha}$: a)$\Pi_{\sigma \alpha} = 2pxls$, and b)$\Pi_{\sigma \alpha} = 4pxls$ has been performed (Fig. 3.) Because of the image tuning, their effect can be directly seen in the 95% image search regions size for the map features.

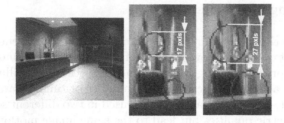

Fig. 3. Pure rotation image search regions. Left: sample image. Centre: $\Pi_\alpha = 2pxls$. Right:$\Pi_\alpha = 4pxls$.

It is important to notice that, in the previous paragraph, neither 3D scene assumptions nor time between frames Δt are needed in the filter. The tuned values are the allowed image motion between frames due to camera linear and angular acceleration and image noise.

6.3 The Same Image Tuning for Different Sequences

Two translational sequences have been recorded walking along a corridor and looking at the wall. In the first one, the distance from the wall was 2.5 metres. In the second, the distance from the wall was twice (5 metres), the distance walked along the corridor the same, and the walking velocity was double (therefore, the number of frames of the second sequence is half the first one). Although they are two different experiments, the image motion in both sequences is the same, and dimensionless monocular SLAM has to be tuned with same values. In this experiment, these values were: $\sigma_z = 1pxl$, $\sigma_a = 2pxl$ and $\sigma_\alpha = 2pxl$. Notice again the simplicity of image tuning compared with 3D tuning, in which you

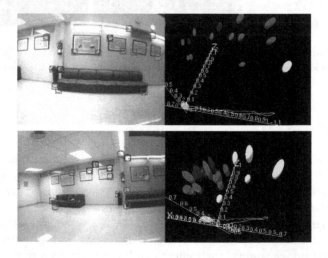

Fig. 4. Two equivalent sequences. First and last images and 3D estimated geometry.

have to imagine the depth prior and the 3D accelerations, unobservable with a single camera. Figure 4 shows the results of both estimations.

The dimensionless estimated translation can be interpreted as the translation in units of the initial depth prior. As the wall is twice as far in the second sequence, the second sequence's estimated translation is half. It can also be noticed that, as the normalized translation is smaller in the second experiment, the normalized 3D point positions are estimated with less accuracy and have larger uncertainty regions.

7   Conclusions

Up-to-scale results from real-time, EKF based monocular SLAM without an initialisation target are presented. As no known points are included in the estimation, the real size of the scene cannot be recovered. Nevertheless, a scaled estimation is obtained, its size depending on priors introduced to the filter.

In order to represent the non-observability of the real size of the scene, a new monocular SLAM parameterisation is presented. This approach separates the geometric problem of estimating a point map and camera motion up to scale from the unobservable real size of the map and motion. A parameter that codes the real size of the scene is added to the state vector, but single-camera measurements do not involve this value. As a consequence, its value cannot be estimated with single camera measurements.

Buckingham's theorem was used to build the dimensionless state vector in this new EKF approach. A geometrical interpretation of the dimensionless parameters as angles allows a simplified tunning of the filter: the number of tuning parameters is reduced and no 3D assumptions of the scene are made.

References

1. Buckingham, E.: On physically similar systems; illustrations of the use of dimensional equations. Phys. Rev. 4(4), 345–376 (1914)
2. Castellanos, J.A., Tardós, J.D.: Mobile Robot Localization and Map Building: A Multisensor Fusion Approach. Kluwer Academic Publishers, Dordrecht (1999)
3. Davison, A.J.: Real-time simultaneous localization and mapping with a single camera. In: Proc. International Conference on Computer Vision (2003)
4. Eade, E., Drummond, T.: Scalable monocular SLAM. In: Proceedings of the IEEE Conference on Computer Vision and Pattern Recognition (2006)
5. Hartley, R.I., Zisserman, A.: Multiple View Geometry in Computer Vision, 2nd edn. Cambridge University Press, Cambridge, ISBN: 0521540518 (2004)
6. Montiel, J., Civera, J., Davison, A.: Unified inverse depth parametrization for monocular slam. In: Proceedings of Robotics: Science and Systems, Philadelphia, USA (August 2006)
7. Smith, R., Cheeseman, P.: On the representation and estimation of spatial uncertainty. Intl. Journal of Robotics Research 5(4), 56–68 (1986)

Improved Camera Calibration Method Based on a Two-Dimensional Template

Carlos Ricolfe-Viala and Antonio-Jose Sanchez-Salmeron

Polytechnic University of Valencia
Camino de Vera s/n, 46120, Valencia, Spain
{cricolfe,asanchez}@isa.upv.es

Abstract. Camera calibration is necessary to obtain 3D information from 2D images of a scene. Different techniques exist which are based on photogrammetry or self-calibration. As a result of the calibration the intrinsic and extrinsic camera parameters are computed. A lot of work has been done in camera calibration and also in data pre- and post-processing techniques. From a practical point of view, it is quite difficult to decide which calibration method produces the best results and even whether any data processing at all is necessary.

This paper defines the best performance camera calibration algorithm. Based on the state of the art of all camera calibration processes, including pre- and post-processing data, a camera calibration method is chosen on the grounds of robustness and ease of handing. After, the calibration method is improved adding pre- and post-processing statements. Data treatment reduces the noise of the measurements and optimum performance is thus achieved. Its performance is tested with both simulated and real data and best results are always computed. The aim is to define a complete method which will allow all camera calibration situations to be easily resolved.

Keywords: Camera calibration, 2D template, distortion rectification, data normalization, non-linear calibration.

1 Introduction

Camera calibration is necessary in order to resolve applications in which it is necessary to obtain quantitative data from images with certain accuracy. Precise calibration provides distance measurements of the scene from images or allows locating an object in absolute to the coordinate axes of the scene or relative to any other object. Consequently, it is possible to resolve industrial applications of part assembly or obstacle avoidance in robot navigation. This information is very useful in path planning or robot control. On the other hand, if 3D reconstruction is carried out, using several images of the same scene without movement, it is possible to relate both optical rays to compute the position of the point 3D in the scene.

Camera calibration computes the intrinsic and extrinsic camera parameters. Intrinsic parameters model the geometry of the camera and the optical features of the sensor and also define image distortion due to imperfections intrinsic to the camera.

J. Martí et al. (Eds.): IbPRIA 2007, Part II, LNCS 4478, pp. 420–427, 2007.

Extrinsic parameters provide the position and orientation of the camera with respect to the coordinate axes of the scene.

Several methods are now being used for camera calibration. These methods can be classified following different criteria. If the template features are taken into account, there are methods which use three, two and one-dimensional templates and others that do not use any template. If a three-dimensional template is used, only one image of the template; however it requires complex planning to reduce the errors in the template [6]. When two-dimensional templates are used, several images should be taken of it from different positions and orientation. The camera can change its position or the two-dimensional template can be moved. It is not necessary to know the positions from where the images are taken [7]. This method is more versatile, since the creation of the template is easy. Calibration methods based on one-dimensional templates are useful if systems with several cameras are to be calibrated. Since it is necessary to take images of the template with all the cameras, if three or two-dimensional templates are used, it is very difficult to locate the template where it can be seen with all the cameras at the same time. The template should be transparent. This is because using a one-dimensional template is very useful if a system with several cameras has to be calibrated [8]. Take into account the set of algorithms which compute the distortion of the camera, there are methods which use epipolar and trilineal restrictions between pairs and triplets of images respectively, to define the radial distortion and other which are based on the perspective ideal projection criterion [1].

The paper is structured as follows. Section 2 gives decides which camera calibration methods obtain best performance according with existing comparisons. Section 3 describes the base of the calibration method. Section 4 describes how it can be improved using data pre- and post-processing techniques like data correction and normalization and how radial distortion can be avoided. Section 5 shows experimental results and the paper ends with some conclusions.

2 Calibration Methods

The state of the art of the calibration process does not provide much help in choosing an efficient method of camera calibration in all situations. Salvi [4] compares the calibration methods developed between 1982 and 1998 and the Tsai method shows better performance, in spite of the fact that it requires high precision in the input data. On the other hand Zhang's method [7], which is not included in Salvi's comparison [4], represents a new era in the camera calibration process. This method uses images of a 2D template taken from different camera positions and orientations. In this way, the advantages of camera self calibration are combined with the points coordinate-based calibration. This calibration method is very flexible; since the camera and the template can be moved freely and also as many images as are wanted can be taken without measuring any point in the template. Sun [5] compares the Tsai method with Zhang's method. On one hand, Tsai produces a precise estimation of camera parameters if the input data are not very corrupt. Since 100 point in the template is necessary and its coordinates should be referred to a fixed origin, careful design of the calibration template and a very accurate coordinate measurement are necessary. Nevertheless, errors are committed and in practice results are not as accurate as expected. This is shown by Sun [5]. On the other hand, Zhang's method based on a 2D template does not require either a special design or precise measurement of the points. Sun obtains camera calibration with a hand-made template and better results are computed with Zhang's method. Also, the sensibility of the calibration algorithm to errors in the measures can be improved by increasing the spotted number in the template, simply by printing a chessboard with more corners. The results of the comparison show the flexibility and adaptability of Zhang's method since it can be performed on any scene.

From the point of view of the computed model, experiments with medium quality cameras realized by Salvi [4] and Sun [5] suggest that it is reasonable to consider tangential distortion, zero misalignment and second-rate radial distortion. Considering a fourth-rate radial distortion can be useful if the input data is not very corrupt. If radial distortion is not considered, results can be improved by including tangential distortion and image decentring components.

Taking into account the results of all of these authors, Zhang's method is used as a reference for camera calibration. A version of this method uses circles to avoid coordinate measurement in the template. On the other hand, Zhang's method can include data normalization as defined by Hartley [2], or points corrections in the template established by Lavest [3]. It can also be improved by correcting distortion in the image before using data from it as is suggested by Ahmed [1]. In order to improve Zhang's camera calibration method, data normalization and distortion correction will be used to achieve best performance of camera calibration with the aim of defining a calibration method based on Zhang's that includes all improvements in order to establish the best performance calibration method to date.

3   Camera Calibration with Planar Pattern

Camera calibration estimates the camera model. In this case, only the lineal model without distortions will be computed:

$$q_i = \lambda \cdot K \cdot [R \quad t] p = \lambda \cdot K \cdot [r_1 \quad r_2 \quad r_3 \quad t] p_i \qquad (1)$$

Matrix K contains internal camera parameters. Vector t and matrix R are the external camera parameters. Zhang in [7] presented a novel camera calibration method based on the homographies between a planar calibration pattern and its images from several camera locations. The method assumes the planar pattern situated at $z_w = 0$ of the scene coordinate system. Denoting r_i as the ith column of the rotation matrix of the camera R and t its the translation vector in the scene coordinates system, the initial model is transformed in the homography H. This homography H defines the coordinates $q_i = (u_i, v_i, 1)^T$ in the image of a point $p_i = (x_i, y_i, 1)^T$ of the planar pattern. This is $q_i = H \cdot p_i$. Several images are taken of the planar template and a homography H is computed for each one. Given m homographies, its elements can be arranged in a expression $V \cdot b = 0$ where V is a $2m \times 6$ matrix and vector b contains intrinsic camera parameters. At least three images are necessary $m \geq 3$, in order to obtain a unique solution. Once b is estimated the camera internal parameters can be computed. When K is known, the external parameters for each image can be computed knowing the corresponding homography. See [7] for details.

3.1 Non Linear Camera Calibration Step

The algorithm described in the previous subsection gives values for camera parameters solving a linear equation. If non linear parameter estimation is carried out, the residual error is minimized. In the case of camera calibration, error e represents the geometrical error between measured points coordinates in the image $q_i^{\#}$ ($^{\#}$ represents noisy data) and projecting points coordinates of the template with the estimation of camera parameters at this moment $q_i^* = M^{\#} \cdot p_i^{\#}$. In this case, camera parameters are computed directly, $a = (\alpha_u, \alpha_v, u_0, v_0, t_{x1}, t_{y1}, t_{z1}, \theta_1, \varphi_1, \psi_1, \ldots t_{xm}, t_{ym}, t_{zm}, \theta_m, \varphi_m, \psi_m t_x, t_y, t_z)$. The index to minimize is:

$$I = \sum_{i=1}^{n} \left(u_i - \alpha_u \frac{r_{11}x_i + r_{12}y_i + r_{13}z_i + t_x}{r_{31}x_i + r_{32}y_i + r_{33}z_i + t_z} - u_0 \right)^2 + \left(v_i - \alpha_v \frac{r_{21}x_i + r_{22}y_i + r_{23}z_i + t_y}{r_{31}x_i + r_{32}y_i + r_{33}z_i + t_z} - v_0 \right)^2 \quad (2)$$

This index depends on 4+6 parameters, where 4 correspond to intrinsic and 6 to extrinsic camera parameters.

4 Improving the Camera Calibration Method

In the previous section linear and non linear camera calibration using a two-dimensional template is described. In order to compute the optimal parameters p^* which satisfy function f for a set of measurement x', initial values p_0 close to the best values are computed in the linear step and are used as the starting point in the non linear searching. To obtain a set of parameters very close to the real ones in the linear step, two data pre-processing techniques will be used. These data pre-processing techniques developed by Hartley [2] and by Ahmed [1] reduce the noise level in the measurements and therefore parameters computed with this data are closer to the real parameters by using only linear techniques.

Hartley normalizes point's coordinates to obtain a well conditioned matrix A [2] and to increase the robustness of the computing process. Ahmed [1] makes an estimation of the image distortions produced by the camera. The distortion is first computed and then is used to correct the image. This process decreases the noise of the data from images. The aim is to pre-process the data before it is used to calibrate the camera.

4.1 Camera Distortion Calibration

Section 3 gives a brief description on how to estimate the camera linear model using only a few images of the planar template. Now a method to estimate the camera distortions is used. Mainly, radial distortion is considered although tangential or decentring distortion can be considered. If distortion is corrected previously, noise is reduced and calibration process improves its results. If camera distortion parameters are known beforehand, image distortion can be rectified, but unfortunately, this information is not available. This is because lens imperfections are different in each one and it also depends on how they are mounted and focused. Therefore manufacturers cannot give standard values for distortion parameters that model a set of lenses. Consequently, it is necessary to define a method to estimate camera distortion parameters based on invariant geometric features of the image. In this case, the method of Ahmed [1] is used. It is based on the principle that an image of straight lines is always straight. Since the planar pattern is a chessboard which has a lot of straight lines, image distortion can be computed using non linear techniques. In this case, it is expressed as a function of the deformation of the straight lines.

4.2 Data Normalization

Regarding the robustness of camera calibration, the results must not depend on a point's situation either in the scene or in the image. Formally it could be said that given a set of points p_i in the scene, and its images q_i, its positions can change using two transformation matrices T_p and T_q obtaining $p_i{}^o=T_p \cdot p_i$ and $q_i{}^o=T_q \cdot q_i$. If both set of points are related with the homography such as $q_i=H \cdot p_i$, this expression is transformed with the new set of points in $q_i{}^o=T_q \cdot H \cdot T_p{}^{-1} \cdot p_i{}^o$. This equation gives a new homography H^o which relates both sets of transformed points $p_i{}^o$ and $q_i{}^o$ and which is $H^o=T_q \cdot H \cdot T_p{}^{-1}$. If a point's position does not affect the calibration process, the camera model H can be computed using an alternative method. It consists of transforming the initial set of points p_i and q_i into $p_i{}^o=T_p \cdot p_i$ and $q_i{}^o=T_q \cdot q_i$ using two transformation matrices T_p and T_q. H^o is computed with T_p and T_q and the camera model H is obtained using $H=T_q{}^{-1} \cdot H^o \cdot T_p$, which can be directly computed with the initial sets of points p_i and q_i. This procedure may appear feasible, however it is not accurate. Hartley [2] shows that algorithms based on algebraic error minimization are affected by the points position. This is because restrictions are not the same for $|h|=1$ and $|h^o|=1$. Since, algebraic error minimization is used to compute homographies data normalization is necessary. The Hartley data normalization consists of translating them so that centroide is the origin of the reference system. Translation is different for points in the template than for those in the image. Moreover, coordinates are scaled so that the average length is one. Scaling is the same in both axes but differs in the image and template.

4.3 Camera Parameters and Points in the 2D Template from Different Positions

In the non linear step of camera calibration, only camera parameters were searched in subsection 3.1. Since the points coordinates in the template $p_i{}^\#$ are corrupted with noise, camera parameters can be searched together with them. In each iteration, a new set of estimated points $p_i{}^*$, will decrease their noise level from $p_i{}^\#$ since they generate a smaller geometrical error. In this case points coordinates in the template $p_i{}^\#$, are included with the camera parameters in the vector to be estimated. Since the calibration method defined by Zhang [7] is used, the template is two dimensional and the parameter vector is changed to $a=(\alpha_u, \alpha_v, u_0, v_0, t_{x1}, t_{y1}, t_{z1}, \theta_1, \varphi_1, \psi_1, \ldots t_{xm}, t_{ym}, t_{zm}, \theta_m, \varphi_m, \psi_m, x_1, y_1, x_2, y_2, \ldots x_n, y_n)$. m is the number of template images and n corresponds to the number of points. In this case, the searching dimension is $4+6m+3n$.

5 Experimental Results

Camera calibration based on a two-dimensional template is improved as follows. First, image distortion is estimated in order to correct the point coordinates and to reduce the noise level. Second, once image distortion is corrected, data is normalized to obtain a robust estimation in the linear camera calibration step. With this data pre-processing, the performance of linear camera calibration improves considerably. Referring to the non linear camera calibration step, point coordinates in the template are included in the index. As will be seen in the experimental results section and Lavest [3], if point coordinates in the template are corrected, errors in camera calibration depend only on noise of point coordinates in the images. Since noise in the image has been greatly reduced with data pre-processing, the estimated parameters are very close to the real ones. Following figure 3 of [7], calibrating results are improved if angles between the pattern and image planes are between $50°$ and $70°$. Concerning the number of images, figure 2 of [7] shows that starting from 7 or 8 images, the improvement of results is not significant.

The effect of distorted points is tested first. What is done is to test how results are improved when image distortion is corrected before calibrating the camera with a planar pattern. Since simulated data is used, method efficiency is tested by changing the conditions of the calibration process. The next step is to simulate how distortion correction and data normalization improves the calibration result. Using real values of the previously computed k_1, k_2, p_1 y p_2, the intrinsic camera parameters α_u, α_v, u_0, v_0, are calibrated with pre-processed data and then compared with calibration without pre-processing. Point coordinates in the image and the template are corrupted with noise separately in order to test the effects in both cases.

Figure 1 shows the results of the linear camera calibration of α_u, u_0 using corrected and non-corrected images. Obviously, the results with corrected images are better. In the case of performing a linear camera calibration only, this is a necessary step in order to compute the best results. If non-linear camera calibration is performed, image correction should also be performed, since non-linear searching improves the results if the starting searching point is close to the best parameters. In addition, better results will be obtained if the image is not distorted.

The last step in the camera calibration process is the non-linear parameter searching. Initial values for the camera parameters are used to start a non linear searching which minimizes a given index. Initial searching values are computed previously in the linear step. It does not matter if data normalization has been carried out, since point coordinates are the same and therefore no linear searching converges to the same value. However, if starting values are computed using data normalization, non-linear searching ends earlier, since the initial values are closer to the best ones. If image distortion is corrected, non-linear calibration reaches results similar to the real ones. This is because the data used is closer to the real data. From the point of view of the index to be minimized, figure 2 shows the results of non-linear searching when the noise level in the point coordinates in the template is changed. Image coordinates are corrupted with Gaussian noise of $\sigma=0.5$. Here, two results are compared. In one case, the index is minimized looking for camera parameters only and in the other, the

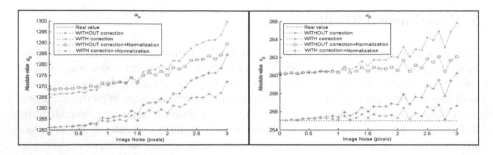

Fig. 1. Effect of image distortion correction and data normalization with linear estimation of camera parameters

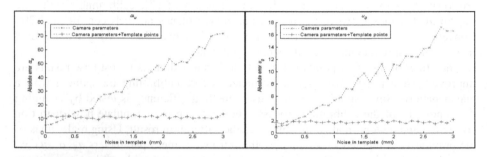

Fig. 2. Effect of noise in the template with non-linear camera calibration. Points in the image have a noise level of $\sigma=0.5$ pixels.

camera parameters are computed together with the point coordinates in the template. When template point coordinates are included in the index, the algorithm rectifies its coordinates, noise is minimized and errors depend only on the noise of point coordinates in the image. This fact indicates that the point coordinates in the template should be included in the non-linear searching index.

Table 1 shows the results of calibration a camera model VCM50. It has been calibrated using all possibilities presented in the paper. It is assumed than better results are computed with the non linear searching of camera parameters together with points coordinates in the template since simulated results gives betters results.

Table 1. Camera parameters for a real camera VCM50

	Without data normalization		Data Normalization		No linear	
		Dist. correction		Dist. correction		Parameters +coordinates
α_u	931.2	932.2	933.5	929.3	932.1	930.4
α_v	947.2	942.2	945.4	941.5	942.5	940.1
u_0	312.5	318.5	326.8	322.4	323.5	317.5
v_0	238.7	237.9	242.5	242.9	242.8	241.9
φ	1.12	1.45	1.12	1.45	1.11	0.98

6 Conclusions

The robustness of the calibration process depends on the quality of measurements, the model to be computed and the calibration method. Based on an exhaustive review of the state of the art in camera calibration and techniques which can improve calibration methods, the most effective estimation method to resolve all the problems involved in camera calibration has been defined. The method is based on Zhang [7]. It can be improved adding data pre-processing and improvement of the non-linear searching of camera parameters. Data pre-processing consisted of correcting errors in point coordinates corrupted by image distortion and data normalization in order to increase the robustness of the computing process. With regard to the non-linear camera calibration step, it is very important to include point coordinates of the template in the non-linear searching process, since they are corrected and noise decreases.

Acknowledgments. The authors gratefully acknowledge the support from the Comisión Interministerial de Ciencia y Tecnología (CICYT), the local government of the "Generalitat Valenciana" and the European Commission for partial funding of this work, under projects number DPI2005-09133-C03-01 and DPI2005 08732-C02-02, project reference GV06/115, European Project number 500095-2 and Fondo Europeo Desarrollo Regional (FEDER). We would like also, to thank the R+D+i Linguistic Assistance Office at the Universidad Politecnica of Valencia for their help in revising this paper.

References

1. Ahmed, M., Farag, A.: Non metric calibration of camera lens distortion: Differential methods and robust estimation. IEEE Transactions on image processing 14(8), 1215–1230 (2005)
2. Hartley, R.: In defence of the eight point algorithm. IEEE Transactions on pattern analysis and machine intelligence, vol. 19(6) (1997)
3. Lavest, J., Viala, M., Dhome, M.: Do we really need accurate calibration pattern to achieve a reliable camera calibration. European Conference on Computer Vision, vol. I (1998)
4. Salvi, J., Armangué, X., Batlle, J.: A Comparative review of camera calibrating methods with accuracy evaluation. Pattern recognition 35, 1617–1635 (2002)
5. Sun, W., Cooperstock, J.: An empirical evaluation of factors influencing camera calibration accuracy using three publicly available techniques. In: Machine Vision and Applications, vol. 17(1), pp. 51–67. Springer, Heidelberg (2006)
6. Tsai, R.: A versatile camera calibration technique for high-accuracy 3D machine vision metrology using off-the-self TV camera lenses. IEEE Journal of Robotics and Automation RA-3(4), 323–344 (1997)
7. Zhang, Z.: A flexible new technique for camera calibration. Technical Report MSR-TR-98-71, Microsoft Research (1998)
8. Zhang, Z.: Camera calibration with one-dimensional objects. Technical Report MSR-TR-2001-120, Microsoft research (2002)

Relative Pose Estimation of Surgical Tools in Assisted Minimally Invasive Surgery

Agustin Navarro, Edgar Villarraga, and Joan Aranda

Technical University of Catalonia, ESAII Department, Barcelona, Spain
agustin.navarro@upc.edu, edgar.alberto.villarraga@upc.edu,
joan.aranda@upc.edu

Abstract. Minimally Invasive Surgery (MIS) is one of these applications where usually only 2D information is available to perform a 3D task. It requires a high degree of sensory-motor skills to overcome the disengagement between action and perception caused by the physical separation of the surgeon with the operative site. The integration of body movements with visual information serves to assist the surgeon providing a sense of position. Our purpose in this paper is to present a solution to the exterior orientation problem based on computer vision, as a tool in assisted interventions, locating the instruments with respect to the surgeon. Having knowledge of the 3D transformations applied to the instrument and its projections in the image plane, we show it is possible to estimate its orientation with only two different rotations and also its relative position if scale information is supplied. Experimental results show some advantages of this new algorithm such as simplicity and real-time performance.

1 Introduction

The visual sense in the Minimally Invasive Surgery (MIS) environment is very limited. It imposes a 2D window of the operative site. Thus, approaches focused to assist the surgeon are fundamentally based on image content recognition and presentation. Dutkiewicz et al. [1] reported an experimental verification of surgical tool tracking to be presented in the center of the image. Sun et al. [2] studied the distribution of markers to accurately track the instruments, and Payandeh et al. in [3] established models for the lens distortion. These are examples of emergent techniques to assist the surgeon.

Healey in [4] describes the mediation between action and perception in the MIS environment. There he states that it is necessary to effectively link action to perception in egocentric coordinates to overcome the indirect cognitive mediation. It can be seen in Fig. 1 an application where exterior orientation is used and presented through enhanced visual information to assist the surgeon. This presentation is commonly performed by augmented reality. From early approaches as the one by Milgram et al. [5] in different kinds of applications, to more specialized in surgery as the works of Devernay [6], recognizing objects seen by the endoscope in cardiac MIS, or Pandya and Auner [7], designing a system for surgical guidance, this visual enhancement has served as a human-machine interface.

J. Martí et al. (Eds.): IbPRIA 2007, Part II, LNCS 4478, pp. 428–435, 2007.

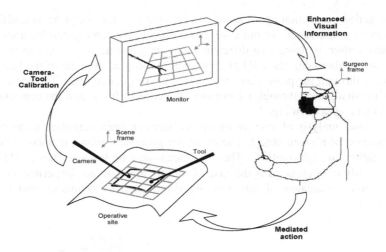

Fig. 1. Application of the exterior orientation as a tool to assist the surgeon in MIS through perception enhancement to control the action

We suggest that the estimation of the position and orientation of the surgery instruments with respect to the camera is capable to provide this egocentric information. Computer vision issues as the 2D-3D pose estimation and exterior orientation deal with this problem and can be applied to aid the surgeon in this kind of procedures.

Several methods have been proposed to estimate the orientation of a rigid object. The first step of these algorithms consists in the identification and location of some kind of features that represent an object in the image plane. Most of them rely on feature points and apply either closed-form or numerical solutions, depending on the number of objects and image feature correspondences. Some works dealing with a small number of correspondences apply iterative numerical techniques as [8] and [9]. Other methods apply a direct linear transform (DLT) for a larger number of points as [10] or reduce the problem to close-form solutions, as [11] applying orthogonal decomposition.

In this work the features of interest will be lines associated to object direction. There are several approaches that use this kind of features to estimate motion parameters. Some early works solve a set of nonlinear equations, as the one in [12], or use iterated extended Kalman filters, as show in [13], through three perspective views. Works by [14] combine sets of lines and points for a linear estimation, and [15] discuss the estimation of motion and structure parameters studying the inherent stability of lines and explain why two views are not enough.

An important property of using lines, as reported in [16], is the angular invariance between them. Then, our goal is to study this property to provide a robust method that solves orientation estimation problems. It is possible to compute the orientation of an object through the analysis of angular variations in the image plane induced by its 3D rotations with respect to the camera. It can be seen as an exterior orientation problem where objects in the scene are moved to calculate their pose.

Some action-perception applications can be seen as a fixed camera visualizing the objects to be manipulated. In our case, these objects are represented by lines. Three views taken after applying two different rotations generate three lines in the image plane. Each of them defines a 3D plane called the projection plane of the line. These planes pass through the projection center and their respective lines. Their intersection is a 3D line that passes through the origin of the camera frame and the centroid of the rotated object, as seen in Fig. 2.

The motion analysis of angular variations between lines permitted us to estimate the orientation of a given object. Therefore, we propose a robust method to compute the orientation through rotations. These rotations must be known. They could be just sensed or fully controlled, as is the case of robotic applications. Experimental results showed some advantages of this new algorithm such as simplicity and real-time performance.

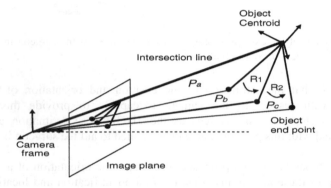

Fig. 2. A 3D line through the origins is the intersection of the projection planes after two rotations of the object

2 Orientation Estimation Algorithm

Motion analysis of feature lines is the base of our orientation estimation algorithm. In this case known 3D rotations of a line and its subsequent projections in the image plane are related to compute its relative orientation with respect to a perspective camera. Vision problems as feature extraction and line correspondences are not discussed and we assume that the focal distance f as known. Our goal is, having this image and its associated motion information, to estimate the orientation of an object represented by feature lines, with the minimum number of movements and to identify the patterns that permit to compute a unique solution without defined initial conditions.

2.1 Mathematical Analysis

The result of the projection of a line in the image plane is called the projection plane. It passes through the projection center of the camera and the 3D line. This 3D line is the representation of an object. From three views taken after applying two different rotations of the object, three lines are projected in the image plane. Thus three projection planes can be calculated. These planes are P_a, P_b and P_c, and their intersection is a 3D line that passes through the projection center and the centroid of the rotated object, being the centroid the point of the object where it is rotated. Across this line a unit director vector v_d can be determined easily by knowing f and the intersection point of the projected lines in the image plane. Our intention is to use this 2D information to formulate angle relations with the 3D motion data.

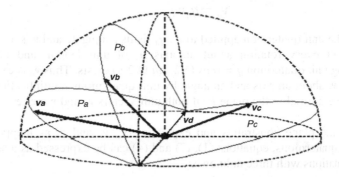

Fig. 3. Unit vectors Va, Vb and Vc are constrained to lie on planes Pa, Pb and Pc respectively. Their estimation can be seen as a semi sphere where their combination must satisfy the angle variations condition.

Working in the 3D space permits to take advantage of the motion data. In this case where the object is represented by a 3D line, the problem could be seen as a unit vector along the line direction that is rotated twice. In each position of the three views this unit vector lies in one of the projection planes as seen in Fig. 3. It is first located in P_a, then it rotates an angle α_1 to lie on P_b and ends in P_c after the second rotation by an angle α_2. To estimate the relative orientation of the object we first obtain the location of three unit vectors, v_a, v_b and v_c, that coincide with the 3D motion data and lie on their respective planes. To do this we know that the scalar product of:

$$v_a.v_b = \cos\alpha_1 \tag{1}$$

$$v_b.v_c = \cos\alpha_2 \tag{2}$$

Calculating the angle γ between the planes formed by $v_a v_b$ and $v_b v_c$ from the motion information, we have

$$\left(v_a \times v_b\right)\left(v_b \times v_c\right) = \cos\gamma \tag{3}$$

And applying vector identities

$$v_a.v_c = \cos\alpha_1 \cos\alpha_2 - \cos\gamma \tag{4}$$

With the set of equations conformed by (1), (2) and (4) we have to calculate the three unit vectors. However, since there is not a unique solution, some constraints must be applied.

2.2 Projection Planes Constraint

There are many possible locations where the three unit vectors can satisfy the equations in the 3D space. To obtain a unique solution unit vectors v_a, v_b and v_c must be constrained to lie in their respective planes. Unit vector v_a could be seen as any unit vector in the plane P_a rotated through an axis and an angle. Using unit quaternions to express v_a we have

$$v_a = q_a v q_a^*$$ (5)

where q_a is the unit quaternion applied to v_a, q_a^* is its conjugate and v is any vector in the plane. For every rotation about an axis n, of unit length, and angle Ω, a corresponding unit quaternion $q = (cos\ \Omega/2,\ sin\ \Omega/2\ n)$ exists. Thus v_a is expressed as a rotation of v, about an axis and an angle by unit quaternions multiplications. In this case n must be normal to the plane P_a if both unit vectors v_a and v are restricted to be in the plane.

Applying the plane constraints and expressing v_a, v_b and v_c as mapped vectors through unit quaternions, equations (1), (2) and (4) can be expressed as a set of three nonlinear equations with three unknowns

$$q_a v_d q_a^* q_b v_d q_b^* = \cos \alpha_1$$ (6)

$$q_b v_d q_b^* q_c v_d q_c^* = \cos \alpha_2$$ (7)

$$q_a v_d q_a^* q_c v_d q_c^* = \cos \alpha_1 \cos \alpha_2 - \cos \gamma$$ (8)

The vector to be rotated is v_d, which is common to the three planes, and their respective normal vectors are the axes of rotation. Extending the equations (6), (7) and (8), multiplying vectors and quaternions, permits to see that there are only three unknowns which are the angles of rotation Ω_a, Ω_b and Ω_c.

Applying iterative numerical methods to solve the set of nonlinear equations, the location of v_a, v_b and v_c with respect to the camera frame in the 3D space are calculated. Now we have a simple 3D orientation problem that can be solved easily by a variety of methods as least square based techniques. However, in the case where motions could be controlled and selected movements applied, this last step to estimate the relative orientation would be eliminated. Rotation information could be obtained directly from the numerical solution. If we assume that one of the coordinate axes of the object frame coincide with the moving unit vector and apply selected motions, as one component rotations, a unique solution is provided faster and easier.

3 Experimental Results

Real world data was used to validate the algorithm. Experiments were carried out through a robotic test bed that was developed in order to get high repeatability. It consists on an articulated robotic arm with a calibrated tool frame equipped with a surgery instrument, which is presented in different precisely known orientations to a camera. The camera field of view remains fixed during the image acquisition sequence.

An endoscopic camera with known focal length optics has been used. This generates a wide field of view that is sampled at 768x576 pixels resolution. After image edge detection, Hough Transform is used in order to obtain the tool contour and the straight line in the image plane associated to it. Tool contour is supposed to have the longest number of aligned pixel edges in the image. Fig. 4 shows this process.

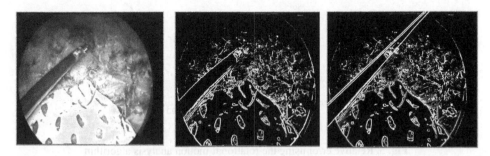

Fig. 4. Image processing to obtain straight boundaries from the surgery instrument

Feature lines were identified and located in a sequence of images. Once the equations of the lines projected in the image plane were acquired, unit vectors normal to the constraint planes and v_d could be calculated. This unit vectors and the motion angles α_1 and α_2 served as the input to the proposed algorithm. The intersection of the lines was needed to calculate v_d. This calculation is prone to errors due to be located out of the field of view. It means the intersection of a different number of lines is not usually the same point. Table 1 shows the standard deviation in pixels of the intersection points calculated through different motion angles. The intersections converge to a single point when the angles between lines are higher.

Table 1. Standard deviation of intersecting lines through different motion angles; with the intersection point defined by Xint and Yint

Degrees (α_1, α_2)	Xint	Yint	σ
5	895,81	264,11	62,31
10	928,28	278,91	35,65

The 3D transformation resultant from the algorithm was tested projecting 3D lines, derived from new tool rotations, in the image plane and comparing them with the line detected by the vision system. Tests for motion angles between 5 and 20 degrees were carried out. Fig. 5 shows the error between lines through different angles. There can be seen how the error is minimum at the position where the transformation was calculated, it means at its second motion or third image. This error varies depending on the position of the tool; it increases with higher angles, when the position of the tool separates from the minimum error position. Fig. 6 compares the algorithm performance for 5 and 20 degrees motion angles. There the error varies differently. In the case of 5 degrees the error increases greatly with each motion that separates the tool from the minimum error position. While for 20 degrees this error also increments, but remains stable.

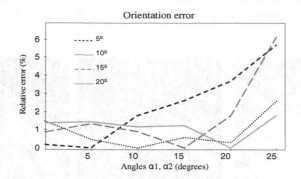

Fig. 5. Relative error using the rotational motion analysis algorithm

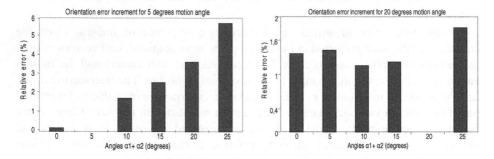

Fig. 6. Algorithm performance comparison between 5 and 20 degrees, with a first rotation α1 followed by a second α2 of the same magnitude

These results validate the line-based algorithm and its simplicity demonstrates its real-time performance. The error increment with large position separations is mainly product of the deviation at the intersection point. It can be seen that the calculation of v_d has a great impact in the result and future work should be focused in this issue.

4   Conclusions

A robust method to estimate the relative orientation of a surgical instrument with respect to a camera has been proposed. The instrument has been reduced to a single line indicating its orientation. We showed that with only two known rotations the angular variation between lines provides sufficient information to estimate the relative orientation. This motion analysis led to address questions as the uniqueness of solution for the minimum number of movements and possible motion patterns to solve it directly. In the case of controlled motions, one component rotations through normal axes simplify calculations to provide a robust technique to estimate the relative orientation with no initial conditions defined.

References

1. Dutkiewicz, P., Kielczewski, M., Kowalski, M., Wroblewski, W.: Experimental Verification of Visual Tracking of Surgical Tools. Fifth International workshop on Robot Motion and Control (2005)
2. Sun, J., Smith, M., Smith, L., Nolte, L.P.: Simulation of an Optical-Sensing Technique for Tracking Surgical Tools Employed in Computer-Assisted Interventions. IEEE Sensors Journal, vol. 5(5) (2005)
3. Payandeh, S., Xiaoli, Z., Li, A.: Application of Imaging to the Laparoscopic Surgery. IEEE Int. Symp. Computer Intelligence in Robotics and Automation, pp. 432–437 (2001)
4. Healey, A.: On Mediating Action and Perception in a Surgical Wonderland. In: Presence: Teleoperators and Virtual Environments, MIT Press, Cambridge, MA (2004)
5. Milgram, P., Zhai, S., Drascic, D., Grodski, J.: Applications of Augmented Reality for Human-Robot Communication. In: Proc. Int. Conf. on Intelligent Robotics and Systems, pp. 1467–1472 (1993)
6. Devernay, F., Mourgues, F., Coste-Maniere, E.: Towards Endoscopy Augmented Reality for Robotically Assisted Minimally Invasive Cardiac Surgery. IEEE Proc. Int. Workshop on Medical Imaging and Augmented Reality, pp. 16–20 (2001)
7. Pandya, A., Auner, G.: Simultaneous Augmented and Virtual Reality for Surgical Navigation. IEEE Annual Meeting of the North American Fuzzy Information Processing Society (2005)
8. Lowe, D.G.: Three-dimensional Object Recognition from Single Two-dimensional Images. Artificial Intelligence, vol. 31(3) (1987)
9. Haralick, R.M., Lee, C., Ottenberg, K., Nölle, M.: Analysis and Solutions of the Three Point Perspective Pose Estimation Problem. IEEE Conf. Computer Vision and Pattern Recognition (1991)
10. Hartley, R.I.: Minimizing Algebraic Error in Geometric Estimation Problems. In: Proc. Int. Conf. Computer Vision, pp. 469–476 (1998)
11. Fiore, P.: Efficient Linear Solution of Exterior Orientation. IEEE Trans. Pattern Analysis and Machine Intelligence 23, 2 (2001)
12. Yen, B.L., Huang, T.S.: Determining 3-D Motion and Structure of a Rigid Body using Straight Line Correspondences. In: Image sequence Processing and Dynamic Scene Analysis, Springer, Heidelberg (1983)
13. Faugeras, O., Lustran, F., Toscani, G.: Motion and Structure from Point and Line Matches. In: Proc. First Int. Conf. Computer Vision (1987)
14. Ansar, A., Daniilidis, K.: Linear Pose Estimation from Points and Lines. IEEE Trans. Pattern Analysis and Machine Intelligence 25, 578–589 (2003)
15. Weng, J., Huang, T.S., Ahuja, N.: Motion and Structure from Line Correspondences; Closed-form Solution, Uniqueness, and Optimization. IEEE Trans. Pattern Analysis and Machine Intelligence 14(3), 318–336 (1992)
16. Mitiche, A., Seida, S., Aggarwal, J.K.: Interpretation of Structure and Motion using Straight Line Correspondences. In: Proc. Int. Pattern recognition (1986)

Efficiently Downdating, Composing and Splitting Singular Value Decompositions Preserving the Mean Information

Javier Melenchón and Elisa Martínez

Communications and Signal Theory Department,
Enginyeria La Salle, Universitat Ramon Llull,
Pg. Bonanova, 8, 08002 Barcelona, Spain
jmelen@salle.url.edu, elisa@salle.url.edu

Abstract. Three methods for the efficient downdating, composition and splitting of low rank singular value decompositions are proposed. They are formulated in a closed form, considering the mean information and providing exact results. Although these methods are presented in the context of computer vision, they can be used in any field forgetting information, combining different eigenspaces in one or ignoring particular dimensions of the column space of the data. Application examples on face subspace learning and latent semantic analysis are given and performance results are provided.

1 Introduction

Process analysis can be carried out by means of the observation of its related data. In general, the more data obtained, the more detailed the analysis can be; however, redundancy is also increased. The latter effect is specially important when managing high dimensional data, e.g., video sequences, images, audio waveforms and document sets, which makes the analysis harder; nevertheless, this kind of data can usually be approximated by a subspace of low dimension. Working with these subspaces in the analysis process has two main advantages: i) the laws or rules of the system are described in a more intuitive way; ii) processing algorithms tend to be faster and require less memory space. Therefore, dimensionality reduction techniques [1] are welcome to remove all possible redundant information of high dimensional data. The reader is referred to [2], [3] and [4] for some examples involving data analysis in low dimensional spaces.

Given a data set, the well-known Karhunen-Loève expansion [5] can find its optimal orthogonal basis, which is the expression of its underlying subspace. This expansion has received different names in the literature, e.g., principal component analysis (PCA) [6], and can be computed with the singular value decomposition (SVD) [7], which is a powerful mathematical tool of linear algebra. Therefore, the SVD can be used to find the subspace of any data set, e.g., the low dimensional subspace for video and image sequences of natural scenes.

J. Martí et al. (Eds.): IbPRIA 2007, Part II, LNCS 4478, pp. 436–443, 2007.
© Springer-Verlag Berlin Heidelberg 2007

However, SVD computation is rather expensive, specially when using a batch algorithm [7], requiring the whole data matrix at once. For high dimensional data such as video sequences, this last fact is a key point, as they can easily exhaust memory resources. Incremental schemes have recovered importance in the last decade, with the increasing interest in video and image sequence processing. Most efforts have been directed to incremental computation of SVD, but little attention has been given to other cases, as SVD downdating (or decremental SVD), composing little subspaces into a higher dimensional one or splitting an existing subspace into little ones.

1.1 Related Work

The first work introducing an incremental computation of SVD in the field of computer vision was [8]; although it is an efficient algorithm based on eigenvalue decomposition (EVD), it can only update one vectorized image per iteration (or column update), it does not account for the mean information and has some potential numerical instability; moreover, only the left singular vectors and singular values are obtained. Chandrasekaran et al. [9] proposed a more stable update algorithm based on the work of Gu et al. [10], where a direct SVD readjustment was given, also updating the right singular values; however it still cannot update more than one column per iteration and does not take into account the mean information. Fortunately, Hall et al. [11] included it in the incremental computation of SVD, also allowing for multiple columns update (or block update). This work is based on EVD, achieving a method to merge and split subspaces, which can be seen as updating and downdating the SVD; however, they only offer the left singular vectors and singular values. Later, these authors presented another approximation [12] based on direct SVD updating, obtaining the right singular vectors and achieving better numerical stability; nevertheless, they claimed that SVD downdate was impossible to achieve in closed form with their formulation. Brand [13] proposed a highly efficient and stable incremental SVD algorithm with block update and also pointed out a way of adapting the eigenspace defined by the SVD to nonstationary systems by means of decaying singular values; however, he did not take into account the mean information. The work of Skocaj et al. [14] is very similar to that of [11]; eigendecomposition is used, mean information update is taken into account and robust features are presented, however block update is not considered. Melenchon et al. [15] extended the work of [13] proposing a novel incremental algorithm through a reorthonormalization process, allowing block update with the stability and efficiency of [13] and mean update like in [12]; however, SVD downdating is not addressed in their work. Finally, Lim et al. [16] presented a new alternative based on R-bidiagonalization SVD (RSVD) [7]; mean update is taken into account, block update is offered and a forgetting factor is introduced, based on [17] and similarly to [13]. However, old information is progressively forgotten but never removed in [13] and [16]. The reader is referred to table 1 for a summary about the described works. Additional SVD early history can be read in [18].

Table 1. Evolution about incremental computation of SVD in computer vision fields. Main features of past and proposed methods. Note the decaying singular values of [13], the robust features of [14], and the forgetfulness of [16].

Work	Year	Method	Update columns	Mean update	Down-date	Miscellanea
[8] Murakami et al.	1982	EVD	single	no	no	
[9] Chandrasekaran et al.	1997	SVD	single	no	no	
[11] Hall et al.	2000	EVD	multiple	yes	yes	
[12] Hall et al.	2002	SVD	multiple	yes	limited	
[13] Brand	2002	SVD	multiple	no	no	decaying
[14] Skocaj et al.	2003	EVD	single	yes	no	robust
[15] Melenchón et al.	2004	SVD	multiple	yes	no	
[16] Lim et al.	2005	RSVD	multiple	yes	no	forgetful
This paper	2006	SVD	multiple	yes	yes	$\begin{cases} \text{splitted} \\ \text{composed} \end{cases}$

1.2 Contributions

Three novel methods for efficiently downdating the SVD (section 2.1), composing different SVD's (section 2.2) and splitting existing ones (section 2.3) are proposed in this work. They are presented in closed form, preserve the mean information and are based on the reorthonormalization process and mean extraction of [15]. Moreover, they become extremely efficient for low rank SVD's. Their application to video sequence data is shown in section 3. Additional experiments have been conducted with textual information in the Latent Semantic analysis (LSA) framework [3] to test the methods with sparse matrices. Concluding remarks and future work are provided in section 4.

2 SVD Computation

Let $\mathbf{D}_{m \times n}$ be a real matrix of full rank $r = min\,(m, n)$, then its singular value decomposition can be expressed as a sum of r rank one matrices (matrix size will only be shown when necessary for clarity purposes):

$$\mathbf{D}_{m \times n} = \mathbf{U}'_{m \times m} \mathbf{\Sigma}'_{m \times n} \left(\mathbf{V}'_{n \times n}\right)^T = \sum_{i=1}^{r} \sigma'_i \mathbf{u}'_i \left(\mathbf{v}'_i\right)^T . \tag{1}$$

where $\mathbf{U}' = [\mathbf{u}'_1 \cdots \mathbf{u}'_m]$ and $\mathbf{V}' = [\mathbf{v}'_1 \cdots \mathbf{v}'_n]$ are orthonormal matrices containing the eigenvectors of $\mathbf{DD}^T$ and $\mathbf{D}^T\mathbf{D}$, respectively (a.k.a. right and left singular vectors of $\mathbf{D}$), and $\mathbf{\Sigma} = diag\,(\sigma_1, \ldots, \sigma_r)$ is a diagonal matrix with the eigenvalues of both $\mathbf{DD}^T$ and $\mathbf{D}^T\mathbf{D}$ (a.k.a. singular values of $\mathbf{D}$) in descending order. The SVD finds the best rank k approximation matrix of $\mathbf{D}$. Any other rank k matrix $\mathbf{B}$ that is not the rank k SVD approximation will have greater error:

$$\underset{rank(\mathbf{B})=k}{argmin} \ \|\mathbf{D}_{m \times n} - \mathbf{B}_{m \times n}\|_2 = \mathbf{A}_{m \times n} = \mathbf{U}'_{m \times k} \mathbf{\Sigma}'_{k \times k} \left(\mathbf{V}'_{n \times k}\right)^T . \tag{2}$$

where $\|\mathbf{D} - \mathbf{A}\|_2 = \sigma'_{k+1}$. The reader is referred to [7] for a proof of (2). The SVD of $\mathbf{A}$ (2) is known as the truncated SVD of $\mathbf{D}$ and also as its compact version when $\mathbf{D}$ is a rank k matrix.

The SVD is often used when computing the PCA of a dataset $\mathbf{D}$ approximated by $\mathbf{A}$, which needs the extraction of the mean information; moreover, it is needed in statistical methods used in classification problems, like mahalanobis distance. Let the mean be $\bar{\mathbf{a}}_{m\times 1} = m^{-1}\mathbf{A}_{m\times n} \cdot \mathbf{1}_{n\times 1}$, it is often required to obtain a mean centered dataset $\overline{\mathbf{A}} = \mathbf{A} - \bar{\mathbf{a}} \cdot \mathbf{1}$ with the following truncated SVD:

$$\mathbf{A}_{m\times n} = \overline{\mathbf{A}}_{m\times n} + \bar{\mathbf{a}}_{m\times 1} \cdot \mathbf{1}_{1\times n} = \mathbf{U}_{m\times k}\mathbf{\Sigma}_{k\times k}\left(\mathbf{V}_{n\times k}\right)^T + \bar{\mathbf{a}}_{m\times 1} \cdot \mathbf{1}_{1\times n} . \quad (3)$$

2.1 Decremental SVD

In this section, the problem of downdating the SVD preserving the mean information is addressed. Dropping columns of any data matrix can be considered as a radical forgetting action. Given (3), if p columns are removed from $\mathbf{A}$, a new matrix $\mathbf{A}^d_{m\times l}$ is obtained, where $l = n - p$. The SVD of $\mathbf{A}^d_{m\times l}$ can be updated efficiently with (4), without recomputing it from scratch.

$$\mathbf{A} = \mathbf{U}\mathbf{\Sigma}\mathbf{V}^T + \bar{\mathbf{a}}\cdot\mathbf{1} \Rightarrow \mathbf{A}^d = \mathbf{U}\mathbf{\Sigma}\tilde{\mathbf{V}}^T + \bar{\mathbf{a}}\cdot\mathbf{1} = \mathbf{U}\mathbf{\Sigma}\hat{\mathbf{V}}^T + \mathbf{U}\mathbf{\Sigma}\bar{\mathbf{v}}^T\cdot\mathbf{1} + \bar{\mathbf{a}}\cdot\mathbf{1} =$$
$$= \mathbf{U}\mathbf{\Sigma}\mathbf{R}^T\mathbf{Q}^T + \left(\mathbf{\Delta}\bar{\mathbf{a}}^d + \bar{\mathbf{a}}\right)\cdot\mathbf{1} = \mathbf{U}^d\mathbf{\Sigma}^d\mathbf{V}^T_t\mathbf{Q}^T + \bar{\mathbf{a}}^d\cdot\mathbf{1} =$$
$$= \mathbf{U}^d_{m\times k}\mathbf{\Sigma}^d_{k\times k}\left(\mathbf{V}^d_{l\times k}\right)^T + \bar{\mathbf{a}}^d_{m\times 1}\cdot\mathbf{1}_{1\times l} = \mathbf{A}^d_{m\times l} . \quad (4)$$

here, matrix $\tilde{\mathbf{V}}^T$ is not orthonormal and contains the columns of $\mathbf{V}^T$ corresponding to the non-dropped columns of $\mathbf{A}$. It is centered around its mean row $\bar{\mathbf{v}} = l^{-1}(\mathbf{1}_{1\times l} \cdot \tilde{\mathbf{V}}_{l\times k})$, obtaining matrix $\hat{\mathbf{V}}$. The mean update $\mathbf{\Delta}\bar{\mathbf{a}}^d$ is computed as $\mathbf{U}\mathbf{\Sigma}\bar{\mathbf{v}}^T$. The updated mean $\bar{\mathbf{a}}^d$ is obtained as $\bar{\mathbf{a}} + \mathbf{\Delta}\bar{\mathbf{a}}^d$. Finally, the expression $\mathbf{U}\mathbf{\Sigma}\hat{\mathbf{V}}^T$ is reorthonormalized as $\mathbf{U}^d\mathbf{\Sigma}^d(\mathbf{V}^d)^T$ with the QR decomposition of $\hat{\mathbf{V}} = \mathbf{Q}\mathbf{R}$, the SVD of $\mathbf{U}\mathbf{\Sigma}\mathbf{R}^T = \mathbf{U}^d\mathbf{\Sigma}^d\mathbf{V}^T_t$ (with lower cost than that of $\mathbf{U}\mathbf{\Sigma}\hat{\mathbf{V}}^T$, since $k < n$) and the identity $\mathbf{V}^d = \mathbf{Q}\mathbf{V}_t$.

2.2 Composed SVD

Given matrices $\mathbf{A}$, $\mathbf{B}$ and their compact SVD's (5), (6), that of $\mathbf{C} = [\mathbf{A}^T \ \mathbf{B}^T]^T$ (7) can be obtained efficiently from them (8), if $m = q + p$ and $k = r + s$.

$$\mathbf{A}_{q\times n} = \mathbf{U}^A_{q\times r}\mathbf{\Sigma}^A_{r\times r}\left(\mathbf{V}^A_{n\times r}\right)^T + \bar{\mathbf{a}}^A_{q\times 1} \cdot \mathbf{1}_{1\times n} . \quad (5)$$

$$\mathbf{B}_{p\times n} = \mathbf{U}^B_{p\times s}\mathbf{\Sigma}^B_{s\times s}\left(\mathbf{V}^B_{n\times s}\right)^T + \bar{\mathbf{a}}^B_{p\times 1} \cdot \mathbf{1}_{1\times n} . \quad (6)$$

$$\mathbf{C}_{m\times n} = \mathbf{U}^C_{m\times k}\mathbf{\Sigma}^C_{k\times k}\left(\mathbf{V}^C_{n\times k}\right)^T + \bar{\mathbf{a}}^C_{m\times 1} \cdot \mathbf{1}_{1\times n} . \quad (7)$$

$$\mathbf{C} = \begin{bmatrix} \mathbf{A} \\ \mathbf{B} \end{bmatrix} = \begin{bmatrix} \mathbf{U}^A\mathbf{\Sigma}^A\left(\mathbf{V}^A\right)^T \\ \mathbf{U}^B\mathbf{\Sigma}^B\left(\mathbf{V}^B\right)^T \end{bmatrix} + \begin{bmatrix} \bar{\mathbf{a}}^A \\ \bar{\mathbf{a}}^B \end{bmatrix} = \begin{bmatrix} \mathbf{U}^A\mathbf{\Sigma}^A\mathbf{R}^T_A \\ \mathbf{U}^B\mathbf{\Sigma}^B\mathbf{R}^T_B \end{bmatrix}\mathbf{Q}^T_t + \begin{bmatrix} \bar{\mathbf{a}}^A \\ \bar{\mathbf{a}}^B \end{bmatrix} =$$
$$= \mathbf{U}^C\mathbf{\Sigma}^C\mathbf{V}^T_t\mathbf{Q}^T_t + \bar{\mathbf{a}}^C = \mathbf{U}^C\mathbf{\Sigma}^C\left(\mathbf{V}^C\right)^T + \bar{\mathbf{a}}^C . \quad (8)$$

where the QR decomposition of $\begin{bmatrix} \mathbf{V}^A & \mathbf{V}^B \end{bmatrix}$ is $\mathbf{Q}_t \begin{bmatrix} \mathbf{R}_A & \mathbf{R}_B \end{bmatrix}$ and the SVD is done to matrix $[(\mathbf{U}^A\boldsymbol{\Sigma}^A\mathbf{R}_A^T)^T \ (\mathbf{U}^B\boldsymbol{\Sigma}^B\mathbf{R}_B^T)^T]^T$, obtaining $\mathbf{U}^C\boldsymbol{\Sigma}^C\mathbf{V}_t^T$ (with lower cost than computing the SVD of $[\mathbf{A}^T\mathbf{B}^T]^T$), as $k < n$); finally, matrix $\mathbf{V}^C$ is computed as $\mathbf{Q}\mathbf{V}_t$ and $\overline{\mathbf{a}}^C$ is obtained as the vertical concatenation of $\overline{\mathbf{a}}^A$ and $\overline{\mathbf{a}}^B$. Any SVD's of matrices with the same number of columns can be composed.

2.3 Splitted SVD

This case is the opposite of that in section 2.2: given a SVD (7), the desire is to obtain two (or more) SVD's, (5) and (6), splitting the subspace definition of the starting one (in this case $k = r = s$). It can be achieved as follows, using the reorthonormalization process proposed in section 2.1:

$$
\mathbf{C} = \begin{bmatrix} \mathbf{U}_s^A \\ \mathbf{U}_s^B \end{bmatrix} \boldsymbol{\Sigma}^C \left(\mathbf{V}^C\right)^T + \begin{bmatrix} \overline{\mathbf{a}}^A \\ \overline{\mathbf{a}}^B \end{bmatrix} = \begin{bmatrix} \mathbf{Q}^A\mathbf{R}^A\boldsymbol{\Sigma}^C \left(\mathbf{V}^C\right)^T \\ \mathbf{Q}^B\mathbf{R}^B\boldsymbol{\Sigma}^C \left(\mathbf{V}^C\right)^T \end{bmatrix} + \begin{bmatrix} \overline{\mathbf{a}}^A \\ \overline{\mathbf{a}}^B \end{bmatrix} =
$$

$$
= \begin{bmatrix} \mathbf{Q}^A\mathbf{U}_t^A\boldsymbol{\Sigma}^A \left(\mathbf{V}^A\right)^T \\ \mathbf{Q}^B\mathbf{U}_t^B\boldsymbol{\Sigma}^B \left(\mathbf{V}^B\right)^T \end{bmatrix} + \begin{bmatrix} \overline{\mathbf{a}}^A \\ \overline{\mathbf{a}}^B \end{bmatrix} = \begin{bmatrix} \mathbf{U}^A\boldsymbol{\Sigma}^A \left(\mathbf{V}^A\right)^T + \overline{\mathbf{a}}^A \\ \mathbf{U}^B\boldsymbol{\Sigma}^B \left(\mathbf{V}^B\right)^T + \overline{\mathbf{a}}^B \end{bmatrix} = \begin{bmatrix} \mathbf{A} \\ \mathbf{B} \end{bmatrix}. \quad (9)
$$

where $(\mathbf{U}^C)^T = [(\mathbf{U}_s^A)^T \ (\mathbf{U}_s^B)^T]^T$ and $(\overline{\mathbf{a}}^C)^T = [(\overline{\mathbf{a}}^A)^T \ (\overline{\mathbf{a}}^B)^T]^T$; QR decomposition is done to $\mathbf{U}_s^A = \mathbf{Q}^A\mathbf{R}^A$ and $\mathbf{U}_s^B = \mathbf{Q}^B\mathbf{R}^B$; the SVD is computed to $\mathbf{R}^A\boldsymbol{\Sigma}^C(\mathbf{V}^C)^T = \mathbf{U}_t^A\boldsymbol{\Sigma}^A(\mathbf{V}^A)^T$ and $\mathbf{R}^B\boldsymbol{\Sigma}^C(\mathbf{V}^C)^T = \mathbf{U}_t^B\boldsymbol{\Sigma}^B(\mathbf{V}^B)^T$ with lower cost than those of $\mathbf{U}_s^A\boldsymbol{\Sigma}^A(\mathbf{V}^A)^T$ and $\mathbf{U}_s^B\boldsymbol{\Sigma}^B(\mathbf{V}^B)^T$, since $k < m$; finally, $\mathbf{U}^A = \mathbf{Q}^A\mathbf{U}_t^A$ and $\mathbf{U}^B = \mathbf{Q}^B\mathbf{U}_t^B$. Rows of matrix $\mathbf{C}$ can be reordered with some permutation matrix $\mathbf{P}$, obtaining $\mathbf{C}_r$; therefore, $\mathbf{U}^C$ and $\overline{\mathbf{a}}^C$ can also be reordered by the same $\mathbf{P}$, further obtaining $\mathbf{U}_r^C$ and $\overline{\mathbf{a}}_r^C$ in (10). Consequently, rows of matrix $\mathbf{C}$ can be splitted into any desired groups: first, row grouping can be achieved with (10); second, (9) can be applied to the reordered SVD.

$$
\mathbf{C}_r = \mathbf{P}\mathbf{C} = \mathbf{P}\mathbf{U}^C\boldsymbol{\Sigma}^C \left(\mathbf{V}^C\right)^T + \mathbf{P}\overline{\mathbf{a}}^C = \mathbf{U}_r^C\boldsymbol{\Sigma}^C \left(\mathbf{V}^C\right)^T + \overline{\mathbf{a}}_r^C. \quad (10)
$$

3 Results

The proposed algorithms of decremental, composed and splitted SVD have been applied to computer vision and LSA fields. Datasets and tests are presented in sections 3.1 and 3.2. A 3GHz processor with 2GB of RAM has been used.

3.1 Test Data Used

A video data sequence with a size of 320 × 240 and 482 frames (at 25 fps) has been recorded for the testing of the performance of given algorithms, similarly to [14,15,16]. This sequence shows a human face while it is speaking and making different gestures. Using a tracking algorithm like in [15] and [16], the face in each frame can be aligned w.r.t. the first one, so pixel value variations are due only to appearance changes. Collecting all face pixels into columns (one per frame), a matrix $\mathbf{F}$ can be obtained; if the face pixels are classified into R regions, then R matrices $\mathbf{F}_r$ can be built, one per facial region. Here, the forehead, both eyes and mouth have been considered. Moreover, a big textual sparse matrix $\mathbf{T}$ [19] related to LSA has been also considered. The columns represent its 600 documents and the rows offer its 12018 possible words. Efficient SVD algorithms can be applied to this kind of matrices [20]; however, they are outperformed by the proposed algorithms (see 3.2).

3.2   Experiments

The computational cost of the three proposed methods is $O\left(k^2\left(k+m+n\right)\right)$, while the memory requirements are $O\left(km+kn\right)$. Direct batch computation algorithms for the decremental, composed and splitted schemes have been considered for comparison purposes and involve recomputing original matrices and obtaining the desired SVD's directly. They have the same computational and memory costs, $O(m^2n+n^2m)$ and $O(mn)$, which are higher than the proposed ones when $n \gg k$ and $m \gg k$. In all the experiments, the results offered by both approaches were practically the same (spectral norms of difference matrices are less than 10^{-13}). Figure 1 shows the executed experiments.

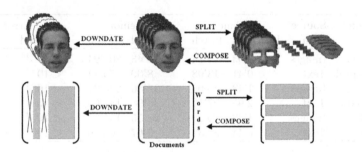

Fig. 1. Description of the experiments on facial appearance (up) and textual data (bottom), both represented by a matrix; the former has faces in its columns and pixels in its rows and the latter has documents in its columns and words in its rows. From left to right: the original data without some faces or documents left; the whole grouped data; the splitted data into 4 facial regions or 3 word sets. Every case has a SVD or set of SVD's; the left decompositions can be provided by downdating the central ones with the decremental SVD; the right ones can be achieved dividing the central decompositions with the splitted SVD, which can also be obtained with the composed SVD from the right ones.

Starting from the truncated SVD of the four matrices $\mathbf{F}_r$ of ranks 17, 10, 9 and 14, corresponding to forehead, both eyes and mouth, respectively, the intention is to compose them in order to obtain the truncated SVD of rank $50 = 17 + 10 + 9 + 14$ of the whole matrix $\mathbf{F}$. Using the composed SVD algorithm (sect. 2.2) both time and memory requirements are reduced w.r.t. the batch approaches. If this matrix was to be divided into the original four facial regions $\mathbf{F}_r$, the splitted SVD of section 2.3 obtains the original truncated SVD's faster and with less memory requirements than the batch process; note that each truncated SVD keeps its original rank. Next, considering the SVD of $\mathbf{F}$, the information of the first 52 frames and the ones from 266 to 325 are removed; the decremental SVD stated in section 2.1 can be executed, obtaining the result far sooner than with the batch scheme and with less memory resources (see table 2).

Regarding the textual data matrix $\mathbf{T}$, a truncated SVD of rank 40 is initially computed. First, the intention is to forget the last 200 documents (as if they had never been observed); with the explained decremental SVD, the time and memory resources spent are of smaller orders of magnitude than those of the batch method. Second, the original truncated SVD of $\mathbf{T}$ is divided into three textual LSA, grouping the first 6437 words, the next 1814 ones and the rest; with the proposed splitted SVD, the result is obtained in less time and with less memory requirements than with the batch process. Joining the resulting SVD's can be done with the composed SVD, which, like before, takes less time and memory than the batch method (table 2).

Table 2. Computational, memory resources and relative errors of the proposed algorithms and their batch counterpart. The latter are obtained with the norm $\|\cdot\|_2$.

Operation	Source data	Time Proposed	Batch	Memory Proposed	Batch	Error Proposed	Batch
Decremental	Images	1'53	30'14	24'43	201'94	$< 10^{-14}$	$< 10^{-13}$
Decremental	Text	0'41	13'08	8'00	79'84	$< 10^{-14}$	$< 10^{-13}$
Composed	Images	1'48	46'09	39'86	245'27	$< 10^{-14}$	$< 10^{-13}$
Composed	Text	2'95	27'19	38'98	131'62	$< 10^{-14}$	$< 10^{-14}$
Splitted	Images	1'42	79'00	28'55	141'27	$< 10^{-14}$	$< 10^{-14}$
Splitted	Text	0'44	38'33	9'67	64'66	$< 10^{-13}$	$< 10^{-14}$

4   Concluding Remarks and Future Work

In this work, three novel methods for SVD computation have been presented. One for downdating the SVD, another one for joining or composing SVD's, increasing the dimension of the final column space, and a last one for dividing or splitting a SVD, obtaining smaller SVD's. They are very efficient for truncated SVD's and for compact ones of low rank matrices, with sublinear computational and memory costs w.r.t. the amount of data (and cubic and linear w.r.t. the rank, which is of smaller orders of magnitude than the size). Moreover, they are solved in closed form and do not provide additional error terms. Some application examples of face subspace learning and LSA have been provided. Future work involving the application of these methods to face segmentation, tracking and synthesis will be carried out.

Acknowledgments. Thanks to G. Cobo and X. Sevillano for the LSA data.

References

1. Kirby, M.: Geometric Data Analysis. In: An empirical Approach to Dimensionality Reduction and the Study of Patterns, John Wiley and Sons, Inc. New York (2001)
2. Sirovich, L., Kirby, M.: A low-dimensional procedure for the characterization of human faces. Journal of the Optical Society of America A 4, 524–529 (1987)
3. Deerwester, S.C., Dumais, S.T., Landauer, T.K., Furnas, G.W., Harshman, R.A.: Indexing by latent semantic analysis. Journal of the American Society of Information Science 41(6), 391–407 (1990)
4. Turk, M., Pentland, A.: Eigenfaces for Recognition. Journal of Cognitive Neuroscience 3(1), 71–86 (1991)
5. Loève, M.: Probability Theory, Van Nostrand. Princeton, New Jersey (1955)
6. Jolliffe, I.T.: Principal Component Analysis. Springer, Heidelberg (1986)
7. Golub, G.H., Van Loan, C.F.: Matrix Computations. Johns Hopkins University Press, Baltimore, MD (1983)
8. Murakami, H., Kumar, V.: Efficient calculation of primary images from a set of images. Trans. on PAMI 4(5), 511–515 (1982)
9. Chandrasekaran, S., Manjunath, B., Wang, Y., Winkeler, J., Zhang, H.: An Eigenspace Update Algorithm for Image Analysis. Graphical Models and Image Processing 59(5), 321–332 (1997)
10. Gu, M., Eisenstat, S.T.: A stable and fast algorithm for updating the singular value decomposition. Tech. report YALEU/DCS/RR-966. Department of Computer Science, Yale University, New Haven (1993)
11. Hall, P.M., Marshall, A.D., Martin, R.R.: Merging and Splitting Eigenspace Models. Trans. on PAMI 22(9), 1042–1049 (2000)
12. Hall, P.M., Marshall, A.D., Martin, R.R.: Adding and subtracting eigenspaces with eigenvalue decomposition and singular value decomposition. Image and Vision Computing 20(13–14), 1009–1016 (2002)
13. Brand, M.: Incremental Singular Value Decomposition of Uncertain Data with Missing Values. In: Proc. of ECCV'02, vol. 1, p. 707 (2002)
14. Skocaj, D., Leonardis, A.: Weighted and robust incremental method for subspace learning. In: Proc. of ICCV'03, vol. 2, pp. 1494–1501 (2003)
15. Melenchón, J., Meler, L., Iriondo, I.: On-the-fly Training. In: Perales, F.J., Draper, B.A. (eds.) AMDO 2004, LNCS, vol. 3179, pp. 146–153. Springer, Heidelberg (2004)
16. Lim, J., Ross, D., Lin, R.S., Yang, M.H.: Incremental Learning for Visual Tracking. Advances in Neural Information Processing Systems 18, 793–800 (2005)
17. Levy, A., Lindenbaum, M.: Sequential Karhunen-Loeve basis extraction and its application to images. Trans. on Image Processing 9(8), 1371–1374 (2000)
18. Stewart, G.W.: On the early history of the singular value decomposition. Society for Industrial and Applied Mathematics Review 35, 551–566 (1993)
19. Cobo, G., Sevillano, X., Alías, F., Socoró, J.C.: Técnicas de representación de textos para clasificación no supervisada de documentos. Procesamiento del Lenguaje Natural 37, 329–336 (2006)
20. Lehoucq, R.B., Sorensen, D.C., Yang, C.: ARPACK Users' Guide. Society for Industrial and Applied Mathematics (1998)

On-Line Classification of Human Activities*

J.C. Nascimento[1], M.A.T. Figueiredo[2], and J.S. Marques[1]

[1] ISR-IST
jan@isr.ist.utl.pt, jsm@isr.ist.utl.pt
[2] IT-IST
mario.figueiredo@lx.it.pt

Abstract. In this paper we address the problem of on-line recognition of human activities taking place in a public area such as a shopping center. We consider standard activities; namely, *entering, exiting, passing* or *browsing*. The problem is motivated by surveillance applications, for which large numbers of cameras have been deployed in recent years. Such systems should be able to detect and recognize human activities, with as little human intervention as possible.

In this work, we model the displacement of a person in consecutive frames using a bank of switched dynamical systems, each of which tailored to the specific motion regimes that each trajectory may contain.

Our experimental results are based on nearly 20,000 images concerning four atomic activities and several complex ones, and demonstrate the effectiveness of the proposed approach.

1 Introduction and Problem Formulation

In this paper, we address the problem of (on-line) recognition of human activities in video sequences. Recently, this has become an active research area in computer vision, mainly driven by a large number of potential applications, such as video surveillance, computer-human interfaces, and contend-based video retrieval.

In a surveillance context, the analysis of the human behavior is often split into two parts: tracking and activity recognition [8]. Considering that tracking has seen tremendous recent progress [2,3,5,6,11,14,16], activity recognition has naturally become the next step to be addressed.

Different methods have been used to recognize human activities from the information extracted from video. The most popular techniques rely on *hidden Markov models* (HMM) and *coupled HMM* [12]. Both approaches are used to characterize the evolution of the person's mass center along the video sequence. A model termed *abstract HMM* was used to recognize human indoor motion patterns [10]. Other types of techniques have also been successfully used for gesture and activity recognition; e.g., Bayesian networks [7], neural networks [15], finite state machines (FSM) [1,4] and syntactic recognition [9].

---

* This work was supported by Fundação para a Ciência e a Tecnologia (ISR/IST pluri-anual funding) through the POS Conhecimento Program which includes FEDER funds.

J. Martí et al. (Eds.): IbPRIA 2007, Part II, LNCS 4478, pp. 444–451, 2007.
© Springer-Verlag Berlin Heidelberg 2007

In this work, we consider that a tracking system computes the active region (bounding box) of the person along the video sequence. We also assume that the measurements provided by the tracker are corrected using the image to ground plane projective transformation, thus achieving viewpoint invariance and removing perspective distortion. Fig. 1 shows an example of an observed trajectory, before and after the projective transformation.

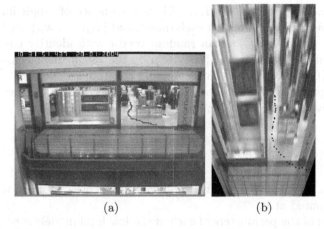

(a)   (b)

Fig. 1. Original (left) and resulting transformed (right) images of the shopping center scenario

Our fundamental assumption is that the human (motion) activity can be inferred from the sequence of positions of the centroid of the person throughout the video sequence, which is provided by the tracker. After the projective transformation is applied, this sequence is denoted $\mathbf{x} = (\mathbf{x}_1, \ldots, \mathbf{x}_n)$, where $\mathbf{x}_t \in \mathbb{R}^2$, for $t = 1, \ldots, n$, is the position at time instant t.

Our approach categorizes human activities using a two-level hierarchical system. At the lower-level, we have *dynamic models*, which are short term coherent units of movement; at the higher level, we consider *activities*, which are linearly ordered sequences of lower level *dynamic models*. In this paper, we consider five low level *dynamic models*: "moving left", "moving right", "moving up", "moving down", "stopped". Four activities are considered: "passing", "entering" "leaving" and "browsing". Of course, this hierarchy could be extended to more complex arrangements of activities, but this will not be pursued in this paper.

Finally, our problem can be formulated as follows: *given a trajectory* $\mathbf{x} = (\mathbf{x}_1, \ldots, \mathbf{x}_n)$, *observed in a length-n time window, segment it into a sequence of low level dynamic models and classify it into one of the high level activities.*

The paper is organized as follows. Section 2 describes the adopted low level model and the parameter estimation method. Section 3 addresses the segmentation criterion. Section 4 describes the high level classification of sequences. Section 5 describes experimental results and Section 6 concludes the paper.

2   Statistical Model and Parameter Estimation

A trajectory is a sequence of positions, $\mathbf{x} = (\mathbf{x}_1, ..., \mathbf{x}_n)$ with $\mathbf{x}_i \in \mathbb{R}^2$. This sequence is modeled by a switched dynamical system, which is allowed to switch among the 5 low level models above defined. Formally, the state equation is

$$\mathbf{x}_t = \mathbf{x}_{t-1} + \boldsymbol{\mu}_{k_t} + \mathbf{Q}_{k_t}^{1/2}\mathbf{w}_t, \tag{1}$$

where $\{k_1, ..., k_n\}$, with $k_t \in \{1, ..., 5\}$, is a sequence of labels indicating the active low level dynamic model at each time t, and $\{\mathbf{w}_1, ..., \mathbf{w}_n\}$ are independent samples of a zero-mean Gaussian random vector with identity covariance; the parameters of this system are $\{\boldsymbol{\mu}_1, ..., \boldsymbol{\mu}_5\}$, the mean displacements of each model, and $\{\mathbf{Q}_1, ..., \mathbf{Q}_5\}$, the corresponding covariances.

The joint probability density of a sequence $\mathbf{x} = (\mathbf{x}_1, ..., \mathbf{x}_n)$, generated according to (1), given a sequence of model labels $\{k_1, ..., k_n\}$ is thus

$$p(\mathbf{x}_1, ..., \mathbf{x}_n | k_1, ..., k_n) = \prod_{t=2}^{n} \mathcal{N}(\mathbf{x}_t - \mathbf{x}_{t-1} | \boldsymbol{\mu}_{k_t}, \mathbf{Q}_{k_t}), \tag{2}$$

where $\mathcal{N}(\mathbf{v}|\mathbf{u}, \mathbf{P})$ denotes a multivariate Gaussian density of mean $\mathbf{u}$ and covariance $\mathbf{P}$, computed at $\mathbf{v}$.

Estimation of the parameters of each of the low level models is performed in a supervised fashion using training trajectories which were previously segmented and classified by a human observer. These parameters are set to the standard maximum likelihood estimates, given the training data.

3   Segmentation and Classification

3.1   Segmentation with a Known Number of Segments

For segmentation purposes, we assume that the sequence of labels $\{k_1, ..., k_n\}$ is piece-wise constant, with T segments, that is,

$$\{k_1, ..., k_n\} = \{m_1, ..., m_1, m_2, ..., m_2, ..., m_T, ..., m_T\}. \tag{3}$$

Let us denote as $\{s_1, ..., s_{T-1}\}$ the switching times between segments, where s_j is the time instant where switching from model m_j and m_{j+1} occurs. Obviously, the sequence of models $\{m_1, ..., m_T\}$ and switching times $\{s_1, ..., s_{T-1}\}$ contains exactly the same information as the sequence of labels $\{k_1, ..., k_n\}$. This allows writing the segmentation log-likelihood, which is simply the logarithm of (2), as

$$L(m_1, ..., m_T, s_1, ..., s_{T-1}) = \log p(\mathbf{x}_1, ..., \mathbf{x}_n | m_1, ..., m_T, s_1, ..., s_{T-1})$$
$$= \sum_{j=1}^{T} \sum_{t=s_{j-1}}^{s_j} \log \mathcal{N}(\mathbf{x}_t - \mathbf{x}_{t-1} | \boldsymbol{\mu}_{m_j}, \mathbf{Q}_{m_j}) \tag{4}$$

where we take $s_0 = 1$.

Assuming that T is known, we can "segment" the sequence (i.e., estimate $\{m_1, \ldots, m_T\}$ and $\{s_1, \ldots, s_{T-1}\}$) by the maximum-likelihood criterion:

$$\{\hat{m}_1, \ldots, \hat{m}_T, \hat{s}_1, \ldots, \hat{s}_{T-1}\} = \arg\max L(m_1, \ldots, m_T, s_1, \ldots, s_{T-1}) \quad (5)$$

The maximization with respect to the switching times can be expressed as

$$\hat{s}_1, \ldots, \hat{s}_{T-1} = \arg\max_{s_1, \ldots, s_{T-1}} \left\{ \max_{m_1, \ldots, m_T} L(m_1, \ldots, m_T, s_1, \ldots, s_{T-1}) \right\}. \quad (6)$$

The inner maximization in (6), that is, with respect to $\{m_1, \ldots, m_T\}$, for some fixed $\{s_1, \ldots, s_{T-1}\}$, can be decoupled into

$$\max_{m_1, \ldots, m_T} L(m_1, \ldots, m_T, s_1, \ldots, s_{T-1}) = \sum_{j=1}^{T} \max_{m_j} \sum_{t=s_{j-1}}^{s_j} \log \mathcal{N}(\mathbf{x}_t - \mathbf{x}_{t-1} | \boldsymbol{\mu}_{m_j}, \mathbf{Q}_{m_j}).$$
$$(7)$$

Notice that the maximization with respect to each of m_j is a simple maximum likelihood classifier of the sub-sequence $(\mathbf{x}_{s_{j-1}-1}, \ldots, \mathbf{x}_{s_j})$ into one of the 5 low level models. Finally, the maximization with respect to $s_1, \ldots, s_{T-1}$ is done by exhaustive search, which is never too expensive, since we are considering short segments of the trajectory, with up to a maximum of $T = 3$ segments.

3.2   Estimating the Number of Segments: MDL Criterion

In the previous section, we derived the segmentation criterion assuming that the number of segments T is known. It is well known that the same criterion can not be used to select T, as this would always return the largest possible number of segments. We are thus in the presence of a model selection problem, which we address by using the minimum description length (MDL) criterion [13]. The MDL criterion for selecting T is

$$\hat{T} = \arg\min_T \Big\{ -\log p(\mathbf{x}_1, \ldots, \mathbf{x}_n | \hat{m}_1, \ldots, \hat{m}_T, \hat{s}_1, \ldots, \hat{s}_{T-1})$$
$$+ M(\hat{m}_1, \ldots, \hat{m}_T, \hat{s}_1, \ldots, \hat{s}_{T-1}) \Big\} \quad (8)$$

where $M(\hat{m}_1, \ldots, \hat{m}_T, \hat{s}_1, \ldots, \hat{s}_{T-1})$ is the number of bits required to encode the selected model labels and switching times. Notice that we do not have the usual $\frac{T}{2} \log n$ term because the real-valued model parameters (means and covariances) are assumed fixed (previously estimated). Finally, it is easy to conclude that

$$M(\hat{m}_1, \ldots, \hat{m}_T, \hat{s}_1, \ldots, \hat{s}_{T-1}) \approx T \log_2 5 + (T-1) \log_2 n \quad (9)$$

where $T \log_2 5$ is the code length for the T model labels $m_1, \ldots, m_T$, since each belongs to $\{1, \ldots, 5\}$, and $(T-1) \log_2 n$ is the code length for the $T-1$ switching times, $\hat{s}_1, \ldots, \hat{s}_{T-1}$, because each belongs to $\{1, \ldots, n\}$; we ignore the fact that two switchings can not occur at the same time, a reasonable approximation because $T \ll n$. The maximization in (8) is solved simply by trying all allowed numbers of segments (1, 2, or 3, in all the experiments below).

In a classical MDL-based segmentation method, we would simply estimate the segment parameters along with the segmentation, and use the MDL criterion in the standard way to select the number of segments. However, without the supervised training scheme, we wouldn't be able to assign a semantic to each model, e.g., *"moving right"*, *"moving left"*. In short, supervised training is needed when, in addition to segmenting, one wishes to classify and interpret activities. This leads to the use of the MDL with fixed parameters, as propose in this work.

4 On-Line Identification of the Sequence

To identify the (high level) activity present in a given sequence of positions, each possible sequence of 1, 2, or 3, low-level models (produced by the segmentation algorithm) is mapped to an activity according to a simple look-up table (which we omit due to lack of space). For example, a sequence segmented into only one segment ($\hat{T} = 1$) with model "walking right" or "walking left" is classified as "passing"; a sequence segmented into two segments ($\hat{T} = 2$), as "walking right" - "walking up", or "walking left" - "walking up", is classified as "entering"; a sequence segmented into three segments ($\hat{T} = 3$), as "walking right" - "stopped" - "walking left" is classified as "browsing". For the 5 considered models, there are 5 possible 1-segment segmentations, $5 \times 4 = 20$ possible 2-segment segmentations, and $5 \times 4 \times 4 = 80$ possible 3-segment segmentations, thus our look-up table has a total of 105 entries.

To perform on-line classification, the segmentation/classification algorithm is not applied to the whole observed trajectory of a given person, but to the positions inside a fixed length sliding window. For each window position, the segmentation and classification algorithm is applied and the system outputs a high-level activity class.

5 Experimental Results

The proposed algorithm was tested with real data collected in the context of a EU-funded project[1]. This section shows the performance of the proposed algorithm applied to about 20 movies. The duration of the movies ranges from 30 seconds up to two minutes, with a frame rate of 25 frames/second. The data was collected and the ground truth was hand-labeled for 50 video sequences. These sequences include indoor plaza and shopping center observations of individuals and small groups of people. The sequences are hand labeled with the activity of each track person, frame by frame. The total data consists of nearly 20,000 images.

---

[1] More information about the CAVIAR project can be found at http://homepages.inf.ed.ac.uk/rbf/CAVIAR/

Table 1. Confusion matrix for the classification of high level activities in the shopping

		Output			
		Entering	*Exiting*	*Passing*	*Browsing*
	Entering	81	0	0	0
True	*Exiting*	0	72	5	0
Classes	*Passing*	1	0	462	3
	Browsing	1	0	1	180

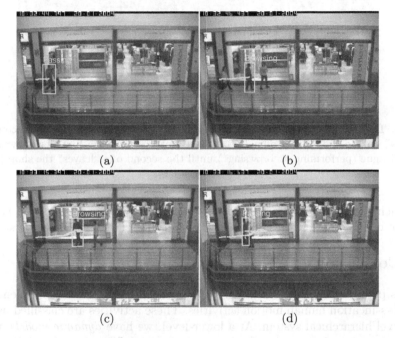

(a)   (b)

(c)   (d)

Fig. 2. A person "passing" in a front of a shop (a) (frame 21), starts to "browse" while the second one "enters" to the shop (b) (frame 62). He waits ("browsing") until his colleague leaves the shop (c) (frame 786). Finally they go together leaving the scenario ("passing") (frame 817).

Table 1 shows the confusion matrix for the tested activities. The evaluation is made at every window position. The samples of the trajectories varies from 300 (shorter sequences) to 1200 (longer sequences).

Figures 2 and 3 show some results obtained using the proposed approach. Each image shows the successive positions of the person up to the time instant

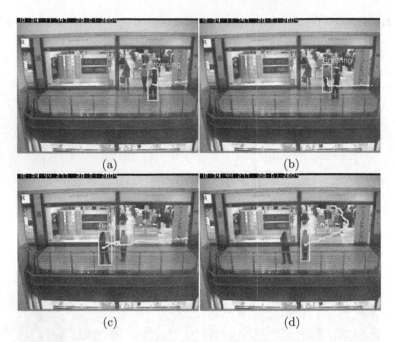

Fig. 3. The first row shows a person who starts to "browse" (a) while the second one "enters" to the shop (b) (frame 157). In the bottom row, the first person waits for his colleague (performing a "browsing") until the second one "leaves" the shop (frame 969).

in which the classification is being output, the current bounding box. For the sake of clarity, these figures only show the activity class for a single person.

6   Conclusion

In this paper we have proposed and tested an algorithm for online segmentation and classification human motion activities. These activities are classified using a two-level hierarchical system. At a lower-level, we have *dynamic models*, which are short units of movement (such as "moving right") and at the higher level, we have the target *activities*, which are sequences of lower level models. We introduce probabilistic generative low-level models and a minimum description length criterion to segment each observed trajectory into a sequence of low-level models. Each possible sequence of low-level models is then translated into a high-level activity, via a look-up table. We have reported extensive experiments, which testify for the good performance of the proposed methodology.

We plan to extend our work to higher semantic levels. For instance, in the example shown in the Fig. 2, we may hope to infer that the person is waiting for another person, while that other person goes to the shop. In the future, we hope to bring this higher level descriptions (such as "waiting") by considering interactions among the trajectories of different people.

References

1. Ayers, D., Shah, M.: Monitoring human behavior from video taken in an office environment. Image and Vision Computing 19, 833–846 (2001)
2. Bobick, A., Davis, J.: The recognition of human movement using temporal templates. IEEE Trans. on Patt. Anal. and Machine Intell. 23, 257–267 (2001)
3. Davis, J.: Sequential reliable inference for rapid detection of human actions. IEEE Conf. on Advance Video and Signal Based Surveillance, pp. 169–176 (2003)
4. Davis, J., Shah, M.: Visual gesture recognition. IEEE Proc. Vision, Image and Signal Processing 141, 101–106 (1994)
5. Efros, A., Berg, A., Mori, G., Malik, J.: Recognizing action at a distance. In: IEEE Int. Conf. on Comp. Vision, Nice, France, pp. 726–733 (2003)
6. Haritaoglu, I., Harwood, D., Davis, L.S.: W^4: real-time surveillance of people and their activities. IEEE Trans. on Patt. Anal. and Machine Intell. 22, 809–830 (2000)
7. Hongeng, S., Nevatia, R., Bremond, F.: Video-based event recognition: activity representation and probabilistic recognition methods. Computer Vision and Image Understanding 96, 129–162 (2004)
8. Hu, T., Tan, T., Wang, L., Maybank, S.: A survey on visual surveillance of object motion and behaviors. IEEE Trans. on Systems and Cybernetics: Applications and Reviews 34, 334–352 (2004)
9. Ivanov, Y., Bobick, A.: Recognition of visual activities and interactions by stochastic parsing. IEEE Trans. on Patt. Anal. and Machine Intell. 22, 852–872 (2000)
10. Liao, L., Fox, D., Kautz, H.: Learning and inferring transportation routines. In: Proc. National Conf. on Artificial Intelligence (2004)
11. Okuma, K., Taleghani, A., de Freitas, N., Little, J.J., Lowe, D.G.: A bosted particle filter: Multitarget detection and tracking. In: Pajdla, T., Matas, J(G.) (eds.) ECCV 2004. LNCS, vol. 3021, pp. 28–39. Springer, Heidelberg (2004)
12. Oliver, N., Rosario, B., Pentland, A.: A Bayesian computer vision system for modeling human interactions. IEEE Trans. on Patt. Anal. and Machine Intell. 22, 831–843 (2000)
13. Rissanen, J.: Stochastic Complexity in Statistical Inquiry. World Scientific, Singapore (1989)
14. Rosales, R., Sclaroff, S.: 3D trajectory recovery for tracking multiple objects and trajectory guided recognition of actions. In: Proc. IEEE Conf. on Comp. Vision and Patt. Recognition, vol. 2, pp. 2117–2123 (1999)
15. Rosenblum, M., Yacoob, Y., Davis, L.S.: Human expression recognition from motion using a radial basis function network architecture. IEEE Trans. Neural Networks 7, 1121–1138 (1996)
16. Zhao, T., Nevatia, R.: Tracking multiple humans in complex situations. IEEE Trans. on Patt. Anal. and Machine Intell. 26, 1208–1221 (2004)

Data-Driven Jacobian Adaptation in a Multi-model Structure for Noisy Speech Recognition

Yong-Joo Chung[1] and Keun-Sung Bae[2]

[1] Department of Electronics, Keimyung University
[2] School of Electrical Engineering and Computer Science,
Kyungpook National University Daegu, S. Korea

Abstract. We propose a data-driven approach for the Jacobian adaptation (JA) to make it more robust against the noisy environments in speech recognition. The reference hidden Markov model (HMM) in the JA is trained directly with the noisy speech for improved acoustic modeling instead of using the model composition methods like the parallel model combination (PMC). This is made possible by estimating the Jacobian matrices and other statistical information for the adaptation using the Baum-Welch algorithm during the training. The adaptation algorithm has shown to give improved robustness especially when used in a multi-model structure. From the speech recognition experiments based on HMMs, we could find the proposed adaptation method gives better recognition results compared with conventional HMM parameter compensation methods and the multi-model approach could be a viable solution in the noisy speech recognition.

1 Introduction

Noise robustness in the automatic speech recognition is essential to prevent the performance degradation in real environments where the background noise causes the mismatch between the training and testing conditions. Various methods have been developed to solve the robustness problem and they can be summarized into a few categories, namely, speech enhancement, noise-robust front ends and model compensation. In the model compensation approaches based on the HMM, the model parameters are updated using the statistics of the noise signal in the testing speech [1][2][3]. Among them, the PMC and JA have shown to be effective compared with other approaches. In particular, the JA is quite useful when we have HMMs which have been already trained in a similar condition as the target environment [3]. In the JA, the trained (reference) HMM parameters can be easily adapted to the testing speech by using the Jacobian matrices. The reference HMM in the JA is usually constructed by the model combination methods like the PMC [1]. The model composition approach makes it easy to associate the Jacobian matrix for each mixture component of the continuous density HMM with the mean vector of the clean speech HMM. However, it is well known that the composite HMM will not perform better than the HMM which has been directly trained with the noisy speech in the target

J. Martí et al. (Eds.): IbPRIA 2007, Part II, LNCS 4478, pp. 452–459, 2007.
© Springer-Verlag Berlin Heidelberg 2007

environment. We think that the use of the model composition approach in constructing the reference HMM makes it difficult for the JA method to outperform the PMC. In this paper, we propose to train the reference HMM directly with the noisy speech. But, as this will make the state/mixture alignment between the Jacobian matrices and the clean speech HMM parameters obscure, the Jacobian matrices and other statistical information for the adaptation are estimated during the training along with the HMM parameters by using the Baum-Welch algorithm [6]. We also suggest to use the proposed adaptation algorithm in a multi-model structure using multiple reference HMM sets corresponding to the various Signal-to-Noise ratio (SNR) values and the noise types [4]. By using the multiple reference HMM sets in recognition, the approximation errors occurring in the JA can be significantly reduced compared with the single reference HMM set, thus improving the recognition performance. In section 2, we explain in detail the proposed adaptation method and experimental results are given in section 3. Finally, the conclusions are given in section 4.

2 Data-Driven Jacobian Adaptation in a Multi-model Structure

2.1 Data-Driven Jacobian Adaptation (D-JA)

In this section, we explain the proposed data-driven JA (D-JA) method where the reference HMM is trained directly with the noisy speech. We will need to estimate some statistical information as well as the Jacobian matrix during the training along with the HMM parameters by using the Baum-Welch algorithm.

In general, the noise-corrupted speech vector $\mathbf{y}$ in the mel-frequecy cepstral coefficients (MFCCs) is characterized by the following nonlinear equation.

$$\mathbf{y} = \mathbf{C}[\log\{\exp(\mathbf{C}^{-1}\mathbf{x}) + \exp(\mathbf{C}^{-1}\mathbf{n})\}] \tag{1}$$

where $\mathbf{x}$ and $\mathbf{n}$ represents respectively the clean speech and additive noise in the MFCCs. $\mathbf{C}$ is the matrix representing the discrete cosine transformation (DCT).

In an HMM-based speech recognition, the HMM parameters are usually estimated by the Baum-Welch algorithm [6]. For example, in the continuous density HMM, the re-estimation formula for the mean vector $\boldsymbol{\mu}_{x,jk}$ in the state j and mixture component k is as follows.

$$\boldsymbol{\mu}_{x,jk} = \frac{\sum_{t=1}^{T} \gamma_t(j,k) \mathbf{x}_t}{\sum_{t=1}^{T} \gamma_t(j,k)} \tag{2}$$

Here, $\gamma_t(j,k)$ is the probability of being in state j at time t with the k-th mixture component accounting for the cepstral feature vector $\mathbf{x}_t$ in the HMM.

When the noisy speech vector $\mathbf{y}_t$ in Eq. (1) is affected by the small changes in the cepstral noise vector $\mathbf{n}_t$, it can be expressed using the Jacobian matrix $\partial \mathbf{y}_t / \partial \mathbf{n}_t$ as follows.

$$\tilde{\mathbf{y}}_t = \mathbf{y}_t + \frac{\partial \mathbf{y}_t}{\partial \mathbf{n}_t}(\mathbf{n}_t - \tilde{\mathbf{n}}_t) \tag{3}$$

Based on Eq. (2) and (3), the mean vector $\tilde{\mathbf{y}}_t$ of the noisy speech can be written as follows.

$$\mu_{\tilde{y}, jk} = \frac{\sum_{t=1}^{T} \gamma_t(j,k)(\mathbf{y}_t + \frac{\partial \mathbf{y}_t}{\partial \mathbf{n}_t}(\mathbf{n}_t - \tilde{\mathbf{n}}_t))}{\sum_{t=1}^{T} \gamma_t(j,k)} \tag{4}$$

If we make the assumption that the difference $\Delta \mathbf{n} (\equiv \mathbf{n}_t - \tilde{\mathbf{n}}_t)$ in the noise vectors can be substituted for its mean value (i.e., independent of the time), the above equation can be rewritten as follows.

$$\mu_{\tilde{y}, jk} = \frac{\sum_{t=1}^{T} \gamma_t(j,k)\mathbf{y}_t}{\sum_{t=1}^{T} \gamma_t(j,k)} + \frac{\sum_{t=1}^{T} \gamma_t(j,k)\frac{\partial \mathbf{y}_t}{\partial \mathbf{n}_t}}{\sum_{t=1}^{T} \gamma_t(j,k)} \Delta \mathbf{n} \tag{5}$$

$$\mu_{\tilde{y}, jk} = \mu_{y, jk} + \mu_{J, jk} \Delta \mathbf{n} \tag{6}$$

The Jacobian matrix $\partial \mathbf{y}_t / \partial \mathbf{n}_t$ in Eq. (5) can be easily calculated from Eq. (1). From Eq. (6), $\mu_{y, jk}$ is the mean vector for the state j and mixture component k of the reference HMM and $\mu_{J, jk}$ is the estimated mean Jacobian matrix. $\Delta \mathbf{n}$ is estimated by finding the difference between the mean values of the reference noise and observed noise in the testing speech. After estimating $\mu_{y, jk}$ and $\mu_{J, jk}$ during the training, the adapted mean vector $\mu_{\tilde{y}, jk}$ in Eq. (6) is calculated in recognition using the noise mean difference $\Delta \mathbf{n}$. The distinctive feature of the proposed method is that Jacobian matrix $\mu_{J, jk}$ is estimated during the training along with the mean vector $\mu_{y, jk}$ of the reference HMM. In a similar approach, the covariance matrix can be adapted as in the following equation using Eq. (3).

$$\Sigma_{\tilde{y},jk} = \frac{\sum_{t=1}^{T} \gamma_t(j,k)((\mathbf{y}_t + \frac{\partial \mathbf{y}_t}{\partial \mathbf{n}_t}(\mathbf{n}_t - \tilde{\mathbf{n}}_t) - \mu_{\tilde{y}}) \cdot (\mathbf{y}_t + \frac{\partial \mathbf{y}_t}{\partial \mathbf{n}_t}(\mathbf{n}_t - \tilde{\mathbf{n}}_t) - \mu_{\tilde{y}})^T}{\sum_{t=1}^{T} \gamma_t(j,k)} \qquad (7)$$

We can see from Eq. (7) that some statistics resulting from the multiplication in the numerator needs to be estimated for the covariance matrix adaptation and they can be estimated directly with the noisy speech. This is contrary to the JA where the adapted covariance matrix is derived analytically by using statistical approximations [3].

The delta-MFCCs in this paper are calculated as follows.

$$\dot{\mathbf{y}}_t = \mu \sum_{k=-K}^{K} k \mathbf{y}_{t+k} \qquad (8)$$

If we substitute Eq. (3) into (8), the mean vector of the delta-MFCCs is calculated as follows.

$$\mu_{\tilde{y},jk} = \mu \sum_{k=-K}^{K} k E(\mathbf{y}_{t+k}) + \mu \sum_{k=-K}^{K} k E(\frac{\partial \mathbf{y}_{t+k}}{\partial \mathbf{n}_t})\Delta \mathbf{n} \qquad (9)$$

From Eq. (9), we can see that the expectation values $E(\mathbf{y}_{t+k})$, $E(\frac{\partial \mathbf{y}_{t+k}}{\partial \mathbf{n}_t})$ should be estimated in the HMM during the training for the delta-MFCCs mean adaptation.

2.2 Multi-model Structure

In the D-JA, we assume that the HMM parameters can be well adapted to the noisy speech using the linear relation in Eq. (3). But, if the spectral characteristics of the noise signal assumed during the training differ significantly with that in the testing speech, the accuracy of Eq. (3) will be poor and it will result in performance degradation. Thus, the performance improvement by the D-JA algorithm employing just a single reference HMM set will have some limitations. We suggest to use the D-JA algorithm in the multi-model structure where we construct multiple reference HMM sets trained on data corresponding to various noise types and SNR values. In recognition, we can select the most suitable one among the reference HMM sets by classifying the input noise signal and estimating the SNR values. With the partitioning of the training data and establishing separate reference HMM sets, we can model more precisely the acoustical variations due to the noise in the testing speech.

In Fig. 1, we show the architecture of the multi-model based noisy speech recognition system. To select the most appropriate reference HMM set, we estimate the SNR values of the testing noisy speech and classify the input noise signal into one of the candidate noise types. The parameters of the selected reference HMM set will be compensated by using the D-JA.

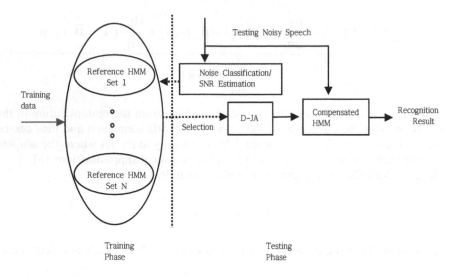

Fig. 1. The architecture of the multi-model based noisy speech recognition system

3   Experiments and Results

In this section, the performance of the proposed method of compensating the HMM parameters is evaluated on speaker-independent isolated word noisy speech recognition. The vocabulary consists of 75 phoneme-balanced Korean words and the basic recognition unit is the set of 32 phoneme-like units that are modeled by the left-to-right continuous density HMM. Utterances from 80 speakers are used in these experiments and each speaker uttered the 75 words once. A jack knife approach is used in the recognition experiment. We divided the speakers into 4 sets with 20 speakers in each set. Each set is successively used as the testing set and the remaining three as the training sets. The noisy speech was obtained by adding noise signal to the clean speech at various signal-to-noise ratios (SNRs). The noise signal was taken from the noise files contained in the AURORA 2 database [5]. The types of the noise signals are car, babble, exhibition hall, subway, restaurant, street, airport and train station. 13-th order mel-frequency cepstral coefficients (MFCC) and their time derivatives (delta-MFCC) are used as the feature vectors.

In Table 1, we compare the recognition rates of the D-JA in the car noise case with the conventional model compensation methods such as the PMC and JA. As shown in the table, the recognition performance of the baseline recognizer with no compensation dropped severely at 10dB or below. For a detailed investigation of the compensation results, the HMM parameters were compensated in sequences. First, only the static mean vector of the MFCC is compensated and then the mean vector of the delta-MFCC was adapted as well. And, finally the covariance matrix of the MFCC was added in the compensation process. The results are shown in the separate rows of the table and we can see that the recognition rates generally increase as we include more feature vectors in the compensation process. The JA shows marginal improvement over the PMC. The JA seems to have the ability to correct the approximation errors occurring in the model compensation process of the PMC.

As shown in the table, the results of D-JA outperformed both the PMC and JA at all SNRs. The use of the reference HMM which has been trained directly with the noisy speech at the SNR of the testing speech may have contributed a lot to the superior performance. The recognition error rate reduction ratio was about 50(%) at 0dB and 10dB and it was about 40(%) at 20dB.

Table 1. Performance comparison in word recognition rates(%) of the proposed method (D-JA) with the previous model compensation methods (car noise)

		0dB	10dB	20dB	clean
Baseline		12.6	60.7	92.5	98.6
Matched Conditions		82.1	95.0	97.5	98.6
PMC	Static mean	59.8	87.8	95.3	98.6
	+delta mean	62.7	88.3	95.4	98.3
	+covariance	66.6	88.6	95.4	98.3
JA	Static mean	59.9	87.8	95.4	98.6
	+delta mean	62.4	88.2	95.5	98.4
	+covariance	68.6	89.5	95.8	98.4
D-JA	Static mean	82.4	95.0	97.4	98.6
	+delta mean	82.0	95.0	97.4	98.6
	+covariance	82.0	94.8	97.5	98.6

The superior performance of the D-JA in Table 1 is obtained when we have a separate reference HMM set for each SNR of the testing noisy speech. As it is not practical to take many reference HMM sets in the recognition, we investigated the robustness of the proposed approach when the reference HMM set was trained at a specific SNR condition.

Table 2. Performance comparison in average word recognition rates(%) of the proposed method (D-JA) in the multi-model structure with the previous model compensation methods when the reference HMM set was trained at the SNR of 10 and 20 dB (car/babble/exhibition hall/subway noise)

Testing — Training		0dB	5dB	15dB	25dB
D-JA	10dB	77.2	89.6	95.2	93.5
	20dB	66.8	84.8	95.7	97.5
JA	10dB	60.5	77.4	91.2	90.1
	20dB	62.8	79.2	92.3	96.4
MCT		65.2	84.1	94.1	96.1
PMC		61.2	76.8	91.8	96.6

In Table 2, we show the recognition results of the D-JA in the multi-model structure as the SNR of the testing speech changes when the selected reference HMM sets have been trained at the SNR of 10 and 20 dB, respectively. There are 4 reference HMM sets corresponding to the noise types (car, babble, exhibition hall, subway) at each SNR. In recognition, we classify the type of the noise signal in the testing speech to select the most appropriate reference HMM set. For the noise classification, a GMM (Gaussian mixture model) based noise classifier with 5 mixtures was trained for each type of the noise signal [4]. The first 20 frames (200ms) of the non-speech segments of the testing noisy speech are used for the noise classification. We could find that the noise classification results for the 4 types of noise signals were very high and it makes the multi-model structure in the noisy speech recognition quite feasible.

There are also four sets of testing data corresponding to the different noise types. The recognition experiments have been done for each set of the testing data and their recognition rates are averaged to give the results in the table.

The recognition results of the proposed method are compared with the JA, PMC and the MCT (Multi-condition training). The MCT was originally introduced with the AURORA database, where 4 different noise types at 5 different SNRs are considered in constructing the training data [5]. The HMM obtained from MCT may be thought to be able to well represent the acoustical effects due to the various SNRs and noise types. The training data for the MCT in this paper was also organized in a similar way. For the JA, the reference HMM was obtained by the PMC during the training.

The covariance matrices as well as the static and delta-mean vectors of the HMM are compensated. As we can see in Table 2, the D-JA is far more robust than the other approaches. For example, when the reference HMM is trained at 10 dB, it attains the word recognition rates of 77.2(%) and 93.5(%) at the testing SNR of 0 dB and 25 dB, respectively while the JA has the recognition rates of 60.5(%) and 90.1(%) at the same condition. The error rate reduction ratio is about 40 (%). Also, when the reference HMM is trained at 20 dB in the D-JA, it performs better than all the other methods at all testing SNRs.

From the results in Table 2, we can conclude that the D-JA method will perform much better than the conventional methods by constructing the reference HMM sets only at the SNR of 10 and 20 dB in the multi-model structure. For example, when the SNR of the testing speech is 15 dB, the D-JA outperforms the other methods even if we choose any one between the reference HMM set trained at 10 and 20 dB. This is true for all the testing SNRs except for 25dB. But, in this case, we may easily choose the reference HMM set trained at 20 dB by the SNR estimation process.

In the above results, we only considered the 4 types of the noise signals in the testing. For practical purposes, we also investigated the robustness of the proposed method when unknown types of noise signal are given in testing speech. In this case, the testing noisy speech may contain noise signals which type was not assumed during the training as usually happens in real environments.

For the unknown types of noise signal, the restaurant, street, airport and train station noise signals from the AURORA 2 database were employed. The recognition experiments have been done for each set of testing data corresponding to the unknown types of noise signals and the average word recognition rates are shown in Table 3. The results do not show much difference with that in Table 2. The D-JA outperformed

Table 3. Performance comparison in average word recognition rates(%) when unknown types of noise signal are given in the testing speech (restaurant/street/airport/train station)

Testing Training		0dB	5dB	15dB	25dB
D-JA	10dB	80.4	90.0	94.6	92.4
	20dB	72.9	86.2	95.6	97.1
MCT		71.6	85.2	94.0	96.1
PMC		69.4	81.3	93.0	97.0

both MCT and PMC and we could confirm that the proposed D-JA method shows superior noise robustness even in the case of unknown noise types.

4 Conclusion

In this paper, we proposed a data-driven adaptation method to improve the performance of the JA in noisy speech recognition. By using the reference HMM set trained directly with the noisy speech, the adapted HMM could more effectively represent the acoustical variations due to the noise. We could be confident from the experimental results that the proposed adaptation method would be quite effective in the multi-model structure by using only a few reference HMM sets for each type of noise even in the presence of unknown types of noise signals in the testing speech.

Acknowledgments. This work was supported by grant No. R01-2003-000-10242-0 from the Basic Research Program of the Korea Science & Engineering Foundation.

References

[1] Gales, M.J.F.: Model Based Techniques for Noise-Robust Speech Recognition, Ph.D. Dissertation. University of Cambridge, Cambridge (1995)

[2] Moreno, P.J.: Speech Recognition in Noisy Environments, Ph. D. Dissertation, Carnegie Mellon University (1996)

[3] Sagayama, S., Yamaguchi, Y., Takahashi, S.: Jacobian Adaptation of Noisy Speech models. IEEE Workshop on Automatic Speech Recognition and Understanding 14(17), 396–403 (December 1997)

[4] Xu, H., Tan, Z.-H., Dalsgaard, P., Lindberg, B.: Robust Speech Recognition on Noise and SNR Classification – a Multiple-Model Framework. Interspeech, Lisbon, Portugal (2005)

[5] Pearce, D., Hirsch, H.-G.: The AURORA Experimental Framework for the performance evaluation of speech recognition systems under noisy conditions (ICSLP 2000) Beijing, China (2000)

[6] Baum, L.E., Petrie, G.S.T., Weiss, N.: A maximization technique occurring in the statistical analysis of probabilistic functions of Markov chains. Ann. Math. Statist. 41, 164–171 (1970)

Development of a Computer Vision System for the Automatic Quality Grading of Mandarin Segments

José Blasco, Sergio Cubero, Raúl Arias, Juan Gómez,
Florentino Juste, and Enrique Moltó

Centro de AgroIngeniería. Instituto Valenciano de Investigaciones Agrarias (IVIA),
Ctra. Moncada-Náquera km 5. 46113 Moncada (Valencia), España
jblasco@ivia.es

Abstract. This work focuses on the development of a computer vision system for the automatic on-line inspection and classification of Satsuma segments. During the image acquisition the segments are in movement, wet and frequently in contact with other pieces. The segments are transported over six semi-transparent conveyor belts that advance at speed of 1 m/s. During on-line operation, the system acquires images of the segments using two cameras connected to a single computer and process the images in less than 50 ms. Extracting morphological features from the objects, the system identifies automatically pieces of skin and row material and separates entire segments from broken ones, discriminating between those with slight or large breaking degree. Combinations of morphological parameters were employed to decide the quality of each segment, classifying correctly 95% of sound segments.

Keywords: automatic inspection, machine vision.

1 Introduction

In the Spanish industry, the economic importance of the processed fruit is low in comparison with the fresh fruit. For this reason most of the researches related with machine vision applied to the agricultural produces are focused in the field fresh fruit [1],[2],[3]. In the same way, manufacturers of automatic fruit sorters are centred in the development of machines for grading fresh fruit, being the market of the processed fruit minor. This is the case of the canned peaches [4], [5] or the mandarin segments [6]. In this industry, when the mandarins come into the production line they are peeled, the segments are then separated, peeled, inspected and canned. All the operations are performed automatically, but the inspection which is the only part of the process that has not already been automated [7]. In this industry, operators carry out visual inspections for broken segments or those that contain pips as they go pass on a conveyor belt. When a defective segment is detected, it is removed from the conveyor belt manually. Problems related to subjectivity, fatigue or the disparity of criteria among operators as to how to decide which are broken and which are not decrease the quality of the inspection and, consequently, the final product.

This article presents a contribution to introduce the computer vision in this industrial sector designing computer vision techniques for the automatic estimation of

J. Martí et al. (Eds.): IbPRIA 2007, Part II, LNCS 4478, pp. 460–466, 2007.

the quality of mandarin segments. This paper shows the image analysis algorithms developed for the inspection of the segments. The algorithms are intended to allow on-line detection of the presence of pips in the segments and to analyze the shape of the segments in order to detect broken segments in order to classify the segments in different commercial categories. Also pieces of skins or doubles segments (which are those that were not properly split in previous processes) have to be detected.

2 Objective

The objective is to develop image analysis algorithms for the on-line estimation of the quality of mandarin segments. The algorithms use morphological features extracted from the images of the segments to identify those broken or containing pips, as well as being capable of detecting the presence of raw material while the fruit travels on a conveyor belt; an added difficulty is the fact that there are a random number of wet segments in each image without a known position. The system have to be capable of inspecting 1 T of segments per second.

3 Material and Methods

The satsuma segments entered to the inspection machine coming from a vibrating plate that spread them along the width of the machine. Then, the high speed of the conveyor belts facilitates their separation. Being the averaged weight of the segments about 5 g, to achieve the requirements of 1 T per second, the machine must inspect about 55 segments per second. Two consecutive segments in the conveyor belt should be separated about 30 mm for increasing the performance.

To get the performance requirements, the speed of the conveyor belts using only one camera would be very high and the segments could be damaged due to mechanical operations. The computer vision system consists of two progressive scan cameras that acquires RGB images format with a resolution of 0.65 mm/pixel. Both cameras are connected to a single personal computer trough a frame grabber. The images of the segments were acquired using a satsuma mandarin sorter prototype, particularly developed for this work (Fig. 1), placed in a satsuma segments producer company. Six semi-transparent conveyor belts transport the segments, which allow the backlighting of them, thus facilitating the detection of pips and the segmentation of the shape of the segments. Each camera is capable of acquiring a scene with three conveyor belts. The processing of the image acquired with one camera is overlapped with the acquisition of the image with the second camera, which allow saving the 40 ms required to acquire one image.

Specific algorithms for detecting the pips and analysing the shape of the segments were developed and implemented in C programming language. The first step consists on segmenting the image to separate the product from the background. When backlighted, objects presented high contrast respect the translucent conveyor belts. In the acquired images, the colour of the segments has a small contribution of blue component respect to the background which allows separating between them using a thresholding in this colour band. However, the objects found include segments, seeds and skin pieces.

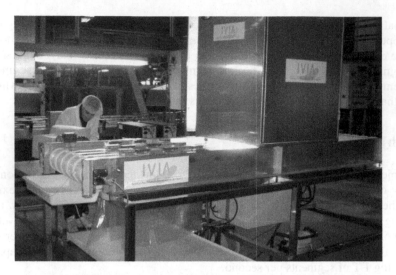

Fig. 1. Prototype for the automatic sorting of satsuma segments

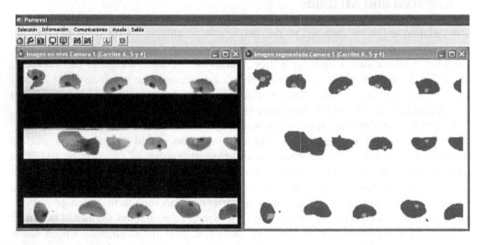

Fig. 2. Original image and the result of the image segmentation

A second segmentation within the area of these objects is performed to discriminate between them (fig. 2). In this case, the red image is used because the seeds and the skin pieces are more opaque than segments, having lower values of red. Also double segments, which are those that had not been properly split in previous processes, are detected using this second segmentation.

This second segmentation separates between segments by one hand and seeds and skins by other. Being the seeds normally very smaller than skins, a threshold of size was established. The threshold is set a value of area 50% greater that the estimated area of the largest seed found in the training set. The area of each object is estimated by counting the number of pixels belonging to it. In the case of the double segments, they are normally detected as large opaque objects inside an area of good segment. Segments with seeds and skins will be rejected by the prototype and no further processing is performed with them.

The shape of the remaining objects is analysed to estimate morphological features that allow determining if they are complete, broken or pieces of segments. The sequence of the shape analysis starts with the extraction of the perimeter (P) of the objects (the close contour), that is formed by those pixels belonging to the object having some neighbour belonging to the background. Then, the centroid is calculated as the averaged x and y coordinates of the pixels of the perimeter. The area (A) is calculated as the number of pixels inside the perimeter. The moments of inertia are calculated following the equations 1 to 3. The principal axis of inertia is used to estimate the length and the orientation of the object (fig. 3).

$$M_{xx} = \sum_x \sum_y (x - \bar{x})^2 I(x, y) \tag{1}$$

$$M_{yy} = \sum_x \sum_y (y - \bar{y})^2 I(x, y) \tag{2}$$

$$M_{xy} = \sum_x \sum_y (x - \bar{x})(y - \bar{y}) I(x, y) \tag{3}$$

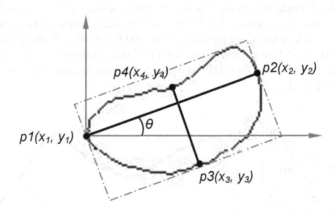

Fig. 3. Representation of the axis of inertia

In the next step the elongation is calculated using the equation (4). The elongation (E) provides information about the ration between the length (L) and width (W) of the object.

$$E = W \times L^{-1} \tag{4}$$

A shape factor (R) is calculated to estimate the relative shape of the object against a circumference with a perimeter equal to the object. The values of this factor ranges between 0 and 1 and was calculated using the equation 5 [8].

$$R = 4 \times PI \times A \times P^{-2} \qquad (5)$$

The compactness (C) is used to analyse the presence of concavities and convexities in the contour caused by breakings in the segment. It is calculated using the equation (6)

$$C = P^2 \times A^{-1} \qquad (6)$$

Supposedly, a perfect segment is symmetric while a broken one is irregular. The estimation of the distribution of the mass at both sides of the secondary axis of inertia can be used as an estimation of the symmetry. The ratio between the number of different pixels in both parts respect the total area is calculated. Fig. 4 (left) shows an entire segment where the contour of the left part has been projected over the right part to check visually the symmetry. Fig. 4 (right) shows the symmetry of a broken segment.

Fig. 4. Representation of the symmetry of the segments

Finally, the boundary is coded using the polar signature, represented as a one-dimensional array that contains the Euclidean distances between the centroid of the object (C) and each point of the perimeter p(i) i=[0,P] [9]. Fig. 5 shows this signature graphically. The fast Fourier transform (FFT) of this signature is calculated since it provides information about their profile that can be used as estimation of the shape of the objects [10], [11].

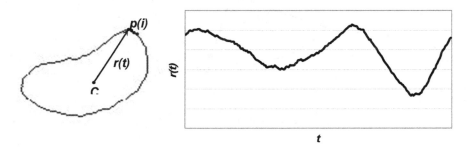

Fig. 5. Polar signature of the boundary of the segment

To test the performance of the algorithms, the inspection prototype was put to work in a satsuma segments producer for one season, acquiring and inspecting more than 15.000 images of mandarin segments randomly chosen from the product lines. All the segments were manually analysed and classified by experts from the quality laboratory of the producer company. Attending to the experience of these experts, the good segments represent about the 78% of the production, the broken segments the 18%, double segments 3% and segments with seeds 1%. The distribution of the 15.000 segments analysed followed this distribution. The results of the proposed system were compared with the visual classification of the experts.

As described above, segments with seeds and double segments are detected and classified in a previous process. The rest of the segments were classified through a discriminant analysis classification model. To generate the model, a set of 620 segments (including good and broken segments) were randomly chose from the production line, labelled as good or broken and imaged. The morphological parameters described above (shape factor, compactness, elongation, length, area, symmetry and, following the methodology proposed in [12], the first 10 harmonics obtained from the FFT of the polar signature) were calculated for each segment and stored. A discriminant analysis was performed using the calculated parameters as independent variables and the label as the grouping variable, to classify the segments between the classes *entire* and *broken*. Discriminant functions were obtained from the analysis and implemented in the classification algorithm. The model was then applied to the 15.000 images of segments to obtain the performance of the prototype classifying segments on line.

The processing time of the images was measured using an oscilloscope connected to the parallel port of the computer. Starting and ending events were triggered to the oscilloscope and the time employed for the operation registered.

4 Results

This classification of the segments as entire or broken was joined with the skin pieces, seeds and double segments detection to obtain a global view of the machine vision performance. The results show the performance of the Image analysis algorithms developed for the quality inspection of mandarin segments when they travelled by the inspection machine at a speed of 1 m/s. The results of the classification given by the image processing algorithm were compared with the visual inspection of the producer company experts to obtain success ratios for each category (table 1). The system was capable of detecting 94% of the segments that contained pips and 94% of pieces of skin that were travelling on the conveyor belt. The algorithms' rate of success in separating out sound segments was 95% while the detections of broken ones was only 77% due, mainly, to the fact that most of breakages in many segments correspond with small fragments in one extreme, difficult to detect by the actual system. The

Table 1. Confusion matrix

Category	Complete	Broken	Seeds	Skins	Doubles
Complete	95,2%	4,0%	0,7%	0,0%	0,0%
Broken	23,2%	76,8%	0,0%	0,0%	0,0%
Seeds	4,8%	1,2%	94,1%	0,0%	0,0%
Skins	1,9%	3,9%	0,0%	94,2%	0,0%
Doubles	21,4%	0,0%	0,0%	0,0%	78,6%

average of success in the detection reach 78%. Specific algorithms have to be developed to detect these small breakages. The averaged processing time of the images was 48 ms.

Acknowledgements. This work was partially funded by the *Instituto Nacional de Investigación y Tecnología Agraria y Alimentaria* (INIA) through project RTA03-105. Authors are grateful for the collaboration of the satsuma segment producer company, Agriconsa, S.A.

References

1. Blasco, J., Aleixos, N., Moltó, E.: Machine vision system for automatic quality grading of fruit. Biosystems Engineering 85(4), 415–423 (2003)
2. Blasco, J., Aleixos, N., Moltó, E.: Computer vision detection of peel defects in citrus by means of a region oriented segmentation algorithm. Journal of Food Engineering, doi:10.1016/j.jfoodeng.2007.03.027 (2007)
3. Aleixos, N., Blasco, J., Navarrón, F., Moltó, E.: Multispectral inspection of citrus in realtime using machine vision and digital signal processors. Computers and Electronics in Agriculture 33(2), 121–137 (2002)
4. Aranda, J.D., Tomás, L.M.: Automatic process for the stoning peach inspection and classification phase in a packaging fruits factory using artificial vision techniques. Robotics and automated machinery for bio-productions, BIO-ROBOTICS 97. Gandía (Valencia), Spain, pp. 77–82 (1997)
5. Vizmanos, J.G., Fuentes, L.M., Gutierrez, J.A.: Splinter detection in half-cut peaches. SPIE 3208, 277–286 (1997)
6. Tomás, L.M., Torres, R., López, J.A., Doméénech, G.: Colour image processing and artificial vision techniques, used for detection, segmentation and identification of satsuma slices. Third international conference on automation, robotics and computer vision III, 1955–1959 (1994)
7. Blasco, J., Arias, R., Cubero, S., Alegre, S., Alamar, M.C., Juste, F., Moltó, E.: Automatic inspection of satsuma slices using machine vision. In: AgEng 04. Leuven (Belgium) EurAgEng Paper N 243 (2004)
8. Gonzalez, R.C., Wintz, P.: Digital Image Processing, 2nd edn, pp. 396–397. Addison Wesley, New York (1987)
9. Throop, J.A., Aneshansely, D.J.: Improvements in an image processing algorithm to find new and old bruises. International Winter Meeting of the American Society of Agricultural Engineers, ASAE Paper No. 93-6534 (1993)
10. Miao, Z.J., Gandelin, M.H., Yuan, B.Z.: A new image shape analysis approach and its application to flower shape analysis. Image and vision computing 24(10), 1112–1115 (2006)
11. Zhang, D.S., Lu, G.: A Comparative Study on Shape Retrieval Using Fourier Descriptors with Different Shape Signatures. In: Proc. of ICIMADE 01, Fargo, ND, USA, pp. 1–9 (2001)
12. Tao, Y., Morrow, C.T., Heinemann, P.H., Sommer, H.J.: Fourier-Based Separation Technique for Shape Grading of Potatoes Using Machine Vision. Transactions of the ASAE 38(3), 949–957 (1995)

Mathematical Morphology in the *HSI* Colour Space

M.C. Tobar, C. Platero, P.M. González, and G. Asensio

Grupo de Bioingeniería Aplicada de la Universidad Politécnica de Madrid
Dpto. de Matemática Aplicada y Dpto de Electrónica,
Automática e Informática Industrial
m.carmen.tobar@upm.es

Abstract. Mathematical Morphology is a powerful non-linear image analysis techniques based on lattice theory. The definitions of morphological operators need an ordered lattice algebraic structure. In order to apply these operators to the colour images it is required, on one hand the choice of a suitable colour space representation and on the other hand, to establish an order in the colour space providing an ordered lattice algebraic structure. The *HSI* space represents the colour in terms of physical attributes that separate the achromatic component from the chromatic one and it yields a more intuitive description of the colour properties than the *RGB* space. The suggested order weighs the hue and the intensity according to the saturation level: it has a lexicographical order in which the intensity has priority if the saturation is high, and the hue has priority if the saturation is low.

1 Introduction

The techniques of Artificial Vision have been developed initially for binary and grayscale images, where the information is codified by 2 and $2^n - 1$, $n \in \mathbb{N}$ levels, respectively. Nevertheless, the colour is an important source of information. For this reason, during the last years these techniques are being developed for colour images. However, at present, both the representation and the treatment of colour images continue to be open problems.

Mathematical Morphology is the natural arena for a rigorous formulation of many problems in image analysis and powerful non-linear techniques including operators for the filtering, texture analysis, shape analysis, edge detection or segmentation. Nevertheless, to define the basic morphological operators, erosion and dilation, it is necessary to define before an order on the space used for processing the images.

For grayscale images, this order comes from the usual order of $\mathbb{R}$. For colour images two problems arise. On one hand, the chromatic space in which the image is processed, and on the other hand, the order that settles down on it.

This paper is structured as follows. First, in Section 2, the basic operators in Morphology, erosion and dilation, are defined in sets and binary images. The natural generalization to grayscale and colour images needs the lattice structure.

J. Martí et al. (Eds.): IbPRIA 2007, Part II, LNCS 4478, pp. 467–474, 2007.

In Section 3, in the HSI space a family of orders is suggested that comes defined by a cost function, and makes use of the lexicographical order in the RGB space. In section 4 one of these orders is chosen. It allows to define a lexicographical order with weight in the hue component when the image has high saturation and a with priority in the intensity component when the image has low saturation. Finally, conclusions are included in Section 5.

2   Mathematical Morphology and Lattices

Mathematical Morphology is a well-known non-linear technique for the signal processing. It was initiated in the sixties with the works by Matheron [1] and Serra [2] guided by the works on sets by Minkowski. In the eighties, Matheron and Serra proposed the ultimate mathematical formulation of Morphology within the algebraic framework of the lattices [3].

The structuring element in the morphological operations is a finite subset $E \subset \mathbb{Z}^2$ with $(0,0) \in E$. The erosion (resp. dilatation) of $A \subset \mathbb{Z}^2$ by E is defined by the formula $\varepsilon_E(A) = \{x \in \mathbb{Z}^2 \;/\; E_x \subseteq A\} = \bigcap_{s \in E} A_{-s}$ (resp. $\delta_E(A) = \{x \in \mathbb{Z}^2 \;/\; (-E)_x \cap A \neq \emptyset\} = \bigcup_{s \in E} A_s$). Here $A_s = \{x + s \;/\; x \in A\}$. Hence the erosion is an infimum and the dilation is a supremum in the lattice $P(\mathbb{Z}^2)$ (Parts of $\mathbb{Z}^2$).

A binary image is a map $f : \Omega \subset \mathbb{Z}^2 \to \{0, 1\}$ and therefore it is the characteristic function $f = \chi_A$ of A, where $A = \{x \in \mathbb{Z}^2 \;/\; f(x) = 1\}$. Then we can define the erosion and dilation of $f = \chi_A$ by the structuring element $E \subset \mathbb{Z}^2$ as the characteristic functions of $\varepsilon_E(A)$ and $\delta_E(A)$ respectively. Precisely, $\varepsilon_E(f) = \chi_{\varepsilon_E(A)}$ and $\delta_E(f) = \chi_{\delta_E(A)}$. Note that

$$\varepsilon_E(f) = \inf_{s \in E}(f \circ \tau_s)$$
$$\delta_E(f) = \sup_{s \in E}(f \circ \tau_{-s}) \tag{1}$$

where $\tau_s(x) = s + x \quad \forall x \in \mathbb{Z}^2$. Again, the erosion and dilation are an infimun and a supremum respectively, now in binary images lattice. Punctually,

$$\varepsilon_E(f)(x) = \inf_{s \in E}(f(s + x))$$
$$\delta_E(f)(x) = \sup_{s \in E}(f(-s + x)) \tag{2}$$

A grayscale image is a map $f : \Omega \subset \mathbb{Z}^2 \to \mathbb{Z}$. Since $\mathbb{R}$ is a total order (with its usual order), the grayscale images set is a lattice, which allow us to define the erosion and the dilation of a grayscale image f by the structuring element $E \subset \mathbb{Z}^2$ by (1) and punctually by (2).

For the extension of the basic morphological operations to colour images, we need a lattice structure in colour images set. A colour image can be represented by a map $f : \Omega \subset \mathbb{Z}^2 \to C$, where $C \subset \mathbb{R}^3$ is a colour space. If C has a lattice structure with the order $\leq_C$, then the colour images set is a lattice with the order

$$f \leq g \;\Leftrightarrow\; f(x) \leq_C g(x) \quad \forall x \in \Omega \quad \forall f, g : \Omega \subset \mathbb{Z}^2 \to C \tag{3}$$

This allows to define the erosion and dilation of a colour image $f : \Omega \subset \mathbb{Z}^2 \to C$ by a structuring element $E \subset \mathbb{Z}^2$ by (1) and punctually by (2), where the infimum and the supremum are calculated with the order $\leq_C$ in the colour space.

For binary and grayscale images, in (2) infimum and supremum are minimum and maximum respectively. For colour images, if the colour space has a total order, we also have minimum and maximum. However, if the colour space is partially ordered, infimum and supremum do not have to be minimum nor maximum. This could originate fake colours, i.e., colours that were not in the original image.

Eroding binary images is the same as diminishing white objets and dilating them makes white objets bigger. For grayscale images, eroding is the same as darkening them and dilating is clarifying them. Nevertheless, for colour images erosion and dilation do not have this univocal meaning: they depend on the order relation on the chromatic space. We must select this order depending on the image features or the type of image processing task.

3   Order in the *HSI* Colour Space

In the RGB space, colours are specified as (R, G, B) which give the amount of each red, green and blue primary stimulus in the colour. The transformation from RGB to hue, saturation and brightness coordinates is simply a transformation from a cartesian coordinates system to a cylindrical coordinates system. The achromatic axis is formed by all the achromatic points $(R = G = B)$. The perpendicular plane to the achromatic axis, and intersecting it at the origin, called chromatic plane, contains all the colour information. The hue and saturation coordinates are determined within the achromatic plane. Hanbury and Serra [4], [5], [6] adopt a family of HSI spaces using norms in $\mathbb{R}^3$, and proving the independence between chromatic and achromatic components. The equations of transformation between RGB and HSI using the max-min semi-norm are given by

$$\begin{cases} I = 0.213R + 0.715G + 0.072B \\ S = \max{(R, G, B)} - \min{(R, G, B)} \\ \begin{cases} \theta = \arccos{\left(\dfrac{2R - G - B}{2(R^2 + G^2 + B^2 - (RG + RB + GB))^{\frac{1}{2}}} \right)} \\ H = \begin{cases} 2\pi - \theta & \text{si } B > G \\ \theta & \text{si } B \leq G \end{cases} \end{cases} \end{cases} \quad (4)$$

where I, S and H are the intensity, the saturation and the hue respectively.

All different orders defined in colour spaces are based on other previous orders defined in every component of colour. In the specific case of HSI space, there are two linear components, saturation and intensity; therefore, it is possible to work with the usual order of the real numbers. However, the hue is an angle value, $H \in [0, 2\pi)$, and the unit circle neither has relevant order nor dominant position. In mathematical terms, we cannot construct a lattice on the unit circle if we do not assign it to an arbitrary origin.

Peters [7] and Hanbury [8] fix a reference hue, H_{ref} and establish an order. This reference hue is chosen as the minimum value. The hue circle is ordered by the distance:

$$d(H, H_{ref}) = \begin{cases} |H - H_{ref}| & \text{if } |H - H_{ref}| \leq \pi \\ 2\pi - |H - H_{ref}| & \text{if } |H - H_{ref}| > \pi \end{cases} \quad (5)$$

From this distance we obtain an order for the hue:

$$H_1 \leq_{H_{ref}} H_2 \Leftrightarrow \begin{cases} d(H_1, H_{ref}) < d(H_2, H_{ref}) \\ \text{or} \\ d(H_1, H_{ref}) = d(H_2, H_{ref}) \text{ y } H_1 \leq H_2 \end{cases} \quad (6)$$

It should be observed that the natural order in the linear components, saturation and intensity, agrees with the intuitive order. But there are different orders for hue component depending on the value H_{ref}, so that the intuitive idea of smaller or bigger point disappears. For this reason some rare results can be obtained when an angular component plays an important role in the order defined on the chromatic space.

Fix a (cost) function $c : HSI \to \mathbb{R}$, and consider the following order:

$$(H_1, S_1, I_1) \leq^c_{H_{ref}} (H_2, S_2, I_2)$$

$$\Leftrightarrow \begin{cases} c(H_1, S_1, I_1) < c(H_2, S_2, I_2) \text{ (a)} \\ \qquad \text{or} \\ c(H_1, S_1, I_1) = c(H_2, S_2, I_2) \text{ and } I_1 < I_2 \text{ (b)} \\ \qquad \text{or} \\ c(H_1, S_1, I_1) = c(H_2, S_2, I_2) \text{ and } I_1 = I_2 \text{ and } H_1 <_{H_{ref}} H_2 \text{ (c)} \\ \qquad \text{or} \\ c(H_1, S_1, I_1) = c(H_2, S_2, I_2) \text{ and } I_1 = I_2 \text{ and } H_1 = H_2 \text{ and } S_1 \leq S_2 \text{ (d)} \end{cases}$$
$$(7)$$

Case a) of (7) determines the order almost everywhere. Only for pairs of points over the same surface $c(H, S, I) = c$ the order must be decided via the HSI lexicographical order with priority I, H, S. Certainly, RGB space is the most employed colour space in images acquisition. In addition, if we want to work using the order defined by (7), it requires a high computational cost for calculating the equations of a change of coordinates between the spaces RGB and HSI. However, we can avoid to calculate inverse transform equations if the lexicographical order given by (7) is considered on RGB space.

4   Erosion and Dilation in the HSI Colour Space

The lexicographical orders are total orders with priority of components. In real images, the intensity is the attribute that offers greater definition of scenes, therefore the priority of lexicographic order I, H, S offers good visual results. If the image has a high saturation, it is mainly determined by the hue, so we set the hue as first position in the lexicographical order. [8], [9], [10], [11], [12], [13].

A new order is suggested for HSI space defined by (7), where the cost function is a function of the hue for high saturation level case and a function of the intensity for low saturation.

Fixed a hue reference value H_{ref}, we defined the normalized hue value by the formula

$$h = \frac{d(H, H_{ref})}{\pi} \in [0, 1] \tag{8}$$

The above cost function is defined by

$$c(H, S, I) = a(S)h + (1 - a(S))I \tag{9}$$

where $a : [0, 1] \rightarrow [0, 1]$ is increasing with $a(0) = 0$ and $a(1) = 1$. Initially, it is possible to choose $a(S) = S$ [14], so

$$c(H, S, I) = Sh + (1 - S)I \tag{10}$$

and the order is expressed by

$(H_1, S_1, I_1) \leq_{H_{ref}} (H_2, S_2, I_2)$

$$\Leftrightarrow \begin{cases} (1 - S_1)I_1 + S_1 h_1 < (1 - S_2)I_2 + S_2 h_2 \\ \qquad\qquad \text{or} \\ (1 - S_1)I_1 + S_1 h_1 = (1 - S_2)I_2 + S_2 h_2 \text{ and } R_1 < R_2 \\ \qquad\qquad \text{or} \\ (1 - S_1)I_1 + S_1 h_1 = (1 - S_2)I_2 + S_2 h_2 \text{ and } R_1 = R_2 \text{ and } G_1 < G_2 \\ \qquad\qquad \text{or} \\ (1 - S_1)I_1 + S_1 h_1 = (1 - S_2)I_2 + S_2 h_2 \text{ and } R_1 = R_2 \text{ and } G_1 = G_2 \\ \qquad\qquad\qquad\qquad\qquad \text{and } B_1 \leq B_2 \end{cases}$$

$$\tag{11}$$

where (R, G, B) and (H, S, I) are the components of a point in the RGB and HSI spaces respectively.

We remark that:

- Saturation component S and its complementary value $1 - S$ are weights of the normalized hue and the intensity respectively. To establish the order relation it must be taken into account that the hue component has bigger weight when the saturation is high, whereas the intensity has bigger weight when the saturation is low.
- If the image has a high saturation level, then the fixed reference hue value plays an important role. For example, if the predominant colour is red and we select $H_{ref} = 0$, then eroding (resp. dilating) is the same that increasing (resp. decreasing) the size of saturate red objects.

The image Miro (368×271), used by Hanbury [11], [8] has low saturation (Fig. 1). However, the image Colours (249×245) has medium-high saturation (Fig. 2). These images are used to testing the goodness of the order above suggested. For the image Miro, the order works by intensity level and for the image Colours, the order works by hue level.

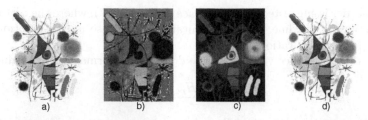

a)   b)   c)   d)

Fig. 1. a) Image Miro b) Distance hue with $H_{ref} = 0°$, c) Saturation d) Intensity

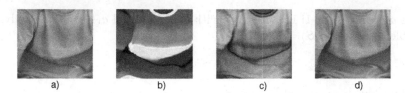

a)   b)   c)   d)

Fig. 2. a) Image Colours b) Distance hue with $H_{ref} = 0°$, c) Saturation d) Intensity

Fig. 3 shows the erosion and dilation of image Miro by a disk of width 4 with the order (11) with $H_{ref} = 0°$ in a) and b) and with $H_{ref} = \pi$ in c) and d). At Fig. 1 c) we can see: the red and yellow shaded regions are areas of high saturation; the blue and green shaded body and the blue and green coloured spots over background have medium saturation; the white background, with green-gray coloured spots and dark border of imagen and dark spots have low saturation values.

Noting that with $H_{ref} = 0°$ the result of erosion increases the size of the image borders and dark spots. In the dilation by a structuring element big enough, these elements with low intensity disappear. Green-gray spots over white background (high intensity), also increase their size after an erosion operation. Finally, the yellow and red coloured spots at the right bottom of the image, over white background, are objects with high saturation that also increase their size. However, yellow and red regions of face with dark border decrease.

Any change of reference hue value give rise to no different behavior of low saturation areas, but we can appreciate some differences at middle-high saturation regions. For example, if we select $H_{ref} = \pi$, close to blue colour, then the red colour has a high hue level. Fig. 3 c) shows at the right bottom of the image that as result of erosion, the edge of the red spot is not enhanced due to green-gray spots over background.

Fig. 4 shows the erosion and the dilation of image Colours by a disk of width 4, with the order (11) with $H_{ref} = 0°$ in a) and b) and with $H_{ref} = \pi$ in c) and d). At Fig. 2 c) we can see that image Colours has middle-high saturation level; therefore, the order works like an intermediate order between the lexicographical order with intensity as priority component and the lexicographical order with

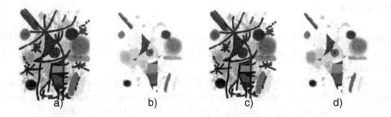

Fig. 3. a) Erosion b) Dilation with $H_{ref} = 0°$ c) Erosion d) Dilation with $H_{ref} = \pi$ of image Miro

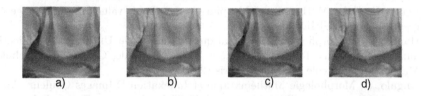

Fig. 4. a) Erosion c) Dilation with $H_{ref} = 0°$ c) Erosion d) Dilation with $H_{ref} = \pi$ of image Colours

hue as priority component. Fig. 4 is agreed with our intuitive perception: the reference hue value has more influence than in the above case.

5   Conclusion

A new order has been presented in the *HSI* colour space in the Mathematical Morphology framework for colour images. This order allows to select the saturation level as a weighting factor for the intensity and the hue.

For low saturation regions, the order works in a lexicographical order with intensity as priority component, whereas if the regions have a high saturation value, the order chooses the hue as priority component, since these components are the right ones to determine the image at every case. When saturation is medium, then the order works like an intermediate order between the lexicographical one with the intensity as priority component and the lexicographical one with the hue as priority component.

It is possible to prove that the fixed hue reference value has a high influence on images with medium-large saturation level, whereas this influence is not significant for images with low saturation level. Another advantage of the order is that it allows to reduce the computational cost that involves the work in colour spaces different the RGB space.

Acknowledgments. This paper has been partially supported by the program "Ayudas Puente a los grupos de investigación" of Comunidad Autónoma de Madrid.

References

1. Matheron, G.: Random Sets and Integral Geometry. Wiley, New York (1975)
2. Serra, J.: Mathematical Morphology, Therorical Advances, vol. 2. Academic Press, San Diego (1988)
3. Bourbaki, N.: Théorie des Ensembles; Élements de Mathématique. Hermann (1977)
4. Hanbury, A., Serra, J.: A 3D-Polar Coordinate Colour Representation Suitable for Image Analysis. Technical report, PRIP-TR-077, TU Wien (2002)
5. Hanbury, A., Serra, J.: Colour Image Analysis in 3D-Polar Coordinates. Pattern Reccognition and Image Processing Group, Vienna
6. Hanbury, A.: The Taming of the Hue, Saturation and Brightness Colour Space. Rapport Technique N-28/02/MM, CMM-École des Mines de Paris (2002)
7. Peters II, R.A.: Mathematical Morphology for Angle-value Images. Image Procesing VIII, vol. SPIE, 3026 (1997)
8. Hanbury, A.: Morphologie Mathématique sur le Cercle Unité avec Applications aux Teintes et aux Textures Orientées. Thése doctorale, Centre de Morphologie Mathématique, École des Mines, Paris (2002)
9. Angulo, J.: Morphologie Mathématique et Indexation D'Images Couleur. Aplication á la Microscopie en Biomédecine. Ph.D. Thése doctorale, Centre de Morphologie Mathématique, École des Mines, Paris (2003)
10. Angulo, J., Serra, J.: Morphological Coding of Color Images by Vector Conected Filters. In: 7 th International Symposium on Signal Processing and its Applications (ISSPA'03), vol. 1, pp. 69–72. IEEE, New Jersey, New York (2003)
11. Hanbury, A.: Lexicographical Order in the HLS Colour Space. Technical report N-04/01/MM, Centre de Morphologie Mathematique. École des Mines de Paris (2001)
12. Ortiz, F., Torres, F., Angulo, J., Puente, S.: Comparative Study of Vectorial Morphological Operations in Different Color Spaces. Intellegent Robots and Computer Vision XX; Algorithms, Techniques, and Active Vision, SPIE, vol. 4572 (2001)
13. Ortiz, F., Torres, F., Juan, E., de Cuenca, N.: Colour Mathematical Morphology for Neural Image Análisis. Real Time Imaging 8, 455–465 (2002)
14. Tobar, M.C, Platero, C., Sanguino, J., Asensio, G.: Estudio Comparativo de Órdenes en los Espacios de Color para su Aplicación en Morfología Matemática. XXVII Jornadas de Automática, Almería (2006)

Improving Background Subtraction Based on a Casuistry of Colour-Motion Segmentation Problems

I. Huerta[1], D. Rowe[1], M. Mozerov[1], and J. Gonzàlez[2]

[1] Dept. d'Informàtica, Computer Vision Centre, Edifici O. Campus UAB,
08193, Bellaterra, Spain
Ivan.Huerta@cvc.uab.es
[2] Institut de Robòtica i Informàtica Ind. UPC, Llorens i Artigas 4-6,
08028, Barcelona, Spain

Abstract. The basis for the high-level interpretation of observed patterns of human motion still relies on motion segmentation. Popular approaches based on background subtraction use colour information to model each pixel during a training period. Nevertheless, a deep analysis on colour segmentation problems demonstrates that colour segmentation is not enough to detect all foreground objects in the image, for instance when there is a lack of colour necessary to build the background model. In this paper, our segmentation procedure is based not only on colour, but also on intensity information. Consequently, the intensity model enhances segmentation when the use of colour is not feasible. Experimental results demonstrate the feasibility of our approach.

1 Introduction

The analysis of human motion in image sequences involves different tasks, such as motion segmentation and tracking, action recognition and behaviour reasoning [6]. However, the basis for high-level interpretation of observed patterns of human motion still relies on *when* and *where* motion is being detected in the image. This kind of information is critical for different applications such as smart video surveillance for intruder detection and suspicious behaviour detection.

To achieve robust detection, many researchers have proposed methods to address segmentation problems, such as illumination changes, shadows, camouflage, background in motion, or deposited and removed objects from the scene [7]. To overcome these difficulties, different techniques can be applied, such as temporal differencing, optical flow and background subtraction [9]. The latter is based on a background model used to compare the current image with such a model. Among these background subtraction methods, statistical approaches are very popular: W^4 [3] use a bimodal distribution; Pfinder uses a single Gaussian to model the background; Stauffer et al. [2] use a mixture of Gaussians; and Elgammal et al. [1] present a non-parametric background model.

On the other hand, several cues are used for segmentation in the literature: Horprasert et al. [4] use colour information to classify a pixel as foreground,

J. Martí et al. (Eds.): IbPRIA 2007, Part II, LNCS 4478, pp. 475–482, 2007.

Case Analysis (Colour Model Casuistry)					
Cues	Chromatic	Equal			Different
	Brightness	Lower	Equal	Higher	-
Description	Base case	Global shadow Local shadow	Background	Global Highlight Local Highlight	Foreground
	Anomalies	Dark Camouflage Dark Foreground	Camouflage	Light Camouflage Light Foreground	Sensitivity of Sensor Change of illuminant Gleaming surface Saturation Minimum Intensity

Fig. 1. This table analyzes the differences between an input image and the background model

background, shadow or highlighted background, while Wallflower [8] uses a three-level categorization, namely pixel, region and frame level. Jabri et al. [5] use colour and edge information, and Shen [10] uses a RGB/HSL colour space plus fuzzy classification.

In this paper, a casuistry of colour-motion segmentation problems is first presented, since colour is not enough to detect all foreground objects. This allows to identify when a colour model can and can not be used. Thus, based upon this casuistry, different colour problems can be then addressed properly. As a result, a novel background subtraction technique is presented, which combines both colour and intensity cues in order to solve colour motion segmentation problems such as saturation or the lack of colour when building the background model.

This paper is organized as follows. Next section presents a casuistry of the problems when using colour information for motion segmentation. This leads to our approach to confront segmentation. Section 3 explains our approach to solve the above aforementioned problems using the colour and intensity cues. Experimental results are described in section 4. Lastly, section 5 concludes this contribution and discusses about future work.

2   Problems on Colour Models

Colour information obtained from the recording camera is based on three components which depend on the wavelength λ: the object reflectance R, the illuminant spectral potency distribution E and the sensor wavelength sensitivity S:

$$Colour = \int_{\lambda} R(\lambda)E(\lambda)S(\lambda)d\lambda. \tag{1}$$

Unfortunately, *sensitivity of the sensor* may depend on intensities for each channel which can cause chromaticity changes. In addition, if the *illuminant*

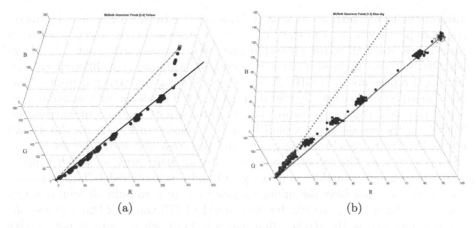

Fig. 2. Intensity RGB values of a) yellow and b) blue colours extracted from a Macbeth board which becomes lighter over time. The dashed line corresponds to a wrong chromaticity line and solid line corresponds to a correct chromaticity line due to: (a) at least one of the RGB channels is saturated, or (b) there is not enough intensity to build a colour model.

changes, the perceived chromaticity changes too, so the colour model can be wrongly built.

Fig. 1 shows a Colour Model Casuistry based on a background model which separates the chromaticity from the brightness component. The Base Case is the correct operation of the theoretical colour model, and the anomalies are problems that may appear. The theoretical base case solves some of the segmentation problems, as sudden or progressive global and local illumination changes, such as shadows and highlights. However, some problems remain. Foreground pixels with the same chromaticity component as the background model are not segmented. If the foreground pixel has the same brightness as the background model appears the *Camouflage* problem. A *Dark Camouflage* is considered when the pixel has less brightness and it cannot be distinguished from a shadow. Next, *Light Camouflage* happens when the pixel is brighter than the model, therefore the pixel cannot be distinguished from a highlight. *Dark Foreground* denotes pixels which do not have enough intensity to reliably compute the chromaticity. Therefore it can not be compared with the chromaticity background model. On the other hand is *Light Foreground* which happens when the present pixel is saturated and can not be compared with the chromaticity background model either.

Further, the perceived background chromaticity may change due to the *sensitivity of the sensor*, or *local* or *global illumination changes*. For instance, background pixels corresponding to shadows can be considered as foregrounds. The *Gleaming Surfaces* as mirrors cause that the reflect of the object is considered as foreground. On the other hand, due to saturation or minimum intensity problems the colour model can not be build correctly. Therefore, a background pixel can be considered foreground erroneously. *Saturation problem* happens when the intensity value of a pixel for at least one channel is saturated or almost saturated. An example can be seen in the Fig. 2 where an experiment which consists on recording a Macbeth board while changing intensity was carried out. The Machbet board is broadly used because it contains a wide range of different colours. Fig. 2.(a) represents the RGB values of the yellow region extracted from a Macbeth board which becomes lighter over time. If the model is built when at least one of the RGB channels is saturated, the chromaticity line becomes erroneous. Therefore, the colour model would be build wrongly. In Fig. 2.(a), the dashed line is the erroneous chromaticity line and the solid line would be the correct chromaticity line. The second one is *minimum intensity problem* which happens when there is not enough chromaticity to build a colour model. This is mainly due to pixels do not have the minimum intensity value to built the chromaticity line, as shown in Fig. 2.(b) which represents the RGB values of Blue. The wrong chromaticity line is the dashed line which is built when there is not enough intensity. Then, a correct chromaticity line will be built when there is enough intensity. See the black solid in Fig. 2.(b).

3   Handling Colour-Based Segmentation Problems

The approach is based on background subtraction and uses either colour or intensity statistics, depending on the casuistry. First, the parameters of the background model are defined, next the colour and intensity models are explained in detail, and finally the segmentation procedure is presented. An sketch of the system can be seen in Fig. 3.

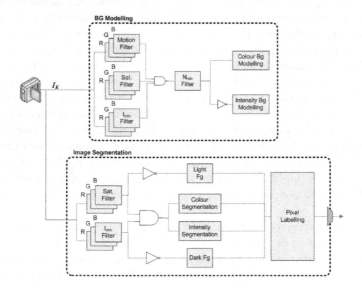

Fig. 3. Overview of the system

3.1 Background Modelling

The background model takes into account the problems depicted before. A motion filter is used to avoid moving foreground pixels of the images acquired during the training period, such as walking people or moving cars:

$$\text{Motion(x, t)} = \begin{cases} 1 & \text{if } |V(x,t) - \lambda(x)| < max(2 * \sigma(x), T_m) \\ 0 & otherwise, \end{cases} \qquad (2)$$

where $V(x,t)$ is the intensity of a pixel location x in the t image of sequence V, $\lambda(x)$ is the median value, and $\sigma(x)$ is the standard deviation computed for all pixels in the image. The threshold T_m is a minimum constant value.

Pixels below a minimum intensity value (N_{Imin}) or pixels over a saturation intensity value (N_{Sat}) are not used to compute the colour model, but to build the intensity model:

$$\text{Imin(x, t)} = \begin{cases} 1 & \text{if } V(x,t) > N_{Imin} \\ 0 & otherwise \end{cases} \qquad (3)$$

$$\text{Sat(x, t)} = \begin{cases} 1 & \text{if } V(x,t) < N_{Sat} \\ 0 & otherwise \end{cases} \qquad (4)$$

Lastly, a Nmin filter is used to know if a pixel position x in the image has enough values to build colour statistics:

$$\text{Nmin(x)} = \begin{cases} 1 & \sum_{t=1}^{N} Motion(x,t) \& Sat(x,t) \& Imin(x,t) > N_{Nmin} \\ 0 & otherwise \end{cases} \qquad (5)$$

As a result, the colour model is built using those pixels which have passed the Nmin filter, without saturation $Sat(x,t)$ neither minimum intensity $Imin(x,t)$ nor motion pixels $Motion(x,t)$ for each frame.

Next, the intensity model is built with those pixels which have not passed the Nmin filter but without considering motion pixels $Motion(x,t)$. Nevertheless, if almost all the pixels corresponding a place x are in motion, then there is not enough statistics to build the model correctly.

3.2 The Colour and Intensity Models

The colour model is based on the algorithm presented in [4], which computes the chromatic and brightness distortion components of each pixel. Furthermore, it can solve local and global shadows and highlights.

Each pixel is modelled by a 4-tuple $< E(x), s(x), a(x), b(x) >$, where $E(x) = [\mu_R(x), \mu_G(x), \mu_B(x)]$ is the expected colour value, μ is the arithmetic mean of the xth pixel's red, green, blue values computed over the training period of N frames, $s(x) = [\sigma_R(x), \sigma_G(x), \sigma_B(x)]$ is the standard deviation of colour value, $a(x)$ is the variation of the brightness distortion, and $b(x)$ is the variation of the chromaticity distortion of the xth pixel. See [4] for more details.

The intensity model is built based on a 2-tuple $< E(x), s(x) >$ for every pixel, where $E(x) = \mu[(R(x) + G(x) + B(x))/3]$ is the arithmetic mean of the xth pixel computed over the training period, and $s(x) = \sigma[(R(x) + G(x) + B(x))/3]$ is the standard deviation of colour value.

Foreground detection is thus achieved by using the normalised brightness and normalised chromaticity measures from colour model and the statistics from the intensity model for every new images, and then applying the pixel classification procedure explained next.

3.3   Image Segmentation

The combination of colour and intensity models allows to cope with different problems. In fact, our algorithm can detect different situations. If the background colour model of the current pixel is not available due to the lack of colour or saturation problems during the training period, then this pixel is segmented using intensity model. A pixel is considered foreground (FI) using a mean filter[1], in other case is considered background (BI):

$$\text{meanfilter}(x, t) = \begin{cases} 1 & \text{if } |V(x, t) - E(x)| < max(2 * s(x), T_i) then Bg. \\ 0 & otherwise foreground, \end{cases} \quad (6)$$

In other case, the colour model is used. When the current pixel has not chromaticity, it can be only segmented using the brightness component from the colour model. A threshold over brightness classifies if this pixel is a *Dark Foreground* (DF) or *Light Foreground* (LF). The thresholds $T_{CD}, T_{\alpha 1}, T_{\alpha 2}$ are given by the colour model defined in [4], and the thresholds $T_{\alpha lo} = k_1 * T_{\alpha 1}$ and $T_{\alpha Hi} = k_1 * T_{\alpha 2}$, where k_1 is a constant value. In other case this pixel is classified as *Background* (BB). Finally, if the pixel have chromaticity, then this will be compared with the background model chromaticity. The pixel is foreground (F) if it has different chromaticity. If the pixel have the same chromaticity, it is classified depending on the brightness as *Shaded Background or Shadow* (S), *Highlighted Background* (H), or *Original Background* (B).

Summarizing all the parameters of the background and colour model explained before, a pixel of the segmented image $M(i)$ is classified as:

$$M(i) = \begin{cases} FI & if & \neg meanfilter & \& & \neg Nmin & then & Fg. \\ BI & else\ if & & \neg Nmin & & then & Bg. \\ DF & else\ if & \hat{\alpha}_i < T_{\alpha lo} & \& & \neg Imin & & \left.\begin{array}{c} \\ \end{array}\right\} Fg. \\ LF & else\ if & \hat{\alpha}_i > T_{\alpha Hi} & \& & \neg Sat & & \\ BB & else\ if & \neg Sat & | & \neg Imin & then & Bg. \\ F & else\ if & & \hat{C}D_i > T_{CD} & & then & Fg. \\ B & else\ if & \hat{\alpha}_i > T_{\alpha 1} & \& & \hat{\alpha}_i < T_{\alpha 2} & & \left.\begin{array}{c} \\ \\ \end{array}\right\} Bg. \\ S & else\ if & & \hat{\alpha}_i < 0 & & \\ H & & & otherwise & & \end{cases} \quad (7)$$

---

[1] The threshold T_i is a minimum constant value.

4   Experimental Results

Our approach has been tested with multiple and different sequences with multiples segmentation problems. The first row of Fig. 4 shows the results obtained using colour model presented in [4]. In these images the saturated sky (blue sky colour) and saturated floor (yellow colour) are detected wrongly as foreground regions due to saturation problem. Furthermore, second image show as a black shadow is detected as foreground erroneously due to lack of colour problem. The second row shows that these problems are solved using our approach. The Fig. 5 shows that our approach works in different datasets, such as PETS and CAVIAR, among others.

Fig. 4. First row shows erroneous blobs wrongly segmented by the colour model [4] due to the lack of colour and/or saturation. Second row shows that these blobs are removed by our approach, using both colour and intensity cues.

Fig. 5. Foreground region segmentation applying our approach to different datasets, such as PETS and CAVIAR, among others

5   Conclusion

In this paper, firstly a casuistry of the possible colour-motion segmentation problems is presented. This allows us to define when the colour model can be used. Then, an approach is proposed to cope with different colour problems as dark foreground and light foreground. Furthermore, it solves saturation problems and minimum intensity problems using intensity cue. The approach reduces the number of false negatives, false positives and increase the detected correct foreground regions as it can be seen in the experimental results. Future Work needs to address news cues, like edges or corners because the intensity model can not work with intense shadows and highlights. Furthermore, these kind of cues can help solving problems related to the sensitivity of sensor and changes of illumination which are not being tackled in this paper. Finally, an object based multilayer background model is required to face problems as ghosts [8].

Acknowledgments. This work has been supported by EC grant IST-027110 for the HERMES project and by the Spanish MEC under projects CICYT SISY-PHUS TIN2006-14606 and DPI-2004-5414. Jordi Gonzàlez also acknowledges the support of a Juan de la Cierva Postdoctoral fellowship from the Spanish MEC.

References

1. Elgammal, A., Harwood, D., Davis, L.S.: Nonparametric background model for background subtraction. In: Proceedings European Conference Computer Vision (ECCV'00), pp. 751–767, Dublin (2000)
2. Grimson, W.E.L., Stauffer, C.: Adaptive background mixture models for real-time tracking. vol. 1, pp. 22–29 (1999)
3. Haritaoglu, I., Harwood, D., Davis, L.S.: W4: Real-time surveillance of people and their activities. IEEE Trans. Pattern Analysis and Machine Intelligence 22(8), 809–830 (2000)
4. Horprasert, T., Harwood, D., Davis, L.S.: A statistical approach for real-time robust background subtraction and shadow detection. IEEE Frame-Rate Applications Workshop (1999)
5. Jabri, H.W.S., Duric, Z., Rosenfeld, A.: Detection and location of people in video images using adaptive fusion of color and edge information. vol. 4, pp. 627–630 (September 2000)
6. Gonzàlez i Sabaté, J.: Human Sequence Evaluation: the Key-frame Approach. PhD thesis (May 2004)
7. Karaman, M., Goldmann, L., Yu, D., Sikora, T.: Comparison of static background segmentation methods. In: Visual Communications and Image Processing (VCIP '05) (July 2005)
8. Toyama, K., Krumm, J., Brumitt, B., Meyers, B.: Wallflower: Principles and practice of background maintenance, vol. 1, pp. 255–261 (1999)
9. Moeslund, T.B., Hilton, A., Krüger, V.: A survey of advances in vision-based human motion capture and analysis. Computer Vision and Image Understanding 104, 90–126 (2006)
10. Shen, J.: Motion detection in color image sequence and shadow elimination. Visual Communications and Image Processing 5308, 731–740 (2004)

Random Forest for Gene Expression Based Cancer Classification: Overlooked Issues

Oleg Okun[1] and Helen Priisalu[2]

[1] University of Oulu, Oulu 90014, Finland
[2] Tallinn University of Technology, Tallinn 19086, Estonia

Abstract. Random forest is a collection (ensemble) of decision trees. It is a popular ensemble technique in pattern recognition. In this article, we apply random forest for cancer classification based on gene expression and address two issues that have been so far overlooked in other works. First, we demonstrate on two different real-world datasets that the performance of random forest is strongly influenced by dataset complexity. When estimated before running random forest, this complexity can serve as a useful performance indicator and it can explain a difference in performance on different datasets. Second, we show that one should rely with caution on feature importance used to rank genes: two forests, generated with the different number of features per node split, may have very similar classification errors on the same dataset, but the respective lists of genes ranked according to feature importance can be weakly correlated.

1 Introduction

Gene expression based cancer classification is a supervised classification problem. However, unlike many other classification problems in machine learning, it is unusual because the number of features (gene expressions) far exceeds the number of cases (samples taken from patients). This atypical characteristic makes this task much more challenging than the problems where the number of available cases is much larger than the number of features.

In gene expression based cancer classification, a subset of the original genes is relevant and related to cancer, but genes constituting this subset are frequently unknown and need to be discovered and selected by means of machine learning methods. As remarked in [1], classification algorithms providing measures of feature importance are of great interest for gene selection, especially if the classification algorithm itself ranks genes. One of such algorithms is random forest.

Random forest has not been frequently utilised in bioinformatics [1,2,3,4,5,6]. However, it has several properties that make it attractive. The most important among them are 1) it does not overfit when the number of features exceeds the number of cases, 2) it implicitly performs feature selection, 3) it incorporates interactions among features, and 4) it returns feature importance. In addition, it was claimed [1,2] that its performance is not much influenced by parameter choices.

J. Martí et al. (Eds.): IbPRIA 2007, Part II, LNCS 4478, pp. 483–490, 2007.

The most significant parameter of random forest is *mtry*, the number of features used at each split of decision tree. In [2] they claimed that the performance of random forest is often relatively insensitive to the choice of *mtry* as long as *mtry* is far from its minimum or maximum possible values (1 or *m*, respectively, where *m* is the total number of features). Another parameter is the number of trees, which should be quite large (say, 500 to several thousands).

In gene expression based cancer classification there are two goals: to achieve as high as possible classification rate with as few as possible genes. Often researchers concentrate on high accuracy while overlooking the analysis of the selected genes. Based on tests with two gene expression datasets, we discovered in this article that although the random forest performance in terms of error rate may be similar or the same for two different values of *mtry*, gene rankings, produced by two forests applied to a certain dataset, can be *weakly correlated*. In other words, genes that are very important in one case can be almost irrelevant in another case. This is the first overlooked issue emphasising that feature importance provided by random forest should be treated with caution.

Another overlooked issue concerns a less severe but nevertheless important problem. It is often said that random forests are competitive with respect to other classifiers used in cancer research. We do not argue against this claim, but would like to emphasise that dataset complexity computed before trying random forest on a certain dataset can provide a useful performance estimate. Again, we demonstrate based on several complexity measures borrowed from [7] that the performance of random forest can be roughly predicted from these measures. Our goal was not to obtain precise numerical predictions but rather to attain a kind of indication of the expected performance without classifying a dataset.

2   Random Forest

A random forest is a collection of fully grown CART-like (CART stands for Classification and Regression Tree) decision trees combined by averaging the predictions of individual trees in the forest. For each tree, given that the total number of cases in a dataset is N, a training set is first generated by randomly choosing N times with replacement from all N cases (bootstrap sample). It can be shown [8] that this botstrap sample includes only about 2/3 of the original data. The rest of the cases is used as a test (or out-of-bag) set in order to estimate the out-of-bag (OOB) error of classification, which serves as a fair estimate of accuracy. If there are m features, a number $mtry \ll m$ is specified such that at each node, *mtry* out of m features are randomly selected (thus, random forest uses two random mechanisms: bootstrap aggregation and random feature selection) and the best split on these *mtry* features is used to split the node. Various splitting criteria can be employed such as Gini index, information gain, node impurity. The value of *mtry* is constant during the forest growing (typical values of *mtry* are chosen to be approximately equal to either $\frac{\sqrt{m}}{2}$ or $\sqrt{m}$, or $2\sqrt{m}$). Unlike CART, each tree in the forest is fully grown without pruning. Each tree is a weak classifier and because of this fact, averaging the predictions of many weak classifiers results in significant accuracy improvement compared to a single tree. In other words, since the unpruned trees are low-bias, high-variance models, averaging over an ensemble of trees reduces variance while keeping bias low.

In addition to being the useful estimate of classification accuracy, the out-of-bag error is also used to get estimates of feature importance. However, based on the out-of-bag error alone, it is difficult to define a sharp division between important and unimportant features.

3   Datasets

Two datasets were chosen for experiments. They differ in technology used to produce a dataset and in dataset complexity. Dataset complexity is discussed in detail below.

3.1   SAGE Dataset

SAGE stands for Serial Analysis of Gene Expression [9,10]. This is technology alternative to microarrays (cDNAs and oligonucleotides). Though SAGE was originally conceived for use in cancer studies, there is not much research using SAGE datasets regarding ensembles of classifiers (to our best knowledge, this is the first research on random forests based on SAGE data). SAGE provides a statistical description of the mRNA population present in a cell without prior selection of the genes to be studied [11]. This is the main distinction of SAGE over microarray approaches (cDNA and oligonucleotide) that are limited to the genes represented in the chip. SAGE "counts" the number of transcripts or tags for each gene, where the tags substitute the expression levels. As a result, counting sequence tags yields positive integer numbers in contrast to microarray measurements.

In the chosen dataset [12], there are expressions of 822 genes in 74 cases (24 cases are normal while 50 cases are cancerous) [13]. Unlike many other datasets with one or few types of cancer, it contains 9 different types of cancer. We decided to ignore the difference between cancer types and to treat all cancerous cases as belonging to a single class. No preprocessing was done.

3.2   Colon Dataset

This microarray (oligonucleotide) dataset [14], introduced in [15], contains expressions of 2,000 genes for 62 cases (22 normal and 40 colon tumour cases). Preprocessing includes the logarithmic transformation to base 10, followed by normalisation to zero mean and unit variance as usually done with this dataset.

4   Dataset Complexity

It is known that the performance of individual classifiers and their ensembles is strongly data-dependent. It is often impossible to give any theoretical bounds on performance or these bounds are limited to few very specific cases and too weak to be useful in practice. To gain insight into a supervised classification problem such as gene expression based cancer classification, one can adopt complexity measures introduced and studied in [7]. Knowing the dataset complexity can help to predict the behaviour of a certain classifier before it is applied to the dataset, though the prediction may be not absolute because of finite dataset size. Complexity measures described below assume two-class problems and they are *classifier-independent*, i.e., they do not rely on a certain classification model. Employing classifier-dependent measures would not provide an absolute scale for comparison. For example, it is well known that a nearest neighbour classifier can sometimes easily classify a highly nonlinear dataset.

The following characteristics were adopted to estimate the dataset complexity.

4.1   Fisher's Discriminant Ratio (F1)

Fisher's discriminant ratio is defined as $f = \frac{(\mu_1 - \mu_2)^2}{\sigma_1^2 + \sigma_2^2}$, where μ_1, μ_2, σ_1^2, σ_2^2 are the means and variances of the two classes, respectively. The higher f ($f \to \infty$ corresponds to two classes represented by two spatially separated points), the easier the classification problem. Hence $F1 = \max\{f_i\}$, $i = 1, \ldots, m$.

4.2   Volume of Overlap Region (F2)

A similar measure is the overlap of the tails of the two class-conditional distributions. Let $\min(g_i, c_j)$ and $\max(g_i, c_j)$ be the minimum and maximum values of feature g_i in class c_j. Then the overlap measure $F2$ is defined to be $F2 = \Pi_{i=1}^m \frac{MIN(\max(g_i, c_1), \max(g_i, c_2)) - MAX(\min(g_i, c_1), \min(g_i, c_2))}{MAX(\max(g_i, c_1), \max(g_i, c_2)) - MIN(\min(g_i, c_1), \min(g_i, c_2))}$. If $F2 \to 0$, it implies that there is at least one feature for which value ranges of the two classes do not overlap. In other words, the smaller $F2$, the easier the dataset to classify.

4.3   Feature Efficiency (F3)

This measure accounts for how much each feature individually contributes to the class separation. Each feature takes values in a certain interval. If there is an overlap of intervals of two classes, there is ambiguity of classification in the overlapping region. The larger the number of cases lying outside this region, the easier class separation. For linearly separated classes, the overlapping region is empty and therefore all cases are outside of it. For highly overlapped classes, this region is large and the number of cases lying outside is small. Thus, feature efficiency is defined as the fraction of cases outside the overlapping region. $F3$ corresponds to the maximum feature efficiency.

5   Experimental Details

In all experiments below we used Random Forest software from Salford Systems (San Diego, CA, USA), version 1.0. The number of trees in the forest was equal to the default value, 500.

5.1 Complexity Measures

As can be seen from the described complexity measures, they are computed *before* classification. Values of all complexity measures are summarised in Table 1 for both datasets. SAGE dataset appears to be more complex for classification than Colon one. It is therefore natural to expect a worse performance of random forest on the SAGE data. A higher complexity of the SAGE data is not very surprising since this dataset comprises nine different types of cancer treated as one class, while the colon data only includes one cancer type. Table 2 confirms this idea as well as the results from Table 1. Hence, it can be good to estimate the dataset complexity *before* applying random forest to the dataset in order to have a rough estimate of classification accuracy which can be achieved. Table 2 points to dramatic performance degradation of random forest occurred on the SAGE data, compared to the Colon data. This in turn implies that random forest might not achieve acceptable performance in complex problems.

Table 1. Summary of dataset complexity measures for both datasets. Italicised values point to a more complex dataset according to each measure.

Dataset	$F1$	$F2$	$F3$
SAGE	*0.35*	*2.86e-154*	*0.34*
Colon	1.39	5.15e-300	0.42

Table 2. OOB error rates. For each dataset, three typical values of *mtry* were tried

$mtry$	SAGE	$mtry$	Colon
14	0.398	22	0.191
28	0.410	44	0.143
56	0.400	88	0.143

5.2 Receiver Operating Characteristic

Except for OOB error, we also utilised a Receiver Operating Characteristic (ROC) for performance evaluation. ROC is a plot of false positive rate (X-axis) versus true positive rate (Y-axis) of a binary classifier. The true positive rate (TPR) is defined as the ratio of the number of correctly classified positive cases to the total number of positive cases. The false positive rate (FPR) is defined as the ratio of incorrectly classified negative cases to the total number of negative cases. Cancer (normal) cases are positives (negatives). TPR and FPR vary together as a threshold on a classifier's continuous output varies.

The diagonal line $y = x$ corresponds to a classifier which predicts a class membership by randomly guessing it. Hence, all useful classifiers must have ROC curves above this line. The best possible classifier would yield a graph that is a point in the upper left corner of the ROC space, i.e., all true positives are found and no false positives are found.

The ROC curve is a two-dimensional plot of classifier performance. To compare classifiers one typically prefers to work with a single scalar value. This value is called the Area Under Curve or AUC. It is calculated by adding the areas under the ROC curve between each pair of consecutive FPR values, using, for example, the trapezoidal rule. Because the AUC is a portion of the area of the unit square, its value will always lie between 0 and 1. Because random guessing produces the diagonal line between (0,0) and (1,1), which has an area of 0.5, no realistic classifier should have an AUC less than 0.5 [16]. In fact, the better a classifier performs, the higher the AUC. The AUC has an important statistical property: the AUC of a classifier is equivalent to the probability that the classifier will rank a randomly chosen positive case higher than a randomly chosen negative case [16]. AUC values for both datasets and typical choices of *mtry* are shown in Table 3.

Table 3. AUC values. For each dataset, three typical values of *mtry* were tried.

mtry	SAGE	mtry	Colon
14	0.667500	22	0.873864
28	0.659167	44	0.873864
56	0.671667	88	0.852273

Looking at Tables 2 and 3, one can notice that the performance of random forest on each dataset remains almost the same as *mtry* varies. This is the expected result just confirming conclusions of other researchers. We went, however, one step further and analysed the gene rankings produced according to the Gini index of feature importance. The Gini index is computed as follows. For every node split by a feature in every tree in the forest we have a measure of how much the split improved the separation between classes. Accumulating these improvements leads to scores that are then standardised. The most important gene always gets a score of 100.00 and a rank of 1. The second most important gene will get a smaller score and a rank of 2, etc.

We used these ranks to compute rank correlation coefficients. We opted for the rank correlation coefficients such as Kendall's τ and Spearman's ρ instead of the linear (Pearson) correlation coefficient, because they provide appropriate results even if the correlation between two variables is not linear. Both Kendall's τ and Spearman's ρ with a correction for ties were computed for all possible pairs of ranked genes lists (for details, see [17]). There were three pairs for each dataset because of three values of *mtry*. Two statistical tests were done: two-tailed test that correlation is not zero and one-tailed test that correlation is greater than zero. For SAGE, positive correlation if existed at significance levels 0.05 and 0.01 was about 0.12-0.17 at maximum, while for Colon its value was even smaller (0.04-0.11). It means that gene ranks turned out to be almost uncorrelated. Hence, given two similar OOB error rates, one should use feature importance provided by random forest with caution in order to avoid spurious conclusions about biological relevance of top ranked genes.

The fact that different subsets of genes can be equally relevant when predicting cancer has been already highlighted in several works [18,19]. It was argued that one of the possible explanations for such multiplicity and non-uniqueness is a strong influence of the training set on gene selection. In other words, different groups of patients can lead to different gene importance rankings due to genuine differences between patients (cancer grade, stage, etc.). In random forest, bootstrap naturally produces different training sets and these sets have a significant overlap. Although there are many trees in random forest, it seems that multiplicity and non-uniqueness still cannot be avoided. This observation implies that for random forest the rank in the list is not necessarily a reliable indicator of gene importance. Despite of this pessimistic conclusion, random forest remains a good predictive method that probably needs to be complemented by more rigorous and careful analysis of the results.

6 Conclusion

We considered the overlooked issues related to random forests for cancer classification based on gene expression. To facilitate biological interpretation, it is important to know which genes are relevant to cancer. It was claimed that random forest can attach importance measure to each gene, which may point to gene relevance. We showed that despite of similar OOB errors for several typical choices of $mtry$, gene importance can significantly vary. Perhaps, one alternative could be to combine *explicit* feature selection and random forest (see, e.g. [1,4]), but it needs extra verification since it was reported in [1] (see "Stability (uniqueness) of results" there) that this strategy does not always lead to very stable results. In addition, dataset complexity computed before running random forest can be a useful performance predictor. Based on it, users can decide whether to apply random forest or not.

References

1. Díaz-Uriarte, R., Alvarez de Andrés, S.: Gene Selection and Classification of Microarray Data Using Random Forest.: BMC Bioinformatics, vol. 7 (2006)
2. Svetnik, V., Liaw, A., Tong, C., Wang, T.: Application of Breiman's Random Forest to Modeling Structure-Activity Relationships of Pharmaceutical Molecules. In: Roli, F., Kittler, J., Windeatt, T. (eds.) MCS 2004. LNCS, vol. 3077, pp. 334–343. Springer, Heidelberg (2004)
3. Wu, B., Abbot, T., Fishman, D., McMurray, W., Mor, G., Stone, K., Ward, D., Williams, K., Zhao, H.: Comparison of Statistical Methods for Classification of Ovarian Cancer Using Mass Spectrometry Data. Bioinformatics 19, 1636–1643 (2003)
4. Geurts, P., Fillet, M., de Seny, D., Meuwis, M.-A., Malaise, M., Merville, M.-P., Wehenkel, L.: Proteomic Mass Spectra Classification Using Decision Tree Based Ensemble Methods. Bioinformatics 21, 3138–3145 (2005)

5. Alvarez, S., Díaz-Uriarte, R., Osorio, A., Barroso, A., Melchor, L., Paz, M.F., Honrado, E., Rodríguez, R., Urioste, M., Valle, L., Díez, O., Cigudosa, J.C., Dopazo, J., Esteller, M., Benitez, J.: A Predictor Based on the Somatic Genomic Changes of the BRCA1/BRCA2 Breast Cancer Tumors Identifies the Non-BRCA1/BRCA2 Tumors with BRCA1 Promoter Hypermethylation. Clinical Cancer Research 11, 1146–1153 (2005)
6. Gunther, E.C., Stone, D.J., Gerwein, R.W., Bento, P., Heyes, M.P.: Prediction of Clinical Drug Efficacy by Classification of Drug-Induced Genomic Expression Profiles in Vitro. Proc. Natl. Acad. Sci. 100, 9608–9613 (2003)
7. Ho, T.K., Basu, M.: Complexity Measures of Supervised Classification Problems. IEEE Trans. Patt. Analysis and Machine Intell. 24, 289–300 (2002)
8. Breiman, L.: Random Forests. Machine Learning 45, 5–32 (2001)
9. http://www.sagenet.org
10. Velculescu, V.E., Zhang, L., Vogelstein, B., Kinzler, K.W.: Serial Analysis of Gene Expression. Science 270, 484–487 (1995)
11. Aldaz, M.C.: Serial Analysis of Gene Expression (SAGE) in Cancer Research. In: Ladanyi, M., Gerald, W.L. (eds.) Expression Profiling of Human Tumors: Diagnostic and Research Applications, pp. 47–60. Humana Press, Totowa, NJ (2003)
12. http://lisp.vse.cz/challenge/ecmlpkdd2004
13. Gandrillon, O.: Guide to the Gene Expression Data. In: Berka, P., Crémilleux, B. (eds.) Proc. the ECML/PKDD Discovery Challenge Workshop, Pisa, Italy, pp. 116–120 (2004)
14. http://microarray.princeton.edu/oncology/affydata/index.html
15. Alon, U., Barkai, N., Notterman, D.A., Gish, K., Ybarra, S., Mack, D., Levine, A.J.: Broad Patterns of Gene Expression Revealed by Clustering Analysis of Tumor and Normal Colon Tissues Probed by Oligonucleotide Arrays. In: Proc. Natl. Acad. Sci. 96, 6745–6750 (1999)
16. Fawcett, T.: An Introduction to ROC Analysis. Patt. Recogn. Letters 27, 861–874 (2006)
17. Sheskin, D.J.: Handbook of Parametric and Nonparametric Statistical Procedures. Chapman & Hall/CRC, Boca Raton, London, New York, Washington, DC (2004)
18. Ein-Dor, L., Kela, I., Getz, G., Givol, D., Domany, E.: Outcome Signature Genes in Breast Cancer: Is There a Unique Set? Bioinformatics 21, 171–178 (2005)
19. Michiels, S., Koscielny, S., Hill, C.: Prediction of Cancer Outcome with Microarrays: a Multiple Random Validation Strategy. Lancet 365, 488–492 (2005)

Bounding the Size of the Median Graph

Miquel Ferrer[1], Ernest Valveny[1], and Francesc Serratosa[2]

[1] Computer Vision Center, Dep. Ciències de la Computació
Universitat Autònoma de Barcelona, Bellaterra, Spain
{mferrer,ernest}@cvc.uab.es
[2] Departament d'Enginyeria Informàtica i Matemàtiques
Universitat Rovira i Virgili, Tarragona, Spain
francesc.serratosa@urv.cat

Abstract. Median graphs have been presented as an useful tool for capturing the essential information of a set of graphs. The computation of the median graph is a complex task. Exact algorithms are, in the worst case, exponential both in the number of graphs and their size. The known bounds for the minimum and maximum number of nodes of the candidate median graphs are in general very coarse and they can be used to achieve only limited improvements in such algorithms. In this paper we present more accurate bounds based on the well-known concepts of maximum common subgraph and minimum common supergraph. These new bounds on the number of nodes can be used to improve the existing algorithms in the computation of the median graph[1].

1 Introduction

In object prototyping, finding the median is an important issue for capturing the global information of a set of patterns. When objects are represented by graphs, the element representing the mean is called the median graph. Given a set of graphs, the median is defined as the graph that has the smallest sum of distances to all graphs in the set [1]. The computation of the median graph is exponential both in the number of input graphs and their size [2]. As a consequence, in order to make the practical use of the median-graph concept possible, we have to resort to approximate solutions. In [1], a genetic algorithm has been used to synthesize good approximations of the median graphs. The same authors computed the median graph using the same algorithm in [3] and applied their results to the synthesis of graphical symbols. Other approximate algorithms have been presented for the computation of median graphs [4,5].

In addition, in [1] some properties have been derived concerning median graphs. Such properties include the bounds for the median graphs related to both the number of nodes and the sum of distances. These bounds turn out to be useful in assessing the quality of the approximate solutions of the median graph. In this work we will focus our attention on the bounds for the median

---

[1] This work was sponsored research Fellowship number 401-027 (UAB) / Cicyt TIN2006-15694-C02-02 (Ministerio Ciencia y Tecnología).

J. Martí et al. (Eds.): IbPRIA 2007, Part II, LNCS 4478, pp. 491–498, 2007.

related to the number of nodes. The bounds given in [1] are very coarse and may not be very useful for the existing algorithms in the computation of the median graph. Using the well-known concepts of maximum common subgraph and minimum common supergraph, we present a reduction in these bounds that may be useful to improve the efficiency of such algorithms and consequently may help us in the computation of median graphs. In particular, we show that the number of nodes of the median graph must be in between the number of nodes of the maximum common subgraph and the number of nodes of the minimum common supergraph of a set of graphs. We prove this result from a theoretical point of view and we also give a detailed example to validate and clarify the theoretical results.

The rest of the paper will be as follows. In sections 2 and 3, we introduce the basic terminology used in the paper. Section 4 contains the new contribution on the bounds of the size of the median graph. In section 5 a detailed example and some results are presented. Finally, some discussions conclude the paper.

2   Definitions and Notation

2.1   Basic Definitions

Definition 1. *Given L, a finite alphabet of labels for nodes and edges, a graph is a triple $g = (V, \alpha, \beta)$ where, V is the finite set of nodes, α is the node labeling function $(\alpha : V \longrightarrow L)$, and β is the edge labeling function $(\beta : V \times V \longrightarrow L)$.*

We assume that our graphs are fully connected, i.e., $E = V \times V$. Consequently, the set of *edges* is implicitly given. Such assumption is only for notational convenience, and it doesn't impose any restriction in the generality of our results. In the case where no edge exists between two given nodes, we can include the special label *null* in the set of labels L. The number of nodes of a graph g is denoted by $|g|$.

Definition 2. *Given two graphs $g = (V, \alpha, \beta)$, and $g' = (V', \alpha', \beta')$, g' is a subgraph of g, denoted by $g' \subseteq g$ if,*

- $V' \subseteq V$
- $\alpha'(x) = \alpha(x)$ *for all $x \in V'$*
- $\beta'((x, y)) = \beta((x, y))$ *for all $(x, y) \in V' \times V'$*

From definition 2 it follows that, given a graph $g = (V, \alpha, \beta)$, a subset $V' \subseteq V$ of its vertices uniquely defines a subgraph, called the subgraph *induced* by V'.

Definition 3. *Given two graphs $g_1 = (V_1, \alpha_1, \beta_1)$, and $g_2 = (V_2, \alpha_2, \beta_2)$, a graph isomorphism between g_1 and g_2 is a bijective mapping $f : V_1 \longrightarrow V_2$ such that,*

- $\alpha_1(x) = \alpha_2(f(x))$ *for all $x \in V_1$*
- $\beta_1((x, y)) = \beta_2((f(x), f(y)))$ *for all $(x, y) \in V_1 \times V_1$*

In the real world, when encoding objects into graph-based representations some degree of distortion may be introduced due to multiple reasons. Hence, graph representations of two identical objects may not have an exact match. Therefore, it is necessary to introduce some degree of error tolerance into the matching process. Hence, we need an algorithm for error-correcting graph matching [6] or equivalently, a method to compute a similarity measure between two given graphs.

Definition 4. *Let* $g_1 = (V_1, \alpha_1, \beta_1)$ *and* $g_2 = (V_2, \alpha_2, \beta_2)$ *be two graphs. An error-correcting graph matching (ecgm) from* g_1 *to* g_2 *is a bijective function* $f : \hat{V}_1 \longrightarrow \hat{V}_2$, *where* $\hat{V}_1 \subseteq V_1$ *and* $\hat{V}_2 \subseteq V_2$.

We say that node $x \in \hat{V}_1$ is substituted by node $y \in \hat{V}_2$ if $f(x) = y$. If $\alpha_1(x) = \alpha_2(f(x))$ then the substitution is called identical. Otherwise it is called non-identical. In addition, any node from $V_1 - \hat{V}_1$ is deleted from g_1 and any node from $V_2 - \hat{V}_2$ is inserted in g_2 under f. Indirectly, the mapping f implies the same edit operations on the edges of g_1 and g_2 (see [7] for more details).

Definition 5. *The cost of an ecgm* $f : \hat{V}_1 \longrightarrow \hat{V}_2$ *from a graph* $g_1 = (V_1, \alpha_1, \beta_1)$ *to a graph* $g_2 = (V_2, \alpha_2, \beta_2)$ *denoted by* $c(f)$ *is the sum of the costs of insertion, deletion and substitution of both nodes and edges. These costs are represented by* $c_{ni}(x), c_{nd}(x), c_{ns}(x), c_{ei}(e), c_{ed}(e), c_{es}(e)$ *respectively.*

All costs are real non-negative numbers and are used to model the probability of errors and distortions that may change the original model. Usually, the higher the probability of a distortion is to occur, the lower is its cost. Normally, it is assumed that the cost of an identical node/edge substitution is zero, while the cost of any other edit operation is greater than zero. The set of all costs is the *cost function* γ and it is usually written in a tuple form, i.e. $\gamma = \{c_{ni}, c_{nd}, c_{ns}, c_{ei}, c_{ed}, c_{es}\}$. If the cost function γ is explicitly given the notation $c_\gamma(f)$ for the *ecgm* is used instead of $c(f)$.

Definition 6. *Given a cost function* γ, *and an ecgm* f *from* g_1 *to* g_2, *f is called an optimal ecgm under* γ *if there is no other ecgm* f' *from* g_1 *to* g_2 *such that* $c_\gamma(f') < c_\gamma(f)$. *The cost of an optimal ecgm,* $c_\gamma(f)$ *is also called the* edit distance *between* g_1 *and* g_2 *denoted by* $d(g_1, g_2)$, *and it can be seen as the sequence of graph edit operations that transforms* g_1 *into* g_2 *with the minimum cost.*

$$d(g_1, g_2) = min(c_\gamma(f)) \tag{1}$$

Notice that for a given cost function γ there are usually more than one optimal ecgm from a graph g_1 to another graph g_2.

2.2   Maximum Common Subgraph

Definition 7. *Let* $g_1 = (V_1, \alpha_1, \beta_1)$ *and* $g_2 = (V_2, \alpha_2, \beta_2)$ *be two graphs, and* $g_1' \subseteq g_1$, $g_2' \subseteq g_2$. *If there exists a graph isomorphism between* g_1' *and* g_2' *then, both* g_1' *and* g_2' *are called a* common subgraph *of* g_1 *and* g_2.

Definition 8. *Let $g_1 = (V_1, \alpha_1, \beta_1)$ and $g_2 = (V_2, \alpha_2, \beta_2)$ be two graphs. A graph g_M is called a* maximum common subgraph *(MCS) of g_1 and g_2 if g_M is a common subgraph of g_1 and g_2 and there is no other common subgraph of both g_1 and g_2 having more nodes than g_M.*

2.3   Minimum Common Supergraph

Definition 9. *Let $g_1 = (V_1, \alpha_1, \beta_1)$, $g_2 = (V_2, \alpha_2, \beta_2)$ and $d\ g' = (V', \alpha', \beta')$ be three graphs. If both g_1 and g_2 are subgraphs of g' then g' is called a* common supergraph *of g_1 and g_2.*

Definition 10. *Let $g_1 = (V_1, \alpha_1, \beta_1)$ and $g_2 = (V_2, \alpha_2, \beta_2)$ be two graphs. A graph g_m is called a* minimum common supergraph *(mcs) of g_1 and g_2 if g_m is a common supergraph of both g_1 and g_2 and there is no other common supergraph of g_1 and g_2 having less nodes than g_m.*

2.4   Generalized Median Graph

Definition 11. *Let U be the set of graphs that can be constructed using labels from L. Given $S = \{g_1, g_2, ..., g_n\} \subset U$, the generalized median graph $\bar{g}$ of S is defined as follows:*

$$\bar{g} = arg \left(\min_{g \in U} \sum_{g_i \in S} d(g, g_i) \right) \tag{2}$$

In other words, the generalized median graph is a graph $g \in U$ which minimizes the sum of distances (SOD) from g to all the graphs in S.

3   Important Results Based on the Previous Definitions

In this section we present the three basic elements that we will use to demonstrate the new and more accurate bounds on the size of the median graphs: 1. A particular cost function; 2. A distance measure based on the maximum common subgraph; and 3. The known bounds for number of nodes of the median graph.

A particular cost function: We will use a particular cost function given in [7], where the cost of node deletion and insertion ($c_{nd}(x)$ and $c_{ni}(x)$) is always 1, the cost of edge deletion and insertion ($c_{ed}(e)$ and $c_{ei}(e)$) is always 0 and the cost of node and edge substitution ($c_{ns}(x)$ and $c_{es}(e)$) takes the values 0 or ∞ depending on whether the substitution is identical or not, respectively.

Relation between edit distance and MCS: In [7], it has been proven that, using the cost function given before, the edit distance between two graphs can be expressed in terms of their MCS in the following way:

$$d(g_1, g_2) = |g_1| + |g_2| - 2|g_M| \tag{3}$$

Bounds on the size of the median graph: Let U be the set of graphs that can be constructed with labels from L and $S = \{g_1, ..., g_n\} \in U$. In [1] it is shown that the minimum and maximum number of nodes of the median graph is:

$$0 \leq |\bar{g}| \leq \sum_{i=1}^{n} |g_i| \tag{4}$$

4   Reducing the Bounds on the Size of the Median Graph

In this section we present and demonstrate the new minimum and maximum bounds on the number of nodes of the median graph using the concepts of *maximum common subgraph* and *minimum common supergraph* of a set of graphs.

Definition 12. *Let $S = \{g_1, g_2, ..., g_n\}$ be a set of graphs. A graph g_{M_S} is called a* maximum common subgraph *of S if g_{M_S} is a common subgraph of $\{g_1, g_2, \cdots, g_n\}$ and there is no other common subgraph of $\{g_1, g_2, \cdots, g_n\}$ having more nodes than g_{M_S}.*

Definition 13. *Let $S = \{g_1, g_2, ..., g_n\}$ be a set of graphs. A graph g_{m_S} is called a* minimum common supergraph *of S if $\{g_1, g_2, \cdots, g_n\}$ are subgraphs of g_{m_S} and there is no other common supergraph of $\{g_1, g_2, \cdots, g_n\}$ having less nodes than g_{m_S}.*

Theorem 1. *The number of nodes of $\bar{g}$ is in the limits,*

$$0 \leq |g_{M_S}| \leq |\bar{g}| \leq |g_{m_S}| \leq \sum_{i=1}^{n} |g_i| \tag{5}$$

Proof. To demonstrate the first part of the equation (5) (i.e. $|g_{M_S}| \leq |\bar{g}|$), suppose that $|\bar{g}| < |g_{M_S}|$. If we compute the term $SOD(g_{M_S})$, we will arrive to the next expression:

$$SOD(g_{M_S}) = \sum_{i=1}^{n} d(g_i, g_{M_S}) = \sum_{i=1}^{n} |g_i| + |g_{M_S}| - 2|y_{M_S}| = \sum_{i=1}^{n} |g_i| - n|g_{M_S}| \tag{6}$$

Notice that g_{M_S} is the maximum common subgraph of S and, then, it is a subgraph of any graph g_i in S. Therefore, if we compute $d(g_i, g_{M_S})$ using expression (3) the term $|g_M|$ is exactly $|g_{M_S}|$.

For the computation of $SOD(\bar{g})$ we will follow a similar reasoning. Assuming that $|\bar{g}| < |g_{M_S}|$, we can determine the minimum value that $SOD(\bar{g})$ can take:

$$SOD(\bar{g}) = \sum_{i=1}^{n} d(g_i, \bar{g}) \geq \sum_{i=1}^{n} |g_i| + |\bar{g}| - 2|\bar{g}| = \sum_{i=1}^{n} |g_i| - n|\bar{g}| \tag{7}$$

Notice that, in this case, if $|\bar{g}| < |g_{M_S}|$ then $|\bar{g}| < |g_i|$. Consequently the maximum value for $|g_M|$ in (3) will be precisely $|\bar{g}|$ and the minimum value for $SOD(\bar{g})$ will be obtained when $|\bar{g}| = |g_M|$ as expressed in equation 7.

At this point, using equations (6) and (7) and assuming that $|\bar{g}| < |g_{Ms}|$ we arrive to the following conclusion:

$$SOD(\bar{g}) \geq \sum_{i=1}^{n} |g_i| - n|\bar{g}| > \sum_{i=1}^{n} |g_i| - n|g_{Ms}| = SOD(g_{Ms}) \qquad (8)$$

This is a contradiction because, by definition of the median, $SOD(\bar{g})$ must be minimum. Thus $|\bar{g}|$ must be greater or equal than $|g_{Ms}|$.

Let's now proof the second part of equation (4) (i.e. $|\bar{g}| \leq |g_{ms}|$). Suppose now that $|\bar{g}| > |g_{ms}|$. In this case the term $SOD(g_{ms})$ will take this value:

$$SOD(g_{ms}) = \sum_{i=1}^{n} |g_i| + |g_{ms}| - 2|g_i| = n|g_{ms}| - \sum_{i=1}^{n} |g_i| \qquad (9)$$

Again, equation 9 holds because if g_{ms} is the minimum common supergraph of S, then any g_i will have precisely g_i as a maximum common subgraph between itself and g_{ms} and consequently the term $|g_M|$ in (3) is exactly $|g_i|$.

To compute the minimum value of $SOD(\bar{g})$, if $|\bar{g}| > |g_{ms}|$ then every graph g_i can share at most $|g_i|$ nodes with $\bar{g}$ and then the maximum value for $|g_M|$ in (3) is $|g_i|$. Then:

$$SOD(\bar{g}) \geq \sum_{i=1}^{n} |g_i| + |\bar{g}| - 2|\bar{g}_i| = n|\bar{g}| - \sum_{i=1}^{n} |g_i| \qquad (10)$$

Then, from equations (9) and (11), and assuming that $|\bar{g}| > |g_{ms}|$ we obtain:

$$SOD(\bar{g}) \geq n|\bar{g}| - \sum_{i=1}^{n} |g_i| > n|g_{ms}| - \sum_{i=1}^{n} |g_i| = SOD(g_{ms}) \qquad (11)$$

Again, this is a contradiction and, thus $|\bar{g}|$ must be less or equal than $|g_{ms}|$. □

5   Practical Example

Consider the situation where $S = \{g_1, g_2, ..., g_n\}$. In this framework, basically 3 situations may arise regarding the size of MCS and mcs (figure 1 shows an example of each of these situations for $S = \{g_1, g_2, g_3, g_4\}$):

1. At least one MCS of all graphs in S exists: $|g_{Ms}| \neq 0$ (figure 1(a)). Notice that, in this case, $|g_{ms}|$ is always less than $\sum_{i=1}^{n} |g_i|$.
2. No MCS between all graphs in S exists ($|g_{Ms}| = 0$) and $|g_{ms}| = \sum_{i=1}^{n} |g_i|$ (figure 1(b)).
3. No MCS between all graphs in S exists ($|g_{Ms}| = 0$) and $|g_{ms}| < \sum_{i=1}^{n} |g_i|$ (figure 1(c)).

For each case in figure 1, the true median $\bar{g}$, the maximum common subgraph g_{Ms} of S and the minimum common supergraph g_{ms} of S were manually obtained and $|\bar{g}|$, $|g_{Ms}|$ and $|g_{ms}|$ were also computed. The results are summarized

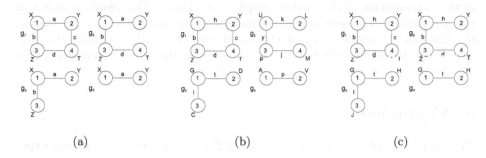

$$\begin{array}{ccc}(a) & (b) & (c)\end{array}$$

Fig. 1. A set $S = \{g_1, g_2, g_3, g_4\}$ of graphs and the 3 possible situations: 1 (a), 2 (b) and 3 (c)

in table 1. Each row corresponds to one of the three examples in figure 1. Notice that the values of the reference bounds of previous works for $|0|$ and $|\sum_{i=1}^{n} |g_i|$ (expression (4)) are 0 and 13 respectively for all situations.

First, notice that our hypothesis $(0 \leq |g_{M_S}| \leq |\bar{g}| \leq |g_{m_S}| \leq \sum_{i=1}^{n} |g_i|)$ holds in all cases. But there are some differences in the reduction of the bounds depending on the situation. The maximum reduction of the bounds is achieved when a g_{M_S} exists. In this case there is a reduction in both the minimum and the maximum number of nodes of the median graph and the possible improvement

Table 1. Results for g_{M_S}, $\bar{g}$, g_{m_S}, $|g_{M_S}|$, $|\bar{g}|$ and $|g_{m_S}|$ for the situations of figure 1

Situation	g_{M_S}	$\bar{g}$	g_{m_S}	$|g_{M_S}|$	$|\bar{g}|$	$|g_{m_S}|$
1				2	3	5
2	$\varnothing$	$\varnothing$		0	0	13
3	$\varnothing$			0	4	8

in the computation of the median graph is maximum. This result is shown in row 1 of table 1. The reduction in the bounds in the other cases is lower than in the first case. Concretely, no reduction in the lower bound is achieved (because $g_{M_S} = \varnothing$), but some reduction can be achieved in the upper bound depending on whether g_{m_S} exists (row 3) or not (row 2).

6 Conclusions

The median graph is an alternative and useful concept to represent prototypes of a set of graphs. However, the computation of both exact and approximate solutions have been shown very hard. In this paper we have shown that under a certain cost function, the bounds on the minimum and maximum number of nodes od the median graph can be reduced using the concepts of maximum common subgraph and minimum common supergraph. In order to show the practical usefulness of this result, a detailed example has been presented.

The results show that, in general, some reduction in the minimum and maximum number of nodes of the median graph can be introduced. This result could be interesting beyond the theoretical point of view. We are convinced that the existing algorithms for the computation of the median graph could be improved using these bounds to reduce the space where the median is searched for. Therefore, we are currently working on the development of more efficient algorithms for the computation of both exact and approximate solutions for the median graphs.

References

1. Jiang, X., Münger, A., Bunke, H.: On median graphs: Properties, algorithms, and applications. IEEE Trans. Pattern Anal. Mach. Intell. 23(10), 1144–1151 (2001)
2. Bunke, H., Münger, A., Jiang, X.: Combinatorial search versus genetic algorithms: A case study based on the generalized median graph problem. Pattern Recognition Letters 20(11-13), 1271–1277 (1999)
3. Jiang, X., Münger, A., Bunke, H.: Synthesis of representative graphical symbols by computing generalized median graph. In: Chhabra, A.K., Dori, D. (eds.) GREC 1999. LNCS, vol. 1941, pp. 183–192. Springer, Heidelberg (2000)
4. Hlaoui, A., Wang, S.: A new median graph algorithm. In: Hancock, E.R., Vento, M. (eds.) GbRPR 2003. LNCS, vol. 2726, pp. 225–234. Springer, Heidelberg (2003)
5. Ferrer, M., Serratosa, F., Sanfeliu, A.: Synthesis of median spectral graph. In: Marques, J.S., de la Blanca, N.P., Pina, P. (eds.) IbPRIA 2005. LNCS, vol. 3523, pp. 139–146. Springer, Heidelberg (2005)
6. Bunke, H., Allerman, G.: Inexact graph matching for structural pattern recognition. Pattern Recognition Letters 1(4), 245–253 (1983)
7. Bunke, H.: On a relation between graph edit distance and maximum common subgraph. Pattern Recognition Letters 18(8), 689–694 (1997)

When Overlapping Unexpectedly Alters the Class Imbalance Effects

V. García[1,2], R.A. Mollineda[2], J.S. Sánchez[2], R. Alejo[1,2], and J.M. Sotoca[2]

[1] Lab. Reconocimiento de Patrones, Instituto Tecnológico de Toluca
Av. Tecnologico s/n, 52140 Metepec, México
[2] Dept. Llenguatges i Sistemes Informàtics, Universitat Jaume I
Av. Sos Baynat s/n, 12071 Castelló de la Plana, Spain

Abstract. This paper makes use of several performance metrics to extend the understanding of a challenging imbalanced classification task. More specifically, we refer to a problem in which the minority class is more represented in the overlap region than the majority class, that is, the overall minority class becomes the majority one in this region. The experimental results demonstrate that the use of a set of appropriate performance measures allows to figure out such an atypical case.

1 Introduction

The class imbalance problem has received considerable attention in areas such as Machine Learning and Pattern Recognition. A data set is said to be imbalanced when one of the classes (the minority one) is heavily under-represented in comparison to the other class (the majority one). This issue is particularly important in real-world applications where it is costly to misclassify examples from the minority class, such as the diagnosis of rare diseases and the detection of fraudulent telephone calls, among others. Because of examples of the minority and majority classes usually represent the presence and absence of rare cases, respectively, they are also known as positive and negative examples.

The research in this topic has been mainly addressed to find solutions for learning from imbalanced data [1,2,4,9]. This constitutes a challenging task because standard discriminant learning tends to bias towards the most represented class [9]. A closely related issue that has also received much attention refers to the evaluation of the classifier performance in these domains [5,6]. The usual method consists of measuring the fraction of test examples correctly (or incorrectly) classified. Numerous investigations have demonstrated that this metric is not the most appropriate in imbalance problems because it may produce good overall performance, but ignoring (and hiding) results on the minority (and usually the most important) class [6,8,10,11].

Alternative measures have been proposed to evaluate classifiers, which are especially useful in the presence of two-class imbalanced data [5,8,9,11]. Their common characteristic is that they are based upon performance indexes over each individual class, being able to find out skewed behavior of classifiers in

J. Martí et al. (Eds.): IbPRIA 2007, Part II, LNCS 4478, pp. 499–506, 2007.

favor of a specific class. Some widely known examples are Receiver Operating Characteristic (ROC) curve, area under the ROC curve, g-mean, sensitivity, specificity, and precision. Apart from being useful for classifier evaluation, these measures could help to characterize the data complexity so as to find out the reasons that affect the classifier behavior.

It is generally accepted that imbalance is the main responsible for a significant degradation of the performance on individual classes, even under the presence of other difficulties, such as overlapping. It seems to be true in cases where the imbalance ratio in the overlap region(s) is similar to the overall imbalance ratio. In these common situations, alternative metrics have been exhaustively analyzed and their values, easily interpreted. Nevertheless, less frequent but possible cases in which the minority class is more represented than the majority class in the overlap region, have not been studied enough. Considering that classification errors come mostly from overlap, how would the performance measures evaluate those atypical scenarios? How can they be explained by these measures?

The ultimate aim of this paper is to answer those questions. For such a purpose, we have designed two classification experiments over two-class synthetic data sets with a fixed overall imbalance ratio in order to make results not dependent on this parameter. The first experiment considers a typical situation in which both the imbalance in the overlap region and the overall imbalance are identical while overlapping changes. This will establish a baseline to analyze the results of the next part. The second experiment operates on data sets where the minority class is locally denser than the majority class in the overlap region. This situation leads to obtain values different from those expected, considering the only a priori knowledge (the overall imbalance). Discussion of new results will focus on the difficulty of figure out such particular data complexity, which is not usually taken into account in general studies.

2   Performance Measures in Class Imbalance Problems

Most of performance measures for two-class problems are built over a 2×2 confusion matrix as illustrated in Table 1. From this, four simple measures can be directly obtained: TP and TN denote the number of positive and negative cases correctly classified, while FP and FN refer to the number of misclassified positive and negative examples, respectively.

The most widely used metrics for measuring the performance of learning systems are the *error rate* and the *accuracy*, which can be computed as $(TP + TN)/(TP + FN + TN + FP)$. Nevertheless, researchers have demonstrated that,

Table 1. Confusion matrix for a two-class problem

	Positive prediction	Negative prediction
Positive class	True Positive (TP)	False Negative (FN)
Negative class	False Positive (FP)	True Negative (TN)

when the prior class probabilities are very different, these measures are not appropriate because they do not consider misclassification costs, are strongly biased to favor the majority class, and are sensitive to class skews [6,8,10,11].

Thus, several metrics that measure the classification performance on positive and negative classes independently can be derived from Table 1. The *true positive rate*, also referred to as *recall* or *sensitivity*, $TPrate = TP/(TP + FN)$, is the percentage of correctly classified positive examples. The *true negative rate* (or *specificity*), $TNrate = TN/(TN + FP)$, is the percentage of correctly classified negative examples. The *false positive rate*, $FPrate = FP/(FP + TN)$ is the percentage of misclassified positive examples. The *false negative rate*, $FNrate = FN/(TP+FN)$ is the percentage of misclassified negative examples. Finally, the *precision* (or *purity*), $Precision = TP/(TP + FP)$, is defined as the proportion of positive cases that are actually correct.

A way to combine the TP and FP rates is by using the ROC curve. The ROC curve is a two-dimensional graph to visualize, organize and select classifiers based on their performance. It also depicts trade-offs between benefits (true positives) and costs (false positives) [7,11]. In the ROC curve, the TP rate is represented on the Y-axis and the FP rate on the X-axis. To assess the overall performance of a classifier, one can measure the fraction of the total area that falls under the ROC curve (AUC) [8]. AUC varies between 0 and +1. Larger AUC values indicate generally better classifier performance.

Kubat et al. [9] use *the geometric mean* (*g*-mean) of accuracies measured separately on each class, $g-mean = \sqrt{recall \times specificity}$. This measure relates to a point on the ROC curve and the idea is to maximize the accuracy on each of the two classes while keeping these accuracies balanced. An important property of the *g*-mean is that it is independent of the distribution of examples between classes. Another property is that it is nonlinear, that is, a change in recall (or specificity) has a different effect on this measure depending on the magnitude of recall (or specificity). An alternative metric that does not take care of the performance on the majority class corresponds to the geometric mean of precision and recall, which is defined as $gpr = \sqrt{precision \times recall}$. Like the *g*-mean, this measure is higher when both precision and recall are high and balanced.

3   Experimental Results and Discussion

Here, we try to show the utility of several performance measures as a tool to characterize the data complexity in class imbalance domains. To this end, we employ two distinct overlapping scenarios, both using two-dimensional synthetic data sets. Pseudo-random bivariate patterns have been generated following a uniform distribution in a square of length 100. There are 400 negative examples and 100 positive patterns, in all cases keeping the overall majority/minority ratio equal to 4. It should be pointed out that, although only one dimension appears as discriminant, inclusion of two dimensions is with the aim of making easier the interpretation of the results.

From the two scenarios employed in the experiments, the first constitutes a typical class imbalance problem with overlapping, in the sense that imbalance equally affects to the whole representation space. The second experiment refers to a more challenging situation, where the imbalance ratio in the overlap region is inverse to the overall imbalance ratio, that is, the majority and minority classes have interchanged their roles.

We have adopted a 10-fold cross-validation method: each data set was divided into ten equal parts, using nine folds as the training set and the remaining block as an independent test set. This process has been repeated ten times. The experiments consist of computing the performance metrics reported in Sect. 2, when using several classifiers of distinct natures: a nearest neighbor (1-NN) classifier, a multilayer perceptron (MLP), a naïve Bayes (NBS) classifier, a radial basis function (RBF), and a C4.5 decision tree.

3.1   Experiment I: A Typical Class Imbalance Situation

The first experiment has been over a series of six data sets with increasing class overlap. In all cases, the positive examples are defined on the X-axis in the range [50..100], while those belonging to the majority class are generated in [0..50] for 0% of class overlap, [10..60] for 20%, [20..70] for 40%, [30..80] for 60%, [40..90] for 80%, and [50..100] for 100% of overlap. Note that the overall imbalance ratio matches the imbalance ratio corresponding to the overlap region.

In Fig. 1, we have plotted the average values of g-mean, gpr, TN rate, TP rate, precision and AUC obtained by each classifier when varying the overlapping degree. First, we concentrate our analysis on the mid case of 40% of class overlap, supposing that the only a priori knowledge refers to the presence of class imbalance, ignoring the overlapping degree. From the results, it is possible to remark some observations. In particular, while the TN rates for all classifiers (except 1-NN) are 97-100%, the TP rates are close to 60%, relation that can be expected in an imbalance scenario. This, jointly with the fact that there are not relevant differences in the behavior of the distinct classifiers (i.e., the results are independent of the classifiers), suggest that measures are revealing a certain level of overlapping between both classes and more importantly, that the percentage of positive examples in the overlap region has to be approximately equal to the error on the minority class (i.e., $100\% - \text{TP rate} \approx 40\%$). This hints that the TP rate and the TN rate can be viewed as good descriptors of the data complexity.

Indeed, all these comments can be now corroborated by making use of the whole knowledge about the artificial data sets. Thus it is possible to see that in the previous case of study, about 40% of positive examples are inside the overlap region. Even, we can observe that very similar effects appear on the rest of cases. On the other hand, focusing on the geometric means (see Fig. 1(c-d)), one can observe that both decrease as the overlapping degree increases, despite the imbalance ratio does not vary along the different data sets. When analyzing Fig. 1(e), the high values of precision indicate that almost all classifiers produce very few false positives. In a scenario with class imbalance, this should be fully expected because most of the negative examples will result correctly classified

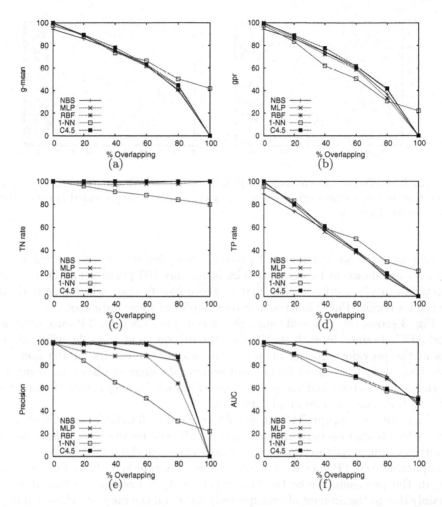

Fig. 1. Classifier performance metrics for Experiment I: (a) g-mean, (b) gpr, (c) TN rate, (d) TP rate, (e) precision, and (f) AUC

(in fact, this can also be observed in the TN rates). The close to 0% of precision in the case of 100% of class overlap means that almost all positive examples have been misclassified, thus corroborating the previous results of the TP rate.

3.2 Experiment II: An Unexpected Practical Case

The second experiment has been carried out over a collection of five artificial data sets in which the number of elements in the overlap region varies in such a way that the overall minority class becomes majority in this region. To this end, the negative examples have been defined on the X-axis to be in the range [0..100] in all data sets, while the positive cases have been generated in the ranges [75..100], [80..100], [85..100], [90..100], and [95..100]. The first means that both

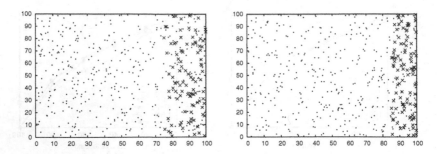

Fig. 2. Two different cases in Experiment II: [75..100] and [85..100]. For this latter case, note that in the overlap region, the majority class is under-represented in comparison to the minority class

classes have the same number of patterns (and density) in the overlap region (i.e, no imbalance in this region). The latter has 100 positive and 20 negative examples in the overlap region, that is, the minority class appears as majority in such a region. Fig. 2 illustrates two examples of these data sets.

Fig. 3 shows the averaged values of g-mean, gpr, TN rate, TP rate, precision and AUC obtained by each classifier for the five different cases described above. As in the previous experiment, we firstly discuss the results for the mid case [85..100], with the aim of finding out some data characteristics by using the performance metrics and the (only) a priori knowledge concerning the presence of a high imbalance ratio in all data sets.

Values of g-mean, gpr, TP rate and TN rate in Fig. 3 indicate significant errors (close to 10-20%) on both classes. Surprisingly, the results reveal that, despite addressing an imbalance problem, for each classifier the TP and TN rates are comparable: the TP rate is 80-100% and the TN rate is 85-90%. On the other hand, the precision, unlike the first experiment, is low enough (about 65%), mainly due to the amount of (unexpected) errors on the majority class. All these observations suggest high overlapping between the two classes. Nevertheless, the fact that the overlapping affects both positive and negative examples, can be deemed as contradictory to our a priori knowledge (the existence of an important class imbalance) since this effect is more likely to be produced in a balanced set. Finally, a deeper analysis of the comparable values of TP and TN rates in absolute terms, considering this strongly imbalance scenario, concludes that there are many more errors on the majority class than on the minority one. Thus, taking all these into account, it can be guessed that the different classifiers have identified the overlapping region as belonging to the minority class. In other words, in such an overlap region there exists a majority of positive examples.

The full knowledge of class distributions confirms again our suspects. Figure 3 shows the performance measures used while the minority class becomes denser along with the decrease of the overlapping region. Despite the full overlapping (of the minority class) and the strong imbalance, all the measures reveal an improvement of classifier performances. This is due to the change of the imbalance ratio

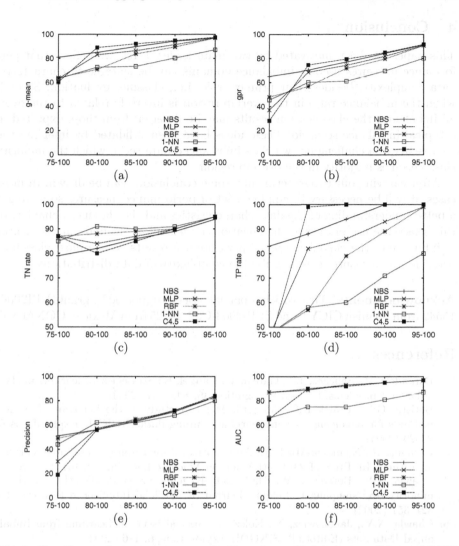

Fig. 3. Classifier performance measures for Experiment II: (a) g-mean, (b) gpr, (c) TN rate, (d) TP rate, (e) Precision, and (f) AUC

in the overlapping region which benefits both classes, that is, the increase of the density of the positive examples and the reduction of the number of (affected) negative examples.

The discussion just exposed should provide some guidelines of how to predict these rare situations through a number of classifier performance measures. In this way, when individual errors in a two-class imbalance domain are significant and similar (for more than one classifier), there likely exists an overlapping region where the minority class is more represented than the majority one.

4   Conclusion

This paper has been motivated by two main issues. First, we believe that performance measures used in imbalance domains can be suitable to characterize data complexity, besides their primary role, i.e., classifier evaluation. Second, when the imbalance ratio in the overlap region is inversely related to the overall imbalance, the classification results may be different from those expected in a typical imbalance scenario. These ideas have been validated by inferring the complexity of a challenging two-class imbalanced data set in which the minority class becomes majority in the overlap region.

After carrying out two experiments, some conclusions can be drawn. In most cases, it will be necessary to employ a set of performance measures so as to get a better understanding of the data characteristics and the classifier behavior. In this sense, the use of diverse classification models allows to find out the degree of influence of the classifiers on the performance results. When most classifiers coincide, the measures can describe the complexity of data distributions.

Acknowledgments. This work has partially been supported by grants DPI2006-15542 from Spanish CICYT and SEP-2003-C02-44225 from Mexican CONACyT.

References

1. Barandela, R., Sánchez, J.S., García, V., Rangel, E.: Strategies for learning in class imbalance problems. Pattern Recognition 36, 849–851 (2003)
2. Batista, G.E., Pratti, R.C., Monard, M.C.: A study of the behavior of several methods for balancing machine learning training data. SIGKDD Explorations 6, 20–29 (2004)
3. Caruana, R., Niculescu-Mizil, A.: An empirical comparison of supervised learning algorithms. In: Proc. of 23rd Intl. Conf. on Machine Learning, pp.161–168 (2006)
4. Chawla, N.V., Bowyer, K.W., Hall, L.O., Kegelmeyer, W.P.: SMOTE: synthetic minority over-sampling technique. Journal of Artificial Intelligence Research 16, 321–357 (2002)
5. Chawla, N.V., Japokowicz, N., Kolcz, A.: Special Issue on Learning from Imbalanced Data Sets (Editorial). SIKGDD Explorations 6, 1–6 (2004)
6. Daskalaki, S., Kopanas, I., Avouris, N.: Evaluation of classifiers for an uneven class distribution problem. Applied Artificial Intelligence 20, 381–417 (2006)
7. Fawcett, T.: ROC graphs with instance-varying costs. Pattern Recognition Letters 27, 882–891 (2006)
8. Huang, J., Ling, C.X.: Using AUC and accuracy in evaluating learning algorithms. IEEE Trans. on Knowledge and Data Engineering 17, 299–310 (2005)
9. Kubat, M., Matwin, S.: Adressing the curse of imbalanced training sets: one-sided selection. In: Proc. of 14th Intl. Conf. on Machine Learning, pp. 179–186 (1997)
10. Landgrebe, T.C.W., Paclick, P., Duin, R.P.W.: Precision-recall operating characteristic (P-ROC) curves in imprecise environments. In: Proc. of 18th Intl. Conf. on Pattern Recognition, pp. 123–127 (2006)
11. Provost, F., Fawcett, T.: Analysis and visualization of classifier performance: Comparison under imprecise class and cost distributions. In: Proc. of 3rd Intl. Conf. on Knowledge Discovery and Data Mining, pp. 43–48 (1997)

A Kernel Matching Pursuit Approach to Man-Made Objects Detection in Aerial Images

Wei Wang, Xin Yang, and Shoushui Chen

Institute of Image Processing and Pattern Recognition, Shanghai Jiaotong University,
Shanghai, 200240, P.R. China
{wangwei2002,yangxin,sschen}@sjtu.edu.cn

Abstract. This paper describes a new aerial images segmentation algorithm. Kernel Matching Pursuit (KMP) method is introduced to deal with the nonlinear distribution of the man-made objects' features in the aerial images. In KMP algorithm, a lot of training samples containing substantive information are used to detect the man-made objects. With KMP classifier, pixels in large aerial images will be labeled as different prediction values, which can be classified linearly. Then the modified Mumford-Shah model, which comprises the features of the KMP prediction values, is built to segment the aerial image by necessary level set evolution. The proposed method is proven to be effective by the results of experiments.

1 Introduction

Nowadays, many remotely sensed image processing algorithms have appeared for the purpose of the segmentation or classification of man-made objects. Some aerial image segment algorithms based upon modified Mumford-Shah model[1] have been proposed recently, but the experiment result is still frustrating when dealing with nonlinear distribution of man-made objects' features in aerial images. However, the methodology proposed in this paper, which is based upon the Kernel Matching Pursuit (KMP) method[2], can solve the problems effectively.

KMP method, one of the sparse classifier approaches, requires far fewer support points than SVM[3] does, and it has no constraint on the form of kernels in a certain instance. KMP classifier usually requires a threshold to label samples as different classes, but it is challenging to select a proper threshold. In light of that, the modified Mumford-Shah model is introduced to integrate the features of the KMP prediction values, so the remotely sensed images can be segmented into different classes automatically, and the level set method is responsible for the image evolution.

This paper is organized as follows: Section 2 introduces the modified Mumford-Shah model, which comprises the mapped features. Linear distribution in high dimensional spaces, which is equivalent to non-linear distributions in the input space by the kernel methods, is obtained. Section 3 introduces the KMP method, including the overview of the method, and the detailed description on how the algorithm implements in the aerial image segment. Section 4 elaborates on the new aerial images segmentation algorithm. The outputs of experiments are presented and illuminated in Section 5 and the conclusions are listed in Section 6.

J. Martí et al. (Eds.): IbPRIA 2007, Part II, LNCS 4478, pp. 507–514, 2007.
© Springer-Verlag Berlin Heidelberg 2007

2 Mumford-Shah Model and the Modification

2.1 Mumford-Shah Model

Mumford-Shah model[1] is a commonly used model in image segmentation. Based on it, Chan and Vese [4] applied the active contour evolving method to minimize the Mumford-Shah function. The energy function in Chan and Vese's two-phase model is given by

$$F\left(C, c_o, c_b\right) = u \cdot \text{Length}\ (C) + \lambda_1 \cdot \int_{inside\ (C)} |I - c_o|^2\, dxdy$$
$$+ \lambda_2 \cdot \int_{outside\ (C)} |I - c_b|^2\, dxdy \tag{1}$$

where $I(x, y)$ is the grey level in (x, y), and C is the curve which indicates the border of the different regions, c_o and c_b are the mean of grey levels of the object region and the background region, u, λ_1 and λ_2 are the parameters. When C is the border of optimal classification, the value of the energy function is at a minimum.

2.2 Modified Mumford-Shah Model and the Improvement

The active contour evolving method can combine other features besides the grey level features. Jean-Francois Aujol, Gilles Aubert, and Laure Blanc-Féraud[5] presented a supervised classification model based upon a variational approach. The wavelet features are taken into consideration in their model. Cao Guo[6] proposed a simplified Mumford-Shah model, in which the features of fractal error metric and DCT coefficients of texture edges are considered. Based upon the knowledge of image multi-scale geometric analysis, which can capture the image's intrinsic geometrical structure effectively, the contourlet features are also selected in recent model[10].

Modified Mumford-Shah models are effective in most situations. However, when dealing with non-linear distribution of the features in the input space, all these techniques become less effective.

Non-linear distribution of the features also exists in the aerial images, especially for man-made objects. After mapping the original features, we can obtain the energy function as follows:

$$F\left(C, f(c_o), f(c_b)\right) = u \cdot \text{Length}\ (C) + \lambda_1 \cdot \int_{inside\ (C)} |f(I) - f(c_o)|^2\, dxdy$$
$$+ \lambda_2 \cdot \int_{outside\ (C)} |f(I) - f(c_b)|^2\, dxdy \tag{2}$$

where $f(x)$ is a non-linear function.

3 Kernel Matching Pursuit

Since Pascal Vincent and Yoshua Bengio introduced Kernel Matching Pursuit method[2] in 2002, this new classification technique has achieved rapid development. K- MP Classifier has the advantage over SVM method as KMP usually requires far fewer support points and permits different forms of kernels in one instance. Vlad Popovici etc. [7] developed the algorithm to enable KMP Classifier to be applied in large datase- ts. Moreover, Licheng Jiao and Qing Li[8] introduced an ensemble method to overco- me KMP Classifier's drawbacks in practical application. In [9], S.Sathiya Keerthi and Wei Chu successfully applied KMP method in sparse GP regression models.

KMP Classifier indicates that the target function is an approximation of the classi-fication function, which can be calculated as follows.

$$f_N = \sum_{n=1}^{N} a_n g_n \tag{3}$$

where N is the number of basis functions in the expansion, $\{g_1, \cdots, g_N\}$ are basis functions selected from the dictionary in a Hilbert space. $\{a_1, \cdots, a_N\} \in R^N$ are the co- efficients corresponding to the set of $\{g_1, \cdots, g_N\}$.

In this paper, KMP method described by S.Sathiya Keerthi and Wei Chu is sele-cted. The algorithm is matching pursuit with back-fitting and has lower calculating complexity when dealing with large datasets.

The procedure of KMP Classifier developed by Wei Chu can be described as follows[9]:

● Selection of basis functions

Step1: Randomly select c samples from the n training samples;

Step2: Calculate the corresponding selection score Δ_i of each selected sample;

Step3: Sort the selected samples by their Δ_i values;

Step4: Select the sample with the biggest Δ_i values as a basis function, and save it in-to the basis list.

Step5: Randomly reselect κ samples from the n training samples. Replace the one with the biggest Δ_i value and the $\kappa - 1$ samples with the lowest Δ_i value in the orig-inal c samples.

Step6: Repeat the steps of 2~5, until the criterion of termination is met.

The selection score Δ_i can be calculated as follows:

$$\Delta_i = \frac{1}{2}(\alpha_i^*)^2 (\sigma^2 \kappa(x_i, x_j) + K_{i,.}^T K_{i,.}) \tag{4}$$

where α_i^* is defined by equation (5); σ^2 refers to the parameter of the noise variance; $K_{i,.} = [\kappa(x_1, x_i), \cdots, \kappa(x_n, x_i)]^T$, $\{x_1, \cdots, x_n\}$ refers to n training samples.

$$\alpha_i^* = \frac{K_{i,.}^T (y - K_{i,.}^T \alpha_i^*) - \sigma^2 \tilde{k}_i^T \alpha_i^*}{\sigma^2 \kappa(x_i, x_i) + K_{i,.}^T K_{i,.}} \tag{5}$$

where α_i^* is defined by equation (6); $\tilde{k}_i = [\kappa(\tilde{x}_1, x_i), \cdots, (\tilde{x}_d, x_i)]^T$, $\{\tilde{x}_1, \cdots, \tilde{x}_d\}$ refers to d selected basis samples.

● Calculation of the coefficients corresponding to the basis functions

The set of the coefficients α_I^* can be obtained as follows:

$$\alpha_I^* = \left(\sigma^2 K_I + K_{I,.} K_{I,.}^T \right)^{-1} K_{I,.} \, y \tag{6}$$

where
$$K_I = \begin{bmatrix} \kappa(\tilde{x}_1, \tilde{x}_1) & \cdots & \cdots \\ \cdots & \kappa(\tilde{x}_i, \tilde{x}_j) & \cdots \\ \cdots & \cdots & \kappa(\tilde{x}_d, \tilde{x}_d) \end{bmatrix}, \; K_{I,.} = \begin{bmatrix} \kappa(\tilde{x}_1, x_1) & \cdots & \kappa(\tilde{x}_1, x_n) \\ \cdots & \kappa(\tilde{x}_i, x_j) & \cdots \\ \kappa(\tilde{x}_d, x_1) & \cdots & \kappa(\tilde{x}_d, x_n) \end{bmatrix}$$

$y = [y_1, \cdots, y_n]^T$, $\{y_1, \cdots, y_n\}$ refer to the target of n training samples.

● The target function and the KMP prediction

$$\tilde{f} = \tilde{k}^T \alpha_I^* \tag{7}$$

where $\tilde{k} = [\kappa(\tilde{x}_1, x), \cdots, (\tilde{x}_d, x)]^T$, x refers to the test sample.

In this paper, we also use the ARD Gaussian kernel defined by equation (8):

$$\kappa(x_i, x_j) = v_0 \exp\left(\sum_{l=1}^{m} v_l (x_i^l - x_j^l)^2 \right) + v_b \tag{8}$$

where $v_0, v_l, v_b > 0$, x_i^l is the l-th element of x_i.

We can set the value of v_l to control each element's influence to KMP Classifier.

In aerial image, the elements of middle-high frequency in the feature vector usually have higher weight values.

4   KMP Approach to Man-Made Objects Detection

4.1   Feature Extraction

The features of aerial images are mainly concentrated in the middle and high frequency components, while the low-frequency components usually contain the gray scale information. So we only need to extract the features of the middle and high frequency components in which we are interested. Using the Discrete Cosine Transform, the Wavelet Transform or the Contourlet Transform to extract features, satisfactory experiment results[6][10] have been achieved.

Manesh Kokare[11] proposed a new rotationally invariant feature extraction method, in which the images are decomposed into different sub-bands by DT-CWT and DT-RCWF. Then the final rotation invariant wavelet features are obtained from these sub-bands. Referring to Manesh Kokare's method, the rotation invariant contourlet features can also be extracted.

In this paper, we will use the rotation invariant wavelet. To calculate the features of a certain point in a remotely sensed image, we select a block sized 16×16 or 32×32 , with a certain point located in the center of the block. Then we decompose this block into three levels by the wavelet transform. The wavelet features are sequentially extracted from three levels wavelet decompositions. Supposing that the size of sub-band is $M \times N$ in ith level, the value of mean and standard deviation of the HL and LH channel's coefficients are calculated as shown in equation (9) and (10). Then the rotation invariant features are given by equation (11) and (12). Finally, the six-dimensional rotation invariant wavelet features are obtained.

$$e_i = \frac{1}{MN} \sum_{m=1}^{M} \sum_{n=1}^{N} |x(m,n)| \tag{9}$$

$$e_{istd} = \frac{1}{MN} \sqrt{\sum_{m=1}^{M} \sum_{n=1}^{N} (|x(m,n)| - e_i)^2} \tag{10}$$

$$E_i = 0.5 * [e_{iHL} + e_{iLH}] \tag{11}$$

$$E_{istd} = 0.5 * [e_{istdHL} + e_{istdLH}] \tag{12}$$

4.2 Modified Mumford-Shah Model with KMP Prediction Feature

After extracting the KMP prediction features, which equals to mapping the rotation invariant wavelet features by non-linear function, we can obtain the energy function as follows:

$$F(C, c_o, c_b) = u \cdot Length(C) + \lambda_1 \cdot \int_{inside(C)} |feature - \overline{feature}_o|^2 dxdy + \lambda_2 \cdot \int_{outside(C)} (|feature - \overline{feature}_b|^2) dxdy \tag{13}$$

where *feature* are the KMP prediction features of point (x, y), $\overline{feature}_o$ denotes the mean value inside of the curve C, $\overline{feature}_b$ is the mean value outside of the curve C.

Function (13) can be represented in another form as follows:

$$F(\phi, c_o, c_b) = u \cdot \int_{\Omega} \delta(\phi) |\nabla \phi| dxdy + \lambda_1 \cdot \int_{\Omega} |feature - \overline{feature}_o|^2 H(\phi) dxdy + \lambda_2 \cdot \int_{\Omega} (|feature - \overline{feature}_b|^2) [1 - H(\phi)] dxdy \tag{14}$$

where ϕ is the level set function, Ω is the domain of definition of $feature(x, y)$,.

The associated Euler-Lagrange equations to (14) give the following expression:

$$\begin{cases} \overline{feature}_o = \dfrac{\int_{\Omega} feature(x,y) H(\phi) dxdy}{\int_{\Omega} H(\phi) dxdy}, \quad \overline{feature}_b = \dfrac{\int_{\Omega} feature(x,y)(1 - H(\phi)) dxdy}{\int_{\Omega} (1 - H(\phi)) dxdy} \\ \\ \dfrac{\partial \phi}{\partial t} = \delta(\phi) \left[u\nabla \cdot \dfrac{\nabla \phi}{|\nabla \phi|} - \lambda_1 \cdot [feature(x,y) - \overline{feature}_o]^2 + \lambda_2 \cdot [feature(x,y) - \overline{feature}_b]^2 \right]; \\ \\ \phi(0, x, y) = \phi_0(x, y); \end{cases} \tag{15}$$

where $H(Z) = \begin{cases} 1 & Z > 0 \\ 0 & Z < 0 \end{cases}$, $\delta(x)$ is the Dirac function.

4.3 Description of the Aerial Images Segment Algorithm

The aerial image segmentation algorithm proposed in this paper is a supervised method. The algorithm contains two parts, namely training part and prediction part. The procedure of segmentation can be described as follows:

● The algorithm of the KMP samples training part:

Step1: Randomly select the representative sections of different classes from the aerial image and save these sections into the original training samples dataset.

Step2: Calculate the rotation invariant wavelet features of each training sample. Then combine the features with the target value as the input training vector.

Step3: The training procedure begins. The proper basis functions are selected sequentially by matching pursuit with back-fitting. Finally, the classification function is acquired as a linear combination of some basis functions.

● The algorithm of the man-made objects prediction part:

Step1: Calculate rotation invariant wavelet features of every point in the aerial image. Save the features as $feature_{wav}$.

Step2: Load the classification function. Then predict every point in the aerial image. Save the KMP prediction values as $feature_{KMP}$.

Step3: Referring to Chan and Vese[12], initial closed curves in the aerial image are given in this algorithm, just as Fig. 1(c) show.

Step4: The curve begins to evolve as described in the equation (15).

Step 5: Update and evolve the level set function ϕ and check whether the criterion of termination is met or not. If the criterion of termination is met, the area inside the closed curves is the area of the object.

5   Experiment Results and Discussion

In the experiment, the criterion of termination is set as below:

The difference between two evolving steps is smaller than a pre-defined threshold as 0.015 or the evolution reach 20 times.

Set the parameters as $\lambda_1 = \lambda_2 = 0.1$.

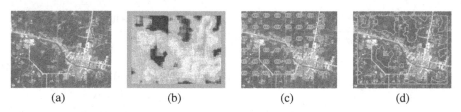

| (a) | (b) | (c) | (d) |

Fig. 1. Aerial image to be classified. (a) The aerial image. (b) KMP prediction values. (c) Initial conditions. (d) Result of evolution.

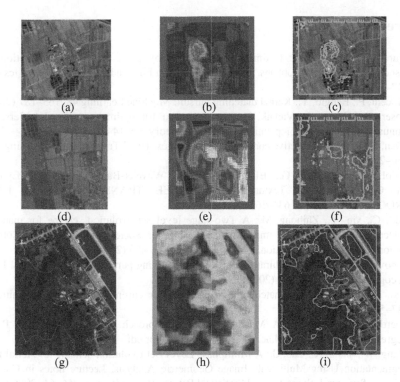

Fig. 2. Segmentation results. (a) The aerial image a. (b) KMP prediction values of a. (c) Segmentation result of a. (d) The aerial image d. (e) KMP prediction values of d. (f) Segmentation result of d. (g) The aerial image g. (h) KMP prediction values of g. (i) Segmentation result of g.

The original aerial image is shown in Fig. 1(a). 50 training samples are randomly selected from the image. 20 selected samples belong to man-made objects, with target value set as 5; The rest samples are part of the nature areas, with target value set as 1. The target function is acquired by KMP training procedure, then the whole aerial image can be predicted. The pixels in large aerial imagery are labeled as different prediction values as shown in Fig. 1(b). Initial closed curves in the aerial image are shown in Fig. 1(c), while the segmentation results are shown in Fig. 1(d).

More experiment results are shown as Fig. 2. The statistics of the errors is about 0.19.

6 Conclusion

In this paper, a new aerial images segmentation algorithm is proposed. It is built upon the basis of the modified two-phase Mumford-Shah model with the calculated features constraint. The features are obtained via the KMP prediction values. In order to achieve better aerial images segmentation results, kernel matching pursuit method is included to solve the problem of the feature's nonlinear distribution. Finally, the proposed method is proven to be effective by the results of experiments.

References

1. Mumford, D., Shah, J.: Optimal approximation by piece wise smooth functions and associated variational problems. Communications on Pure and Applied Mathematics 42(5), 577–685 (1989)
2. Vincent, P., Bengio, Y.: Kernel matching pursuit. Machine Learning 48, 165–187 (2002)
3. Boser, B., Guyon, I., Vapnik, V.: An algorithm for optimal margin classifiers, Fifth Annual Workshop on Computational Learning Theory, pp. 144–152 (1992)
4. Chan, F.T., Vese, L.: Active contours without edges. IEEE Trans Image Processing 10(2), 266–277 (2001)
5. Aujol, J.-F., Aubert, G., Blanc-Féraud, L.: Wavelet-Based Level Set Evolution for Classification of Textured Images. IEEE TRANSACTIONS ON IMAGE PROCESSING 12(12), 1634–1641 (2003)
6. Guo, C., xin, Y., Zhihong, M.: A Two-stage level set evolution scheme for man-made objects detection in aerial images. IEEE Computer Society Conference on Computer Vision and Pattern Recognition, CVPR 2005, pp. 474–479 (2005)
7. Popovici, V., Bengio, S., Thiran, J.-P.: Kernel matching pursuit for large datasets. Pattern Recognition 38, 2385–2390 (2005)
8. Jiao, L., Li, Q.: Kernel matching pursuit classifier ensemble. Pattern Recognition 39, 587–594 (2006)
9. Keerthi, S.S., Chu, W.: A Matching Pursuit Approach to Sparse Gaussian Process Regression. www.gatsby.ucl.ac.uk/~chuwei/paper/sgpr.pdf
10. Wang, W., Yang, X., Cao, G.: A Multiphase Level Set Evolution Scheme for Aerial Image Segmentation Using Multi-scale Image Geometric Analysis, Lecture notes in Computer Science, Structural, Syntactic, and Statistical Pattern Recognition, pp. 56–64 (2006)
11. Kokare, M., Biswas, P.K., Chatterji, B.N.: Rotation Invariant Texture Features Using Rotated Complex Wavelet For Content Based Image Retrieval. International Conference on Image Processing(ICIP), pp. 393–396 (2004)
12. Vese, L.A., Chan, T.F.: A Multiphase Level Set Framework for Image Segmentation Using the Mumford and Shah Model. International Journal of Computer Vision 50(3), 271–293 (2002)

Anisotropic Continuous-Scale Morphology

Michael Breuß, Bernhard Burgeth, and Joachim Weickert

Mathematical Image Analysis Group, Faculty for Mathematics and Computer
Science, Building E11, Saarland University, 66041 Saarbrücken, Germany
{breuss,burgeth,weickert}@mia.uni-saarland.de

Abstract. We describe a new approach to incorporate adaptivity into
the partial differential equations (PDEs) of morphological dilation and
erosion. By multiplication of the image gradient with a space-variant
matrix, the speed of the evolution is locally adapted to the data. This is
used to create anisotropic morphological evolutions that enhance coherent, flow-like image structures. We show that our adaptive method can
be implemented by means of a simple modification of the classical Rouy-
Tourin finite difference scheme. Numerical experiments confirm that the
proposed dilations and erosions are capable of real anisotropic behaviour
that can be used for closing interrupted lines.

1 Introduction

Mathematical morphology is concerned with image analysis of shapes. It is one
of the oldest and most successful areas of digital image processing; see e.g. the
textbooks [6,9,17,18,19] for an overview. Its fundamental operations are called
dilation and erosion. They form the basis of many other morphological processes
such as openings, closings, top hats and morphological derivative operators.

Dilation and erosion are frequently implemented by algebraic set operations,
see e.g. [19] for a detailed overview. However, for convex structuring elements
tB with a mask B and a scaling parameter $t > 0$, there is also an alternative formulation in terms of partial differential equations (PDEs) [1,2,5,16,20]: Consider
some initial greyscale image $f(x, y)$, a disk

$$B := \left\{ \mathbf{z} \in \mathbb{R}^2, \ |\mathbf{z}| \leq 1 \right\}, \tag{1}$$

and the evolution equations

$$\partial_t u = \pm |\nabla u|, \tag{2}$$

where $\nabla = (\partial_x, \partial_y)^\top$ denotes the spatial nabla operator. Moreover, assume that
at "time" $t = 0$, the evolution is initialised with $f(x, y)$:

$$u(x, y, 0) = f(x, y). \tag{3}$$

Then the solution $u(x, y, t)$ at time $t > 0$ gives the dilation (for the plus sign) or
erosion (for the minus sign) with a disk of radius t.

J. Martí et al. (Eds.): IbPRIA 2007, Part II, LNCS 4478, pp. 515–522, 2007.

PDEs of this type using a continuous scaling parameter t for the structuring element create a *continuous-scale morphology*. They offer advantages when non-digitally scalable structuring elements such as disks or ellipses are desirable, or subpixel accuracy is required.

So far continuous-scale morphology is mainly used in a non-adaptive fashion where all locations are treated equally. In other image analysis areas such as diffusion filtering, however, interesting results have been obtained by replacing homogeneous processes by space-variant [13] or even direction-variant *(anisotropic)* ones [21]. The latter ones can be used for processing anisotropic image features such as coherent, flow-like structures. Some first attempts have been made to extend such anisotropic ideas into morphological shock filters that switch locally between dilation or erosion processes [23]. However, even in this case the underying morphological processes use a nonadaptive structuring element, and adaptivity only results from the fact that the shock fronts limit dilation and erosion. Similar shape restrictions are used for the recently introduced *morphological amoebae* [10] that are described in a set-theoretic framework.

The goal of the present paper is to introduce a space-variant anisotropic behaviour directly into the PDEs of dilation and erosion. In this way one benefits from the advantages of continous-scale morphology, and creates real anisotropic behaviour without the need to impose explicit or implicit shape restrictions.

We study a generalisation of (2) enabling the implementation of dilation or erosion processes adapted to the local structure of a given image. To this end, we consider *adaptive norms* by multiplying ∇u with a suitable matrix $\mathbf{D}$, yielding the new PDEs

$$\partial_t u = \pm |\mathbf{D}\nabla u| . \tag{4}$$

The purpose of (4) is to obtain a morphological approach to *coherence-enhancement*. This is of importance in order to reconstruct interrupted anisotropic image structures. We introduce a corresponding model of the matrix $\mathbf{D}$ using information from local structure tensors [4,8,15].

Our paper is organised as follows. After a detailed discussion of the interpretation of (4) and the modeling of $\mathbf{D}$ in Section 2, we present a numerical approximation of (4) as well as some numerical experiments in Section 3 and 4, respectively. The paper is finished by concluding remarks in Section 5.

2   Interpretation and Modelling

As can easily be shown, the introduction of a matrix $\mathbf{D}$ in (4) is equivalent with the multiplication of $|\nabla u|$ with a function $\kappa \geq 0$, where κ is defined by the deformation of the unit circle by $\mathbf{D}$ in direction of the normalised gradient:

$$|\mathbf{D}\nabla u| = \left| \mathbf{D}\frac{\nabla u}{|\nabla u|} |\nabla u| \right| = \underbrace{\frac{|\mathbf{D}\nabla u|}{|\nabla u|}}_{=: \kappa} |\nabla u| . \tag{5}$$

So, in effect, we have

$$\partial_t u\,(x,y,t) = \pm \kappa\,(x,y,t)\,|\nabla u\,(x,y,t)| \tag{6}$$

with a scaling function κ. However, the formulation using the matrix $\mathbf{D}$ is appropriate for our purpose since we will incorporate directional information into our model by the use of structure tensors.

Important modeling ingredients are the following. As the norm of a matrix $\mathbf{D}$ is defined by considering the deformation of the unit circle, we obtain

$$0 \leq \kappa = \frac{|\mathbf{D}\nabla u|}{|\nabla u|} \leq \max_{\mathbf{v} \neq \mathbf{0}} \frac{|\mathbf{D}\mathbf{v}|}{|\mathbf{v}|} = \|\mathbf{D}\|. \tag{7}$$

Now, instead of stretching the unit circle in a desired direction, we consider *normalised matrices* $\mathbf{D}$, so that we (i) keep a maximal signal speed by $\|\mathbf{D}\| = \|\mathbf{I}\| = 1$, and (ii) attenuate the flow given by $|\nabla u|$ at non-coherent image structures.

This desired behaviour is modeled by use of the *structure tensor* $\mathcal{S}$, see [4,8,15]. It is given by the 2×2-matrix

$$\mathcal{S} := \mathcal{K}_\rho * \left(\nabla u_\sigma \nabla u_\sigma^T \right), \tag{8}$$

where ∇u_σ is the gradient of the image u pre-smoothed by a Gaussian kernel with variance σ, and where $\mathcal{K}_\rho *$ describes an analogous, element-wise convolution with a Gaussian. In this context, ρ is the so-called *integration scale*.

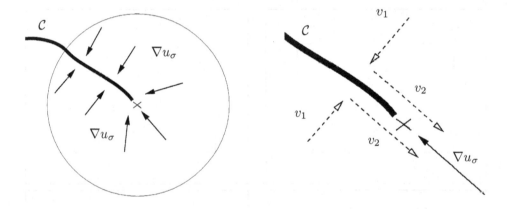

Fig. 1. (a) Left: Coherent structure $\mathcal{C}$ (thick line) together with image gradients (black arrows) and integration scale (circle) around marked point. **(b) Right:** Zoom into region around marked point, with representants of v_1, v_2 (dotted arrows) and image gradient ahead of $\mathcal{C}$ (black arrow).

Choosing, without a loss of generality, $\lambda_1 \geq \lambda_2$ for the two eigenvalues of $\mathcal{S}$, important information about the structure of the image u is then inferred from the two eigenvectors v_1, v_2: v_1 describes the orientation of highest contrast variation within the window given by the integration scale ρ, and $v_2 \perp v_1$.

Let us stress that the purpose of the structure tensor is robust estimation of directional information in an image. The pre-smoothing of u is done to attenuate sensitivity to noise. The decisive step in the construction of the structure tensor is the subsequent averaging over a neighborhood conveniently achieved by componentwise convolution with a Gaussian of width ρ, the *integration scale* as displayed in (8). This especially has the effect that the eigenvector for the larger eigenvalue of S is a reliable estimate of the direction of features in the neighborhood, more robust than the direct average of the gradients itself.

What is the role of the integration scale? Let us stress explicitly, that v_1 and v_2 are supposed to incorporate orientation information on a *larger scale*, determined by ρ in (8), in comparison to the more *local* gradient information given by ∇u_σ. The parameter σ determining the pre-smoothing is usually chosen relatively small (≤ 1), while typical integration scales we have employed for numerical testing are $\rho \geq 3$. The idea followed in this paper is to compare pointwise an *average orientation* given by v_1, v_2 (where we make use, especially, of v_2), with *local orientations* given by ∇u_σ, compare Figure 1.

Is the selection of the integration scale related to the size of gaps in coherent structures? The answer is *no*. The integration scale is only of importance in its role computing (8). This is confirmed by a simple illusory contour type experiment in Figure 2: while the integration scale is given by

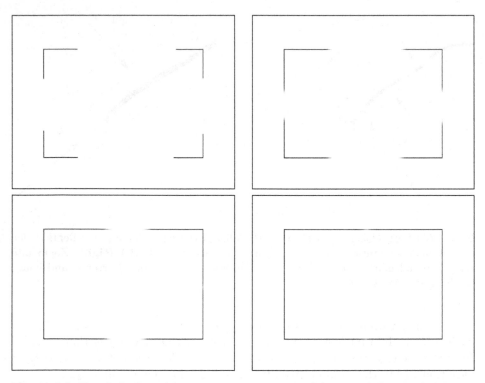

Fig. 2. (a) **Top left:** Initial image, 385 × 300 pixels. (b) **Top right:** Eroded image after 40 time steps. (c) **Bottom left:** After 100 time steps. (d) **Bottom left:** After 170 time steps.

$\rho = 4$, i.e., practically, it is limited by 12 pixels after truncating the Gaussian convolution kernel, the gaps that are going to be closed have widths of about $100 - 200$ pixels. The figure displays the temporal evolution of an anisotropic erosion process.

How do we implement orientation information in our model? As illustrated by Figure 1 (b), directly at the end of a coherent structure the vectors v_2 and ∇u_σ have approximately the same *orientation*, but they do not necessarily point in the same direction. In this situation, the function η,

$$\eta\,(v_2, \nabla u_\sigma) := |\cos \angle (v_2, \nabla u_\sigma)| = \left| \frac{\langle v_2, \nabla u_\sigma \rangle}{|v_2| \cdot |\nabla u_\sigma|} \right| , \tag{9}$$

where $\langle \cdot, \cdot \rangle$ denotes the inner product of vectors, is close to 1. Note, that we suppressed for the sake of brevity the dependence of η on space and time variables. If ∇u_σ is evaluated at points not too close to the end of $\mathcal{C}$, then $0 \leq \eta \ll 1$ will hold. In order to enforce a strong damping of the function η in this case, we exponentiate η by a nonnegative integer μ. The influence of μ on the quality of numerical results is shown in Figure 3: if μ is chosen too small, then the propagated coherent structures will be diffused.

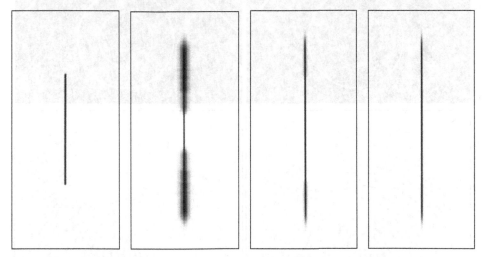

Fig. 3. From left to right: (i) Initial image, 106×238 pixels, (ii) eroded image after 50 time steps with $\Delta t = 0.5$, $\mu = 1$, (iii) analogously, but with $\mu = 2$, (iv) analogously, with $\mu = 4$

We then define

$$\kappa \equiv \kappa\,(x, y, t) := \eta\,(v_2, \nabla u_\sigma)^\mu , \tag{10}$$

compare the discussion of (5)-(7). Because of $|\cos(\cdot)| \leq 1$ it is guaranteed that $\|\mathbf{D}\| \leq 1$. Note, that $\|\mathbf{D}\| = 1$ holds if and only if v_2 and ∇u_σ have identical orientations (which is not likely in a numerical computation).

3   The Numerical Method

The PDEs (2) are of *hyperbolic type* [7]. This means, in analogy to the Huygens principle of wave propagation, object boundaries are moved with or against the direction of their normal vector, depending on the given grey values. Thus, numerically, the task is to accurately approximate *moving fronts* given by the dilated/eroded object boundaries. A standard method for this purpose which we use here in a slight variation is the *Rouy-Tourin (RT) scheme*, see [14]. With the usual abbreviation $U_{ij}^n \approx u(i, j, n\Delta t)$, the method reads:

$$U_{i,j}^{n+1} = U_{i,j}^n + \kappa_{i,j}^n \Delta t \Big(\big[\max \big(0, U_{i+1,j}^n - U_{i,j}^n, U_{i-1,j}^n - U_{i,j}^n \big) \big]^2$$

$$+ \big[\max \big(0, U_{i,j+1}^n - U_{i,j}^n, U_{i,j-1}^n - U_{i,j}^n \big) \big]^2 \Big)^{1/2}. \quad (11)$$

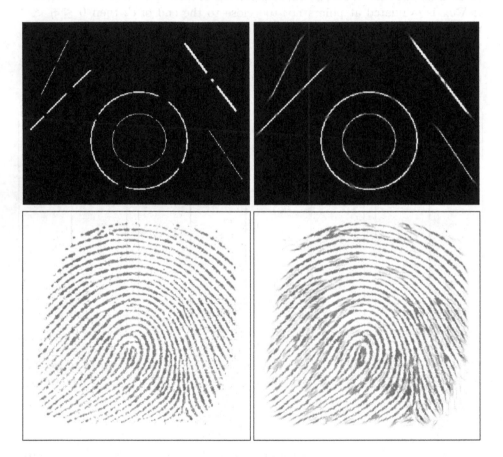

Fig. 4. (a) Top left: Synthetic image, 393×278 pixels. **(b) Top right:** Anisotropic dilation after 50 time steps. **(c) Bottom left:** Original image of a fingerprint with interrupted coherent structures, 300×300 pixels. **(d) Bottom right:** Anisotropic erosion of fingerprint after 20 time steps.

Specifying $\kappa_{i,j}^n = 1$ for all i, j, n, we retreive the original RT method. For more information on numerical methods for hyperbolic equations and more details concerning (11), we refer the interested reader to [3,11,12,14].

4   Numerical Experiments

We show two more experiments illuminating the capability of our method to enhance coherent image structures, supplementing the previous simple tests.

For the computation of κ, we use the procedure described in Paragraph 2, see especially (10). The parameters we use within the numerical experiments are set as $\sigma = 0.5$, $\rho = 4$, $\mu = 4$ and $\Delta t = 0.5$. For the computation of gradients, we use central differences for computing $\mathcal{S}$ and the Sobel operator for all other local gradients, respectively. These choices yield an accurate and efficient method.

We consider first an *synthetic image* featuring linear and round structures of several, randomly chosen orientation, and its anisotropic dilation, see Figure 3 (top row). We especially observe that interrupted lines are closed.

This desired outcome is also observable in real-world images, see Figure 3 (bottom row). The displayed image of a fingerprint is used as the initial condition for an anisotropic erosion process. Note, that our morphological anisotropic process does not introduce additional smoothing into the processed image.

5   Concluding Remarks

We have shown that our method yields morphology-based anisotropic enhancement of images. In our ongoing research, we study extensions of the method for image areas where structures cross, which is a hard problem for algorithms for coherence enhancement. Furthermore, we investigate possibilities to make the scheme more accurate with respect to the estimation of local flow directions, so that even very large gaps in thin image structures (i.e., width of, effectively, one pixel) oblique to the grid orientation can be closed without directional deviation.

References

1. Alvarez, L., Guichard, F., Lions, P.-L., Morel, J.-M.: Axioms and fundamental equations in image processing. Archive for Rational Mechanics and Analysis 123, 199–257 (1993)
2. Arehart, A.B., Vincent, L., Kimia, B.B.: Mathematical morphology: The Hamilton–Jacobi connection. In: Proc. Fourth International Conference on Computer Vision, Berlin, pp. 215–219. IEEE Computer Society Press, Washington, DC, USA (1993)
3. Breuß, M., Weickert, J.: A Shock-Capturing Algorithm for the Differential Equations of Dilation and Erosion. Journal of Mathematical Imaging and Vision 25, 187–201 (2006)
4. Bigün, J., Granlund, G.H., Wiklund, J.: Multidimensional orientation estimation with applications to texture analysis and optical flow. IEEE Transactions on Pattern Analysis and Machine Intelligence 13(8), 775–790 (1991)

5. Brockett, R.W., Maragos, P.: Evolution Equations for Continuous-Scale Morphological Filtering. IEEE Transactions on Signal Processing 42(12), 3377–3386 (1994)
6. Dougherty, E.R.: Mathematical Morphology in Image Processing. Marcel Dekker, New York (1993)
7. Evans, L.C.: Partial Differential Equations. Graduate Studies in Mathematics, vol. 19. American Mathematical Society, Providence (1998)
8. Förstner, W., Gülch, E.: A fast operator for detection and precise location of distinct points, corners and centres of circular features. In: Proc. ISPRS Intercommission Conf. on Fast Processing of Photogrammetric Data (Interlaken, June 2-4, 1987) pp. 281–305 (1987)
9. Heijmans, H.J.A.M.: Morphological Image Operators. Academic Press, Boston (1994)
10. Lerallut, R., Decencière, E., Meyer, F.: Image processing using morphological amoebas. In: Proc. 5th Int. Symp. on Mathematical Morphology, Kluwer Academic Publishers, Dordrecht (2005)
11. LeVeque, R.J.: Finite Volume Methods for Hyperbolic Problems. Cambridge University Press, Cambridge (2002)
12. Osher, S., Sethian, J.A.: Fronts propagating with curvature-dependent speed: Algorithms based on Hamilton–Jacobi formulations. Journal of Computational Physics 79, 12–49 (1988)
13. Perona, P., Malik, J.: Scale space and edge detection using anisotropic diffusion. IEEE Transactions on Pattern Analysis and Machine Intelligence 12, 629–639 (1990)
14. Rouy, E., Tourin, A.: A viscosity solutions approach to shape-from-shading. SIAM Journal on Numerical Analysis 29, 867–884 (1992)
15. Rao, A.R., Schunck, B.G.: Computing oriented texture fields. CVGIP: Graphical Models and Image Processing 53, 157–185 (1991)
16. Sapiro, G., Kimmel, R., Shaked, D., Kimia, B.B., Bruckstein, A.M.: Implementing continuous-scale morphology via curve evolution. Pattern Recognition 26, 1363–1372 (1993)
17. Serra, J.: Image Analysis and Mathematical Morphology, vol. 1. Academic Press, London (1982)
18. Serra, J.: Image Analysis and Mathematical Morphology, vol. 2. Academic Press, London (1988)
19. Soille, P.: Morphological Image Analysis, 2nd edn. Springer, Heidelberg (2003)
20. van den Boomgaard, R.: Mathematical Morphology: Extensions Towards Computer Vision. PhD thesis, University of Amsterdam, The Netherlands (1992)
21. Weickert, J.: Anisotropic Diffusion in Image Processing. Teubner, Stuttgart (1998)
22. Weickert, J.: Coherence-enhancing diffusion filtering. Int. J. Comput. Vision 31, 111–127 (1999)
23. Weickert, J.: Coherence-enhancing shock filters. In: Michaelis, B., Krell, G. (eds.) Pattern Recognition. LNCS, vol. 2781, pp. 1–8. Springer, Heidelberg (2003)

Three-Dimensional Ultrasonic Assessment of Atherosclerotic Plaques[*]

José Seabra[1], João Sanches[1], Luís M. Pedro[2], and J. Fernandes e Fernandes[2]

[1] Instituto Superior Técnico, Instituto de Sistemas e Robótica
[2] Faculdade de Medicina de Lisboa, Instituto Cardiovascular de Lisboa

Abstract. Carotid atherosclerosis is the most common life-threatening neurological disease and therefore an accurate assessment of atheromatous plaques is clinically important. Several studies were developed to characterize plaques from two-dimensional (2D) ultrasound images that are associated with high risk of stroke. However, 2D characterization may not be very accurate because it depends on the selection of a representative ultrasound image of the plaque by an experimented physician. In this paper we present a novel approach for diagnosis based on 3D ultrasound, which only requires a common ultrasound equipment without need of any additional and expensive devices like spatial locators. The semi-automatic algorithm uses medical guidance to obtain a 3D representation of the carotid artery and plaque and automatically generates measures to characterize the plaque in terms of dimensions and texture. A useful analysis tool is provided to allow the identification of vulnerable *foci* within the plaque.

1 Introduction

In the majority of western countries, atherosclerosis is the most prevalent and main cause of death. It is a disease of the large and medium size arteries, being characterized by plaque formation due to sub-endothelial accumulation of lipid, protein, and cholesterol esters. The most frequent location of the atherosclerotic lesion in the cerebrovascular sector is the common carotid bifurcation where plaque formation tends to produce stenosis which reduces the blood flow to the brain. Therefore, a significant effort has been done in the development of new techniques to assess the atherosclerosis state of the carotid artery.

Up to now the degree of stenosis has been targeted as the main indicator for plaque vulnerability and is the primary factor for deciding a surgical intervention [1]. This decision presents relevant clinical and financial consequences and therefore accurate diagnosis tools are needed. To increase the accuracy of the diagnosis, parameters aiming to identify vulnerable lesions have been studied using 2D B-mode ultrasound (US) imaging with computer-assisted analysis [2].

---

[*] This work was supported by Fundação para a Ciência e a Tecnologia (ISR/IST pluri-anual funding) through the POS Conhecimento Program which includes FEDER funds.

J. Martí et al. (Eds.): IbPRIA 2007, Part II, LNCS 4478, pp. 523–531, 2007.
© Springer-Verlag Berlin Heidelberg 2007

The ultrasound images are used to extract the carotid contours and measure the stenosis severity, to automatically or semi-automatically segment the intima-media layer thickness and to segment and classify the plaques with respect to their instability, based on intensity and texture [3]. However, 2D characterization is difficult and not very accurate because it depends on the selection of a representative ultrasound image of the plaque by an experimented physician. The classical methods do not allow a global visualization of the carotid anatomy nor the global extension and morphology of the plaques. For this reason an increasing amount of work has been published where 3D reconstructions of the carotid and plaques are used to better assess the risk of stroke.

Usually, in 3D ultrasound, a spatial locator is attached to the ultrasound probe to measure its position and orientation. The manipulation of the probe can be performed by mechanical devices or in a free-hand basis by the medical doctor. These devices are expensive and not usually provided with the traditional ultrasound equipment. Hence, 3D ultrasound algorithms usually require specialized experimental setup which is only available in academic laboratories or highly technological equipped medical centers.

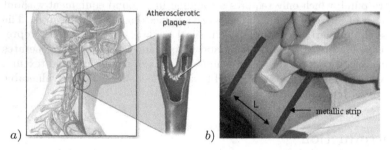

Fig. 1. a) Carotid anatomy. b) Acquisition protocol.

In this paper we propose an acquisition protocol that does not need spatial locators to obtain the 3D reconstruction. The anatomy and location of the carotid makes it possible to keep a uniform sweep velocity of the ultrasound probe allowing the acquisition of a set of nearly parallel cross sections. Furthermore, the paper proposes a volume based analysis algorithm of the atherosclerotic plaques in order to classify them with respect to its instability in a global and local basis. This new local approach analysis leads to significant and important improvements in the assessment of the atherosclerotic disease, primarily in concerning the risk of stroke.

2   Problem Formulation and Acquisition Protocol

The carotid is the major vessel which supplies the brain and face with blood. It is located in the lateral side of the neck, along its longitudinal axis and branches off in the external and internal carotids along the upward direction (see Fig.1a).

This paper is focused on the bifurcation region where the plaque formation is more frequent. The goal is to acquire parallel cross-sections of the carotid to build a 3D mesh representing its anatomy. Since no spatial locators are being used the acquisition protocol is a critical process to guarantee the quality of the results. The ultrasound probe should be manipulated as uniformly as possible from the base of the neck up to the base of the skull keeping its orientation as static as possible. In a typical acquisition session, 60 images are acquired with a 5 to 12 MHz dynamic range linear transducer. Small variations on the orientation of the ultrasound probe are not critical because the algorithm performs the alignment of the images. This acquisition protocol is performed using two metallic strips (see Fig.1b), which come apart by a known distance, that are used as landmarks for signaling the limits of the probe course. Small variations on the sweep velocity, $V = V_0 + \Delta_V$ with $\Delta_V < 0.1V_0$ and $V_0 = 8cm/2sec = 4cm/sec$, leads to position errors $\leq 0.02cm$, which are small when compared with the total length of the probe course, $d = 8cm$ (for details see [4]).

3 Three-Dimensional Reconstruction

The reconstruction of the carotid and plaques is performed using a surface rendering approach where the contours of both structures are extracted from each image of the data sequence. To produce the final meshes these contours are regularized, linked, aligned and longitudinally smoothed. Since the spatial information inside the plaque is clinically relevant, volume rendering is also performed, only inside the plaques, to allow the assessment of its global and local instability. The overall mesh generating process is performed in the following steps:

1) Pre-processing. This step is used to attenuate the speckle noise present in the ultrasound images. The Bayesian denoising process is based on the *maximum a posteriori* (MAP) criterion and in the *total variation* (TV) edge preserving prior, being the optimization achieved by solving the Lyapounov equation [5] for which there are fast and efficient solvers described in the literature. Fig.2a-c displays an example of application of the pre-processing in a 346×440 pixel ultrasound noisy image (fig.2a), the filtered image using a combination of median and gaussian filters (fig.2b) and the filtered image using the MAP method (fig.2c). This image demonstrates the edge-preserving nature of this type of filter.

2) Contour extraction. The extraction of contours from the pre-processed images is done by using the active contours algorithm described in [6], based on the *Gradient Vector Flow* (GVF). The algorithm is used to automatically segment the anatomic objects under medical supervision. That is, under regular conditions the initialization of the GVF algorithm for a given image is obtained from the previous one, as displayed in fig.2d-f. However, the medical doctor may interfere with the process. He may change the initial contour or the default parameters, such as the internal and external energies of the contour. This functionality is useful when the algorithm wrongly converges due to bad initialization or, more important, when topological modifications arise. The need for accuracy and precision during the segmentation makes it necessary to use semi-automatic methods because the results are relevant for surgery taking decisions. Two situations need a special initialization: 1) the beginning of the bifurcation, where two contours must be merged into a single one. Both contours (fig.2d) intersect, after convergence, in the bifurcation plane (fig.2e). The new single contour results from these two contours by removing the intersection region; finally, the composed contour is used as initialization to segment the carotid in the bifurcation region (fig.2f); 2) in the first image containing the plaque, which must be manually defined (fig.2g). In the next images, the plaque segmentation is made automatically. However, in order to force consistency of both contours, carotid and plaque, a post processing is needed. This procedure consists in the extraction of the plaque region from the intersection between the new contour defined for the plaque and the already existing one for the carotid, as well as, the correction of the carotid artery wall, by removing the region of the plaque.

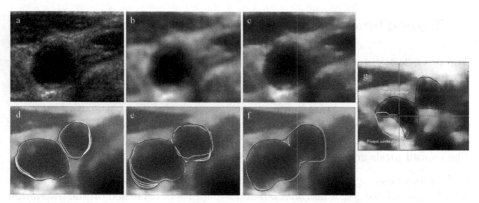

Fig. 2. a-c) Pre-processing. d-f) Segmentation of the carotid artery in the bifurcation. g) Manual detection of the plaque.

3) Contour re-sampling, smoothing and linking. The contours of the carotid and plaques are described by a set of control points not evenly spaced. These must be linked to build the 3D mesh representing the anatomy of the carotid and plaques. Therefore, a re-sampling is needed and smoothing is desirable. In this step a continuous vectorial function depending on scalar parameter s, describing each contour is estimated from the corresponding control points.

Let $c(s) = [x(s), y(s)]$ be the closed continuous contour where $0 \leq s \leq 1$. The control points describing this contour are $p_i = [x_i(s_i), y_i(s_i)]$ where s_i are the normalized positions of each point, along the contour, that is $s_0 = 0$ and $s_{M-1} = 1$. The M control points are considered noisy observations of the unknown curve, $c(s) = [\Phi(s)^T A, \Phi(s)^T B]$, where $\Phi(s) = [\phi_0, \phi_1, ..., \phi_{N-1}]^T$ is a column vector of the N basis functions, computed at position s, and $A = [a_0, ..., a_{N-1}]^T$ and $B = [b_0, ..., b_{N-1}]^N$ are vectors of coefficients to be estimated. The estimation of

A (B is estimated in the same way) is performed by minimizing the following quadratic energy function,

$$E = (X - \Theta A)^T (X - \Theta A) + \alpha(\theta A)^T(\theta A) \tag{1}$$

with

$$\theta = \begin{pmatrix} 1 & 0 & 0 & \dots & 0 & -1 \\ -1 & 1 & 0 & \dots & \dots & 0 \\ \dots & \dots & \dots & \dots & 1 & 0 \\ 0 & 0 & 0 & \dots & -1 & 1 \end{pmatrix}, \Theta = \begin{pmatrix} \phi_0(s_0) & \phi_1(s_0) & \dots & \phi_{N-1}(s_0) \\ \phi_0(s_1) & \phi_1(s_1) & \dots & \phi_{N-1}(s_1) \\ \dots & \dots & \dots & \dots \\ \phi_0(s_{M-1}) & \phi_1(s_{M-1}) & \dots & \phi_{N-1}(s_{M-1}) \end{pmatrix},$$

where θ is a difference operator and Θ is $M \times N$ matrix depending on the location of the control points. The vector $\hat{A}$ that minimizes (1) is

$$\hat{A} = (\Theta^T \Theta + \alpha \theta^T \theta)^{-1} \Theta^T X. \tag{2}$$

The vector $\hat{B}$ is obtained as $\hat{A}$ by replacing X by Y. From $\hat{A}$ and $\hat{B}$ the new evenly spaced control points are computed from

$$q_i = [\Phi(s_i)^T \hat{A}, \Phi(s_i)^T \hat{B}] \tag{3}$$

where $s_i = i/(L-1)$, $0 \leq i \leq L-1$ and L is the number of the new control points which will be used in the sequel of the segmentation process.

The re-sampled contours are linked in a pairwise basis, i.e. the contours on the second image are linked with the homologous in the first one, the contours on the third are linked with the homologous in the second one and successively, up to the last image. However, it is necessary to match them to allow a correct pairing of homologous control points. This is done by using the Iterative Closest Point (ICP) [7] algorithm which estimates a rigid transformation applied to the second set of points in order to minimize the distance between them. Once paired the linking of both set of points is possible.

4) Vertical alignment and smoothing. In order to compensate the small lateral displacements of the ultrasound probe during the acquisition process an alignment procedure of the contours is needed. In this step, the contours are aligned with the homologous ones in the previous image. After the alignment, a smoothing operation is applied to the vertical lines to attenuate discontinuities in the final mesh. This procedure is similar to the one applied to the contours in step 3. The alignment of two consecutive images is achieved by minimizing an energy function involving translation vectors associated with each image, i.e.

$$E_i = \sum_{k=0}^{L-1} [p_i(k) - p_{i-1}(k) - t_i]^2 \tag{4}$$

where $p_\tau(k)$ is the k-th control point of the i-th contour and t_i is the compensation vector related to the i-th image. Using matrix notation leads to

$$E_i = (P_i - P_{i-1} - \theta t_i)^T (P_i - P_{i-1} - \theta t_i) \tag{5}$$

with $P_\tau = [p_{\tau x}(0), p_{\tau y}(0), ..., p_{\tau x}(L-1), p_{\tau y}(L-1)]^T$, $t_i = [t_{ix}, t_{iy}]^T$ and $\theta = \begin{pmatrix} 1\ 0\ 1\ ...\ 0\ 1 \\ 0\ 1\ 0\ ...\ 1\ 0 \end{pmatrix}^T$. The vector that minimizes (5) is

$$t_i = (\theta^T \theta)^{-1} \theta^T (P_i - P_{i-1}) \qquad (6)$$

5) VRML generation. The final step of the reconstruction algorithm consists in the creation of a finite-element mesh, by applying different luminescence and transparency codes to the defined elements in order to facilitate the anatomy inspection. This information and criteria are used to create 3D virtual reality models of both carotid artery and atherosclerotic plaque, like shown in Fig.4.

4   Plaque Classification

The morphology and texture of the plaques have prognostic relevance [8]. For instance, a smooth surface and a homogenous texture indicates a stable plaque, while an irregular surface and a heterogeneous texture are typical in unstable plaques. Studies comparing plaque histology with ultrasonography have suggested that echolucent (darker) plaques have more lipid and hemorrhage, which indicates inflammatory activity and therefore instability. Conversely, echogenic (brighter) plaques are associated with the presence of more calcium and fibrous tissue, which are stable components. Therefore, a method is proposed for computational analysis of atherosclerotic disease, either based on global or local data. In the former approach, plaque volume and extension, level of stenosis, grayscale median (GSM) and percentage of echolucent pixels (PEP) are used. In the local analysis, statistical measures, such as mean, median, variance, standard deviation, skewness and curtosis, are computed for each location inside the plaque. Global measures characterize heterogeneity and echogenicity of plaques and local statistics allow the identification of possible active and unstable *foci* whithin the plaque. This new local analysis methodology improves the diagnosis based only on global characterization of the plaque. Fig.3a shows the plaque segmentation

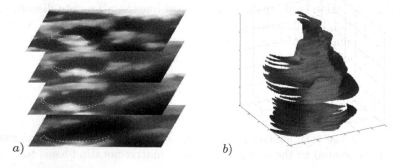

a)   b)

Fig. 3. a) Extraction of plaque US information. b) 3D US reconstruction.

results. Fig.3b displays a 3D view of an entire reconstructed plaque which may be inspected using opaque or semi-transparent visualization techniques.

5   Experimental Results

In this section examples of reconstructions using real data from two clinical studies are presented. Fig.4 shows 3D views of a healthy (a) and a diseased carotid (b) where the plaque is well observed. In this framework is easy and fast to evaluate the geometry and extension of the plaques and its precise localization inside the carotid. The local assessment of plaque severity is also available by using the program interface, as shown in Fig. 5. The results for plaque characterization are based on a third clinical study. Besides the carotid anatomy, the program also gives important global information. The example presents a diseased carotid containing a moderately echogenic plaque (GSM of 37), with a considerable level of stenosis (61% at most and 51% in average), PEP of 53% and a smooth surface. The estimated plaque volume of $1,352 mm^3$ is also important, but its relevance depends on the plaque extension. Even more important than the volume itself is the respective evolution along the time. This application is particularly suitable for this type of prospective clinical approach, allowing the comparison of the atherosclerotic plaque volume and extension at different stages of the disease.

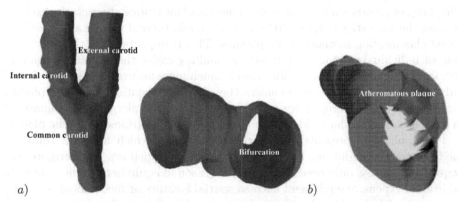

Fig. 4. 3D realistic models of normal (a) and diseased (b) carotid arteries

The plaque echogenic analysis, in particular the GSM, determines whether (or not) the plaque is stable, considering the consensual threshold given in the literature $(GSM = 32)$. This binary classification is however very simplist because it does not take into account if the GSM is closer to the threshold and, even worst, it does not give any information about the extension of the unstable regions inside the plaque.

Local assessment is needed to obtain information not provided by the global measurements. Fig. 5b shows the local analysis of the plaque using two different criteria to identify the unstable regions: first, the most echolucent regions at the

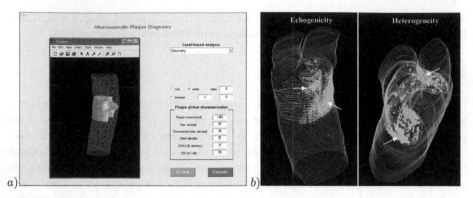

Fig. 5. a) User-interface for plaque classification. b) Local detection of unstable regions within the plaque.

central core (on the left), where the median values are below 20, and the most heterogeneous regions (on the right), where the standard deviation is above 20, mainly in the peripheral locations of the plaque.

6   Conclusion

This project proposes a new computer-based tool for plaque characterization, involving the reconstruction of a 3D mesh of the carotid and plaque and a volume based classification method of the plaques. This is important for the identification of individuals at high risk of stroke, making easier the clinical decision of surgical intervention. This classification is much more accurate than those based only on 2D images, since it considers the entire information from the plaque. Furthermore, the heterogeneity and echogenicity of the plaque is also analyzed in a local basis, in order to identify possible unstable locations inside the plaque.

The application presents a user-friendly interface which allows a complete medical exam in about one hour, including image acquisition. Furthermore, the acquisition process only needs a common ultrasound equipment without need of additional expensive equipment such as spatial locators or mechanical scanners. Automatic global and local evaluation of textural parameters in conjunction with its 3D integration in the carotid artery anatomy, leads to significant improvements of the current state-of-the-art atherosclerosis diagnosis tools.

References

1. ECST. Randomised trial of endarterectomy for recently symptomatic carotid stenosis: final results of the mrc european carotid surgery trial. Lancet, vol. 351, pp. 1379–1387 (1998)
2. Pedro, L.M.: Computer-assisted carotid plaque analysis: characteristics of plaques associated with cerebrovascular symptoms and cerebral infarction. Eur. J. Vasc. Endovasc. Surg. 19, 118–123 (2000)

3. Stoitsis, J., Golemati, S., Nikita, K.S., Nicolaides, A.N.: Characterization of carotid atherosclerosis based on motion and texture features and clustering using fuzzy c-means. In: Proceedings of the 26th Annual International Conference of the IEEE EMBS, pp. 1–5 (September 2004)
4. Seabra, J.C.: Reconstrução e diagnóstico 3d ecográfico da lesão aterosclerótica. Master thesis (2007)
5. Nascimento, J., Sanches, J.M., Marques, J.S.: A method for the dynamic analysis of the heart using a lyapounov based denoising algorithm. In: Proceedings IEEE EMBC 2006, New York City, USA (August 30-September 3 2006)
6. Xu C., Prince J.L.: Snakes, shapes, and gradient vector flow. In: IEEE Transactions on Image Processing, vol. 7(3) (March 1998)
7. Besl, P., McKay, N.: A method for registration of 3-d shapes. Trans. PAMI, vol. 14(2) (1992)
8. Christodoulou, C.I., Pattichis, C.S., Pantziaris, M., Nicolaides, A.: Texture-based classification of atherosclerotic carotid plaques. IEEE Transactions on Medical Imaging, vol. 22(7) (2003)

Measuring the Applicability of Self-organization Maps in a Case-Based Reasoning System

A. Fornells, E. Golobardes, J.M. Martorell, J.M. Garrell, E. Bernadó, and N. Macià

Research Group in Intelligent Systems
Enginyeria i Arquitectura La Salle, Ramon Llull University
Quatre Camins 2, 08022 Barcelona, Spain
{afornells,elisabet,jmmarto,josepmg,esterb,nmacia}@salle.url.edu
http://www.salle.url.edu/GRSI

Abstract. Case-Based Reasoning (CBR) systems solve new problems using others which have been previously resolved. The knowledge is composed of a set of cases stored in a case memory, where each one describes a situation in terms of a set of features. Therefore, the size and organization of the case memory influences in the computational time needed to solve new situations. We organize the memory using Self-Organization Maps, which group cases with similar properties into patterns. Thus, CBR is able to do a selective retrieval using only the cases from the most suitable pattern. However, the data complexity may hinder the identification of patterns and it may degrade the accuracy rate. This work analyses the successful application of this approach by doing a previous data complexity characterization. Relationships between the performance and some measures of class separability and the discriminative power of attributes are also found.

Keywords: Statistical and Structural Pattern Recognition, Data Complexity, Neural Networks, Self-Organization Maps, Case-Based Reasoning, Soft Computing.

1 Motivation

Case-Based Reasoning (CBR) [1] is an approach based on solving new problems using others which have been previously solved. The knowledge is represented by a case memory, where each case is defined by a set of features that describe the problem. The way in which CBR works can be summarized in the following steps: (1) it retrieves the most similar cases from the case memory, (2) it adapts them to propose a new solution, (3) it checks if this solution is valid, and finally, (4) it stores the solution according to a learning policy. The CBR performance, in terms of computational time, is related to the size of the case memory because CBR has to explore it in the retrieval phase. Therefore, its organization can help to improve this issue by avoiding the selection of useless cases. There are mainly two organization strategies: (1) The identification of patterns for using only the cases from the best matching patterns [2,3], and; (2) The rejection of cases in

J. Martí et al. (Eds.): IbPRIA 2007, Part II, LNCS 4478, pp. 532–539, 2007.

function of their features' values [4]. However, the use of fewer cases may imply a reduction of the solving capabilities.

The SOMCBR (Self-Organization Map in a Case-Based Reasoning) [5] system is a CBR framework where the case memory has been organized by a Self-Organization Map (SOM) [6]. SOM is a clustering technique that defines patterns by highlighting the most important features of the data. These patterns allow SOMCBR to do a selective retrieval based on using only the cases from the most suitable pattern instead of all the cases. Thus, the computational time is reduced obtaining a meaningful property for real time environments [9]. Nevertheless, the SOMCBR success depends on the existence of reliable data patterns.

The goal of this paper is to show how a previous data complexity [11] analysis can help us to predict the SOMCBR applicability by evaluating the presence of useful data patterns.

The paper is organized as follows. Section 2 explains the previous work on SOMCBR. Section 3 briefly describes the data complexity analysis and proposes a set of metrics as predictors of the SOMCBR applicability. Section 4 summarizes the experiments and the results. Finally, we present the conclusions and further work.

2   Self-organization Map in a Case-Based Reasoning System

SOM is an unsupervised clustering technique from the neural network approach. It defines a topology map, where the cases are grouped in patterns. This ability is used to organize the CBR case memory in the SOMCBR approach [5]. Figure 1 illustrates a case memory organized by a 2-dimensional map of $M \times M$ patterns. The SOM has two layers: (1) The input layer is composed of N neurons, where each neuron represents one of the N-dimensional features of the input case, and; (2) The output layer is composed of $M \times M$ neurons, where each neuron contains a set of similar cases represented by a director vector. Each input neuron is connected to all the output neurons. When a new input case C is introduced in the input layer, each neuron from the output layer computes a degree of similarity between the input case C and its director vector applying a similarity function. In our approach, we use the complementary of the normalized Euclidean distance (see Eq. 1). A value closer to 1 means that the input case C should be similar to the elements from the Xth pattern (M_X). Otherwise, it should be different.

$$
similarity(C, M_X) = \left| 1 - d(\overline{C}, \overline{M_X}) \right| = \left| 1 - \sqrt{\frac{\sum_{n:1..N}(C(n) - M_X(n))^2}{N}} \right| \quad (1)
$$

The retrieval consists in: (1) Looking for the most similar pattern, and; (2) Comparing with the cases from the selected pattern. Consequently, SOMCBR reduces the computational time because only a subset of the cases are used. Nevertheless, the patterns definition can be compromised due to the data complexity.

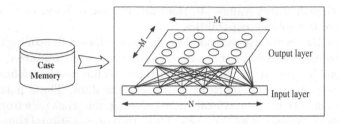

Fig. 1. The case memory is organized by the SOM in order to define $M \times M$ groups of cases with similar properties. This organization allows the CBR system to improve the computational time in the retrieval phase.

3 Data Complexity Measures

The study of data complexity addresses the characterization of the intrinsic complexity of the dataset, and to what extent this complexity is related to the classifier's performance [10]. Although dataset complexity may be related to three main causes (class ambiguity, boundary complexity, and training set sparsity) the previous studies in this matter have been focused on the characterization of boundary complexity, due to the difficulty to determine class ambiguity and the real sparsity of a training set. Ho & Basu [11] proposed a measurement space to identify the different aspects of boundary complexity: the discriminant power of attributes, the separability of classes, and the topology of classes such as the degree of overlap and the geometry of classes distributed as hyperspheres. Based on this previous study, we select those measures that are most relevant to identify meaningful structures in the dataset that could be correlated with SOMCBR clusters. We find that measures related to the separability of classes are the most useful to predict SOMCBR's success. Also measures detecting the degree of class overlap with respect to the feature space are useful to explain SOMCBR's behaviour. Other types of measures given in [11] do not reveal any structure as seen by SOMCBR's clusterization. In the following, we briefly describe these relevant metrics.

Feature efficiency (F3): it defines the efficiency of each feature individually and describes to what extent the feature takes part in the class separability. For each feature, the measure uses a local continuity heuristic which supposes that all the points belonging to the same class are included in the interval between the minimum and maximum value of that feature. Thus, if two instances of opposite classes have the same value for an attribute, there is an overlap and the instances are considered ambiguous for this dimension. The ambiguity is solved removing these instances. The efficiency is then assessed as the ratio of the remaining (non-overlapping) points to all the training points. The measure of feature efficiency is the maximum feature efficiency of all dimensions.

Length of class boundary (N1): it measures the number of training points located near the class boundary. It is based on building a minimum spanning tree

(MST) connecting all training points, using Euclidean distances between each pair of points. Then, the measure computes the number of points of opposite classes that are connected in the MST with respect to the total number of points. N1 is an indicator of class separability and cluster tendency; the higher the measure, the greater the presence of points of different classes on the boundary.

Intra/inter class nearest neighbour distances (N2): it describes the dispersion within classes with respect to the separability of classes. It is based on computing the Euclidean distance of each point with the nearest neighbour within the same class and the nearest neighbour of the opposite class. N2 is the ratio between the average within-class nearest neighbour distances and the average opposite-class nearest neighbour distances. A low value indicates a major degree of clustering and higher separability among different classes.

4   Results and Discussion

4.1   Testbed and Results

Several datasets of different domains and characteristics from the UCI Repository [13] are considered for studying the relation between the data complexity and the SOMCBR applicability. Due to the way in which the complexity measures are implemented [11], the datasets of N-class are split in N datasets of two classes: each class versus all other classes. The name and the number of features and instances are described in table 1.

The experimentation is performed in two parts. First, we compute the data complexity of each normalized dataset for several measures. Next, CBR and SOMCBR are executed applying a 10-fold stratified cross-validation with the following configuration: (1) The retrieve phase uses the Euclidean distance as similarity function; (2) The reuse phase proposes a solution using the most similar case, and; (3) The retain phase does not learn. Additionally, the SOMCBR is tested with 10 random seeds. All these results are also summarized in table 1: N1, N2 and N3 are the complexity measures; %AR and σ are the accuracy rate and its standard deviation for CBR, and for the best configuration of SOMCBR; %R is the reduction in the number of operations between CBR and SOMCBR; p-value is the probability to reject the null hypothesis assuming equal values for %AR of both approaches [14]. Small values of p-value imply a high probability of significant difference between both %AR.

Table 1 is divided (by an horizontal line) in two categories ordered by p-value. **Type 1** represents situations where the computational time is improved and the accuracy rate is at least maintained. On the other hand, **type 2** is produced when the accuracy rate is proportional to the number of cases retrieved and, consequently, the accuracy rate depends on the number of cases used. Therefore, the difference between both types indicates if the SOM is capable or not to splitting the domain in well defined patterns.

Table 1. Summary of the dataset description (number of instances and attributes), the results from CBR and SOMCBR (accuracy rates (%AR) with their standard deviation (σ)) and, the results from the comparison between CBR and SOMCBR (percentage of reduction (%R) and the probability of CBR and SOMCBR being equal (p-value)). The horizontal line divides datasets into type 1 and 2, which are ordered by the p-value.

Dataset			Measures			CBR	SOMCBR	Statistics	
Name	Inst.	Attr.	N1	N2	F3	%AR(σ)	%AR(σ)	%R	p-value
Waveform c1	5000	41	0.24	0.86	0.23	83.2 (1.2)	81.1 (1.2)	89.2	0.00
Vehicle c1	846	19	0.12	0.42	0.46	93.4 (2.4)	87.5 (4.7)	86.9	0.00
Vehicle c4	846	19	0.09	0.54	0.22	96.0 (4.2)	89.2 (3.6)	87.7	0.00
Balance c2	625	5	0.20	0.62	0.00	87.0 (3.1)	81.8 (4.1)	89.7	0.00
Waveform c2	5000	41	0.27	0.90	0.15	80.2 (1.4)	78.8 (1.6)	89.7	0.01
Pim	768	9	0.44	0.84	0.01	71.3 (3.4)	69.9 (3.4)	87.9	0.03
Wpbc	198	34	0.42	0.91	0.18	73.7 (7.1)	73.2 (9.2)	82.5	0.03
Waveform c3	5000	41	0.23	0.85	0.24	83.6 (1.8)	82.7 (1.6)	89.3	0.03
Balance c3	625	5	0.20	0.62	0.00	86.9 (3.7)	82.3 (6.5)	89.5	0.04
Tao	1888	3	0.07	0.16	0.36	95.4 (1.3)	94.9 (1.6)	81.8	0.06
Wdbc	569	31	0.07	0.56	0.52	95.1 (3.2)	95.3 (2.7)	80.2	0.09
Wbcd	699	10	0.06	0.34	0.12	95.3 (2.2)	94.6 (2.6)	86.9	0.09
Vehicle c3	846	19	0.37	0.74	0.06	73.9 (4.1)	73.4 (4.5)	82.5	0.11
Vehicle c2	846	19	0.37	0.71	0.04	75.3 (3.4)	75.4 (2.9)	81.9	0.11
Bpa	345	7	0.58	0.91	0.03	62.9 (6.0)	63.2 (5.1)	52.6	0.17
Heart-Statlog	270	14	0.37	0.67	0.01	74.1 (6.4)	76.3 (8.3)	87.1	0.19
Balance c1	625	5	0.21	0.65	0.00	83.7 (2.2)	86.1 (4.9)	89.0	0.21
Wisconsin	699	10	0.06	0.33	0.12	96.1 (2.0)	96.9 (2.4)	84.5	0.33
Ionosphere	351	35	0.23	0.63	0.19	86.9 (4.1)	88.1 (3.6)	64.0	0.41
Iris c2	150	5	0.01	0.10	1.00	100.0 (0.0)	100.0 (0.0)	56.3	0.00
Thyroids c2	215	6	0.06	0.23	0.81	98.1 (3.3)	97.2 (4.0)	52.8	0.01
Thyroids c1	215	6	0.05	0.23	0.85	98.1 (3.3)	96.3 (4.3)	51.4	0.02
Iris c1	150	5	0.09	0.17	0.75	95.3 (4.3)	93.3 (5.9)	60.7	0.04
Wine c1	178	14	0.05	0.43	0.72	98.3 (3.7)	97.2 (5.1)	68.6	0.05
Wine c2	178	14	0.07	0.49	0.76	97.2 (4.3)	97.2 (4.3)	67.9	0.05
Thyroids c3	215	6	0.10	0.31	0.67	97.2 (4.0)	95.8 (4.4)	54.2	0.08
Iris c3	150	5	0.10	0.21	0.56	94.7 (5.8)	93.3 (6.6)	60.9	0.08
Wine c3	178	14	0.12	0.57	0.58	94.9 (5.2)	95.5 (4.9)	65.3	0.09

4.2   Relationship Between Data Complexity and SOMCBR

We establish a classification where the datasets are divided into the two types previously explained. Regarding type 2 datasets, the computational time does not improve in a great percentage (%R < 70%) and the probability defined by the p-value is small (p-value < 10%). Figure 2(a) shows the relationship between the p-value and the percentage of reduction of the computational time, %R, for all datasets tested. The perpendicular lines delimit the region of type 2 datasets.

Even so, the goal is to find a representation on the complexity space to distinguish between types 1 and 2. Thus, this should indicate *a priori* the applicability of SOMCBR according to the defined threshold values of p-value and %R. The

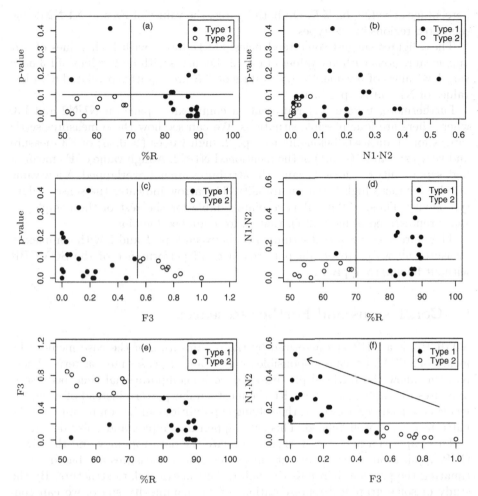

Fig. 2. The charts show how the combination of p-value, %R, and complexity measures are useful tools for distinguishing the behaviour of type 1 and 2. The chart (f) allow us to predict the SOMCBR applicability.

F3, N1, and N2 complexity measures present interesting properties to distinguish between both types. Because the N1 and N2 separability measures have a similar behaviour, we can work with their product in order to promote extreme behaviours, especially in the case of datasets with low values.

Figures 2(b, c, d, e) depict the complexity measures (F3 and N1·N2) with the previously defined p-values and %R. In Figure 2(b), we observe that all datasets of type 2 are near to the origin, with low values of N1·N2 and p-value, but there are some overlaps with the location of type 1 datasets. On the other hand, Figure 2(c) shows that type 2 problems are separated from type 1 with respect to F3. Moreover, type 2 problems are mainly related to high values of F3. Figures 2(d) and 2(e) show similar results, where we also plot the complexity measures and the percentage of reduction %R. On both figures, the values of F3 and N1·N2 define separated regions in two types.

These figures suggest some tendencies: (1) Datasets with high values of %R appear in regions with low values of F3. (2) Datasets with high values of F3 have very low values of p-value. (3) Low values of %R are slightly correlated with low values of N1 and N2 product.

Furthermore, Figure 2(f) represents a complexity space on N1·N2 and F3, where there are four possible situations. We can see how these measures settle ranges for all datasets belonging to type 2: high values (> 0.55) of F3 measure and very low values (< 0.1) of the mentioned N1·N2. A high value of F3 means a high separability of classes because the attributes are not overlapped. A low value of N1·N2 implies high linear separability. The arrow indicates the sense of data complexity. Thus, SOMCBR is recommendable for the rest of the complexity space represented in figure 2(f), that is, for complex domains.

Therefore, the *a priori* discrimination between type 1 and 2 with complexity measures allows us to obtain patterns of good performance of the SOMCBR without having to apply it.

5   Conclusions and Further Research

SOMCBR is a CBR characterized by the organization of the case memory by means of a SOM, which is responsible for grouping the cases into patterns. These patterns allow the retrieval phase to reduce its computational time because it only uses the cases associated with the most similar pattern instead of using the whole case memory. However, the solving capabilities can be compromised if the patterns are not well defined. This can happen in complex and noisy domains.

This paper is a first step in trying to relate the data topology and the SOM-CBR application using complexity measures. These measures are based on estimating the problem hardness through the geometrical data structure. By the study of some graphical representations of the complexity space, we can conclude that the F3 measure and the product of N1 and N2 measures are useful to determine when the SOMCBR should be used, namely, for complex domains. Therefore, these complexity measures help us to predict *a priori* the performance of the SOMCBR without applying it.

Further work involves two issues. First, extending the analysis of the effects of other complexity measures and more datasets. Second, studying others ways of retrieving cases from SOMCBR in order to avoid losing useful cases if clusters are not well defined.

Acknowledgements. We would like to thank the Spanish Government for the support under grants TIN2006-15140-C03-03, TIN2005-08386-C05-04 and the *Generalitat de Catalunya* for the support under grants 2005SGR-302 and 2006FIC-0043. Also, we would like to thank *Enginyeria i Arquitectura La Salle* of Ramon Llull University for the support to our research group.

References

1. Aamodt, A., Plaza, E.: Case-based reasoning: Foundations issues, methodological variations, and system approaches. IA Communications 7, 39–59 (1994)
2. Wess, S., Althoff, K.D., Derwand, G.: Using k-d Trees to Improve the Retrieval Step in Case-Based Reasoning. In: Wess, S., Richter, M., Althoff, K.-D. (eds.) Selected papers from the First European Workshop on Topics in Case-Based Reasoning. LNCS, vol. 837, pp. 167–181. Springer, Heidelberg (1994)
3. Lenz, M., Burkhard, H.D., Brückner, S.: Applying Case Retrieval Nets to Diagnostic Tasks in Technical Domains. In: Smith, I., Faltings, B.V. (eds.) Advances in Case-Based Reasoning. LNCS, vol. 1168, pp. 219–233. Springer, Heidelberg (1996)
4. Vernet, D., Golobardes, E.: An Unsupervised Learning Approach for Case-Based Classifier Systems. Expert Update. The Specialist Group on Artificial Intelligence 6(2), 37–42 (2003)
5. Fornells, A., Golobardes, E., Vernet, D., Corral, G.: Unsupervised case memory organization: Analysing computational time and soft computing capabilities. In: Roth-Berghofer, T.R., Göker, M.H., Güvenir, H.A. (eds.) ECCBR 2006. LNCS (LNAI), vol. 4106, pp. 241–255. Springer, Heidelberg (2006)
6. Kohonen, T.: Self-Organization and Associative Memory. Series in Information Sciences, vol. 8. Springer, Heidelberg (1989)
7. Oja, M., Kaski, S., Kohonen, T.: Bibliography of Self-Organizing Map (SOM) Papers: 1998-2001. Neural Computing Surveys 3, 1–156 http://www.cis.hut.fi/research/refs/ (2003)
8. Kaski, S., Kangas, J., Kohonen, T.: Bibliography of Self-Organizing Map (SOM) Papers: 1981-1997. Neural Computing Surveys 1, 102–350 http://www.cis.hut.fi/research/refs/ (1998)
9. Fornells, A., Golobardes, E., Vilasís, X., Martí, J.: Integration of strategies based on relevance feedback into a tool for retrieval of mammographic images. In: Corchado, E., Yin, H., Botti, V., Fyfe, C. (eds.) IDEAL 2006. LNCS, vol. 4224, pp. 116–124. Springer, Heidelberg (2006)
10. Basu, M., Ho, T.K.: Data Complexity in Pattern Recognition. Springer, Heidelberg (2006)
11. Ho, T.K., Basu, M.: Complexity measures of supervised classification problems. IEEE Transaction on Pattern Analysis and Machine Intelligence 3(24), 289–300 (2002)
12. Bernadó-Mansilla, E., Ho, T.K.: Domain of competence of XCS classifier system in complexity measurement space. IEEE Transaction Evolutionary Computation 1(9), 82–104 (2005)
13. Blake, C.L., Merz, C.J.: UCI repository of machine learning databases (1998)
14. Sheskin, D.J.: Handbook of Parametric and Nonparametric Statistical Procedures. CRC Press, Boca Raton (1997)

Algebraic-Distance Minimization of Lines and Ellipses for Traffic Sign Shape Localization

Pedro Gil-Jiménez, Saturnino Maldonado-Bascón, Hilario Gómez-Moreno,
Sergio Lafuente-Arroyo, and Javier Acevedo-Rodríguez

Dpto. de Teoría de la Señal y Comunicaciones,
Universidad de Alcalá, 28805 Alcalá de Henares (Madrid), Spain
{pedro.gil,saturnino.maldonado,hilario.gomez,sergio.lafuente,
javier.acevedo}@uah.es

Abstract. In traffic sign recognition systems, one of the normal approaches is the identification of the shape of the sign prior to the recognition itself. Normally, the recognition process needs an accurate localization of the sign for a good performance. If we are dealing with triangular, rectangular and circular signs, this means the accurate localization of the vertices of the triangle and the rectangle, or the parameters of the ellipse. In this paper we have developed a system which searches the above mentioned parameters from the signature of the blob using techniques of algebraic-distance minimization. Comparisons with previous works show good improvements in the localization of the shape, especially in the presence of slight occlusions. This work is part of a traffic sign recognition system, and in this paper we focus on the shape localization step.

1 Introduction

A traffic sign recognition system consists of a video camera mounted on a vehicle recording the road at usual speed, and an image processing system implemented in a computer. The goal of these systems is the detection and recognition of the traffic signs of the road. Some examples can be found in [1,2,3]. In [4], the image processing system consists of three steps, namely, the segmentation, detection and the recognition blocks. The objective of the segmentation block is the isolation of possible blobs which are candidates to be a traffic sign from the background. The output of this block is the list of connected components for each color mask. The block also performs a filtering of the blobs according to the size of its bounding box and area.

The detection block can be divided into two sub-blocks. The shape classification sub-block performs the identification of the shape of the blob comparing the signature of the blob (defined as the distance from the mass center to the edge of the blob as a function of the angle [5]) with the signature of the theoretical shapes of an equilateral triangle, a square and a circle. The main advantages of the implemented algorithm are its invariance to object translation, scaling, rotations and a great robustness to camera projection deformation. A complete description of this block can be found in [6]. The output is the blob list returned

J. Martí et al. (Eds.): IbPRIA 2007, Part II, LNCS 4478, pp. 540–547, 2007.

by the segmentation step updated with its estimated shape. The other sub-block achieves the localization of the shape. For a triangle and a rectangle, localization means the estimation of the position of its three or four vertices respectively. For a circle, it means the estimation of the coordinates of the center, the major and minor axes and the orientation of the major axis of the corresponding ellipse.

Finally, the recognition block performs the identification of the meaning of the sign according to its content. This is achieved using a series of Support Vector Machines (SVMs) trained with samples previously selected from each category. A complete description of the system can be found in [4]. In this paper, we will focus in the improvement of the localization sub-block, increasing the accuracy in estimating the position of the shapes. Since we are dealing with three different shapes, three different algorithms must be designed, one for each shape.

2 Shape Localization

Shape localization is a fundamental process when we are dealing with geometric distortions, like object rotation, scaling, shifts and projection deformation, for a correct performance of the recognition step. In most of the previous works found in the literature, including the one developed in this project, the recognition is based on a pixel wise comparison of the candidate blob with the reference samples previously stored. Here, comparison means the use of correlations, SVMs, neural networks or whatever other kind of classifier. This kind of algorithms is highly dependent on geometric distortions. Even a slight displacement of two pixels between the current blob and the samples can make the algorithm fail. For this reason, an accurate localization of the shape is needed for a proper operation of the recognition block. Once the shape has been localized, a planar affine transformation allows the system to place the blob on a reference position, undoing any possible geometric distortion. This transformation, called homography, is computed through a 2D Direct Linear Transformation (DLT) [7], and implies the design of three different algorithms, one for each shape.

2.1   Triangle and Rectangle Cases

For the triangle case, the three vertices of the triangle must be found. Our previous work tries to find these vertices directly from the signature of the blob previously computed for the shape classification task. As can be seen in Fig. 1, the vertices of the triangle match the three peaks of the signature. Therefore, a peak-search algorithm would be enough to find the position of the vertices. For the rectangle case, it is easy to see that the algorithm is essentially the same to the one designed for the triangle except from being 4 peaks instead of 3. Because of this, hereafter we will only describe the algorithm for triangular shapes, having into account that the algorithm for the rectangle is very similar.

Although this method is a good strategy in the theoretical case, as can be seen in Fig. 1, when applied to real images the results become very inaccurate. This is due to two main reasons. First of all, we rely on the information of only

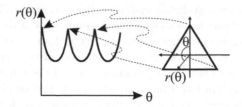

Fig. 1. Correspondences between the vertices and the peaks of the signature

one pixel, which can be corrupted with noise. Secondly, if an occlusion makes disappear one of the vertex, the estimated coordinates of the hidden vertex will be located at a very different position. We also need to have into account that the system does not yield sub-pixel precision, since the output of the algorithm is the position of the three pixels corresponding to the peaks of the signature.

The first problem may be overcome if we consider more than one pixel. Therefore, instead of determine directly the coordinates of the pixels corresponding to the vertices, we can estimate the parameters of the three straight lines which compose the triangle. This estimation can be performed using a number of pixels from the contour of the blob. The easiest way of doing this is using directly the samples of the signature. Considering that the three peaks of the signature have already been localized, all the pixels between two peaks compose one straight line. Using homogeneous coordinates [7], a point $\mathbf{x_i} = (x_i, y_i, 1)^T$ belongs to a straight line $\mathbf{l} = (l_a, l_b, l_c)^T$ if:

$$\left(x_i,\, y_i,\, 1 \right) \left(l_a,\, l_b,\, l_c \right)^T = 0 \,. \tag{1}$$

Stacking the equation for all the available points for a particular line, we get:

$$\mathbf{X} \cdot \mathbf{l} = \begin{pmatrix} x_1 & y_1 & 1 \\ x_2 & y_2 & 1 \\ \vdots & \vdots & \vdots \\ x_N & y_N & 1 \end{pmatrix} \left(l_a\ l_b\ l_c \right)^T = \mathbf{0} \,, \tag{2}$$

which implies the computation of the null-space of matrix $\mathbf{X}$. Since the number of rows of $\mathbf{X}$ is, in general, greater than two, and are affected by noise, (2) defines an over-determined system, and must be solved using some minimization techniques. Although the use of iterative geometric-distance minimization techniques should be used to get the most accurate solution, simple algebraic-distance minimization is accurate enough for our purpose, taking advance of its less computational complexity. Geometric-distance minimization is suitable in the presence of outliers, or when the data is highly affected by noise. Note, however, that in our case neither there are outliers nor the noise is high. Otherwise, the shape detection algorithm would have failed and none of this would make sense.

Before go on, at this point we can estimate the degree of confidence of the computed line. Computing the mean geometric error of the points according to:

$$e = \frac{1}{N} \sum_{i=1}^{N} \left| \frac{l_a x_i + l_b y_i + l_c}{\sqrt{l_a^2 + l_b^2}} \right| , \tag{3}$$

allows us to evaluate the degree of fitting of the list of points to the line. The mean geometric error of each line can be thresholded, and if one of the errors exceeds the given threshold, the blob can be considered as a false alarm. That is, the shape classification algorithm classified the blob as a triangle but, actually, the blob is not a triangle because it is not composed of straight lines, according to our threshold. Once the three lines of the triangle have been correctly obtained, the vertices of the triangle can be computed using:

$$\mathbf{x}_{ij} = \mathbf{l}_i \times \mathbf{l}_j = \begin{vmatrix} a & b & c \\ l_{ia} & l_{ib} & l_{ic} \\ l_{ja} & l_{jb} & l_{jc} \end{vmatrix} = \left(l_{ib}l_{jc} - l_{ic}l_{jb}, \, l_{ic}l_{ja} - l_{ia}l_{jc}, \, l_{ia}l_{jb} - l_{ib}l_{ja} \right) , \tag{4}$$

and so, the three vertices have been estimated. After this step, three (four in the rectangle case) points correspondences have been obtained, and the computation of the homography of the affine transformation between the current blob and the reference shape (an equilateral triangle of side 1 or a square of side 1), is straightforward using the standard DLT algorithm, as it is described in [7].

2.2 Circle Case

Although many algorithms have been described in the literature for fitting points to ellipses [8], they focus on the computation of the parameters of the ellipse. Our novel approach however computes directly the homography required for the re-orientation of the shape without any other extra computation. In our previous work we compute the parameters of the ellipse directly from the moments of the mask. The main drawback of this approach is that occlusions can modify the moments of the blob, mistaking the localization of the circle. Taking into account only blob contour pixels, or equivalently, the samples of the signature, instead of all pixels of the blob, we can improve considerably the accuracy. If we consider the ellipse as a conic [7], it can be described by a symmetric matrix of the form:

$$\mathbf{C} = \begin{bmatrix} a & b/2 & d/2 \\ b/2 & c & e/2 \\ d/2 & e/2 & f \end{bmatrix} , \tag{5}$$

with five degrees of freedom, accounted for the six elements of a symmetric matrix less one for scaling, and therefore, a minimum of 5 points are required to define an ellipse. Any point laying on the ellipse must fulfill:

$$\mathbf{x}_i^{\mathsf{T}} \mathbf{C} \mathbf{x}_i = 0 , \tag{6}$$

or equivalently:

$$\left(x_i^2, \, x_i y_i, \, y_i^2, \, x_i, \, y_i, \, 1 \right) \mathbf{c} = 0 \, , \tag{7}$$

where $\mathbf{c} = (a, b, c, d, e, f)^{\mathrm{T}}$ is the conic $\mathbf{C}$ represented as a 6-vector. Stacking the equation for all the available points of the signature of the blob we get the following system:

$$\begin{pmatrix} x_1^2 & x_1 y_1 & y_1^2 & x_1 & y_1 & 1 \\ x_2^2 & x_2 y_2 & y_2^2 & x_2 & y_2 & 1 \\ \vdots & \vdots & \vdots & \vdots & \vdots & \vdots \\ x_N^2 & x_N y_N & y_N^2 & x_N & y_N & 1 \end{pmatrix} \mathbf{c} = \mathbf{0} \, . \tag{8}$$

If the number of points N is greater than 5, (8) implies the computation of the null-space of an over-determined system, which can be solved easily using algebraic-distance minimization techniques. Once the conic $\mathbf{C}$ has been computed, the following step is the computation of a 2D homography which transforms the ellipse into a reference circle, of radius 0.5 centered at the coordinates origin, according to [7]:

$$\mathbf{C}' = \mathbf{H}^{-\mathrm{T}} \mathbf{C} \mathbf{H}^{-1} \, , \tag{9}$$

where $\mathbf{C}' = \mathrm{diag}\,(4, 4, -1)$ is the reference circle represented as a 3×3 diagonal matrix with diagonal entries 4, 4 and -1. Taking the inverse transformation, and decomposing $\mathbf{H}$ into a product of matrices:

$$\mathbf{C} = \mathbf{H}_R^{\mathrm{T}} \mathbf{H}_P^{\mathrm{T}} \mathbf{H}_D \mathbf{C}' \mathbf{H}_D \mathbf{H}_P \mathbf{H}_R \, , \tag{10}$$

where $\mathbf{H}_R$ is an orthogonal matrix. Furthermore $\mathbf{C} = \mathbf{H}_R^{\mathrm{T}} \mathbf{C}_D \mathbf{H}_R$, where $\mathbf{C}_D$ is a diagonal matrix, can be seen as the Singular Value Decomposition (SVD) of $\mathbf{C}$, which can be solved using standard SVD algorithms. Matrix $\mathbf{H}_P$ is a permutation matrix to ensure that $\mathbf{C}_D = \mathbf{H}_P^{\mathrm{T}} \mathbf{C}_E \mathbf{H}_P$, being $\mathbf{C}_E$ a diagonal matrix with entries e_{11} and e_{22} positive, and entry e_{33} negative. Finally, $\mathbf{H}_D$ is a diagonal matrix with entries:

$$d_{11} = \sqrt{e_{11}}/2; \quad d_{22} = \sqrt{e_{22}}/2; \quad d_{33} = \sqrt{-e_{33}} \, . \tag{11}$$

Matrix $\mathbf{H} = \mathbf{H}_D \mathbf{H}_P \mathbf{H}_R$ is then the 2D homography matrix which transforms the ellipse $\mathbf{C}$ into the reference circle $\mathbf{C}'$ of radius 0.5 centered at the origin of coordinates. We can measure the mean geometric error for all points of the signature according to:

$$e = \frac{1}{N} \sum_{i=1}^{N} |d\,(\mathbf{H}\mathbf{p}_i, \mathbf{0}) - 0.5| \, , \tag{12}$$

where $d\,(\mathbf{x}_1, \mathbf{x}_2)$ is the euclidean distance between points $\mathbf{x}_1$ and $\mathbf{x}_2$, $\mathbf{x}' = \mathbf{H}\mathbf{x}_i$ are the original points of the signature mapped to the reference plane, $\mathbf{0}$ are the coordinates of the circle center (0,0), and 0.5 is the radius of the circle. The mean geometric error, then, can be thresholded to discard false alarms.

3   Experimental Results

The algorithm described in this paper was implemented using VC++ 6.0, taking as input the results of the shape detection algorithm of the traffic sign recognition system developed in our project. This input comprises the kind of shape (i.e. triangle, square or circle) and the 64-sampled signature of the blob. The output will be the 3×3 matrix corresponding to the 2D planar affine transformation. Since the goal of this section is the evaluation of the accuracy in locating the parameters of the shape, the evaluation is different for each kind of shape. Although the whole system can work with real images, in this section we are going to evaluate errors between the estimated position and the real one, which implies that we must know the real position of the shape. Since this would be impossible for real images, even it we did it by hand, we finally decided to generate synthetic figures, obviously with known position, to this end.

For the triangle case, we constructed a synthetic triangle with known vertices, $v = \{\mathbf{p}_1, \mathbf{p}_2, \mathbf{p}_3\}$, or equivalently, composed of the lines $\mathbf{l}_{ij} = \mathbf{p}_i \times \mathbf{p}_j$ for $i, j = (1, 2), (2, 3), (3, 1)$. If the vertices of the triangle are defined clockwise, a pixel of the image belongs to the triangle if its scalar product with the three lines $\mathbf{l}_{ij}$ is negative for all lines, that is $\mathbf{l}_{ij}^{\mathrm{T}} \mathbf{p} < 0$ for $\mathbf{l}_{12}, \mathbf{l}_{23}$ and $\mathbf{l}_{31}$. To simulate the effect of the noise introduced by the camera, we generated a random distance d_n of gaussian probability with zero mean and particular standard deviation, so that a point finally belongs to the triangle if $\mathbf{l}_{ij}^{\mathrm{T}} \mathbf{p} + d_n < 0$ for the three lines. With a further close operation (i.e. an erosion followed by a dilation) finally we get a mask very similar to that we would obtain from a real noisy camera. In Fig. 2(a) and (b) we can see some examples for different values of the standard deviation of the random distance d_n. The construction of noisy rectangles is similar than the one for triangles, except that four vertices are needed instead of three. Figure 2(a) and (b) shows some examples.

We have also evaluated the performance of the algorithm in the presence of slight occlusions. To this end, we manually delete some parts of a triangle

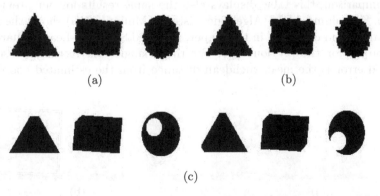

(a)   (b)

(c)

Fig. 2. Examples of shapes generated for evaluation: (a-b) Noisy shapes with standard deviation of d_n equal to: (a) 2 pixels, (b) 4 pixels. (c) Partially hidden shapes.

Table 1. Comparison between ADM (Algebraic-Distance Minimization), and NLSM (Non-Least Square Minimization) algorithms. In (a), σ is the standard deviation for random distance d_n. The results shown are the mean error distance measured in pixels.

	ADM			NLSM		
σ (pixels)	1	2	4	1	2	4
Triangle	1.06	1.50	1.92	2.85	3.00	5.29
Rectangle	1.03	1.56	2.17	1.56	2.96	4.92
Ellipse	1.21	1.78	2.16	1.47	2.23	4.18

(a) Results for noisy samples

	ADM	NLSM
Triangle	2.28	6.84
Rectangle	3.22	5.10
Ellipse	2.15	5.36

(b) Results for occlusion samples

or rectangle with known vertices, as can be seen in Fig. 2(c). We have paid attention specially to occlusions in the vertices, since occlusions in the straight parts of the shape do not cause any problem neither in the detection nor in the localization of the shape. The occlusion must be slight since quite strong occlusion would make the shape classification algorithm fail. Generally, most of the shape classification algorithms described in the literature fail in the presence of important occlusions.

The circle localization accuracy has been also evaluated. In this case, an ellipse with random noise can be constructed from:

$$f(x,y) = \sqrt{(x - x_c)^2 + \left(\frac{y - y_c}{k}\right)^2} - r + d_n \,, \tag{13}$$

where (x_c, y_c) is the center of the ellipse, r is the major semi-axis and kr the minor semi-axis with $0 < k < 1$, and d_n is a random distance with particular standard deviation. A pixel belongs to the ellipse if $f(x,y)$ in (13) is negative. Figure 2(a) and (b) show some examples of ellipses with different standard deviation for parameter d_n. We have also evaluated the effect of occlusions on ellipses. In Fig. 2(c) are shown some occlusion examples for ellipses.

In Table 1 the accuracy results of the proposed method are shown. To make some comparison, this table displays also the same results for our previous algorithm. So, column ADM (Algebraic-Distance Minimization) shows the results for the algorithm described in this paper, while NLSM (Non-Least Square Minimization) is for the previous one. For the triangle and rectangle cases, the measured error is the mean euclidean distance from the estimated coordinates

(a)   (b)

Fig. 3. Results using real images

of each vertex $\mathbf{p}'_i$ of the triangle or rectangle to the true one $\mathbf{p}_i$. For the circle case, the measured error is the mean of the sum of the euclidean distance from the coordinates of the center of the estimated ellipse to the true one, plus the difference in distance between both the estimated axes and the true ones.

Finally, in Fig. 3 some examples for a triangle, a circle and a rectangle using real images are shown to test the performance of the whole system in real environments. In Fig. 3(a), the real images are shown, while (b) corresponds with the output of the detection block printed over the original images.

4 Conclusion

This paper describes a method to accurately localize the position of a traffic sign within the image. Accurate localization is fundamental for a successful achievement of the sign recognition. The accuracy is reached using algebraic-distance minimization techniques applied to the samples of the signature of the blob. Comparison with our previous work shows a great improvement in accuracy, specially in the presence of occlusions. From the evaluation of the whole system, the work described here has proved to be accurately enough when working in outdoor normal conditions, such as sunny days, rain or at night.

Acknowledgments. This work was supported by the project of the Ministerio de Educación y Ciencia de España number TEC2004/03511/TCM.

References

1. de la Escalera, A., Armingol, J.M., Mata, M.: Traffic sign recognition and analysis for intelligent vehicles. Image and Vision Computing 21, 247–258 (2003)
2. Janssen, R., Ritter, W., Stein, F., Ott, S.: Hybrid approach for traffic sign recognition. In: IEEE International Conference on Intelligen Vehicles, pp. 390–397. IEEE, NJ, New York (1993)
3. Ritter, W.: Traffic sign recognition in color image sequences. In: Intelligent Vehicles Symposium, Detroit, USA, pp. 12–17. IEEE, NJ, New York (1992)
4. Maldonado, S., Lafuente, S., Gil, P., Gómez, H., López, F.: Road-sign detection and recognition based on support vector machines. IEEE Trans. on Intelligent Transportation Systems (Accepted) (2005)
5. González, R., Woods, R.: Digital Image Proccesing. Addison-Wesley, London (1993)
6. Gil-Jiménez, P., Lafuente-Arroyo, S., Gomez-Moreno, H., López-Ferreras, F., Maldonado-Bascón, S.: Traffic sign shape classification evaluation II: FFT applied to the signature of blobs. In: Proc. IEEE Intelligent Vehicles Symposium, Las Vegas, USA, pp. 607–612 (2005)
7. Hartley, R., Zisermann, A.: Multiple view geometry in computer vision, 2nd edn. Cambridge University Press, Cambridge (2003)
8. Gander, W., Golub, G.H., Strebel, R.: Least-squares fitting of circles and ellipses. BIT 34, 558–578 (1994)

Modeling Aceto-White Temporal Patterns to Segment Colposcopic Images

Héctor-Gabriel Acosta-Mesa[1], Nicandro Cruz-Ramírez[1],
Rodolfo Hernández-Jiménez[2], and Daniel-Alejandro García-López[1]

[1] Faculty of Physics and Artificial Intelligence, Department of Artificial Intelligence,
University of Veracruz, Sebastián Camacho # 5, 91000, Xalapa, Ver. México
{heacosta,ncruz}@uv.mx, dalexgarcia@gmail.com
[2] Obstetrician and Gynaecologist, Diego Leño # 22, C.P. 91000, Xalapa, Ver. México

Abstract. Colposcopy test is the second most used technique to diagnose cervical cancer disease. Some researchers have proposed to use temporal changes intrinsic to the colposcopic image sequences to automatically characterize cervical lesion. Under this approach, every single pixel on the image is represented as a Time Series of length equal to the sampling frequency times acquisition points. Although this approach seems to show promising results, the data analysis procedures have to deal with huge data set that rapidly increase with the number of cases (patients) considered in the analysis. In the present work, we perform principal component analysis (PCA) to reduce the dimensionality of the data in order to facilitate similarity measures for classification and clustering. The importance of this work is that we propose a model to parameterize the dynamics of the system using an efficient representation getting a 1.11% data compression ratio and similarity on clustering of 0.78. The feasibility of the proposed model is shown testing the similarity of the clusters generated using the k-means algorithm over the raw data and the compressed representation of real data.

1 Introduction

Cervical cancer is one of the most common cancers affecting women. If it is detected early, the probability of cure is very high. After Pap smear test, colposcopy is the most used technique to diagnose this disease because, although it is more economically expensive, it has a higher sensitivity and specificity [1, 2]. Basically, the colposcopic test consists of the evaluation of the level of white color intensity that the cervical tissue reaches after acetic acid application. Some researchers have suggested to use the temporal patterns intrinsic to the color changes [7-9], but as far as we know, at the time in which this publication was made, there is not a complete understanding of how to represent the dynamic of the whitening occurred after acetic acid application and how to use these temporal patterns to automatically segment the image, far from only subtracting images before and after acetic acid application [7, 8]. Moreover, none of the Time Series Data Mining methods has been used to approach this application.

J. Martí et al. (Eds.): IbPRIA 2007, Part II, LNCS 4478, pp. 548–555, 2007.
© Springer-Verlag Berlin Heidelberg 2007

In the present work we propose a methodology analysis to segment the colposcopic image using the temporal changes regarding reflection of light in tissue, that is the essence of the analysis made by the colposcopist. The hypothesis is that not only color changes are important to categorize the lesion, but also, the temporal component of this change (dynamics) is important to be considered in the analysis. The importance of this work is that we propose a model to parameterize the dynamics of the system and a way to segment the image with respect to these parameters.

2 Materials and Methods

2.1 Subject Preparation

Six women with abnormal Papanicolaou, aged from 22 to 35 years participated in the experiment. All of them gave informed written consent. Before colposcopy, the cervical mucus was cleaned using a cotton-wool swabs. The colposcopic tests were made spreading three milliliters of acetic acid (3%) over the cervix using a needle for fast application. A cotton-wool was put in the low part of the cervix to absorb the remaining acetic acid that drops after the application. A leg-holder structure was used to make the patient feel comfortable and to reduce movements. After colposcopy, a biopsy was taken for histological analysis and PCR test [10].

2.2 Data Acquisition

Images were acquired using a colposcope dfv Vasconsellos model CP-M7 with magnification 16 X without any optical filter. The viewing distance was 20 cm. Images were acquired using a color camera Sony SSC-DC50A and a frame grabber Matrox Meteor-II/Standard driven by a HP workstation XW6000 running Matlab 7.0 image acquisition toolbox. During the first ten seconds of the image acquisition 10 images (640x480) were taken as base line reference (1 frame/second), then after acetic acid application, three hundred and sixty images were taken in 6 minutes using the same sampling frequency. Control images taken at the beginning of each trial have a double purpose, the first one is to have a base reference to assess the signal percentage of change and the second one is to estimate the amount of signal noise. Each image was saved independently as a BMP file. In order to simplify the image analysis the images were processed in gray scale.

3 Data Analysis

Our data consist of a sequence of 2D images of the reflectance of the surface of the cervix taken over a period of time, before and after acetic acid application.

The colposcopic image sequence can be represented as a sequence of t 2D images $I_t(x,y)$ with acquisition time t with $t < t+1$. The color variation over time of each pixel in the image provides a time series. The resulting image sequence can be viewed as a 3D image block $I(x,y,t)$ defined on the spatio-temporal domain. The methodology proposed in this paper to analyze the colposcopic sequences involves 3 main processes: preprocessing, feature extraction and classification. Those processes are explained in detail in the following sections.

3.1 Preprocessing

The acquisition process of colposcopic images spans over 6 minutes and even though that the patient is fixed some small random movements are unavoidable. They have often local character (patient's breathing, movements due to the muscle tonus etc.). To be able to analyze the sequence of the images, i.e. compare and evaluate corresponding structures, the structures in the images should be brought into the same position by removing the differences due to the patient movements - the colposcopic images have to be registered. This step is very important in this application, the goal of the 2D image spatial alignment, is to enable comparison between corresponding anatomical positions. There are various registration methods, a good overview can be found in [11] or in [12]. Medical registration methods are covered in more detail for example in [13]. The appropriate method has to be chosen with respect to the expected geometric differences and the type of processed data. Our previous experimental assessment suggests that the main source of the misalignments in colposcopic sequences can be modeled by simple translation. The method can transform the whole data using the same parameters, or can be local, depending on the local variations. It can be based directly on the image intensity values (area-based methods) or can be done using some features computed from the images (feature-based methods). Because colposcopic images do not contain many distinctive details, an area-based method was chosen. The classical representative of the area-based methods is the normalized cross-correlation (CC), this method exploits for matching directly image intensities, this measure of similarity is computed for window pairs from the input and reference images and its maximum is searched [12].

The input and the reference images are actualized continuously starting with the first and second images of the sequence respectively, then the input and the reference images are redefined by the second and the third images and so on. The starting points to initialize the search are updated by the last position in which the pattern window was found. This registration strategy allows not only to contend with the fact that the searched pattern changes over time, but also, to reduce the spatial space over which to develop the search. Because cervical lesions are spread over the tissue as regions (forming areas with homogeneous tissue), a high spatial resolution is not needed. Then after registration the spatial resolution was reduced at 20% of the original size. The intensity value of each pixel over time was used to construct a time series, which we call, the Aceto-white response function (Awrf).

3.2 Parametric Modeling

Time Series Data Mining (TSDM) is a very active area of research interested in the preprocessing, representation, and interpretation of temporal data stored in a data base. More specifically, this area of research investigates efficient representations of time series, change point detection, and similarity measures for time series classification and clustering [14]. A colposcopic data set can be seen as a time series data base, the segmentation task consists of finding the similar temporal patterns with regular shapes. The shape of the Awrf is determined by the aceto white dynamical process occurred on tissue. The most frequently used methods in TSDM are techniques that perform dimensionality reduction on the data, then use this compact representation to show the data in a parameter space, facilitating similarity search and clustering. Some goodnesses of the time series transformation are data compression, temporal smooth, outliers detection and feature extraction among others.

The most used time series representations reported in the literature are Discrete Fourier Transforms (DFT), Discrete Wavelet Transforms (DWT), Principal Component Analysis (PCA), Dynamic Time Warping (DTW), Clipped representations, Polynomial Models, Picewise Linear Approximations (PLA) and Symbolic Aggregate Approximations (SAX). The appropriate technique to use depends on the particular application [15, 16]. For the application reported in this work and because we are interested in a data adaptive model representation, the Principal Component Analysis (PCA) technique was used. PCA is a multivariate statistical method which, given a set of correlated variables, finds a reduced set of orthogonal variables (principal components) from which the observations can be explained as a linear combination [17]. This transformation can be thought of as a data rotation such that maximum variabilities are projected onto certain axes called eigenvectors. After data rotation, the eigenvectors can be ordered with respect to the data variability that each one explains (*eigenvalues*). The m-th eigenvalue λ_m represents the variance of data along the m-th principal eigenvector v_m. Since most of the data can be explained in terms of the linear combination of the firsts eigenvectors, PCA is used as a dimensionality reduction method. For our application, each Awrf can be represented as a discrete-time multivariable stochastic system.

$$Awrf = \alpha_1 G_1 + \alpha_2 G_2 + ... + \alpha_n G_n + \varepsilon \qquad (1)$$

Where G are the orthogonal axes and α are the projections of data over those axes, plus some differences (ε) than can not be explained by the regresors. The colposcopic set of images can be thought of as a spatiotemporal data matrix. Let $\mathbf{Awrf}(m,n,t)$ represent a stack of t images of size (m,n). Thus there are $(m*n)$ pixels, each of which is a time series of length t. Let $p(i,j)$ represent the colour of the pixel (i,j), i=1, ..., m, j=1, ..., n. The PCA can be carried out by treating each image as a variable and each pixel as an observation. The objective of the analysis is to find the set matrix $\mathbf{G}$ which explains the $\mathbf{Awrf}$ volume in order to reduce the dimensionality of the data. Using this compressed representation, every single Awrf can be approximated through a linear regression of the data on the principal components.

This model not only reduces the dimensionality of the data, but also provides a feature vector on which a similarity measures can be done to facilitate time series clustering and image segmentation. Additionally, it can be used as a temporal low pass filter.

3.3 Image Segmentation

Given the parametric model obtained from using PCA, a parametric fashion repre sentation can be used to visualize the colposcopic image as a parametric Maps. Parameters can be computed using the General Linear Model [17], in which:

$$Awrf = \alpha G + \varepsilon \qquad (2)$$

Where **Awrfs** is the spatiotemporal data matrix, **G** is the design matrix (for our case is represented by k first principal components computed as explained above), α is the parameter matrix corresponding to the projections of **Awrf** in **G**, and ε is the error. Parameter estimation can be done using least square:

$$\alpha = \frac{G^T Awrf}{G^T G} \qquad (3)$$

Once the parameters have been computed, they can be used as a features to segments the image according with the different temporal patterns represented by the values of α. The fitted model can be easily recovered using (2). The goodness of fit of the model can be assessed comparing the signal noise with the error (ε) computed as the difference between the Awrf and its model.

3.3.1 Clipped Representation

Colposcopic image sequences can contain outliers due to errors in the registration process or due to illumination inhomogeneities in the surroundings, so knowing the characteristic shape expected from the data, a generic representation can be used as a lower bounding estimator to make an early detection of outliers. The dynamics of the system can be captured through the rate of change on the Awrf, it is assessed using the first derivative which is equivalent to the instantaneous velocity:

$$Awrf' = \frac{d_{Awrf}}{dt} = \frac{Awrf(t + \Delta t) - Awrf(t)}{\Delta t} \qquad (4)$$

For analytical purposes the Awrf can be divided in two sets: the "upwards" part and the "downwards" part. The first part ($Awrf' > 0$) represents that the signal reaches the maximum level at some time from the base line and the second one, represents the dynamics of how the signal goes back from the maximum to the base line ($Awrf' < 0$).

Clipped representation serves as a mean of outlier detection and a method of identifying model misspecification through the use of learned constraints, rather than use the raw data, we used the local derivatives computed as velocities [18, 19]. Where clipped(i) = 1 if Awrf(i)' > 0 or clipped(i) = 0 if Awrf(i)' < 0. Under this representation, Run Length Encoding (RLE) can be used to get a compressed representation of the Awrf [20]. RLE is a compressed form to represent binary sequences, under this representation the number of consecutive positions (bits) with the same value are counted to form a vector of $n+1$ positions, where the first element represents the parity bit, i.e. [1, $x_1, x_2 \ldots, x_n$]. Using RLE clipped representation the outlier detection can be done using *apriori* constrains known about the Awrf expected shape [21].

4 Results

Image registration was made using the cross-correlation technique explained above [23]. The search window was defined selecting a region feature over which some anatomical features show high contrast boundaries, e.g. cervical hole. For the lack of space, motion correction results are not shown, see [23]. Once the data set was registered, PCA was applied to the database conformed by the volumes of the six subjets included in this study. The four principal components were selected to explain the 98.78% of the variance (figure 1). This transformation provides a data compression ratio of 1.11% (4/360).

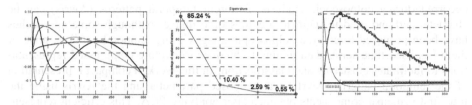

Fig. 1. Principal component analysis. At the left are shown the first four eigenvectors obtained after to apply PCA. Their corresponding eigenvalues shows the percentage of variance explained by each of them (meddle). At the right, an Awrf is presented in blue with its corresponding fitted model in red. Clipped representation is also shown on this graph.

Although the nature of this application requires to use a supervised learning algorithm to learn from the expert the classification criteria, as an exploratory analysis to investigate the viability to use the proposed model to represent the raw data, an unsupervised learning algorithm (k-means) was used to compare the similarity of the clusters obtained using raw data versus those obtained using model parameters. The algorithm was run asking to form two clusters (k=2) suggested by the expert (colposcopist). The input of the algorithm was the observations (n*m), represented as a raw data or as a feature vector of parameters (α). The criteria defined in [22] was used to measure the similarity between the clusters found using both data bases. The similarity measure is computed following the formula:

$$Sim(C_i^r, C_j^p) = \frac{|C_i^r \cap C_j^p|}{|C_i^r| + |C_j^p|}$$

(5)

and

$$Sim(C^r, C^p) = \left(\sum_i \max_j Sim_j\left(C_i^r, C_j^p\right)\right)$$

(6)

Where C^r refers to raw data (complete time series) and C^p refers to the compressed representation proposed. This similarity measure will return 0 if the two clusterings are completely dissimilar and 1 y they are the same. The algorithm was run 10 times per each data set. Table 1 shows the average values obtained per each patient.

Table 1. Similarity results obtained doing clustering over raw data against feature vectors expressed as parametric values obtained using (3). The number of clusters (k) used to run k-mean algorithm over each patient (P) was suggested by the expert.

	P1,k=2	P2,k=2	P3,k=2	P4,k=2	P5,k=2	P6,k=3
Similarity	0.58	0.71	0.88	0.82	0.96	0.70

5 Conclusion and Future Work

Preliminary results using 6 data sets, show that different acetowhite temporal patterns can be discriminated using the temporal information intrinsic to the change of color occurred during colposcopic analysis. Different temporal patterns (Awrfs) can be characterized and used to segment a colposcopic image. Although some approaches have been proposed to analyze colposcopic images using temporal patterns, none of them has used time series data mining techniques to explore compressed representations to facilitates clustering and classification. In this work, a compact representation of the temporal patterns (Awrfs) was proposed parameterising the Awrfs using the four first principal components obtained after applying PCA. This efficient representation can approximate and store the raw data with a compression ratio less than 2% and acceptable similarity results when compared against raw data (0.78). It was shown that the clipped representation of the first derivative is a good signature to detect outliers. Our results about the segmentation obtained using the k-means algorithm suggests that automatic segmentation can be possible. However, it is necessary to train a supervised algorithm in order to correlate the Awrf parameters with the class of lesion. As a continuation of this work we are working with a group of colposcopist experts who are manually segmenting the images and to explore other time series representations. Using this information we are going to be able to train a supervised algorithm under the structure proposed in [23], to automatically associate the Awrf with precancerous cervical lesions.

References

1. Erich Burghardt, H.P., Girardi, F.: Primary care Colposcopy, (ed.) Thieme, pp. 167 (2004)
2. Ronne, M.: Chromosome preparation and high resolution banding techniques. Dairy of Science, pp. 363–1377 (1989)
3. Craine, B.L., Cynthia, E.R.C., O'Toole, J., Ji, Q.: Digital Imaging Colposcopy: Corrected Area Measurements Using Shape-from-Shading. IEEE Transactions on Medi-cal Imaging 17(6), 1003–1010 (1998)
4. Anne-Thérèse, V. M., Richards-Kortum, R.: PhD, Andres Zuluaga, PhD, and Michele Follen, MD, PhD, New approaches to cervivcal cancer screening. Contem-porary Ob/Gyn, pp. 87–103 (2002)
5. Claude, I., Huault, S., Boulanger, C.: Integred Color and Texture Tools For Colposcopic Image Segmentation. IEEE Transactions on Medical Imag-ing (2001)
6. Ji, Q., E, J., Craine, E.: Texture Analysis for Classification of Cervix Lesions. IEEE Transactions on Medical Imaging 19(11), 1144–1149 (2000)
7. Balas, C.: Novel Optical Imaging Method for the Early Detection, Quantitative Grading, and Mapping of Cancerous and Precancerous Lesions of Cervix. IEEE Transactions in Biomedical Engineering 48(1), 96–104 (2001)
8. Stefanaki, I., et al.: In Vivo Detection of Human Papilloma Virus-Induced Lesions of Anogenital Area after Application of Acetic Acid: a Novel and Accurate Approach to a Trivial Method. Journal of Photochemistry and Photobiology 65, 115–121 (2001)
9. Pogue, B., et al.: Analysis of Acetic Acid-induced Whitening of High-grade Squamous Intra-epitelial Lesions. Journal of Biomedical Optics 6(4), 397–403 (2001)

10. Anderson, M., j, A.M., Sharp, F.: A Text and Atlas of Integrated Colposcopy. Mosby (1993)
11. Brown, L.G.: A survey of Image Registration Techniques, pp. 1–60 (1992)
12. Zitova Barbara, F.J.: Image Registration Methods: a Survey. Image and vision computing (2004)
13. Hill, D.L.: Medical Image Registration. Physics in Medicine and Biology 1(46), R1–R45 (2001)
14. Last, M., Kandel, A., Bunke, H.: Data Mining in Time Series Databases. World Scientific, Singapore (2004)
15. Keogh, E., et al.: Dimensionality Reduction for Fast Sililarity Search in Large Time Series Databases. Knowledge and Information System 3(3), 263–286 (2000)
16. Keogh, E., Ratanamahatana, C.: Exact Indexing of Dynamic Time Warping. Knowledge and Information Systems. In: Proceedings of the 28th International Conference on Very Large Data Bases, pp. 406–417 (2004)
17. Tabachnick, Using Multivarieate Statistics. Fourth ed, A.a. Bacon. (ed.): Allyn and Bacon (2001)
18. Keogh, E., Ratanamahatana, C.: Making Time-series Classification More Accurate Using Learned Constraints. In: Proceedings of hte SIAM International Conference on Data Mining, pp. 11–22 (2004)
19. Ratanamahatana, C., et al.: A Novel Bit Level Time Series Representation with Implications for Similarity Search and Clustering. Data Mining and Knowledge Discovery (accepted for publication) (2005)
20. Gonzalez, C., Woods, R., Eddins, S.: Digital image processing. Prentice-Hall, Englewood Cliffs (2004)
21. Keogh, E., Pazzani, M.: Dynamic Time Warping with Higher Order Features. In: First SIAM International Conference on Data Mining (2001)
22. Larsen, B., Aone, C.: Fast and effective text mining using linear-time document clustering. In: Zaki, M.J., Ho, C.-T. (eds.) Large-Scale Parallel Data Mining. LNCS (LNAI), vol. 1759, pp. 16–22. Springer, Heidelberg (2000)
23. Acosta-Mesa Héctor-Gabriel, Z.B., Ríos-Figueroa, H., Cruz-Ramírez, N., Marín-Hernández, A., Hernández-Jiménez, R., Cocotle-Ronzón, B., Hernández Galicia, E.: Cervical Cancer Detection Using colposcopic Images: a Temporal Approach. In: Proceedings of the Sixth International Conference on Computer Science, pp. 158–164. IEEE Computer Society Press, Washington 0-7695-2454-0 / 1550-4069 (2005)

Speech/Music Classification Based on Distributed Evolutionary Fuzzy Logic for Intelligent Audio Coding

J.E. Muñoz Expósito, N. Ruiz Reyes, S. Garcia Galán, and P. Vera Candeas

Telecommunication Engineering Department, University of Jaén
Polytechnic School, C/ Alfonso X el Sabio 28, 23700 Linares, Jaén, Spain

Abstract. Automatic Speech/Music Discrimination (SMD) has become a research topic of interest in the last years. This paper present a new approach for such goal, which is mainly based on a distributed expert system that incorporates fuzzy rules into its knowledge base. The proposed SMD scheme consists of two stages: 1) features extraction, 2) classification of parameters. Classification is performed by cascading a GMM-based classifier with an Evolutionary Fuzzy Expert (EFE) system. The EFE system improves the accuracy rate provided by the GMM-based classifier taking into account information of current and past audio frames. Testing the kindness of new fuzzy rules for the expert system has a high computacional cost. For that reason, a distributed learning approach based on web services has been implemented.

1   Introduction

There are several situations that can benefit from efficient SMD. This tool can be used to perform a content-based selection of broadcast programs [1]. An example of this kind of application is the selection of radio stations that are actually playing music. The SMD is also a basic part in Automatic Speech Recognition (ASR) [2][3] and Automatic Music Transcription (AMT) [4], which often need to analyze unstructured or unknown audio data. In the case of ASR, only speech segments must be considered, whereas AMT must process only music excerpts. Modern hearing-aid devices often include algorithms that change the operation of the devices according to the type of sound that reaches the ear [5]. Finally, another application that can benefit from distinguishing speech from music is low bit-rate audio coding. A challenging approach is to design a multi-mode coder that can accommodate different signals. The appropriate module is selected using SMD [6]. For all applications, it is important that the signal be segmented properly before being submitted to the corresponding tool.

Soft Computing [7][8] is a methodology with high uncertainty tolerance. It includes, among other issues, fuzzy logic, evolutionary computation, neural networks and probabilistic reasoning. Using partial truths, the behavior of the involved systems is improved with a reasonable computational cost. Concretely, fuzzy logic controllers [9] are expert systems which incorporate human knowledge in its knowledge bases using fuzzy rules [7][10]. One of the most important

J. Martí et al. (Eds.): IbPRIA 2007, Part II, LNCS 4478, pp. 556–563, 2007.

features of this kind of expert systems is its facility or working in uncertainty environments (classification, systems modelling, control systems, robotics,...). Evolutionary computation constitutes a class of search and optimization methods which imitates the principles of natural evolution [11].

Finally, web services [12] are modular applications that can be published, located and invoked from any part of the Web or within any local network based on Internet standards. Software systems may interact with web services in a way prescribed by its definition, using XML-based messages conveyed by Internet protocols.

This work deals with SMD based on an EFE system for intelligent audio coding (a suitable audio coder is selected every 23 ms according to the decision of the expert system). We propose to cascade a standard Statistical Pattern Recognition (SPR) classifier with the EFE system in order to improve the classification accuracy rate. Furthermore, the knowledge base for the EFE system is obtained in a distributed way using web services technology with the aim at reducing the associated computational cost. For testing the proposed approach, we have considered some commonly used timbral features.

2 Speech/Music Discrimination

Speech/music discrimination involves a suitable processing for two main tasks: audio feature extraction and classification of the extracted parameters. Five commonly used timbral features are considered for assessing the proposed SMD scheme. It assumes that classification is performed by cascading a SPR classifier with an EFE system. A decision is taken every 23 ms from the features extracted during the last one second. The intelligent audio coder chooses the suitable coder every 23 ms according to the decision of the cascaded classifier. The proposed scheme is represented in figure 1.

2.1 Analysis Stage: Features Extraction

The literature describes a wide variety of features that can be used to classify audio segments. Comparative view of different types of features in speech music discrimination is provided in [13][14], where different types of features are compared for discriminating speech and music signals. Mel Frequencies Spectral or Cepstral Coefficients (MFSC or MFCC) are very often used features for audio classification tasks, providing quite good results. MFCC [3] are a compact representation of the spectrum of an audio signal taking into account the nonlinear human perception of pitch, as described by the Mel scale. They are one of the most used features in speech recognition and its use to separate speech and music has recently been explored in [15].

The first step of the feature extraction process is the division of the signal into frames, which is performed using a Hanning window of 23 ms, with an overlap of 50% between consecutive frames. The signals used in this work are sampled at 44.1 kHz, resulting in frames of 1024 samples. In our approach, each 23 ms-length Hanning-windowed frame is called *analysis frame*. We also define frames

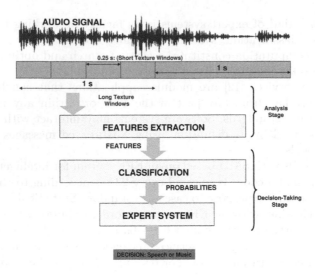

Fig. 1. SMD general scheme for intelligent audio coding

of 1 second and 250 ms, which are called *long texture frames* and *short texture frames*, respectively. Note that each long texture frame of 1 seconds contains 43 analysis frames. Taking overlapping into account, the vector for describing each considered feature, when using long texture frames, consists of 85 values, which are updated every 23 ms. This large dimensional feature vector is difficult to be handled for classification tasks. Therefore, it is required to reduce the feature space to a few statistical values. In this work, the mean and variance of each feature vector are only computed.

Once the feature extraction process has been described, we focus on the features to be extracted. In this paper, the following timbral features are considered: Mel Frequencies Cepstral Coefficients (MFCC), Spectral Centroid (SC), Spectral Rolloff (SR), Spectral Flux (SF) and Time Domain Zero Crossings (ZC) are used. Analysis comparative between them is provided in section 3.

2.2   Classification Stage: Gaussian Mixture Model-Based Classifier

For classification purposes, a number of standard SPR classifiers [16] have been evaluated. The basic idea behind SPR is to estimate the probability density function (pdf) for the feature vectors of each class. In the simple Gaussian (GS) classifier, each pdf is assumed to be a multidimensional Gaussian distribution whose parameters are estimated using a labelled training set. In the Gaussian Mixture Model (GMM) classifier, each class pdf is assumed to consist of a mixture of a specific number K of multidimensional Gaussian distributions. Unlike the k-NN classifier, which needs to store all the training feature vectors in order to compute the distances to the input feature vector, the GMM classifier only needs to store the set of estimated parameters for each class. The iterative

Expectation-Maximization (EM) algorithm is used to estimate the parameters of each Gaussian component and the mixture weights.

In this work a three-component GMM classifier with diagonal covariance matrices is used because it has showed a slightly better performance than other SPR classifiers. The performance of the system does not improve when using a higher number of components in the GMM classifier. The GMM classifier is initialized using the K-means algorithm with multiple random starting points. Modern classification techniques, such as Neural Networks (NN), Support Vector Machines (SVM), and dynamic programming, could also be used. Other statistical techniques, such as Hidden Markov Models (HMMs) and n-grams could be of interest to deal with the classification based on sequences. We decided to use standard SPR classifiers because this work is mainly focussed on SMD for intelligent audio coding using an EFS system.

2.3 Classification Stage: Evolutionary Expert Fuzzy System

We are interested in discriminating between speech and music for intelligent audio coding. A suitable coder must be selected each 23 ms-length analysis frame according to the decision of the SMD system (i.e. a HVXC coder can be applied to speech frames, whereas the ACC coder is used for music frames). If the audio coder selection is only based on current analysis frame data, the GMM classifier obtains low success rate. It is very important to assure a robust performance of the SMD scheme for intelligent audio coding. Hence, we propose to cascade the 3-GMM classifier with an EFE system for selecting the suitable coder every 23 ms. The EFE system takes into account information not only of the current frame but also of past frames. The inclusion of the evolutionary fuzzy system within the classification stage produces an improvement on the classification accuracy rate regarding the case of only using the GMM classifier, as shown in section 3.

How does the EFE system take the final decision?. The EFE system takes the final decision from four input parameters. The input parameters (p_0, p_1, p_2 and p_3) represent the probabilities obtained by the 3-GMM classifier for the last four consecutive 250 ms-length short texture frames. The last of them includes the current 23 ms-length analysis frame, as shown in figure 2. Using these probabilities and a knowledge base, the EFE system selects the suitable coder (a coder adapted to speech or music) for intelligent audio coding. The general structure of the EFE system appears in figure 2.

All inputs has been calculated using the 3-GMM classifier from the mean and variance of the vector associated to each 250 ms-length short texture frame. This vector consists of the considered feature values computed for all 23 ms-length analysis frames contained within the corresponding 250 ms-length short texture frame. All probabilities range from 0 to 1. There is only one output variable, called *Coder*, which also ranges from 0 to 1. If the output value is higher than 0.5, a speech coder is selected. Otherwise, a music coder is selected.

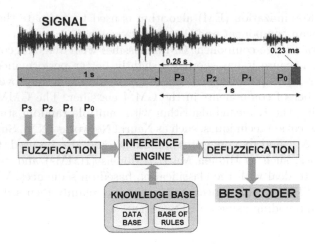

Fig. 2. EFE system general structure

How is the knowledge base obtained?. The new rules added to the knowledge of the EFE system base have been calculated using evolutionary computation. The learning algorithm is based on random rules generation with consequent mutation. A new rule is incorporated into the knowledge base whether an improvement in the classification accuracy rate is achieved when the EFE system takes that rule into account. The learning process for the EFE system uses different audio signals with an approximated duration of 1000 seconds, which implies a high computational cost.

To reduce the high computacional cost derived from building the knowledge base, a distributed learning process based on web services technology is proposed. In this sense, two approaches have been explored: 1) each computer evaluates a different rule; 2) each rule is evaluated in a distributed way. The first approach involves a synchronization mechanism for the rules, because they are evaluated in different environments. In the second approach each computer processes a certain audio fragment according to its computation power. Since the second approach is more simple, it has been chosen in this work. The audio signal is divided in so many parts as computers (*agents*) have the web services provider. Hence, each agent does a partial evaluation of the rule behavior. The agents are acceded by a client (*scheduler*), which coordinates the global evaluation of each rule.

The EFE system takes a decision every 23 ms. Two types of error can appear: an audio frame is labelled as speech when it is a music frame and the opposite. The first one (Music as Speech Error, MSE) is considered more serious than the second one (Speech as Music Error, SME), since it gives rise to a higher loss of audio quality. The SME error is less critical, because it implies an increase in the necessary bandwidth to transmit the signal, but no loss of audio quality is produced. In order to design and evaluate the EFE system, a fitness function which considers both types of error is proposed:

$$Ev = a \cdot MSE + b \cdot SME \tag{1}$$

The values for parameters a and b in (1) are chosen aiming to reduce MSE as much as possible. In this work, we have chosen the following values: $a = 0.8$ and $b = 0.2$. The fitness function in (1) penalizes MSE more than SME, since the first type of error is more critical than the second.

3 Experimental Evaluation

First of all, the audio test database is carefully prepared. It consists of a continuous 1-hour audio signal representative of the two audio classes (speech and music). The speech data come from news programs, dialogs and announcing of radio and TV stations. The speakers involve male and female with different ages. The music data come from musical programs of radio and TV stations too, and consist of songs and instrumental music. The songs cover as more styles as possible (rock, pop, folk, funky,...) and they are sung by male and female in English and Spanish. The instrumental music covers different instruments (piano, violin, cello, pipe, clarinet) and styles (symphonic music, chamber music, jazz, electronic music). We have attempted that the data set is representative of the two classes to be classified (speech and music) so that the results are indicative of the discrimination performance with real-world unknown signals.

The classification results are calculated using a ten-fold cross-validation evaluation where the data set to be evaluated is randomly partitioned so that 10% is used for testing and 90% is used for training. The process is iterated with different random partitions and the results are averaged. The results presented in this section are obtained with 50 iterations. This ensures that the calculated accuracy will not be biased because of a particular partitioning of the whole data set for training and testing.

Table 1 shows the improvement in the classification accuracy rate (averaged results) due to the inclusion of the EFE system within the classification stage regarding the case of only using the GMM classifier. Note that equation (1) has been used for the learning process, but not for computing the percentages in table 1.

From table 1, we can see that the EFE system gives rise to a better performance of the proposed SMD system. Concretely, the fuzzy system leads to a reduction of about 6% in the total error rate.

To assess the performance of the proposed distributed scheme, the following experiment is performed: first, only one computer is used. Later, this number is increased by 1 up to reach 9. In all cases, the processing time for building the knowledge base using evolutionary computation is determined. In figure 3, the processing time for the learning process appears as a function of the number of computers.

Table 1. Classification accuracy percentage

FEATURE	CLASSIFIER	SPEECH (%)	MUSIC (%)	TOTAL (%)
SC	GMM	93.98	86.55	90.26
SC	GMM + EFES	95.64	95.47	95.55
SR	GMM	96.99	71.69	84.34
SR	GMM + EFES	95.49	88.56	92.02
SF	GMM	67.34	75.19	71.26
SF	GMM + EFES	70.20	78.16	74.18
ZC	GMM	95.18	85.51	90.34
ZC	GMM + EFES	96.09	92.41	94.25
MFCC	GMM	98.12	84.55	91.33
MFCC	GMM + EFES	98.80	94.43	96.61

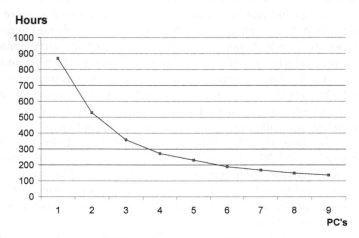

Fig. 3. Processing time evolution

4 Conclusion

This work proposes to use evolutionary fuzzy logic for designing an improved SMD scheme. Cascading the proposed the EFE system with a GMM-based classifier an improvement of about 6% is achieved regarding the case of only using the GMM-based classifier. Experiment results demonstrate the robustness of the proposed SMD scheme. A classification accuracy percentage higher than 96% is obtained for a wide range of audio samples. The new rules incorporated to the knowledge base of the expert system have been calculated using evolutionary computation. Since this process makes the computational cost expensive, we have implemented a Web services-based distributed approach to achieve time-saving in the fuzzy rules learning process. The proposed SMD scheme is intended for intelligent audio coding, and it is evaluated using commonly used timbral features.

Acknowledgments. This work was supported by FEDER and the Spanish Ministry of Education and Science under Project TEC2006-13883-C04-03.

References

1. Saunders, J.: Real-time discrimination of broacast speech/music. In: Proc. IEEE ICASSP'96, Atlanta, USA, pp. 993–996 (1996)
2. O'Shaughnessy, D.: Speech Communcations: Human and Machine, 2nd edn. IEEE Press, Piscataway, NJ (2000)
3. Rabiner, L.R., Juang, B.H.: Fundamentals of Speech Recognition. Prentice-Hall, Englewood Cliffs, NJ (1993)
4. Klapuri, A.: Automatic music transcription as we know it today. J. New. Music Research 33, 269–282 (2004)
5. Greenberg, J.E., Desloge, J.D., Zurek, P.M.: Evaluation of array-processing algorithms for a head-band hearing aid. J. Acoustic Soc. Am. 113, 1646–1657 (2003)
6. Tancerel, L., Ragot, S., Ruoppila, V.T., Lefebvre, R.: Combined speech and audio coding by discrimination. In: Proc. IEEE Workshop on Speech Coding, pp. 17–20 (2000)
7. Cordon, O., Herrera, F., Hoffmann, F., Magdalena, L.: Genetic fuzzy systems. Evolutionary tuning and learning of fuzzy knowledge bases. Advances in fuzzy systems. Applications and theory, vol. 19 (2001)
8. Dote, Y., Ovaska, S.: Industrial Applications of Soft Computing: A review. Proceedings of the IEEE (Special Issue on Industrial Innovations using soft Computing), vol. 89(9) (2001)
9. Lee, C.C.: Fuzzy Logic in Control Systems: Fuzzy Logic Controller, Part I-II. IEEE Transactions on Systems, Man. and Cybernetics 20(2), 404–435 (1990)
10. Magdalena, L., Velasco, J.R.: Fuzzy Rule-Based Controllers that Learn by Evolving their Knowledge Base. In: Herrera, F., Verdegay, J.L. (eds.) Genetics Algorithms and Soft Computing, Physica-Verlag (1996)
11. Goldberg, D.E.: Genetic Algorithms in Search, Optimization and Machine Learning. Addison-Wesley, London (1989)
12. Alonso, G., Cassati, F., Kuno, H., Machiraju, V.: Web services. Concepts. Architectures and Applications. Springer, Heidelberg (2004)
13. Carey, M.J., Parris, E.S., Lloyd-Thomas, H.: A comparison of features for speech, music discrimination. In: Proc. IEEE ICASSP'99, Phoenix, USA, pp. 1432–1435 (1999)
14. Vinton, M., Robinson, C.: Automated speech/other discrimination for loudness monitoring. 118th AES Convention, Barcelona, Spain, vol. 6437 (preprint) (2005)
15. Logan, B.: Mel frequency cepstral coefficients for music modelling. In: Proc. Int. Symp. Music Information Retrieval (2000)
16. Duda, R., Hart, P., Stork, D.: Pattern classification. John Wiley, New York (2000)

Breast Skin-Line Segmentation Using Contour Growing

Robert Martí, Arnau Oliver, David Raba, and Jordi Freixenet

Computer Vision and Robotics Group, University of Girona
Av. Lluís Santaló 17071, Spain
{marly,aoliver,draba,jordif}@eia.udg.es
http://vicorob.udg.es

Abstract. This paper presents a novel methodology to obtain the breast skin line in mammographic images. The breast edge provides important information of the breast shape and deformation which is posteriorly used by other processing techniques, typically mammographic image registration and abnormality detection. The proposed methodology is based on applying edge detection algorithms and scale space concepts. The proposed method is a particular implementation (application focused) of a growing active contour with common considerations. Quantitative and qualitative evaluation is provided to show the validity of the approach.

1 Introduction

Breast cancer is one of the most devastating and deadly diseases in women [1]. X-ray mammography remains currently the most effective method for early signs of breast cancer. Although the estimation of the breast skin-line (the boundary between breast tissue in the mammogram and the background) has not received much attention in the field of mammographic image analysis, it should be regarded as an important initial step for achieving an specific task. This includes the delimitation of the region of interest for the detection of abnormalities (microcalcifications and/or masses) in Computer Aided Detection systems or the estimation of breast deformation for image registration. In addition, the removal of non interesting regions in images would also reduce image storage and transmission sizes.

Most of the methods found in the literature are based on combining histogram thresholding techniques (which provides a fair initial estimate of the breast area) with other more elaborated approaches. In contrast, the aim of this paper is to investigate the feasibility of applying an edge detection approach for extracting the breast skin-line. This is based on the combination of edge detection using scale-space representation and active contours concepts.

The paper is structured as follows. The following section explains in more detail the difficulty of extracting the breast skin-line, as well as describes typical approaches for such task, underlining the main key works. Subsequently, the proposed method is described in Sect. 3 and results are shown in Sect. 4. The paper ends with the conclusions and future work.

J. Martí et al. (Eds.): IbPRIA 2007, Part II, LNCS 4478, pp. 564–571, 2007.

2   Skin-Line Segmentation

Although skin-line segmentation might be naively regarded as a simple task, obtaining an accurate segmentation is not often straightforward. This is mainly due to the projective nature of the acquisition process. Even though compression is applied to the breast, the thickness of the breast is not constant and decreases along the skin boundary toward the nipple, this fact decreases film contrast in this area. Besides, an added difficulty is the amount of noise found in the background. This might be due to different reasons involving the acquisition (i.e. scattering) and to the digitalisation process. This latter factor is more pronounced in mammographic films which have been digitised using a film scanner compared to full field digital acquisition systems, in which the heterogenous nature of the background is less prononounced. However, the number of film mammograms being used for diagnosis is still important, as well as the contrast problem still persists in the digital world.

A common approach to breast skin-line segmentation is thresholding algorithms. Their main drawback is that they do not account for the non-homogeneity of the mammographic background and usually low contrast parts of the breast are being considered background. This is partially solved by using post-processing strategies. Thus, in the works of Sallam et al. [2] and Yin et al. [3], the post-processing operations include morphology and line smoothing. In contrast, in the work of Méndez et al. [4] a tracking of the boundary is done using gradient information. In addition, Wirth [5] used active contours and fuzzy classification. A kindly different approach was adopted by Chandrasekhar [6], who modelled the breast background using a polynomial form and, subsequently, subtracted this from the original image obtaining the breast profile. A deeper review of these techniques can be found in [7]. In 2006, Pan et al. [8] presented a novel approach based on incorporating phase, amplitude and orientation from multiscale analysis obtaining very successful results.

3   Method

The idea behind the proposed method is based on finding the skin-line by using a contour growing technique. The growing process is stated following similar concepts of attraction and regularisation found in active contours. The method starts by computing an scale space representation of the image in order to perform edge detection using different scales. Subsequently, an initial seed point lying in the skin-line contour is located based on a robustly estimation process. Using this seed point, a contour growing process starts based on enlarging and adapting a contour using different criteria. Basically, and following the simile of active contours or snakes we adapt the concept of attraction forces (which make the contour enter a region) and what we refer to regularisation forces which penalises rapid curvature and position changes. An overview of the method is illustrated in the Fig. 1.

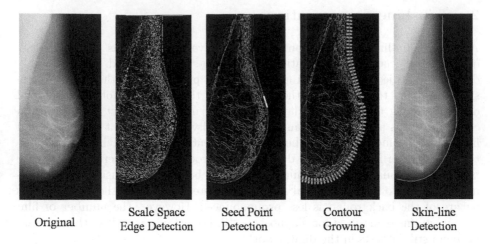

	Scale Space	Seed Point	Contour	Skin-line
Original	Edge Detection	Detection	Growing	Detection

Fig. 1. Overview of the proposed skin-line segmentation method

3.1 Skin-Line Detection in Scale Space

The scale-space representation [9] describes an image as its decomposition at different scales. This is achieved by the convolution of the image with a Gaussian smoothing function at various scales (given by the σ value of the Gaussian function). This representation has been used in conjunction with edge detection in order to automatically extract edges at their optimum scale. If a small scale is used, the edge localisation is accurate but results are sensitive to noise. On the other hand, edges at larger scales have a better tolerance to noise but poor edge localisation. The motivation of using scale space edge detection is given by the nature of the breast skin-line: a low contrast edge often affected by noise. Various approaches to automatic scale selection have been proposed [9]. A simple and common approach is to select as the optimum scale the one which obtains a maximum response from scale invariant descriptors. This is in general given by normalised derivatives, for instance Lindeberg [9] defines

$$L_{norm} = \sigma^{\alpha/2}(L_x^2 + L_y^2) \tag{1}$$

as an edge strength measure for scale σ. L_x is the convolution of the image function with a first derivative Gaussian function. Here α is a parameter used as an additional degree of freedom for edge and ridge detection. A typical value of 1 is generally used in the definition of normalised derivatives for edge detection. Edge points are obtained detecting zero-crossing points of the second derivative in the scale-space representation. The final edge strength of a zero crossing will be given by the maximum normalised strength measure along the different scales. This maximum scale is regarded as the edge scale at that particular point.

3.2   Seed Point

The first step of the method focuses on finding the starting point (or seed point) from which the contour will start growing. Special care has to be taken on estimating this point which directly affects the accuracy of the segmentation. As stated before, mammographic image segmentation presents difficulties mainly due to the low contrast in the skin-line and to the non-homogeneous background. From our experience this lower contrast is less severe for points close the nipple. Therefore a seed point can be easily detected in points at this area. An initial guess of a seed point is obtained as the first local maxima of the gradient in the scale space representation along the x axis at half the height of the image. Obviously, this first estimation lacks of robustness if this first local maxima does not correspond to the skin-line. That could be the case if the point lies inside the breast area (due to a low contrast of the skin-line) or in the background (due to noise, label and other image artifacts). A more robust approach is adopted based on analysing the position of various seed points at close the same position (at a small range in the y coordinate). The final seed point is obtained using a least median error estimation. Edge direction will also provide an important information in the contour growing process. Therefore the estimation of the initial angle it is also important. In this case a similar least median error estimation is adopted for the angle measure. Figure 2a shows an example of seed detection.

3.3   Contour Growing

Once the seed point has been obtained a contour growing process starts based on the combination of different criteria. For each point, a set of candidate growing points are obtained situated in a normal line along the gradient direction. A measure of affinity or cost C_i is computed for all points and the value with the minimum cost is taken as the next growing point. This iterative process is illustrated in the Fig. 2b.

As one may note from the figure, the growing scheme incorporates several parameters which need to be defined. These include a kernel size K, normal to the previous point, and a growing step S. Those values have been empirically determined (i.e. typical values are $K = 51$ and $S = 20$) and kept constant trough all the experiments.

Also from the experiments we noted that a more robust approach should be used for the process of selecting the next candidate point as it was often affected by noise and outliers. Instead of evaluating only a set of normal points at a given distance and obtain the candidate with a minimum cost over C_i, several sets of points on the normal are evaluated at different positions close to the desired position of the candidate point. A set of cost functions C_i^k is then obtained for each set of normal points. Using this approach the candidate point will be the one with the minimum cost over all the different sets C^k. One should note that in the different cost functions, the same (or nearly the same) point can lie in a shifted position. In order to make those cost functions comparable the cost functions are iteratively right and left shifted. The global minimum cost for each

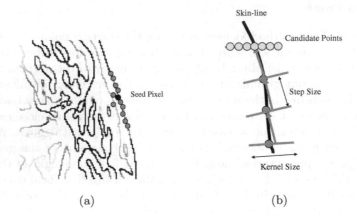

(a)   (b)

Fig. 2. Contour growing scheme: (a) Initial seed point and (b) contour growing process

point is obtained as the minimum using those shifted functions and the original cost. Figure 3 shows the minimum cost function of candidate points with and without cost shifting. Note that transportation effects have been minimised when costs are shifted allowing a better estimation of the minimum cost.

Candidate points are obtained from the zero crossing points along the normalised gradient using the scale space representation described earlier. The cost of choosing a candidate point i is given by a weighted function C_i, following the typical snake additive model formulation. This includes gradient, intensity, contour curvature and position information. Hence, the contour tends to grow finding areas of increasing intensity keeping minimal position and direction changes.

$$C_i = \alpha G_i + \beta D_i + (1 - \alpha - \beta)A_i \tag{2}$$

where G_i refers to an attraction factor (i.e. intensity or gradient), while the other two respond to regularisation terms penalising position differences (D_i) and direction changes (A_i). The factors α and β are scalar constants which will weight the importance of each term. As in many other approaches using weighted cost functions, it is important to obtain a good estimation of those factors in order to achieve a satisfactory segmentation. The selection of those factors will be later discussed in the paper (see the results section). Different attraction factors can be stated based on the represented information and how it is computed. Here two commonly used attraction factors are evaluated based on gradient and intensity information.

$$G_i = 1 - \exp(-1/f) \tag{3}$$

where f is the gradient or intensity image function, depending on the factor used. Gradient is obtained from the gradient of the zero crossing pixels while intensity information is given by the median intensity value in a local small window (i.e. 5x5 pixels).

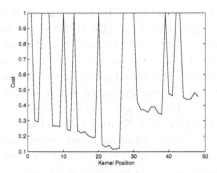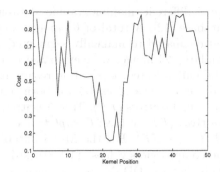

Fig. 3. Cost functions for robust candidate selection: (a) cost without shifting and (b) with cost shifting

The segmented breast skin-line should be continuous without having abrupt changes. This obviously corresponds to the continuous nature of the breast. A way to ensure this continuity is to impose some regularisation conditions to the contour growing process. This continuity assumption might not hold in all cases (i.e. when the nipple appears in the skin-line) but in this case the attraction factors described earlier will be able to adapt the contour to those changes. The first regularisation factor D_i biases the cost to points closer to the centre of the kernel of size K. This means that between two similar points the factor will select as a better point the one with a closer distance to the kernel centre. This factor is independent of the image contents and is given by,

$$D_i = \exp(-1/abs((i-1) - (K-1)/2)/((K-1)/2)) \tag{4}$$

The last regularisation term is defined computing the curvature change in a local neigbourhood. Curvature values at each pixel are obtained with a similar approach as used in [10]. Curvature (or directional change) between two pixels i and j is defined by the scalar product of their normal vectors. Hence, the curvature measure of a given pixel i is obtained by computing the scalar product between i and its neighbouring pixels,

$$A_i = \frac{1}{N} \sum_{j=1}^{N} \exp(-d_{ij}^2)(1 - \cos(\phi_i - \phi_j)) \tag{5}$$

where ϕ_i is the angle of the normal at a pixel i. N is the number of points in a local neighbourhood and d_{ij} is the Euclidean distance between points i and j. The distance factor is used here to weight the curvature of each point j, in order to incorporate a bias to points closer to i.

4   Results and Discussion

In this section we show initial results obtained using the proposed skin-line segmentation algorithm. Evaluation has been carried out in several experiments using different mammographic databases: the MIAS [11] and the DDSM database [12]. A total of 65 images were segmented from the MIAS database and compared to manually segmented images, regarded here as ground truth. Similarly, 24 images were evaluated from the DDSM database. All images were randomly selected. Evaluation results have been computed using *completeness* and *correctness* measures for both databases. Those measures are related to the True Positives (TP), True Negatives (TN), False Negatives (FN) and False Positives (FP) values: $Completeness = TP/(TP + FN)$ and $Correctness = TP/(TP + FP)$. For the MIAS database we have obtained mean correctness and completeness values of 0.9697 (std: 0.0507) and 0.9547 (std: 0.0618), respectively. For the DDSM case the mean correctness and completeness values were 0.9524 (std: 0.0557) and 0.9744 (std: 0.0103), respectively. Special care has to be taken when looking at those values as they tend to be too optimistic. For instance, it is accepted that values over 0.95 can be considered as good segmentation but also results below 0.90 were often regarded in our experiments as unacceptable. Those results are slightly lower compared to other approaches [5] for the case of the MIAS database but also interestingly better for the DDSM, which has been generally perceived as more difficult to segment due to the larger amounts of noise. Moreover, one has to keep in mind that those are initial results and are likely to be improved in the future. In addition to the DDSM and MIAS database and although not quantitatively evaluated, we have tested the algorithm using full field digital mammograms from our local database. As expected, and due to the less noise found in the background, the segmentation results were all considered satisfactory.

In some cases the algorithm does not obtain what could be considered an acceptable segmentation. Those are mainly related to a large amount of noise in the image which lead to a poor estimate of the initial seed point and to non-uniform breast intensity distribution which yields undersegmented images. On the other hand, it is also important to notice that the performance of the algorithm does not substantially depend on the database used which usually has been reported with other approaches [5]. The weighting factors of the growing criteria described in the methodology section were established empirically, experiencing that extreme values of any of the factors did not obtain satisfactory results and that the attraction factor (intensity and gradient information) were the most important in order to reach more accurate segmentation. However, additional experiments will be carried out in order to asses the information aported by each factor.

5   Conclusions

A novel approach to the segmentation of the skin-line in digital mammograms has been presented based on a novel contour growing technique using scale-space edge detection and attraction and regularisation terms. Although we have presented initial evaluation results these have shown that our method can robustly obtain an accurate segmentation in most of cases using different databases. Future work will focus in further evaluating our method using a larger number of cases and additional databases, including full field digital mammograms. In addition, this evaluation will be compared to other recent approaches [8] for which we have been unable to include in this work.

Acknowledgments. Work partially supported by MEC grant nbs. TIN2005-08792-C03-01 and TIN2006-08035.

References

1. American Cancer Society: Breast cancer: facts and figures. 2003-04. ACS (2003)
2. Sallam, M., Bowyer, K.: Registration and difference analysis of corresponding mammogram images. Medical Image Analysis 3(2), 103–118 (1999)
3. Yin, F., Giger, M., Doi, K., Vyborny, C., Schmidt, R.: Computerized detection of masses in digital mammograms: automated alignment of breast images and its effect on bilateral-subtraction technique. Med. Phys. 21(3), 445–452 (1994)
4. Mendez, A., Tahoces, P., Lado, M., Souto, M., Correa, J., Vidal, J.: Automatic detection of breast border and nipple in digital mammograms. Comput. Methods Programs Biomed. 49(3), 253–262 (1998)
5. Wirth, M., Nikitenko, D., Lyon, J.: Segmentation of the Breast Region in Mammograms using a Rule-Based Fuzzy Reasoning Algorithm. ICGST International Journal on Graphics, Vision and Image Processing,vol. 05(2) (2005)
6. Chandrasekhar, R., Attikiouzel, Y.: Gross segmentation of mammograms using a polynomial model. In: Proc. Eng. Med. and Biol. Soc. 3, 1056–1058 (1996)
7. Raba, D., Oliver, A.: Breast segmentation with pectoral muscle suppression on digital mammograms. In: Iberian Conference on Pattern Recognition and Image Analysis, Estoril, Portugal, pp. 471–478 (2005)
8. Pan, X., Brady, M., Highnam, R., Declerck, J.: The use of multi-scale monogenic signal on structure orientation identification and segmentation. In: Astley, S.M., Brady, M., Rose, C., Zwiggelaar, R. (eds.) IWDM 2006. LNCS, vol. 4046, pp. 601–608. Springer, Heidelberg (2006)
9. Lindeberg, T.: Edge detection and ridge detection with automatic scale selection. International Journal of Computer Vision 30(2), 117–154 (1998)
10. Deschênes, J., Ziou, D.: Detection of line junctions and line terminations using curvilinear features. Pattern Recognition Letters 21, 637–649 (2000)
11. Suckling, J., Parker, J., Dance, D., Astley, S., Hutt, I., Boggis, C., Ricketts, I., Stamatakis, E., Cerneaz, N., Kok, S., Taylor, P., Betal, D., Savage, J.: The Mammographic Image Analysis Society digital mammogram database. In: International Workshop on Digital Mammography, pp. 211–221 (1994)
12. Heath, M., Bowyer, K., Kopans, D., Moore, R., Kegelmeyer, P.: The digital database for screening mammography. In: International Workshop on Digital Mammography (2000)

New Measure for Shape Elongation

Miloš Stojmenović[1] and Joviša Žunić[2,*]

[1] SITE, University of Ottawa, Ottawa, Ontario, Canada K1N 6N5
mstoj075@site.uottawa.ca
[2] Computer Science, Exeter University, Exeter EX4 4QF, U.K.
J.Zunic@ex.ac.uk

Abstract. Shape elongation is one of the basic shape descriptors that has a very clear intuitive meaning. That is reason for its applicability in many shape classification tasks. In this paper we define a new method for computing shape elongation for shapes with polygonal boundaries. The measure is the ratio of the maximal and minimal of the sums of squared lengths of the projections of all of the edges of the polygonal boundary onto a line which has a particular slope. We express the measure with a closed formula. This measure finds the elongation for shapes whose boundary is not extracted completely, which is impossible to achieve with existing area based measures.

Keywords: Shape, elongation, orientation, image processing, computer vision.

1   Introduction

This paper introduces a new shape elongation measure. Elongation has an intuitively clear meaning and is hence a very common shape descriptor. In literature, shape orientation and shape elongation are strongly connected, and usually considered together ([2,3,4]). The standard measure of shape elongation is derived from the definition of shape orientation that is based on the axis of the least second moment of inertia. Precisely, the axis of the least second moment ([2,3,4]) is the line which minimises the integral of the squares of distances of the points (belonging to the shape) to the line. The integral is

$$I(S, \varphi, \rho) = \iint\limits_{S} r^2(x, y, \varphi, \rho) dx dy \qquad (1)$$

where $r(x, y, \varphi, \rho)$ is the perpendicular distance from the point (x, y) to the line given in the form

$$x \cdot \cos \varphi - y \cdot \sin \varphi = \rho.$$

---

* The author is also with the Mathematical institute of Serbian Academy of Sciences and Arts, Belgrade.

J. Martí et al. (Eds.): IbPRIA 2007, Part II, LNCS 4478, pp. 572–579, 2007.

The angle φ for which the above integral reaches a minimum defines the orientation of the shape S. This angle is easy to compute and it can be shown that such an angle φ satisfies the following equation:

$$\frac{\sin(2\varphi)}{\cos(2\varphi)} = \frac{2 \cdot \overline{m}_{1,1}(S)}{\overline{m}_{2,0}(S) - \overline{m}_{0,2}(S)}, \tag{2}$$

where $\overline{m}_{p,q}(S)$ are centralised moments of the shape S defined as

$$\overline{m}_{p,q}(S) = \int\!\!\int_S \left(x - \frac{\iint_S x\,dx\,dy}{\iint_S dx\,dy}\right)^p \cdot \left(y - \frac{\iint_S y\,dx\,dy}{\iint_S dx\,dy}\right)^q dx\,dy. \tag{3}$$

The minimum and maximum of $I(S, \varphi, \rho)$ are also easy to compute. They are:

$$\max_{\substack{\rho \geq 0 \\ \varphi \in [0, 2\pi]}} \{I(S, \varphi, \rho)\} =$$

$$\frac{\overline{m}_{2,0}(S) + \overline{m}_{0,2}(S) + \sqrt{4 \cdot (\overline{m}_{1,1}(S))^2 + (\overline{m}_{2,0}(S) - \overline{m}_{0,2}(S))^2}}{2}$$

and

$$\min_{\substack{\rho \geq 0 \\ \varphi \in [0, 2\pi]}} \{I(S, \varphi, \rho)\} =$$

$$\frac{\overline{m}_{2,0}(S) + \overline{m}_{0,2}(S) - \sqrt{4 \cdot (\overline{m}_{1,1}(S))^2 + (\overline{m}_{2,0}(S) - \overline{m}_{0,2}(S))^2}}{2}.$$

Next, the ratio between $\max_{\varphi \in [0,\pi)} I(S, \varphi, \rho)$ and $\min_{\varphi \in [0,\pi)} I(S, \varphi, \rho)$

$$\mathcal{E}_s(S) = \frac{\max\{I(S, \varphi, \rho) \mid \varphi \in [0, 2 \cdot \pi], \ \rho \geq 0\}}{\min\{I(S, \varphi, \rho) \mid \varphi \in [0, 2 \cdot \pi], \ \rho \geq 0\}} \tag{4}$$

is the standard measure of elongation of the shape S. Some generalisation of the standard method for measuring shape elongation can be found in [8]. Let us mention that there are also some naive measures of elongation. For example, shape elongation can be measured as the ratio of the longer and shorter edges of the minimum area bounding rectangle for the measured shape. It is worth mentioning that such bounding rectangles are easy to compute ([1,5]).

The standard measure (4) of shape elongation is area based because all points belonging to the shape are involved in the computation (area moments are used). Our new shape elongation measure is boundary based, because only the boundary points are used in its computation. In this paper we will use the above given idea while considering a recently disclosed method [9] for computing shape orientation for deriving the new measure for shape elongation.

The restriction to polygonal shapes is not strictly enforced since real image processing applications deal with discrete data that are a result of a particular discretization process. In order to enhance the data manipulation, the boundaries of the original shapes are usually approximated with canonical arc sections (circular arcs, parabolic arcs, straight line segments, etc.). Approximating boundaries by straight line sections (i.e., polygonal approximation) is used most frequently and many algorithms for the polygonal shape approximation already exist – see [6].

The new elongation measure defined in this paper takes into account all the boundary points – not only those that belong to the convex hull or to bounding rectangles of the shape, for example.

2   Boundary Based Shape Orientation

As mentioned, we will derive a new shape elongation measure from a recent boundary based method for computing the orientation of polygonal shapes. We will first give a short sketch of the main result from [9]. Let us start with the following definition from the same paper.

Definition 1. *Let P be a planar shape with a polygonal boundary, and let $\overrightarrow{a} = (\cos\alpha, \sin\alpha)$ denotes the unit vector with direction α. Then, the orientation of the shape is defined by the angle α such that the total sum*

$$F(\alpha, P) = \sum_{e \text{ is an edge of } P} |\mathbf{pr}_{\overrightarrow{a}}(e)|^2 \tag{5}$$

of squared lengths of projections of all the edges of P onto a line having the slope α is maximal possible.

Since the length of the projection $\mathbf{pr}_{\overrightarrow{a}}(e_i)$ of the edge e_i onto a line having the slope α is

$$|\mathbf{pr}_{\overrightarrow{a}}(e_i)| = |e_i||(\cos\alpha_i \cos\alpha + \sin\alpha_i \sin\alpha)| = |e_i||\cos(\alpha_i - \alpha)|,$$

the function $F(\alpha, P)$ that should be maximised (in order to compute the orientation of P) can be expressed as

$$F(\alpha, P) = \sum_{i=1}^{n} |\mathbf{pr}_{\overrightarrow{a}}(e_i)|^2 = \sum_{i=1}^{n} |e_i|^2 \cos^2(\alpha_i - \alpha). \tag{6}$$

By setting the first derivative $dF(\alpha, P)/d\alpha$ equal to zero it can be shown that both angles for which $F(\alpha, P)$ reaches its minimum and maximum satisfy

$$\frac{\sin(2\alpha)}{\cos(2\alpha)} = \frac{\sum\limits_{i=1}^{n} |e_i|^2 \sin(2\alpha_i)}{\sum\limits_{i=1}^{n} |e_i|^2 \cos(2\alpha_i)}. \tag{7}$$

Once again, for a detailed proof and more details we refer to [9].

3   New Shape Elongation Measure for Polygonal Shapes

Following the idea of the standard method for measuring shape elongation we define the new elongation measure as the ratio of the maximum and minimum value of the function that has been used for computing the shape orientation.

Definition 2. *Let P be a shape with a polygonal boundary. Then, the elongation of P is defined as the ratio*

$$\mathcal{E}(P) = \frac{\max\{F(\alpha, P) \mid \alpha \in [0, 2 \cdot \pi]\}}{\min\{F(\alpha, P) \mid \alpha \in [0, 2 \cdot \pi]\}} \tag{8}$$

of the maximum and minimum of the function $F(\alpha, P)$.

The new definition seems well motivated. For practical applications it would be a desirable property if $\mathcal{E}(P)$ is easily computable. We will show that the computation is straight forward, and more over it turns up that there is a closed formula for computing shape elongation as defined by (8).

Theorem 1. *Let P be a shape with a polygonal boundary. Then the new elongation measure of P can be expressed as*

$$\mathcal{E}(P) = \frac{\sum\limits_{1 \leq i \leq n} |e_i|^2 + \sqrt{\left(\sum\limits_{1 \leq i \leq n} |e_i|^2 \cos(2\alpha_i)\right)^2 + \left(\sum\limits_{1 \leq i \leq n} |e_i|^2 \cdot \sin(2\alpha_i)\right)^2}}{\sum\limits_{1 \leq i \leq n} |e_i|^2 - \sqrt{\left(\sum\limits_{1 \leq i \leq n} |e_i|^2 \cdot \cos(2\alpha_i)\right)^2 + \left(\sum\limits_{1 \leq i \leq n} |e_i|^2 \cdot \sin(2\alpha_i)\right)^2}} \tag{9}$$

where e_i ($1 \leq i \leq n$) are edges of the boundary of P and α_i ($1 \leq i \leq n$) are angles between the edges e_i and the x-axis.

Proof. By using a simple trigonometric identity $\cos^2(\alpha) = \dfrac{1 + \cos 2\alpha}{2}$ we can transform the optimising function $F(\alpha, P)$ from the form (6) into:

$$F(\alpha, P) =$$

$$\frac{1}{2} \cdot \sum\limits_{1 \leq i \leq n} |e_i|^2 + \frac{1}{2} \cdot \sum\limits_{1 \leq i \leq n} |e_i|^2 (\cos(2\alpha_i) \cos(2\alpha) + \sin(2\alpha_i) \sin(2\alpha)). \tag{10}$$

As already proved (see (7)), the angle values γ for which $F(\alpha, P)$ reaches its

minimum and maximum satisfy $\dfrac{\sin(2\gamma)}{\cos(2\gamma)} = \dfrac{\sum\limits_{i=1}^{n} |e_i|^2 \sin(2\alpha_i)}{\sum\limits_{i=1}^{n} |e_i|^2 \cos(2\alpha_i)}$. Now, using the

trigonometric identities: $\sin(2\varphi) = \dfrac{\pm \tan(2\varphi)}{\sqrt{1 + \tan^2(2\varphi)}}$ and $\cos(2\varphi) = \dfrac{\pm 1}{\sqrt{1 + \tan^2(2\varphi)}}$

we derive that $\cos(2\gamma)$ and $\sin(2\gamma)$ at the extreme points of $F(\alpha, P)$ can be expressed (together) as

$$\cos(2\gamma) = \frac{\pm \sum\limits_{1 \le i \le n} |e_i|^2 \cos(2\alpha_i)}{\sqrt{\left(\sum\limits_{1 \le i \le n} |e_i|^2 \cos(2\alpha_i)\right)^2 + \left(\sum\limits_{1 \le i \le n} |e_i|^2 \sin(2\alpha_i)\right)^2}}$$

$$\sin(2\gamma) = \frac{\pm \sum\limits_{1 \le i \le n} |e_i|^2 \sin(2\alpha_i)}{\sqrt{\left(\sum\limits_{1 \le i \le n} |e_i|^2 \cos(2\alpha_i)\right)^2 + \left(\sum\limits_{1 \le i \le n} |e_i|^2 \sin(2\alpha_i)\right)^2}}.$$

Entering the last two equalities into (10) we derive that the minimum and maximum of $F(\alpha, P)$ can be expressed as

$$\frac{1}{2} \sum\limits_{1 \le i \le n} |e_i|^2 + \frac{1}{2} \sum\limits_{1 \le i \le n} |e_i|^2 \cdot \frac{\pm \cos(2\alpha_i) \cdot \sum\limits_{1 \le i \le n} |e_i|^2 \cos(2\alpha_i)}{\sqrt{\left(\sum\limits_{1 \le i \le n} |e_i|^2 \cos(2\alpha_i)\right)^2 + \left(\sum\limits_{1 \le i \le n} |e_i|^2 \sin(2\alpha_i)\right)^2}}$$

$$+ \frac{1}{2} \sum\limits_{1 \le i \le n} |e_i|^2 \cdot \frac{\pm \sin(2\alpha_i) \cdot \sum\limits_{1 \le i \le n} |e_i|^2 \sin(2\alpha_i)}{\sqrt{\left(\sum\limits_{1 \le i \le n} |e_i|^2 \cos(2\alpha_i)\right)^2 + \left(\sum\limits_{1 \le i \le n} |e_i|^2 \sin(2\alpha_i)\right)^2}}$$

or equivalently as

$$\frac{1}{2} \cdot \sum\limits_{1 \le i \le n} |e_i|^2 \pm \frac{1}{2} \cdot \frac{\left(\sum\limits_{1 \le i \le n} |e_i|^2 \cos(2\alpha_i)\right)^2 + \left(\sum\limits_{1 \le i \le n} |e_i|^2 \sin(2\alpha_i)\right)^2}{\sqrt{\left(\sum\limits_{1 \le i \le n} |e_i|^2 \cos(2\alpha_i)\right)^2 + \left(\sum\limits_{1 \le i \le n} |e_i|^2 \sin(2\alpha_i)\right)^2}}.$$

Thus, we derived that the maximum and minimum of $F(\alpha, P)$ are as follows:

$$\max\{F(\alpha, P) \mid \alpha \in [0, 2\pi]\} =$$

$$\frac{1}{2} \cdot \sum\limits_{1 \le i \le n} |e_i|^2 + \frac{1}{2} \cdot \sqrt{\left(\sum\limits_{1 \le i \le n} |e_i|^2 \cdot \cos(2\alpha_i)\right)^2 + \left(\sum\limits_{1 \le i \le n} |e_i|^2 \cdot \sin(2\alpha_i)\right)^2}$$

and

$$\min\{F(\alpha, P) \mid \alpha \in [0, 2\pi]\} =$$

$$\frac{1}{2} \cdot \sum_{1 \leq i \leq n} |e_i|^2 - \frac{1}{2} \cdot \sqrt{\left(\sum_{1 \leq i \leq n} |e_i|^2 \cdot \cos(2\alpha_i) \right)^2 + \left(\sum_{1 \leq i \leq n} |e_i|^2 \cdot \sin(2\alpha_i) \right)^2}.$$

This establishes the proof.   □

Lemma 1 considers two properties that encompass the new elongation measure. The proof is omitted because it follows directly from the definitions.

Lemma 1. *The new elongation measure satisfies the following properties:*

- *$\mathcal{E}(P) \in [1, \infty)$ for each polygonal shape P;*
- *$\mathcal{E}(P)$ is invariant with respect to similarity transformations.*

Remark. It is worth mentioning that the new elongation measure is valid for both open and closed polygons, as it considers the boundary of the polygonal shape. It can be applied to open polygonal lines, but also to the set of several polygonal lines. This enables the method to be applicable to shapes whose boundaries are not completely extracted. The reasons for an incomplete extracted boundary could be: the shape is partially overlaid, there are large similarities between background pixels and pixels belonging to the shape, etc.

4   Experiments

In the previous section we proposed a new shape elongation measure. It is naturally motivated and simple to compute. There is a closed formula (9) that expresses the elongation of a given polygonal shape as a function of the boundary edges and angles that those edges made with the x-axis. It performs well in some canonical cases. For example, let us consider a rectangle $T(a)$ having edge lengths a and 1. In accordance with (9) its measured elongation is

$$\mathcal{E}(T(a)) = \frac{1 + a^2 + \sqrt{(a^2 - 1)^2}}{1 + a^2 - \sqrt{(a^2 - 1)^2}} = \begin{cases} a^2 & \text{if} \quad a > 1 \\ 1 & \text{if} \quad a = 1 \\ 1/a^2 & \text{if} \quad a < 1 \end{cases}$$

which is acceptable. In the limit cases where $a \to \infty$ and $a \to 0$ the rectangle degenerates into a line segment while the measured elongations tend to infinity. This behaviour is expected, and in fact preferred. In the case of $a = 1$ the measured elongation is equal to 1. In this case the rectangle degenerates into a square which is a 4-fold rotationally symmetric shape. Problems arising when working with manyfold rotationally symmetric shapes are discussed in [7,8].

Next we give several shapes with their measured elongations. The new measure $\mathcal{E}$ is boundary based and it is more sensitive to noise or to boundary defects (e.g.

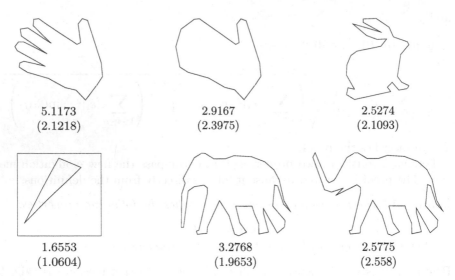

5.1173   2.9167   2.5274
(2.1218)   (2.3975)   (2.1093)

1.6553   3.2768   2.5775
(1.0604)   (1.9653)   (2.558)

Fig. 1. Computed elongations by the new method. Elongations computed by the standard method are in brackets.

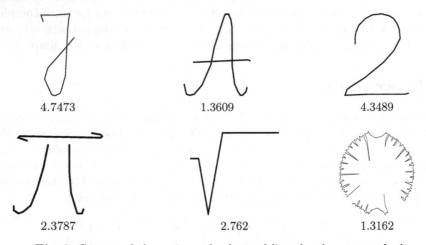

4.7473   1.3609   4.3489

2.3787   2.762   1.3162

Fig. 2. Computed elongations of polygonal lines by the new method

intrusions on the boundary) than the standard measure $\mathcal{E}_s$. That is illustrated by the first two examples from Fig.1. There is an essential difference between the measured elongations if the new measure $\mathcal{E}$ is used. On the other hand, there is only a small difference if those shapes are measured by the standard elongation measure $\mathcal{E}_s$. Such "sensitivity" is not necessarily a disadvantage – particularly when working in high precision (inspection) tasks.

The last two shapes in Fig.1 illustrate how shape deformations could affect the measured elongation. In those examples the rankings given by $\mathcal{E}$ and $\mathcal{E}_s$ are different.

An advantage of the method is that it can be applied to shapes whose boundary consists of several polygonal lines (see the fourth shape in Fig.1.) or to shapes with missing parts on their boundaries (see the last example on Fig.2). The fourth shape in Fig.1 presents a square with a triangular hole. It has a measured elongation $\mathcal{E}_s$ very close to one. It is not surprising, because results from [7,8] imply that all N-fold rotationally symmetric shapes (if $N > 2$) have the same, minimal possible, measured elongation which is equal to 1. Since the percentage of pixels that correspond to the triangular hole is relatively small, it does not lead to an essential change in the measured elongation $\mathcal{E}_s$. If the new measure $\mathcal{E}$ is applied then the impact of the hole is more significant. That can be understood as a desirable property.

Several shapes that are presented usually by a curved line (or several of them) are given in Fig.2.

5   Conclusion

The traditional shape elongation measure is area based. It is therefore defined only for closed shapes. In this article, we proposed a shape boundary based measure, with a closed formula. Using our new method, elongation can be measured for any open shape, including shapes composed of several components. The measure is invariant with respect to rotation, translation and scaling.

References

1. Freeman, H., Shapira, R.: Determining the Minimum-Area Encasing Rectangle for an Arbitrary Closed Curve. Comm. of the ACM 18, 409–413 (1975)
2. Horn, B.K.P.: Robot Vision. MIT Press, Cambridge (1986)
3. Jain, R., Kasturi, R., Schunck, B.G.: Machine Vision. McGraw-Hill, New York (1995)
4. Klette, R., Rosenfeld, A.: Digital Geometry. Morgan Kaufmann, San Francisco (2004)
5. Martin, R.R., Stephenson, P.C.: Putting Objects into Boxes. Computer Aided Design 20, 506–514 (1988)
6. Rosin, P.L.: Techniques for Assessing Polygonal Approximations of Curves. IEEE Trans. PAMI 19(6), 659–666 (1997)
7. Tsai, W.H., Chou, S.L.: Detection of Generalized Principal Axes in Rotationally Symmetric Shapes. Pattern Recognition 24, 95–104 (1991)
8. Žunić, J., Kopanja, L., Fieldsend, J.E.: Notes on Shape Orientation where the Standard Method Does not Work. Pattern Recognition 39(5), 856–865 (2006)
9. Žunić, J.: Boundary Based Orientation of Polygonal Shapes. In: Chang, L.-W., Lie, W.-N. (eds.) PSIVT 2006. LNCS, vol. 4319, Springer, Heidelberg (2006)

Evaluation of Spectral-Based Methods for Median Graph Computation*

Miquel Ferrer[1], Francesc Serratosa[2], and Ernest Valveny[1]

[1] Computer Vision Center, Dep. Ciències de la Computació
Universitat Autònoma de Barcelona, Bellaterra, Spain
{mferrer,ernest}@cvc.uab.es
[2] Departament d'Enginyeria Informàtica i Matemàtiques
Universitat Rovira i Virgili, Tarragona, Spain
francesc.serratosa@urv.cat

Abstract. The median graph is a useful tool to cluster a set of graphs and obtain a prototype of them. The spectral graph theory is another approach to represent graphs and find "good" approximate solutions for the graph-matching problem. Recently, both approaches have been put together and a new representation has emerged, which is called Spectral-Median Graphs. In this paper, we summarize and compare two techniques to synthesize a Spectral-Median Graph: one is based on the correlation of the modal matrices and the other one is based on the averaging of the spectral modes. Results show that, although both approaches obtain good prototypes of the clusters, the first one is slightly more robust against the noise than the second one.

1 Introduction

Graphs, specially labelled or attributed relational graphs, are general and powerful data structures for object representation in structural pattern recognition and computer vision applications. When objects are represented by graphs, *graph matching* is used to compare such objects. Algorithms for graph matching include graph and subgraph isomorphism [1]. However, due to errors and noise in the input data, many times it is not possible to find a perfect match between two elements and then, algorithms for approximate or error-tolerant matching must be considered. These algorithms compute a similarity measure between two given graphs. An excellent survey on graph matching algorithms and applications to pattern recognition is [2].

In some of these applications it may be necessary to obtain the prototype of a set of objects. Given a set of noisy samples of a certain object, error-tolerant graph matching can be useful to infer a representative model that captures the essential information of the class while rejecting small distortions due to noise. In this context the concept of median graph [3] can be very useful and it has already been applied to the synthesis of a prototype of a set of graphical symbols [4].

---

* This work was sponsored research Fellowship number 401-027 (UAB) / Cicyt TIN2006-15694-C02-02 (Ministerio Ciencia y Tecnología).

J. Martí et al. (Eds.): IbPRIA 2007, Part II, LNCS 4478, pp. 580–587, 2007.

It is well-known that one of the drawbacks of graph matching is its computational complexity. However, in the last years, spectral graph theory have been applied to graph matching as an alternative way to obtain approximate solutions in a reasonable time [5]. In this paper, we perform an evaluation and compar ison between two spectral-based methods for the computation of the median graph. The first one [6] is based on the correlation of the modal matrices and the latter [7] is based on the averaging of the spectral modes. Concretely, we have applied such methods to compute the representative prototype of a set of graphical symbols. Thus, we first define a graph-based representation of symbols that is suitable for applying spectral techniques. Then we evaluate both methods performing two experiments: 1) the similarity of the approximate solutions to the ideal median graph 2) the recognition rate. Finally, such methods are compared based on these experiments. The results show that with both methods good prototypes are obtained. However the method based on the correlation of the modal matrices is slightly more robust against the distortions than the method based on the spectral modes average.

The rest of the paper is organized as follows. In section 2, we present the methods for the spectral-median graph computation. In section 3 we introduce the representation of graphical symbols used to perform the tests. Section 4 presents the experiments and the results obtained. We terminate with some conclusions and possible future research lines.

2   Synthesis of Spectral-Median Graphs

Given a set of graphs, the generalized median is defined as the graph that has the smallest sum of distances to all graphs in the set. Formally speaking, median graph can be defined as follows:

Let Z be the set of graphs that can be constructed using labels from L_V and L_E. Given $S = \{G_1, G_2, ..., G_n\} \subset Z$, the generalized median graph $\bar{g}$ of S are defined as follows:

$$\bar{g} = arg \left(\min_{G \in Z} \sum_{G_i \in S} d(G, G_i) \right) \tag{1}$$

In the following lines we present two methods for the synthesis of spectral-median graphs. The first one is based on the correlation of the modal matrices while the latter is based on the averaging of the spectral modes.

2.1   Modal Matrix Correlation Method (C-Method)

The first method is that presented in [6]. Merging the concepts of median graph [3] and spectral graph theory and using the Umeyama's method [5] to solve the weighted graph matching problem, they presented the concept of spectral median graph. Concretely, they used an incremental algorithm to compute the generalized spectral median graph. Let $\{\Phi_1, \Phi_2, \ldots, \Phi_n\}$ be the set of modal matrices which represents the spectral counterpart of S in definition 1. If $\Phi = (\phi_1|\phi_2|\ldots|\phi_{|V|})$ is the modal matrix of a graph $G = (V, E)$ with ordered eigenvectors and $\Lambda = diag(\lambda_1, \lambda_2, \ldots, \lambda_{|V|})$ the diagonal matrix containing the ordered eigenvalues, they first perform a maximization of the correlation between the modal matrices of two graphs in the set using the procedure explained in [5]. In this step they obtain an intermediate median graph. Then, the modal matrix of this intermediate median graph is used to maximize the correlation to the next graph in the set, and the process is repeated iteratively until the last graph in the set is processed, giving the final spectral-median graph. The median graph is obtained in each iteration computing the adjacency matrix by means of the eigenvalues and eigenvectors applying $G = \Phi\Lambda\Phi^T$. The reader is referred to [6] for more details.

2.2 Spectral Modes Averaging Method (*M-Method*)

The second approach has been presented in [7]. They propose the direct mixing or averaging of spectral modes. If $\Phi = (\phi_1|\phi_2|\ldots|\phi_{|V|})$ is the modal matrix of a graph $G = (V, E)$ with ordered eigenvectors and the diagonal matrix of ordered eigenvalues is $\Lambda = diag(\lambda_1, \lambda_2, \ldots, \lambda_{|V|})$, the first step before mixing the two representations of two graphs is to align the rows of Φ. This can be done using the methods proposed in [5,6]. Once aligned a sign correction must be done on each modal matrix in order to mix correctly the eigenmodes. First they must find the largest magnitude component for each mode. Then, they have to correct the sign of the eigenvectors by ensuring that the largest component is positive for each mode in all modal matrices. Once aligned the spectral matrices may be merged by simply taking the average of the matrices, $\Phi_m = (\widehat{\Phi}_1 + \widehat{\Phi}_2)/2$ and $\Lambda_m = (\widehat{\Lambda}_1 + \widehat{\Lambda}_2)/2$. The reconstruction of the graph can be done performing a reverse eigendecomposition $X_m = \Phi_m\Lambda_m\Phi_m^T$ as in the previous described method. As we are working with adjacency matrices, we will obtain in general consistent results and the last step (projection of the obtained graph onto the nearest graph) described in [7] is not necessary.

3   Representation of Graphical Symbols and the Dataset

In this paper we have applied such methods to the computation of the prototype of a given set of graphical symbols. We have chosen a subset of the symbols used in the *Sixth IAPR International Workshop on Graphics Recognition - GREC 2005* [8]. This subset contains 80 different symbols (classes), extracted from architectural, electric and other technical fields. Some representative symbols of such subset are shown in figure 1. Notice that all of them are composed of a set of straight lines. Each segment terminates either with a terminal point or a junction point (confluence point between two or more segments). For convenience, from now to the end of this work, we will refer to these kinds of points as TP and JP respectively.

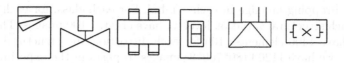

Fig. 1. Six symbols corresponding to *GREC 2005* database

Graph-based representation: In order to compute the prototypes a graph-based representation of the symbols must be defined. We have defined two different representations, namely *node-based* representation and *edge-based* representation. In both of them a symbol is represented as an undirected labeled graph, where the TPs and JPs are represented as nodes. Edges correspond to the segments connecting those points. The information associated to nodes or edges are their coordinates (x, y). As labels can only be real numbers we have created two adjacency matrices for each symbol, one of them containing x-coordinates and the other containing y-coordinates. In the *edge-based* representation, information associated to nodes is always 0 while edge labels are the coordinates (x, y) of the mid point of the segment. In the *node-based* representation, labels of nodes are the coordinates (x, y) of the point while labels of edges are always 1. In both cases we store a 0 when no edge exists between two nodes. The distance between two symbols will be the mean between the x and y distances. Figure 2 shows the two representations of a symbol.

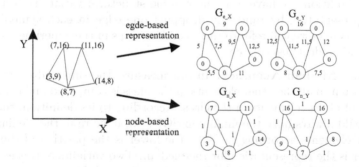

Fig. 2. Two graph-based representations of a graphical symbol

Generation of the dataset: In order to prove the robustness of the prototypes against noise, 7 different levels of distortion have been introduced. Distortion is generated moving each TP or JP randomly within a circle of radius r, given as a parameter for each level, centered at original coordinates of the point. If a JP is randomly moved, all the segments connected to it are also moved. With such distortion, gaps in line segments, missing line segments and wrong line segments are not allowed. But the number of nodes of each symbol is not changed. Figure 3 shows an example of such distortions. In addition we have generated another set of symbols using the same distortion and adding structural variations by randomly dropping an edge in each symbol. For each class, for each distortion, and for each structural variation level we have created 100 images. Thus for each class we have 1400 elements (100 for each distortion and structural variation). Therefore, we have 11200 (80*700*2) images to perform the experiments.

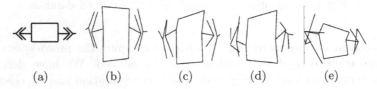

(a)   (b)   (c)   (d)   (e)

Fig. 3. Original model (*a*) and distorted models (levels: 1 (b), 3 (c), 5 (d) and 7 (e))

4   Experiments and Results

In this section the experiments we have performed will be further explained. Concretely, we propose two measures in order to test the accuracy and the robustness of the two methods explained in section 2 to compute the prototype of a set of a given models. This measures are *Intra-class Median Accuracy* and *Recognition Rate*. Recall that for each class and distortion we have generated 100 elements. For the experiments mentioned before we have defined, for each class and distortion, a training set composed of 25 symbols used to compute the medians and a test set composed of the remaining 75 symbols. Both methods explained in section 2 have been tested using the two representations explained above. In addition, we have introduced some structural variations in the node-based representation by randomly dropping one edge in each symbol. Due to space constraints we will refer to these combinations in the experiments as Edge, Node-0 and Node-1 respectively.

Intra-class Median Accuracy: In this measure, the sum of distances (SOD) of the median to all the other elements in the class is computed and compared to the SOD of all the elements in the class. According to its definition, the median graph would always have the minimum SOD. So, if we rank the median and all the other elements according to SOD, the lower is the position of the median, the better is the representation for the median. Two variants of this experiment were performed. In both cases the Spectral-median graphs were computed using 1, 10 and 25 symbols from the training set. While in the first variant, the *Intra-class Median Accuracy* was computed using the 25 symbols in the training set, in the second variant, the *Intra-class Median Accuracy* was computed using the 75 symbols in the test set. These two variants were designed in order to prove the goodness of the obtained Spectral-median graphs. The results for these two variants are shown in figures 4 and 5 respectively.

Regarding the first variant, the results show that when the median is computed with only one model, the position of the SOD of the median with respect to the rest of the elements in the class is distributed randomly. As a consequence, the accumulative frequency tends to be linear from 0 to 100. For the

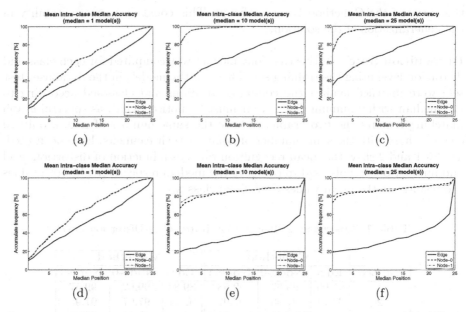

Fig. 4. Intra-class median accuracy of C-method ((a)-(c)) and M-method ((d)-(f)) for the training set

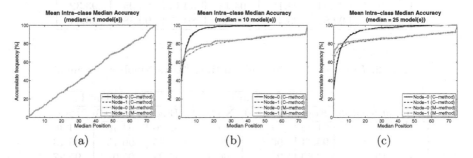

Fig. 5. Intra-class median accuracy for the test set

other cases we can see that both methods have better behavior. However these results show that the representation of the median obtained with the C-method (figure 4 (b)-(c)) outperforms the results of M-method (figure 4 (e)-(f)). In addition, the results obtained in both methods for the node-based representations are better with respect to those obtained in the edge-based representation. For this reason we performed the second variant only taking into account the node-based representation. Results for this variant (figure 5) show similar behavior of the methods as in the first variant. It is interesting to notice that for the M-method the curves for the training and the test set are more similar than in the case of the C-method. This fact means that the median obtained using the M-method is more general and therefore, it represents better the class. However, the curve of the C-method is more abrupt. This could mean more stability in the generalization of the solution.

Recognition Rate: In this case, one median was computed for each class and distortion level using the training set. Then, all the models in the database (test set) were matched against the computed medians and classified according to the median with minimum distance. It must be noticed, that, as spectral graph matching requires the two graphs to have the same number of nodes, only 20 classes, those with the same number of nodes in their elements, have been used. Tables 1 and 2 show the mean recognition rates as a function of distortion level and number of symbols used to compute the median respectively. In both tables the results are the mean values over all 20 classes.

Table 1. *Experiment 2:* Recognition Rate [%] vs Distortion Level

Dist. Level	C-method			M-method		
	Edge	Node-0	Node-1	Edge	Node-0	Node-1
1	95.90	99.67	99.68	89.83	99.62	99.57
2	93.18	97.96	97.97	92.21	97.97	97.95
3	93.63	97.12	97.11	88.18	97.12	97.15
4	93.11	95.93	95.92	90.01	95.63	95.91
5	91.81	95.55	95.56	91.68	95.01	95.01
6	93.54	94.14	94.14	90.15	93.05	93.32
7	92.81	93.40	93.40	80.77	90.88	90.64

Table 2. *Experiment 2:* Recognition Rate [%] vs Number of symbols

Num. of Symbols	C-method			M-method		
	Edge	Node-0	Node-1	Edge	Node-0	Node-1
1	91.49	94.40	94.40	92.26	94.40	94.40
5	93.44	96.45	96.43	88.95	96.15	96.13
10	92.80	96.27	96.28	87.98	95.01	95.27
15	93.91	96.66	96.67	87.77	96.10	96.12
20	95.05	96.85	96.85	88.20	95.77	95.86
25	93.85	96.88	96.88	88.70	96.24	96.11

Results show that both methods have similar recognition rates. Nevertheless, concerning the results obtained regarding the distortion levels the C-method is slightly better than M-method specially in high levels of distortion and using the edge-based representation. The results regarding the number of symbols used to compute the median are very similar for both methods, except in the case of the edge-based representation. It is to be noted too that the node-based representation obtains better results in all cases.

5   Conclusion

The median graph concept as an alternative to represent prototypes of a set of graphs has been turned out very useful, but the computation of both exact and approximate solutions has been shown very hard.

In this paper we have applied two different schemes for the computation of spectral-median graphs. In particular they have been applied to the computation of approximate solutions for the mean graph to the graphical symbol recognition problem. Intra-class median accuracy experiment shows some differences between the methods regarding the generalization and the stability of the solutions they provide. The results for the recognition rate experiment show that the two methods have similar results, but some differences have been detected regarding the level of distortion. In particular we have shown that the C-method outperforms the M-method when high distortion is introduced in the symbols. We have defined two graph representations of graphical symbols, obtaining better results with the node-based representation in both algorithms. These results suggest that a deep study of the influence of the representation and the structure of the adjacency matrix should be done in order to characterize as well as possible the behavior of spectral techniques.

References

1. Ullman, J.R.: An algorithm for subgraph isomorphism. Journal of ACM 23(1), 31–42 (1976)
2. Conte, D., Foggia, P., Sansone, C., Vento, M.: Thirty years of graph matching in pattern recognition. IJPRAI 18(3), 265–298 (2004)
3. Jiang, X., Münger, A., Bunke, H.: On median graphs: Properties, algorithms, and applications. IEEE Trans. Pattern Anal. Mach. Intell. 23(10), 1144–1151 (2001)
4. Jiang, X., Münger, A., Bunke, H.: Synthesis of representative graphical symbols by computing generalized median graph. In: Chhabra, A.K., Dori, D. (eds.) GREC 1999. LNCS, vol. 1941, pp. 183–192. Springer, Heidelberg (2000)
5. Umeyama, S.: An eigendecomposition approach to weighted graph matching problems. IEEE Transactions on Pattern Recognition and Image Analysis 10(5), 695–703 (1988)
6. Ferrer, M., Serratosa, F., Sanfeliu, A.: Synthesis of median spectral graph. In: Marques, J.S., de la Blanca, N.P., Pina, P. (eds.) IbPRIA 2005. LNCS, vol. 3523, pp. 139–146. Springer, Heidelberg (2005)
7. White, D., Wilson, R.C.: Mixing spectral representations of graphs. In: ICPR (4), pp. 140–144. IEEE Computer Society Press, Los Alamitos (2006)
8. Dosch, P., Valveny, E.: Report on the second symbol recognition contest (to appear in lncs series) (2006)

Feasible Application of Shape-Based Classification

A. Caro[1], P.G. Rodríguez[1], T. Antequera[2], and R. Palacios[3]

[1] University of Extremadura, Computer Science Dept.
Escuela Politécnica, Av. Universidad s/n, 10071 Cáceres, Spain
andresc@unex.es, pablogr@unex.es
[2] University of Extremadura, Food Technology.
Facultad Veterinaria, Av. Universidad s/n, 10071 Cáceres, Spain
tantero@unex.es
[3] "Infanta Cristina" University Hospital, Radiology Service, Badajoz, Spain
ramon.palacios@ses.juntaex.es

Abstract. This paper reports the results obtained by analysing some of the most well-known features used in Computer Vision to describe and classify shapes in an appealing real application. We aim to demonstrate the applicability of shape descriptors to classify muscles on Magnetic Resonance Imaging (MRI). The mechanized classification of ham muscles could help the industries to automate the ripening process for Iberian ham. The excellent classification percentages obtained in our experiments suggest the real viability of the feature vector developed in this paper to recognize and classify muscles.

1 Introduction

In the last decades, a large number of techniques have been developed to extract image features which are invariant under translation, scale change and rotation caused by the image formation process. These invariant features have been used in object recognition and image classification processes [14].

Moment invariants, boundary chain coding, geometric features and Fourier descriptors [4] [12] have been used in this paper to obtain a large feature vector that can be used to characterise objects within images [6] [8]. A great deal of research has been conducted to identify and classify patterns in images. However, none of work done, as far as we know, has focused on feature extraction of ham muscles and their later classification. In this respect, the applicability of muscular pattern recognition and evaluation of usefulness have become desirable tasks for ham industries. This is especially due to the fact that nowadays physical-chemical and sensorial methods evaluate the different parameters in relation to the quality of Iberian ham; such procedures tend to be destructive, expensive and tedious [1]. In contrast, the application of Computer Vision and Magnetic Resonance Imaging (MRI) offers great capabilities to non-invasive explorations into the tissues. A pattern recognition system designed to identify muscles at different maturation stages could help the industries both to control the ripening process of the hams and to cut down on the production costs.

J. Martí et al. (Eds.): IbPRIA 2007, Part II, LNCS 4478, pp. 588–595, 2007.
© Springer-Verlag Berlin Heidelberg 2007

The experiments have been carried out to recognize and classify the shapes of two muscles, *biceps femoris* (B) and *semimembranosus* (S), acquiring MR images at four stages during the ripening of the ham (raw, post-salting, semi-dry and cured stages). In our research, the shape categories (classes) are especially unclear and the problem requires the classification of a particular shape (a muscle) into a general class of similar object shapes. To prove the effectiveness of the pattern vector obtained by the automatic feature extraction, four different statistical classifiers have been implemented [2]: Euclidean classifier (EC), discriminant analysis (DA), multinomial logistic regression (MLR) and Bayesian multinomial logistic regression (BMLR). A Principal Component Analysis (PCA) has also been computed to reduce the computational time required for classification [9].

The practical viability of the feature vector has been demonstrated by applying the above methods. Optimal results have been achieved by reducing the dimensionality of this vector, while the computational performance of the classification process has increased. Finally, the recognition percentages reached by means of this feature vector exceed by 75% for any of the classifier developed. Therefore, we may conclude that the shape classification based on the feature vector developed is highly reliable.

2 Materials

Our experimental study has been carried out with a total of six Iberian hams. They were scanned over four stages during their ripening time. The MRI volume data set was obtained using the "body" antenna of a Philips Gyroscan NT Intera 1.5 T scanner, from sequences of T1 images with a FOV (*field-of view*) of 120x85 mm and a slice thickness of 2 mm, i.e. a voxel resolution of 0.23x0.20x2 mm. As a result, a large image database is obtained: 960 shapes (muscles) have been considered. A total of 480 shapes per muscle (120 shapes in each of the four stages) have been processed.

3 Shape Descriptors

Active Contours [13] was applied to recognise the two main muscle forms of Iberian ham (*biceps femoris* and *semimembranosus*).

An experiment was designed to study the ripening process of the hams. Four stages during the maturation process were selected: *raw*, *post-salting*, *semi-dry* and *dry-cured*, acquiring MR images of the six hams in each of the stages. These images were processed using non-destructive computer vision techniques (Active Contours) [3]. Once the Active Contours recognised the muscles in the MR images, a complete database of shapes was formed. Figure 1 contains MR images with the final snake for both *biceps femoris* (a) and *semimembranosus* (b) muscles, as examples of the obtained shapes.

In image analysis, statistical object description uses elementary numerical descriptions called features. The feature vector (or pattern) describes an object as a vector of elementary descriptions. These shape descriptors should be invariant to translation, rotation and scale [14].

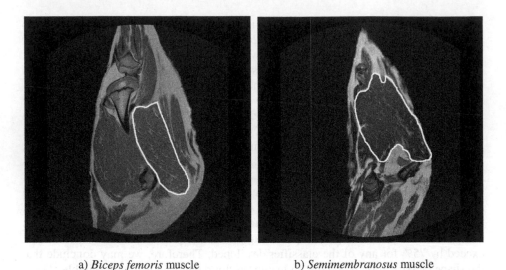

a) *Biceps femoris* muscle   b) *Semimembranosus* muscle

Fig. 1. Illustration of Iberian ham MR images, which include the detection of the muscles

The feature vector used in this paper consists of 104 features, and is based on invariant moments (positions 0-58 of the vector), Fourier descriptors (positions 59-74), geometric features (positions 75-103) and boundary chain codes (positions 95-101). Figure 2 presents the set of these features.

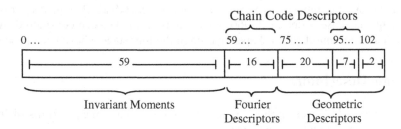

Fig. 2. The vector of 104 features, grouped in invariant moments, Fourier descriptors, geometric descriptors and chain code features

Invariant moments can provide characteristics of an object that uniquely represent its shape. Features from 0 to 58 of the vector shown in Figure 2 belong to this type of shape descriptors. In detail, the invariant moments and their positions in the feature vector were: general moments m_{00}, m_{01}, m_{10}, m_{11}, m_{02}, m_{20}, m_{12}, m_{21}, m_{03}, m_{30} (positions 0-9), central moments μ_{00}, μ_{01}, μ_{10}, μ_{11}, μ_{02}, μ_{20}, μ_{12}, μ_{21}, μ_{03}, μ_{30} (positions 10-19), normalised central moments η_{00}, η_{01}, η_{10}, η_{11}, η_{02}, η_{20}, η_{12}, η_{21}, η_{03}, η_{30} (positions 20-29), moments invariant to rotation θ_{00}, θ_{01}, θ_{10}, θ_{11}, θ_{02}, θ_{20}, θ_{12}, θ_{21}, θ_{03}, θ_{30} (positions 30-39), Hu's moments [7] (positions 40-46), Flusser and Suk invariant moments [14] (positions 47-50) and Zernike's moments [11] (positions 51-58).

Two approaches have been used to compute the feature vector: descriptors based on object regions (region-based, internal description) and descriptors based on object boundary information (contour-based, external description) [14]. Approaches based on object regions consider binary images to compute the descriptor values. Thus, a double loop is needed to process these binary images, which requires a large number of iterations [6]. On the other hand, boundary-based computations of moments consider the contour of the shape. Since the data dimension of the boundary representation is substantially smaller than that of the region representation, the boundary-based computation of moments is more efficient than region-based approaches [6]. A disadvantage of this method is its insufficient flexibility. If moments of the highest order are needed, new formulas have to be worked out and programmed [6].

Features from 59 to 74 represent the lower-order Fourier descriptors of the feature vector (Figure 2). They were computed by using boundary chains. Fourier descriptors numerically describe shapes and are normalised to make them independent of translation, scale and rotation. These Fourier descriptor values produced by the Fourier transformation of a given image represent the shape of the object in the frequency domain. The lower frequency descriptors store the general information of the shape and the higher frequency the smaller details. Therefore, the lower frequency components of the Fourier descriptors define a rough shape of the original object [12]. The high-quality boundary shape representation obtained using only a few lower-order coefficients is a favourable property, common to Fourier descriptors.

Examples of geometric descriptors are the features from 75 to 103 of the vector showed in Figure 2. Particularly, the following geometric features were used in this paper: centroid (positions 75 and 76), angle of minimum inertia (position 77), area and perimeter (positions 0 and 78), ratio of area and perimeter (position 79), compactness and roundness (positions 80 and 81), major and minor axis of fitted ellipse (positions 82 and 83), diameter (positions 84), ratio medium, major and minor (positions 85-87), rates of changes (positions 88-90), curvature (position 91), bending energy (position 92), thickness and rate of thickness (positions 93-94), chain code histogram (positions 95-101), ratio major to minor axis of fitted ellipse (position 102), aspect ratio (position 103) and number of image (position 104). These descriptors are based on scalar features derived from the boundary of an object. They use several characteristics of the object for performing shape recognition.

Eventually, boundary chain coding encodes piecewise linear curves as a sequence of directed straight-line segments called links. Features 91, 92, 95 to 101 and even 59 to 74 (Fourier descriptors) are descriptors based on chain codes that have been added to the developed feature vector.

4 Dimensionality Reduction and Classification Process

Indexing a vector typically turns to a complex task when the size of the vector is high. Computational problems tend to arise when the recognition process is performed in a high-dimensional space. Significant improvements can be achieved by first mapping the data into a lower-dimensionality space. Principal Component Analysis (PCA) has been used to reduce the dimensionality of the feature vector. The goal of the PCA is to reduce the dimensionality of the data while retaining as much as possible of the variation present in the original dataset. PCA allows us to compute a linear transformation that maps data from a high dimensional to lower dimensional space. In our experiments, the original vector of 104 features was redimensioned by PCA to 18 variables.

Different statistical classifiers are implemented in order to compare the performance of the feature vector. These classifiers are based on the concept of similarity: similar patterns are assigned to the same class [2]. Even though this methodology produces satisfactory results, a convenient metric of similarity is required. In our research, experiments are carried out with Euclidean- (E), discriminant analysis- (DA), multinomial logistic regression- (MLR) and Bayesian multinomial logistic regression- (BMLR) classifiers. These are some best-known classifiers [5] [10], and the results achieved by using them could help to study the feasibility of the feature vector developed.

5 Results and Discussion

This paper aims to study the shape of the muscles and their evolution during the maturation process. In an attempt to check the usefulness of the feature vector to recognize and classify muscles, the four different classifiers presented are applied in our experiment. A Principal Component Analysis (PCA) is carried out on DA- and MLR-classifiers to prove effectiveness or dimensionality reduction in the classification process. All the shapes of the database are used as test images. The experimental design consists of three different tests:

Test 1: shape classification on *biceps femoris* or *semimembranosus*. Food technology experts deem muscle distinction as a noteworthy option. The first test is designed to verify this crucial issue. Thus, the 960 shapes are classified by the four classifiers into two classes (muscles), having 480 shapes per class. Table 1 shows the results obtained for this test. The results display a high percentage of true positives in the classification process. The good separation achieved between classes, using any of the classifiers, entails an excellent performance of the feature vector to discriminate between these two muscles.

Table 1. Percentage of true positives for the classification of muscles (B:*biceps femoris*; S:*semimembranosus*)

Class	EC	DA	DA + PCA	MLR	MLR + PCA	BMLR
B	88,8	88,5	88,1	100,0	92,1	89,8
S	91,5	95,0	91,5	99,4	93,8	92,7
Average	**90,1**	**91,8**	**89,8**	**99,7**	**93,0**	**91,2**

Test 2: classification on four classes, distinction among muscles considering two maturation stages. This test is run as a first approach to check the possibility that the feature vector adequately sort out the two muscles, considering their initial maturation stage (*raw*) and the last one (*cured*). Four classes are considered, two for muscles at the raw stage, and the other two for muscles at the cured stage. There were 480 shapes and, consequently, 120 shapes per class. The results achieved for the second test are

shown in Table 2. The high percentage of true positives achieved determines the high performance of the feature vector to discriminate among muscles at their initial and final maturation stages.

Table 2. Percentage of true positives for classification into raw and cured muscles (RB:*raw biceps femoris*; CB:*cured biceps femoris*; RS:*raw semimembranosus*; CS:*cured semimembranosus*)

Class	EC	DA	DA + PCA	MLR	MLR + PCA	BMLR
RB	84,2	92,5	90,0	100,0	91,7	93,3
CB	85,8	87,5	90,8	100,0	76,7	91,7
RS	78,3	87,5	91,7	100,0	96,7	95,8
CS	83,3	96,7	87,5	99,2	87,5	94,2
Average	**82,9**	**91,1**	**90,0**	**99,8**	**88,2**	**93,7**

Test 3: distinction among muscles considering all the maturation stages, with a classification into eight classes (two muscles at the four maturation stages). Considering the positive results obtained for the second test, the next step involves increasing the number of classes accounted by the classifiers. Eight classes are thus considered for these two muscles at all four ripening stages. A total of 960 shapes are used in this experiment, with 120 shapes per class. The results for test 3 are shown in Table 3. Again, the percentages of true positives ensure that the feature vector could discriminate among the two main muscles at all their ripening stages.

Table 3. Percentage of true positives for the classification of two muscles and their maturation stages (RB:*raw biceps femoris*; PB:*post-salting biceps femoris*; SB:*semi-dry biceps femoris*; CB:*cured biceps femoris*; RS:*raw semimembranosus*; PS:*post-salting semimembranosus*; SS:*semi-dry semimembranosus*; CS:*cured semimembranosus*)

Class	EC	DA	DA + PCA	MLR	MLR + PCA	BMLR
RB	92,5	86,7	97,5	70,0	97,5	94,2
PB	59,2	51,7	54,2	86,7	72,5	65,0
SB	59,2	45,8	50,0	75,0	60,8	57,5
CB	40,0	78,3	65,8	71,7	75,8	75,0
RS	75,0	70,8	87,5	52,5	99,2	95,8
PS	69,2	65,0	73,3	77,5	81,7	76,7
SS	74,2	40,8	56,7	60,8	67,5	55,8
CS	74,2	38,3	65,0	70,8	78,3	80,8
Average	**67,9**	**59,7**	**70,6**	**75,1**	**79,2**	**75,1**

The average percentages of true positives retrieved in the four tests are summarized in Table 4. For our classification process, 75% may be an acceptable percentage of true positives (three in every four). For our experiment, nearly all the obtained percentages are higher than this value. Hence, the results in this paper are analysed as optimal. In turn, results below 70% could be caused by the high number of classes and covariables. Two classes in Statistic are usually considered in the most part of the classification process [2]. The higher the number of classes, the higher the possibility for a biased classification. In spite of the amount of classes used in the experiments (two, four and eight), high percentages are given for classes (when they are two and four), and acceptable results are reached for eight classes.

Table 4. Average percentage of true positives for each of the tests

Classifier	Test 1	Test 2	Test 3	Average
EC	90,6	83,5	67,9	**80,3**
DA	93,9	92,0	59,7	**80,9**
DA + PCA	90,3	92,2	70,6	**83,5**
MLR	99,7	99,7	75,1	**91,5**
MLR + PCA	93,5	86,1	79,2	**86,8**
BMLR	91,8	94,4	75,1	**86,7**
Average	**92,6**	**91,0**	**71,3**	

Regarding the most suitable method, discriminant analysis leads to the good results, perhaps because its simplicity (with or without PCA), whereas logistic regression (multinomial or Bayesian) yields best average values.

In relation to the PCA, the average results are quite similar to the averages obtained by considering all the variables of the feature vector. Lower percentages may be a consequence of the high number of classes and covariables. There are some variations among the percentages because there are classes with patterns that are very different from one another. Likewise, there exists elements from one class that are very similar to others from other classes. In spite of the large number of classes, the results from using all the features remain high while the percentages for each test are promising.

6 Conclusion

This paper presents a direct application of classification techniques to an appealing real problem, in order to get an automatic shape-based classification of ham muscles in MRI. The method considers large amount of features that are used by different classifiers. The extended validation demonstrates the feasibility of shape-based feature vectors. Highly positive values have been obtained by the pattern vector for two and four classes. These significant results demonstrate the robustness of the given feature vector. In addition, the method to reduce cardinality in the pattern vector while keeping its discriminant capability has proved to be an interesting aspect of the research. Eventually, the feasibility of applying Computer Vision techniques to automate the ripening process of the Iberian ham constitutes a cornerstone in our research.

Acknowledgments

The authors wish to acknowledge and thank for the support of the "Dehesa de Extremadura" brand and the "Hermanos Alonso Roa" company from Villar del Rey (Badajoz). This research has been funded by the Junta de Extremadura (Regional Government Board) under the IPR98A03P-, 2PR01C025- and 3PR05B027-labeled projects.

References

1. Antequera, T., López-Bote, C.J., Córdoba, J.J., García, C., Asensio, M.A., Ventanas, J., Díaz, Y.: Lipid oxidative changes in the processing of Iberian pig hams. Food Chem. 54, 105 (1992)
2. Berry, D.A., Lindgren, B.W.: Statistics. Theory and method, Duxbury (1996)
3. Caro, A., Rodríguez, P.G., Durán, M.L., Ávila, M.M., Antequera, T., Gallardo, R.: A Comparison of Algorithm Design Paradigms in Active Contours for Muscle Recognition. In: Perales, F.J., Draper, B. (eds.) AMDO 2004. LNCS, vol. 3179, pp. 249–258. Springer, Heidelberg (2004)
4. Castleman, K.: Digital Image Processing. Prentice-Hall, Englewood Clifss, New Jersey (1996)
5. Gelman, A., Carlin, J.B., Stern, H.S., Rubin, D.B.: Bayesian Data Analysis. Chapman&Hall, Boca Raton, Florida (2004)
6. González, R.C., Woods, R.E.: Digital Image Processing. Addison-Wesley, London (1992)
7. Hu, M.K.: Visual Pattern Recognition by Moment Invariants. IRE Transactions on Information Theory IT-8, 179–187 (1962)
8. Jähne, B.: Digital Image Processing. Springer, Heidelberg (1997)
9. Jain, A., Duin, R., Mao, J.: Statistical Pattern Recognition: A Review. IEEE Transactions on Pattern Analysis and Machine Intelligence 22(1), 4–37 (2000)
10. Jobson, J.D.: Applied Multivariate Data Analysis. Springer, Heidelberg (1991)
11. Khotanzad, A., Hong, Y.H.: Invariant Image Recognition by Zernike Moments. IEEE Transactions on Pattern Analysis and Machine Intelligence 12(5), 489–1997 (1990)
12. Persoon, E., Fu, K.S.: Shape Discrimination Using Fourier Descriptors. IEEE Transactions on Pattern Analysis and Machine Intelligence 8(3), 388–397 (1986)
13. Singh, A., Goldgof, D., Terzopoulos, D.: Deformable Models in Medical Image Analysis. IEEE Computer Society Press, Los Alamitos (1998)
14. Sonka, M., Hlavac, V., Boyle, R.: Image Processing, Analysis and Machine Vision. PWS Publishing, Pacific Grove, CA (1998)

3D Shape Recovery with Registration Assisted Stereo Matching

Huei-Yung Lin, Sung-Chung Liang, and Jing-Ren Wu

Department of Electrical Engineering,
National Chung Cheng University,
168 University Rd., Min-Hsiung
Chia-Yi 621, Taiwan, R.O.C.

Abstract. A novel method for simultaneously acquiring and registering range data of a real object from different viewpoints is presented. Currently, most 3D model reconstruction techniques do not cooperate with the existing range data for shape recovery of future viewpoints. In this work, a stereo vision system is developed for 3D model acquisition. To reduce the computation and increase the accuracy of stereo matching algorithms, the recovered range data from previous viewpoints are registered and then used to provide additional constraints for 3D acquisition of the next viewpoint. Experiments have shown that our approach gives better performance on both execution time and stereo matching results.

1   Introduction

3D model acquisition of real-world objects is an active research area with applications in reverse engineering, pattern recognition, industrial inspection, computer graphics and multimedia systems, etc. Most commonly used approaches for obtaining a 3D model acquire partial 3D shapes of an object from different viewpoints and then fuse the range data sets into a common coordinate system. Thus, the procedure for 3D model reconstruction usually consists of the following four stages: (i) data acquisition, (ii) data registration, (iii) surface integration, and (iv) texture mapping. The data acquisition stage is to acquire the partial 3D shapes and the texture information of an object. The acquired range images are registered to a common reference frame based on their acquisition viewpoints. The registered range images are then integrated into a single surface representation. Finally, the texture information is mapped onto the surface to create a textured 3D model.

Most 3D model reconstruction methods use passive camera systems or laser range scanners to collect partial 3D shapes of an object. Data registration for multiple views either heavily relies on the accuracy of 3D measurements or requires significant manual assistance. The separation of data acquisition and registration not only restricts the applicability to many systems, but also lacks data correction functionality from the registration stage. For example, Pulli et al. presented a complete system for scanning the range and color information of a 3D object from arbitrary viewpoints [1]. Albamont and Goshtasby designed a scanner

J. Martí et al. (Eds.): IbPRIA 2007, Part II, LNCS 4478, pp. 596–603, 2007.

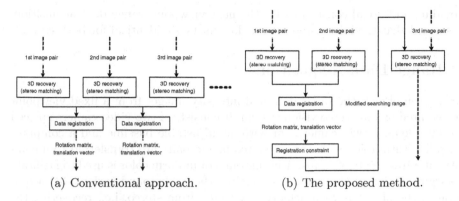

(a) Conventional approach.　　　　　　(b) The proposed method.

Fig. 1. Flowcharts of the conventional 3D model acquisition approach and the proposed registration assisted method

system using four synchronous camera heads equipped with laser line generators to obtain the 3D structure of the object [2]. Reed and Alan built a robotic system consisting of a laser range finder attached to a robot arm to acquire range images [3]. Lin and Subbarao developed a stereo vision system using a single camera for range data acquisition by rotating the object [4]. Although some of the above work used incremental shape acquisition approach for view planning and range image registration, all of them separated the data acquisition stage from the data registration stage.

In this work, we present a novel method to integrate the partial shape acquisition stage and range data registration stage for different viewpoints. It is basically an incremental method for 3D model acquisition, but the main focus is on the assistance of partial shape recovery rather than data registration from predetermined range images. Intensity images and the corresponding range data of a viewpoint are acquired by our stereo vision system. Different from conventional stereo-based techniques for 3D shape recovery, stereo pairs recorded from different image frames are not processed independently in our approach. 3D shapes recovered from the previous image frames are first registered to find the rotation matrix and translation vector of the transformation and generate a larger 3D surface. 3D reconstruction of the current viewpoint is then based on the information to reduce the computation and increase the accuracy and robustness of the stereo matching algorithms.

Figure 1(a) shows the conventional 3D model acquisition approach used in the earlier research. Partial 3D shapes acquired by stereo based approaches or laser range scanning techniques are registered and integrated to create a more complete 3D model. Range data acquisition for the present viewpoint does not utilize any information from the previous viewpoints. Thus, error correction and processing speedup are not possible with this method. Figure 1(b) illustrates the proposed registration assisted stereo matching for range data acquisition. The major difference is that the registration constraint available after the first two sets of range data are obtained and registered. The information is then used for providing additional constraints for the next viewpoint range data acquisition. It is noted that the initial steps of the flowcharts are identical for both cases.

2   Range Data Acquisition

For a given object, the range data and intensity images from a fixed viewpoint are acquired by our stereo vision system. It consists of two video cameras placed side-by-side on a twin camera bar with an adjustable baseline and a computer controlled turntable. Sequences of stereo image pairs are transferred to a computer at a frame rate of 15 fps. A background of uniform color is used to facilitate the segmentation of the real object against the background regions. 3D acquisition of the object is then achieved by shape from stereo, i.e., recovering the depth information using triangulation. Multiple partial 3D shapes of the object for different viewpoints are collected by rotating the turntable gradually.

In our earlier work, *multiple base-angle rotational stereo* concept has been proposed to achieve multi-baseline stereo by rotating the object placed on the turntable [4]. This technique, however, requires fairly accurate rotation angle to establish the epipolar geometry. In this research we are more interested in recovering range data using the assistance of previous registration information, rather than 3D shape reconstruction with precise rotation angle calibration. Thus, two cameras are installed to meet the conventional stereo configuration, i.e., the optical axes are parallel and the image planes are coplanar, for range range data acquisition. Furthermore, the rotation axis of the turntable is estimated by Tsai's calibration method [5] using a planar checkerboard pattern aligned with the axis. With a fixed angle of rotation, the matches of the control points on the calibration pattern are used to estimate the corresponding transformation.

3   Multi-view Range Data Registration

The goal of registration is to find the spatial transformation between the range images taken from an object at different viewpoints, so that the points found in different range image views that represent the same surface point are aligned. A popular method for refining a given registration is the iterative closest point (ICP) technique, first introduced by Besl and McKay [6]. It uses a nonlinear optimization procedure to further align the data sets from coarse registration. Most ICP based registration algorithms require a fairly good initial rotation matrix and translation vector between the data sets to avoid the registration result stuck in a local minimum. In our data acquisition system, since the difference between two consecutive viewpoints is very small, the rotation matrix and translation vector are given by identity matrix and zero vector, respectively.

To obtain a more complete 3D model of an object, multi-view registration of the partial 3D shapes is required. If a pair of range data from two consecutive viewpoints are registered at a time, it is clear that the registration errors will accumulate. General approach to this problem is to consider the network of views as a whole and minimize the registration errors of all views simultaneously, such that the registration errors are equally distributed [7]. Since our vision system focuses on 3D model acquisition, multi-view registration up to the n-th viewpoint (n-th frame) only depends on the previous $n-1$ viewpoints. To reduce the processing time and take the advantage of small changes between the viewpoints, the registration approach for newly added data set is implemented as follows.

First, the registration is based on the modified ICP algorithm [6], but with m range data sets considered at a time. Suppose $\mathcal{S}_i, \mathcal{S}_{i+1}, \cdots, \mathcal{S}_{i+m-1}$ are the consecutive data sets, and $\mathcal{T}_{i-1}$ represents the initial transformation (rotation and translation) to the data sets. Then the algorithm for the block of m data sets is given by

---

Algorithm 1. BLOCK REGISTRATION

1: $\mathcal{S}'_i \leftarrow \mathcal{T}_{i-1} \circ \mathcal{S}_i$
2: $j = 1$
3: **while** $j < m$ **do**
4:     $\mathcal{S} \leftarrow \mathcal{S}_{i+j}$
5:     **for** $k = -1$ to $j - 2$ **do**
6:         $\mathcal{S} \leftarrow \mathcal{T}_{i+k} \circ \mathcal{S}$
7:     **end for**
8:     $\mathcal{S}'_{i+j} \leftarrow \mathcal{S}$
9:     $\mathcal{T}_{i+j-1} \leftarrow$ Apply ICP on $\{\mathcal{S}'_{i+j-1}, \mathcal{S}'_{i+j}\}$
10:     $j + +$
11: **end while**

It is clear that $m < n$, and the computation and correctness of the registration simultaneously increase with m.

After the registration has been done for the 3D data sets from newly added viewpoints, there might exist some *isolated* points due to data acquisition error. Those points are considered as noise and will be removed if the following two criteria are met: (i) the distances between the point and any other points are larger than a threshold, (ii) for a partitioned working volume, the point belongs to a cube with density lower than a threshold. Since the overlapping parts of the object surface accumulate as the the number of acquisition viewpoints increases, the error points can be removed efficiently without affecting the points belonging the true object surface.

4   Registration Assisted 3D Shape Recovery

3D reconstruction using correlation based stereo algorithms is usually time-consuming due to template matching and the unknown searching areas. In addition to the commonly used constraints for stereo matching (such as ordering constraint, epipolar constraint), we propose a registration constraint to reduce the computation and increase the accuracy of 3D shape recovery. The basic idea

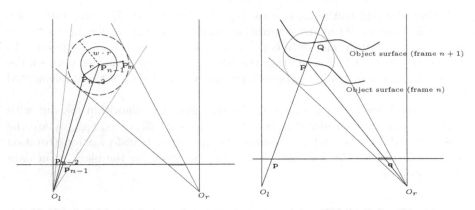

Fig. 2. Searching range   **Fig. 3.** Projected circles

is to use the recovered and registered 3D shapes from previous image frames (viewpoints) to restrict the searching areas of the current stereo image pair. Under the assumption of slow object motion between different image frames, the corresponding motion vectors are bounded by some constants predicted from previous 3D registration.

Suppose the 3D data are obtained and registered for image frames $n-2$ and $n-1$, and the registration is given by rotation matrix $\mathbf{R}_{n-1}$ and translation vector $\mathbf{t}_{n-1}$, respectively. If the corresponding 3D point of an image point $\mathbf{p}_{n-1}$ with respect to image frame $n-1$ is $\mathbf{P}_{n-1}$, as illustrated in Fig. 2, then the same 3D point with respect to image frame $n-2$ is given by

$$\mathbf{P}_{n-2} = \mathbf{R}_{n-1}^{-1}(\mathbf{P}_{n-1} - \mathbf{t}_{n-1}) \tag{1}$$

Thus, the displacement of the 3D point between the image frames is given by $\mathbf{P}_{n-1}-\mathbf{P}_{n-2}$. If we assume the object motion (both the rotation and translation) is smooth, then the same 3D point with respect to image frame n should be bounded by a sphere with radius $w \cdot r$ centered at $\mathbf{P}_{n-1}$, where r is given by $\|\mathbf{P}_{n-1} - \mathbf{P}_{n-2}\|$ and w is a weighting factor. Therefore, the searching areas corresponding to the 3D point $\mathbf{P}_n$ are the projections of the sphere onto the left and right images.

There is a sphere associated with each image point in frame $n-1$, and the spheres can be constructed based on the previous registration result. As shown in Figure 2, for a given image point $\mathbf{p}_n$ of the left image from viewpoint n, the searching area in the right image is given by the projections of the spheres which intersect the ray passing through the optical center and the image point $\mathbf{p}_n$. More precisely, suppose the spheres are given by S_j, for $j = 1, 2, ..., n$, where n is the total number of image pixels. B_j and $\hat{B}_j$ are the projections of S_j onto the left and right images, respectively. Then for a given point $\mathbf{x}$ in the left image with $\mathbf{x} \in \cap_{j=1}^{k} B_j$, the stereo correspondence $\hat{\mathbf{x}}$ in the right image is given by $\hat{\mathbf{x}} \in \cup_{j=1}^{k} \hat{B}_j$. Consequently, the searching range is bounded by the union of the projected circles of the spheres.

The above observations on the stereo searching range and the required computation can be further reduced for the overlapping foreground (object) region of two consecutive image frames. As shown in Figure 3, suppose the projection of an object point $\mathbf{P}$ onto the left image is given by $\mathbf{p}$ for the n-th image frame, and there exists a foreground image point at the same image point $\mathbf{p}_l$ in the $(n+1)$-th image frame. Then there must exist a point $\mathbf{Q}$, after the object motion, such that the projection of $\mathbf{Q}$ onto the left image in the $(n+1)$-th image frame is also given by $\mathbf{p}$. Thus, the searching range for the object point $\mathbf{Q}$ from image frame $(n+1)$ can be fully determined by a *single* sphere centered at the point $\mathbf{P}$. Consequently, the searching range for the left image point $\mathbf{p}_l$ given by the n-th frame is bounded by a single circle centered at $\mathbf{p}_r$, the correspondence of $\mathbf{p}_l$ in the n-th image frame.

Since the motion of the object or the cameras is relatively slow compared to the video frame rate during image acquisition, the foreground and background difference between two consecutive image frames is usually small and happens near the object boundary. In the experiments, the searching range of more than 80% of the object region in the left image can be covered by a single circle centered at the matching point in the previous image frame. The radius of the circle is given by a weighting factor times the motion vector derived from range data registration with previous two image frames. If the object motion (rotation and translation) is fairly uniform, a constant weighting factor can be used for the whole image sequence. In practice, smaller weighting (less than one, for instance) is preferred since both the possibility of stereo mismatch and computation time can be reduced. For the rest of the object regions which do not exist in the previous image frame, the union of projected circles has to be used for the searching region.

5 Experimental Results

The described algorithms have been implemented on a stereo vision system, and tested on a number of real objects. The baseline of the stereo cameras is set as 60 mm and the pose of the test object is changed slowly in front of a static background. A blue screen technique is used to segment the background, and only the foreground regions are used for stereo matching. The foreground regions of two consecutive image frames are also used to identify their common image area for single circular stereo searching regions. In the implementation, the epipolar constraint is applied and the searching range is given by the intersection of the union of the circles and the epipolar line. One interesting observation is that the resulting searching range varies for different image positions.

Figure 4 shows the first set of experimental results. The test object is manufactured via rapid prototyping without additional texturing. The disparity maps of the 3D reconstruction without registration information are shown in the second rows, followed by those obtained with registration assistance using weighting factors of 0.6, 0.8, 1, and 2, respectively. It can be seen that the disparity maps obtained from registration assistance with weighting factor of 0.8 give the

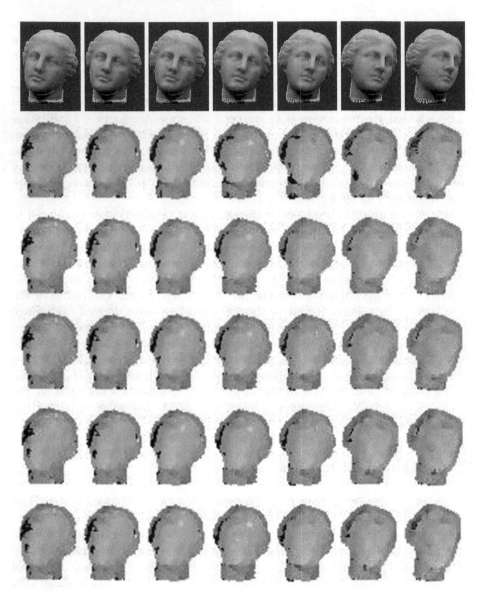

Fig. 4. From top to bottom: the acquired intensity images from the left sequence, the disparity maps obtained without registration information, the disparity maps obtained with registration assistance using weighting factors of 0.6, 0.8, 1, and 2, respectively

best results in terms of smoothness and correctness. Table 1 shows the execution times (in seconds) of the results in Figure 4. The processing time for stereo reconstruction is speeded up about five times with the assistance of data registration.

Table 1. Execution times of the results shown in Figures 4 (in seconds)

Frame No.	1	2	3	4	5	6	7
without registration assistance	1.25	1.24	1.23	1.22	1.22	1.20	1.20
with registration (weighting = 0.6)	1.25	1.24	0.22	0.22	0.22	0.23	0.30
with registration (weighting = 0.8)	1.25	1.24	0.24	0.25	0.25	0.25	0.31
with registration (weighting = 1)	1.25	1.24	0.30	0.28	0.28	0.34	0.38
with registration (weighting = 2)	1.25	1.24	0.39	0.47	0.42	0.44	0.52

6 Conclusion and Future Work

Most of the existing 3D model acquisition techniques lack data correction functionality due to the separation of range data registration and 3D data collection stages. In this work, we have presented a novel method to simultaneously acquire and register range data of an object from different viewpoints. A stereo vision system was developed to acquire the 3D shapes of an object. The range data obtained from previous viewpoints are first registered and then used to provide additional geometric constraints for the 3D acquisition of the next viewpoint. Experiments have shown that the proposed approach gives better performance on both execution time and 3D reconstruction result. In the future work, more sophisticated prediction model based Kalman filter should be adopted to further reduce the correspondence searching time. The possibility of extending current research to deal with generically shaped object will also be investigated.

References

1. Pulli, K., Shapiro, L.: Surface reconstruction and display from range and color data. Graphical Models 62(3), 165–201 (2000)
2. Albamont, J., Goshtasby, A.: A range scanner with a virtual laser. Image and Vision Computing 21(3), 271–284 (2003)
3. Reed, M.K., Allen, P.K.: 3-d modeling from range imagery: An incremental method with a planning component. Image and Vision Computing 17(2), 99–111 (1999)
4. Lin, H.Y., Subbarao, M.: A vision system for fast 3d model reconstruction. In: CVPR (2), pp. 663–668. IEEE Computer Society Press, Los Alamitos (2001)
5. Tsai, R.: A versatile camera calibration technique for high-accuracy 3d machine vision metrology using off-the-shelf tv cameras and lenses. IEEE Trans. Robotics and Automation 3(4), 323–344 (1987)
6. Besl, P.J., McKay, N.D.: A method for registration of 3-D shapes. IEEE Transactions on Pattern Analysis and machine Intelligence 14(2), 239–258 (1992)
7. Bergevin, R., Soucy, M., Gagnon, H., Laurendeau, D.: Towards a general multi-view registration technique. IEEE Trans. Pattern Analysis and Machine Intelligence 18(5), 540–547 (1996)

Blind Estimation of Motion Blur Parameters for Image Deconvolution[*]

João P. Oliveira, Mário A.T. Figueiredo, and José M. Bioucas-Dias

Instituto de Telecomunicações, Instituto Superior Técnico, T.U. Lisbon,
Av. Rovisco Pais, 1049-001 Lisboa, Portugal
{joao.oliveira,mario.figueiredo,jose.bioucas}@lx.it.pt

Abstract. This paper describes an approach to estimate the parameters of a motion blur (direction and length) directly form the observed image. The motion blur estimate can then be used in a standard non-blind deconvolution algorithm, thus yielding a blind motion deblurring scheme. The estimation criterion is based on recent results about the general spectral behavior of natural images. Experimental results show that the proposed approach is able to accurately estimate both the length and orientation of motion blur kernels, even for small lengths which are traditionally difficult.

1 Introduction

In image deconvolution/deblurring problems, the goal is to estimate an original image $f = \{f(x,y), \ x = 1,...,N, \ y = 1,...,N\}$ from an observed image $g = \{g(x,y), \ x = 1,...,N, \ y = 1,...,N\}$, assumed to have been produced according to

$$g = f * h + w, \tag{1}$$

where $h = \{h(x,y), \ x = 1,...,N, \ y = 1,...,N\}$ is the blur point spread function (PSF), $w = \{w(x,y), \ x = 1,...,N, \ y = 1,...,N\}$ is a set of independent samples of zero-mean Gaussian noise of variance σ^2, and $*$ denotes the discrete two-dimensional (2D) convolution,

$$(f * h)(x,y) \equiv \sum_u \sum_v h(u,v) \, f(x-u, y-v). \tag{2}$$

After collecting the elements of f, g, and w into vectors $\mathbf{f}, \mathbf{g}, \mathbf{w} \in \mathbb{R}^{N \times N}$, usually in lexicographic order, (1) can be written in vector notation as

$$\mathbf{g} = \mathbf{Hf} + \mathbf{w}, \tag{3}$$

where $\mathbf{H}$ is a matrix representing the blur operator. This makes clear that (1) is a particular case of the general problem of signal/image restoration from linear and

---

[*] This work was supported by Fundação para a Ciência e Tecnologia, under project POSC/EEA-CPS/61271/2004.

J. Martí et al. (Eds.): IbPRIA 2007, Part II, LNCS 4478, pp. 604–611, 2007.

noisy observations. For most non-trivial blur kernels, the corresponding matrix is severely ill-conditioned, or even singular, making deconvolution an ill-posed inverse problem.

It's well known that the ill-posed nature of image deconvolution demands some kind of regularization to be used. Among the state of the art methods, we find those based on *total variation* (TV) regularization (see [3,4,8] and further references therein) which favors images of bounded variation, without penalizing possible discontinuities, as well as wavelet-based methods [2,9,10], which also provide regularization without overly penalizing image discontinuities.

In standard deconvolution problems, it is assumed that $\mathbf{H}$ (equivalently h) is fully and exactly known. In *blind* deconvolution, the goal is to deblur an image with (total of partial) lack of knowledge about the blurring operator [13,14]. Blind deconvolution is significantly more difficult than its non-blind counterpart [1]. The problem is now ill-posed both with respect to the unknown original image and to the blur operator. Simply put (and because convolution can be expressed as a product in the Fourier domain), blind deconvolution can be seen as the problem of recovering two functions from their product; a clearly hopeless goal, in the absence of some rather strong assumptions or prior knowledge about the underlying image and blur. Assumptions about the blur PSF which have been used are positiveness, known shape (*e.g.*, Gaussian blur) or known support.

There are essentially two alternative approaches to blind deconvolution: **(i)** simultaneously estimate the image and the blur [1,7]; **(ii)** perform a previous step of blur estimation and then feed this blur estimate to a classical non-blind image deblurring algorithm [6]. In this paper, we introduce a blur estimation technique to be used in an approach of type **(ii)**. More specifically, we introduce a method to estimate the parameters of a "motion blur" from the noisy blurred image, with weak assumptions on the underlying original image.

The particular class of blur operators herein considered, known as motion blur, arises when there is relative motion between the acquisition device (*i.e.*, the camera) and the scene being acquired. For simplicity, we assume that the camera is moving with constant speed and direction, with respect to the scene. The resulting blur kernel/filter has a linear support in the spacial domain and a sinc-like (recall that $\text{sinc}(x) = \sin(x)/x$) behavior in the Fourier domain, leading to well pronounced valleys in the logarithm of the magnitude of the spectrum of the observed image. The method proposed in this paper, exploits the identification of the parameters characterizing this sinc-like behavior (namely, the orientation and period, which correspond to the orientation and length of the blur kernel) using the Radon transform [5]. As will be shown in the experimental results, the proposed algorithm is able to accurately estimate the motion blur parameters (orientation and length) for motion blurs with lengths as short as three pixels.

This paper is organized as follows. In Section 2 we define the motion blur and corresponding parameters for the continuous and the discrete cases. We also define the blur kernel structure used in this work. In Section 3.1, we review some of the state of the art methods and present the proposed algorithm. In section 4 we report experimental results on the performance of the proposed method. Finally, section 5 draws some conclusions.

2   Motion Blur Parameters

In the continuous case, the motion blur PSF is characterized by a normalized delta function, supported on a line segment with length L and an angle θ (say, with respect to the horizontal). The angle gives the direction of motion, and the length L is proportional to the motion speed. To deal with digital images, we need a discrete version of this motion blur, defined on the discrete pixel grid. To produce a straight line segment on a digital grid, we use a standard algorithm (well known in computer graphics): the digital differential analyzer (DDA) [11]. The length L is assumed to be, for all angles, the number of pixels, and is directly proportional to the motion speed. As can be easily verified, there is no way to exactly produce lines with one pixel width in all possible directions.

One big limitation of this DDA-based discrete PSF approximation, or any discrete representation in general, is that it cannot distinguish between two blur kernels with nearby angles. This effect is stronger for shorter motion blur kernels. For example, a three pixels long kernel can only have five different directions between $0°$ and $90°$. With all these assumptions and limitations in hand, our goal is to estimate the motion angle and speed parameters from an observed image, without knowledge of the underlying original image.

3   Estimation of Motion Blur Parameters

3.1   Natural Image Models

Let us denote as $F(\xi, \eta)$ the 2D Fourier transform of a natural image $f(x, y)$. As pointed out in [6], the behavior of $\log |F(\xi, \eta)|$ along lines $\eta = \xi \tan \theta$ in the (ξ, η) plane, is roughly the same for most natural images. While local behavior may be irregular, the coarse/global behavior is essentially monotonically decreasing with $|\xi|$. In [6], the approximate model $\log |F(\xi, \xi \tan \theta)| \simeq -a |\xi|^b$, with $a, b > 0$, was proposed. Although a and b can vary for different images, this global behavior is approximately true, regardless of the considered angle.

If we take the Fourier transform of equation (1), we obtain

$$G(\xi, \eta) = F(\xi, \eta)H(\xi, \eta) + W(\xi, \eta), \tag{4}$$

where F, G, H, and W are the Fourier transforms of f, g, h, and w, respectively. As is common in deconvolution problems, assuming the noise is weak, we have

$$\log |G(\xi, \eta)| \approx \log |F(\xi, \eta)H(\xi, \eta)|, \tag{5}$$

so the coarse behavior of the $G(\xi, \eta)$ depends essentially on $F(\xi, \eta)H(\xi, \eta)$. Since the coarse behavior $F(\xi, \eta)$ along lines $\eta = \xi \tan \theta$ in the (ξ, η) plane is approximately independent of θ, the sinc-like structure of $H(\xi, \eta)$ is preserved in $G(\xi, \eta)$.

In the presence of noise, the zeros of this sinc function become local minima. In order to capture these coarse behaviors, we will use the Radon transform (RT) of $\log |G(\xi, \eta)|$, as described in the following subsections.

3.2   The Radon Transform

Recall that the Radon transform (RT) of a real-valued function $\phi(x, y)$ defined on $\mathbb{R}^2$, at angle θ and distance ρ from the origin, is defined as

$$\mathcal{R}(\phi, \rho, \theta) = \int_{-\infty}^{\infty} \int_{-\infty}^{\infty} \phi(x, y)\, \delta(\rho - x \cos\theta - y \sin\theta)\, dx\, dy, \tag{6}$$

where δ denotes the Dirac delta function. Equivalently,

$$\mathcal{R}(\phi, \rho, \theta) = \int_{-\infty}^{\infty} \phi(\rho \cos\theta - s \sin\theta, \rho \sin\theta + s \cos\theta)\, ds. \tag{7}$$

The Radon transform $\mathcal{R}(\phi, \rho, \theta)$ is equal to the integral of ϕ along a line that forms an angle θ with the x-axis and is at a distance ρ from the origin [5].

3.3   Angle Estimation

The RT has been recently proposed for motion blur estimation in [12,15]. In [15], the angle estimate is the one for which the maximum of the RT occurs; naturally, this only works for rather long blurs, so that the image gets flat, leading to a maximum of the RT. In [12], the angle estimate is that for which $\mathcal{R}(\phi, \rho, \theta)$, as a function of ρ, has highest entropy. The authors claim to have a problem at 45° (due to the finite support of the images): at this angle, the entropy is maximum because the length of the integral is maximum, thus picking up the largest amount of noise (according to the authors' explanation). To circumvent this problem, they normalize the RT of the image with the RT of a matrix of 1's of the same dimension as the image. However, this explanation is not true; the true reason is related to the implementation of RT for digital images.

Our approach circumvents these limitations and allows excellent angle estimation performance, even for very short lengths. We use an exact RT for digital images, the details of which can be found in [16]. As explained above, for natural images, $\log |G(\xi, \eta)|$ has an approximate coarse behavior along radial lines, independent of the angle; thus the RT obtained by integrating on similar intervals, that is, with the same area for any direction, will also be approximately equal. Accordingly, instead of computing the RT for the whole image, we integrate in the maximum inscribed square,

$$\mathcal{R}_d(f, \rho, \theta) = \int_{-d}^{d} f(\rho \cos\theta - s \sin\theta, \rho \sin\theta + s \cos\theta)\, ds, \tag{8}$$

with $d = \frac{\sqrt{2}}{2}N$. This RT of $\log |G(\xi, \eta)|$ has approximately the same variance, independently of θ, thus avoiding the angle-dependence problem pointed out

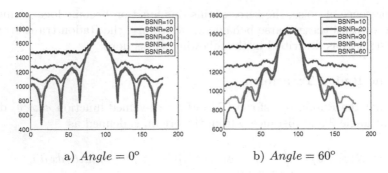

a) $Angle = 0°$ b) $Angle = 60°$

Fig. 1. Radon transform of the blurred cameraman ($L = 10$)

in [16]. Consequently, the variance of $\mathcal{R}_d(\log|G(\xi,\eta)|, \rho, \theta)$, as a function of θ, depends fundamentally on the orientation of the blur kernel.

The observations made in the previous paragraph lead to our proposed estimate for the angle of the motion blur kernel, which is given by

$$\widehat{\theta} = \arg\max_{\theta} \text{var}\{\mathcal{R}_d(\log|G(\xi,\eta)|, \rho, \theta)\} \tag{9}$$

where var$\{\}$ is the variance of the set of values obtained by varying ρ.

3.4 Length Estimation

Once we have $\widehat{\theta}$ (the estimate of the motion blur direction), we proceed to estimate the length of the motion blur kernel. Given that the sinc-like behavior is preserved in the RT at angle $\widehat{\theta}$, we base the estimation of the blur length on $\mathcal{R}_d(\log|G(\xi,\eta)|, \rho, \widehat{\theta})$. This line of attack is also followed in [15] using fuzzy sets and in [12] exploiting cepstral features. Figure 1 illustates this behaviour. The RT of the "cameraman" image, for angles $\theta = 0°$ and $\theta = 60°$ and blur length $L = 10$ exibits a clear sinc-like pattern.

In the present work, we propose an heuristic algorithm simpler than those introduced in [15,12], yet accurate. Let's denote $\Pi(\omega) = \mathcal{R}_d(\log|G(\xi,\eta)|, \omega, \widehat{\theta})$. From the above rationale, we conclude that the minima of $\Pi(\omega)$ are the minima of the Fourier transform of a rectangular pulse of size L. Let's then assume for a while that $\Pi(\omega)$ is indeed the Fourier transform of a rectangular pulse of length L_S, i.e,

$$\Pi(\omega) = e^{j\psi(\omega)} \frac{\sin(\frac{\omega L_S}{2})}{\sin(\frac{\omega}{2})}. \tag{10}$$

Our goal is to find L_S by seeking for the first positive zero of $\Pi(\omega)$ given by $\omega_0 = \frac{2\pi}{L_S}$. Since we have determined $\mathcal{R}_d$ based on an M point FFT, we approximate $\omega_0 = \frac{2\pi}{L_S}$ with the frequency $\frac{2\pi}{M}i$ corresponding to the minima of the FFT magnitude. We have then $\widehat{L}_S = \text{round}(M/i)$.

Algorithm 1 shows the pseudo-code for the estimation of the length $\widehat{L}$, where lines 2, 3, and 4 implement a robust estimator of the first minimum. Line 5 converts distance to number of pixels. Figure 2 illustrates the working of Algorithm 1 with two different RTs.

Algorithm 1. Length Estimation Algorithm

1: Compute the differences $\Delta_i = \Pi(\omega_i) - \Pi(\omega_{i-1})$ (only for $\omega > 0$)
2: Compute

$$\Delta_i^* = \begin{cases} p\,\Delta_i, & if\ \Delta_i > 0 \\ \Delta_i, & otherwise \end{cases} \tag{11}$$

where $p = 3$.
3: Compute the cumulative sums $\{S_1, S_2, ...\}$ where $S_i = \sum_{j=1}^{i} \Delta_i^*$.
4: Find the minimum $\hat{L}_S = \min\{S_1, S_2, ...\}$.
5: Compute

$$\hat{L} = \frac{N}{\hat{L}_S} C \tag{12}$$

where C is correction term is given by

$$C = \begin{cases} \cos(\hat{\theta}), & if\ |\hat{\theta}| \leq \pi/4 \\ \sin(\hat{\theta}), & if\ \pi/4 < |\hat{\theta}| \leq 3\pi/4 \end{cases} \tag{13}$$

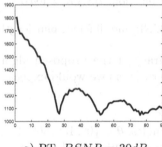 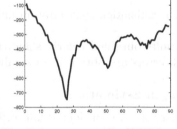

a) RT, $BSNR = 30dB$ b) Cummulative sums S_i, $BSNR = 30dB$

Fig. 2. Radon transform and cummulative sums S_i for motion blur of *length* = 10 pixels, *angle* = 0°

4 Experimental Results

In this section we evaluate the performance of the proposed algorithm in terms of the root mean squared error (RMSE) of the estimated parameters. We considered a set of 7 well known images: cameraman, Lena, Barbara, boats, mandrill, goldhill and peppers, all of size 256 by 256 pixels. RMSE is computed based on 70 runs, 10 for each image.

4.1 Angle Estimation

The use of DDA-based discrete PSF approximations makes it impossible to distinguish two kernels with nearby angles. Given a blur length L, we compute the intervals and respective middle angle, $\theta_m(L)$, that leads to the same blur kernel. For each test angle, we choose the closest $\theta_m(L)$ and use this value in the simulations. We proceed in the same way for the estimated angle, which leads to the error defined by

$$\text{error} = \hat{\theta}_m(L) - \theta_m(L). \tag{14}$$

Since we can not evaluate all possible scenarios, we considered six different motion blur lengths, $L \in \{4, 12, 20, 24, 32, 40\}$ pixels, with two different blur-signal-to-noise ratios (BSNR) of 10dB and 40dB. The obtained results are shown in figure (3).

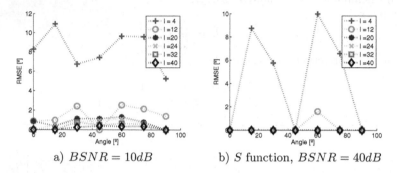

a) $BSNR = 10dB$ b) S function, $BSNR = 40dB$

Fig. 3. Estimation angle error for different BSNR and different blur length

The results obtained clearly show the accuracy of the proposed algorithm. The worst errors are obtained for small blur kernels, as we would expect.

4.2   Length Estimation

In a similar way, we considered four different angles, $\theta \in \{0°, 15°, 30°, 45°\}$, and two different BSNR, 15 and 40 (dB). The obtained results are shown in figure 4.

The results again show the accuracy of the proposed algorithm, even in the worst BSNR. For large blur lengths, the errors are bigger, given that the first zero of $\Pi(\omega)$ is close to the origin and $\hat{L}$ is inversely proportional to this frequency. Then, small errors in this location are very amplified. For short blurs, the proposed algorithm fails when the BSNR is low. In this situation, the RT is too noisy, and the heuristic value of p used in Algorithm 1 leads to poor estimate.

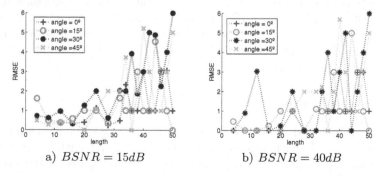

a) $BSNR = 15dB$ b) $BSNR = 40dB$

Fig. 4. Estimation length error for different BSNR and different blur angle

5 Conclusion

This paper introduced a robust algorithm to infer motion blur parameters, namely the motion direction and the motion length. The angular quasi-invariance of natural images spectrum was exploited in the Radom transform domain. The effectiveness of the method was illustrated in a set of experiments.

References

1. Bar, L., Sochen, N., Kiryat, N.: Variational pairing of image segmentation and blind restoration. In: Pajdla, T., Matas, J(G.) (eds.) ECCV 2004. LNCS, vol. 3024, Springer, Heidelberg (2004)
2. Bioucas-Dias, J.: Bayesian wavelet-based image deconvolution: a GEM algorithm exploiting a class of heavy-tailed priors. IEEE Transactions on Image Processing 15, 937–951 (2006)
3. Bioucas-Dias, J., Figueiredo, M., Oliveira, J.: Total variation-based image deconvolution: A majorization-minimization approach. IEEE International Conference on Acoustics, Speech, and Signal Processing - ICASSP'2006, Toulouse, France (2006)
4. Bioucas-Dias, J., Figueiredo, M., Oliveira, J.: Adaptive Bayesian/total-variation image deconvolution: A majorization-minimization approach. European Signal Processing Conference - EUSIPCO'2006, Florence, Italy (2006)
5. Bracewell, R.: Two-Dimensional Imaging. Prentice-Hall, Englewood Cliffs (1995)
6. Carasso, A.: Direct blind deconvolution. SIAM Journal of Applied Mathematics 1, 1980–2007 (2001)
7. Chan, T., Wong, C.: Total variation blind deconvolution. IEEE Transactions on Image Processing 7, 370–375 (1998)
8. Combettes, P., Pesquet, J.: 'Image deconvolution with total variation bounds. In: Proceedings of the Seventh International Symposium on Signal Processing and Its. Applications,Paris, France 1, 441–444 (2003)
9. Figueiredo, M., Nowak, R.: An EM algorithm for wavelet-based image restoration. IEEE Trans. on Image Processing 12, 906–916 (2003)
10. Figueiredo, M., Nowak, R.: A bound optimization approach to wavelet-based image deconvolution. IEEE Intern. Conf. on Image Processing – ICIP'05, Genoa, Italy (2005)
11. Harrington, S.: Computer Graphics: A Programming Approach. McGraw-Hill, New York (1985)
12. Krahmer, F., Lin, Y., McAdoo, B., Ott, K., Wang, J., Widemannk, D., Wohlberg, B.: Blind image deconvolution: motion blur estimation. Technical Report, Institute of Mathematics and its Applications, University of Minnesota (2006)
13. Kundur, D., Hatzinakos, D.: Blind image deconvolution. Signal Processing Magazine 13, 43–64 (1996)
14. Kundur, D., Hatzinakos, D.: Blind image deconvolution revisited. Signal Processing Magazine 13, 61–63 (1996)
15. Moghaddam, M., Jamzad, M.: Motion blur identification in noisy images using fuzzy sets. In: Proceedings of the Fifth IEEE International Symposium on Signal Processing and Information Technology, pp. 862–866 (2005)
16. Oliveira, J.: Implementation of an exact Radon transform. Technical Report, Instituto de Telecomunicações, Lisboa (2006)

Dependent Component Analysis: A Hyperspectral Unmixing Algorithm

José M.P. Nascimento[1] and José M. Bioucas-Dias[2,*]

[1] Instituto Superior de Engenharia de Lisboa and Instituto de Telecomunicações
zen@isel.pt
[2] Instituto de Telecomunicações and Instituto Superior Técnico, T.U. Lisbon
bioucas@lx.it.pt

Abstract. Linear unmixing decomposes a hyperspectral image into a collection of reflectance spectra of the materials present in the scene, called endmember signatures, and the corresponding abundance fractions at each pixel in a spatial area of interest.

This paper introduces a new unmixing method, called Dependent Component Analysis (DECA), which overcomes the limitations of unmixing methods based on Independent Component Analysis (ICA) and on geometrical properties of hyperspectral data.

DECA models the abundance fractions as mixtures of Dirichlet densities, thus enforcing the constraints on abundance fractions imposed by the acquisition process, namely non-negativity and constant sum. The mixing matrix is inferred by a generalized expectation-maximization (GEM) type algorithm. The performance of the method is illustrated using simulated and real data.

1 Introduction

Spaceborn and airborne hyperspectral sensors acquire images of ground surface radiance in hundreds of narrow contiguous bands simultaneously [1]. The radiance, collected in a spectral vector, are mixtures of spectra from the substances present in the respective pixel coverage.

Given a set of mixed hyperspectral vectors, linear unmixing aims at estimating the number of reference substances, also called endmembers, their spectral signatures, and their abundance fractions.

Linear spectral unmixing considers that a mixed pixel is a linear combination of endmember signatures weighted by the correspondent abundance fractions [2]. Under this model, the observations from a scene are in a simplex whose vertices correspond to the endmembers.

Several approaches such as *vertex component analysis* (VCA) [3], *pixel purity index* (PPI) [4], and N-FINDR [5] have exploited geometric features of hyperspectral mixtures to determine the smallest simplex containing the data. Those

---

* This work was supported by the FCT, under the projects POSC/EEA-CPS/61271/2004 and PDCTE/CPS/49967/2003 and by IPL under project IPL-5828/2004.

J. Martí et al. (Eds.): IbPRIA 2007, Part II, LNCS 4478, pp. 612–619, 2007.

methods assume the presence in the data of at least one pure pixel of each endmember. This is a strong requisite that may not hold in some data sets.

Independent Component Analysis (ICA) has recently been proposed as a tool to blindly unmix hyperspectral data [6, 7, 8]. However, ICA applicability is compromised by the statistical dependence existing among abundances [9]. This dependence results from the constant sum constraint imposed on the abundance fractions by the acquisition process [2]. In ICA jargon, sources are not independent. Thus, the central assumption of ICA is not satisfied.

This paper proposes a new method to blindly unmix hyperspectral data, termed *dependent component analysis* (DECA), where abundance fractions are modelled by a mixture of Dirichlet densities, thus automatically enforcing source nonnegativity and constant sum constraints. DECA is in the vein of works [10, 11] replacing independent sources represented by Mixtures of Gaussians (MOGs) with mixtures of Dirichlet (MODs) sources. The mixing matrix is inferred by a generalized expectation-maximization (GEM) type algorithm. The resulting scheme is suited to hyperspectral unmixing since abundance fractions dependence is ensured. Whereas works [10, 11] assume independent sources (abundance fractions), which is not the hyperspectral data case. Compared with the geometric based approaches, the advantage of DECA is that there is no need to have pure pixels in the observations.

The paper is organized as follows. Section 2 describes the fundamentals of the proposed method. Sections 3 and 4 illustrate aspects of the performance of DECA approach with experimental and real data, respectively. Section 5 ends the paper by presenting a few concluding remarks.

2 Statistical Modelling and Unmixing Algorithm

Assuming the linear observation model, each pixel $\mathbf{r}$ of an hyperspectral image can be represented as a spectral vector in $\mathbb{R}^L$ (L is the number of bands) and is given by $\mathbf{r} = \mathbf{Ms}$, where $\mathbf{M} \equiv [\mathbf{m}_1, \mathbf{m}_2, \ldots, \mathbf{m}_p]$ is a $L \times p$ mixing matrix ($\mathbf{m}_i$ denotes the ith endmember signature), p is the number of endmembers present in the covered area, and $\mathbf{s} = [s_1, s_2, \ldots, s_p]^T$ is the abundance vector containing the fractions of each endmember (notation $(\cdot)^T$ stands for vector transposed).

To be physically meaningful [2], abundance fractions are subject to nonnegativity and constant sum constraints, *i.e.*, $\{\mathbf{s} \in \mathbb{R}^p : s_j \geq 0, \sum_{j=1}^{p} s_j = 1\}$. Note that only $p - 1$ components of $\mathbf{s}$ are free, *i.e.*, $s_p = 1 - \sum_{j=1}^{p-1} s_j$. Therefore the spectral vectors are in a $p - 1$ dimensional simplex in $\mathbb{R}^L$.

Usually the number of endmembers is much lower than the number of bands ($p \ll L$). Thus, the observed spectral vectors can be projected onto the signal subspace. The identification of the signal subspace improves the SNR, allows a correct dimension reduction, and, thus, yields gains in computational time and complexity [12]. Let $\mathbf{E}_p$ be a matrix with orthonormal columns, spanning the signal subspace. The coordinates of the spectral vector $\mathbf{r}$ with respect to $\mathbf{E}_p$ are

$$\mathbf{x} \equiv \mathbf{E}_p^T \mathbf{r}$$
$$= \mathbf{E}_p^T \mathbf{M} \mathbf{s}$$
$$= \mathbf{A} \mathbf{s}, \tag{1}$$

where $\mathbf{A}$ is a $p \times p$ square mixing matrix and $\mathbf{x} = [x_1, x_2, \ldots, x_p]^T$ is a $p \times 1$ vector. Let's assume that $\mathbf{W} \equiv \mathbf{A}^{-1}$ exists. Then, we have $\mathbf{s} = \mathbf{W} \mathbf{x}$.

Consider that each vector $\mathbf{x}$ represents one particular outcome of a p-dimensional random variable $\mathbf{X} = [X_1, \ldots, X_p]^T$. Given a set of N independent and identically distributed samples $\mathcal{X} = \{\mathbf{x}^{(1)}, \ldots, \mathbf{x}^{(N)}\}$, then, we may write the likelihood of the unmixing matrix $\mathbf{W}$ and of the set of parameters $\boldsymbol{\theta}$ as

$$\mathcal{L}_N(\mathbf{W}, \boldsymbol{\theta}) \equiv \frac{1}{N} \log p_X(\mathcal{X}|\mathbf{W}, \boldsymbol{\theta})$$
$$= \mathbb{T}[\log p_X(\mathbf{x}|\mathbf{W}, \boldsymbol{\theta})]$$
$$= \mathbb{T}[\log p_S(\mathbf{s}|\boldsymbol{\theta})] + \log|\det \mathbf{W}|, \tag{2}$$

where we have used the fact that $p_X(\mathbf{x}) = p_S(\mathbf{s})|\det(\mathbf{W})|$ and $\mathbb{T}[\mathbf{x}] \equiv 1/N \sum_{i=1}^{N} \mathbf{x}^{(i)}$, *i.e.*, $\mathbb{T}[\mathbf{x}]$ is the sample average of $\mathbf{x}$.

Assume that the abundance fractions follow a K-component Dirichlet finite mixture given by

$$p_S(\mathbf{s}|\boldsymbol{\theta}) = \sum_{q=1}^{K} \epsilon_q \underbrace{\frac{\Gamma(\sum_{j=1}^{p} \theta_{qj})}{\prod_{j=1}^{p} \Gamma(\theta_{qj})} \prod_{j=1}^{p} s_j^{\theta_{qj}-1}}_{D(\mathbf{s}|\boldsymbol{\theta}_q)}, \tag{3}$$

where the complete set of parameters is $\boldsymbol{\theta} = \{\epsilon_1, \ldots, \epsilon_K, \boldsymbol{\theta}_1, \ldots, \boldsymbol{\theta}_K\}$ with $\epsilon_1, \ldots, \epsilon_K$ being the weight of the Dirichlet modes and $\boldsymbol{\theta}_q = \{\theta_{q1}, \ldots, \theta_{qp}\}$, for $q = 1, \ldots, K$, the q-component parameters. Replacing expression (3) in to (2), it follows that

$$\mathcal{L}_N(\mathbf{W}, \boldsymbol{\theta}) = \mathbb{T}\left[\log \sum_{q=1}^{K} \epsilon_q D(\mathbf{s}|\boldsymbol{\theta}_q)\right] + \log(|\det \mathbf{W}|). \tag{4}$$

The maximum likelihood (ML) estimate $\left(\widehat{\mathbf{W}}, \widehat{\boldsymbol{\theta}}\right) = \arg\max_{\mathbf{W}, \boldsymbol{\theta}} \mathcal{L}_N(\mathbf{W}, \boldsymbol{\theta})$ can not be found analytically [13]. The usual choice for obtaining the ML estimates of the parameters is the EM framework [14], which relies on the so-called incomplete data and missing data. In our setup, $\mathcal{X}$ denotes the incomplete data and $\mathcal{Z} = \{\mathbf{z}^{(1)}, \ldots, \mathbf{z}^{(N)}\}$ the missing data. Each label $\mathbf{z}^{(i)} = \left[z_1^{(i)}, \ldots, z_K^{(i)}\right]$ is a binary K-vector, where only one component z_q^i is set to one indicating which mode produced the i-sample. The complete log-likelihood is then

$$\mathcal{L}_C(\mathbf{W}, \boldsymbol{\theta}) = \frac{1}{N} \log[p_{X,Z}(\mathcal{X}, \mathcal{Z}|\boldsymbol{\theta})]$$
$$= \mathbb{T}\left[\sum_{q=1}^{K} z_q \log \epsilon_q D(\mathbf{s}|\boldsymbol{\theta}_q)\right] + \log(|\det \mathbf{W}|). \tag{5}$$

The EM algorithm iterates between the E-step and the M-step [14, 15]:

- **E-step:** Computes the conditional expectation of the complete log-likelihood, given the samples and the current estimate $\widehat{\theta}^{(t)}$. The result is the so-called Q-function

$$Q(\theta, \widehat{\theta}^{(t)}) = \mathbb{T}\left[\sum_{q=1}^{K} \underbrace{\mathbb{E}\left[z_q | \mathbf{s}, \widehat{\theta}^{(t)}\right]}_{\beta_q^{(t)}} \log\left[\epsilon_q^{(t)} D\left(\mathbf{s} | \theta_q^{(t)}\right)\right]\right] + \log\left(|\det \mathbf{W}|\right), \quad (6)$$

where

$$\beta_q^{(t)}(\mathbf{s}) = \frac{\widehat{\epsilon}_q^{(t)} D\left(\mathbf{s} | \widehat{\theta}_q^{(t)}\right)}{\sum_{l=1}^{K} \widehat{\epsilon}_l^{(t)} D\left(\mathbf{s} | \widehat{\theta}_l^{(t)}\right)}. \quad (7)$$

- **M-step:** Updates the parameter estimates according to

$$\widehat{\theta}^{(t+1)} = \arg\max_{\theta}\left\{Q\left(\theta, \widehat{\theta}^{(t)}\right)\right\}. \quad (8)$$

The maximization of Q in (8) is still a hard problem. Instead of computing $\widehat{\theta}^{(t+1)}$, we maximize $Q(\theta, \widehat{\theta}^{(t)})$ with respect to θ_j, for $j = 1, \ldots, p$, resulting in the following learning rules for the mixing probabilities and for the mixture of Dirichlet source parameters (see [16, 18]):

$$\epsilon_q^{(t)} = \mathbb{T}\left[\beta_q^{(t)}(\mathbf{s})\right], \quad (9)$$

$$\widehat{\theta}_{qj}^{(t+1)} = \mathrm{psi}^{-1}\left(\mathrm{psi}\left(\sum_{l=1}^{p} \widehat{\theta}_{ql}^{(t)}\right) + \frac{\mathbb{T}\left[\beta_q^{(t)}(\mathbf{s}) \log \widehat{s}_j^{(t)}\right]}{\mathbb{T}\left[\beta_q^{(t)}(\mathbf{s})\right]}\right), \quad (10)$$

for $q = 1 \ldots, K$ and $j = 1 \ldots, p$, respectively[1].

The resulting algorithm is of the generalized expectation-maximization class (GEM) [14]: the learning rule (9) maximizes Q-function with respect to $\epsilon_q^{(t)}$, whereas expression (10) assures that the Q-function does not decrease (see [16, 17] for details).

To solve the equation $\partial Q / \partial \mathbf{W} = 0$ we implement an iterative gradient type learning rule is derived for the unmixing matrix $\mathbf{W}$:

$$\mathbf{W}^{(t+1)} = \mathbf{W}^{(t)} + \tau^{(t)} \left(\frac{\partial Q}{\partial \mathbf{W}}\right)^{(t)}, \quad (11)$$

---

[1] $\mathrm{psi}(\cdot)$ and $\mathrm{psi}^{-1}(\cdot)$ denote the psi function (logarithmic derivative of the Gamma function) and its inverse, respectively.

where $\tau^{(t)}$ determines the learning rate on iteration t and

$$\left(\frac{\partial Q}{\partial \mathbf{w}_j}\right)^{(t)} = \mathbb{T}\left[\sum_{q=1}^{K}\beta_q^{(t)}\left(\frac{(\widehat{\theta}_{qj}^{(t)}-1)}{\widehat{s}_j} - \frac{(\widehat{\theta}_{qp}^{(t)}-1)}{\widehat{s}_p}\right)\mathbf{x}^T\right] + \left[\mathbf{W}^{-T}\right]_{j,:} - \left[\mathbf{W}^{-T}\right]_{p,:},$$

(12)

where $\mathbf{w}_j$, for $j = 1,\ldots,p-1$ denotes the jth row of matrix $\mathbf{W}$ and $\left[\mathbf{W}^{-T}\right]_{j,:}$ denotes the jth row of the inverse of $\mathbf{W}$ transposed.

3   Evaluation with Simulated Data

In this section DECA is tested in simulated scenes. The data is generated according to expression (1), where three signatures where selected from the USGS digital spectral library The scene is composed by 10^5 pixels partitioned into two regions; region A has the half size of the region B. The abundance fractions follow a Dirichlet distribution with $\boldsymbol{\theta}_a = [9, 2, 9]$ and $\boldsymbol{\theta}_b = [2, 15, 7]$ for regions A and B of the scene, respectively. Pure pixels were removed from the data set in order to illustrate the robustness of DECA to the absence of pure pixels.

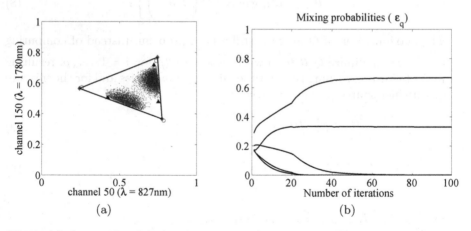

(a)   (b)

Fig. 1. (a) Scatterplot (bands $\lambda = 827nm$ and $\lambda = 1780nm$) of the three endmembers mixture: true endmembers (circles); VCA estimate (triangles); DECA estimate (diamonds); (b) Dirichlet mixing probabilities

In this experiment the number of modes is set to $K = 5$, the Dirichlet parameters are randomly initialized, and the mixing probabilities are set to $\epsilon_q = 1/K$, for $q = 1,\ldots,K$. This setting reflects a situation in which no knowledge of the size and of the number of regions in the scene exist. Fig. 1(a) presents a scatterplot (bands $\lambda = 827nm$ and $\lambda = 1780nm$) of the simulated scene, where dots represent the pixels. The two clouds correspond to the two regions A and B, respectively. It is also presented the true endmembers (circles), the endmembers estimation (diamonds), and, for comparison purposes the endmembers estimation by VCA (triangles) which, has shown in [3], performs better than PPI and better or equal than N-FINDR.

The estimates provided by the DECA algorithm are very close to the true endmembers, whereas those provided by VCA are not. The reasoning behind this behavior is that DECA searches for the smallest simplex that contains all data, whereas VCA finds the most pure pixels in data (see triangles in Fig. 1(a)). Since there is no pure pixels in data, VCA performs worse than DECA.

Fig 1(b), presents the evolution of the Dirichlet mixing probabilities (ϵ_q, for $q = 1, \ldots, K$) as function of the number of iterations of the algorithm. Note that three modes tend to zero and the remaining modes have the values of 0.65 and 0.33, corresponding to the weight of the region B and region A respectively. Table 1 presents the Dirichlet parameters and their estimates. Although the estimated values are near from the true parameter values, we note that this does not have to happen necessarily, since the same distribution can be modelled with different MODs. We note that the main purpose of the DECA algorithm is the estimation of the unmixing matrix $\mathbf{W}$ and not the estimation of the MOD parameters.

Table 1. Estimated Dirichlet parameters

region	A			B		
θ	9	2	9	2	15	7
$\widehat{\theta}$	9.0	2.2	10.0	2.5	14.8	9.7

The result of the separation process is illustrated trough the product of the unmixing matrix $\mathbf{W}$ and square mixing matrix $\mathbf{A}$ which would be, in an ideal scenario, the identity matrix $\mathbf{I}_p$, apart from a permutation. In this experiment, we obtained

$$\mathbf{WA} = \begin{bmatrix} \mathbf{0.97} & 0.02 & -0.02 \\ 0.03 & \mathbf{0.93} & -0.02 \\ 0.00 & 0.04 & \mathbf{1.03} \end{bmatrix}. \tag{13}$$

The same pattern of behavior was, however, found on a set of simulated experiments for different endmember signatures, different number of endmembers, and different abundance fraction distributions.

4   Experiments with Real Hyperspectral Data

In this section, DECA is applied to real hyperspectral data collected by the AVIRIS sensor over Cuprite, Nevada[2]. This site has been extensively used for remote sensing experiments over the past years and its geology was previously mapped in detail [19]. This site has become a standard test site for comparison of unmixing and endmember extraction algorithms.

Fig. 2 (a) presents the subimage (50 × 90 pixels and 224 bands) for this experiment. Due to several degradation mechanisms normally found in hyperspectral applications (namely signature variability, topography modulation, and noise),

---

[2] Available at http://aviris.jpl.nasa.gov/html/aviris.freedata.html

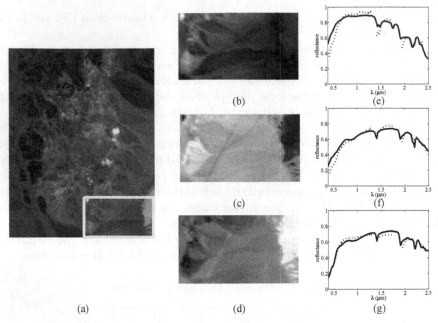

Fig. 2. (a) Band 30 (wavelength $\lambda = 667.3nm$) of the subimage of AVIRIS cuprite Nevada data set (rectangle denotes the image fraction used in the experiment);(b)-(d) Alunite, Kaolinite, and Montmorillonite abundance fractions; (e)-(g) Alunite, Kaolinite, and Montmorillonite spectra (solid line) and DECA estimated signatures (dotted line)

the observed data is not in a simplex. To obtain a simplex, a projective projection of data onto a hyperplane $\mathbf{y}^T\mathbf{u} = 1$ is implemented as a pre-processing step (see [3] for more details). A visual comparison between the abundance fractions estimates on the cuprite data set and the ground truth presented in [19] shows that first, second, and third extracted endmembers are predominantly Alunite, Kaolinite, and Montmorillonite, respectively (see Fig. 2 (b)-(d)).

A comparison of the estimated endmember signatures with laboratory spectrum is presented in Fig. 2. The signatures provided by DECA are scaled in order to minimize the mean square error between them and the respective library spectra. The estimated signatures are very close to the laboratory spectra reflectances.

5   Conclusion

Blind hyperspectral linear unmixing aims at estimating the number of endmembers, their spectral signatures, and their abundance fractions at each pixel, using only the observed data (mixed pixels). In this paper, a new method is proposed to blindly unmix hyperspectral data, where abundance fractions are modelled as Dirichlet sources. This model forces abundance fractions to be nonnegative and to have constant sum on each pixel. The mixing matrix is inferred by an EM type algorithm. The main advantage of this model is that there is no need to have pure pixels in the observations.

The performance of the proposed model is illustrated with simulated and real hyperspectral data. Comparisons with pure pixel estimation methods are conducted. The results achieved show the effectiveness of DECA on hyperspectral data unmixing. In future work, the proposed algorithm shall be improved in order to account for sensor noise.

References

1. Lillesand, T., Kiefer, R., Chipman, J.: Remote Sensing and Image Interpretation, 5th edn. John Wiley & Sons, Inc, New York (2004)
2. Keshava, N., Mustard, J.: Spectral unmixing. IEEE Sig. Proc. Mag. 19(1), 44–57 (2002)
3. Nascimento, J., Dias, J.: Vertex component analysis: A fast algorithm to unmix hyperspectral data. IEEE Trans. Geosci. Rem. Sens. 43(4), 898–910 (2005)
4. Boardman, J.: Automating spectral unmixing of AVIRIS data using convex geometry concepts. In: JPL Pub. 93-26, AVIRIS Workshop, Vol. 1, pp. 11–14 (1993)
5. Winter, M.: N-findr: an algorithm for fast autonomous spectral end-member determination in hyperspectral data. In: Olsen, O.F., Florack, L.M.J., Kuijper, A. (eds.) DSSCV 2005. LNCS, vol. 3753, pp. 266–275. Springer, Heidelberg (2005)
6. Tu, T.: Unsupervised signature extraction and separation in hyperspectral images: A noise-adjusted fast independent component analysis approach. Opt. Eng. of SPIE 39(4), 897–906 (2000)
7. Lennon, M., Mouchot, M., Mercier, G., Hubert-Moy, L.: Spectral unmixing of hyperspectral images with the independent component analysis and wavelet packets. In: Proc. of IEEE IGARSS (2001)
8. Parra, L., Mueller, K., Spence, C., Ziehe, A., Sajda, P.: Unmixing hyperspectral data. Advances in Neural Information Processing Systems 12, 942–948 (2000)
9. Nascimento, J., Dias, J.: Does independent component analysis play a role in unmixing hyperspectral data? IEEE Trans. Geosci. Rem. Sens. 43(1), 175–187 (2005)
10. Attias, H.: Independent factor analysis. Neural Computation 11(4), 803–851 (1999)
11. Moulines, E., Cardoso, J., Gassiat, E.: Maximum likelihood for blind separation and deconvolution of noisy signals using mixture models. In: Proc. of the IEEE ICASSP 5, 3617–3620 (1997)
12. Nascimento, J., Dias, J.: Signal subspace identification in hyperspectral linear mixtures. In: Marques, J.S., Pérez de la Blanca, N., Pina, P. (eds.) IbPRIA 2005. LNCS, vol. 3523, pp. 207–214. Springer, Heidelberg (2005)
13. McLachlan, G., Peel, D.: Finite Mixture Models. John Wiley & Sons, Inc, New York (2000)
14. McLachlan, G., Krishnan, T.: The EM Algorithm and Extensions. John Wiley & Sons, Inc, New York (1996)
15. Optimization: Kenneth Lange. First edn. Springer (2004)
16. Dias, J.: An EM algorithm for the estimation of dirichlet parameters. Technical report, Instituto de Telecomunicações, http://www.lx.it.pt/~bioucas/ (2005)
17. Nascimento, J., Dias, J.: Unmixing Hyperspectral Data: Independent and Dependent Component Analysis. In: Hyperspectral Data Exploitation: Theory and Applications(in press), John Wiley & Sons, Inc, Chichester (2006)
18. Minka, T.: Estimating a dirichlet distribution. Technical report, M.I.T (2000)
19. Swayze, G., Clark, R., Sutley, S., Gallagher, A.: Ground-truthing aviris mineral mapping at cuprite, nevada. JPL Pub. AVIRIS Workshop 1, 47–49 (1992)

Synchronization of Video Sequences from Free-Moving Cameras

Joan Serrat, Ferran Diego, Felipe Lumbreras, and José Manuel Álvarez

Computer Vision Center & Computer Science Dept.
Edifici O, Universitat Autònoma de Barcelona,
08193 Cerdanyola, Spain

Abstract. We present a new method for the synchronization of a pair of video sequences and the spatial registration of all the temporally corresponding frames. This is a mandatory step to perform a pixel wise comparison of a pair of videos. Several proposals for video matching can be found in the literature, with a variety of applications like object detection, visual sensor fusion, high dynamic range and action recognition. The main contribution of our method is that it is free from three common restrictions assumed in previous works. First, it does not impose any condition on the relative position of the two cameras, since they can move freely. Second, it does not assume a parametric temporal mapping relating the time stamps of the two videos, like a constant or linear time shift. Third, it does not rely on the complete trajectories of image features (points or lines) along time, something difficult to obtain automatically in general. We present our results in the context of the comparison of videos captured from a camera mounted on moving vehicles.

1 Introduction

Image matching or registration has received a considerable attention for many years and is still an active subject for its role in segmentation (background subtraction), recognition, sensor fusion, construction of panoramic mosaics, motion estimation, etc. Video matching shares with still image matching a great deal of potential applications. It requires simultaneous alignment in the temporal and spatial dimensions. Temporal alignment or synchronization means to find out a mapping from the time domain of the first sequence to the second one, such that corresponding frame pairs, each from one sequence, show 'similar content'. The simplest notion of similar content is that a warping can be found which spatially aligns one frame with the other, to the extent that they can be compared pixel wise. But it is not unique, as we will comment.

Several solutions to the problem of video synchronization can be found in the literature. Here we briefly review those we consider the most significant. This is relevant to put into context our work, but also because, under the generic label of temporal alignment, they try to solve rather different problems. The distinction is based on the assumptions made by each method. For instance, some methods [1,2,3,4,5,6] assume the temporal correspondence to be a simple constant time

J. Martí et al. (Eds.): IbPRIA 2007, Part II, LNCS 4478, pp. 620–627, 2007.

offset $c(t_1) = \beta$ or linear [7,8] $c(t_1) = \alpha t_1 + \beta$, the later due to the different frame rate of the two cameras, whereas others [9,10] let it be of free form. More importantly, some methods [1,2,3,7,4,5] are tailored to videos acquired simultaneously, in order to show exactly the same motion or keep constant the relative position and orientation of the two cameras. Others [10,9,8,6], instead, can also deal with sequences recorded at different times, showing slightly different object motions, like one same action performed by different people. A few works [9,4] address the case of free moving cameras, where no fixed geometric relationship exists among them. Each method needs some input data which can be more or less difficult to obtain and hamper its practical applicability. For instance, feature–based methods require tracking one or more characteristic points along the two whole sequences [7,3,10,5,6], or points and lines in three sequences [4]. In contrast, direct methods are those built just on the image intensity values [7,9,8]. What's more, some methods need to estimate quantities for which not very robust techniques exist, like the fundamental matrix [2,6] and the trifocal tensor [4].

Concerning the basis of these methods, most of them rely on the existence of a geometric entity which somehow constraints the relationship between the coordinate systems of two frames *if* they are corresponding: an affine transform [8], a plane–induce homography [1,7], the fundamental matrix [2,6], the trifocal tensor [4], and a deficient rank condition on a matrix made of the complete trajectories of tracked points along a whole sequence [10,3,5]. This fact allows either to formulate some minimization over the time correspondence parameters (e.g. α, β), to perform an algorithmic search for them, or at least to directly look for pairs of corresponding times. A few methods, in our opinion more realistic from the point of view of practical applicability, are based on the image intensities instead of point trajectories [7,9,8].

Our goal is to synchronize videos recorded simultaneously or at different times, which can thus differ in intensity and even in content, i.e., show different objects or actions (motion), up to an extent. Videos can be recorded by a pair of free moving cameras, but their motion is not completely free. For the video matching to be possible, there must be some overlapping in the field of view of the two cameras, when they are at the same or close positions. Thus, we require that they follow *approximately* coincident trajectories and, more importantly, that the relative camera rotations between corresponding frames are not too large. Note that, even in this case, free motion precludes the use of a constant epipolar constraint. The scene is 3D: we do not impose the condition of planar or very far away scenes, so that the constant homography constraint can not be applied. Neither do we want to depend on error–free and complete feature trajectories, provided manually or by an ideal tracker. Finally, the time correspondence is free form: anyone of the cameras can stop while the other keeps moving.

Our work is most closely related to [9] in the sense of striving for generality and applicability. Beyond this, each of the former steps is completely different. For instance, they do not adopt any explicit motion field model for corresponding frames, as we do. Also, their frame matching measure is based on point (Harris corners) correspondences, computed with an EM–like algorithm plus a Kanade–Lucas–Tomasi local motion optimization. We guess this makes their method dependent on having a number of such characteristic points evenly distributed on the images, along the whole sequences, as shown in their results. In contrast, we will be able to synchronize videos with a much more sparse structure (e.g. night sequences).

We propose a method which replaces the former constraints on the coordinates of every pair of corresponding frames (provided by a certain *fixed* affine transform, homography, fundamental matrix or trifocal tensor) by a specific image motion field model (Sect. 2.1). Its five parameters can vary from pair to pair due to the free moving cameras assumption, but some dependencies exist among them that we enforce. For each candidate pair of frames, the estimation of these parameters allows to compute an spatial alignment error (Sect. 2.2). Based on it, an efficient divide–and–conquer procedure searches the corresponding frame in the second video for all the frames in the first one (Sect. 2.3). We present some results in the context of a realistic and challenging application (Sect. 4). Imagine a car, equipped with a forward facing camera, which repeatedly drives along one same track, for building surveillance. We want to compare two videos, at different times, because differences are potential signs of intruders: office lights switched on or off, parked cars etc. which have changed from the previous round. Finally, Sect. 5 draws the conclusions.

2   Method

2.1   A Motion Model for Corresponding Frames

Two frames, one from each video sequence, are corresponding if the cameras were on the same 3D location at the time they were recorded. Thus, ideally, only the camera pose could vary, that is, their relative orientation which is expressed by a rotation matrix R. Let be $P_1 = K_1 [I \mid 0]$ and $P_2 = K_2 [R \mid 0]$ the projection matrices of the two cameras, having centered the reference coordinate system in the first camera. It can be seen then that the coordinates of the two frames are related by the homography $H = K_2 R K_1^{-1}$.

We aim at defining a simple, linear parametrized model for the image coordinate difference (or motion vector) of two corresponding points, both in space and time. To this end, we are going to state several simplifying, yet reasonable assumptions:

1. The two cameras have the same intrinsic parameters, that is, $K_1 = K_2 = K$. Then $H = KRK^{-1}$, a conjugate rotation.
2. The principal point (the origin of the image coordinate system) is at the image center, and the focal lengths for the x and y axis are equal, $f_x = f_y = f$. Hence, $K = \text{diag}(f, f, 1)$.
3. Let the rotation R be parametrized by the Euler angles $\Omega_x, \Omega_y, \Omega_z$ (respectively pitch, yaw and roll). If they are all small enough, R can be substituted by its first order approximation, $R = [(\Omega_x, \Omega_y, \Omega_z)]_\times$. Accordingly,

$$H = \begin{bmatrix} 1 & -\Omega_z & f\Omega_y \\ \Omega_z & 1 & -f\Omega_x \\ -\Omega_y/f & \Omega_x/f & 1 \end{bmatrix} \tag{1}$$

Note that the relationship between coordinates of corresponding frames is linear but in homogeneous coordinates. Thus, the motion vector between a point $\mathbf{x}$ from the first to the second frame is

$$\mathbf{u}(\mathbf{x}) = \mathbf{x}_2 - \mathbf{x}_1 = \begin{bmatrix} u(\mathbf{x}) \\ v(\mathbf{x}) \end{bmatrix} = \frac{1}{H_3\mathbf{x}} \begin{bmatrix} (H_1 - xH_3)\mathbf{x} \\ (H_2 - yH_3)\mathbf{x} \end{bmatrix} \tag{2}$$

where H_i denotes the i-th row of H. Let us add a final assumption to obtain a linear dependence in non–homogeneous coordinates.

4. For f large enough (that is, a medium to narrow camera field of view), since the rotation angle is small, $H_3\mathbf{x} = -x\Omega_y/f + y\Omega_x/f + 1 \approx 1$.

Finally, we obtain a parametric motion field model which is called quadratic for its dependence on the terms x^2, y^2 [11] but linear with regard its parameters p_i:

$$\mathbf{u}(\mathbf{x}; \mathbf{p}) = X\mathbf{p} = \begin{bmatrix} 1 & y & x^2 & xy & 0 \\ 0 & -x & xy & y^2 & 1 \end{bmatrix} \begin{bmatrix} p_1 \\ p_2 \\ p_3 \\ p_4 \\ p_5 \end{bmatrix}, \mathbf{p} = S\Omega = \begin{bmatrix} 0 & f & 0 \\ 0 & 0 & -1 \\ 0 & 1/f & 0 \\ -1/f & 0 & 0 \\ -f & 0 & 0 \end{bmatrix} \begin{bmatrix} \Omega_x \\ \Omega_y \\ \Omega_z \end{bmatrix} \tag{3}$$

2.2 Spatial Frame Matching

We need a measure of spatial registration of a pair of frames, in order to choose the frame K in the second sequence that best matches a given frame J from the first one. To this end, we have devised the motion field model of Eq. (3), which parametrizes the motion field between frames if they are corresponding. Consequently, we need to estimate the parameters $\mathbf{p}$ that minimize some registration error measure and use its magnitude. We have chosen the sum of squared *linearized* differences (i.e., the linearized brightness constancy):

$$\sum_{\mathbf{x}} \left(K(\mathbf{x}) - J(\mathbf{x} + \mathbf{u}(\mathbf{x}; \mathbf{p})) \right)^2 \approx \sum_{\mathbf{x}} \left(K(\mathbf{x}) - J(\mathbf{x}) - \nabla J(\mathbf{x})^T X\mathbf{p} \right)^2 \tag{4}$$

where $\nabla J(\mathbf{x}) = (\frac{\partial J}{\partial x}(\mathbf{x}), \frac{\partial J}{\partial y}(\mathbf{x}))^T$ is the spatial gradient of J. It has been widely used in the past in the context of image matching, for instance to build panoramic mosaics or matching neighbour frames in sequences of planar scenes [12,13]. The reason to choose this technique is that it does not depend on characteristic points/regions, that is, we do not require images to have a prominent structure (distinct objects well distributed on the image). In addition, we intend to synchronize sequences recorded at night, where often there is not much 'content'.

The error minimization is achieved by deriving with respect to the unknown $\mathbf{p}$ and setting to zero. This leads to a system of five linear equations in the five unknowns

$$\mathbf{C}\,\mathbf{p} = \mathbf{b}, \quad \mathbf{C} = \sum_{\mathbf{x}} X^T \nabla J(\mathbf{x}) \nabla J(\mathbf{x})^T X, \quad \mathbf{b} = \sum_{\mathbf{x}} (K(\mathbf{x}) - J(\mathbf{x})) X^T \nabla J(\mathbf{x}) \tag{5}$$

In practice, we can not directly solve for $\mathbf{p}$ because the first order approximation of Eq. 4 holds only if the motion field $\mathbf{u}(\mathbf{x}; \mathbf{p})$ is small. Instead, $\mathbf{p}$ is successively estimated in a coarse–to–fine manner. A Gaussian pyramid is built for both J and K and at each resolution level $\mathbf{p}$ is re–estimated based on the value of the previous level. This means that K is successively warped towards J. At the same time, at each pyramid level, several iterations of this process are performed. For a detailed description we refer the reader to [12,13,7].

2.3   Correspondence Finding

In the former section we have explained how to assess the matching between a pair of frames. But how to use it to determine the correspondence c from the first to the second sequence ? Obviously, the brute force approach of an exhaustive test of all possible pairs is infeasible since our target videos may have hundreds to thousands of frames. Less costly, trying a fixed number of frames in the second sequence, for every frame in the first one, misses out the chance to cut down the number of comparisons, as we will see. We propose for this task a divide–and–conquer procedure.

Let be S_1 and S_2 two sequences m and n frames long, respectively. We impose the condition that the first sequence is contained within the second one S_2, that is, first and last frames of S_1 have some corresponding frame within S_2. The mapping c must be defined for all the time instants $t_1 = 1 \ldots m$ and be monotonically increasing, $c(t_1 + 1) - c(t_1) \geq 0$. Equality accounts for the fact that the first camera may move slower than the second one, or even stop while the other keeps moving. The reverse case is $c(t_1 + 1) > c(t_1) + 1$. Suppose that, somehow, we decide frames $S_1(t_1)$ and $S_2(t_2)$ are corresponding. Then necessarily, $1 \leq t \leq t_1 \Rightarrow 1 \leq c(t) \leq t_2$ and $t_1 \leq t \leq m \Rightarrow t_2 \leq c(t) \leq n$. This means that each time we augment c with a pair of corresponding time instants, the possible pairs may be strongly reduced. Consider the particular case that each camera was moving at (may be different) constant speed and we already know the corresponding frames of $t_1 = 1, m$. Then c would be the line $t_2 = c(1) + t_1(c(m) - c(1))/m$ (Fig. 1a). The largest possible reduction, to a half, is achieved by looking for the correspondence of $t_1 = m/2$. In Fig. 1a the possible correspondences prior to this decision are within the lighter rectangle and posterior to it the two darker ones. Based on it, the procedure for correspondence finding, illustrated by Fig. 1b, is:

1. Set a maximum time offset ΔT (height of thin bars)
2. For $t_1 = 1$ try $t_2 = 1 \ldots \Delta T/2$ and for $t_1 = m$, $t_2 = n - \Delta T/2 \ldots n$, and choose in each case the one of minimum error as $c(1)$ and $c(m)$, respectively
3. Look for the corresponding frame to $t_1 = m/2$: first interpolate a line $l_{1,m}(t)$ between $(1, c(1))$ and $(m, c(m))$ and then try $t_2 = \max\{c(1), l(m/2) - \Delta T/2\} \ldots \min\{c(m), l(m/2) + \Delta T/2\}$, taking the time of minimum error as $c(m/2)$
4. Repeat step 3 for the two resulting intervals (now $[1, m/2], [m/2, m]$) if the interval length is greater than 2.

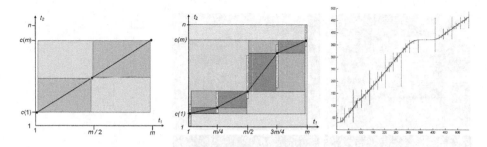

Fig. 1. Divide–and–conquer correspondence search, see text

Fig. 1b shows the intervals and their bounds for the first two subdivisions, the darker the later. Fig. 1c illustrates a real case: vertical bars represent the tried pairs and $\Delta T = 120$. In another experiment, for $m = 521, n = 421$ frames and $\Delta T = 200$ the number of evaluated pairs was only 3423.

3   Efficiency

Efficiency can not be an afterthought in this problem. For the method to be of practical use, it must be able to synchronize videos of hundreds or thousands of frames in a reasonable time. We briefly report two ways to improve efficiency, without an important loss of precision. The first is to speed up the spatial registration of a pair of frames. It can be done by not iterating the linear system of Eq. 3 at the lowest level of the image pyramid, that is, at maximum resolution. This achieves a gain because at each iteration one of the images must be warped according to the newly computed parameters **p**. The second way is to reduce the number of frame pairs to match by sampling the temporal dimension of the first video: instead of finding the correspondence for each frame in the first video, do it just for each tenth, for instance, and interpolate the correspondence and parameters for frames in between. Just to provide some specific figures, with our current Matlab implementation two videos of 720×288 pixels/frame, around 720 frames each, were synchronized in 3 hours 45 min. With the former two approximations the computation time was reduced to 24 min.

4   Results

The application motivating this research was to compare videos recorded at night from a moving vehicle, with the camera forward facing. This may be a complement to the surveillance of parkings, warehouses or widespread facilities. We have successfully synchronized relatively long parts of day and night videos (hundreds of frames), even with significant differences in content. The main limitation of our method is the ability to deal with large initial misalignments due to significant camera translation and/or relative rotation, which may give rise to synchronization errors. The reason is that, to deal with this situation,

Fig. 2. Registration of corresponding frames. From left to right: frame of first video, warped frame of the second video and contrast inverted difference.

we rely only on the hierarchical estimation of the motion parameters. Another source of synchronization errors is the hard (irreversible) decisions of the correspondence finding algorithm: wrong correspondences introduce errors locally because they determine a bound for the following correspondences to be found. And the sooner they are computed, the wider their influence. Fig. 2 shows some examples from which small differences could be detected by substraction. Figures however, are a poor reflex of synchronized videos. They can be viewed at www.cvc.uab.es/adas/projects/sincro/IbPRIA07.html.

5 Conclusion

We have presented a new method for video synchronization, which includes spatial in addition to temporal registration. Compared to most of the previous works, we try to solve an under constrained version of this problem: free camera motion and no need of tracked features or geometric entities difficult to estimate like the fundamental matrix. Efficiency is an issue in this problem, which we address through the correspondence search procedure, the interpolation of the correspondence and motion parameters along time and the fast registration of frame pairs. The main limitation of our method is the registration errors due to large misalignments. In spite of this, it can synchronize many sequences without paying special care to the camera motion (driving speed and style), including night sequences where the structure is sparse.

Acknowledgments. This research has been partially funded by grant TRA2004-06702/AUT of the Spanish *Ministerio de Educación y Ciencia*.

References

1. Stein, G.: Tracking from multiple view points: self calibration of space and time. In: Proc. DARPA Image Understanding Workshop, pp. 521 527 (1998)
2. Carceroni, R., Pádua, F., Santos, G., Kutulakos, K.: Linear sequence–to–sequence alignment. In: Proc. IEEE Conf. on Computer Vision and Pattern Recognition, Washington DC, pp. 746–753 (2004)
3. Tresadern, P., Reid, I.: Synchronizing image sequences of non–rigid objects. In: British Machine Vision Conf., Norwich, UK, pp. 629–638 (2003)
4. Lei, C., Yang, Y.: Trifocal tensor–based multiple video synchronization with sub-frame optimization. IEEE Trans. Image Processing 15(9), 2473–2480 (2006)
5. Wolf, L., Zomet, A.: Wide baseline matching between unsynchronized video sequences. Int. Journal of Computer Vision 68(1), 43–52 (2006)
6. Tuytelaars, T., VanGool, L.: Synchronizing video sequences. In: Proc. IEEE Int. Conf. Computer Vision and Pattern Recognition, Washington DC,Vol. 1, pp. 762–768 (2004)
7. Caspi, Y., Irani, M.: Spatio–temporal alignment of sequences. IEEE Trans. Pattern Analisys and Machine Intelligence 24(11), 1409–1424 (2002)
8. Ukrainitz, Y., Irani, M.: Aligning sequences and actions by maximizing space–time correlations. In: Proc. European Conf. on Computer Vision, Graz, Austria (2006)
9. Sand, P., Teller, S.: Video matching. ACM Transactions on Graphics (Proc. SIG-GRAPH) 22(3), 592–599 (2004)
10. Rao, C., Gritai, A., Sha, M., et al.: View–invariant alignment and matching of video sequences. In: Proc. IEEE Int. Conf. Computer Vision, Nice, France, pp. 939–945 (2003)
11. Irani, M.: Multi–frame correspondence estimation using subspace constraints. Int. Journal of Computer Vision 48(3), 173–194 (2002)
12. Szeliski, R.: Image alignment and stitching: A tutorial. Technical Report MSR-TR-2004-92, Microsoft Research (2006)
13. Zelnik-Manor, L., Irani, M.: Multi–frame estimation of planar motion. IEEE Trans. Pattern Analisys and Machine Intelligenc 22(10), 1105–1116 (2000)

Tracking the Left Ventricle in Ultrasound Images Based on Total Variation Denoising*

Jacinto C. Nascimento, João M. Sanches, and Jorge S. Marques

Instituto de Sistemas e Robótica - Instituto Superior Técnico
{jan,jmrs,jsm}@isr.ist.utl.pt

Abstract. Tracking the Left Ventricle (LV) in ultrasound sequences remains a challenge due to speckle noise, low SNR and lack of contrast. Therefore, it is usually difficult to obtain accurate estimates of the LV cavities since feature detectors produce a large number of outliers. This paper presents an algorithm which combines two main operations: i) a novel denoising algorithm based on the Lyapounov equation and ii) a robust tracker, based on an outlier feature model. Experimental results are provided, showing that the proposed algorithm is computationally efficient and leads to accurate estimates of the LV.

1   Introduction

The left ventricle (LV) boundary estimation plays an important role in clinical diagnosis since it allows to extract relevant measures of the heart dynamic behavior, among which the ejection fraction and local wall motion.

Ultrasound imaging is a popular technique to observe the dynamical behavior of the heart. However, the low signal-to-noise ratio (SNR) and the multiplicative nature of the noise (speckle) corrupting the ultrasound images, make the LV segmentation a difficult task.

The major edge detection algorithms fail due to the presence of multiplicative noise in heart ultrasound imagery. The strongest edges are often not located on the endocardium. In [1] it is proposed the instantaneous coefficient of variation (ICOV) providing good segmentation results, but the so called problem of "edge dropout" still remains (this is typical in the diastole phase). Therefore, noise reduction must be applied before edge detection. Several techniques have been proposed to reduce the speckle noise without distorting the relevant clinical details, e.g., Bayesian methods [2], mixture distribution of the Rician pdf with the inverse Gaussian as a mixture distribution (RiIG) [3], soft thresholding [4], wavelet based methods [5], wavelet soft-shrinking [6], median filtering [7], and anisotropic diffusion [8].

* This work was supported by Fundacao para a Ciência e a Tecnologia (ISR/IST pluri-anual funding) through the POS Conhecimento Program which includes FEDER funds.

J. Martí et al. (Eds.): IbPRIA 2007, Part II, LNCS 4478, pp. 628–636, 2007.

Even though the denoising algorithms significantly reduce the speckle noise, advanced tracking techniques are needed to segment the LV boundary. Prior art in segmentation of echocardiographic sequences of the heart includes active shape models [9], or level set techniques [10].

In this paper we join a novel edge preserving total variation (TV) based denoising algorithm and a robust tracker [11]. The denoising algorithm must process a large number of ultrasound images in an efficient way. This is obtained by formulating the filtering operation as the solution of a Sylvester/Lyapunov equation for which there are fast and computationally efficient algorithms described in the literature.

The robustness of the tracker is obtained by using feature grouping (line segments), which are labeled as valid or invalid. Since the labels are unknown they are replaced by their probabilities computed using a probabilistic model of the observations. A data association filter is then used to update the contour parameters under the presence of outliers.

The tracking algorithm proposed in the paper was assessed using a set of image sequences, segmented by medical doctors. These images, are used as a ground truth to compute FOM (figures of merit).

The paper is organized as follows: Section 2 describes the overall system. Sections 3, 4 and 5 describe the pre-processing, feature detection and tracking steps respectively. Section 6 describes experimental and section 7 concludes the paper.

2   System Overview

The proposed system aims is to track the boundary of the left ventricle during the cardiac cycle. The system input is a sequence of ultrasound images sampled at 25Hz.

The system performs three main operations: i) *denoising* : to reduce the speckle noise and enhance the contrast; due to the large amount of data to be processed a novel algorithm was developed to perform this task, ii) *feature detection* : detects intensity transitions along orthogonal lines radiating from the contour. Transitions are obtained by applying a matched filter to the intensity profiles and computing the local maxima [12], and iii) *tracking* : based on a robust tracking algorithm which fits a deformable curve (quadratic B-spline) to the points detected in the image. This algorithm must be able to deal with a large number of outliers and to interpolate the boundary when no features are detected due to low contrast of the heart boundary. This is specially important close to the apex and in the presence of sudden motion changes (e.g., in the mitral valve). A recent tracking algorithm is used in this step.

3   Pre-processing

The performance of the tracker depends on the SNR of the input images which have multiplicative noise.

The goal of the pre-processing step is to reduce the noise without losing relevant information. In this paper a MAP criterion is used to estimate the original images from the noisy ones. This approach is usually slow and computationally demanding, furthermore, there is a large number of images to process.

A Bayesian framework is used with the MAP criterion, and the optimization algebraic problem is formulated as Sylvester/Lyapunov equation for which there are fast em computationally efficient algorithms described in the literature.

The denoising algorithm estimates the original image, X, by minimizing the following energy function $E(Y, X) = -\log[p(Y|X)p(X)]$ where Y is the noisy image, $p(Y|X)$ is the observation model and $p(X)$ is the prior distribution of the unknown image.

Assuming conditional independence of the observations, leads to $p(Y|X) = \prod_{ij}^{N,M} p[y(ij)|x(ij)]$ where $p(y|x) = \frac{y}{x}e^{-y^2/2x}$ is the Rayleigh distribution [13].

An edge preserving prior $p(X)$ was chosen to avoid over-smoothing the transitions. The prior is based on the total variation (TV) function as $p(X) = \frac{1}{Z}e^{-\alpha\sum_{i,j} g(i,j)}$ where $g(i,j) = |\nabla X(i,j)|$ is the gradient magnitude of X at the (i,j) pixel, α is a parameter and Z is a partition function. This gradient magnitude may be approximated by using the first order differences, $g(i,j) = \sqrt{\delta_{v_{i,j}}^2 + \delta_{h_{i,j}}^2}$ where $\delta_{v_{i,j}} = x(i,j) - x(i,j-1)$ and $\delta_{h_{i,j}} = x(i,j) - x(i-1,j)$.

The denoised image is obtained by solving the following equation

$$\hat{X} = \arg\min_X E(Y, X) \tag{1}$$

where

$$E(Y, X) = \sum_{i,j}\left[\log\left(\frac{y(i,j)}{x(i,j)}\right) - \frac{y^2(i,j)}{2x(i,j)}\right] + \alpha\sum_{i,j} g(i,j) \tag{2}$$

To find out the minimizer of (2), its stationary points must be computed, i.e., $\nabla E(Y, X) = 0$, which is equivalent to

$$\frac{x(i,j) - x^{ML}(i,j)}{x^2(i,j)} + \frac{\partial}{\partial x(i,j)}\sum_{i,j} g(i,j) = 0, \ 0 \le i,j \le N-1, M-1 \tag{3}$$

where $x^{ML}(i,j) = y^2(i,j)/2$ is the *maximum likelihood* (ML) estimate for the Rayleigh distribution. The set of equations (3) is non-linear on X and it is iteratively solved. The fixed point method and the majorize/minimize (MM) algorithm described in [14] leads too the following recursion equation,

$$\frac{x(i,j) - x^{ML}(i,j)}{x_{t-1}^2(i,j)} + \frac{\partial}{\partial x(i,j)}\sum_{i,j}\frac{\delta_{v_{i,j}}^2 + \delta_{h_{i,j}}^2}{w_{t-1}(i,j)} = 0, 0 \le i,j \le N-1, M-1 \tag{4}$$

where $x_{t-1}(i,j)$ and $w_{t-1}(i,j) = 1/g_{t-1}(i,j)$ are the image and gradient magnitude reciprocals, respectively, computed in the $(t-1)$-th iteration.

The set of equations (4) can be written in the following matrix notation as shown in [15]

$$X_{t-1} \circledast (X - X^{ML}) + 2\alpha G_{t-1}^{-1} \circledast [\phi_v X + X \phi_h] = 0 \qquad (5)$$

where $\phi_v = \theta_v^T \theta_v$, $\phi_h = \theta_h^T \theta_h$ and $G_{t-1}^{-1}(i,j) = 1/|\nabla X_{t-1}(i,j)|$ is the matrix whose elements are the reciprocals of the gradient magnitudes of X_{t-1}. The operator $\circledast$ stands for Hadamard product, i.e., element wise product. θ_v and θ_h are $n \times n$ vertical and $m \times m$ horizontal difference operators respectively. Therefore, equation (5) can be rewritten as follows

$$\Phi_v X + X \Phi_h + Q_{t-1} = 0 \qquad (6)$$

where $\Phi_v = \beta I_N/2 + 2\alpha \phi_v$, $\Phi_h = \beta I_M/2 + 2\alpha \phi_h$, $Q_{t-1} = W_{t-1} \circledast (X_{t-1} - X^{ML}) - \beta X_{t-1}$ and $W_{t-1} = G_{t-1} \circledast / [X_{t-1} \circledast X_{t-1}]$. I_N and I_M are N and M dimensional identity matrices respectively and β is a conditioner parameter to improve the stability of the algorithm (typically $\beta = 1$).

The equation (6) is the so called Sylvester equation for which there are efficient and fast solver algorithms. Fig.1 shows an example of denoised ultrasound image using the pre-processing described above.

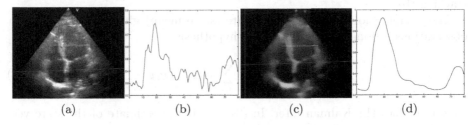

(a)   (b)   (c)   (d)

Fig. 1. (a) Real image, (b) denoised image using the proposed technique, (c) image profile of (a), image profile of (b)

4   Feature Detection

Feature detection detects line segments belonging to the boundary of the LV. This is done in two steps. First we detect intensity transitions along lines orthogonal to the predicted contour. This is done by template matching. Feature detection along the ith direction is performed by computing the local maxima of the function

$$\mathcal{J}(t_0) = \int_t |p_i(t) - T(t,t_0)|^2 dt \qquad (7)$$

where $p_i(t)$ is the image profile taken at the ith direction, t denotes the distance to the object boundary and $T(t,t_0)$ is a template which is obtained off-line. The template T is obtained as follows: $T(t)$ is equal to the typical intensity of the object for $t \leq t_0$ and $T(t)$ is equal to the background intensity for $t > t_0$. In the second step, feature points detected at consecutive lines are grouped, by mutual by mutual favorite pairing, forming image line-segments.

5   Tracking

A deformable curve (B-spline) is used to approximate the LV contour. The parameters of the B-spline at time k, $x_k \in \mathbb{R}$ are estimated from the image features obtained in the previous step using a tracking algorithm.

This is not an easy task since there are many invalid features detected in the ultrasound image and the tracker must able to ignore them and to track valid features only. The Kalman filter fails in this problem since it is not able to separate valid features from invalid ones.

In this paper we have used a data association filter which was recently proposed in [11]. This method considers all the hypothesis of valid/invalid features, H_i, and assigns a probability to each of them (see [11] for the details).

To avoid an exponential growth of hypothesis at different time instants, a simplifying assumption is adopted: it is assumed that the state distribution given past observations is Gaussian, i.e.,

$$p[x_k \mid Y^{k-1}] = \mathcal{N}[x_k; \hat{x}_{k|k-1}, P_{k|k-1}] \tag{8}$$

where $\hat{x}_{k|k-1}$, $P_{k|k-1}$ are the mean and covariance of x_k given past observations Y^{k-1}. This hypothesis was proposed by Bar-Shalom in the context of target tracking [16].

The computation of the state estimate (state mean) given current and past observations is done considering all the hypothesis

$$\hat{x}_{k|k} = \hat{x}_{k|k-1} + \sum_{i=1}^{m_k} \alpha_{ik} K_{ik} \nu_{ik} \tag{9}$$

This resembles the Kalman filter. In (9) $\hat{x}_{k|k}$ is the estimate of the state vector, K_{ik}, ν_{ik} are the Kalman gain and the innovation respectively, and $\alpha_{ik} \triangleq p(H_{ik} \mid Y^k)$ is the *a posteriori* probability of the i-th hypothesis H_{ik}. The interpretation of equation (9) suggests that we have a bank of Kalman filters each one specialized to each ith data hypothesis.

A recursive equation can also be derived for the covariance matrix (see details in [11])

6   Experimental Results

This section shows experimental results obtained with the proposed method. A echocardiographic sequence of the left ventricle is used in this study. The length of the sequence has 490 frames comprising 27 cardiac cycles and each image has 320×240 pixels.

The experiments involve three main steps: i) the LV boundary is manually defined by an expert (ground-truth) in several images; ii) the sequence is automatically processed by the tracker; iii) metrics between automatic and manual boundaries are computed for the sequence. The tests are performed under three options: i) without, ii) median, iii) and Lyapounov pre-processing.

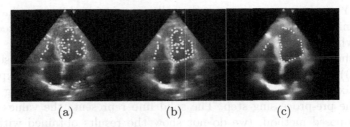

(a)	(b)	(c)

Fig. 2. Features (dots) detected in three situations: without pre-processing (a), median filtering (b), proposed algorithm (c)

6.1   Ground Truth

To obtain the ground truth, an observer provides a hand-labeled contours for the sequence. Four images in each cardiac cycle are selected for hand labeling: two images in the systole phase and two images in the diastole phase. A total number of 108 contours were manually generated (54 in each phase). The tracker-generated boundaries are compared to the ground truth resulting in an error measurement in each image.

6.2   Error Metrics

Three error metrics are used to compare the tracker-generated boundaries against the boundaries outlined by the observer.

The two curves are represented as sets of points $\mathcal{X} = \{\mathbf{x}_1, \mathbf{x}_2, \ldots, \mathbf{x}_{N_x}\}$, and $\mathcal{Y} = \{\mathbf{y}_1, \mathbf{y}_2, \ldots, \mathbf{y}_{N_y}\}$, where $N_y > N_x$. Each $\mathbf{x}_i$ and $\mathbf{y}_i$ is a pair of coordinates of the point in the image plane.

The distance from a point $\mathbf{x}_i$ to the curve $\mathcal{Y}$ is

$$d(\mathbf{x}_i, \mathcal{Y}) = \min_j \|\mathbf{y}_j - \mathbf{x}_i\| \tag{10}$$

The average distance from the contour model $\mathcal{X}$ to the ground truth boundary $\mathcal{Y}$ (ideal contour) is

$$d_{av} = \frac{1}{N_x} \sum_{i=1}^{N_x} d(\mathbf{x}_i, \mathcal{Y}) \tag{11}$$

The Hausdorff distance between the two curves is defined as the maximum distance from a point to the other curve

$$d_{max}(\mathcal{X}, \mathcal{Y}) = \max\left(\max_i \{d(\mathbf{x}_i, \mathcal{Y})\}, \max_j \{d(\mathbf{y}_j, \mathcal{X})\} \right) \tag{12}$$

The third metric is the Hammoude [17] measure proposed in the context of ultrasound images and given by

$$d_H = \frac{\sharp((X \cup Y) - (X \cap Y))}{\sharp(X \cup Y)} \tag{13}$$

where X, Y are binary images such that all pixels inside the curves have label 1 and remaining pixels have label 0. This metric computes the normalized number of pixels which receive different labels.

Fig. 3 shows the evolution of the metrics for the sequence. The first measure (Fig. 3 (a)) belongs to the interval $[0, 1]$, the remaining ones are expressed in terms of pixels. The dashed line refers to the results obtained by using a median filter in the pre-processing step. The solid line represents the values obtained by the proposed method, (we do not show the results obtained without pre-processing since they are much worse). Fig. 3 shows the results at specific frames. These frames correspond to the time instants when the cardiac phase switch from systole to the diastole and vice-versa. This figure also shows the situation when the tracker has difficulties to represent the *apex* of the ventricle.

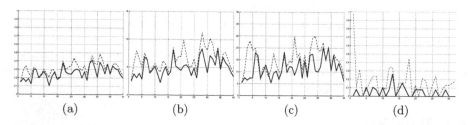

| (a) | (b) | (c) | (d) |

Fig. 3. Metric statistics for the heart sequence, (a) d_H, (b) d_{av}, (c) d_{max}, (d) number of outliers without pre-processing and with the proposed technique. Median filtering (dashed line), proposed method (solid line).

Fig. 3 shows that the denoising technique proposed herein has a much better performance compared with the median filter (the solid line is under the dashed line). The first and second order statistics of the contour metrics are shown in Table 1. Here, it is shown the average computation time associated to the tracker in seconds. We conclude that the proposed pre-processing method is twofold: i) the mean and variance error of the shape estimates is smaller than in the other cases; ii) it allows a faster tracking since less outlier features are detected in the image. See Fig. 2 where it is clearly shown that the number of outliers decrease

Table 1. Mean and variance values for the metrics shown in the Fig. 3 and the computation time (average per frame) for the three different cases

	Hammoude metric-d_H			Average Distance-d_{av}			Hausdorff Distance-d_{max}		
	without	Median	Denoising	without	Median	Denoising	without	Median	Denoising
E[.]	0.29	0.28	**0.26**	6.1	5.7	**5.2**	14.2	13.7	**11.7**
var[.]	0.01	0.01	**0.008**	5.5	4.6	**4.0**	38.0	26.5	**22.9**

	without	Median	Denoising
Time$_{av}$	0.87	0.86	**0.76**

from (a) (without pre-processing) through (c) (proposed algorithm), the latter preserving the contour.

7   Conclusion

This paper proposes a system for tracking the left ventricle using two key operations. The first is a novel denoising algorithm based on the Lyapounov equation. The second is a robust tracker used to estimate the evolution of the LV contour. The robustness is achieved by using data-association within the detected line-segments.

It is concluded from the experimental results that the proposed algorithm manages to accurately track the heart motion in images with a low contrast between the heart cavity and the miocardium. It is also concluded that the denoising algorithm plays an important role and significantly reduces the number of outliers.

References

1. Yu, Y., Acton, S.T.: Edge detection in ultrasound imagery using the instantaneous coefficient of variation. IEEE Trans. Med. Imag. 13(12), 1640–1655 (2004)
2. Zeng, Z., Cumming, I.: Bayesian speckle noise reduction using the discrete wavelet transform. In: Int. geosc. and rem. sens. symp. pp. 6–10 (1998)
3. Eltoft, T.: Modeling the amplitude statistics of ultrasonic images. IEEE Trans. Med. Imag. 25(2), 229–240 (2006)
4. Gupta, S., Kaur, L., Chauhan, R.C., Saxena, S.C.: A wavelet based statistical approach for speckle reduction in medical ultrasound images. In: Med. and Biol. Eng. and computing 42, 189–192 (2004)
5. Duskunovic, I., Pizurica, A., Stippel, G., Philips, W., Lemahieu, I.: Wavelet based denoising techniques for ultrasound images. In: Proc. of the IEEE Eng. in Medicine and Biol. Soc. Conference 4, 2662–2665 (2000)
6. Yue, Y., Croitoru, M.M., Bidani, A., Zwischenberger, J.B., Clark, J.W.: Ultrasonic speckle suppression using robust nonlinear wavelet diffusion for LV volume quantification. In: Proc. of the Int. Conf. of the IEEE EMBS, pp. 1609–1612 (2004)
7. Loupas, T., McDicken, W., Allan, P.: An adaptive weighted median filter for speckle suppression in medical ultrasonic images. IEEE Trans. Circuits Syst. 36, 129–135 (1989)
8. Montagnat, J., Sermesant, M., Delingette, H., Malandain, G., Ayache, N.: Anisotropic filtering for model-based segmentation of 4d cylindrical echocardiographic images. Pattern Recognition Letters - Special Issue on Ultrasonic Imag. Proc. and Anal. 24, 815–828 (2003)
9. amd, X.H., Paragios, N., Metaxas, D.: Establishing local correspondences towards compact representation of anatomical structures. Med. Imag. Comp. and Computer-Assisted Intervention (2003)
10. Osher, S., Paragios, N.: Geometric Level Set Methods in Imag. Vision and Graphics. Springer, Heidelberg (2003)
11. Nascimento, J., Marques, J.S.: Robust shape tracking in the presence of cluttered background. IEEE Trans. Multimedia 6(6), 852–861 (2004)

12. Blake, A., Isard, M.: Active Contours. Springer, Heidelberg (1998)
13. Burckhardt, C.: Speckle in ultrasound b-mode scans. IEEE Trans. on Sonics and Ultrsonics SU-25(1), 1–6 (1978)
14. Dias, J.M.B.: Fast GEM wavelet-based image deconvolution algorithm. IEEE Int. Conf. on Image Proc. pp. 961–964 (2003)
15. Sanches, J., Marques, J.S.: Image denoising using the lyapunov equation from non-uniform samples. In: ICIAR (2006)
16. Bar-Shalom, Y., Fortmann, T.: Tracking and Data Association. Academic Press, San Diego (1988)
17. Hammoude, A.: Computer-assited endocardial border identification from a sequence of two-dimensional echocardiographic images. Ph.D. dissertation, Univ. Washington, Seatle (1988)

Bayesian Oil Spill Segmentation of SAR Images Via Graph Cuts*

Sónia Pelizzari and José M. Bioucas-Dias

Instituto de Telecomunicações, I.S.T., TULisbon,Lisboa, Portugal
soniap@lx.it.pt, bioucas@lx.it.pt

Abstract. This paper extends and generalizes the Bayesian semi-supervised segmentation algorithm [1] for oil spill detection using SAR images. In the base algorithm on which we build on, the data term is modeled by a finite mixture of Gamma distributions. The prior is an M-level logistic Markov Random Field enforcing local continuity in a statistical sense. The methodology proposed in [1] assumes two classes and known smoothness parameter. The present work removes these restrictions. The smoothness parameter controlling the degree of homogeneity imposed on the scene is automatically estimated and the number of used classes is optional. Semi-automatic estimation of the class parameters is also implemented. The maximum a posteriori (MAP) segmentation is efficiently computed via the α-expansion algorithm [2], a recent graph-cut technique, The effectiveness of the proposed approach is illustrated with simulated (Gaussian or Gamma data term and M-level logistic classes) and real ERS data.

1 Introduction

Segmentation of dark patches in SAR images is an important step in any oil spill detection system and many different approaches to the problem have been proposed so far. These approaches are built on off-the-shelf segmentation algorithms such as 'Adaptive Image Thresholding', 'Hysteresis Thresholding', 'Edge Detection' (see [3] and references therein) and entropy based methods like the 'Maximum Descriptive Length' technique [4].

Work [1] introduces a Bayesian segmentation algorithm where the observed data (oil and water) data is modeled by a finite Gamma mixture, with a given predefined number of components. To estimate the parameters of the class conditional densities, an expectation maximization (EM) algorithm was developed. The used prior is a second order Markov Random Field (MRF), more specifically an isotropic Ising Model. To estimate the labels, the posterior distribution is maximized (MAP) via graph-cut techniques [5].

---

* The work was supported in part by the Portuguese "Fundação para a Ciência e Tecnologia" (FCT) under the grant PDCTE/CPS/49967/2003 and by the European Space Agency (ESA) under the grant ESA/C1:2422.

J. Martí et al. (Eds.): IbPRIA 2007, Part II, LNCS 4478, pp. 637–644, 2007.

Notwithstanding the promising results provided by the above described segmentation method, it has restrictions that the present work overcomes. The first restriction concerns the number of classes that is limited to two. The second restriction concerns the smoothness parameter that has to be manually tuned. Furthermore, the class parameters estimation process is completely supervised, requiring an interaction with the user in order to manually select a region containing oil pixels and a region containing water pixels.

In the present work we generalize [1] by: (1) extending the number of segmented classes to a predefined optional number c, (2) automatically estimating the homogeneity parameter β in the MRF, and (3) automatically estimating the class parameters.

To extend [1] to an optional number of classes, the so-called α-expansion algorithm [2] is implemented. In order to estimate the smoothness parameter, two different techniques are tested, namely the Least Squares (LS) Fit and the Coding Method (CD) [6]. A first attempt is carried out to implement unsupervised segmentation using a semi-supervised initialization.

To evaluate the accuracy of the algorithm, different simulations are carried out. The simulations address both the Gamma and the Gaussian data model. For the real images, the Gamma mixture data model proposed in [1] is adopted to model the observed SAR intensity values.

The article is organized as follows: Section 2 gives a short overview of the original algorithm that builds the base to this work; Section 3 describes, in pseudo-code, the main steps of the proposed segmentation methods; Section 4 presents simulation and real results, and finally Section 5 contains concluding and future work remarks.

2 Overview of Base Algorithm

The algorithm proposed in [1] addresses the problem of finding an estimation $\hat{f}$ of a labeling for a set of N pixels $P := \{1, 2, ..., N\}$. When c possible classes are available, a labeling $f := \{f_1, f_2, ... f_N\}$ is a mapping from P to L, where $L := \{l_1, l_2, ..., l_c\}$ is the set of discrete values that the pixels may take. The vector $y := \{y_1, y_2, ... y_N\}$ stands for the observed data, corresponding to the image intensity measurements at the pixels.

In order to infer $\hat{f}$, we adopt the MAP criterion. This amounts to maximize the posterior density of the labeling given the observed data. As described in [1] in detail, this is equivalent to minimizing the objective function

$$E(f_1,...,f_N) = \sum_{p=1}^{N} E^p(f_p) + \sum_{p<j} E^{p,j}(f_p, f_j), \tag{1}$$

where p, j $\in$ P are pixel locations, E^p is the negative likelihood given by

$$E^p(f_p) = -\log(p(y_p \mid f_p)), \tag{2}$$

where $p(y_p|f_p)$ is the conditional density of y_p given f_p, called data model or sensor function, and $E^{p,j}$ is the prior clique potential associated with the clique $\{p,j\}$

containing the pair of neighboring pixels p and j [6]. Since we have adopted an MLL, we have

$$E^{p,j}(f_p, f_j) = -\beta \delta(f_p, f_j),\tag{3}$$

where δ is the discrete delta function and β controls the degree of homogeneity we wish to impose on the scene. Note that

$$\sum_{p<j} E^{p,j}(f_p, f_j) = -\beta \, \text{nrNeighbours}(f),\tag{4}$$

with

$$\text{nrNeighbours}(f) = \sum_{i=1}^{N} n(f_i),\tag{5}$$

where $n(f_i)$ is the number of neighbors in neighborhood N_i having the same label as pixel i.

As demonstrated in [1], $E(f_1, \ldots f_N)$ is graph representable for c = 2 and in these circumstances, the global minimum of the objective function may be computed by applying the graph-cut algorithm described in [5].

3 Proposed Segmentation Methods

In the next Sections we propose supervised and unsupervised approaches to the segmentation. The first approach assumes known class parameters, whereas the second does not. In both methods, the smoothness parameter is assumed unknown.

3.1 Supervised Segmentation with Beta Unknown

In the first segmentation method, we adopt iterative labeling-estimation, with the two steps being performed alternately, inspired by the EM algorithm [6]. The initial values for the labeling and the parameter estimator are optional and don't seem to have a relevant influence on the final performance. Since the class parameters are assumed known, they are omitted from the pseudo-code.

```
Algorithm-1:
1. Start with an arbitrary initial labeling f₀ and arbi-
trary parameter β̂=β₀
2.  While |Δβ̂|≤δ or nrIterations < ItMaxNr do
        2.1 Find f̂ = α_Expansion(f₀, β̂)
        2.2 Find β̂=LS_Estimation(f̂)or CodingMethod(f̂)
3. Return (f̂, β̂)
```

3.2 Unsupervised Segmentation with Semi-supervised Initialization

In this second method, we have also adopted iterative labeling-estimation as in 'Algorithm-1', but now the class parameters are also iteratively estimated. The initialization of the class parameters is performed in a semi-automatic way: the user provides a region of pixels corresponding to one (for example the most frequent) of the classes (class1). This region is then used to estimate the ML (Maximum Likelihood) parameters of the class1 distribution. In a second step, pixels are clustered in two sets, class1 and not-class1, by applying a simple threshold to the estimated distribution. Then, the parameters of the remaining classes are initialized by applying an EM mixture estimation procedure to the pixels clustered in the set not-class1.

Algorithm-2:

1. Start with an arbitrary parameter $\hat{\beta}=\beta_0$ and arbitrary initial labeling f_0

2. Provide initial class parameter estimations $\hat{\theta}=\theta_0$

3. Provide initial $\hat{f}$ = α_Expansion(f_0,β_0,θ_0)

4. While $|\Delta\hat{\beta}|\leq\delta$ or nrIterations < ItMaxNr do

    4.1 Find $\hat{\theta}$= ML_Estimation($\hat{f}$)

    4.2 Find $\hat{f}$ = α_Expansion($f_0,\hat{\beta},\hat{\theta}$)

    4.3 Find $\hat{\beta}$=LS_Estimation($\hat{f},\hat{\theta}$)or CodingMethod($\hat{f},\hat{\theta}$)

5. Return ($\hat{f},\hat{\beta},\hat{\theta}$)

4 Results: Simulated and Real Images

This section presents results for simulated and for real SAR images. In the first case, different test scenarios are provided, corresponding to Gaussian and Gamma data terms. Although simulations have been restricted to one Gamma mode per class, the developed procedure also works with Gamma mixtures as developed in [1].

4.1 Simulated Images

Three different test scenarios have been adopted:

Scenario 1: the simulated image contains three classes generated by an MLL Markov-Gibbs distribution corrupted with Gaussian noise. Segmentation is performed applying "Algorithm-1", described in Section 3.1. The parameter estimation is performed using the LS method and the class parameters are known (same values as used for the simulation). The test is performed for five different images, corresponding to an increasing difficulty grade of segmentation. Each test is run three times and the mean values of the overall accuracies (OA) corresponding the percentage of correct label are computed. For comparison, the estimation of β is performed in a supervised way, applying the LS method to the 'ground-truth' image and running the α-expansion algorithm once with the estimated β.

Scenario 2: here a simulated image of three classes corrupted by Gamma noise is used. The ground-truth is 'hand-made' and contains structures resembling those that may be found in oil-spill scenarios. The same algorithm as in 'Scenario 1' is used, both with the LS and the CD estimation methods. The unsupervised segmentation is compared with the results given by the best achievable segmentation using α-expansion, corresponding to tuning the β parameter manually.

Scenario 3: here, for the same simulated image used in scenario 1, the class parameters estimation is also incorporated in the algorithm, by applying 'Algorithm-2', described in Section 3.2. Initial class parameters estimation is provided by performing a one-class supervised estimation based on one-class clustering.

Scenario 1: To assess the segmentation performance, we compare the OA with that obtained without the MRF prior, *i.e.,* $\beta=0$. For Gaussian classes with equal standard deviation σ, means equally D-spaced, we have

$$OA\ (\beta=0)=\left[1-\left(\frac{c-1}{c}erfc\left(\frac{D/2}{\sqrt{2}\times\sigma}\right)\right)\right]100, \tag{6}$$

where erfc( ) is the complementary error function and c is the number of classes. Figure 1 shows the OA's obtained by segmenting the image using 'Algorithm-1' (legend: unsupervised) and using the supervised estimated beta value (legend: supervised) against the values provided by (6).

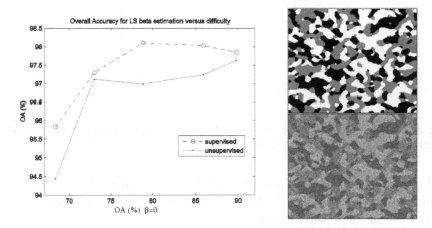

Fig. 1. On the left: overall accuracies against $OA_{MAP}(\beta=0)$. On the right: upper image is the MLL ground-truth with 3 classes; lower image are the simulated intensity values.

Scenario 2: In Figure 2 and 3 as in Scenario 1 but the OA ($\beta=0$) is now estimated by running the algorithm with $\beta=0$, since there is no close expression for it.

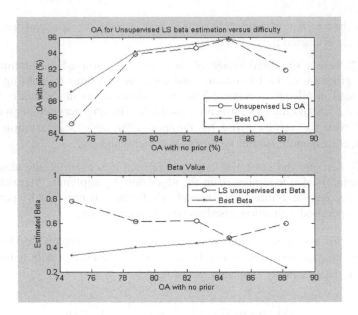

Fig. 2. Upper image: OA's obtained by unsupervised segmentation using LS and best achievable results with manually tuned β. Lower image: LS estimated β and best β.

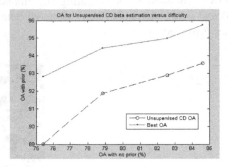

Fig. 3. Overall accuracies obtained by unsupervised segmentation using CD and best achievable results with manually tuned α-expansion

Figure 2 shows the results obtained with the LS method and Figure 3 the results obtained with the CD method. Figure 4 displays an example of simulated image and corresponding segmentation results.

Scenario 3: By applying 'Algorithm-2' to an MLL image like the one adopted in Scenario 1, for a OA(β=0) of 85.9% given by expression (9), the achieved OA value is 94.5% using LS estimation. The Best achievable OA is 99.1%.

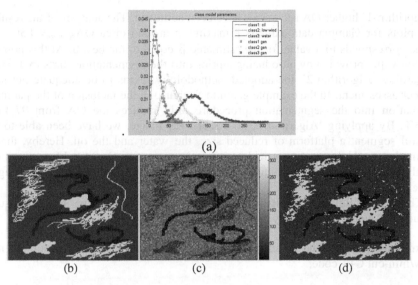

(a)

(b)   (c)   (d)

Fig. 4. (a) Density functions used to generate the simulated image with superimposed histogram of generated data set. (b) Ground-truth (c) Simulated image (d) Segmentation result using 'Algorithm-1': unsupervised LS estimated $\beta = 0.4213$, OA = 95.3%. The best achievable OA for this image was determined to be 95.4% . The OA for $\beta = 0$ is 83.2%.

4.2 Real Images

The 'Algorithm-1' has been applied to a real ERS-1 SAR image fragment. The scene (frame 2367, orbit 17211) containing the fragment has been acquired on 30 October 1994, and covers several oil platforms in the Norwegian and British sector of the North Sea. The image has been radiometric calibrated and corrected for the incidence angle effect. We have assigned a class to 'oil', a class to 'water' and a class to 'platform' and learned the class parameters using the supervised method described in [1]. Figure 5 displays the obtained results after applying 'Algorithm-1'.

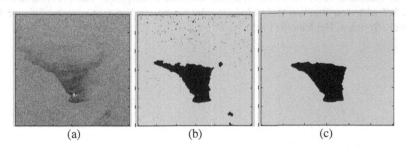

(a)   (b)   (c)

Fig. 5. (a) ERS image: intensity values (b) Segmentation with LS (c) Segmentation with CD

5   Conclusion

The first results of applying the proposed methodology to simulated images with Gaussian and Gamma data models and to real ERS SAR data are promising. With

'Algorithm-1' higher OA accuracies have been achieved. The analysis of the resulting OA plots for Gamma data exhibits a maximum around circa $OA_{no\ prior}= 85\%$. This value corresponds to a value for the estimated β equal to the best β. At this point the add-on value provided by introducing a prior into the segmentation starts to decrease. Regarding 'Algorithm-2', the adopted methodology seems to be adequate but needs further assessment. In the example given in Scenario 3, the inclusion of the parameter estimation into the segmentation procedure only reduces the OA from 97,3% to 94,5%. By applying 'Algorithm-1' to a real ERS image, we have been able to successful segment a platform of reduced size, the water and the oil. Hereby, the CD estimation method seems to provide a better segmentation than the LS method, contrarily to what happened for simulated images, where the LS method provided slightly better results.

These are preliminary results and more tests, with more trials per test, are required to fully determine the accuracy of the proposed methods..

Acknowledgments. The authors acknowledge Vladimir Kolmogorov for the max-flow/min-cut C++ code.

References

1. Pelizzari, S., José, M. B.: Dias: Bayesian Adaptive Oil Spill Segmentation of SAR Images via Graph Cuts. In: Proceedings of the SeaSAR 2006, Frascati, Italy (2006)
2. Boykov, Y., Veksler, O., Zabih, R.: Fast Approximate Energy Minimization via Graph Cuts. IEEE Transactions on Pattern Analysis and Machine Intelligence, Vol. 23, No.11 (2001)
3. Montali, A., Giacinto, G., et al.: Supervised Pattern Classification Techniques for Oil Spill Classification in SAR Images: Preliminary Results. In: Proceedings of the SeaSAR 2006 (2006)
4. Galland, F.: Synthetic Aperture Radar oil spill segmentation by stochastic complexity minimization. IEEE Geoscience and Remote Sensing Letters, Vol. 1, issue 4 (2004)
5. Kolmogorov, V., Zabih, R.: What Energy Functions Can Be Minimized via Graph Cuts? IEEE Transactions on Pattern Analysis and Machine Intelligence, Vol. 26, No.2 (2004)
6. Li, S.Z.: Markov Random Field Modeling. In: Computer Vision, Computer Science Workbench, Springer, Heidelberg (1995)

Unidimensional Multiscale Local Features for Object Detection Under Rotation and Mild Occlusions

Michael Villamizar, Alberto Sanfeliu, and Juan Andrade Cetto

Institut de Robòtica i Informàtica Industrial, CSIC-UPC
Llorens Artigas 4-6, 08028 Barcelona, Spain
{mvillami,sanfeliu,cetto}@iri.upc.edu

Abstract. In this article, scale and orientation invariant object detection is performed by matching intensity level histograms. Unlike other global measurement methods, the present one uses a local feature description that allows small changes in the histogram signature, giving robustness to partial occlusions. Local features over the object histogram are extracted during a *Boosting* learning phase, selecting the most discriminant features within a training histogram image set. The *Integral Histogram* has been used to compute local histograms in constant time.

1 Introduction

Color histograms are often used as local features for object identification and tracking [1,2], specially, given its invariance to pose change. However its main drawback is its sensitivity to illumination conditions. Schiele and Crowley [3] have extended the idea of representing the object by histograms, incorporating other local image features like the gradient magnitude, orientation and laplacian, resulting in a multidimensional histogram representation. This approach performs robust object recognition under different viewing conditions, such as, orientation, scale and view points changes.

With the propose of attaining object detection for real time applications, many methods have arisen that tackle the feature computation cost. One simple and effective method is based on the use of integral images. Viola and Jones [4] presented their integral image based on accumulation of pixel intensities over the image axes. Other extensions have been proposed to calculate other local properties efficiently. Villamizar *et al.* [5] and Porikli [6] developed the Integral Histogram, with which is possible to compute rapidly any local histogram independently of its size and location.

2 Proposed Method

In this paper we combine the benefits of speed from the integral image computation with the invariant properties that color histograms give, and build on top

J. Martí et al. (Eds.): IbPRIA 2007, Part II, LNCS 4478, pp. 645–651, 2007.

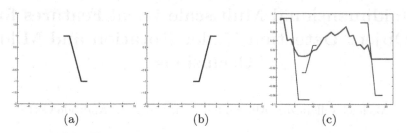

Fig. 1. Haar features a) sign + b) sign − c) Haar description

of our previous work on Boosting algorithms to produce a fast and robust object recognition system. The major benefit of the proposed method relies on its robustness to partial occlusions, since the histogram matching is performed locally, using a robust boosted classifier based on the combination of local features.

The work reported here introduces a novel multiscale unidimensional histogram representation based on a linear combination of Haar features, that follows the spirit of other typical feature sets learned via Boosting. These histograms are efficiently computed using our previously reported integral histogram image [5] and we compare on its use for object detection against the Swain and Ballard histogram intersection metric.

2.1   Local Features

We propose to describe objects by means of intensity level histograms, in order to achieve viewpoint invariance [1,3]. However, our similarity measurement relies on a linear boosted classifier that uses Haar local features over the histogram signature. Histogram matching is carried out locally.

Those local features that are more discriminant during the Boosting learning phase are selected as weak hypothesis or classifiers, and their linear combination gives a strong hypothesis, called strong classifier. The Haar local features showed in Figure 1 represent a simple and suitable form to describe a histogram signal. They encode the inflexions in the histogram at any location, width, and sign. Consequently, the object can be modelled as a Haar decomposition of its histogram signature using the more relevant coefficients (see Figure 1c).

Intensity level histograms are computed from both the patch training images (30x30 pixels) for the Boosting stage, and patches extracted from test images.

2.2   Boosting Classifier

Feature selection is performed via AdaBoost [7]. AdaBoost extracts in each iteration the weak classifier (feature width, location and sign) that best discriminates objects from background training histogram images. A weak classifier can be expressed as

$$h(s) = \begin{cases} 1 & : \quad s*f > t \\ 0 & : \quad \text{otherwise} \end{cases} , \tag{1}$$

where s is a training sample histogram, f is the feature being tested, with all its parameters (width, location and sign), $*$ indicates the convolution operation, and t is the response threshold. The algorithm selects the most discriminant weak classifier h, as well as its contribution α in classifying the entire training set, as a function of the classification error ϵ.

$$\alpha = \frac{1}{2} \ln \frac{1 - \epsilon}{\epsilon} \tag{2}$$

At each iteration, the algorithm also updates a set of weights over the training set. Initially, all weights are set equally, but on each round, the weights of missclassified samples are increased so that the algorithm is forced to focus on such hard samples in the training set the previously chosen classifiers missed. In a certain way, the technique is similar to a Support Vector Machine, in that both search for a class separability hyperplane, although using different distance norms, l_2 for SVMs, and l_1 for boosting [8]. The dimensionality of the separating hyperplane in AdaBoost is given by the number N of weak classifiers that form the strong classifier:

$$H(s) = \begin{cases} 1 & : \quad \sum_{i=1}^{N} \alpha_i h_i(s) \geq \frac{1}{2} \sum_{i=1}^{N} \alpha_i \quad \text{object} \\ 0 & : \quad \text{otherwise} \qquad\qquad\qquad\quad \text{no-object} \end{cases} . \tag{3}$$

2.3   Integral Histogram

An integral image is a representation of the image that allows fast computation of features because it does not work directly with the original image intensities. Instead, it works over an incrementally built image that adds feature values along rows and columns. Once computed this image representation, any one of the local features can be computed at any location and scale in constant time [4].

Extending the idea of having cumulative data at each pixel in the integral image, we have proposed to store on it the histogram data instead of intensity sums [5]. The integral histogram stores intensity level histograms which, once constructed, allow for the computation of histogram within a rectangular area in constant time.

The value of the integral histogram s at coordinates u, v contains the intensity histogram of the region above and to the left of u, v, inclusive,

$$s(u, v) = \sum_{i \leq u, j \leq v} s(i, j) . \tag{4}$$

then, it is possible to compute for example, the intensity histogram in a rectangular region, called *Area*, simply by adding and subtracting the cumulative histograms at its four corners in the integral histogram representation (see figure 2),

$$histogram(Area) = s(A) + s(D) - s(B) - s(C) \tag{5}$$

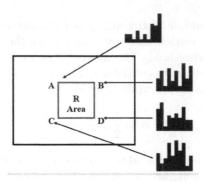

Fig. 2. The integral histogram

Furthermore, the construction of the integral histogram is computed iteratively with

$$s(u, v, bin) = bin(I(u, v)) + s(u - 1, v, bin) + s(u, v - 1, bin) - s(u - 1, v - 1, bin)$$
(6)

where

$$bin(I(u, v)) = \begin{cases} 1 & : & I(u, v) \in bin \\ 0 & : & \text{otherwise} \end{cases}$$
(7)

3   Object Detection

We have decided to compare our proposed method with the known Swain and Ballard method [1] in terms of classification. The tests are based on patch images of both object and background outdoor scenes. The Swain and Ballard color intersection metric is defined as

$$\bigcap(H, T) = \sum_{i=1}^{m} \min(H(i), T(i))$$
(8)

where $H(i)$ is the new class test histogram, $T(i)$ the reference histogram associated to the object image and m the number of bins. This method makes the comparison with such specific object histogram $H(i)$, that is, it only uses one canonical image to perform object detection.

Conversely, our method performs a object detection in a local manner, taking into account possible changes in the histograms, due to small object translation, non uniform illumination, scale and partial occlusions. As the learning process is carried out over a set of training histogram images, the selected weak classifiers become robust to small image transformations present in the training set. Some of the training histogram images that have been used for our proposed method are shown in the Figure 3a-l.

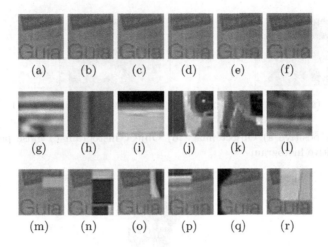

Fig. 3. Training set images. a-f) Object g-l) Background m-r) Occluded object.

The first experiment consists in applying the measurement over a validation set of 30 object patch images. In the proposed method, we required a training set of 50 object images and 100 background images. The number of bins selected was of 12 as tradeoff between reliability and computation burden. The results appear in table.

The second experiment is carried over 300 background patch images, extracted from outdoor and indoor scenes, (none with the object). This test is performed to show the method performance to background scenes and its discrimination. One false positive is detected for our method (figure 4).

The third experiment was aimed at evaluating the descriptor robustness to mild occlusions. The table shows the results for the occluded object shown in Figure 3(m-r). Thanks to the local matching property of the proposed method, the correct detection is high.

Method	Correct	False negatives	False positives	Test
Proposed method	96%	4%	0%	Validation
Swain & Ballard	93%	6%	0%	
Proposed method	99%	0%	1%	Background
Swain & Ballard	85%	0%	15%	
Proposed method	90%	10%	0%	Occlusions
Swain & Ballard	73%	27%	0%	

The detection is performed by applying the strong classifier $H(s)$ over the entire test image, at every location and scale. Therefore the use of the integral histogram is of utmost importance in this hard task.

Some detection results are shown in Figure 5. We can appreciate that the detection is achieved even when the object presents several scales, locations and rotations in the plane.

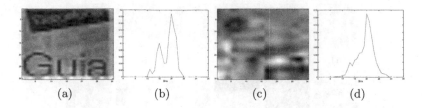

(a)   (b)   (c)   (d)

Fig. 4. False positive a) Object image b) Object histogram c) False positive patch d) False positive histogram

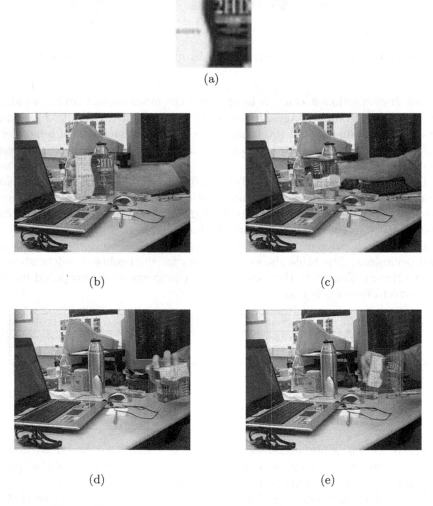

(a)

(b)   (c)

(d)   (e)

Fig. 5. Object detection a) Box object b-e) Object detection

4   Conclusions

We have presented an appearance method to perform object detection invariant to object scale and orientation changes, and robust under partial occlusions. The classification rule is based on Haar local features extracted during a Boosting training phase, giving a local measurement that accounts for small changes in the object histogram signature. In order to reduce the computational cost of performing object detection, the integral histogram has been incorporated.

References

1. Swain, M., Ballard, D.: Color indexing. Int. J. Comput. Vision 7(1), 11–32 (1991)
2. Moreno, F., Andrade-Cetto, J., Sanfeliu, A.: Fusion of color and shape for object tracking under varying illumination. In: Perales, F.J., Campilho, A.J., Pérez, N., Sanfeliu, A. (eds.) IbPRIA 2003. LNCS, vol. 2652, pp. 580–588. Springer, Heidelberg (2003)
3. Schiele, B., Crowley, J.L.: Object recognition using multidimensional receptive field histograms. In: Buxton, B.F., Cipolla, R. (eds.) ECCV 1996. LNCS, vol. 1065, pp. 610–619. Springer, Heidelberg (1996)
4. Viola, P., Jones, M.: Rapid object detection using a boosted cascade of simple features. In: Proc. 15th IEEE Conf. Comput. Vision Pattern Recog, pp. 511–518, Kauai (December 2001)
5. Villamizar, M., Sanfeliu, A., Andrade-Cetto, J.: Computation of rotation local invariant features using the integral image for real time object detection. In: Proc. 18th IAPR Int. Conf. Pattern Recog. Hong Kong, vol. 4, pp. 81–85 (August 2006)
6. Porikli, F.: Integral histogram: a fast way to extract histograms in cartesian spaces. In: Proc. 19th IEEE Conf. Comput. Vision Pattern Recog. vol. 1, pp. 829–836, San Diego (June 2005)
7. Freund, Y., Schapire, R.E.: A decision-theoretic generalization of on-line learning and an application to boosting. J. Comput. Syst. Sci. 55(1), 119–139 (1997)
8. Rätsch, G., Schölkopf, B., Mika, S., Müller, K.-R.: SVM and Boosting: One class. Technical report, GMD First (November 2000)

4 Conclusions

We have presented an approach to the local feature for object detection invariant to rotation scale and orientation change... robust under partial occlusions. The feature detection rule is based on local... features... during a Boosting training phase giving a local invariant... that accounts for small changes in the object based on significant... a... to reduce the computational cost of performing object detection, the integral histogram has been incorporated...

References

Author Index

Lecture Notes in Computer Science

For information about Vols. 1–4409

please contact your bookseller or Springer

Vol. 4472: M. Haindl, J. Kittler, F. Roli (Eds.), Multiple Classifier Systems. XI, 524 pages. 2007.

Vol. 4471: P. Cesar, K. Chorianopoulos, J.F. Jensen (Eds.), Interactive TV: a Shared Experience. XIII, 236 pages. 2007.

Vol. 4470: Q. Wang, D. Pfahl, D.M. Raffo (Eds.), Software Process Dynamics and Agility. XI, 346 pages. 2007.

Vol. 4465: T. Chahed, B. Tuffin (Eds.), Network Control and Optimization. XIII, 305 pages. 2007.

Vol. 4464: E. Dawson, D.S. Wong (Eds.), Information Security Practice and Experience. XIII, 361 pages. 2007.

Vol. 4463: I. Măndoiu, A. Zelikovsky (Eds.), Bioinformatics Research and Applications. XV, 653 pages. 2007. (Sublibrary LNBI).

Vol. 4462: D. Sauveron, K. Markantonakis, A. Bilas, J.-J. Quisquater (Eds.), Information Security Theory and Practices. XII, 255 pages. 2007.

Vol. 4459: C. Cérin, K.-C. Li (Eds.), Advances in Grid and Pervasive Computing. XVI, 759 pages. 2007.

Vol. 4453: T. Speed, H. Huang (Eds.), Research in Computational Molecular Biology. XVI, 550 pages. 2007. (Sublibrary LNBI).

Vol. 4452: M. Fasli, O. Shehory (Eds.), Agent-Mediated Electronic Commerce. VIII, 249 pages. 2007. (Sublibrary LNAI).

Vol. 4451: T.S. Huang, A. Nijholt, M. Pantic, A. Pentland (Eds.), Artifical Intelligence for Human Computing. XVI, 359 pages. 2007. (Sublibrary LNAI).

Vol. 4450: T. Okamoto, X. Wang (Eds.), Public Key Cryptography – PKC 2007. XIII, 491 pages. 2007.

Vol. 4448: M. Giacobini et al. (Ed.), Applications of Evolutionary Computing. XXIII, 755 pages. 2007.

Vol. 4447: E. Marchiori, J.H. Moore, J.C. Rajapakse (Eds.), Evolutionary Computation,Machine Learning and Data Mining in Bioinformatics. XI, 302 pages. 2007.

Vol. 4446: C. Cotta, J. van Hemert (Eds.), Evolutionary Computation in Combinatorial Optimization. XII, 241 pages. 2007.

Vol. 4445: M. Ebner, M. O'Neill, A. Ekárt, L. Vanneschi, A.I. Esparcia-Alcázar (Eds.), Genetic Programming. XI, 382 pages. 2007.

Vol. 4444: T. Reps, M. Sagiv, J. Bauer (Eds.), Program Analysis and Compilation, Theory and Practice. X, 361 pages. 2007.

Vol. 4443: R. Kotagiri, P.R. Krishna, M. Mohania, E. Nantajeewarawat (Eds.), Advances in Databases: Concepts, Systems and Applications. XXI, 1126 pages. 2007.

Vol. 4440: B. Liblit, Cooperative Bug Isolation. XV, 101 pages. 2007.

Vol. 4439: W. Abramowicz (Ed.), Business Information Systems. XV, 654 pages. 2007.

Vol. 4438: L. Maicher, A. Sigel, L.M. Garshol (Eds.), Leveraging the Semantics of Topic Maps. X, 257 pages. 2007. (Sublibrary LNAI).

Vol. 4433: E. Şahin, W.M. Spears, A.F.T. Winfield (Eds.), Swarm Robotics. XII, 221 pages. 2007.

Vol. 4432: B. Beliczynski, A. Dzielinski, M. Iwanowski, B. Ribeiro (Eds.), Adaptive and Natural Computing Algorithms, Part II. XXVI, 761 pages. 2007.

Vol. 4431: B. Beliczynski, A. Dzielinski, M. Iwanowski, B. Ribeiro (Eds.), Adaptive and Natural Computing Algorithms, Part I. XXV, 851 pages. 2007.

Vol. 4430: C.C. Yang, D. Zeng, M. Chau, K. Chang, Q. Yang, X. Cheng, J. Wang, F.-Y. Wang, H. Chen (Eds.), Intelligence and Security Informatics. XII, 330 pages. 2007.

Vol. 4429: R. Lu, J.H. Siekmann, C. Ullrich (Eds.), Cognitive Systems. X, 161 pages. 2007. (Sublibrary LNAI).

Vol. 4427: S. Uhlig, K. Papagiannaki, O. Bonaventure (Eds.), Passive and Active Network Measurement. XI, 274 pages. 2007.

Vol. 4426: Z.-H. Zhou, H. Li, Q. Yang (Eds.), Advances in Knowledge Discovery and Data Mining. XXV, 1161 pages. 2007. (Sublibrary LNAI).

Vol. 4425: G. Amati, C. Carpineto, G. Romano (Eds.), Advances in Information Retrieval. XIX, 759 pages. 2007.

Vol. 4424: O. Grumberg, M. Huth (Eds.), Tools and Algorithms for the Construction and Analysis of Systems. XX, 738 pages. 2007.

Vol. 4423: H. Seidl (Ed.), Foundations of Software Science and Computational Structures. XVI, 379 pages. 2007.

Vol. 4422: M.B. Dwyer, A. Lopes (Eds.), Fundamental Approaches to Software Engineering. XV, 440 pages. 2007.

Vol. 4421: R. De Nicola (Ed.), Programming Languages and Systems. XVII, 538 pages. 2007.

Vol. 4420: S. Krishnamurthi, M. Odersky (Eds.), Compiler Construction. XIV, 233 pages. 2007.

Vol. 4419: P.C. Diniz, E. Marques, K. Bertels, M.M. Fernandes, J.M.P. Cardoso (Eds.), Reconfigurable Computing: Architectures, Tools and Applications. XIV, 391 pages. 2007.

Vol. 4418: A. Gagalowicz, W. Philips (Eds.), Computer Vision/Computer Graphics Collaboration Techniques. XV, 620 pages. 2007.

Vol. 4416: A. Bemporad, A. Bicchi, G. Buttazzo (Eds.), Hybrid Systems: Computation and Control. XVII, 797 pages. 2007.

Vol. 4415: P. Lukowicz, L. Thiele, G. Tröster (Eds.), Architecture of Computing Systems - ARCS 2007. X, 297 pages. 2007.

Vol. 4414: S. Hochreiter, R. Wagner (Eds.), Bioinformatics Research and Development. XVI, 482 pages. 2007. (Sublibrary LNBI).

Vol. 4412: F. Stajano, H.J. Kim, J.-S. Chae, S.-D. Kim (Eds.), Ubiquitous Convergence Technology. XI, 302 pages. 2007.

Vol. 4411: R.H. Bordini, M. Dastani, J. Dix, A.E.F. Seghrouchni (Eds.), Programming Multi-Agent Systems. XIV, 249 pages. 2007. (Sublibrary LNAI).

Vol. 4410: A. Branco (Ed.), Anaphora: Analysis, Algorithms and Applications. X, 191 pages. 2007. (Sublibrary LNAI).